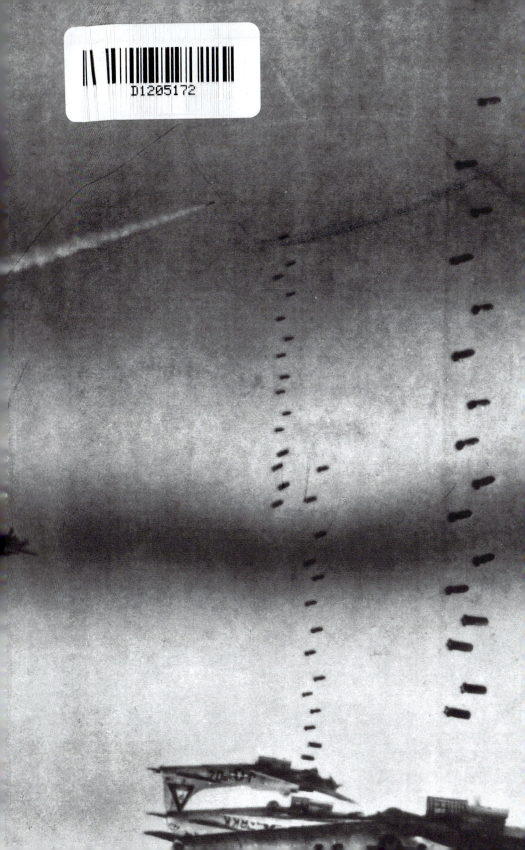

THE FIRE

FIRE

The Bombing of Germany, 1940–1945

COLUMBIA UNIVERSITY PRESS
Publishers Since 1893

New York   Chichester, West Sussex
Translation copyright © 2006 Columbia University Press
Der Brand © Ullstein Heyne List GmbH and Co. KG, Munich
Published in 2002 by Propyläen, Munich

Library of Congress Cataloging-in-Publication Data

Friedrich, Jörg, 1944–
    [Brand. English]
    The fire : the bombing of Germany, 1940–1945 / Jörg Friedrich ;
translated by Allison Brown.
        p. cm.
    Includes bibliographical references and indexes.
    ISBN 978-0-231-13380-7 (cloth : alk. paper)
    ISBN 978-0-231-13381-4 (pbk. : alk. paper)
    1. World War, 1939–1945—Aerial operations.   2. Bombing, Aerial—Germany.
3. Germany—History—1939–1945.   I. Title.   II. Title: Bombing of Germany,
1940–1945.

D785.F7513 2008
940.54'213—DC22

                                                                2006010408

∞ Columbia University Press books are printed on permanent and
durable acid-free paper. Printed in the United States of America

Designed by LINDA SECONDARI & VIN DANG. Assistance from KABIR DANDONA.

CONTENTS

THE FIRE

1. WEAPON

"The bomber will always get through."
—PRIME MINISTER STANLEY BALDWIN

The bomb does not take a precise path when finding its target. So the target becomes whatever the bomb can find—a city. No city can be reduced to ruins with the three thousand tons of explosives that a bomber fleet carries, but incendiary ammunition can create damage that keeps feeding upon itself. Developing this kind of spreading damage requires expertise in two fields of science: fireraising and radio navigation. Fire-prevention engineers and physicists spent three years developing systems, techniques, and strategies that could locate inflammable structures in settled areas, mark them with colored lights, and burn them to the ground. Loaded with fuel and bombs, the airplane en route to its target is itself an extremely sensitive target. Pursued by flak artillery and interceptors, the bomber's crewmembers, with their mission of mass killing, are almost exclusively concerned with their own survival.

LOOKING THROUGH THE BOMBSIGHT of a four-engine Lancaster from an altitude of almost twenty thousand feet, it was impossible to see a city such as Wuppertal. The residents blacked out their city, and its basin was shrouded in a veil of mist. The pilot crossed the long, narrow town in one minute. The suburbs did not concern him. The size of his target region allowed him a ten-second window for the drop. This brief moment arrived about two hours after taking off from the southern English coast, but he did not know precisely when it would come without the aid of the pathfinder force flying ahead of him, about six thousand feet lower. A bomb cannot be dropped as the bomber is crossing the target. A bomb's flight is not vertical. It follows a parabolic path, as inertia and gravity pull it in different directions. By the time the bomb hit the ground, the plane was already a couple miles away.

The pathfinder group arrived two minutes late in their Mosquito aircraft, which were fast and out of the reach of German interceptors.[1] German listening posts had located them forty-five minutes earlier, at the mouth of the Schelde, and followed their course over Maastricht and Mönchengladbach. When they crossed the Rhine at 12:40 a.m., flying eastward toward Solingen, Wuppertal became a possible target. Sirens had already blasted in the Ruhr Valley at around midnight on this May evening in 1943, but without disturbing Wuppertal. The British bombers had not yet succeeded in finding the cleft of the Wupper River valley, as it was covered by clouds of industrial smog. From the air, the haze could have been taken for a lake. Thus the people of Wuppertal nurtured the reputation of being the "Ruhr Valley air-raid shelter." And anyway, theirs was a god-fearing city.

The main force had deviated from its course. Wind, antiaircraft fire, or navigation errors moved it too far south, so it approached Wuppertal not as planned, but from the direction of Remscheid. The Mosquitos in the pathfinder force of No. 109 Squadron were the first from the Rheine rendezvous point to reach Wuppertal from the north. At six-minute intervals, they marked the district of Barmen with red flare bombs. At about 3,300 feet above the target, these marker bombs then broke apart, each one dropping sixty flares that fell in clusters. On the ground, the flares glowed red for ten minutes. This wave was then followed by a subsequent wave of green marker bombs. Then came fifty-five fireraisers, dropping incendiaries into the dense wreath of color. The sky became very bright. The red and green markers were set with precision on either side of the residential quarter, the main force having been given instructions to aim for red as long as it was still visible, otherwise to aim for green. The planes rumbled as they approached, stretching out across 150 miles of sky. Over six miles across and almost two miles deep, the six hundred planes discharged their loads, about ten per minute.

The first attack wave of forty-four planes dropped only incendiary sticks, which made a sound like a waterfall as they wailed their way down to the city. Far more than 300,000 bombs fell that night. It was an unprecedented density. From above, it looked like the bombs were rolling down a slope. At 1:20 a.m., Barmen was sealed off by a fire stretching from the theater to the Adler Bridge.

The typical half-timbered buildings, the narrow and twisted alleyways, the valley basin—which acted as a chimney—and a treacherous wind all served to fan the flames. With the smoke filling everything, the crashing of the "cookie" or "blockbuster" bombs that tore away entire buildings, the din of the collapsing roofs and façades, and the racing speed of the flames, it was impossible to tell what could still be saved. Building residents fled to the coolness of their cellars, while the flames continued to spread for three or four hours. Mile after mile, building after building was ablaze—some only in the attics, some all the way down to the ground floor. At 2:30 a.m., the fires had not yet all merged into one. It can take a while for individual blazes to fuse into the carpet that might eventually become a firestorm, drawing everything that moves into an oven from which there is no escape.

The pathfinders were directed both during the approach to Wuppertal and during the actual bomb drop by a train of radar pulses called Oboe. The British Bomber Command had been using this system since the beginning of 1943. The marker pilots listened to a series of tones in their headphones. If the plane was on course, the ground station sent a continuous oboelike tone that would change to a kind of Morse code signal if there were any deviations from course. As the squadron approached the target, the pilots heard a second signal: a quick series of short and long tones followed by a series of short tones. When the tones ceased, the bombardier pressed the trigger. The signals were broadcast from England and barely reached the Ruhr basin, which had been involved in the Ruhr battle since March.

By the time that battle was concluded in July, Oboe had guided to their targets 18,500 airplanes, which dropped a total of 34,000 tons of bombs.

The streets bustled on that early summer evening in Wuppertal. Only a small staff was on duty at the fire department; most had already left for the weekend and were out in the countryside. Guests celebrated a wedding party at the forest villa in the Hardt.[2] The bridal couple so enjoyed the singing and speeches that they delayed by an hour their departure to the Wuppertaler Hof hotel—a lucky break. While they danced, the lights went out. Over the noise of the festivities, no one had heard the air-raid alarm. Controlling the confusion, the restaurant manager asked all the guests to proceed to the air-raid shelter.

In the town of Barmen, Luise Rompf woke to the sound of the sirens. She slipped into the clothing she had set out and took her child Uli in her arms. The building residents all ran down to the cellar, some shouting, others in tears. The slatted cellar partitions had previously been removed, and at the end of the corridor, a loosely closed-up hole in the wall led to the neighboring cellar. "Before we reached the cellar, we could already smell the fire, and through the window in the stairway, we could see it blazing in different shades of yellow and red."[3] Just before the bombs hit, a whirring sound could be heard. An elderly man and woman nestled together and whispered prayers to the Virgin Mary; a tipsy childless woman shouted "Dammit! Shit!" relentlessly. Luise's husband came in from outside, smoke pouring through the door as he entered. "We have to get out of here!"

Hidden in another cellar, Sybill Bannister, an Englishwoman, trusted in the vaulting of German ceilings, which were, as she put it, "strong as a church crypt."[4] Her friend had quickly gone upstairs to grab her jacket from the ground floor, and saw that the stairwell was in flames from top to bottom. "We couldn't fathom how the fire could spread so quickly through the four-story building, even if a hundred firebombs had penetrated the attic." If the stairwell collapsed, said the air-raid warden, then burning rubble would fall onto the cellar steps and everyone would die from the heat and smoke. He led the women through the small opening in the wall into the cellar next door. "It was pitch black and the hole was very small. I was horrified at the thought of getting closed into this dreadfully narrow passageway."

Two girls dared to cross the yard to climb over the wall, but the wall was gone. Since flames were coming from all directions they ran into the swimming center across the street. Flames shot out of the building, but there was nowhere else to go. Twenty people were trapped inside. In order to escape the intense heat, they kept jumping into the pool and wrapping wet clothing around their heads and bodies. The natatorium was burning down all around them; the ceramic tiles were as hot as an oven.

Surrounded by fire, many sought protection in the Wupper River. They did not jump in but instead slid down the embankment walls. Elisabeth Stark, a physician on duty in the first-aid center, was called in by firefighters and let down on rope ladders to help the burn victims out of the water. "Half their bodies were one giant wound, with shreds of clothing sticking to it." Dr. Stark treated the wounds and gave morphine injections to ease the pain.

Luise Rompf crawled with her family through to the laundry room of the neighboring cellar. "The laundry room was filled with a chaotic babble of sobbing, praying, and loud scolding. The mother of a baby girl only a few months old was holding a wet cloth over her daughter's face to help her get some air. I did that with Uli too; the caustic smoke made it harder and harder to breathe."

Even though the ceiling held up, in the public air-raid shelters under the burning factory on Adolf Hitler Strasse, Ruth Adamsen worried about the air. "I didn't feel very safe anymore, so I convinced my mother and aunt to try to find shelter elsewhere. Luckily, the street was very wide." Hot ashes and sparks flew around above them. The flames shot out of windows on both sides of the street and joined together "like a tall cathedral." Twenty-four-year-old Ruth held her Aunt Lene's arm, and her mother ran beside her with her eyes closed. "When we got to Erichstrasse we heard horrific screams coming out of the fire. 'Help me, I'm burning!' Later I found out it was Herr Döring, who used to sell me my notebooks for school."

The smoke in the laundry room forced the Rompf family to leave. They opened up the bricked-up hole leading to the third cellar, since it was getting too crowded for all the residents from three buildings. "Everyone was silent and listened to what was going on outside. The sky was quiet now. We heard only the crackling and seething of the columns of fire around us that were surging up to the sky." The planes were gone; the people climbed out of the cellars and "stared in bewilderment into the sky, where yellow, red, and gray cloud formations were billowing." Confused children with small bags stood around dumbly; people ran past "with distorted or empty expressions, some with dulled looks on their faces."

The eleven families from the wedding party hurried out of the shelter; seven of them

> had nothing left. I accompanied my cousin, who was sobbing quietly, onto the "Rott" where she had left her three small children in the neighbor's care. She ran straight ahead without stopping and didn't even let the firemen stop her, as they warned that buildings were in danger of collapsing. When she saw the apartment house she lived in, she fainted; the building was in flames. But we found the children in the cellar of the building next door, safe and sound.

Mrs. Bannister, who climbed out into the open when the bombardment stopped, realized that though the airplanes had gone, the attack had just begun.

> As far as we could see, every single building was on fire. I tried to walk in the middle of the street, because flames were licking out of every window and the trees at the edge of the sidewalks were also burning and throwing down their glowing branches. The heated and softened tarmac on the streets made it difficult to walk.

As they ran out to the street from their cellars, people often got stuck in the melted asphalt, making it hard to avoid the burning debris raining down all around them.

Old wooden buildings started to topple; the smoke got denser and the path narrower. "Now the way back was blocked and the fire had surrounded me. I looked for a place where the flames didn't reach all that high, only about to my knees." Mrs. Bannister ignored the burns on her legs and the caustic smoke in her eyes, mouth, and throat that was starting to suffocate her. "I was just overcome by a growing, dreadful drowsiness." No oxygen was reaching her brain. She thought to herself that this might be the end of both her and the child in her arms.

"When my knees gave out, I couldn't hold Manny anymore, and he rolled out of my arms. He was lying there, still wrapped in the blanket with only his legs poking out. Whenever the flames touched them, he screamed with pain and rolled and thrashed about on the ground in front of me." It was his screaming that stirred her deadened senses; a patrolling rescue vehicle picked up the two of them and took them to police headquarters, where injured people blackened with soot were being sent to receive medical care. "The rescue operations seemed very well organized." Mrs. Bannister suffered burned calves, and she was given "a bandage soaked in some liquid to prevent the chemicals from burning deeper into the flesh."

On her way, she noticed the clear-cut edge of the destruction. "On one side of the line was hell, and on the other side was a normal city; though the air was full of smoke and there was unusual bustling in the middle of the night, the buildings were still standing. It was truly precision work." When the bombers returned four weeks later, they started at that edge of Wuppertal-Barmen and destroyed Wuppertal-Elberfeld.

A foul smell of gas, fire, and earth permeated the city. The smoke obscured the sun; an orange-colored sky hung over the valley. About three hundred yards from Dr. Stark's first-aid center was the Fischer-tal Hospital. Inside, thirty mothers and their newborns had been incinerated. Dark gray smoke poured out of the houses in the valley as Luise Rompf crossed the fields. "At the center of these buildings was the burning obstetrics clinic, with a big red cross marked on the roof." Some patients had managed to get out. "I saw women from the clinic lying all over the meadows—sick women, pregnant women, women giving birth." Nurses ran back and forth, spreading out blankets. Between the groans and screams were the pleasant sounds of newborn babies crying.

Nine-year-old Wilfried Picard had observed the attack from an attic window in Elberfeld in the south of Wuppertal. The next morning in Barmen, he confronted "death for the first time in my life."[5] He had heard stories that the corpses of the people who burned to death shrunk down to the size of dolls, so he was surprised by the normal size of "a woman, lying face down close to the curb, undressed and with totally blackened skin."

Heinrich Biergann, a sixteen-year-old trainee with the German railroad, had a truck driver's license and was assigned to recover corpses:

> They'd say: here are six corpses, there are twenty, etc. Sometimes the people lay there totally at peace, as if asleep. They had been asphyxiated due to a lack of oxygen. Others had been completely incinerated. The charred bodies measured about twenty inches. We recovered them in zinc bathtubs and washtubs. Three fit into one washtub and seven or eight in a bathtub.[6]

It was hard for Biergann to look at those who were partially burned. An arm, for instance, that lay under the rubble was left uncharred.

"Corpses of the normal burn victims didn't resemble human beings very much; they were like black packages. But if an undamaged body part was attached, you were suddenly aware again that these were people. We often had to down a potent gulp in order to cope with the strain."

Fischertal, a densely built-up quarter of Barmen, suffered the most severe losses. On one property on Zeughausstrasse, a whole neighborhood of thirty-two people had been erased. Identification of the corpses was difficult if entire families had been exterminated. In such a case, the cemetery administration simply noted descriptive details on their casualty list:[7] "Female, blue-and-white checkered dress, wedding ring, no teeth, black lace shoes"; "female, charred (torso), petticoat, gold tooth"; "boy, roughly thirteen years old, black wide-wale corduroy trousers, russet jacket, herringbone pattern, and girl, charred"; "two skulls of adults and two children's skulls."

The May 1943 Wuppertal operation was regarded in England as the most successful mission thus far. "No industrial city in Germany," wrote the *Times*, "has ever before been so completely wiped off the map." More than 10 percent of the aircraft had missed the city and bombed Remscheid and Solingen to the south. But the other five hundred planes had hit within a three-mile radius of the target. It took weeks to recover all the bodies. Eighty percent of the residential land area was destroyed and 3,400 people were killed. That was five times the previous record set with the same bomb tonnage—693 deaths—which had been set shortly earlier in Dortmund. Four other cities suffered more than two hundred civilian deaths in 1943. Munich lost 208 people on the night of March 9, Duisburg lost 272 in the early morning hours of May 13, Essen lost 461 on March 6, and Stuttgart lost 619 on April 15.

News spread quickly about the disaster in Wuppertal. The estimated number of deaths ranged from 4,000 to 40,000. There were no reliable reports in the media, but people sensed that the air war had taken on a new form: fire. People had previously assumed that sooner or later in the war, gas would be dropped; as it turned out, a different chemistry was used. The shift from explosive bombing to the incendiary fire war was interpreted by observers on the ground as a "phosphorus rain," which was a trivial error. The sparkling cascades of the flares and markers were confused with the incendiary material, a mixture in which phosphorus was added as an ignition source.

Since the beginning of 1943, researchers at Britain's Air Ministry were working diligently to develop the annihilating potential of fire. The damage caused by explosive bombs, which are laborious to transport, did little to impress the enemy. Light fuels could be loaded in virtually unlimited quantities and, provided they hit their targets, gave rise to a multiplicative evil that could be far more destructive. Under the right circumstances, a load of four-pound incendiary bombs could ravage more land area than the one- or two-thousand-times heavier explosive bombs. Perfection of this method required a closer analysis of the exact nature of the target of attack. For two whole years, thermite sticks were indiscriminately dropped out of the bombers without any clear idea of a city's flammability, because the air commanders lacked expert knowledge of the science of fireraising.

When the researchers at the Air Ministry consulted engineers from the fire departments, a new science was born.[8] The occupation of fighting fires and that of setting fires both dealt with the same subject: the flammability of the materials. Fireraising required knowledge of the physical composition of the German settlement. The bomb had to burn for between eight and thirty minutes at the point of impact. That was the time needed for the seed to germinate. Determining how that seed spread, how the fire grew, how it passed over obstructions, crossed areas without streets, and caught hold of an area for miles were the jobs for the mathematicians, statisticians, and operation evaluators.

Fire engineers investigated the properties of German furnishings, since the first things to catch fire were the contents of the houses. Junk in attics, food in pantries, clothing, cushions. This inventory in turn set the building on fire. The engineers ordered fire-insurance maps and prepared stereometric images of aerial photographs in order to draw conclusions about the locations of fire cells and firewalls, which are the barriers that slow a fire down. A city with a lot of them, like Berlin, was difficult to set on fire. First, the firewalls had to be collapsed, a preparatory task carried out by the blockbuster bomb.

With general-purpose demolition or high-explosive bombs, the explosive material shatters the massive steel shell. The shrapnel destroys human bodies. These fragments are projectiles with a velocity that only reinforced concrete, two-foot-thick brickwork, or gravel and sand deposits can withstand. Bomber Command had little regard for the high-explosive bomb, even though they dropped more than 800,000 of them.[9] They needed too much metal, were heavy, and contained too little explosive. Their function was similar to that of an artillery grenade: it caused a lot of damage in trenches, but very little harm to the bodies and homes of seventy million Germans when detonated in the open air.

The high-capacity or blockbuster bombs were different. Their shells were thin, with a charge-to-weight ratio of 70 percent. Its impact created shock waves. The detonation converted its high explosive share into an equal volume of gas, which expanded under high pressure, compressing the surrounding air and creating a supersonic thrust. If that blast wave met a vertical barrier standing perpendicular to it, such as a building, it reduced it to rubble. At a greater radius, it tore off roofs and shattered windows. The standard bomb of aerial warfare was the 4,000-pound blockbuster, which could destroy entire blocks of apartment houses. The Germans also called them *Badeöfen*, or "boilers," because of their cylindrical shape. The British dropped 68,000 of them.[10]

In order to blow up concrete constructions, railroad facilities, bridges, viaducts, and canals, a medium-capacity bomb was created that balanced its shock wave and explosive impact. A total of 750,000 were dropped, in a number of weight classifications, ranging from 500 pounds to 22,000 pounds. At the start of the war, Bomber Command considered its explosive and high-explosive bombs to be its main weapons. Not until 1942 did they realize that a bombing war could not be fought with explosives. Explosives were simply one element, which only in combination with another element, the incendiary, created the most powerful weapon ever experienced. The destructive capability of this new weapon depended on the precise mixture, sequence, and density in which the high-explosive fragmentation bombs, blockbusters, and incendiary ammunition were delivered to the target.

In 1940 and 1941, the bomber pilot had two terms for his drop: hit or miss. Two years later, a different war was being waged. Research staffs studied survey maps of developed areas and aerial photographs of built-up areas, marked the fire cells in color, and calculated the necessary tonnage combinations that had to be dropped for the respective cities. Afterward, they evaluated pictures of that raid and adjusted those combinations before the next. When a bomber

1. Five-hundred-pound high-explosive bombs.

Source: Bildarchiv Preussischer Kulturbesitz.

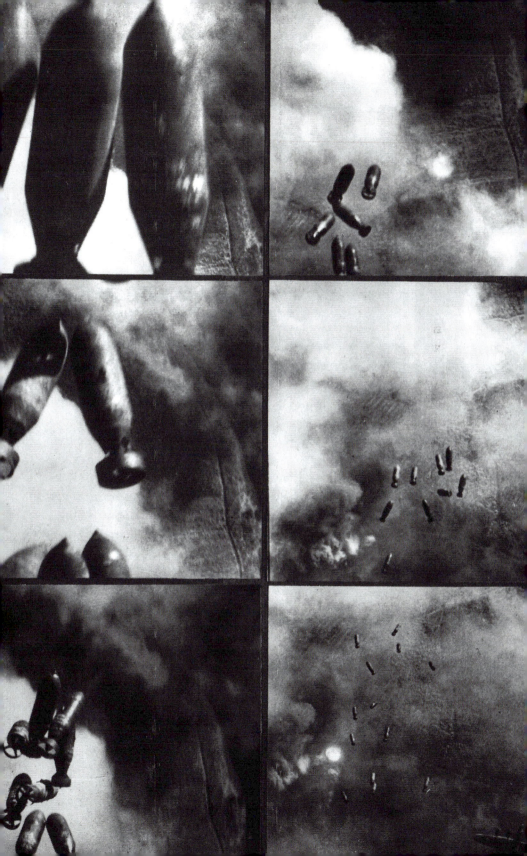

released its load, a photoflash bomb was also dropped, which activated a camera. The next day, reconnaissance planes photographed the results. The war of strategists and warhorses had always consisted of a combination of factual experience, ideas, and intuition. Now the precision of the laboratory was added to that mixture.

As it turned out, it was indeed possible to burn down entire cities from the air, even German cities solidly built of brick. As regards ignition, the relevance of a city increased as one moved from the periphery to the center. The outer ring was built in the nineteenth and twentieth centuries using modern construction techniques. It contained the industrial area and residential developments. Steel girders were used, fire cells were built, and wide spaces were surrounded by buildings. That was the outer ring. Further in toward the center of the major German metropolises were sprawling neighborhoods of unsound and substandard buildings, often hastily built during the period of rapid industrial expansion in the late 1800s. These dismal buildings let in little air, absorbed heat well, and burned quickly. Within that was the eighteenth-century city, with its gridlike pattern of streets and three- to six-story buildings with shared separating walls. They were built with wooden beams, and the ceilings between the floors were stuffed with filling material. Roof ridges ran parallel to the streets and overlapped. Within that was the Old Town, the city hub, whose layout traced back to medieval or early modern building patterns. The streets were narrow, crooked, and winding. Beam frames held the buildings rigid; they were filled in with brick, replacing the loam that had originally been used. That loam still remained in patches. Separating walls were crafted together such that they could easily spread fire from neighbor to neighbor. The attics were partitioned using large amounts of wood. Wherever such Old Town "hubs" existed, they were a natural target, and they served as the kindling for the surrounding areas.

The city block was recognized to be the Achilles' heel of the extended inner district. Originally a row of residential apartments, it evolved into a hybrid design, with shops and commercial enterprises on the ground floor. The buildings quickly expanded, taking

2. The Old Town of Hamburg.

Source: Landesmedienzentrum—Behörde für Bildung und Sport—
Freie Hansestadt Hamburg.

over what had previously been courtyards and open space. Overfilled warehouses and workshops, often made of wood, made excellent fire bridges. A flame needs tight spaces and streets that are far narrower than the buildings are high. The bomb's chances of falling onto an inflammable area increased as open spaces, front yards, and undeveloped sites disappeared.

The buildings fatefully placed their most ignitable part on top, facing the bombardier's sights directly. With its brick and timberwork structure, the roof made it possible to set a fire that worked downward. It took a long time: about three hours per floor. It was also possible to set the detonation point lower. It all depended on the fuse settings. The bomb could crash through three or four floors with its weight, then ignite on the wooden floors. All that was missing was a draft. After the 4,000-pound blockbuster blew away all the roofs and windows for miles around, the buildings became chimneys, and the incendiaries dropped in.

The German cellar provided a safe refuge, built either with brick vaulting or with concrete casting and steel girders. The cellar ceilings offered excellent protection against explosions. It was defenseless only against the seeping in of combustion gases and the subsequent loss of oxygen. At first, the attackers did not know what was happening in the cellars.

Well known, on the other hand, were the effects of intervention by firefighters. If they arrived in time, the fire never crossed beyond the block in which it started. A wide-area fire resulted only if the fire department failed. Firemen needed access to two things: the fire, and water. Explosive bombs kept the firemen from both. With overly heavy heads at the front and guidance fins in the back, the explosive bombs drilled deep into the earth, tearing apart the water mains. They also cratered the street, making it impassable. However, these effects lasted only for a short time: water could be tapped from rivers and from reservoirs set up as a precaution, and rubble could be cleared away. So lighter, duller shrapnel bombs with a timed fuse were also used. They lay on the ground, detonating and hurling their bulletlike fragments for hours after the attacker had left the scene. These time bombs forced firefighters to remain in the shelters or be wiped out.

Bomb researchers were unceasingly concerned with the complex process of mixing and calibrating the materials to be dropped. The flammability of the target over time and across space was one thing. There was also the effect of natural elements such as temperature, humidity, and wind to consider. And human nature confused everything. The pilots could not be programmed as perfectly as the chemical mixtures of the bombs. Incalculable portions of their load regularly landed on unintended sites. It did not help much to calculate behavioral variables into the plans; the pilots were too unpredictable. Quantity was the bombers' quality assurance: the targets were hopelessly inundated with bombs, and dozens of sorties were flown. Postwar inspections described the country as "overbombed."

Before fire raids, never in the history of war had the development of a weapon been guided totally by scientists, and in a sense, the air war *was itself* the research and development of the weapon. Without such a comprehensive extermination strategy, the fire weapon would have never had a chance to be tested, adjusted, and refined. Through trial and error, the weapon groped its way toward perfection; by the time technology and capability fully meshed, the war ended.

Fires were initially started not to damage, but to illuminate the target area for the explosive bombs. However, postraid aerial photographs showed that although seven thousand tons of explosive ammunition could damage a radius of almost twenty miles, the damage caused by the same amount of incendiary materials could extend more than ninety miles. By the summer of 1943, it had been empirically determined that a city was easier to burn down than to blow up, and that both the explosive and incendiary bombs were needed to produce a sufficient blaze. Before that, a whole range of bombs had been dropped; some of them worked, some did not.

Among the failures were the minuscule Razzle and Decker incendiary devices, which were wooden and cloth strips coated with white phosphorus. In the summer of 1940, the Royal Air Force dropped vast numbers of these on forests and fields in order to destroy the German harvest and burn down the High Harz and the Black and Thuringian forests. In the summer of 1941, the trial was repeated with a fifty-pound canister of a rubber-phosphorus solution. Trials in England had been somewhat promising, and tens of thousands of canisters that broke open upon impact with the ground were produced. The yellow-gray liquid ignited upon exposure to the oxygen in the air. As it turned out, the German forests and fields did not catch fire because they were too green and moist. The bomb required tinder-dry vegetation. Rather than scrap the entire supply, they were dumped on the cities, including, on September 8, 1941, Lichtenberg and Pankow, two districts of Berlin. Thirty thousand fell on Wuppertal.

A great success, on the other hand, was the dark red, thirty-pound liquid-incendiary bomb. It was invented in 1940, constructed in 1941, and by 1944, three million of them had been dropped. It was thirty-three inches long, shaped like a cigar with a tail fin, and it cut through three stories. In a small blast, each one hurled seven pounds of viscous incendiary material over about half an acre. The benzole-rubber solution fed an intense half-hour-long fire that could not be extinguished with household means. Lübeck and Rostock in particular suffered from this bomb. The incendiary panel in the Air Ministry nonetheless discontinued their use in late 1944, because its charge-to-weight ratio was only one-quarter that of the four-pound incendiary stick.

There were differences of opinion regarding the next attempt to outdo those four-pounders: the thirty-pound flame-jet bomb. Because of its flaming jet of fire—about fifteen feet long and two feet wide—that sprayed for sixty seconds, many commanders thought of it as a pyrotechnic display that was impressive in laboratory testing but too complex to work in the field. More than 413,000 were manufactured and dropped, owing to the fact that its production required neither magnesium nor rubber, which were in short supply. It used a gallon and a half of gasoline, and since its methane-gas igniter was unreliable, the bomb was highly appreciated by the German firefighters, who dumped the payloads of the numerous duds into their gas tanks. In 1944, the year they were mass produced, an undamaged city was sought for systematic testing, but no such city was found. Brunswick was selected as the second-best choice. On the night of April 22, 32,000 were dropped on the city, but the results were unclear, as were the subsequent trials on Kiel (July 24), Stuttgart (July 24–29), Stettin (August 17), and Königsberg (August 30). Only in Kaiserslautern was there a sweeping success, on the night of September 27, 1944. Thirty-six percent of the built-up area was destroyed, and 144 civilians, mostly women and children, were burned alive. Stick-type incendiaries were also used in that raid, however, and ultimately, Bomber Command decided to discontinue use of the flame-jet bomb, especially since toward the end of the war there was not much left to burn. The four-pound sticks remained the perfect, ideal bomb of this war. German cities were turned into burning ruins by the eighty million incendiary sticks that were dropped. Never before had a single weapon caused such destruction over such a large area. About 650,000 of them showered down on Dresden alone.

The stick-type incendiaries were thin rods 21.74 inches long, with a magnesium-zinc alloy casing. The hexagonal shape was selected to facilitate packing, so they fit better into the small bomb containers (SBCs). The sticks separated easily after being dropped, attaining high velocity and penetration due to their narrow cross-section. But they did not keep to a predetermined trajectory and tended to spin. Their ballistic advantages were tested in the summer of 1936 and were not changed for war use. In mid-1942, small amounts of explosives were added because the fragments kept firefighters at a distance.

A simple firing-pin striker ignited seventeen thermite pellets using percussion caps, touch paper, igniter elements, and ignition pellets. A tongue of flame shot out of the end of the stick, and the magnesium alloy shell melted into an incandescent mass. This extinguished after eight minutes. In the open air, the process did not do much damage, but if put in proximity to the flammable objects in a house, conflagrations ensued that could stretch for miles. The magnesium alloy–thermite stick incendiary transformed the building into a combustion mass that burned street and city. All the stick required was direct access to the flammable materials of the house— access provided by the high-explosive blockbusters.

In 1936, Imperial Chemical Industries, in conjunction with the Royal Air Force, tested the device from many different altitudes; it ignited every time and never broke apart. The government ordered four and a half million of them in October. When war broke out, five million had already been stockpiled. The robustness, intense fire, and astronomical count of the magnesium-thermite stick was combined with the blockbuster to form the invincible weapon of the fire war. A simple addition in 1944 gave it the final touch: The sticks were no longer poured out of the planes from SBCs; instead, they were bundled in targetable clusters that broke apart shortly before impact. The bomb density thus increased considerably and made possible the firestorms that consumed Darmstadt, Heilbronn, Pforzheim, and Würzburg. Bombardment continued for days, with flaming mixtures of gasoline, rubber, synthetic resins, oil, liquid asphalt, gels, and small amounts of metal soaps, fatty acids, and phosphorus, unfurling a destructive force outstripped only by nuclear weapons.

For the purpose of multiplying fires in an urban area, U.S. forces tested vulnerabilities in a model analysis. They set up German and

Japanese test cities in order to determine specifics. It was soon apparent from these tests that civilian, residential neighborhoods were extremely vulnerable to concentrated incendiary bombing from the air. Thus it was resolved to engage in said bombing; destruction had never seemed easier. Transportation of the bombs, on the other hand, proved more difficult. A fleet of several thousand aircraft designed to drop their tonnage on targets over a wide area required industrial reserves other than just the thermite stick. Nevertheless, the 2.7 million tons of bombs that the Western Allies dropped on European theaters of war—1,356,828 tons of which fell on Germany—represented an enormous production battle.[11] The entire Allied apparatus of science, technology, industry, and logistics put bombers in the air 1,440,000 times and put escort fighter planes into the air 2,680,000 times over this theater of war. This was the greatest military entity of all time. In the period from 1944 to 1945, the European air war involved more than 1.8 million personnel. In the British Bomber Command, the true air fleet of the fire war, bomb carriers or fighter planes flew 389,809 sorties. Bomber Command flew operations on 1,481 nights and 1,089 days.[12] Britain spent almost half of its war expenses on the air force; the United States spent 35 percent.

The aircraft that made the British and American air offensive possible was the heavy bomber. In England, its design had been worked on since 1924; the bomber types used in World War II were almost all produced or designed in the 1930s. The task of the heavy bomber was to penetrate deep into enemy territory. Its weight came from its load as well as from the large tanks of fuel needed for extended round-trip flights. Armor-plating and aircraft cannons were also necessary, for defense against attacks from fighter planes and anti-aircraft fire. The two best bomber planes at the end of the war, the American B-17 and the British Lancaster, weighed twenty-five tons when fully loaded.

The disadvantages of the "heavies" were slow speed, a low flying altitude, and limited maneuverability. The apparatus that built such a lumbering fleet harbored a particular conception of war. It acquired the power for an offensive over the most remote enemy territory possible, was convinced it could find its way, and reckoned with little effective resistance. In concrete terms, that meant that it would fly during the day and had to see its target in order to hit it. It might be seen by its targets, but even so, it would not be hit. Nothing of the sort is what really happened. But these were the idealized, utopian, prewar notions of how the air war would proceed.

Pacifists and militarists alike had the same misguided notion that "the bomber will always get through," as Prime Minister Stanley Baldwin asserted. The Whitley, the Hampden, and the Wellington could carry hardly a ton, at a top speed of only 200 or 250 miles per hour and a maximum altitude of 23,000 feet. They were suited perhaps for political deterrence, but not for an offensive like the one that was to be deterred, which involved compact formations that soared to the enemy and eliminated their fighter planes with massive mutual covering fire. The gunner would man a machine-gun station in a rotating Plexiglas bubble, cupola, or turret at the tail, and, using his double or multiple artillery and superior .303 caliber ammunition, shake off the pursuer.

In case the heavy black colossi did not to survive the air battle, despite the heavy artillery, Bomber Command supplemented them with medium bombers, especially the wayward Blenheim. Because it was smaller, it was hit by antiaircraft artillery less often; because it was faster—almost as fast as a fighter plane—it needed neither artillery nor gunners. The concept presumed that the Germans would never develop fast fighter planes. But they did. As long as the fighter plane remained a functioning weapon, the contest of various aircraft designs would continue.

The bomber was a highly vulnerable vehicle by day and even by night. As a bringer of fire it was by no means fireproof, filled as it was with 2,500 gallons of high-octane fuel and a load of high-explosive and incendiary bombs, machine-gun ammunition, and flares and markers. With its limited speed and maneuverability, it had little hope of getting away if sighted by a fighter plane, and certainly no chance of prevailing in a dogfight. The plan to fly in squadrons and in closed formations was not implemented until May 1942, because for a long time it seemed more logical that individual planes could slip through unnoticed—and thus unscathed—under cover of night and in the vastness of the sky.

The United States had the largest head start in constructing four-engine bombers. As a power surrounded by two oceans, it was most firmly able to resist civilian bombardment. The Boeing B-17 Flying Fortress and the B-24 Liberator bristled with weapons that could fire in all directions. Starting in 1943, they flew in frightening squadron blocks three levels high, which the British had avoided doing. The

Liberator carried a bomb load of five thousand pounds and a crew of twelve, and was armed with ten .50 caliber machine guns.

The air fortresses initially intimidated the German fighter planes, until the fighters realized they could withstand the bombers' fire density. The bombers were weakest if the lead plane was attacked in a frontal approach. The fighter group engaged the head in battle, and individual planes filtered into the interior of the bomber formation. The maneuverability and boldness of the fighters could then give the ponderous monsters a fatal blow. The bomber remained a supersensitive creature.

Not until they suffered losses that threatened to eliminate their weapon entirely did the Americans realize that war could be waged *from* the air only if it could be won *in* the air. The barbaric, brute strength of bombs on the ground had to be married to delicate ultratechnology in the sky. Otherwise, the bomber and its payload were doomed. The bomber fleet, on its mission of annihilation, is paradoxically almost exclusively concerned with saving itself from annihilation. The plan of sending aircraft to the Germans to get them to surrender by dropping bombs on them proved to be more complicated than it seemed at first. No matter how good the abstract strategy was, the actual attack procedure failed. First and foremost, a weapon capable of surviving had to be anchored in the sky. The weapon was actually a system. It required not just a single type of aircraft, but an entire suite of planes, armaments, and bombs.

The British gave the bombers a fleet of radar-guided escort planes called the pathfinder force. The pathfinders flew in special aircraft, the light, fast Mosquito bomber. The Americans provided cover for their bomber streams with the Mustang, an innovative, unexpectedly long-range escort fighter plane. The Germans managed to respond with the rocket and the jet fighter, but these weapons never had a chance to prove their superiority, since at that point in the war, German industry was no longer capable of mass production.

The Mustang and the Mosquito, each in its own way, revised the prewar fallacy that the bomber will always get through. Up to then, the bombers did not get through for two reasons. First, it did not always find its target, and second, it was shot down while looking for it. Clumsy and sensitive, the blind gunner of the air campaign needed intelligent guidance and agile protection.

The mechanical war opened up a new arena in the sky—one that brought back the classic man-to-man duel, the test of strength between hunters. First, a plane was required that eliminated a serious flaw, the hunter's short-windedness. Before the Mustang, fighter planes were incapable of carrying enough fuel to venture into the depths of the Reich. The additional weight would have made them less maneuverable, diminishing their fighting strength. In June 1944, Rolls-Royce's Merlin engine finally managed to bring a fighter on a par with the German Messerschmitt Bf 109G and the Focke Wulf 190A all the way to Berlin. From then on, the Boeings could do their job, bombing *from* the air, undisturbed, while the Mustangs fought the war *in* the air. This all happened during the day—the day sky belonged to the United States. Britain's Bomber Command appeared under cover of darkness, which raised other difficulties: navigation and aiming.

The British Mosquito was a twin-engine fighter and light bomber in one. Initially with a bomb load of .8 tons (this was later increased to 1.8), it could reach an altitude of 40,000 feet. Its maximum speed of almost 400 mph could not be met by any German fighter aircraft until the brief appearance of the Messerschmitt Me 262 jet engine. The Mosquito was built largely of wood, so it reflected hardly any radar signals, and therefore could not be spotted. Apart from its ability to fly small nuisance raids virtually undisturbed, it also served to guide the bomber stream. Equipped with the precious Oboe and H2S radar navigation systems, it set turn markers on its approach in yellow and target markers in red and green for bombing. The Mosquitos provided the heavy bombers with orientation at night and a view of the target. But they had to defend themselves on their own.

The British needed more than three years—until the fall of 1943, at the time of the Battle of Berlin—to solve the basic air-war problem of bringing the bombers into bombardment position. By 1940, it had become clear that during the day targets were visible, but a bomber was vulnerable in the light. The next year it was discovered that while bombers could seldom be located at night, it was even more rare that they found what they were looking for. Of the forty attacks that had been made on Hamburg by that time, twenty were actually supposed to hit Lübeck and Kiel. Due to their proximity to rivers and the coast, these three cities were the easiest of all navigation points to find. When it was merely a matter of luck whether or not a city could be identified, it was pointless to look for targets within the city. At best, the city itself was the target, but still, most bombs fell on open land.

Systems were refined in 1943 and 1944 to illuminate the targets with a pattern of colored lights. Like a huge highlighter pen, target-indicator bombs, or TIs, sketched targets in the dark. The ammunition carriers then dropped their bombs onto these marks. It was the outline of destruction. The bombardier was not at all interested in what lay within those illuminated contours. He simply placed a drop inside a frame. This frame was drawn where the city center was presumed to be. The markers who did this had nothing to do with the bombers; the outline of the target region in turn was of no concern to the bombardier—nor to the markers, since they marked the target but did not define it. The targets were determined by the leaders back at Bomber Command. And the link between the leaders and the markers was the master bomber. He was in charge of the marking mission; he circled in his plane, far above the target-indication procedure that determined whether the mission would be successful or not. The master bomber, at an altitude of 26,000 feet, communicated by radio to synchronize the work of the markers and bombardiers working 13,000 feet below him.

The master bomber had a number of different techniques at his disposal. At first, a blind marker would fly by and set red flares according to information from airborne radar or Oboe signals. The RAF's elite No. 5 Bomber Group, however, began by dropping illuminators that lit up the night sky with intensely shining cascades of light that the Germans called "Christmas trees." If there was a heavy cloud cover over a city, parachute flares were used. After this rough marking or illumination, the visual marker took over, facing great personal risk. He would swoop down to 6,500 feet, decide in a matter of seconds which of the red rough marker flares was closest to the city center, drop a green flare on top of it, and move back up to a higher altitude.

From high above, the master bomber reviewed the picture. If it seemed effective to him, he gave instructions to the main bomber stream regarding flare pattern and colors. At one-minute intervals, between forty and sixty planes would assume bombing positions. The individual waves carried loads of different bomb types, which had to be dropped in a predetermined order.

3. B-24 Liberator over Germany.

Source: Bildarchiv Preussischer Kulturbesitz.

After seven to twelve minutes, the TIs faded and extinguished. Then the follow-up marker took over. Major fires were now burning on the ground. They lit up the scene well, and either it became possible to mark more precisely, or else everything was buried in smoke and the bombers were more blind than before. If there was a strong wind, then the first and second target indicator markers drifted away. The master bomber monitored all of this, and passed corrections on to the follow-up markers. They dropped flares in a correction color to adjust and fine tune the coordinates of the first set of flares—unless these correction flares were caught in the smoke and thus placed imprecisely. After the flares were replaced and corrected for, the next wave began and the process repeated.

The master bomber, also called the master of ceremonies by his men, was sometimes absent in the elite groups; every person could feel the attack rhythm for himself. But a bombing war is fundamentally imprecise, and someone is needed to coordinate its execution. After the drops, explosions and fires gave off considerable smoke, causing the follow-up markers to miss the smoky initial indicators, and the final wave of bombers would demolish some unlucky village in the vicinity.

The bomber raced across the heavens; the town below was stationary. When the bomb fell, it needed thirty to forty seconds to reach the ground. Because it continued to travel in the direction of the plane's motion, the bomb had to be released a few seconds before the target was reached. But the ballistics of a bombing war were not totally understood, and the wind also had a great effect. Since they were lighter, the incendiary bombs had a more complex trajectory, so they were bundled into clusters to add weight. But the cluster's curve as it fell to earth was not the same curve as that of a 4,000-pound blockbuster mine. And the pilot had a reflex that had to be taken into account, a reflex that caused him to drop the bomb a bit prematurely, just to get it over with, since his life had never been in such jeopardy as it was just then, in the hail of bombs over the target. These split seconds added up from wave to wave to create a "creep-back" effect. The bombers crept back along the approach path for miles. It could not be avoided. This creep-back effect was accounted for in the plans, so the indicator marking was placed ahead of the actual target. During the July 1943 attack on Hamburg, the region around the City Hall was marked so that with the creep-back effect, the working-class residential area of Hammerbrook would be hit. Blind destruction was avoided in every conceivable way.

The bombers, the pathfinders, and the master bomber could all see the targeted city at best as a blurry silhouette in the moonlight. The silver ribbon of the Elbe River could be identified, but it might also have been the Weser. Bombs were dropped into total darkness, marked out by a template of acoustic or light signals. The airborne radar that was later used indicated light-dark contrasts on the cathode ray tube, indicating flat water surfaces and contoured, built-up areas. The bombers dropped their load into this abstraction. Someone else did the aiming. Aiming and destroying were in different people's hands. No one saw the actual target, even though a division of economists, intelligence officers, and aerial-photograph evaluators had compiled an anatomy of Germany, "The Bomber's Baedeker,"[13] a travesty of the well-known Baedeker series of city guidebooks.

In January 1943, shortly before the Battle of the Ruhr, Britain's Ministry of Economic Warfare had issued a catalog by that name. It included a complete inventory of all German cities with more than 15,000 inhabitants. The city target encompassed a circle with a three-mile radius, which at the time was Bomber Command's smallest unit of measure. The catalog listed everything that was produced, stored, and transported; all that was settled, collected, defended, and fortified in the Reich; and the locations of raw materials, books and archives, art treasures, and shrines.

Some kind of connection between the list of targets and the bomb bay was necessary. The air force squadrons leaving their airfields in the evening hours and the operational apparatus that gave them the name of a city and the flight route in a closed room had to remain connected by some thread. Most important, however, was to make sure that no one could intercept that contact. If that happened, it could direct the German fighters to the location of the bombers, which would mean the bombers' certain demise. Until the start of the war, there was no way to create this connection.

The principle of radar positioning was discovered by the British by chance in 1935. A research committee in the British Air Ministry was the first to work with an idea that captured the public imagination: deadly rays against penetrating enemy fliers. It was ascertained that an electromagnetic pulse directed at airplanes did not kill the pilot but was reflected. The metal fuselage bounced it back to the transmitting antenna. If the time this took was multiplied by the velocity of the signal, divided by two, and oriented along the transmission angle, it was possible to identify the point in the air where the plane was located. If the pulse followed it, the course of the plane could be transmitted onto a screen by means of a cathode ray tube.

The fighter units knew they would have no difficulty whatsoever shooting down an approaching bomber with conventional weapons once it had been located. The difficulty was not in hitting it, it was in seeing through fog, clouds, rain, or night. In the summer of 1939, a screen was developed that was compact and light enough to be built into a fighter plane. This first airborne radar system had a range of almost three miles and, in the spring of 1941, raised the British shoot-down rate abruptly. The Germans noticed that their bombing raids on southern England and the Midlands were failing, but they did not understand why. If they had, the German fighters would have quickly come up with their own airborne radar system; those things were copied in no time.

The radio signal that gave away the bomber's position to the fighter pilot also revealed the fighter's own position to the bomber. Radar helped in both aiming and navigating, depending on whether the signal was reflected off one's own aircraft or that of the enemy. The transmission station that sent a pulse to the pilot told him where he was and where he should go. The British absolutely refused to believe their enemy was capable of having radar-guided bombers. A short-frequency signal that reached from Germany to England was technically impossible. No tube in existence could supply enough energy for wavelengths under fifty centimeters.

In the spring of 1940, documents were salvaged from a shot-down Wehrmacht plane that referred to a "Knickebein beam," under the direction of which, according to the documents, one could fly from dusk until dawn. Remote control was an impossibility, as the two most eminent defense physicists, Henry Tizard and Lord Cherwell, knew. Meanwhile, M. L. E. Oliphant, a young Australian, was working in Birmingham on a tube that could supply 9.8 cm shortwaves. That sealed the fate of German cities east of the Weser River; they had only another three years to live.

In June 1940, the British suspected that German attacks might indeed be controlled by some type of radio navigation system. Intercepted conversations between captured pilots alluded to something in their wrecks that under no circumstances was to be found. So the British tried to find it, and the receiver was found right where it belonged, in the blind-landing device. Radar originally served no other purpose than to guide the airplanes to the runways in bad weather.

The technology behind the German blitz, the bombardment of Britain's industrial cities in southern England and the Midlands, was now clear to the British. The enemy used two radio-beam navigation devices, Knickebein and X, the first providing a general direction and the latter, the precise position. The more sensitive X device was used in the aircraft of the German KGr 100, a specially trained pathfinder bomber wing. X was used to identify the target and mark it with flares, so the later waves of bombers could drop their load without having to do much looking around. This was used most successfully in the bombing of Coventry, an attack that Bomber Command never tired of studying.

It took almost two years before the British Gee and Oboe radar navigation models were ready for use. The latter was splendidly accurate; the former provided only rough bearings, but these could be supplied much faster. Both operated using several widely spaced ground stations that transmitted three (Gee) or two (Oboe) beams. An onboard receiver transformed them into an optical or acoustic signal, respectively. Thus the fighter pilot knew approximately where he was in the night sky.

Gee's range was very limited. At an altitude of 23,000 feet, the last signals were received 375 miles from England, and then the aircraft disappeared behind the curvature of the earth. The lower the crew flew, the faster the signal was swallowed up by the horizon. The British managed at best to locate the Ruhr basin, but not any individual cities.

Gee could not be used as an aiming device for bombs, in contrast to Oboe. Operational Research recommended the procedure tested by the KGr 100 pathfinder group. Similar to Knickebein, Gee could provide guidance to a roughly outlined area. During a full moon, it was also possible to make out the contours of built-up areas from a safe altitude. Dropping flare markers offered a target of sorts. Additional fire-raising bombs lit up the target itself, which could then be destroyed with blast munitions. Initially, fire was used just as an indicator, not as the goal in and of itself. In February 1942, Bomber Command practiced this technique over Wales, and in March they took it to Essen.

The Ruhr basin was a sprawling urban landscape with cities practically nested within one another. It was itself a huge target, and Essen, with the centrally located Krupp Works, held a particular fascination.

From December 1941 to February 1942, Bomber Command limited its activities to forty-three night raids because they were waiting for the Gee equipment. And then within four and a half weeks in March and April 1942, 1,500 bombers closed in on the Ruhr, on a mission to level Essen.

By a full moon, the large, reflective surface of Lake Baldeney is Essen's major landmark. Ninety percent of the mechanically flashed photographs after eight raids showed ground elevations outside Essen. There was one fire at Krupp and a few bombs had ruined the nearby railroad lines, but that was the only industrial damage.[14] A small number of apartments were destroyed and sixty-three civilians died; the popular Blumenhof Restaurant in the Gruga Park was reduced to ashes. It had been used as quarters for foreign workers and forced laborers. Twenty-four other cities were unknowingly bombarded. The attack on the night of March 9 alone brought bitter suffering to Hamborn and Duisburg, killing seventy-four people outside of Essen.

Fifty to 75 percent of all bombs dropped in Gee-guided operations did not fall on the intended cities. It was impossible to increase the accuracy. At the limit of its range, Gee had an error tolerance of roughly six miles. Nonetheless, the beams directed the planes to targets and proved that war from the air could tear apart cities, which at the time was more important than which particular city was being torn apart. At least there was some kind of navigation system that marked out an area at night for high-flying bombers. And the bombers could also find their way back to England after the raids.

In addition to the Ruhr, the Baltic and North Sea cities were also Gee territory, which covered Emden, Wilhelmshaven, and Bremen. Lübeck and Rostock were beyond the 350–375-mile range, but there was safe passage up to that point. And from there on out, the moonlight and easily identifiable coastal shapes marked what was soon popularly referred to as the "bomber road."

Bomber Command, which had already tested Gee in May 1941, knew the problems of the radio navigation system from the outset, and delayed its installation. The transmitting beam that told the airplane where it was also betrayed the airplane's position to the enemy—provided they knew the transmission frequency. Because large numbers of airplanes were being shot down (sixty-four planes were lost during the attack on Essen alone), all equipment at some point ended up in enemy hands. And if it proved impossible to determine everything by analyzing the equipment, then attempts were made to press it out of the captured troops. Gee was decoded eight weeks after it had been introduced. Three months later, the Germans learned how to intercept and jam the signal. As of August 1942, the airwaves were so blanketed with jamming signals that Gee could no longer be used for navigation over German territory. In January 1943, the British produced Oboe, which let the destruction of the Ruhr basin resume.

The battle for radar supremacy, a major front in World War II, revealed the cross-border nature of science. The phantom world of radio-beam guidance in the bombing war developed virtually out of nothing. The air was no longer empty; it became a theater. Under the pressure of to be or not to be, the two sides inspired and robbed each other, caught up with and passed each other by, and in the end, aviation became fit to fight a war. Remote guidance was the lynchpin that enabled the creation of the bomber weapon, the destructiveness of which the world had never seen. Everything was now within range. Science, which before and during World War II became such an integral part of warfare for the first time, had doubted from the very beginning that it would decide the war. At most, scientists on both sides hoped for head starts, to stay one step ahead of the enemy.

Over the course of the European air war, there were numerous head starts, but not all of them were enjoyed by the same side. An improved Knickebein became Oboe, Oboe became Würzburg, Würzburg became Window, Window became SN2, which was tricked by H2S. H2S in turn was followed by Naxos and Korfu, which was tripped up by Tinsel. Every radio-guidance device leading to the target met another device blocking the way. This would lead to a new device that worked around the blockage; the enemy quickly captured that one and used it to track down the user, and so on.

Just as cities were the targets of Bomber Command, the bombers were the targets of the fighter force. Neither could see well in the dark. A bomber is camouflaged in the depths of the night sky, and the fighter looks into nothing but a black hole, even at close range. So the Germans swapped the eye for the radio beam. Between the fall of 1940 and the summer of 1943, they created a defensive belt of radar antennae, sound detectors, and searchlights. This belt, hundreds of miles deep, and above it the patrolling fighter wings constituted the "Kammhuber line." In principle, it was supposed to make an old dream come true, rendering the Reich invulnerable.

Inverting the Baldwin motto, no bomber would ever get through: German Luftwaffe chief Göring had staked his reputation on that. The grid of radio and light beams would reveal the attacker. The shell of darkness had been broken; fast as lightning, the fighters would set the slow bomb carriers on fire with a single shot.

On the North Sea coast, from Denmark to the mouth of the Schelde, the Kammhuber line consisted at first of a radar belt. The Freya radar, which had been positioned there since September 1940, sent out signals and could measure distances up to seventy-five miles, but it could not give any information about altitude. It offered a general picture of everything that approached within a range of five vertical miles. Within a year, Freya was supplemented by Würzburg, an antenna mirror that transmitted and received a pencil-thick beam with a 560 MHz frequency—that is, a never-before-attained 53.3 cm wavelength. Würzburg followed flight movements in every dimension, but it was nearsighted. Its twenty-mile range was doubled in 1942 by the Würzburg Giant, with its twenty-foot-diameter parabolic reflector. Both Freya and Würzburg were coupled with searchlights. Whatever they positioned could be bathed in light, provided the night was cloudless.

The farthest distances were penetrated by the radio detection system, which intercepted take-off preparations 335 miles away. In succession, Freya and Würzburg radar trackers picked up the trail of the attackers; that was the first level of the defense system. Incoming data were projected for evaluation by the fighter-control officer onto the "Seeburg table," a translucent glass pane with green and red spots of light. The red light depicted the approaching bomber and the green, a fighter plane circling in the nearest night-fighter sector. The night-fighter sectors were the second level of defense.

General Josef Kammhuber was appointed by Göring to organize an efficient German night-defense system. He divided the airspace off the coast into zones or "boxes" with a radius of about twenty-two miles, which he code-named *Himmelbetten* (literally, "sky beds"). In each of them, a Würzburg mirror monitored the English Channel, while the fighters circled in the sector, awaiting attackers. The night-fighter control officer connected the plots tracking the course of the red and the green spots on the Seeburg table and directed his pilots via radio to the point where the bomber would cross the searchlights. From that point on, the fighter had three minutes to register his target visually and destroy it. If an air battle ensued, it was usually decided in the fighter's favor within at most ten minutes. If the fighter lost the trail, he was not supposed to pursue.

The bomber then got caught in the third level of defense, a chain of searchlights to the east. They covered an area about eighteen miles deep, starting west of Münster and extending into the Ruhr basin. By July 1943, Kammhuber had extended this chain from the Skagerrak Strait between Norway and Denmark to the Marne River in northeastern France. It was in turn divided into quadrants, each of which had three searchlight departments equipped with nine sixty-inch searchlights. The main searchlight in the center formed a cone of light which, together with those around it, could rotate 360 degrees, its movements guided by a Würzburg Giant. Its illumination extended straight upward for eight miles. Behind this belt of light, the *Helle Nachtjagd* (illuminated night hunt) was waiting: fighter squadrons ready to spot the enemy, who would be lit up by the searchlights for about three minutes.

The Kammhuber line, a strategic defense initiative of an unprecedented scale, utterly failed to protect the Reich. It caused the British 4 percent losses, which meant that on average, a crew was brought down after twenty-five sorties. In order to plug the gaps in the line, Kammhuber organized his barriers into echelons, both in width and depth. Each of the roughly one hundred *Himmelbetten* required a service crew of one hundred men. The Seeburg table became too small, so planetariums of the Kammhuber sky were set up. These were mammoth command posts near Arnhem and in Stade, Metz, Döberitz, and Schleissheim. A map of the Reich was superimposed onto a gigantic translucent glass pane marked with a network of quadrants for fighter-plane guidance. On one side of the panel sat intelligence assistants at ascending, bleacherlike rows of desks; on the other side were the fighter-control officers. The approximately forty-five women collecting intelligence were in telephone contact with the radar stations. Using colored spots of light, they projected bomber squadrons that had been detected and located onto the glass pane; the current positions of German planes were also tracked. The officers seated opposite had telephone connections with all the fighter squadrons. On a balcony above them sat the commanding officer, who kept an eye on the overall air operations.

The planetarium of the air war was not seen as a model of the mechanics in the sky; instead, the celestial bodies fighting and bombing outside were the manifestation of the pattern of lights on the glass screen. The concrete of the ceiling of this command bunker was fifteen feet thick and considered bombproof. And yet the Kammhuber system cracked not because it was hit by a bomb but because of millions of metallic foil strips, one inch wide and ten inches long, that were dropped on July 24, 1943. That was the most consequential blow of the entire radar war, and tens of thousands of Hamburg residents paid for it with their lives.

On July 25, 1943, shortly after midnight, the inhabitants of the combat bunker in Stade caught their breath: The coastal radar stations were reporting the unprecedented approach of 11,000 aircraft. The screens were covered with countless blinking blips. The sky must have been littered with speeding bombers, and the Würzburgs at the *Himmelbetten*, the blocks of searchlights, and the flak could not identify where. A cloud of unidentifiable radar echoes had rendered them useless. The fighter planes, fighter-control officers, searchlight companies, and antiaircraft batteries did not know how to respond. For lack of data from the Würzburgs, they were paralyzed and blinded.

The commotion had been caused by strips of tinfoil that the bomber crews had thrown from the bomb bays with their bare hands. They created dipoles that were effective for fifteen minutes, but only on a very narrow frequency band. The dipoles measured half the wavelength of the jammed radar signal—that information had to have been known beforehand. Before the war started, the British had lined their own coast with a chain of radar stations they called the Chain Home. Since the fall of 1940, they had been observing with great interest the installations on the opposite coast. Würzburg radar, the backbone of the Kammhuber line, had been reconnoitered before it even went into service. They had learned of its development and were keen on seeing it in action.

Reconnaissance photos had shown a conspicuous spot on an isolated building façade on a coastal cliff eleven miles northeast of Le Havre. It turned out to be a Würzburg dish. In a daring February 1942 commando action that certainly had the most serious consequences of any throughout the war, the dish was taken down, brought to Britain, and measured. At the same time, the fantastic possibilities of the dipole had been discovered in both England and Germany. The terrible effect that a measly wire or tinfoil strip had on the most elaborate equipment made both countries uneasy. Using it would at the same time inform the enemy of its effects, so it had to be taken into account whether or not the user could handle having it used against him. In January 1943, Göring had prohibited further experiments with this horrific weapon, for which there was no remedy if the enemy were to learn of it. That was plausible to the extent that the Germans had used their radar as a defense against British bombing raids, while the reverse seldom occurred.

The British had a delicate point that they had to protect at all costs against a radar collapse: the Anglo-American landing in Sicily. After having conquered half the island—up to Catania—by mid-July, Winston Churchill now permitted use of the dipole. It could finally be set loose against Kammhuber's air fortification. Waiting had cost 2,200 airplanes, the number of planes shot down by the Kammhuber line between discovery and use of the dipole. The first trial saved one hundred planes that, based on the usual rate of loss, would have been shot down over Hamburg. The Kammhuber line became useless literally overnight, and was scrapped.

The Germans never flew a dipole counterattack, but the final result of the tinfoil operation is nevertheless questionable. Their fighter pilots viewed the Kammhuber line as a liability. It chained them to the control officers, locked them into boxes in the air, and was calibrated for approach tactics that the British had long since changed. In the awkward *Himmelbetten*, only single fighters could be directed against bombers attacking on their own. The technically wonderful ground-control procedure mobilized too little firepower. Meanwhile, the British were advancing in closed formations of five hundred to a thousand airplanes, so a few losses at the defense line was not really cause for all that much worry.

In early 1942, Bomber Command had hardly more than 400 bombers at its disposal; in the battle of Berlin, which started in August 1943, 1,670 airplanes participated.[15] In the second half of 1943, U.S. forces assembled with 1,823 aircraft ready for action in July, and with 2,893 by the end of the year. The Kammhuber line could not stop such an invasion, even if it had covered all of Germany. British fliers ran 36,000 night missions in 1943, and the Americans flew 12,000 during the day. The fighter force needed a more flexible defense, one that took advantage of the abilities and boldness of the pilots. The dipole disaster forced an immediate change. It paid off.

The campaign's first attack on Berlin, on August 23 and 24, 1943, cost Bomber Command the greatest losses—7.9 percent—it had suffered to date. The Eighth U.S. Air Force lost one-third of the planes that had flown the double attack on Schweinfurt and Regensburg on August 17. The next attempt against Stuttgart, on September 6, brought 13 percent losses; the attack on Münster on October 10 and a renewed attack on Schweinfurt on October 14 each brought losses of 20 percent. The U.S. missions were daytime raids. The fighters, wrote Lieutenant Carlyle Darling, were shooting straight from the sun. No one could see them. Others circled the B-17s "like Indians round a wagon-train."[16]

Before taking off, Darling was told the bombs could be dropped anywhere in Germany, even onto a farm. After the introduction of the dipole, it was also true that a plane could be shot down anywhere. The number of planes downed in this phase of the fighting caused Bomber Command, for the second time since 1941, and the Eighth U.S. Air Force, before it had hardly gotten started, to calculate how much its weapon could withstand. The Americans produced 76,985 airplanes between 1942 and 1944;[17] the British, 26,461 in 1943, and another 26,461 the following year. But it was not possible to produce the 100,000 crew members, train them sufficiently, and send them off on missions. Bomber Command had a flying personnel of more than 125,000 men at its disposal throughout the entire war, and 73,741 were lost due to death, injury, or capture.[18] The most casualties it suffered were in 1943, when its losses reached 14,000. According to conventional standards, this was not the upper limit of what could be accepted—it was far beyond that point.

To free the war in the air from its fetters on the ground, both sides had already introduced airborne radar devices toward the end of 1942. The Luftwaffe's Lichtenstein surrendered to the dipole; the Germans disassembled the British H2S after the second time it was used, from a wreck shot down near Rotterdam. The shelf life of technological head starts in the radar war had diminished to six months. But some secrets remained, as well as each side's hopes of developing new secret weapons. The dipole-resistant German airborne radar system SN2 was never studied by the enemy, who had unceasingly jammed Lichtenstein, which therefore was hardly used anymore. Until January 1944, the Germans in turn could not find anything to counter Oboe, the most precise bomb-aiming device of those times, because they simply could not figure it out. When they finally got their hands on the device from a downed plane near Kleve, they constructed eighty interference transmitters within three days, whereupon Oboe always missed the mark. The British Oboe users noticed that they were being jammed, and broadcast over the device's frequency, "Achtung! Achtung! You are a Schweinhund."[19] That made the Germans proud rather than reflective. They knew the enemy knew. They presumed the British would switch to the 9 cm

(3.3 GHz) band, which was considered unjammable. But the British continued to broadcast on the old wavelength; the Germans took them for idiots and thought no more of it. But that signal on the old wavelength was a decoy; Oboe was switched to the short frequency and remained operational.

Oboe, developed in twenty days during the desperate weeks of the spring of 1941 by A. H. Reeves and S. E. Jones, achieved a theoretical target accuracy of almost 300 feet. In practice, it raised the hit quota within a three-mile radius from 20 to 60 percent, though that was only at a distance of 280 miles from the coastal station, which was barely close enough to cover the Ruhr basin. The Ruhr, however, had been leveled to such a degree by thousands of raids that, by the end of the war, bombing it did not really require a precision instrument.

The attack on Hamburg in the summer of 1943 used H2S, which used a revolutionary magnetron tube. H2S was a less precise navigation and aiming radar system, but it functioned independently of the ground. The sample found by the enemy in a wreck near Rotterdam was sent to Telefunken in Berlin but then destroyed in an H2S bombardment. And so developments were put on hold until another H2S system could be captured. The H2S antidote arrived in September 1943: Korfu, a ground-based receiver, and its airborne counterpart, Naxos-Z. They were so sensitive that they started receiving the H2S signals while the English bomber crews were simply warming up the devices twenty minutes before takeoff. All of western Germany was soon totally blanketed by a Korfu network centered in Berlin that monitored the pathfinders, the advance guard of the bomber stream.

The Germans, meanwhile, had 15,000 people employed in the radar war—a war that brought advantages to one side or the other, but for neither a breakthrough. The turning point came not due to the technological perfection of a radar system but when the German fighter fleet ran out of gasoline and men. What the flying aces, worshipped by the masses, managed with their skill and self-sacrifice, the British made up for with curious ideas like Operation Corona. They took advantage of the fact that England was home to many German anti-Nazi emigrants and refugees—speakers of every German dialect. In the ground-to-air radio transmissions that sent, for example, Korfu data on H2S squadrons, confusing voices intervened. They accused the control officers of being British agents who sent the fighters on the wrong course, countermanded orders and redirected night fighters, claiming the true course was an entirely different one.

A small station in the county of Kent that used a captured German transmitter-receiver to transmit phantom courses and orders to return on the high-frequency band proved exceptionally crafty. The headphones of the German pilots hummed with absurd bickering, in which two Germans accused each other of being English frauds. To avoid being tricked, the fighters were given password questions to ask, frequencies were changed, and women and dialect speakers were used in communications, but no matter what the Germans did, the emigrants followed suit. It took a long time before the fighter pilots, who had other things on their minds, could tell the difference between the real orders and the impostors. Until the end of the war, their ears rang with infernal beeping, whistling, Hitler recordings, and march music on all frequencies.

Both sides recognized the ether as the means of directing the transporters to and from their targets. The death and ruin brought by bombers and fighters found their targets solely through ethereal channels. The H2S beams reflected from the enemy aircraft could be traced by Naxos defenders, provided they had the scientific capability to read the data. Strangely enough, it was easier for the current technology to help two minuscule projectiles find each other at an altitude of 20,000 feet while soaring across the night sky than it was to enable identification of an urban district, such as Berlin-Frohnau, or even a city itself, such as Hamburg.

The H2S airborne radar scanned the ground and reflected its elementary features on a cathode ray tube. Water appeared dark, countryside was light, and built-up cities shone brightly on the screen. The navigator could compare the flickering screen with an H2S ground atlas to determine which bright contours contrasted with which light countryside at which dark bodies of water. If the profile that was entered in the atlas resembled that on the flickering screen, then the pilot was over the city that was the intended target.

But in November 1943, it was still a matter of chance if, within Berlin's 350 square miles, an industrial region covering only 5.8 square miles on the eastern end was hit. When the pathfinders were looking for the city on the night of November 26, their turning point was Frohnau, the bulge at the northwestern end of the built-up area adjacent to the Tegel Forest. Because the navigators reacted nervously when they could not shake the antiaircraft searchlights, they missed the bulge and consequently did not mark a target. Completely disoriented, they hoped to find their bearings based on the city's large lake regions, which would show up as dark areas on the radar screen. When at first one and then many dark areas started to appear, they released the first target-indicator flares. The photo evaluation showed that some other industrial area had been marked, miles from the intended target. During the next raid on Berlin on December 2, pathfinders tried to use the radar echoes of three smaller cities in the vicinity for orientation. But they confused Stendal, Rathenow, and Nauen with the very similar-looking reflections of Genthin, Potsdam, and Brandenburg, and ended up marking an area fourteen miles farther south than they had been instructed.

Berlin was still hit, owing to its sheer size. Things went differently on March 3, 1943, when the master bomber approaching from the coast misinterpreted the signals on his H2S, thinking the bare sand banks of the Elbe River during low tide were the Hamburg harbor. He was also led astray by a decoy facility ten miles downstream that had been erected and illuminated by the Germans. It was supposed to look like the Inner Alster Lake and divert the bombardment away from there. Added together, these two errors doomed the small neighboring town of Wedel, which was razed to the ground.

Interpreting H2S signals called for the talents of a born navigator. These were few and far between, and many in Bomber Command claimed that the good crews had already been wiped out by late 1943. The Battle of the Ruhr had consumed a thousand planes, and five thousand men had been killed or, as occasionally happened, captured. By around mid-1943, a total of twenty thousand crew members had fallen, and 3,448 bombers had not returned from enemy territory. By Christmas, those who had managed to survive so far had slim hopes that their luck would continue.

Compared to their colleagues, navigators were callous, sarcastic characters. Surrounded by exploding, crashing airplanes, they scribbled time, position, and altitude of the flak into their logbooks, as well as the hits of the enemy fighters on their now lost comrades. An aluminum capsule in the air is a bad place to fight a war, especially for a bombardier. Faced with a fighter attack, one navigator wrote to his wife, "There isn't a thing you can do about it except fly through it at 30 degrees below zero with the sweat running off your face and freezing on your clothes and the exploding shells blowing the ship around like a cork in a stormy sea."[20]

A bomber crew consisted of a pilot and copilot, bombardier, radio operator, mechanic, and two gunners, all around twenty-one years of age. Even commanding officers were often still in their twenties. Service in the Royal Air Force was mandatory for anyone who received call-up papers, but serving in Bomber Command was voluntary. No one was forced to fly bombing missions. The first pilot had command over the aircraft. He felt responsible for whether the plane returned home or crashed, if not actually, then at least psychologically. He was prepared for all of the kinds of pilot errors that could get the plane and its crew blown to pieces. He could not be concerned with what was happening on the ground; his domain was strictly the air. If the crew grew into a team and studied and tested their equipment, their chances of staying alive increased. Training and prayer were all that helped.

The plane could not go off course, and contact with the other aircraft had to be maintained. The instruments had to be monitored, and the night fighter needed to be sighted at the latest before he dropped into the blind spot and fired. Squeezed into a very tight space and overtired, on a monotonous night approach that might or might not become deadly at any moment, everyone had to remain vigilant and understand their instruments. Some pilots forbade talking on board. At bombing altitude, the temperature dropped to under minus fifty degrees, so that even the U.S. airmen with their heated uniforms suffered frost damage. The heated cockpit helped little, and was of no help in the machine-gun turrets.

The aerial gunner sat for six to eleven hours with arms and legs pressed together in a Plexiglas turret dome, peering motionless into the night. The copilot shared the pressure that weighed on the pilot; both of them could not let their eyes leave the instrument panel. Besides the cold, fatigue was the bitter enemy, especially on the way home after the bomb drop. The profound need for rest led pilots or gunners to doze off, and their fate met them in their sleep. Because of the much higher internal pressure of the body than the atmosphere of the plane, a wounded airman bled very heavily. If a crew tried to replace a wounded or killed pilot, the situation often ended with a crash.

The bombardier did his job lying on his stomach, getting a fix on the target indicator through the bombsight. U.S. Lieutenant William Lockhart of the 381st Bomb Group reported that he was hit while getting up. "It was like being hit in the face by a brick, like someone hitting you with a baseball bat; the physical impact of being hit and stopping it with your body was considerable. A piece of shell hit me in the chin, passed through the cheek, and lodged behind the left eye."[21] Lockhart found the escape hatch to bail out. Many did not, because the airplane would lose its horizontal position as it went down and would start to spin. Sergeant Bert Nixon, aerial gunner in No. 199 Squadron RAF, said the hit on his plane was like "a giant hand [that] took hold of us and there was a huge shuddering and shaking sensation, just like a massive dog shaking a rat."[22] Nixon was thrown across his machine guns, which started firing; he saw huge flames spurting from the fuse panel between himself and the mid-upper turret, managed to put on his parachute, and was the only member of his crew to abandon the plane before it crashed. That was his first raid. During the same attack on Berlin, on August 23, 1943, a comrade from No. 158 Squadron had been hit in the face, and the blood obscured his vision, preventing him from finding the hatch.

The aerial gunner was positioned in the tail, had no cover, and was at the mercy of fighter planes approaching from the rear. In the second half of 1943, the Germans had practiced a method of shooting down planes that they called *Schräge Musik* ("jazz" or, literally, "oblique music"). A pair of twenty-millimeter cannons were mounted on the aft fuselage of the fighter plane at an angle of sixty-five to eighty degrees, so the pilot could aim upward through a reflector sight and fire. This firing angle allowed him to slip into the blind spot beneath the bomber. When he fired, the entire length of the bomber flew into the burst of fire.

The crew did not notice what was happening until the shots hit. The fighter aimed at the point between the two wing engines, near the fuel tanks. After a few seconds they ignited, and the flaming trail then set the tail on fire. The only chance the pilot had was to go into a nosedive and hope to smother the flames. That was not successful very often; a bomber is a far more effective incendiary than the city it is supposed to set on fire. All crews were familiar with the orange blaze of a burning Lancaster transforming into surges of fire rolling over and overtaking one another like balls. Getting grazed on the wing by these unlucky comrades was itself a serious problem.

The scene that the attacker confronted over heavily defended areas such as Berlin or the cities in the Ruhr basin was total disaster. In a cauldron of deafening noise and flames, the crew was held captive by antiaircraft fire from below, fighters behind or above, and the danger of collision ahead. After a neverending flight through a dark void, the sky above the target was suddenly filled with airplanes, bright as day from searchlights, and charged with a barrage of flak fire, a salvo of machine-gun fire from the fighter planes, bombs whooshing down, and sparkling colored markers and flares.

Bombers had a strong dislike for anything coming from above. On overcast nights, the light from flak battery searchlights struck the cloud cover from below, not penetrating it but flooding it with light. The night fighters called the bright white surface the "shroud." If they climbed to an altitude above the bomber stream, it looked black against the brightness. The fighters marked the area with tongues of flame, which sank down attached to parachutes. Seeing those flares caused a shudder among the bomber crews, as they felt like they had been ambushed; the fighters knew they were coming and were lying in wait. The crews said it felt like running naked through a busy train station, hoping not to be seen. "It was like suddenly coming out of a dark country lane into a brightly lit main street."[23] There was heavy fire from above. Being marked was apparently much worse than being fired on.

The same was true regarding the antiaircraft artillery. It caused less damage than the fighter planes but inspired greater fear. The eighty-eight-millimeter (3.46") standard flak gun shot a 16.5-pound shrapnel grenade about four miles into the air. At detonation, it burst into 1,500 jagged fragments that flew in all directions at a high velocity. A plane about ten yards from the detonation point could be downed, and at a distance of two hundred yards it could be severely damaged. Aiming a shot from a flak cannon and carrying out a well-aimed bombardment were both difficult for the same reason. A grenade needed six seconds to reach a bomber flying at 13,000 feet. When flying at a velocity of 180 mph, for instance, the plane moved almost a third of a mile while the grenade was in the air. A device on the cannon calculated this factor and corrected the target coordinates, but a barrage brought even better results. It was carpet bombing in reverse. The statistical probability of getting hit was low in both cases, but for the air crews, passing through a hail of shrapnel was nerve-wracking, as U.S. Air Force staffs were well aware.

The flak made it difficult to take aim precisely, forced the squadrons to higher altitudes, and pressed them to turn back before completing the mission. The approach corridor had been calculated in

4. Flares and flak fireworks, Berlin, January 1945.
Source: Bildarchiv Preussischer Kulturbesitz.

advance by the defenders, and they kept up a constant burst of fire. Getting caught in this barrage, as members of the crews reported, was like confronting a giant "giving you a kick up the backside with his seven-league boots."[24] The shock waves alone from the grenades exploding all around made the planes quake.

The dramatics of the flak weaponry impressed the cities that were defended as well as the bomber fleets that were attacked. The searchlights and cannons were the actors. As always, it was the light, the guiding beam, that was the harbinger of death. A large battery in 1943 brought together up to seventy searchlights and 160 flak cannons. The beam of the sixty-inch standard searchlight reached eight miles high, with a luminous intensity of 1.3 billion candle-power. Such a piece of equipment was a weapon in itself, because a plane caught in its glare was blinded and no longer capable of making a precision bomb drop.

The radar-guided lead searchlight stretched up perfectly vertically, and its beam was slightly bluish. Once it made contact with an airplane, the beam slanted toward it, and twenty other searchlights followed. Together they formed a cone of light, and the bomber appeared to ride at its moving vertex. Up to thirteen such cones could be clustered in a city like Essen. Each one could track one airplane—a minuscule portion of the entire force. The bomber riding atop the cone would then either be perforated by the cannons or it wouldn't; but its specific fate did not affect the bombardment.

For the most part, larger formations of bombers demanded larger batteries of antiaircraft artillery and vice versa. This did not affect the loss percentage. But it was the theatrical element that counted, and Hitler and the gauleiters continually pressed to set up fighter and flak defenses in the cities. The bombing war was about enduring the death of others. The next time it will be me. It was a performance geared to inner experiences. Corpses cannot surrender, only people who do not want to die. The air drama of the flak was similar: the urban residents saw not a massacre but a battle taking place, and so did the fliers.

"Suddenly your own little bit of sanctuary in the sky where you thought you were safely hidden was engulfed in brilliant and dazzling light," wrote Sergeant G. K. Powell of No. 102 Squadron RAF.

> The aircraft was caught like a fly in a net trying desperately to extricate itself before the gunners could get a bearing on it. Not many survived such attention from searchlights and flak. The only hope was to get clear before the searchlights could form a cone. On a number of occasions I observed bombers held in cones of searchlights and watched helplessly as the shell bursts got nearer the aircraft until suddenly flames appeared and sometimes a violent explosion.[25]

Lieutenant R. B. Leigh of No. 156 Squadron RAF remembered the mere sight of the flak searchlights surrounding Berlin in rings as "probably the most frightening experience of my lifetime."[26] As a bombardier, lying on his stomach in the nose of the Lancaster in the final approach of a seemingly endless run-up, he saw the city bristling with its flak cannons and awaited instructions from the master bomber who, before the release, would order them to fly "straight and level," not to dive away. And he expected to be blown to pieces. The pilot might instead evade the searchlights out of fear and let the vibrating, howling aircraft drop six or seven thousand feet. That tore at his ears but saved him from the fate that Wing Commander D. H. Burnside ordered his crew from No. 427 Squadron into over Essen.[27] Their Wellingtons flew straight into the flak grenades, shrapnel killed the navigator instantly, the radio operator lost one of his feet, and the load was released.

At times, half the Wellingtons did not return from their missions because they lacked self-sealing fuel tanks and thus caught fire immediately. The crews of such older planes were literally flying in their coffins. For the destruction of Berlin, the heavy Stirlings and Halifaxes were called in once again to carry the tonnage needed for the "Big City." The Halifaxes clattered around relatively low, without the option of escaping to a higher altitude when the hunters attacked.

During the months of the Battle of Berlin, the fighters honed their new tactics, the *Wilde Sau* (Wild Boar) and the *Zahme Sau* (Tame Boar). The fighter pilots saw Kammhuber's radar artistry as a strange black magic. The hunt was a sport, and the hunter and his single-engine bird were together an individual fighter. The bomb transporters moved in armored columns along set routes to set destinations, and they overcame their fear, held out, and offered themselves up. These were challenged by the hunter, the fighter, with the skills of a fencer: a good eye, dexterity, cunning. The pains taken by the bomber to find the target did not worry the fighter. He knew where the bomber was. He did not even have to look for his opponent, because he knew where it had to go. In principle, it could be expected over its target.

Kammhuber had pulled the fighter defense out of the cities because flak does not distinguish between friend and foe. The methods of the Wild Boar again divided the sky into levels. The flak scanned the lower level, since its range was limited anyway. The fighters swept the sky above 15,000 feet. They divided up the spheres with the flak commanders. Either the flak forced the bombers higher into the fighter's hunting grounds, or they were chased down by the fighters into the flak.

In the higher air-combat space, the fighter enjoyed a natural advantage but was outnumbered. This was not a duel. Curving and diving, blinded by the beam of the searchlights, the fighter found himself wedged in between bombers next to and above him. Over the course of months, the battle turned into a slaughter. When the Berlin campaign was launched on August 23, 1943, there had been 149 casualties among bomber pilots, compared to three lost fighters. Throughout all of August, Germans fighters downed 290 bombers.

Six months later, they had to endure almost that many losses themselves, but could not replace them.

By the summer of 1943, the fighter pilots knew what the city they were flying over would look like an hour later on the ground. They pitted themselves against squadrons who made pyres out of cities whose names meant something: Aachen, Münster, Nuremberg. The Luftwaffe put a company of problem cases in charge of the Wild Boar—social misfits, disciplinary cases, old warhorses—people who had nothing to lose and who fought their final battle above the city. The tactics of Tame Boar, introduced in January 1944, on the other hand, involved lining the approach route and the way home. The fighter planes followed the bomber stream, threaded themselves in, overtook their victims, turned around, and raced into them in a frontal attack, firing in the split second before a collision, then going into a steep climb. It forced the bombers to be concerned more with their own survival than with bombardment.

Bomber Command assigned a series of thirty missions to their crews. In 1943, there was a one-in-six chance of coming out alive; in November, 20 percent made it. In statistical terms, a loss rate of 3.3 percent per raid meant that two-thirds would not survive the thirty missions. The crews became fatalists. Either you made it or you didn't. You could improve your odds by staying awake and keeping in contact with one another in order to react quickly if a battle situation suddenly developed. But just as helpful were lucky charms or urinating together against the back wheel before takeoff and upon return, as thanks for an extension of your stay in this world.

The boyish candidates who went on their thirty sorties because they were adventurous and were told that Bomber Command would win the war soon had incredible horror stamped into their features. One hundred silent men walked to takeoff with lips tightly pressed. You could not give up a tour without looking like a weakling and letting down your buddies. In the face of direct death, there seemed not to be any sensibility for the indirect death in the bomb bay. Releasing the bombs did not stir up any feelings of uneasiness. The mission included a handful of ironclad truths: The Germans were the first to kill civilians in London, Birmingham, and Sheffield. They tormented residents in the areas they occupied. Bombing saved the bloodshed that ground operations would bring, and it shortened the duration of the war.

Worrisome words were avoided during briefings prior to takeoff. A participant in the attack on Essen on July 25 and 26, 1943, reported years later: "At that point we were not aware that we were bombing civilians as such, because we had always been given an aiming point like the docks, or a rubber factory, or railway yards. But on this occasion the briefing said that we were to bomb the workers' houses or residential quarters and this came as something of a personal shock."[28]

Pilots and navigators who had entered into their logbooks a season earlier that they left the burning city of Essen as "an immense pot, boiling over,"[29] whose glow of the fires looked like a red sunset even 150 miles away, did not have to be told about the havoc their weapons had wrought down on the ground. But their look back could not be separated from their relief at having escaped the two thousand flak artillery that surrounded Essen, which would be remembered as the best-defended city of all.

Sometimes discontent welled up. The No. 76 Squadron stationed in Yorkshire had misgivings about the mission to Wuppertal because it would hit thousands of evacuees who had fled there after having been bombed out of cities in the Ruhr basin. Such objections were always appeased with reference to the military targets. And there were in fact two textile factories in Wuppertal that produced fabric for parachutes. The navigator's remark during the briefing, "Women and children first again,"[30] was studiously ignored, yet it sank in.

After their mission, the bomber crews returned to their home bases in quiet garrison towns and villages where the residents were warmhearted and well disposed toward the airmen. Landing, of all things, turned out to be a hurdle many of them failed to clear. Overcome with fatigue and fear, with empty fuel tanks, in foggy, overcrowded airspace, many of the returning soldiers were killed in a crash landing after all they had already gone through.

Lying awake at night, they brooded over what had happened. The stress of the battle had faded, the cohesion of the crew that held during the mission was interrupted for a short moment, and the navigators and bombardiers turned into young boys, imagining what it now looked like miles below their battlefield. The target photographs were evaluated as soon as the fliers returned, so crews that knew nothing about what they had fought so hard for could get an idea of their accomplishments. At night, this idea became filled with emotion.

According to surveys, three-quarters of the bomber crews felt no animosity whatsoever toward the German civilian population,[31] or at least no more than that expressed by the empty beer bottles they dropped with the bombs as a sign of disrespect. The five hundred

Essen inhabitants who had been mutilated and burned on the night of July 25 were also by no means too abstract to imagine. It had been the sixth operation over Essen since March, and the reports were full of clouds of smoke that rose to 20,000 feet, and the panorama of fire across the city, which was the most impressive ever seen. A pathfinder who in retrospect claimed to have had considerable qualms about bombing women, children, and hospitals afterwards fittingly asked: "But to whom could you express such doubts? . . . If we believed it morally wrong, should we have spoken out to our squadron commanders and refused to participate? What would have been the result? Court martial!"[32]

Thoughts about legal consequences remained in the subjunctive mood, and went on ad absurdum. The military court punished the legal conscience. A totally acceptable reluctance, on the other hand, was asserted by the master bomber of the attack on Dresden when, three months earlier, he was ordered to lead the attack on Freiburg. He had studied at the University of Freiburg and had many friends who lived around the cathedral, which had been selected as the orientation point for the bombardment. He refused to lead the mission, which everyone could understand. He had never been to Dresden and regretted the destruction of such a beautiful city, but he carried it out because he lacked any personal reasons not to.

2. STRATEGY

"Some . . . are curable and others killable."
—WINSTON CHURCHILL

The attack on civilian housing is supposed to end the war faster. Because it sets its sights on decreasing the enemy's staying power and morale, the strategy is called "morale bombing." Civilians are not military targets, but if they produce anything for the military or live near the production sites, it is a different story. In an industrialized war, all industries are war industries. Whoever works and lives in those surroundings is participating in the war effort. They are producing combat weapons and combat will. Strategic bombing views the seat of those sources of strength as a second battlefield. It is both a piece of ground and a dwelling place. Between 1940 and 1943, ideas take shape to create, from the air, annihilation zones on the ground to destroy both the means and morale to continue the war. Those ideas fail. Ultimately, Germany has to be conquered on the ground, yard by yard, in a seven-month campaign. As tactical support for that bloody campaign, the heretofore greatest volume of bombs by far is dropped on the largest area, with the highest number of human casualties.

THE PERCENTAGE OF THE AIR CREWS who lost their lives exceeded by far the loss ratio of the targets of their attacks. Of Bomber Command's 125,000 crew members, there were 55,000 casualties, or 44 percent. The number of people they killed is uncertain. Figures vary between 420,000 and 570,000.[1] That would represent roughly 1.5 percent of the urban population.

Such a comparison makes no sense, of course, because the crews died in combat with military adversaries: the fighters and the flak. The troops were mustered, either voluntarily or by conscription, according to the customs of war. The residents of the towns and cities were fighting for their survival, but they fought against no one. They were neither willing nor equipped to do so, and up to that time, no customs of war confronted them with the force of arms.

The decision to use the unprecedented and unusual tactic of bombing cities and civilians was made by a small number of men—but not in secret. The means deployed during World War II were approved on all sides by the people, parliaments, and armed forces. Everyone thought that what was done was right. Neither German nor British nor American civilian populations disapproved of the deliberate attack of enemy civilians. Such actions were expected throughout the world, and self-protection was drilled extensively. Cellars, gas masks, sirens, blackouts, and fire-extinguishing drills were emergency procedures familiar to millions and millions of Europeans. They were described in detail in everything from light fiction to military doctrine. This is why, regarding the hell whose arrival had been anticipated for twenty years, it is less surprising that it finally broke out at all than that it confronted such extensive material difficulties. It was supposed to be much easier.

The first two major cities attacked by the German Luftwaffe were Warsaw, on September 25, 1939, and Rotterdam, on May 14, 1940. These raids employed from the outset the very force that would avenge itself so bitterly on the Germans: fire. The report of German Air Fleet Command 4 looked just like instructions from the British Bomber Command: The demolition or high-explosive bomb lays the groundwork for the incendiary bomb.[2] That forces the population into the cellars while the houses burn above their heads. Whoever does not leave the cellars will suffer death by asphyxiation. "Moral strength to resist is totally broken by the direct experiences."

Eliminate the water supply with the initial strike! "Incendiary bombs should be dropped, not little by little but en masse," so more fires start than firefighters can handle.

The fires in Rotterdam merged within four days into a mass conflagration. The Old Town, full of nooks and crannies and mostly wooden buildings, caught fire from explosions, without a single incendiary bomb having been dropped. It spread by itself like a continuous fire bridge. Shocked and caught unawares, the residents did not risk intervening, and the low number of firefighters lacked sufficient equipment.

These two cases familiarized air strategists with the combustion properties of residential districts, but it did not familiarize them with the aerial bombing war. Both cities had already been terrorized by ground operations aimed to force an already defeated enemy to capitulate. In earlier times, these cities would have been besieged and hammered with artillery fire, as General Moltke did in Paris in 1870, during the Franco-Prussian War. Strategic bombing was something totally different; it aimed to win the entire war from the air.

Winston Churchill pioneered this concept. When he was minister of munitions, he had planned a thousand-bomber attack on Berlin, for 1919. If the Germans had held their western front in 1918, a new front would have opened up there, which would have been decisive for the war. He wrote this in 1925, evidently relieved that it had not been necessary. "The campaign of 1919 was never fought; but its ideas go moving along." The use of the air made it possible that "death and terror could be carried far behind the lines of the actual armies, to women, children, the aged, the sick, who in earlier struggles would perforce have been left untouched." For the first time, "one group of civilized men" was afforded "the opportunity of reducing their opponents to absolute helplessness." Helplessness meant being completely at the mercy of the bomb. The forty-nine-year-old Churchill added to the catalog of vulnerabilities imaginary weapons that scientists were only gradually starting to conceive. "Might not a bomb no bigger than an orange be found to possess a secret power to destroy a whole block of buildings—nay to concentrate the force of a thousand tons of cordite and blast a township at a stroke?" An enemy city might be hit hard by flying objects "without a human pilot," or by methodically prepared plague, anthrax, and smallpox viruses. If only one of the warring parties were equipped with this, it could enslave the others. And if all sides had access, the result would be "the ruin of the world." War unfortunately stands "ready, if called on, to pulverize . . . what is left of civilization."[3]

The trials carried out during World War I demonstrated not the possibility but the impossibility of achieving anything even remotely resembling total destruction. On January 19, 1915, German zeppelins dropped explosives along the Norfolk coast wherever they perceived clusters of lights.[4] They thereby killed two men and two women, and injured sixteen others. In the course of the year, they returned nineteen times, and killed a total of 498 civilians and 58 military personnel. London was hit for the first time on the night of May 30, and seven were killed. Twin-engine Gothas and four-engine *Riesen*, or Giants, continued the attacks in 1917 and 1918, killing 836 and injuring 1,994. Half the planes, which flew day raids, failed to find London; one in five was shot down. British reprisal in 1918 killed 746 Germans and injured 1,843. All of these deaths by bombing amounted to just a fraction of the annual number of traffic deaths. Churchill's results were even more modest: on the night of August 25, 1940, his long-contemplated Berlin plan was carried out.

Because he did not have a thousand bombers at his disposal, he sent fifty Hampdens and Wellingtons. They faced strong headwinds, which required more fuel than had been provided for. Consequently, three planes went down and three others crashed into the North Sea on their return trip. With that, 12 percent of the expedition corps had been lost. The Germans lost a wooden shack in the town of Rosenthal, and two people were slightly injured. Churchill had personally ordered Bomber Command to execute the operation as a heavy attack.

The impetus for the attack was a trifle that was given two lines in the diary of Churchill's private secretary John Colville: "*Monday, August 26th*: . . . London has been bombed—by a single aircraft on Saturday night."[5] It later turned out that there had been twelve planes that had gotten lost and, contrary to orders from Hitler and Göring, had dropped a couple of bombs on docks, thereby causing "very minor damage." That was how the *Times* reported it on Monday. "And in retaliation," noted Colville, "we sent eighty-nine bombers over Berlin last night."[6] Bomber Command's report on Churchill's telephone orders said "he wished us to be fully prepared and hoped we had adequate resources 'in the bag' and that there would be no difficulties. He felt that it was no good tackling this job with small forces and was averse to administering 'pin pricks.' "[7]

Chief of Air Staff Sir Cyril Newall had not been prepared for such an operation, especially since the weather was unfavorable. Anyway, an attack on Leipzig was being organized. Newall gave orders to go ahead with everything as planned, with the proviso to avoid "indiscriminate bombing of the civil population."[8] But Arthur Harris, then Air Vice Marshal in Bomber Command, convinced Newall to follow the wishes of the prime minister. It was a unique opportunity for retribution, according to Harris, that would not come again very soon. In fact, however, the attack was hardly noticed in Berlin.

"Enemy aircraft over Berlin," wrote Goebbels in his diary.[9] "Several hours of air-raid alarm. We observed the major flak barrage. A majestic spectacle." But other than that, he was more concerned about the U.S. presidential elections that November. "America fluctuates between resignation and military intervention. If Roosevelt is reelected the United States will certainly enter the war." For the meantime, though, the weather was more important. "Perhaps it will finally improve and give our Luftwaffe its much-longed-for opportunity for a major raid."

France surrendered on June 22, 1940; England fled the continent, leaving its ordnance at the Channel ports. Only the troops—without their arms—could be evacuated. And yet Churchill refused to make peace with Hitler. His last remaining weapons were the fleets, both sea and air. The Germans decided to attempt landing on the island, and they also bombarded the coastal defenses, harbors, airports, and military airfields. Only Britain's Fighter Command could stop them. It cannot not win the war, as Churchill declared, but it can definitely lose it. If the fighter force was worn down by the attackers, the only remaining option would be for the Navy to escape by sea, leaving England defenseless. The Germans who wanted to land could take the ferry. Churchill swore to soften up British beaches with mustard gas in such a case.

In the course of the August battle, the Luftwaffe shot down almost twice as many British airplanes as it lost itself, but the Germans were not able to break the bitter resistance.[10] The losses hit both sides hard, but for the British it exhausted their only remaining defense. It was at this watershed of the war that the decision was made to launch the Strategic Air War. With that, modernity gave itself up to a new, incalculable, and uncontrollable fate, which began to gain momentum. In the summer of 1940, war no longer pit armed forces against each other, but rather pit armed forces against civilian quarters—cities. In contrast to the raids on Warsaw and Rotterdam, the new campaign against the cities was not a desperate measure taken in the chaos of war. It was a deliberate strategy; it was the war. This new war had long existed on paper, but that was all. The strategic weapon was an idea; no one possessed it. The political decision to realize this weapon followed, though it took years to acquire the means to implement it.

The first totally industrialized war, from 1914 to 1918, was followed by a general reflection on the military future. The slaughter at the Belgian-French western front was not to be repeated. The fighters at the front lines were killed off age group by age group, by the ability of both sides to produce a neverending supply of machine guns, ordnance, and artillery munitions. Military strength was no longer based on the military abilities and skills of officers and rank and file but on the capacity of industry to supply the front with more and better weapons. The war of the future would not be decided at the theater of war but far behind the lines, in the factories and dwellings of the workers. Air Marshal Hugh Trenchard, father of the Royal Air Force, could not have expressed it better in 1928:

> To attack the armed forces is . . . to attack the enemy at its strongest point. On the other hand, by attacking the sources from which these armed forces are maintained, infinitely more effect is obtained. In the course of a day's attack upon the aerodromes of the enemy perhaps 50 aeroplanes could be destroyed; whereas a modern industrial state will produce 100 in a day—and production will far more than replace any destruction we can hope to do in the forward zone. On the other hand, by attacking the enemy's factories, then output is reduced by a much greater proportion.[11]

Once military production became a military objective, then all production became military production. What went into an airplane that was not produced in the aircraft factory? Sheet metal, ball bearings, rubber, lubricating oil, display instruments—and in all of this, skilled labor. In short, what went into an airplane was everything located in a city and that which made up its essence. In order not to cut the effectiveness of his weapons in half, Trenchard totally redefined his targets: "Air attacks will be directed against any objective which will contribute effectively towards the destruction of the enemy's means of resistance and the lowering of his determination to fight."

Destroying the means of resistance and determination to fight meant winning the war behind the battle lines. The best instrument for penetrating into this zone without resistance was the bomber. Bombers, cities, and war have since then become inextricably linked. Waging war now means first and foremost bombing cities.

That is the message of the Trenchard Doctrine, the raison d'être of the Royal Air Force.

What was doctrinaire about the doctrine was its tacit presumption, which pacifist British Prime Minister Stanley Baldwin had expressed in the alarming sentence that "the bomber will always get through"—that is, get through to the enemy. This impressive and catchy slogan of 1930s appeasement took air-offense strategists at their word. Militarists and antimilitarists came together in believing the same fallacy. But since time immemorial, everything that has wanted to get through has met up against something that has blocked its way.

When Bomber Command commenced its strategic air war, it quickly became clear that the bombers by no means got through. This is why the strategic air war was launched not by its doctrinaire and prophet but by the thing that managed to get through most easily, without a doctrine, without a strategy or a plan, but simply because it was at the French coast of the English Channel: Göring's Luftwaffe. From there, a bombardment of the cities of southern England and the Midlands was launched in September 1940 that had killed thirty thousand people by March 1941. A threshold of the Modern Age had been crossed, and to now there was no way back. There was a strange explanation for the political mechanics that triggered this step.

When Goebbels reviewed the state of the public mood on August 26, 1940, the day after Churchill's unsuccessful reprisal, he found "all of Berlin up in arms,"[12] since they had endured four hours of air-raid alarm. Luckily, there had been hardly any damage, except for "two incendiary bombs." "But 1,500 bombs fell on England!" He added that "incredible anger towards the British" was brewing. Since the Germans responded to such inconsequential attacks with contemptuous apathy, fits of rage had broken out—artificially—among party and government personnel. Goebbels himself was incredibly pleased: "Now Berlin too is in the midst of the war, and that's a good thing." Churchill, just as interested in the Berlin front, pressed Air Chief Marshal Newall to try again. "Now that they have begun to molest the capital"—they were still referring to the twelve scattered planes from that Saturday night—"I want you to hit them hard. And Berlin is the place to hit them."[13]

On the night of Wednesday, September 4, 1940, the Görlitzer train station in the Kreuzberg district of Berlin was hit, killing ten. Two nights later, some planes reached Siemensstadt in the northwest of the city. Goebbels noted, shaking his head, that no one had felt the urge to go into the air-raid shelters, as Hitler had ordered. Hitler had not gone to a shelter either; he "wants to be right here when Berlin is being bombed. He is really charged up." A decision was made sometime between Saturday and Tuesday: "The air war will perhaps enter its more intensified stage by the end of this week. Then things will start happening over London." Because it was assumed that Churchill would respond, Goebbels added, "the valuable paintings in the Reich Chancellery have been brought to safety. I do not think the British will hold out very long."

Nothing happened by Thursday, September 5. "At the moment, the Führer is still holding back. How much longer?" People reckoned with a victory in the fall. "If the war continues through the winter, then it's almost dead certain that we'll see America enter it. Roosevelt is a slave to the Jews." The day before, Hitler spoke in the Sportpalast about the bombing war: It had been going on for three months already, at night, since no Englishman could make it over the English Channel during the day. The bombs fell indiscriminately and randomly on civilian residences, on train stations, on villages. Wherever a light was burning a bomb was dropped. It had been endured in the hope that this nonsense would stop, but that was misinterpreted as a sign of weakness. Now they would receive a response, night after night.

> And should the Royal Air Force drop two thousand, or three thousand, or four thousand kilograms of bombs, then we will now drop 150,000; 180,000; 230,000; 300,000; 400,000; yes, one million kilograms in a single night. And should they declare they will greatly increase their attacks on our cities, then we will erase their cities! We will put these nighttime pirates out of business, God help us! The hour will come that one of us will crack, and it will not be National Socialist Germany.[14]

Breaking staying power and morale by obliterating cities breathed of pure Trenchard Doctrine. The German airborne forces were not geared for such a strategy; they were a tactical force designed to support ground troops, blaze the trail for motorized armed forces, and maintain the flexibility of the ground war. They never had armed and armored strategic bombers that could cover the entire area of the British island. Only because they took off from airfields near the English Channel were they within reach of the opposite shore, with cover from fighter planes. From the territory of the German Reich,

Hitler could have reached hardly a city. But as the die was cast, he had an offensive weapon at his command that could realize Trenchard's dream at a limited distance. No one else was in a position to do that. It was possible, so it was done.

A thousand-aircraft fleet—three hundred bombers accompanied by fighter planes—thundered toward London in close formation, in two tiers at 13,000 and 19,600 feet. From Calais they reached their destination in no time. It was the afternoon of September 7; Göring had announced the docks and the city center as the targets. The code word was "Loge," the fire god in Wagner's *Rhinegold*.

The bombing shifted and came down on the densely populated East End. Three hundred civilians died and 1,300 were seriously injured. Massive conflagrations lit up the night when the fleet returned and let loose another bombing raid that lasted until daybreak. The British government thought the invasion was approaching and let the church bells ring. In fact, however, the invasion faded more and more into the background during this dense series of air raids over the following days. Hitler's appetite for an air war was whetted, and he told Erich Raeder, naval commander in chief, of his plans. Ships might not be necessary, and victory would be sought from the air.

The German military attaché in Washington cabled that the U.S. Department of War thought the British chances looked dismal and that their imminent collapse was becoming apparent.[15] Morale was suffering tremendously; the effect of the bombing of London was like an earthquake. That is precisely what Göring had doubted at the start of the attack. "Do you think," he asked Luftwaffe General Hans Jeschonnek, his chief of staff, "that Germany would give up if Berlin were in ruins?"[16] Jeschonnek thought British morale was far more fragile than that of the Germans. "That is where you are wrong," countered Göring, who was not convinced that England would be ready to surrender by the end of September, although his opinion changed after Germany's fabulous early results. Hitler was also uncertain. Goebbels, joined by the generals at a meeting with Hitler, affirmed impertinently that "the military shares my standpoint that a city of eight million will not be able to take it very long." Then he asked Hitler, "will England capitulate?"[17] Hitler did not respond; the Führer was unable to make a decision at that time.

The next day, Goebbels, too, was confronted with obvious questions. The British were flying deeper into the Reich. "Main attack objective is still Berlin. And for us it is London. That is the momentary military situation."[18] After only two weeks, the British situation seemed paradoxical: "to attack us at a position in which they themselves are so incredibly vulnerable!" Berlin was at a safe distance, but London was virtually within sight. There had to be a reason for that.

The air battle of British Fighter Command versus the German fighter force was proceeding shakily enough; why did Churchill need to make the capitals into a second front? Goebbels was naïve, declaring, "The British are making error after error."[19] Germany, on the other hand, gloated. The tabloids screamed: "London is Burning Left and Right"; "Death and Ruin in London"; "Reprisal Raids on London Continuing Day and Night." Goebbels noted, "London circles declare that the city will be returning to cave life" and that the city was suffering "the fate of Carthage, little by little."[20] Rich and poor were fighting for space in the air-raid shelters in the underground stations, he continued. "Desperate screams in world public opinion. But nothing will help now."[21]

Starting on September 9, 1940, and continuing for fifty-seven nights, roughly 160 bombers at a time attacked London, sometimes during the day as well. On September 15, the Germans lost one-quarter of the bombers they detailed; on September 27, forty-seven were shot down by RAF fighter planes. In October, Göring ordered fighter pilots to be retrained on fighter-bombers, which could avoid searchlights and antiaircraft artillery by flying at higher altitudes. Because they lacked the necessary load capacity and precision, however, this reduced the effectiveness of the bombing. On November 14, Göring had planes head for Plymouth, Portsmouth, and Southampton on the coast, as well as the cities further north, up to Liverpool. Coventry suffered the worst damage. "That is a city that has truly been eradicated," wrote Goebbels. "It is nothing but ruins."[22]

Of 328,000 residents, 568 died; this ratio corresponds roughly to Dortmund, where 693 of 537,000 residents died from the bombing on May 5, 1943. The number of deaths was to increase tenfold by the end of the war, but in any case, Dortmund's tragedy was not remembered. Coventry, however, was the ultimate rallying cry in 1940. "This case has caused an incredible stir throughout the world,"[23] noted Goebbels. "In the United States people are very upset." In Germany, the event was reviewed less emotionally. After looking at the photographs of destroyed streets and buildings that were published in the Nazi organ *Völkischer Beobachter*, people took note of how little the war had affected them up to now. The summaries of the destruction and the lamenting of the press were treated as propaganda. "They are lying and so are we." The grim fates of Warsaw and Rotterdam provided the standard of measure, and some people still doubted whether the damage to London could be considered comparable to that.

"Germany's national comrades are amazed," wrote SS public opinion researchers, "at how much the British can take." No serious signs of breaking down anywhere! People assessed the pictures of mass quarters set up in the tunnels of the underground and the damages to apartment buildings and began to wonder how much they themselves could take. The civilian population was being put to the test, that much was agreed. By October, the Luftwaffe had lost 1,733 planes since the beginning of the campaign in July; the RAF had lost 915. The battle was interrupted for the time being in December, with a total of 23,000 civilian casualties, 14,000 in London alone.

Nothing can be found about the deliberate bombing of civilian targets in Luftwaffe records. Airfields, aircraft factories, docks, port facilities, and shipyards were destroyed. The term "civilian massacre" was not used even later by Bomber Command. Political leadership, however, knew that their weapons did not distinguish between production and producers, industry and city, the factory and the children of the factory workers. Hitler and Göring viewed the Battle of Britain as an acid test for a nation, and the war of the future that Hugh Trenchard had suggested and all the world had expected seemed to have come. But even though the plans for a murder and the murder itself are certainly related entities, they are by no means the same thing.

Hitler did not have a set plan either for war or for the bombing of England. He responded to certain circumstances in his own way. The killing of 23,000 British by the end of 1940 came as a result of the bogged-down attack on the British fighter fleet. This also caused the planned invasion to fall through, since these air battles were supposed to quickly prepare for ground operations. Subsequently, the peace offers were rejected, so Hitler scrutinized his armaments and resorted to the bomber. Nothing else was available. But he instinctively hesitated, and for good reason. If the bomber failed, then his available options would be exhausted.

Air Vice Marshal Robert Saundby interpreted the same situation from a British viewpoint. The German offensive against British aircraft and Fighter Command's ground operations went miserably for the RAF. By late August, Fighter Command was on the brink of disaster. Lost planes far outnumbered the new production, and they were afraid that fighter reserves could be exhausted within three more weeks of such a war of attrition.

> In these circumstances the Prime Minister decided to play a bold card. On the night of August 24 a number of German bombs were dropped on London—the first since 1918—and the government ordered a heavy raid on Berlin as a reprisal. On the night of August 25, eighty-one aircraft of Bomber Command carried out a successful attack on the German capital, although the night was scarcely long enough to allow the aircraft to go and return in darkness. The German High Command reacted sharply, and within a few days their main air attack had been switched to London and other towns and cities. The pressure on Fighter Command's airfields, which was imperiling the British defense system, was relieved. Although this meant that the civilian population had to suffer, it was a turning point in the battle, and greatly improved the British chances of victory.[24]

Captain Basil Liddell Hart, at the time the most esteemed military authority in the country, expressed himself in a similar manner: "The punishment that the capital and its people suffered was to be the saving factor"[25] for the armed forces, which were close to breaking point.

Of course, the blood of the human shields also sullied those who caused it to be spilled, namely Göring's Luftwaffe. The stalwart qualities of the Londoners became famous: they stuck out the bombing alongside Churchill, even without any tangible prospects of victory. Hitler was at the Channel and was allied with Russia, and in the United States, only 7.7 percent of the population supported entering the war.[26] More than five times that amount were opposed. At least there was a group of 19 percent in the middle that advocated entering the war if European democracies started to falter. This group was Churchill's last card, and it had to assure Roosevelt's reelection on November 5. The president had already given some assistance to the British, but intervention would require a shift in public opinion.

During the days of Churchill's odd attacks on Berlin in the last week of August 1940, he sent off his truly live ammunition with the *Duchess of Richmond*, the steamer that brought Henry Tizard to Washington.[27] In Tizard's luggage were all the secrets and patents that in thirty months would create the most ominous weapon ever to have been aimed at humans, the fleet of the Combined Strategic Bomber Offensive. As advance payment for a future alliance,

Roosevelt received the radar technology, the machine-gun platforms for the B-17, the Rolls-Royce Merlin engine, and the basic research of physicists Rudolf Peierls and Otto Frisch, who had derived the critical mass needed to sustain a nuclear fission chain reaction of uranium. The force of the resulting explosion had also been calculated and was very impressive. Tizard had already been involved with the Katanga mines in the Belgian Congo, which held the world's largest supply of uranium.[28] Not yet produced, but researched and thought out, the weapon would unleash a purgatory whose fire would purge the kingdom of evil.

"A fire in his own backyard," swore Churchill in June 1940, would force Hitler to retreat. "And we will make Germany a desert, yes a desert."[29] He asserted this to the ladies at the luncheon table before Air Marshal Sir Hugh Dowding, commander in chief at RAF Fighter Command, reminded him of their present concern: The Germans had to have some kind of guide beam that led their planes to their targets.

Churchill did not expect to have "air superiority" capable "of great offensive operations on land against Germany" until 1942. Until then, England lacked any prospects and was condemned to stick together and stick it out. "In the last war we kept on saying 'How are we going to win,' and then while we were still unable to answer the question, we quite suddenly and unexpectedly found ourselves in a winning position."[30] Because he could do nothing right, Churchill considered whether Hitler could possibly do something wrong: "to attempt invasion . . . even if he decided against it now and went eastwards; and he would not succeed."[31] Both countries were in limbo, fighting a war of attrition. They should have and could have stopped the war, but instead, each waited for the other side to make a mistake.

It was a mistake for the Germans to move toward Russia because they were unable to bomb the British to their knees, and it was a mistake for them to have bombed England's cities because they could not break their fighters' strength, and it was a mistake for them to have attacked the fighter planes because their peace offer had been rejected. Had Churchill set a trap for Hitler, as Saundby attested, and lured him into the bombing war? Maybe, but that is not really the point. The point is that by melding the British into a defiant community with a shared fate, Germany's bomber offensive failed. It made visible on the world stage the torments that slowly but surely drew the United States into the war. The bombing also eliminated all previous inhibitions against killing. The honor of the warrior, which had once demanded that the defenseless be protected rather than massacred, was fading away.

Germany was the first country in which the fury of war from the sky was comprehensively and consistently taken to the point of devastation. Presumably, everything that happened would have happened anyway. The industrial age led to the bombing war, and Hitler was to blame for Germany's ruin. On the other hand, nothing happens "anyway," and everything takes its form and its course. Inevitabilities are fictions. In the summer of 1940, many things played out fictitiously: what would happen if? The Luftwaffe wondered whether it would be better for them to reduce England's cities to rubble, and the RAF staff concluded that there was nothing else to do but use the only directly offensive weapon at their disposal to "undermine the morale of a large part of the enemy people, shake their faith in the Nazi régime, and at the same time and with the very same bombs, dislocate the major part of their heavy industry and a good part of their oil production."[32] Churchill informed his minister of war production, Lord Beaverbrook (as well as the ladies lunching with him), that there was only one way to fight Hitler. There was no continental army that could defeat the German military power, Churchill said, so if Hitler were to turn eastward, he could not be stopped. "But there is one thing that will bring him back and bring him down, and that is an absolutely devastating, exterminating attack by very heavy bombers from this country upon the Nazi homeland."[33] Those were all figures of speech. Attacks that roughly corresponded to this plan were still three years away for England. In the spring of 1941, the Luftwaffe would kill another 18,000 British before turning its attention to Russia. Not that the British were at all lacking in bloody will; they simply lacked the means.

Once Churchill took office on May 11, 1940, the British cabinet did away with the principle of protecting civilians. The first German city bombed was Mönchengladbach, where thirty-five Hampden and Whitley bombers dropped their loads on streets and railways on the night of May 11. Four civilians died, including one British woman who lived there. As long as the campaign on the western front continued, supply lines and factories were targeted specifically, but there was an internal consensus that bombs could also fall within a certain target area. When six bombs fell on Münster on the night of May 15, it was not a factory nor even the city itself that had been targeted. In response to the bombing of Rotterdam, the Rhine had been crossed; flyers looked for sixteen individual targets between Cologne and Dortmund, but ultimately dropped bombs wherever lights indicated a settled area.

Because of the long approach, pilots preferred flying under cover of darkness. In order to avoid being waylaid, they chose individual routes and appeared in small numbers. Certain ground contours could be made out when there was a moon; if skies were cloudy, the pilots had to drop to lower altitudes. In either case, a point target could only be identified by circling, which took time. By then, a flak had spotted the bomber and begun to take aim. A sparse night-fighter defense arduously came together. In contrast to England, arms-industry locations in Germany were very spread out. They were difficult to find, but could be defended only if the defense forces were likewise spread out, thus thinning their density. Both weapons systems—offensive and defensive alike—were not in the least suited for a campaign that could decide the war.

Bomber Command had fewer than two hundred planes available for night operations. To assure that their bomb loads did not go to waste on open fields if they missed the targeted oil refineries, shipyards, and steelworks, the bombing missions concentrated on at least one urban objective starting in late 1940. Subsequently, on November 17—three nights after Coventry—sixty of 130 planes reached Hamburg, started six fires, killed two people, and left 786 homeless. Only a 134-bomber expedition, the most extensive so far, bound for Mannheim offered a sign of what was to come. This raid was flown on December 16, 1940, under the codename Operation Abigail Rachel.

The city center had neither industrial nor military facilities of any interest. It was purely residential, and therefore poorly protected and well suited as an experimental area. Its characteristic grid-shaped structure also contributed to this, as it was relatively easy to recognize. It had streets that crossed at right angles and rectangular housing blocks surrounding square courtyards, which were practical for the study of the effects of explosive blast waves. Fireraising had not yet become a deliberate tactic. The objective was the city center; the orders were to raze it.

The attack was opened by eight Wellingtons flown by experienced personnel; they carried incendiary bombs exclusively. In contrast to later methods, these were used only for illumination purposes, to mark the bombing area for subsequent waves. Despite the cloudless night and full moon, the fires missed the center and were scattered in adjacent residential areas, where twenty people died. The water main was hit early in the raid, but only a handful of fires started, including one in the jewel of the city, the former electoral palace, the construction of which began in 1720 and was completed in 1760. Modeled after Versailles, it was the third-largest castle in the country; both interior and exterior were truly European masterpieces.

The western central block connected to the Rittersaal (Knight's Hall) caught fire. It spread to the precious stucco ceilings of the Trabantensaal and other adjoining halls. Firefighters arrived but could do nothing. A sudden frost caused the water to freeze, and it hung in long icicles from the ceilings and walls. The attic burned for two days; thanks to the arrival of the Darmstadt fire department, the fire did not consume the building. (It was given a grace period. On April 17, 1943, the western wing containing the palace church burned. The eastern wing was reduced to ruins in two raids in September, each with more than six hundred planes. By the summer of 1944, all that was left of the splendor of the rooms was the Cabinet Library of Electress Elisabeth Augusta.) Bomber Command returned to Mannheim on May 10, 1941, this time with three hundred high-explosive bombs and six thousand incendiaries on board. This raid killed sixty-seven people and demolished twenty-four buildings. A direct hit during the third raid in August destroyed the municipal hospital.

Bomber Command declared two classic armaments targets in the first six months of 1941: Germany's oil supply and its shipyards. The Air Ministry put an end to the nightly flitting about for four or five hours in search of a bomb-drop site. It named nine cities where brown coal liquefaction took place, including Leuna, Gelsenkirchen, and Magdeburg. According to reliable calculations made by the scientific staffs, the German war machine would come to a halt if 80 percent of the domestic production of synthetic oils were destroyed.

On the night of February 14, forty-four Wellingtons set out for Gelsenkirchen to locate the Nordstern oil refinery. Thirty-five found nothing; nine thought they saw and hit something, but had no evidence. Two planes were lost the following night in Sterkrade without having damaged the Ruhrchemie works. Forty planes bombed Homberg because the searchlights indicated the existence of factories, but the light was so blinding that it hampered the precision of the operation.

The staff at Bomber Command concluded that point targets could be hit only on the nine days per month when the moon offered enough light. The sky also had to be clear, but it usually clouded over, thus causing the oil offensive to fail. It did not make sense even to attempt to reach remote cities such as Magdeburg and Leuna, so pilots got accustomed to flying over Düsseldorf or Cologne, since they were closest. Once a rural suburb went up in flames; another time thirteen department stores and two Rhine steamers were hit. That was the end of the oil offensive, which gave way to the submarine offensive.

British commerce on the North Atlantic suffered greatly in early 1941, due to German U-boat packs operating from Norwegian bases. It was as difficult to torpedo them underwater as it was to destroy their shipyards from the air. So Churchill ordered them to try both, in the hopes that at least something would be achieved. New cities were assigned to Bomber Command, including Hamburg, Kiel, and Bremen.

On two consecutive March nights, they succeeded in wreaking havoc in the business and administrative offices of the Blohm & Voss shipyard in Hamburg. A lumber wharf and two docked submarines were also damaged. The second attack on March 14 took fifty-one lives, the highest number of casualties thus far. On the nights of April 7 and 8, the 213 deaths in Kiel broke that record; for the first time in eleven months Bomber Command could claim a victory.

The first raid lasted five full hours, damaging the Germania shipyard. As a result, the night shift had to be sent home, and operations were shut down for several days. The second caused more comprehensive damage, spreading farther into the city center, where a bank, museum, engineering college, and gasworks were hit. Above all, eight thousand people became homeless and residents fled the city in droves, many of them on foot. That came closer to Lord Trenchard's predictions. While Germany's raids on London did not have as profound a demoralizing effect, Trenchard saw a convincing reason for that. The steel nerves and humor of the British were not at all comparable with German self-pity. The Germans were virtually imprisoned in their shelters, wrote the aged Trenchard in May 1941 to Chief of Air Staff Sir Charles Portal. "They remain passive and easy prey to hysteria and panic. . . . There is no joking in the German shelters as in ours, nor the bond which unites the public with the ARP [Air Raid Precautions] and Military services."[34] This weak point, emphasized Trenchard, had to be hit time and time again.

The oil and submarine operations had proved that war-economy targets were vulnerable under favorable conditions. But it turned out that the Germans could cope incredibly well with the industrial losses, and continued to do so until mid-1944. Damages assumed immense proportions, but so did the ability of the enemy to balance them out. They had at their disposal the labor pool of Europe from Calais to Kiev. They could plunder, work people to death, abduct, corrupt, organize, and mobilize; in short, they always knew how to help themselves. Of course, the economic losses ate away somewhat at their fighting strength.

Contrary to the experience gathered from 1914 to 1918, the war economy was by no means Germany's Achilles' heel. But memories of 1918 also kept alive the recollections of mutiny and the collapse of the regime. On July 9, 1941, as the German Wehrmacht was marching through Russia for the third week, Bomber Command was given a third category of military objectives: the transportation system. The supply of war matériel that rolled eastward, especially from the Ruhr basin, had to be blocked, and the Ruhr completely isolated. A chain of destruction was to paralyze Osnabrück, Hamm, Soest, Schwerte, Duisburg, Düsseldorf, and Cologne. Because of the short midsummer nights, night flights could only reach the nearby western German areas anyway, and, during moonless nights, the urban regions along the Rhine, which could always be identified.

The directive of July 9, 1941, expanded the main effort of dislocating the transportation system with an additional clause: "destroying the morale of the civil population as a whole and of the industrial workers in particular."[35] With that, the concept that gave the war in and of the air its form had been introduced in practice: "morale bombing."

Morale, if you will, is also made of air. The bomb was not aimed at physical people, but rather was used to attack their misguided way of thinking—their morale. The bomb is a social surgeon that extirpates unhealthy thinking. As soon as the patient begins expressing healthy views, he will be released from the doctor's care. Churchill pointedly described this occupation in April 1941: "There are less than seventy million malignant Huns, some of whom are curable and others killable."[36] Of course, at the same time, the Huns in question were slaughtering thousands of defenseless people in London. That aside, Churchill made his point well, because it was only possible to understand and justify "morale bombing" through the juxtaposition of curing and killing as a pair of alternatives.

A bomb itself cannot destroy morale. It destroys material, stone, structures, bodies. Once the body has been destroyed, it ceases to have any morale. At best, the morale of one German is cured through the killing of another, and the slaughter continues until the cure is achieved. Thus the fate of one is held in the hand of the other. The slaughterer gives him the choice. The master of the situation decides which morals are valid. At this point in 1941, the British themselves definitely did not think they were masters of the situation. Quite the contrary.

During the oil offensive from February to March 1941, the British lost twenty-six aircraft during their night raids. Between July and November, during the implementation of the Transportation Plan, however, they lost 414, along with their crews. That meant that at least every eight months Bomber Command's entire inventory had to be replaced. Losses can be endured only as long as they yield results, but Bomber Command was inflicting deeper wounds on itself than on the enemy.

In August, an investigation, the Butt Report, was submitted to the government and Parliament. On the basis of aerial photographs, the report concluded that under ideal weather conditions, merely one-third of the attacking planes hit their targets.[37] The "target" was considered a region within a five-mile radius of the aiming point. In the Ruhr basin, the main zone of operations, in poor weather, the hit rate was 10 to 15 percent of the time. During moonless weeks, a hit was nothing but a matter of chance. The British bombers, the only weapon that could administer a blow to the enemy, had dulled to the point of uselessness. They could have been scrapped, but that would have left the British defenseless. That was out of the question. Consequently, all that remained was to try to reinterpret the devastating Butt Report in a constructive way.

Perhaps the definition of "target" needed to be refined. If its target was declared to be whatever it could hit, then Bomber Command did in fact hit its mark. A five-mile radius was an unnecessarily limited area. A major city spreads out much farther. It is so big that it would be impossible even with all available means to hit every building and resident. In principle, a shipyard must be reduced to ashes or it will be repaired within ten days at most. Such pinpoint accuracy is neither necessary nor desirable as regards a city. To decimate it would require such high expenditures and, since it is defended, would cause such losses as to make its total destruction impossible.

However, one could and should destroy perhaps only a part, and the other part could draw its own conclusions from that. From what the British had at their disposal according to the Trenchard Doctrine, the city was the stage for "morale bombing."

Esteemed as a thinker, Chief of Air Staff Portal presented his program to Churchill on September 25, 1941. This program deviated from all previous ones; his objectives were no longer the hydrogenation plant, as they had been in February, or the railway lines, as they had been in July, but rather to attack that ultimate fuel that kept all of the rest moving. It was ubiquitous and therefore easy to hit wherever munitions were dropped on settled areas. The Air Force staff calculated that with four thousand heavy bombers and a monthly load of sixty thousand tons of bombs—tenfold the tonnage up to that point—forty-three German cities with more than 100,000 inhabitants each could be destroyed. The civilian population of these cities totaled fifteen million. Germany was to be forced to its knees within six months through the "destruction of German economic life and morale."[38]

Churchill, who had repeatedly proposed an offensive of this magnitude, responded hesitatingly. He admired Portal, and knew that the outlined path would be the one to be taken. But he was too old and had seen too many ideas—especially his own—that had been sure bets fail abysmally to wager everything on hopes that this one would work. Using bombs to shatter the enemy's will to resist was shown to be just as difficult as using them to destroy production. The British, he wrote, were inspired and toughened by bombing, and at any rate, a war would not be won on the basis of one single method, and certainly not by playing with numbers.

This current of skepticism appears throughout the entire bomber offensive. This was a weapon that delivered a blow like a club but in the end missed its mark. The British continued to use it anyway and even augmented its size and its capabilities, because it was better than doing nothing. Portal's demand for four thousand bombers meant increasing the inventory fourfold. Churchill instead advised increasing the effectiveness of the current fleet and waiting for the United States to enter the war. He was not concerned with the specific reason why Americans would send off an expedition from their distant continent to destroy German cities; any reason was fine with him. The Americans had already acquired the means a year earlier, and the weapon one most likely deploys is the weapon one has. Bomber Command, for example, kept a secret reserve of resources on hand—a reserve partly ready for use and partly almost ready—that was waiting for a strategic decision to be made. The decision was then forced by the depressing conclusions of the Butt Report. Bomber Command had bombers that could carry high tonnages quickly and over long distances, radar navigation that could guide the bombers to cities, a variety of bombs that could cause damage over an extended area, and target-indicator markers that illuminated a zone of concentrated annihilation in the dark. That type of marking had not been used in 1941, as bombing theory dictated that a point target must first be sighted. It did not matter whether it was the bomb, or even before that, the marker, that was dropped. The marker outlined zones that a carpet of bombs filled with the materials of destruction.

The bombardier, whether or not he aimed for a target, caused damage. He fired a shot basically like a cannon's, but vertically. It was all the same whether he fired blindly or aimed. The site where the cannonball hit was a target of some kind. Sometimes it was hit intentionally, sometimes unintentionally. The rules changed, however, when the pathfinders and bombers began to divide up the work. The grammar of shot and target became insignificant. The pathfinder no longer indicated a point but rather outlined an area. It then was not a matter of "hitting" discrete objects within the area—instead, the demarcated area comprised all that was simply not supposed to be and was to be removed from the world. Annihilation is the spatial extension of death. The victim does not die his death, because he does not have one. He finds himself in a sphere in which life has ceased.

Around the beginning of 1942, Bomber Command had not only the will but also the basic technology to create an annihilation zone. This zone was the sector of a city. An act of war was the process by which the sector was brought into a state of annihilation. This could succeed entirely, partially, or not at all. Like everything in a war, it depends on a number of factors and on fate. The former could be influenced, the latter happened. Bomber Command learned from experience as it moved from city to city. On the way from Lübeck to Hamburg, it acquired the ability to set the annihilation process going, as far as it could be calculated in advance. Between Hamburg and Darmstadt, it had to rely on favorable conditions for a burning apocalypse to develop. Between Darmstadt and Dresden, Bomber Command learned how to create the beacon of fire.

In October 1940, surrounded by the conflagrations in London, Churchill and Portal had considered the possibility of destroying population centers through the "maximum use of fire." Apart from his wish to expand the fleet, Portal's presentation to Churchill in September became the British strategy, starting on February 14, 1942. In the Area Bombing Directive that the Air Ministry sent to Bomber Command, the most densely settled urban areas were identified as points of attack: "It has been decided that the primary objective of your operations should now be focussed on the morale of the enemy civil population and, in particular, of the industrial workers."[39] Because Portal evidently wanted to make sure this change in policy was worded with absolute clarity, he added for the record, "I suppose it is clear that the aiming points are to be the built-up areas, *not*, for instance, the dockyards or aircraft factories. . . . This must be made quite clear if it is not already understood."

It was not made quite clear how the attack on morale in the densely populated settlements was to be carried out. Arthur Harris was entrusted with answering this not insignificant question, as he became the new head of Bomber Command on February 22, 1942. After the war, Harris wrote that his superiors, Charles Portal and Sir Archibald Sinclair, secretary of state for air, had set the strategy, target sites, and tactics for the offensive. The objective "was to be achieved by destroying, mainly by incendiary bombs, the whole of the four largest cities in the Ruhr, and thereafter fourteen industrial cities elsewhere in Germany."[40]

Harris, a stubborn but very pragmatic man, suggested for incineration a city that was guaranteed to be a success: Lübeck. First of all, it was located along the easily identifiable coastal contours of Lübeck Bay. Second, there was no industry there that was essential for the war effort so it was not heavily defended. Third, its central Old Town consisted largely of half-timbered buildings, which burned easily. These were the reasons why Lübeck was destroyed: its convenient location, its defenselessness, and its age-old beauty.

Harris waited for the full moon, and on the eve of Palm Sunday dispatched 234 aircraft loaded with four hundred tons of bombs, two-thirds of which were incendiaries. The sector to be destroyed was the winding district of merchants and seamen dating from the Hanseatic period. It was an urban island, enclosed by the rivers Trave and Wakenitz, offering a clear-cut aerial image. When the raid commenced at 10:30 p.m., only a few fires could be seen, but in only twenty minutes they completely devoured their way to the Trave side of the island. Fires surged through warehouses, quays, port cranes, and 1,500 of the historic, high-gabled houses, which had been built without firewalls. Ultimately, eighty miles of street façades were ablaze. Sixty-two percent of all buildings were destroyed or damaged. Two hundred acres of the Old Town had been gutted by fire.

Firefighters needed until 10 o'clock the next morning to contain the fire. The cathedral, for which Henry the Lion had laid the cornerstone in 1173, could not be saved. At 10:30 a.m., the cupola of the north tower broke in two, and at 2:00 p.m., the south tower followed. Two bells in the Church of St. Mary fell and broke; one had been cast in 1745 and the other in 1390. They crashed down, destroying their sister, the great organ made by Arp Schnitger. High-explosive bombs that detonated near the choir shook the arch of the vault; the crown of the choir fell, burying the wooden high altar and the sedilia, which had been installed in 1310.

In addition to the 25,000 incendiary sticks, 250-pound benzol and rubber bombs were also used for the first time. Harris had determined the necessary types and number of bombs by analyzing the German raid on Coventry. Now he learned something else from experience: how a city that seemed to him to be "built more like a fire-lighter than a human habitation"[41] reacted when a carpet of flames descended on it. Of 120,000 residents, 320 lost their lives that night. This was the highest casualty rate to date for a raid in the British offensive.

The attack took place in three waves and lasted two hours. That too was amazing. Just a year earlier, a mission involving one hundred planes was considered a complicated endeavor and took four hours, which gave firefighters some time to respond. In order to paralyze them in the critical phase of the fireraising, the raid had to be quick and intensive. If a huge fleet released enormous amounts of bombs in quick succession and over a limited area, the resulting blaze would be uncontrollable.

Next, Harris presented Operation Millennium to his chief of staff Portal and to Churchill for authorization. They were highly impressed. The glory of perfecting the technical aspects of the air war seemed worth the risk, as crazy as it was. Guided by 6,500 British airmen, a fleet of one thousand bombers loaded with 1,350 blast bombs and 460,000 incendiary bombs was to darken the sky. In order to amass such a large fleet, Bomber Command, with its roughly four hundred aircraft and crews ready for action, had to muster all its reserves, borrow naval aircraft, oil scrapped vehicles, and call up recruits in training to the front. They flew at a tremendous risk. If this operation failed it would have meant the end of the bomber weapon's future. There would be either triumph or disaster. The nightmare scenario that plagued everyone was collision. How could such a swarm be navigated—at night—without planes crashing into one another? The mathematicians from Operational Research placed the odds of a collision at one to one thousand. No one believed the odds could be so low, but in fact, very few planes were lost in collisions.

The moon set the date: the last week of May 1942. Now the city had to be determined; the lot fell to Hamburg. It was the second-largest German city and was the preferred choice of the admiralty, because of the hundred U-boats produced there annually. The full-moon period began on May 26, but so did bad weather. The clouds hung too densely, so the mission was delayed three days. On May 30, the orders came: the city was now Cologne. It had its own natural markings, offered by the Rhine.

The bombers approached from the north and flew southward, following the river upstream. Every second plane was fitted with Gee navigation. Crews with a special knack for target location scouted ahead, leading the raid and setting illumination flares. They were ordered to carry out the bombardment in an inconceivably short ninety minutes. Every five seconds a bomber appeared over the city.

Even if only a fraction of them actually ignited, the immense number of small, light incendiary bombs would start thousands of separate fires. If, on top of that, explosives blocked firefighters from reaching the flames to extinguish them, they would grow into a carpetlike blaze.

Things did not go exactly as planned. About 12,000 individual fires developed into 1,700 major conflagrations, but the water lines remained intact. One hundred and fifty fire departments from Düsseldorf, Duisburg, and Bonn raced to the city, laying hoses from hydrants into the buildings. Huge pipes were submerged into the Rhine to draw out many thousands of tons of water, and motor-driven fire pumps generated the pressure to pump the water for miles to the damaged areas. The vast, spreading conflagration of Lübeck was not repeated. Cologne, a more modern city with wider streets, could defend itself.

The flak batteries and their searchlights caused 3.9 percent losses for the attackers, the highest thus far, but the British bore it with relief. It had been worth it. The Thousand-Bomber Raid was an enormous accomplishment of weapons technology; it demonstrated the successful capability of the force. Bomber Command had finally proved to skeptics that its campaign could grow into a war of its own. England would no longer be merely tolerating war, but waging it, and waging it with considerable staying power. Now the gloves were off, commented Churchill, and he announced to the House of Commons that in the course of that year all German cities, ports, and war-production centers "would face a test so unremitting, severe, and extensive such that no country has ever before experienced."[42]

How can the result be put into words? The bomber crews reported home that from the fifty-fifth minute onward they felt like they were flying over a spewing volcano. The Nazi press railed against the inhuman beasts, the "British gangs of murderers who are waging war against the defenseless." In the morning, when caustic smoke still filled the entire city, reddening eyes and adhering to clothing, the *Kölner Zeitung*, a newspaper whose offices had suffered serious damage, wrote that those "who survived the night and looked at the city the next morning were well aware that they would never again see their old Cologne." There were 3,300 buildings destroyed and 9,500 damaged. This was not major damage for a city with a population of 772,000: It took 262 air raids before 95 percent of the Old Town was finally destroyed.

The amount of alteration to the face of the city cannot be measured as a percentage. It was totally disfigured by the damage to the Hohe Strasse, which followed the course of the former Roman main street, the *Cardo Maximus*; the destruction of the eastern side of the Old Market with its buildings from the late Renaissance; and the loss of the western gallery of St. Mary in the Capitol, one of the most architecturally harmonious buildings of the Western world, which had been erected atop late Roman foundations in the eleventh century on a hill along the Rhine. In the Church of St. Ursula, a triple-nave basilica from the thirteenth century, the remains of the 11,000 virgins continued to lie in stone sarcophagi built into the choir for another thirty-four months, until March 1, 1945, the date that marked the "end of Cologne." Four days after that raid, the 262nd, the U.S. Army entered the city.

The Thousand-Bomber Raid took 480 lives and left five thousand injured, most of whom had been outside the large residential-block cellars that provided stable protection. These figures, too, far surpassed all previous campaigns; the British claimed to have killed

6,000. A four-digit figure was more fitting for an operation named Millennium. Air Secretary Sinclair congratulated the troops with the promise that "the next climax would be even more powerful."[43] Churchill publicly announced to Bomber Command that Cologne was "the forewarning of what one German city after another would have to endure from now on."[44]

In retaliation for Cologne, the Germans dropped a hundred incendiary bombs on another symbol of Christianity, the diocese of Canterbury, on June 1, 1942. Harris repeated Millennium's tactics in early June in Essen and later that month in Bremen, with moderate success in the former and miserable results in the latter. The influence of the weather, teething problems with the radar navigation, and the defenses of the mission targets made every operation risky. In the three Thousand-Bomber raids, a total of 777 men and one-fourth of all aircraft were lost. The lives of hard-to-replace flight instructors and trainees had been wasted.

There were no signs of a debacle as regards German morale. And industrial production did not fall through the floor, either. Two raids against Düsseldorf, the headquarters of the armaments combines, were viewed by the British as highly successful, despite the fact that production there still increased 1.8 percent in the second half of the year, after the city had suffered the impact of more than 1,500 tons of bombs carried by 1,100 aircraft, of which 10.5 percent was lost in the first raid and 7.1 percent in the second.

In August 1942, when the 1st German Panzer Army had reached the northern Caucasus and the 4th Panzer Army pushed through to the Volga River to lay siege to Stalingrad, Churchill promised the disgruntled Stalin that he would surround all of Germany. England "hoped to shatter almost every dwelling in almost every German city."[45] "That would not be bad," replied Stalin. Churchill's scientific advisor Professor Frederick A. Lindemann, Lord Cherwell, had calculated that with ten thousand bombers, they could render 22,000,000 Germans homeless. That would put one in every three Germans out on the street, and it would also mean the end of any will to resist.

Henry Tizard ripped apart these irrational fantasies and resigned after he was accused of being a defeatist. Lord Cherwell, ridiculed behind his back as Churchill's Rasputin, was totally surprised when Charles Portal, the most authoritative voice in the Air Force, trumped him in November. Portal demanded that 1.25 million tons of bombs be dropped in 1943 and 1944; six million apartment buildings and a corresponding number of industrial and administrative buildings would thus be reduced to rubble. "Twenty-five million Germans would be rendered homeless, 900,000 would be killed, and one million seriously injured."[46] Experience had shown that raw materials and reserve stocks could not be adequately replaced, nor could structural damages be adequately repaired, but it would be more difficult to estimate the consequences for morale, since the scale of bombardment "would far transcend anything within human experience." Nevertheless, there could be no doubt that they would be "profound indeed."

How should these statistics be interpreted? By the autumn of 1942, when Portal made his calculations, the RAF had dropped a total of 60,000 tons of bombs. By the end of the war, the total tonnage over five years was estimated at 657,000. It is impossible to comprehend how Portal intended to produce and transport 1.25 million tons within two years. As it was, Bomber Command devoured one-third of all British war expenditures. Perhaps this brilliant and impressive officer's overwhelming will for destruction came from his force's fiasco.

In September, the bomber fleet's casualty rate was 10.6 percent. A crew's expectation of surviving their thirty sorties was approaching zero. The weapon of the Strategic Bomber Offensive had essentially been implemented. It functioned, even if not every mission was a success. Its destructive force grew appreciably; considerations that had tied it down had vanished. It had been unleashed, but unfettered strategy did not deliver on its promise. Arthur Harris admitted that "it never occurred to me that we could reduce the largest and most efficient industrial power in Europe to impotence by a year's bombing with an average striking force of six or seven hundred bombers. . . . Thirty thousand heavy bombers and the war would be over by morning."[47]

Bomber Command had a tacit desire for an apocalyptic strike, but that is not how things went. The city landscapes were leveled, layer by layer, and the British losses were unyieldingly endured. Harris's contribution was to develop further the depth of the weapon's destructiveness. Bomber losses in 1943 were five times greater than the total number of bombers that Harris had at his disposal in 1942, and he never managed to have two thousand aircraft ready for deployment. The number of people killed, however, had increased fourteenfold from 1942 to 1943, from 6,800 to 100,000 civilians.[48]

Bomber Command accomplished the steep increase in the weapon's lethality through advances in the navigation systems. Distant cities in the south and east came within its reach, and familiar conurbations became easier to locate. The four-engine Lancaster could carry more bombs, which exploded with greater force and burned with greater intensity. But more important, Harris also changed the method of attack. The bomber stream and the pathfinder system made it possible to increase the density of bombs dropped both in time and space. The attack no longer came in intervals and in gaps. The pathfinders saved the bombers from having to search for the target.

He came and bombed. Harris had set a rate of twelve bombers per minute in Cologne. This had been viewed as highly risky. In the Battle of Berlin in the fall of 1943, a rate of sixteen bombers per minute continued for forty-five minutes. On the evening of November 23, 1943, 753 Lancasters, Halifaxes, and Stirlings released 2,500 tons of bombs from 7:58 p.m. to 8:20 p.m., at a rate of thirty-four planes per minute—one plane every 1.76 seconds—over the Berlin districts of Tiergarten, Charlottenburg, and Spandau. Berlin-Charlottenburg is not much smaller than the city of Würzburg, which on the night of March 16, 1945, was wiped off the face of the earth in seventeen minutes. That was one of the final performances of a virtuoso that Harris had been breeding since 1942. He was able to accurately reduce a shrine of the European baroque to ashes with the help of 1,100 tons of bombs released at 4.76-second intervals. There was no more war to win; it had already been won. Taking a cityscape that was begun in 1040 and completed seven hundred years later by Balthasar Neumann and devastating it in fifteen minutes with 300,000 incendiary sticks had become old hat. Bombing required a special kind of expertise, and after its bungling in 1941, Bomber Command was proud to have perfected the art.

The enormity of the bomber stream enabled such a rapid bomb drop. The pathfinders set the flares to frame the bombers' concentrated drop. That technique was tested in 1942, and its efficacy led to an ever-accelerating vortex of destruction from 1943 to 1945. The innovation of the bomber stream made it possible, first of all, to penetrate the Kammhuber line. The previous flight-approach method was very relaxed and pulsating, more of an infiltration than an offensive. It offered the night hunt too much flank. The tighter and deeper Kammhuber set up his *Himmelbetten*, radar reflectors, and blocks of searchlights, the more difficult it was for intruding planes to slip through. They groped from night-fighter sector to night-fighter sector, with each hour in the air increasing the probability of getting caught. Once they reached the city, they spent two hours on the lookout for oil tanks and train stations, but the flak artillery had just as much time to find them.

Kammhuber had nothing that could prevent the breakthrough of a hundred boxlike, multitiered formations, each of which was about three miles long, five miles wide, and almost two miles deep. The fighter planes caught a handful of bombers at the edge of the stream, but as they were battling with them, the main force swept through. While the Mosquitos above the flak-controlled zone lit up the outline of the bomb-drop sector, the bombers, releasing their loads, shot through at full speed, thereby shortening the time they were subjected to grenade fire. Harris's method can be seen as self-defense. They were protecting themselves from the Germans. And at least the wind knew what area the marker was illuminating, since it scattered the flares as they parachuted down. There are always some other explanations for a politics of annihilation.

The United States officially became part of the hostilities on December 11, 1941, thanks to Hitler's declaration of war. The strategy that it laid down with the British in January 1943 consisted of a combined bomber offensive of the two air forces. The U.S. Eighth Air Force had already been on British bases for three months, gathering its strength. At the Casablanca Conference, the Point-Blank Directive drafted an air offensive that, except for half a sentence, included about a dozen pages listing the industries to be crushed: U-boat, aircraft, and military transport vehicle manufacture; ball bearings; oil supply; and synthetic rubber and tires. The remaining half-sentence mentioned the "undermining of the morale of the German people to a point where their capacity for armed resistance is fatally weakened."[49] This was listed under point 1, "The Mission."

Point 2, "The Principal Objectives," referred to "seventy-six (76) precision targets" within the six industries mentioned above. Point 6, "Effectiveness of the Eighth Air Force," definitively established "the fact that it is possible to conduct precision-pattern bombing operations against selected precision targets from altitudes of 20,000 to 30,000 feet in the face of anti-aircraft artillery and fighter defenses." Point 5, "The General Plan of Operations," named a radius of 1,000 feet within which the necessary hit accuracy was to be achieved. This basically described the accuracy of the Oboe bomb-aiming system, but its range covered only the Ruhr basin area up to and including Wuppertal. The Casablanca Conference had agreed upon making the Ruhr basin the primary target. While U.S. forces were still drilling, Harris was preparing for the Battle of the Ruhr in the spring.

The offensive against the "Arsenal of the Reich" involved the bombing of twenty-one major cities between March and July 1943. After the raid on Essen on the night of March 12, London papers printed five-column photographs of the destroyed Krupp factory. The correspondent of a Swedish trade and shipping newspaper cabled home that fifteen huge production shops were destroyed or severely damaged. "The administration buildings look like an empty honeycomb. The largest foundry brings to mind aerial photographs of Pompeii."[50] The Krupp factory in Essen spread out over an area of 175 square miles. The grounds were not contiguous, but the thousand-foot radius set in the Point-Blank Directive made it possible to destroy quite a bit of it.

Aerial photographs showed an area of destruction covering 148 acres at Krupp and 7.7 square miles in the city, from the main train station to Altenessen. Krupp was hit by 125 high-explosive bombs and twenty thousand incendiaries.[51] A direct hit struck the fuse factory, whose production was moved to Auschwitz. Panzer construction shop no. 3 was also destroyed, so production of the Panther and Tiger models had to be postponed by two months. Crankshaft production also suffered appreciable delays and was moved to Silesia.

In this case, the armaments economy did not endure a Pompeii, just a neverending series of pinpricks. Parallel to that was a neverending series of repairs. While the military machine was becoming industrialized, industry was also becoming militarized. Losses were part and parcel of it. It was possible to patch things together, relocate battalions, and arrange substitute workers. Industry no longer complained about damages as it would have in peacetime; it had become a war zone. Causing and balancing out damages was itself a raging battle, one with uncertain results. Wars, said Marshal Ferdinand Foch, the victor of 1918, are won with whatever is left.

Bomber Command lost 5 percent over Essen; the crews were horrified to discover precision flak artillery that reached an altitude of 23,000 feet. The flak had a better shoot-down rate this time than the fighters did, whose Focke-Wulf 190s gave the heavy Wellingtons especially a hard time. Two of them collided in midair; another fired 750 shots at a pursuer that attacked three times before it escaped. Speed was everything in the bedlam. No one thought about a point target, in accordance with Casablanca standards, within a thousand-foot radius. Something like that was pure fantasy.

Initially, the pathfinders had taken good measurements and marked out a 7.5-mile sector visible to the first wave of bombers. Subsequent waves, blinded by the searchlight cones chasing them down, saw a smoldering, fiery oven miles below them and, if they were calm enough, aimed into it. "The whole Duisburg area seemed ablaze with incendiaries," reported a Lancaster pilot about the night raid on April 26. "The glare from them was so intense that it was difficult to pick out ground details. We dropped our bombs as the white glare was turning to red, showing that the fires had caught and were beginning to spread."[52]

Oboe's precision was nothing more than manufacturer's specifications, which no one was concerned with during a bombing war. Only the pathfinders were fitted with the aiming device. They heard the signals in their ear when the point was reached, and they released containers with flares. If the skies were clear, these landed on the ground; if it was overcast, they drifted through the clouds from parachutes. The precision target was specifically defined only in the Point-Blank Directive, and it soothed the conscience of the Americans. In accordance with the Atlantic Charter of August 1941, they were leading a "crusade in Europe" to free oppressed peoples—but not free them from their lives. The two March 1943 raids on Essen killed 198 and 470, respectively; the latter was hitherto the highest figure for a single raid. On those two nights, a total of 343,000 incendiary bombs were dropped. Such a huge mass of light, four-pound magnesium alloy–thermite sticks made it impossible to aim them at a point target, but fire was a weapon that worked in a different way. When bombers were loaded with it, the objective was destruction over a wider area.

Air Secretary Sinclair sufficiently answered all the questions of the House of Commons on March 31 as regards definitions: "The targets of Bomber Command are always military, but night-bombing of military objectives necessarily involves bombing the area in which they are situated."[53] Harris considered this to be a roundabout answer, as if they had reason to feel ashamed. The government insisted on publicly denying any indiscriminate bombing of civilian centers. On the other hand, neither did it claim to be destroying only military targets. It was emphasized that the targets they destroyed were of military significance, as Deputy Prime Minister Clement Attlee (Labour) assured: "As has been repeatedly stated in the House, the bombing is of those targets which are most effective from the military point of view."[54]

From a military point of view, it was most effective to destroy a city, including all that lived, worked, and was produced therein. The Battle of the Ruhr, a product of the thousand-foot precision protocol declared in Casablanca, killed 21,000 people. The cities that were set on fire were Düsseldorf, Krefeld, Remscheid, and Wuppertal; each of them mourned more than one thousand casualties. Of the 14,000 buildings in Remscheid, 11,000 had been destroyed or damaged by the end of the last raid in the Ruhr campaign on the night of July 30.[55] Eighty-three percent of this city of 95,000 had been devastated by 273 planes. The antiaircraft teams had been paralyzed by the tinfoil strip. They watched from outside town how the city turned red with flames. When residents staggered out of air-raid shelters at 11:45 p.m., after the all clear had sounded, they saw a city of ruins that could not yet free itself from destruction. The incendiary matter wanted to finish its job; it enveloped the city in a firestorm ninety minutes after Bomber Command had left.

The reports published in the British press, such as "Night Bombers Crush Krefeld" in the *Times* of June 23, 1943, denied the government information regarding the nature of the targets that were bombed.[56] Accounts in the *Times* stated that the city was shrouded in black smoke for miles, extending 15,000 feet high, after five 4,000-pound blockbuster bombs had been dropped on it each minute for three-quarters of an hour. Readers were told the next day that not targets but cities had been crushed. Within Bomber Command, the facts were treated openly: In the immediate assessment of damage report, based on aerial photographs,[57] the balance of the raid on Krefeld on the night of June 21, 1943, was reported as follows: 25,000 residences destroyed; 87,000 people homeless; and 1,450 people killed, 850 by high-explosive bombs and 600 by incendiaries. The casualties were undoubtedly viewed as having contributed to the success of the operation. The estimates were slightly high yet still amazingly accurate. Krefeld actually suffered 1,056 deaths, an area of 925 acres became a closed fire zone, and 47 percent of the built-up area was burned out totally.

The Battle of the Ruhr proved Bomber Command's raison d'être; bombing had become a strategic weapon. The same procedure would be used to destroy more than one-fourth of the most industrialized area of Germany by the end of the year. Arthur Harris started collecting his trophies. He glued the aerial photographs of the skeletal ruins into a blue album that he sent to the government, to Buckingham Palace, and to Josef Stalin. No one in the circle of decision makers had any illusions about the fate suffered by the residents of these ruins, as illustrated by Churchill's witticism that Germans did not need to live in their cities; they should go out to the countryside and watch their homes burn from the hills.

Bomber Command lost five thousand men in the Battle of the Ruhr, but the British coped with this sacrifice. It confirmed that the government was waging war with resolve. Public-opinion polls in April 1941 had already showed a 53 percent approval of bombing civilian targets in Germany.[58] Even more remarkable, however, is that 38 percent disapproved. Over the course of the war, reservations dwindled. Sixty percent of Londoners supported bombing civilian targets and about 20 percent rejected it. This vote complemented the government code of conduct denying both that civilian targets were attacked and, on top of that, that civilian targets still existed. Targets were simply either militarily effective or not.

The British public in 1943 and 1944 demonstrated a widening gap between a general knowledge about the progress of the war and actually knowing what was going on. "Knowing what was going on" involved understanding the complexities that occurred but were generally not supposed to, and which were necessary but not right. The press reported extensively on the massive destruction of German cities and cited RAF communiqués that the columns of smoke could be seen as far away as Holland. Bomber Command's assessments of the successful killing were omitted. But Londoners were veterans of bombing, too. They could figure out on their own the connection between burned-out homes and incinerated inhabitants.

After Bomber Command's beacon of fire in July 1943, the word "Hamburgization" was coined in the fall. Ninety percent of people polled in 1944 nevertheless claimed not to know that German city centers were being bombed. "City center" can mean different things. Harris viewed it as the building material most vulnerable to fire, and well suited for igniting. The mass quarters where the will to resist was most consolidated lay in the ring surrounding the center. Workers had to be softened up; nothing more needed to be said. At a time when human casualties became four- and five-digit figures, statistics stopped being mentioned. Ever since the Germans bombed London, everyone knew how people got buried in rubble.

The dispute of the Church of England marked the final line of Christian defense. As early as 1940, pacifist clerics had asked the Archbishops of Canterbury and York at what point the church would rather lose a war than win it through methods that cannot be reconciled with Christianity. The bishops answered that such a case would be the bombing of undefended cities not as reprisal but as regular policy. Since all cities defended themselves against Bomber Command with at least a couple of antiaircraft cannons, this argument could withstand a lot, but it was not the most serious argument put forth to support the bombing of civilians. When the annihilation bombings got serious in 1943, Archbishop Cyril Garbett of York recited the justification of the "just war" from St. Augustine.

> Often in life, there is no clear choice between absolute right and wrong; frequently the choice has to be made of the lesser of two evils, and it is a lesser evil to bomb a war-loving Germany than to sacrifice the lives of our fellow-countrymen who long for peace, and to delay delivering millions now held in slavery.[59]

The question as to who personified the war-loving Germany and who was to make this definition was posed for all to hear by Bishop George Bell of Chichester. There was quite a turmoil when he announced in the British House of Lords: "To line up the Nazi assassins in the same row with the people of Germany whom they have outraged is to make for more barbarism."[60] That was on February 11, 1943. On February 9, 1944, also in the House of Lords, he attacked head-on the unjust nature of the bomber weapon as it had developed over the course of 1943.

> I desire to challenge the Government on the policy which directs the bombing of enemy towns on the present scale, especially with reference to civilians who are non-combatants, and non-military and non-industrial objectives. I fully realize that in attacks on centres of war industry and transport the killing of civilians when it is the result of bona fide military activity is inevitable. But there must be a fair balance between the means employed and the purpose achieved. To obliterate a whole town because certain portions contain military and industrial establishments is to reject

the balance. The Allies stand for something greater than power. The chief name inscribed on our banner is "Law." It is of supreme importance that we, who, with our Allies, are the Liberators of Europe should so use power that it is always under the control of law. It is because the bombing of enemy towns—this area bombing—raises this issue of bombing unlimited and exclusive that such immense importance is bound to attach to the policy and action of His Majesty's Government.[61]

Bishop Bell considered what he called exaggerated bombing of military targets to be legally questionable, but Freeman Dyson, a physicist at the Operational Research Center in Bomber Command, knew better. "Morale bombing" did not exaggerate the targeting of military complexes. A city was not a target as these were defined in the Casablanca Conference list. It was and is a space where people resided, worked, and lived. And the space was to be damaged such that as little as possible of that space remained. Because the completed weapon as it existed in 1943 could not accomplish that in one fell swoop, Cologne had to suffer 262 times, Essen 272 times, Düsseldorf 243, and Duisburg 299. "I felt sickened by what I knew," wrote Dyson in 1984. "Many times I decided I had a moral obligation to run out into the streets and tell the British people what stupidities were being done in their name. But I never had the courage to do it. I sat in my office until the end, carefully calculating how to murder most economically another hundred thousand people."[62]

Dyson was a lifelong eccentric who could do a job and at the same time consider it a war crime. The normal mind of a scientist, on the other hand, like that of Solly Zuckerman, originator of the bloody Transportation Plan bombing of 1944 and 1945, did not feel the need to subject the weapon as he invented it to any moral scrutiny. The politician who deployed it accepted responsibility for the means of war. The physicist simply created a scientific possibility, and was not even asked about the practical admissibility. "A state of war," wrote Zuckerman, "can stimulate the scientist to great feats of the imagination and to great practical achievement."[63] A scientist's disposition about the world was suddenly expanded in an undreamed-of magnitude, since in wartime, scientists enjoyed "resources on a scale they had never dreamed of in peace."

In the otherwise dull grind that was the Battle of the Ruhr, one innovative, first-rate performance stands out. It did not accomplish what was hoped for, but certainly will continue in the future to inspire people in the war business. A club or axe, if you will, is an extension of the strength of the arm, and a firearm is simply the concentration of the mechanics of a blow. This marks the progression from the crossbow to the artillery of World War I. The principle still links the artillerists on the western front to a pugilist. It is all about a violent person who inflicts a wound on someone else, whether he sees him in front of him or not. Fist, blade, and projectile force themselves deep into a human body. The body in turn either dodges it or strikes, stabs, or shoots back. In a confrontation between two bodies, both want to harm the other; they are each other's adversaries and targets, and they exchange violence. The continuum of weaponry merely represents variations on a theme. However, the invention of the gas grenade was something truly new, because it transformed the air.

In World War I, gas was actually the least lethal weapon used, and it did not cause the hideous physical mutilation that heavy artillery did. But it caused the greatest horror among the troops. Perhaps they sensed that with gas, war had changed. The honest contest of arms represented by the bullet was replaced by the annihilation principle. Now, through heat, radiation, and toxic gases, the very air was being transformed into something unlivable. The incendiary weapon and the subsequent atomic weapon of World War II introduced the notion of extracting a state of destruction from the workings of general laws of nature. Reality was no longer a place in which to dwell or even do battle. Living space became a death zone, the wardens of which suffered from a "Jupiter complex," according to Patrick M. S. Blackett, the father of Operational Research.[64] The Allied airmen saw themselves as gods, hurling bolts of lightning down upon the vileness of the enemy. Only a god can deliver a plague, since he is not subject to any law. He is the law. The questionable means used in the Battle of the Ruhr are part of the still barely tested genre of the environmental war. From fireraising, the mental leap to flooding was simple. The operational researchers confronted the question: What would happen if this new god's wrath were aimed at two dams in the Ruhr valley? Most probably, it would bring a modern-day Flood with a twofold effect: First, the deluge, and second, the subsequent water shortage in the Ruhr basin.

The reservoir dam of the Moehne River, together with the Sorpe dam 10.5 miles away, situated in the rivershed region of the Ruhr

River, formed a single water management unit. The two dams supplied 70 percent of Ruhr basin industry with service water and 4.5 million residents with drinking water. The Eder River dam near Kassel was even larger, retaining about seven billion cubic feet of water. Economists in the Air Ministry had calculated that the loss of the Moehne-Sorpe water reservoirs in mid-May, when the water level was highest, would bring all industry in the Ruhr basin to a standstill in the summer, and the lack of drinking water would cause a serious emergency for the civilian population. Blasting the Eder Valley dam, in turn, would bring shipping on the Upper Weser River to a halt, flooding Kassel and causing farmlands to wither.

The dams were of immense proportions. The Moehne dam was 130 feet high and 112 feet thick at its base. In order to breach it, a four-ton, cylindrical "Upkeep" mine was necessary. The point of explosion had to be thirty feet below the surface. Calculations determined that the bomb had to be dropped from a height of exactly sixty feet above the surface; shortly before release, it would be brought into a reverse spin, and once hitting the water, it would skip along to the wall. This would enable it to elegantly bounce over the antitorpedo netting strung in front of the dam. Then it would roll down the dam vertically, maintaining contact with it due to its backspin, and explode by hydrostatic fuse at the proper depth.

Transport of the "bouncing bomb," which was designed by an engineer with the codename "Professor Jeff," was accomplished by twenty-three custom-built Lancasters. A special mounting was needed to attach the bomb to the underside of the plane, perpendicular to the aircraft's front-rear axis. The most difficult part was determining the precise altitude necessary for bomb release such that it would successfully reach the calculated breach point. The British set up a structure similar to the Moehne dam on a test lake. In 125 trial drops, they devised a system to find the precisely calculated drop height. The best crews in the country participated. An aiming instrument made of two spotlights pointing downward was attached to the nose and fuselage. At an altitude of exactly sixty feet, the reflections from the two angled spotlights merged into one on the surface of the water, causing a flash—the signal to drop the bombs—and the four-tonner rolled and bounced along the surface of the lake.

The effects of the Dambusters Raid were considered decisive for the war effort; it took place on the night of the full moon, May 16, 1943. Two formations flew over the North Sea, the Moehne-Eder formation and the Sorpe formation. The former got caught in flak fire and the planes lost each other; when it reformed, one plane was missing.

In the moonlight, the Moehne dam could be seen from over a mile away. Twelve light flak artillery fired from the banks. Wing Commander Guy Gibson went first, releasing while flying at a speed of 240 mph. The mine reached the dam, the bomber jumped the rail, the explosion shot huge masses of water into the sky, but the dam walls held. Then the second plane approached but released its bomb too late; it impacted behind the wall and took the bomber with it in the explosion. The third and fourth bombers placed their bombs accurately. Mountains of water shot up, but the dam continued to hold, even after the next attempt, though the fifth bomber caused the wall to crack. As the sixth plane was preparing to attack, a leak appeared and the dam was breached. With three bombers remaining, the formation flew across the Sauerland region to the Eder Valley dam, which was hardly visible in the dense night fog. The first aircraft succeeded in creating a crack in the dam. With its last bomb, the third plane finally breached the dam and the lake flooded into the valley. The Sorpe formation failed. Almost all of the planes were downed. The remnants of the formation tried their luck at the Schwelm dam, also without success.

The dambusting raid, Operation Chastise, is considered the most brilliant action ever carried out by the Air Force. Its effect on the area was as devastating as its execution was precise. A tidal wave of 160 million tons of water, with a vertex thirty feet high, flooded into the Eder valley. Headed toward Kassel, it inundated five towns as it went: Hemfurth, Affoldern, Bergheim, Giflitz, and Mehlen. It was impossible to save people from the collapsed buildings because there was a shortage of rubber dinghies. Pioneer divisions arrived on May 18, and dived in the barns, looking for dead livestock. It took two hours to recover each cadaver because some were buried, some inaccessible. Affoldern lost the greatest number of animals: forty horses, 250 cattle, and 290 pigs. On May 21, there was a funeral for three hundred people who died but could not be identified until already in their coffins. A couple of days later, the bodies of two dead children and four live pigs were dug out in Affoldern.

During the first hour, water flooded into the Moehne-Ruhr Valley at a rate of 320,000 cubic feet per second. After thirty-six hours, 4.3 of 4.7 billion cubic feet of water had rushed out. The tidal wave in the mid-Ruhr region reached a peak of six to ten feet above the highest flood level and started flowing the ninety-odd miles to the Rhine. Many farm animals were killed and the entire fish stock was decimated. Five miles down from the Moehne dam lay the town of Neheim-Hüsten. It was hit by the full force of the flood and 859 people were killed. Seven hundred and fifty prisoners in a nearby slave labor camp, mostly female Ukrainian fieldworkers, were also killed.[65] All in all, about 1,300 civilians drowned.

Because the dambusters failed to breach the Sorpe Valley dam, the expected disaster for the Ruhr basin's industry and population failed to materialize. For that to have happened, both reservoirs would have had to drain simultaneously. The flood damage to buildings, bridges, and water and electricity works was repaired within weeks or months. The Eder Valley dam was rebuilt by late September by 20,000 workers; the reconstruction of the Moehne Valley dam followed. No attempts were made to further probe the potential of an environmental attack. The United States repeated a dambusting raid in the Korean War. The unleashed flow of water washed away a thin clay soil layer, destroying North Korean rice paddies and triggering a famine. In principle, the environmental aggressor investigated the region for balanced systems. Whether natural or manmade, the important thing was to find the single component that, when surgically removed, caused the collapse of the whole system by flood, famine, epidemic, or bacteria.

Nine months after the flooding project, Lord Cherwell described to the Prime Minister how anthrax bacteria work. By the winter of 1943, a four-pound bomb filled with anthrax spores given the codename "N" had been designed by the British and built by the Americans. "Half a dozen Lancasters could apparently carry enough, if spread evenly, to kill anyone found within a square mile and to render the area uninhabitable thereafter."[66] Churchill responded without delay—this would solve the bothersome problem of precision targeting. On March 8, 1944, he ordered half a million anthrax bombs from the United States.[67] "Pray let me know when they will be available," he wrote to the Bacteriological Warfare Committee. "We should regard it as a first instalment."[68]

The 1944 invasion with ground forces ruled out the option of contaminating the invasion area; clean incendiary attacks proved more feasible than anthrax and flood disasters. The will to annihilate usually preceded the military necessities.

The precision of the dambusters raid proved that point targets could be hit with accuracy down to the inch if the outlays were sufficient and provided the destruction of the targets subsequently devastated large enough regions. The plan succeeded partly due to the bravura of the squadron, but they never would have made such a brilliant show without the glaring defensive error of the Germans. They allowed the attack to take place as if they were watching a display of aerobatics, because all the flak batteries had been concentrated in the areas they thought were at risk: the Ruhr cities. It was impossible to defend everything and, with that in mind, the British used their imagination to deceive the enemy defenses.

The British used absurd approach routes, so the attack objective was not obvious until the bombers arrived. The defensive forces were frittered away on the wrong sites. Some of the Mosquitos were involved exclusively with diversionary tactics. In order to hit Berlin, the night fighters were lured to Leipzig by a feigned raid. On the night of the dambusters raid, Gibson did not want to be disturbed by fighter planes, so he purposely chose a minimum number of planes for the formation, making it look like a typical diversionary run. He knew the Germans would assume that anyone showing up with only nineteen Lancasters could not do all that much damage.

The U.S. Eighth Air Force preferred to shut down the system with precision strikes on a key location. As of mid-1943, the German sky had been divided up between the British and the Americans. The British flew the night raids and the Americans flew during the day. U.S. aircraft flew at higher altitudes, their aerial gunners fired higher calibers, their squadron formation was large and awe-inspiring, and their convictions humane, so they rejected carpet bombing. In their search for the key ingredient in the manufacture of armaments, the lynchpin whose destruction would cause a standstill in the production of all other parts, the economists decided upon the ball bearing. Because the Germans produced them mostly in Schweinfurt and Regensburg, those cities needed to be targeted in an intelligent way. The bomber force had other talents besides just razing residential districts.

Striking the warrior's Achilles' heel proved to be a suicide mission. The locations were well defended and there were 16 percent losses. The First and Fourth Bombardment Wings turned out to be far more sensitive than the ball-bearing industry. During their "bloody summer," the U.S. Eighth Air Force learned the bloody lesson that of all unstable systems, a bomber fleet in the sky is one of the most unstable. This led the Americans to decide that instead of seeking the enemy's most vulnerable point, they would make themselves invulnerable.

For the most part, the bomber was wounded by the fighter. To fight the fighter, the bomber had to hunt it: its airfields and hangars, its production and the production of its fuel had to be eliminated. If one's own aircraft controlled the air unchallenged, then there was no need to search for key sites on the ground. You could simply bomb everything until the stone started to melt. The enemy whose defenses failed ceased to be an adversary and became instead an object of punishment. A target, an adversary, is hunted down, whereas an object is static. The Germans reached this static state of being at someone's mercy starting in the fall of 1944—and the greatest density of bombs were dropped from that point on.

More than half the British tonnage from sixty months of air war against the cities fell during the last nine months.[69] At that point, the lethality of the bomber weapon also reached its peak.[70] From the beginning of the Battle of the Ruhr until the end of 1943, the weapon killed an average of 8,100 civilians each month, 13,500 starting from July 1944. In between, the U.S. Air Force shut down the German aircraft industry. The ratio of the tonnage dropped for that mission to the total tonnage that fell on cities is one to twelve. When the aircraft industry—a strictly military target—lay in ruins, Germany on the ground was helpless in the face of the force in the sky. Taking advantage of the situation, the British-American fleet dropped 370,000 tons of bombs between January and April 1945, far more than one-fourth of the total amount of bombs dropped.[71] During that time, the British and Americans bombed full time, suffering virtually no losses. The convergence of the British and the American weapons had already taken place in the first half of 1944, when the British continued to burn down cities while the U.S. forces set their sights on what obstructed them the most: the German fighter fleet.

Shutting down the fighter weapon as regards production, airfields, and aircraft was to the bombing war what breaching the Moehne dam was to the Ruhr valley. Much like the bottled-up destructive force unleashed in the flooding of the valley, the flood of bombers would be unstoppable in the absence of enemy fighter squadrons. All that still slowed down the Battle of the Ruhr was the destructibility of the destroyer. The wave that buried everything beneath it did not come from Moehne Lake. That kind of "secret weapon" was an illusion of the professors in the service of the air war. Harris considered such things nonsense, "panacea targets," miracle drugs, cure-alls. No, it was the offensive waves of Lancasters and Boeing 17s, uncountable and unhindered, that would continue to raze cities to the ground until none remained. That is why, in the final stretch before the capitulation, the cities of Freiburg, Heilbronn, Nuremberg, Halberstadt, Worms, Pforzheim, Trier, Chemnitz, Potsdam, Dresden, Danzig, and others had to go.

A steamroller worked its way through Germany one last time from January to May 1945. It was almost totally devoid of military purpose and was free from all tactical risk.

> We had to attack the already devastated cities of the Ruhr . . . in order to finish off such industries as had begun to produce again during the long respite from bombing. . . . In Essen and many other towns almost everything that could be burnt was already reduced to ashes, and we could therefore only attack with high-explosive bombs, which in proportion to their bulk weigh far more than incendiaries.
>
> I had some time ago foreseen . . . that the time might come when we should need an enormously larger supply of heavy case high-explosive bombs than before, when our main weapons had been the 4 lb. incendiary and the 4000 lb. blast bomb—this latter was, of course, essentially a weapon for use against intact buildings and was no great use against already ruined cities in which life was mostly going on in cellars.[72]

The two questions that dominated everything one year earlier— when would German staying power and morale finally break? And might not returning to the oil and transportation targets of 1941 be more effective?—were irrelevant in March 1945. There was no longer any morale, oil, or transportation. The ground invasion of the German Reich was advancing, which demanded its own tactical bombing. Places where resistance had taken cover, or might have taken cover, or could have taken cover had been wiped out from the air—as was anything that had once had functioning railway lines. Every one of these attacks was a case of its own. This razing of towns along the battle line, while related to the war, was not always vital to the war effort. While it might look the same as Harris's devastation of ruins, it differed as regards intention. Harris's aims joined forces with the final military offensives without actually being part of them, because Harris's aims served no purpose. Why was Pforzheim reduced to ashes on the night of February 23, 1945, with a fire zone of 1.7 square miles and twenty thousand casualties? Master Bomber Edwin Swales was posthumously awarded the Victoria Cross for that mission.

In addition to Hamburg, Kassel, and Dresden, Pforzheim is one of the dozen or so other cities in which a firestorm developed. The firestorm is the apotheosis of fireraising. Until September 1944, it could not be deliberately produced. It could only be triggered when human destructive rage coupled perfectly with natural phenomena. Atmospheric reactions could pass an unforeseen, rampant, and aggressive rage on to the incendiary devices. The British welcomed this divine boon and immediately tried to determine a mathematical formula for producing it. That seemed an impossible task, since it involved too many variables and unknowns.

The general phenomenon had already been described in 1927, by Lt.-Col. Wilhelm Siegert, inspector of the Flying Troops in Imperial Germany during World War I. The weekly magazine *Berliner Illustrirte Zeitung* reported:

> If it is possible to start numerous sources of fire in a city such that the existing fire departments cannot extinguish all of them at once, the seeds of catastrophes are thus sown. The individual fires merge into a major blaze. The superheated air shoots upward like a giant chimney. The air that rushes in along the ground creates the "firestorm," which in turn causes the smaller fires to unfurl completely.

The physics of this cycle, the area-wide conflagrations, the vertically flaring hot air, the storm that was sucked in horizontally to fill the vacuum that in turn fanned the area blaze, all this was more powerful than any and all munitions. The casualty figures jumped to five digits, a magnitude that for a single bomb drop seemed exclusive to the atomic bomb. Pforzheim proved that was not the case.

In February 1945, there were 65,000 people in Pforzheim. In August 1945, in Nagasaki, there were more than 300,000, where the attack killed 39,000 people, about one in seven. In Pforzheim, there were 20,277 deaths, almost one in three.[73] Siegert's theory was experienced in practice by the Pforzheimers. Soldier Wilhelm Riecker was among those who fled the deceiving security of the cellars beneath the burning apartment buildings.

> They dunked blankets and towels in the bucket, wrapped them around themselves, and ran through the flames to the Enz River, where they doused themselves again with water, since the heat and flying sparks were

incredible. Sedan Square converged the flames from all the streets leading into it and then let the scorching force escape toward the bridge. The flames shot over it into the city center and there the mushroom rose up steeply, drawing all the fire into its shaft. During this hour the radiant heat was so intense that people were jumping into the wintry cold river.[74]

The city, built at the confluence of the Enz and the Nagold, was rich with water. That was why many drowned in the firestorm. Those who entrusted themselves to the cellar did not know its treachery. Theologian Otto Riecker wrote:

> My brother-in-law leaped down and lit up the room with matches. A relative was leaning against a wall with both hands pressed against the stone; she was facing the escape shaft as if she were alive. Opposite her was a man with his back against the wall and his arms outstretched. There were four women on a bench; they were leaning forward slightly with their arms folded as if sleeping peacefully. All of them had died within a single moment; the blast killed them.[75]

It was the work of the 330 five-hundred-pound aerial mines.

In the morning rain Professor Fritz Löffler looked for the veins of a town, its streets. "Where were there still any streets? You had to climb over rocks and timber and then you'd suddenly see—in an open space or in the windowless storefront of the Palace Café—the bloated, unclothed skeletal remains of the working maidens, charred by the dozens."[76]

Cellars worked like crematoria: "The vaulted cellar was still in good condition," wrote Hermine Lautenschlager.

> There were no doors anywhere. No cabinets or boxes remained, which my sister had used to store her best things. On the floor, and especially along the wall, there were piles of ashes here and there. Part of a human torso that looked like a charred tree stump was in the middle of the cellar. Near a pile of ashes in the corner lay a bag that disintegrated at the slightest touch. The bent metal handle and a keychain were all that remained. They were the bag and keys of my sister. That's where she always sat during the air-raids, that's what my brother-in-law told me. Later they even found a small piece of fabric from her dress.[77]

5. "Our fire engine was out of water." Cologne, May 31, 1942.
Source: Bildarchiv Preussischer Kulturbesitz.

The firestorm created a different atmosphere, which was hostile to life in three ways. First, the heat climbed to almost 1,500°F in the area of the burning blocks of houses. Second, the wind blew at a velocity of fifty feet per second within a radius of 2.5 miles from the column of hot air. The thrust of this air current made it impossible to walk; pedestrians braced themselves, were pulled down, and in the worst of cases, were sucked into the fire source. Third, there was no oxygen. It was simply no longer possible to breathe the scorched, stalking air, reported Maria Lupus:

> Because the maddening heat and oxygen deprivation threatened liter-ally to dry us up, we helped each other climb down into the canal. The monstrous firestorm ripped the air right out of our mouths. Our surviv-al instinct showed us the only way to find some oxygen was to breathe directly above the surface of the water. The child on my arm didn't budge. It was probably almost anaesthetized from the fumes that had developed. Meanwhile the lack of oxygen had also gotten worse down in the canal. The thick smoke penetrated painfully into eyes and lungs. You totally lost sense of time. Had many hours passed? Or just a few? There were some horrific scenes at the river that flowed past the canal. Injured people washed ashore who in mortal fear had jumped out of burning houses into the water. Many were already dead; others had ghastly burns. There was dead silence everywhere.[78]

The 1,551 tons of bombs that rained down on the small jewelry- and clock-producing city were a mighty load, one hundred tons more than the Millennium raid on Cologne. The 1,554 tons that fell four days later on Mainz, a city twice the size, killed 1,122 people. Two years earlier, that was considered a dreadfully high figure; now, dur-ing these concentrated attacks, it was merely average. But in Mainz there was no firestorm. Harris had a plausible explanation: Rubble does not burn well. The heavy attacks on Mainz in September 1944 had created space. The firestorm needed close quarters, intact cities, buildings packed full with the essentials of life: furniture, clothing, food, books. Above all, there had to be enough roof frames and floor-boards. It was for them that the hundreds of thousands of incendiary sticks were intended.

Because Pforzheim was small and irrelevant as regards arma-ments, Bomber Command had not damaged it much earlier in the war. Thus the city's flammability had been preserved. Starting in the fall of 1944, Bomber Command's ability to place its incendiaries on the smallest possible, clearly defined area had been improved by the use of new cluster bombs. But the bombs needed combustibles. The smaller and more militarily insignificant the town, the better the target it had now become. The military value of Pforzheim in February 1945 had grown immensely; this was due exclusively to its total military uselessness. Its attraction was the block-end buildings, the sandstone building material, the narrow and winding alleyways in the center, and the closely built row housing without proper firewalls. The city was virtually undefended, and fire protection was minimal. Master Bomber Swales could carry out his bombardment under laboratory conditions. It lasted from 7:50 p.m. to 8:12 p.m. The typhoon did not get going until later, first with a strong air draft, and then, in the middle of the blaze, an ice-cold storm was sucked in, which needed until 11:30 p.m. to envelop the city in flames. Metal with a melting point of 3,100°F became molten. After twenty-two minutes of work, Swales was shot down as he was leaving by a remaining German fighter plane, and Pforzheim boiled into lava as if struck by the cyclopean fists of another geologic era.

Churchill, Harris, and Portal first heard of a firestorm in July 1943, after Hamburg. They had spent two years trying to overcome the paralyzing technological and financial obstacles to annihilation from the air, and they kept morosely adding up unreal numbers of airplanes, homeless, and dead. In one fell swoop, the unfathomable interaction of their weapon with the force of the elements delivered dimensions of destruction that up to then had existed only on paper. The aviation strategists perceived the forces of nature as their logical allies, and they hoped for further collaboration.

A large part of Bomber Command's efforts were dedicated from then on to the "Hamburgization" of Berlin. Berlin did not burn well. The alliance with the physics of the atmosphere was unreliable, but it became an unscheduled addition to the agenda in Kassel in October 1943. Why Kassel and not Berlin?

Ever since the Battle of the Ruhr, Bomber Command had been constantly experimenting with the ratio of incendiaries in the loads to be dropped. The markedly higher incendiary doses of the bombardments of Wuppertal in late May, Aachen in mid-July, and Remscheid in late July led to conflagrations extending for miles. The three raids on Hamburg in July and August also had considerably varied bomb loads. Determining the proper loads and ratios was a science of its own. The second strike of a raid used five times as many incendiaries as the first.[79] An average of 250,000 incendiary sticks and seven thousand liquid-incendiary bombs were released per square mile. Consequently, the mixture was a condition for the firestorm, as were the tinfoil strips that jammed the radar, blocking the defenses. Hamburg, too, offered laboratory conditions. The weapon unfolded as it wanted, not just as far as the defender allowed. But all the incendiaries and tinfoil strips would not have caused the massive destruction of the firestorm without the contribution of the climate. The climate was the main agent.

In Pforzheim it had been bitter cold; in Hamburg, on the other hand, it was hotter and drier than it had been in ten years. On the sweltering summer night of July 28, the temperature was between 70° and 85°F. The combination of the climate, the incendiary ratio, the collapsed defenses, and the structure of the city blocks created what Harris's codename "Gomorrah" predicted: Like Abraham in Genesis 19:28, Harris looked toward the sinful city "and beheld, and, lo, the smoke of the country went up as the smoke of a furnace." It melted between forty thousand and fifty thousand people. Seventy percent of them were in the Hamburg-Mitte district, where the weapon achieved a kill rate of 5.9 percent. In the strictly residential streets of Hammerbrook, 36 percent of the residents were killed. Seven thousand children and adolescents lost their lives, and ten thousand were orphaned.

The small, close courtyards turned into glowing cells whose inmates could not escape death. At the zenith of the firestorm, the pure heat radiation caused buildings to ignite all at once, from the roof to the ground, like a darting flame. The gale winds drew the oxygen out of the cellars like a gigantic pump. Six hours of firestorm supposedly forced two billion tons of fresh air up more than four miles through the air chimney.[80] This created horizontal wind velocities into the storm of up to 170 miles per hour, causing people to lose their footing. Trees with roots extending yards into the ground broke in half, and their crowns were twisted. Poplars were bent completely horizontally. The rescue crews that later gathered the remains of those who had suffocated from lack of oxygen or had been incinerated by the radiant heat had to let the masses of rubble cool down for ten days.

A firestorm usually developed over hours, but in Hamburg it formed during the raid itself. The firefighters were rendered powerless because they could not move through the cratered streets and had almost no water. The storm was preceded by sunny, hot weather, which had already overheated the urban area.[81] A chimney quickly developed, and only minimal additional heating was necessary to put the immense suction of the draft into motion; this turned the horizontal storm into a torrent. Those who were caught in it were ripped into the furnace like poor souls into perdition.

Neither Harris nor Bomber Command nor anyone else knew the least about the meteorological conditions. They declared the operation a success and thought they had discovered the attack that would be a reference point for future raids to emulate. The weapon had now become what they had hoped it would. Churchill's "maximum use of fire" had ignited within three years. The munitions had been unloaded in forty-three minutes, and they were followed by atmospheric reactions that raged for three hours with the force of a Pacific hurricane. And then there was nothing left to burn. Unable to protect itself, the city consumed itself. Nine hundred thousand people fled the smoldering skeletons of buildings, in which the plague of rats was the only thing left alive.

A weapon that caused this kind of destruction must be a strategic one; it must decide the war. If not, then it served only for continued mass extermination. Churchill's cabinet had assured the public that it destroyed whatever served a military use, but now it welcomed the deaths of forty thousand Hamburg civilians. Therefore, their deaths had to serve some purpose. It was believed that this massacre was best interpreted as a prelude to the Hamburgization of Berlin. A comparable attack on the capital would certainly bring an end to the regime and thus to the war. It was always under the assumption that the premise of "morale bombing" applied. To the end of his days, Harris cited Hiroshima as proof of that.

If the larger city of Berlin had losses of the same scale as Hamburg, then 109,000 people would have lost their lives,[82] one and a quarter times the number of Hiroshima deaths.[83] Since after Hamburg there were more than 340,000 additional deaths in the air war, half of all bombing casualties would have remained alive had there been an immediate, final strike against Berlin. Would the capital have capitulated if it had experienced 3 percent losses? Conceivably. But the actual victims from 1943 to 1945 died without yielding any such return from the aggressor's perspective. They were killed in a slow, relentless machine that ground away day and night in all parts of the Reich. Divided among the six hundred remaining days of the bombing war, the effect on morale was militarily insignificant. What does "national staying power" care about the 244 people who died on January 5, 1944, in Stettin; or the 270 on June 12 in Gelsenkirchen? No one heard about it. The news reached Recklinghausen at most. Such losses were two-thirds of the total.

The Nazi party, like Harris, expected the collapse after slaughters like Hamburg. On August 1, Albert Speer said to Hitler that attacks like that on six more cities would mean the end of the war. Field Marshal Erhard Milch, inspector general of the Luftwaffe, thought: "We have lost the war! Finally lost the war!" Soldiers on the battlefield would just have to dig a hole, he said, crawl into it, and wait until the attack is over. But a hole was no protection from a firestorm. "What the home front is suffering now cannot be suffered very much longer."[84] But Churchill's weapon was not able to pull off six Hamburgs; instead it produced a thousand Gelsenkirchens.

Immediately after the war, the U.S. occupation forces extensively investigated the psyches of the bombing victims. They found that defeatism grew after the shock of the first attack experience. However, the accumulation of experiences tended to dull the effect. The soul did not rebel; it shriveled. Apathy and depression predominated. People felt an overwhelming need for sleep and none at all to overthrow Hitler. If there ever were a chance to do that, then it would be in a series of Hamburg-Hiroshima strikes. The atomic bomb very much resembled the firestorm in its primary impact. They both usually killed by roasting, burning to a cinder, vaporizing. Harris once said that an atom bomb was just the equivalent of a certain number of normal bombs—but only as regards the sum and not the impact. The Anglo-American weapon achieved five-digit casualty figures within a single raid five more times after Hamburg: in Kassel, Darmstadt, Pforzheim, Dresden, and Swinemünde. The five-digit losses, however, amount to only one-third of the total losses.

During the next nine months of the Battle of Berlin, Bomber Command lost the strategic clout it had attained in Hamburg and the Battle of the Ruhr. Berlin would not burn, even if three-quarters of the damages there were due to fire. Much to Churchill's and Harris's dismay, they could not make the city into Hitler's funeral pyre. "There was a good deal of consternation in the Royal Air Forces as to the reason that Berlin didn't burn as well as other German cities," wrote U.S. fire protection engineer James K. McElroy, who was working with the RAF. "The real reason . . . in my opinion, was the fact that the city was honeycombed with parapeted firewalls."[85] It lacked the inner-city structure that existed in medieval fortification walls. Even the tenements had a resistant, stable courtyard structure.

The statisticians in Bomber Command calculated other proportions of bombs and considered double-sized bomb loads. McElroy pored over fire-insurance maps of major German cities in order to determine the relationship between failed incendiary raids and the frequency of firewalls. "None of us who were in this incendiary warfare business were able, at any time, to use our judgment without some sort of statistical background." The British absolutely refused to accept Berlin's resistance to fire.

> Fire spread in German targets was the subject of many of the debates of the [British Incendiary Bomb Tests] Panel. Major Sanborn and I attempted unsuccessfully to end the debate in February and March, 1944, by the use of data collected from the German attacks on London. During that period there was not a single instance of the spread of fire over a parapeted firewall.

The notion that the endurance of firewalls was the decisive factor, whether in Berlin or London, of course did not fit into the belief system of the strategic air war.

The nineteen major raids that made up the Battle of Berlin from August 1943 to March 1944 killed 9,390 civilians and 2,690 airmen.[86] This was an astounding ratio for an operation that was supposed to decide the war. There was definitely no shortage of material: 10,813 bombers dropped 17,000 tons of high-explosive bombs and 16,000 tons of incendiaries. A similar mass of bombs fell on each resident of both Berlin and Hamburg: around eighteen pounds. But they worked in different ways.

On October 22, 1943, Bomber Command succeeded in igniting its second firestorm. On October 3, they had been in Kassel, dismantling the Henschel locomotive works and an ammunition depot west of Ihringshausen, but they missed the center of town. The following night, Frankfurt's city center was damaged. The children's hospital on Gagernstrasse suffered a direct hit to its air-raid shelter. Ninety children, fourteen nurses, and a doctor died, as well as 414 other civilians. The 406 airplanes successfully set fires, but none of those fires even remotely resembled what ten squadrons with 569 planes left behind after the second Kassel raid.

The 416,000 incendiary bombs fell in a density of up to two per square yard, thanks to the high-precision marking. Most buildings in the city center were hit by many incendiary sticks and two liquid incendiaries. Kassel's Old Town became the city's undoing. On this evening in late fall, it was not hot as it had been in Hamburg, though it was very dry. The bomber stream extended for more than ninety miles. When the first wave started bombing at 8:45 p.m., the last wave was flying over Bonn-Koblenz. They managed a direct hit on the intended point, St. Martin's Square and St. Martin's Church, with the tomb of Landgrave Karl of Hesse-Kassel.

A rich ensemble of half-timbered buildings was preserved at the residence of the former landgrave as the unparalleled pride of the local citizenry. That was just what Harris had been looking for. The powerful direct hit on this kindling most likely sufficed to set the entire city center ablaze within fifteen minutes. The liquid-incendiary bombs penetrated through all floors of all the buildings, setting fires from attic to basement; the high-capacity blockbusters tore away all roofs and windows within a radius of more than five hundred yards, the flames moving as if through a chimney with the flue wide open.

It became impossible to pass through stairwells and corridors. Although there were water reserves in cisterns, reservoirs, and especially the Fulda River, all of which were independent of the water mains, once the firestorm established its demesnes, it was absolutely impenetrable. A thousand-year-old city like Kassel was built of materials that accelerated the process. The historical depth of such a construction quickened its inexorable demise. The firestorm required forty-five minutes to reach its peak. It was not bothered significantly by the efforts of six firefighting squads and two turntable ladders.[87] A city in the Ruhr basin with neighboring fire departments that could offer quick aid would not have been as defenseless, but Kassel was isolated. The closest major town or city was a hundred miles away.

One in ten people in the city center died in the raid on Kassel. In all, ten thousand lives were lost.[88] That is a rate of 4.42 percent. In Hamburg it was 2.73 percent. Not until almost a year later were a comparable number of people annihilated, but Darmstadt was only half as large, so the deaths made up 10.6 percent of the population.

Firestorms and wide-area conflagrations are closely related events, though the lethality of the former is far greater and occurred less often. The fire weapon was more likely to evoke firestorms in medium-sized cities with historic centers. The fires in Hamburg and Dresden, which remain in our memories as monuments of the air war, are isolated examples. The air war was a war of attrition, in which the bombing of

Brunswick is probably more characteristic than a Kassel or Dresden: a dozen major raids, 2,905 dead, and 80 percent of housing in the city center destroyed, 33 percent of the housing overall. By far, most of the losses were borne by 158 medium-sized German cities.

The failure to Hamburgize Berlin clearly shifted the strategic focus to the ground invasion of the continent. Roosevelt and Churchill had been putting off the date since 1942. Harris and Portal drew a balance of their civilian terror. At the Cairo and Teheran Conferences, in which Allied powers discussed the unprecedented project to land three million troops in Europe, Portal reported on the results of carpet bombing. This too had involved mobilizing millions. Bomber Command had created six million homeless men and women who were spreading alarm and despondency wherever they wandered throughout the Reich, Portal said. Germany could respond to the shortage of clothing and movable goods only at the expense of the war effort, and he had "no shadow of doubt" that German morale was "at an extremely low ebb." Bomber Command was "at least halfway along the road of industrial devastation towards the point where Germany [would] become unable to continue the war."[89]

In fact, in 1943, German industry had suffered a production decline of 9 percent due to bombing damages, but output had generally increased. In the year of the Battle of the Ruhr, steel production had risen 6.5 percent and coal mining, 7 percent. The armaments industry would achieve its maximum output in the second half of 1944.[90]

Harris had set other priorities. On November 3, 1943, he wrote to Churchill, listing nineteen cities that had been "virtually destroyed" and were thus a liability to Germany. Another nineteen had been "seriously damaged," and nine were "damaged." In thirty-eight towns and cities, at least one-fourth of the built-up area had been razed, and the Ruhr especially was "largely 'out.'" If the program were to be continued and Berlin destroyed, then Germany would inevitably collapse. In December, Harris added that this would be possible by April 1 if 75 percent of all Germans in cities with populations over fifty thousand were attacked. Then, he wrote, "the state of devastation would reduce Germany to capitulation."[91]

Bomber Command and two U.S. Air Forces had ravaged Germany as no civilization had ever before, though it took a year longer than scheduled. The capitulation did not come until two ground offensives had conquered the country from the west and the east. The devastation had paved the way, greatly facilitating the subsequent occupation. Given the prevailing power constellation, Germany would have been conquered even without the devastation, but the conquerors would have then suffered higher losses.

The leadership of the U.S. Army Air Forces believed that the war would be decided not by semiclothed homeless people and terrorized residents of small cities but by the landing of ground troops. The continent had to be bombed from the air to prepare for the invasion. All that prevented that was the fighter arm of the German Luftwaffe, which had grown dangerously in 1943, producing a thousand new planes each month. Its fighters battled over the cities with bitter bravura. The initial raid of the Battle of Berlin on August 28 had decimated the force: 169 men were killed and fifty-three captured. The Allies had three casualties.

From February 20 to 25, 1944, the U.S. Army Air Force prepared for a massive strike against the German aviation industry. For days, the so-called Big Week was a sensation in the Allied press.[92] With six thousand bomber and 3,670 escort fighter sorties, this was the heretofore largest armed force to appear in the German sky. It dropped twenty thousand tons of bombs on the Messerschmitt works in Augsburg and on the ball-bearing production sites in Schweinfurt, Regensburg, Stuttgart, and elsewhere. The combined Anglo-American forces claimed to have destroyed 70 percent of the buildings; on top of that, the Luftwaffe lost 1,500 planes and 366 pilots. U.S. forces accepted daily losses of up to 19 percent; that is, each crew and bomber survived five to six attacks. In January and February, however, the German fighters lost almost one-third of the planes they put into action.

Albert Speer had taken over the responsibility for German fighter production in January. By March after the Big Week, the fleet had already regenerated. The Germans were now producing two hundred more fighter planes than in January, and by June, they had doubled the February inventory. That was the peak performance of the war. Robust German machine tools largely withstood the collapse of the production shops. When the rubble was cleared away, the machines stubbornly continued to operate. Speer also managed to relocate aircraft production from the cities to caves, forests, and subterranean tunnels out of the bomber's reach. Outside of the city, the bomber loses its bearings. A fighter jet assembly plant at the foothills of the Thuringian Forest was beyond the air war.

But personnel was irreplaceable. From June 1941 to October 1944, 44,000 German airmen had been lost,[93] including nine thousand officers. Pilots graduated from flying school with 150 flying hours. Their enemies enjoyed double the training time and outnumbered their German counterparts sevenfold. The German airmen made up for their low numbers by flying more sorties. They repressed their fatigue, but that did not help them learn to fly. Half of them crashed during hasty training given by resigned instructors. Pilots lacked training in instrument flight and landing in inclement weather. They sat half blinded in iced-up cockpits, with lighter arms than the enemy's new Mustangs, and as of March 1944, they were more hunted than hunter.

The Mustangs were less needing of inflexible escort protection, and they plunged into open-air battle in packs, flying daring low raids on airfields. "Things have gone so far that our arm threatens to collapse,"[94] reported Inspector of Fighters Adolf Galland to the morphine-addicted Göring, whom the pilots disparagingly called "Tüte." He said that in the first four months of the year, the day fighters had lost a thousand pilots, including the best officers. The gaps could no longer be filled. On top of that, the massive spring raids on hydrogenation plants hit the mark; by September, only one-sixth of the fuel ration remained. The German fighter arm had become inoperative. Now there was nothing left in the sky to stand between the population and the liberator. On the ground there was still a long way to go.

That way first led the Allied forces across the water. Every man, every weapon, every piece of equipment had to be loaded onto a ship for an amphibious landing under fire. The Germans were at the coast, and everything they needed for their barricade was easily brought to the front by an extensive network of rails and roads. That was their sole advantage. Other than that, they had to guard over three thousand miles of coastline and were fighting a relentless rearguard action in Russia with an army that had been broken and bled white over four and a half years. In the invasion region, they had a hundred fighter planes, compared with the 5,400 fighters of their enemy, who had 12,830 airplanes in all. These were the enemy's sole advantage, since its army was mighty in number but completely green. And its mission was also the most difficult of all: to break through a land front from the water and then push back the enemy in their own territory, yard by yard, supported by supply lines over water.

Four months before the Normandy landing, General Eisenhower issued orders to aim his strongest weapon at the adversary's trump card, the transportation connections to the rear. The Transportation Plan of the Allied Air Forces, which was drafted by Solly Zuckerman, took place in two acts. The beginning in March was set in France and Belgium; the fall act, in Germany. In both of them, railway stations were the target, as were shunting stations, rolling stock, streets, bridges, canals, and rivers. All of these usually hugged close within residential areas, which inevitably had to offer up some victims. For the act in Germany, this was regarded as self-evident, even desirable. In France, the operation worked against French and Belgian civilians.

In Allied headquarters, an uneasiness was felt around having to kill civilians whom the war's mission was to liberate. Eisenhower had been presented with the misgivings of the British war cabinet, who believed that there could conceivably be up to forty thousand casualties and 120,000 injured.[95] This was on the magnitude of Hamburg. Churchill urged President Roosevelt to intervene and ask his commanders to practice moderation.[96] After all, at the beginning of the war, Roosevelt had called for humanitarianism among all the parties: that their—that is, the British, French, and German—air forces should definitely leave the civilian populations untouched. After roughly 120,000 had been killed, the British prime minister, who had essentially made the decision to let them be killed, turned to his closest ally to prevent "the French slaughters." The President answered that he shared distress for the French civilian losses. He felt no possibility should be overlooked for "alleviating adverse French opinion,"[97] always provided it did not interfere with military success. He said he did not want to limit his commanders of the troops from doing what they felt best served the invasion and reduced Allied losses.

Among the critics of the Zuckerman plan was General Carl Spaatz, commander of the U.S. Strategic Air Forces in Europe, and it was largely Spaatz's units that were to carry out the plan. Spaatz and Zuckerman had prepared the invasion of Sicily a year earlier and the problem had been the same. Bombing paved the way for the landing, as the routes of the enemy were blocked from the air. Spaatz later praised what he called the "very coldly analytical and precise"[98] application of the air weapon as it had been calculated. In the modern war, he said, the "mathematical genius" is the best general, and this was the first modern war.

The accuracy of the raid on April 4, 1943, on the port facilities of Naples, surpassed the mathematical leeway by a good extent; 221 Neapolitans were killed. But Zuckerman's calculations did not include any civilians, because he had not dealt with "morale bombing." He was concerned with models of freight volume, the numbers of train cars, shipping space, and supplies needed. The logistics of the German Wehrmacht, Sicily's military backbone, had to bring in 300 to 450 tons of supplies daily for troops at the front, depending on whether it was an infantry or armored division. Zuckerman engaged in counterlogistics; he calculated how many barges, rail lines, and locomotives had to explode on which routes in order to prevent the division from moving. Whatever else remained was not considered by the model, but was up to Spaatz, who had gathered fresh impressions in June of the nature of the aerial weapon.

After a week of bombing, the Italian garrison on Pantelleria, an island in the Strait of Sicily, surrendered because "the human mind cannot adjust itself to bombardment on an ascending scale."[99] This led Spaatz to propose bombarding the Neapolitans and then the Romans, if Italy did not prefer to surrender. Because the possibility of Rome's destruction was a source of concern for American Catholics, Roosevelt refrained from doing that, and a transportation offensive was instead carried out against Messina, Livorno, Reggio di Calabria, and any other transportation crossroads. Human victims were permitted because Italy was classed as the enemy.

As it would turn out, the difference between friend and foe was not significant for civilian bombardment. The modern war did not know how to deal with archaic concepts such as "enemy" or "hostility." They were part of political propaganda, whereas the formulas of the modern war followed the principle of expediency. Spaatz, a wavering man, could not easily reconcile himself with that. "Many thousands of French people will be killed," he wrote to General Eisenhower, his superior, on the occasion of the invading raids,

> and many towns laid waste in these operations. I feel a joint responsibility with you and I view with alarm a military operation which involved such widespread destruction and death in countries not our enemies, particularly since the results to be achieved from these bombing operations have not been conclusively shown to be a decisive factor.[100]

Two days later, on April 24, 1944, U.S. bombers attacked the rail yards at Rouen, a diocesan city since the third century and the capital of Normandy and residence of its dukes since 912. The city, a treasure chest of medieval architecture like no other French city, lost the area between the Seine and the Cathedral of Notre Dame. The bombs destroyed its entire south wing and the rosette of the northern transept. The small Church of St. Vincent suffered a direct hit. That elegant late Gothic creation had the most beautiful stained-glass windows in all of Rouen. Removed in time, they continued to live without the rooms they once illuminated. Rouen had been forewarned by a raid by 273 Lancasters a week earlier. It had already struck the rail yards, very successfully, but not successfully enough. Significantly, the Palais de Justice was bombed. Begun in 1499, with the beautiful Salle des Pas Perdus, the Great Hall of the lawyers, with its lofty, pointed, wooden barrel-vault ceiling, it was completely destroyed. The house of Diane de Poitiers went down, an extremely rare gothic wooden construction with façade ornamentation in the Renaissance style, and the Salle des Assises also fell, the former estates parliament from 1509, with a gilded oak ceiling. Four hundred civilians were killed.

On the night of April 9, 239 Halifaxes, Lancasters, Stirlings, and Mosquitos destroyed 2,124 freight cars in Lille, as well as the Cité des Cheminots, a railroad workers' settlement with friendly, light-weight residential homes. Four hundred fifty-six people died, mostly railroaders. The survivors, who thought they were facing their final hours from the force of the attack, wandered among the bomb craters shouting "bastards, bastards." The next night brought the death of 428 Belgians in Ghent. Six hundred buildings were destroyed or damaged, including several schools, two monasteries, and an orphanage. The night raids followed the same pattern as in Germany, with pathfinders, illuminating target-indicator markers, and a horrifying bomb density.

On the night of April 20, 1,155 British airplanes covered the coastal *départements*. In the two nights from May 11 to 13, Bomber Command bombed Louvain, where thirty years earlier the world was outraged when the emperor's army fired like a storm of Huns into a group of supposed demonstrators. Whether intentional or not, the old library burned down, a replacement for which was provided for by the Treaty of Versailles. Now five blocks of the university as well as the sixteenth-century Abbey of St. Gertrude were reduced to rubble. The church's choir stalls were considered the most magnificent wood carvings in all of Belgium. No provision was made for their replacement, because they were irreplaceable. One hundred sixty residents were killed.

The transportation offensive of the preinvasion weeks took the lives of twelve thousand French and Belgian citizens, nearly twice as many as Bomber Command killed within the German Reich in 1942. In the first three weeks of the invasion, 7,704 soldiers on the Allied side were killed, and ten times that many German soldiers.[101] The unanimous judgment was that there had never been a more perfect military operation.

After the successful landing operation, the air war over France entered its decisive stage. In liberating the friends from the army of the foes it was impossible to distinguish friends from foes, since the bomber weapon still did not separate civilians and military, even five years after it was introduced. Sixty-five percent of the town of Coutances, southwest of Utah Beach, the landing sector of the U.S. VII Corps, was burned down the very night of the landing; on June 14, 1944, fire raged through the Notre Dame district of Le Havre. The raid was aimed against not the city but its harbor, where twenty-three German destroyers threatening British supply lines were wrecked. For the same reason, a raid was flown the following day, in which 297 Lancasters, Halifaxes, and Mosquitos were sent to Boulogne, where German light naval vessels, mostly motor torpedo boats, were anchored. The port and its surroundings were destroyed and two hundred people were killed.

Bomber Command returned three months later, on September 5. The invading troops were at a virtual standstill due to supply difficulties and urgently needed port facilities. Some German hedgehog positions were still holding out around Le Havre, although the Allied advance had long since passed them by and had meanwhile reached the Moselle River. In order to eliminate these cut-off units, 313 Lancasters started an expansive conflagration in Le Havre, killing 2,500 civilians.[102] These numbers were inconsequential compared to Caen, which along with Saint Lô were the most-bombed cities in the recapture of France.

Caen assumed the key position in the invasion area. This had not been intended, because the British commander, General Bernard L. Montgomery, was actually supposed to have taken the city on the eve of the invasion. On the day in question, the Germans, who had expected the invasion at Pas de Calais, had only one notable unit along the coast between Cherbourg and Le Havre, the 21st Panzer Division. Erwin Rommel had positioned them behind Caen in case they were needed. On June 7, they were joined by another Panzer division. Britain's attempt to outflank the city to the southeast got bogged down. The 21st Division had broken through British lines the day before and moved toward the coast. If three divisions had been there, they would presumably have drained some of the vigor from the Allied beachheads.

The Germans fortified themselves near the city in order to block access to the Seine basin and to Paris. On June 7, the British deployed 467 bombers to liquidate some rural German positions north of Caen. Because the known degree of error in the calculations gave them reason to fear hitting their own troops positioned nearby, the focus of attack was moved in closer to the city. They dropped 2,200 tons of bombs, eliminating hardly any Germans but instead hitting the northern suburbs. Two weeks later, the next attempt by Scottish tanks and infantry failed to break through to the west.

Although the Germans had a hard time moving in reinforcements along the torn-up streets, the Allies were stuck fast in Normandy for more than five weeks after landing, though they did manage to consolidate the bridgeheads. Caen, which was supposed to fall on the first day, held out until July 18. For reasons that might have had to do with Montgomery's vanity, the British decided—without contacting Eisenhower—finally to break out near Caen. They gathered three armored divisions, hoping to advance on the flanks toward Paris in an operation named "Goodwood," after the racetrack. There had been no plans for anything of the sort.

Before the tanks waiting on the other side of the Orne River started moving on the morning of July 18, Bomber Command took off with an armada of two thousand bombers, the likes of which no German city had ever encountered. They aimed to eliminate five fortified villages at the breakthrough point, and also to scatter seven thousand tons of bombs over an area of eighty square miles. And so the city of Caen went down too. The Church of St. Gilles, with its unique mixture of Norman Romanesque and Gothic elements, was built starting in 1082. Its construction had continued for over three centuries, and now it fell into nothingness. Guarded by the archetypal Norman church tower, St. Pierre lost its spire, which had been regarded the most flawless in the region. A measly stump remained, and the six-hundred-year-old vaulting of the aisle was blasted away as if in a quarry. Nothing remained of the magnificent French baroque city hall. Two-thirds of the buildings were destroyed, and three thousand bodies scattered throughout the city. Germans taken prisoner were so agonized by what they had seen that they could not be interrogated until twenty-four hours later.

Even by the standards of strategic bombing in the Reich, this was the maximum damage possible below the threshold of a firestorm. No single raid on Berlin achieved such a level of lethality. After the Romanesque vaulting collapsed, Operation Goodwood spent the rest of the afternoon caught in the depths of the German defenses. It was later claimed that this made it all the easier for U.S. troops to break out of Normandy at the edge of Brittany, in Operation Cobra. That occurred on July 31 near Avranches, and led to the colossal turn toward the northeast that pointed directly to the Rhine.

After massive bombardment, the isolated fortifications in the ports of Le Havre, Boulogne, and Calais were taken in September. The blood shed by residents surpassed even the level of Caen. Six thousand civilians died there, but not as a result of actions by Roosevelt, whom Churchill had not all that long before asked to refrain from "the French slaughters." It was Churchill who then proceeded to slaughter far more efficiently than Roosevelt did. Churchill would only have had to express his concern for the people of Boulogne, Le Havre, and Calais to Air Marshal Arthur Tedder, who was in charge of Bomber Command at these three cities as well as Caen. But Montgomery was having trouble taking Antwerp's North Sea access from the Germans, where the Allied forces were hoping to land their supplies. So in their fear of getting bogged down and, lacking supplies, being crushed by the Germans, they abandoned all their humaneness. As Roosevelt had known from the very beginning, that kindness would disappear if it forced the inexperienced Allied troops to confront the Germans without sufficient matériel. If necessary, Frenchmen would be slaughtered. Port cities were desperately needed, and the bombers had long been accustomed to softening up cities through civilian massacres.

Twelve months before these events took place, Churchill had watched a film with a weekend guest, Richard Casey, the Australian representative in the War Cabinet. The film had been shot by Bomber Command during the Battle of the Ruhr. It showed the bombardment being carried out, and the lens saw what the pilot, navigator, and bombardier saw in action. Casey noted in his diary that all at once Churchill "sat bolt upright and said to me 'Are we beasts? Are we taking this too far?' I said that we hadn't started it, and that it was them or us."[103]

The "us" remained the same, but the "them" increased continuously. First "they" were the Germans, then the Italians as well. Now it was also the French, along with Romanians, Hungarians, and Bulgarians.

In the winter of 1943–1944, the Allies drafted plans to wage air war against Hitler's allies in southeastern Europe: Hungary, Romania, and Bulgaria. Sofia was given a rough time between November 1943 and April 1944 by British and American units, according to the method they used in Germany: day-night alternation, destruction of the water system, tearing up of residential blocks, and arson. In April, the areas of Sofia around the train station burned for two days. Air-raid protection was minimal. Sofia lost several thousand residents, as did Bucharest, a railroad objective.

Railroad objectives were always military targets, and they always stretched out in the city centers. "Our attack on the marshaling yards at Bucharest was a bloody affair," wrote General Ira Eaker, temporary head of the Eighth Air Force, in a letter of April 17, 1944, to the Pentagon. "We killed about twelve thousand people," Eaker explained. "Six thousand of them were refugees on trains in the yards; six thousand of them were Rumanians living about the yards."[104] Civilians of the Axis powers and civilians in areas occupied by the Axis powers died by the thousands. Turin, Milan, Genoa, Paris, Nantes, Lille, Amsterdam—none of them could hope for any special consideration. At first, it was a military and a transportation target, such as the U-boat shelters in Lorient on the southern coast of Brittany. American bombers were not able to penetrate the concrete encasement, and General Eaker asked the Pentagon for orders. Assistant Secretary of War for Air Robert Lovett responded that the Royal Air Force had abandoned all restrictions against occupied territory, so the U.S. forces should "wipe out the town as the RAF does."[105]

One place was spared, although many of its inhabitants were the only ones really looking forward to an attack. In the early summer of 1944, four Jewish prisoners from the Auschwitz extermination camp had managed to escape.[106] They told the Jewish community in Slovakia about the use of gas chambers. The news reached Switzerland and later, on June 24, was transmitted to the governments in Washington and London, along with requests to bomb a transportation objective: the railroad lines to Auschwitz. A list with twenty train stations along these tracks was included. Churchill personally read the report on June 27 and wrote to Foreign Minister Anthony Eden, "What can be done? What can be said?"[107] Eden advised what Zionist leaders Chaim Weizmann and Moshe Shertok had told him. It was the same as the news that made its way from Slovakia via Switzerland: bomb another railroad line in Europe. Churchill instructed

Eden: "Get anything out of the Air Force you can and invoke me if necessary." The RAF was skeptical of risking the lives of British airmen "for no purpose." But since it would have required visual bombing, it fell in any case within the responsibility of the U.S. forces, who were in charge of day raids. John J. McCloy in the Pentagon had received four appeals to bomb the railway lines to Auschwitz. As his deputy noted, his answer was to "'kill' this." There never was a raid on this transportation objective nor were plans for it ever drafted.

On June 13, 1944, a week after the landing at Normandy, Hitler started firing the reprisal weapon that had been anticipated for over a year. It was a small, unmanned, guided aircraft that was loaded with 1,830 pounds of explosives that went off upon impact. The launching ramps along France's channel coast had already been installed in the summer of 1943, but they were continually attacked by Bomber Command. The same happened with the testing grounds, the most secret site in the Reich: Peenemünde, on the Baltic Sea island of Usedom. The V1 flying bomb was launched from an inclined catapult track. A piston hurled it into its trajectory using chemically produced steam pressure. Once it reached a velocity of two hundred miles per hour, its pulse jet engine accelerated it to twice that speed, propelling it to London in twenty-two minutes.

The initial launch was slow. Of sixty-three positions, nine missiles took off, four of which reached London. One of them killed six civilians. It was not possible to hit a precision target with this weapon. With a dispersion of ten miles, it struck randomly. It was used in the morning and afternoon hours to kill as many people as possible in the bustle of rush hour. What had not occurred in London during the winter of 1940—or in Germany for three and a half years—was to be accomplished with this weapon: panic and collapse. While the other side resorted to the old, bloody method of ground invasion after hundreds of thousands of dead civilians and airmen had brought no results, German reprisal, without any strategic or tactical prospects, caused the deaths of fifteen thousand.

On the morning of July 6, Churchill reported a lamentable 2,752 casualties to the House of Commons. One million Londoners, mostly women and children, were evacuated that summer. In September, twenty-five thousand buildings were destroyed. Of the 8,839 V1s that targeted London, 27 percent struck residential areas, killing 5,475 people.[108] The government was aware that the Germans possessed another weapon besides the flying bomb. R. V. Jones warned the War Cabinet that these rockets might weigh over eleven tons and that one thousand of them might already exist; flying at an unprecedented velocity of almost four thousand miles per hour, they could reach London in three to four minutes.[109]

Jones had caught the basic gist of Hitler's V2 rocket. It did not differ considerably from the V1 in terms of range, warhead, and accuracy, but it weighed fourteen tons and was about twenty times faster. From the mobile launching ramps at Hoek van Holland, it could in fact reach England in five minutes, and there was no defense. A bomber might not get through, because a fighter could pass it by and inflict damage. The rocket was invulnerable, because even a jet fighter could reach only one-sixth of its velocity.

The imperfection of this weapon was at first its weak destructive force. Three thousand V2 rockets would have been necessary to transport to London a tonnage comparable to what had been used to create the Hamburg firestorm. But in the seven months of deployment of this weapon, only 1,359 were fired at London. Its cyclopean weight caused it to drill several yards down into the ground, and it ignited such that the shock wave spread out both upward and down into the earth. Based on the damages generated day after day in Germany, this damage stayed within the range of what was considered militarily insignificant. The weapon of reprisal was from the outset incapable of just that.

V1s and V2s killed 8,938 people in Britain and injured 22,524.[110] The rocket struck silently and invisibly, since it flew almost a mile per second, and had a profound existential effect. There was no alarm, no duck and cover, no prayer when, on November 25, a V2 hit a Woolworth's store in the London suburb of Deptford, claiming the lives of 160 midday shoppers, including passengers on a bus who, having been killed by the blast, remained sitting lifeless and dust-covered in their seats. Churchill and many British, especially bomber pilots, harbored a particular hatred for the rocket. It was considered a treacherous, cowardly weapon, since the means of annihilation had been stripped of every trace of battle. There was no pilot sitting on board, risking his life.

When Churchill was informed of the qualities of the V2 by Jones on July 18, he told the War Cabinet that he would seek reprisal for the weapon of reprisal. He said that "he was prepared, after consultation with the United States and the USSR, to threaten the enemy with large-scale gas attacks in retaliation, should such a course appear profitable."[111] High-ranking RAF officers and even Portal himself advised moderation. "Those damn silly rockets,"[112] as Harris called them, caused less damage than a single Bomber Command attack on a German city. Churchill would not be swayed, and to be on the safe side, he already had some squadrons trained in the use of gas. Air Marshal Tedder, commander of the air segment of the invasion, raised objections, saying there would be no advantage to initiating a gas war shortly before Allied forces invaded German territory.

Hitler had a majority of the V2s fired not at London but at Antwerp.[113] The 1,610 rockets that, for instance, killed a dozen butchers when they struck an Antwerp slaughterhouse on October 13, and thirty-two nuns in a convent on November 17, were not part of any reprisal mission.[114] Instead, they were aimed at a port city, a transportation objective. Twenty-five V2s hit Liège, nineteen Maastricht, and nineteen Paris. Belgium recorded 6,448 dead and 22,524 injured.

Most of the casualties of the reprisal weapons did not die from the weapons themselves but from their production. The pharaonic brutality of the slaveholders in the underground production sites in the southern Harz mountains worked roughly twenty thousand concentration camp prisoners and forced laborers to death.

Montgomery entered Antwerp in the first week of September with the left arm of the invading army. The forces had been divided into a British half, which moved toward the Lower Rhine and the North Sea coast, and an American half, bound for Lorraine and the Saar valley. The Allied forces and the Germans had suffered approximately equal numbers of casualties, a combined 425,000 up to that point. That corresponded to the losses of the 1916 Battle of Verdun. Neither side had reckoned with France surrendering so quickly. It was a bloody campaign with a clear outcome.

The British and Americans had been hoping to celebrate Christmas at home, but the advance suffered from supply problems. Montgomery and Patton, who set the pace of the invasion, competed over the distribution of fuel. Transportation routes were lacking. The same destruction that blocked German movements westward now slowed down the Allied thrust to the east. More than anything else, there was a shortage of ports that could transfer large volumes of men and matériel. At Hitler's behest, the isolated hedgehog units at Le Havre, Boulogne, and Calais guarded their positions at the English

Channel. Bombardment and seizure had destroyed much but accomplished little. The Allies needed Antwerp because it was less than one hundred miles from the Rhine. Montgomery had succeeded in taking the city but not its access to the sea. In between was the Schelde River, and the Germans were there. In order to supply the invading army, it could have been possible to fight to open up the mouth of the Schelde; that would have been advisable shortly before storming the heavily armed German fortifications of the Siegfried Line, or Westwall. But Montgomery had a rather thoughtful nature and a bolder plan.

The Siegfried Line ended at the Dutch border. Anyone who outflanked it, crossed the Rhine right before its mouth at Arnhem, and swung southward from there ended up in the Ruhr basin or at northern Germany's lowland plain, depending on the point of entry. As a precaution, Montgomery included in the Operational Appreciation M525 of September 14, 1944, the statement that the mission was "to encircle, isolate and occupy the industrial heart of Germany [the Ruhr]." But occupation of the region was actually only "our immediate aim. Occupation of the Ruhr . . . will open the way to a powerful thrust deep into Germany by way of the northern route."[115] While the First U.S. Army was preoccupied with the Siegfried Line near Aachen and Patton's Third Army formed a bridgehead at the Moselle, Montgomery took on the bastion of the German Reich, the Ruhr basin, in a surprise attack. After four years of bombing, production peaks had just been reached. The operation was called Market Garden.

According to the plan, paratroopers were to take a system of bridges that would then open up the corridor to Westphalia for armored divisions to follow. "Market" referred to the Rhine bridge at Arnhem; "Garden," the bridges over the Wilhelmina Canal and the Maas River between Eindhoven and Nijmegen. "Market" failed.

There were two capable German generals on the ground there, Walter Model and Kurt Student, the pioneer of the airborne landing. They mastered the situation with a trained eye. Only the 82nd and 101st U.S. paratrooper divisions, the "Garden" commandos, set up positions between the Maas and the Waal rivers with the British 30th Corps on September 17. The bridges there had been taken, and the front advanced by a wedge extending from Antwerp to Nijmegen. The course was unfavorable since it was threatened on two flanks. The eastern flank bordered on the *Reichswald* (Reich Forest), and the closest larger cities were the hilly Kleve and, on the eastern side of the Rhine, Emmerich. The only train lines and roads that led toward the northwest to the wedge ran through these two cities.

Kleve had a population of 21,000 and had little industry—at least, none that was armament related. On Whitmonday, 1940, shortly after Holland had been invaded, four people were killed by bombs, but since then the town had remained quiet. In the week following the failed landing at Arnhem, one alarm followed the next, day and night. Fighter-bombers circled over the city and its environs. A short time earlier, the Dutch resistance had reported an SS Panzer Corps in the Arnhem area, and British intelligence officers assumed it was being supplied by a tank depot near Kleve.

On September 23 and 26, 1944, bombers hit St. Antonius Hospital, the mint, and the town hall. Subsequently, one-third of the population fled for central Germany. The streets were deserted around midday on October 7, when 351 airplanes appeared in the sky and turned three-quarters of the urban area, which measured 480 acres, to rubble: over one million cubic yards of debris, enough to raise the surface of a road fifty miles long and thirty-three feet wide more than three feet. The town was not defended; one bomber crashed into the five-hundred-year-old Swan Tower of the Swan Castle built by Duke Adolf I. Five hundred people were killed, one in thirty of those in Kleve at the time.

On the same day and for the same reason, the medieval trade city of Emmerich was also destroyed by high-explosive and incendiary bombs. The casualties included 641 civilians and ninety-one soldiers. The two cities experienced another twin fate in February and March 1945, during the Allied crossing of the Rhine. Both towns were among those most destroyed in World War II, a dubious honor claimed, justifiably, by many. History refers to the raids as targeting a transportation objective as opposed to being an exercise in "morale bombing." Kleve and Emmerich thus did not need to abandon their will to defend themselves; they just had to relinquish their militarily useful transportation lines. In the end it was all the same. The transportation offensive shifted from French to German soil, where morale and industry had been bombed for years. From a civilian standpoint, the aims of the raids were of less relevance than the intention to maintain some semblance of civil defense. The firestorm in Hamburg and the transportation raid in Kleve yielded the same rate of loss of human life. The urban destruction in Hamburg, 56 percent, was far lower than it was in Kleve. Even the destruction of two-thirds of all the built-up areas of Aachen was lower, though Aachen endured more than seventy air raids between 1940 and 1945 and was besieged in October and November 1944, with house-to-house fighting on a Berlin-like scale.

The Aachen corridor, the historical gateway of the western conquerors, would also experience the second attempt to blow open the door to the German Reich. The odds were not bad, since in the first half of September the Germans had covered the eighty-mile-long line between Aachen and Metz with eight battalions positioned up to the Ardennes. Along the entire western front, armored divisions stood facing each other in a ratio of one German to every twenty Allied; and the ratio of the air fleets was similarly unbalanced, at one to twenty-four. The Allied forces also enjoyed the optimism that came from twelve weeks of unceasing advance from the Atlantic coast to the Vosges Mountains.

The Siegfried Line, the four-hundred-mile-long concrete barrier of pillboxes and strongpoints, antitank obstacles and gun turrets, and with autobahn lines to the cities of the Rhine, was cause for concern, although at the same time, it was now weakly defended and musty. Toward the south, opposite the French border, the fortification deepened, incorporating some nearby villages into its defense. Homes and public buildings were built with thick bricks; attics and church belfries doubled as lookout towers.

Montgomery withdrew after his September fiasco at Arnhem, and consolidated his supply lines at the mouth of the Schelde, though not before November 28. Patton got bogged down in the south at the Metz fortification, which was bristling with arms. The Prussian army had been especially familiar with this terrain since 1870. Patton's fuel reserves dwindled, as did, noticeably, the energy of the troops. There was a growing desire for some respite.

The front did not budge for two months. Between Montgomery and Patton was the Ninth U.S. Army, under William Simpson, and the First U.S. Army, under Courtney Hodges. Hodges made the third attempt to force through into German territory. The selected route was the corridor between the marshes of lower Belgium in the north and the rough natural barricades of the Huertgen Forest, the Ardennes, and the Eifel region to the south. In the middle was Aachen, where they did not intend to stay for very long.

The city was of no military use and on top of that, it had been radically destroyed by bombing raids on the nights of April 11 and May 24, 1944. The former was the most severe preinvasion raid, killing 1,525 residents, including 212 children. Six hospitals were hit, making them needed all the more. Eighty patients and eleven nurses were killed. The train stations at Aachen-West and Rothe Erde were important for transit routes to France; they were not demolished until the later raid on May 24, when Bomber Command sent 442 planes that leveled more than just the two train stations. In addition to the fifteen thousand left homeless and 207 dead, the raid destroyed several villages, including Eilendorf, with fifty-two casualties, and the old district of Aachen-Burtscheid. Situated at the southern end of the basin, with hot springs and the Imperial Abbey dating back to the early Middle Ages, it was razed on April 12. Among the dead were the air-raid wardens and their Hitler Youth couriers, which meant that the fires were then able to consume the town center virtually unhindered. Considering the extensive preliminary work performed by the air forces, Hodges's First Army had the city surrounded in the north by an infantry division and an armored division. From the south, VII Corps was supposed to complete the encirclement near Würselen. Both were within the deep echelons of the Siegfried Line. The plan was that the city would then surrender, and Allied forces could then push eastward up the Rhine to Bonn, crossing it and continuing toward Düsseldorf, on to the trophy that Montgomery had failed to take.

The northern prong launched a joint raid with tanks, infantry, and fighter-bombers on October 2, in the German blitz style. The pilots could not see very much in the black smoke of artillery fire. The bombs streamed onto open country and villages, and some of them even hit the Siegfried Line. The excellent cooperation between armored and infantry divisions enabled them to outflank the pillboxes and, with the aid of pioneers and engineers, destroy the doors along with the soldiers inside. The Germans fought hard but their resistance slackened when they felt the enemy at their backs. The vanquishing of the invincible took its toll on morale, here as elsewhere in Germany. It was October 7, 1944; a corridor through the Siegfried Line was open north of Aachen. And then a fateful decision was made.

The enemy was weakened but slowly gathering its forces to reinforce the troops defending the Siegfried Line. Countless gaps in the line needed only to be discovered. One was opened by force. Siegfried Westphal, at the time chief of staff to Commander in Chief West, later said that up to mid-October, a rapid advance through a gap at any point would have led directly to the Rhine, whose bridges were still all standing.[116] This would have brought about the speedy collapse of the regime, because there was no way to stop movements from the Rhine to the interior of the Reich. That might have been true; virtually all Wehrmacht commanders thought so.[117] A dizzy, staggering force should not have been given time to gather its strength, but that was precisely what happened. The interruption in the flow of the operation had fateful consequences. The invasion got bogged down for five months. This delay cost the Allied forces two-thirds of their total losses of 750,000 in the European campaign. It threw the German cities into a Mongol hurricane of devastation from the air that went above and beyond all that had been suffered up to that time, and it drew the Soviet Union, which was outside Warsaw in mid-September, to central and southeastern Europe, with all the misery that brought to two generations of people there.

The 30th Infantry Division did not succeed in coming down from the north and joining up with the 1st Infantry Division, which had been waiting two and a half miles away in Würselen. The situation was uncertain. There was resistance coming from the garrison in Aachen. It was possible that the Germans had pulled themselves together for a counterattack, planning to cut off supply lines to the divisions hastening to the Rhine, give them an Arnhem-style debacle of a far greater magnitude, gain fresh vigor from that, and then confront the invading army, with its fuel running out, in a textbook counteroffensive to test its staying power. The involved parties by no means ruled that out; how could they know what the enemy was still capable of? It was not a mistake to first secure a promising position. For the First Army, this meant returning to Aachen and pacifying the city.

As the irony of timing had it, in mid-September the city was defenseless and at the mercy of Hodges. All he would have had to do was to go for it. The local Nazi party had come to dismal conclusions and deserted the city without further ado. Consequently, Hitler sent in the 246th *Volksgrenadier*, or People's Grenadier Division. This was a horde of old men and young boys with a thrown-together arsenal of storm cannons, artillery barrels, tanks, and orders to hold the city down to the last man and, if need be, to find themselves a grave under the rubble. Aachen—residence of Charlemagne, who was respected, with reservations, as a Germanic leader capable of building a world power—was filled with echoes of its history. Defending the city and its roots was a sacred mission to those who let themselves be blown to bits in the process. This concerned Hitler least of all; he also had the most remote Ukrainian piece of steppe defended until the men dropped, and after that the second-most.

Colonel Gerhard Wilck, garrison commander of Aachen, rejected the offer to surrender on October 18, and three days later, a U.S. battalion with armored artillery and bulldozers entered the city to flatten its ruins.

A building complex was conquered as cannon fire and mortar shells first blew holes in the walls, followed by tanks and light bombers adding their bursts of fire. Then the waiting infantryman left his cover, ran to the building, and threw a couple of hand grenades through doors and windows, or let his flamethrower do some damage. Right after the explosion, he went in and emptied his machine gun, screaming at the inhabitants that they should surrender. Building after building was cleaned out in this manner. The defenders did what they could to catch the invaders from behind, making use of the sewer system. They thrashed with rifle butts and bayonets, set traps, played tricks, and took a toll of lives for each building. The Americans crawled into the tanks for cover and radioed artillerists and pilots, informing them where they could find the enemy hideouts.

The cradle of Europe filled with ten thousand dead, Germans and Americans together. If Wilck, with 3,473 survivors, had not tired of the brainless massacre on October 21, the enemy would have kept it up to the last man. Captain Joe Dawson, who directed the bombers and gunners from a position above Aachen to the east, did not want to believe what he saw taking place in the city. "This is the worst I've ever seen. Nobody will ever know what this has been like up here."[118] The cathedral and Charlemagne's coronation throne were all that remained intact. When Lieutenant Colonel John C. Harrison, liaison officer to Corps headquarters, had to list the damages in his report on October 22, he noted in his diary, "If every German city that we pass through looks like this one the Hun is going to be busy for centuries rebuilding his country."[119]

The border battles between Arnhem and Metz in the fall and winter of 1944 taught the Allies what they could not have known. No foreign armies had entered Germany since Napoleon, though before then it had happened constantly. But before Napoleon's time, there had not even been a country bearing that name. Germany qua Germany was only in its third generation, and its first conqueror had now crossed its threshold. For centuries, Prussians, Saxons, Bavarians, Badeners, and Hessians had struck out at one another as partners of France, England, Sweden, or Austria. There had been no domestic and no foreign space as such. Germany was the soil of general discord. This time, would the German tribes defend the Reich, collapsing for the second time, against the invaders, or would they join forces with them? Perhaps they would scatter, at least away from Berlin. The Rhineland could secede, as could southern Germany. But perhaps they would now make up for what had been avoided in 1918, and this time, the victor had to claim his victory bloodily from German territory, yard by yard. In 1944, the invading army learned from Aachen what followed and what they had to expect in the towns of the Reich. The *Volksgrenadier* there was composed of people who, after four years of aerial bombing, had been worn down considerably but evidently not entirely.

As Courtney Hodges ordered his VII Corps to Würselen, he also took precautions on his right flank. The dense Huertgen Forest was there, a triangle covering roughly fifty square miles between Eschweiler, Düren, and Schmidt. Schmidt is a village above reservoirs of the Schwammenauel Dam and the Urft River. Whoever had Schmidt also had the reservoirs. And whoever lacked the reservoirs had no military use for Huertgen Forest. Hodges, his superior General Omar Bradley, and Bradley's superior Eisenhower had overlooked that, but the Germans did not. The Roer (Rur) River flows east of Huertgen Forest, and anyone coming from the west who wants to reach the Rhine must cross it. If the defenders flooded the dams, the invaders would be caught between Roer and Rhine, since the water would crash down the Roer and flood the supply routes. The attacker would drive until he used his last drop of gasoline, fire until he fired his last munitions, and then be slaughtered.

But that is not what happened. During the battle of Schmidt, one of the bloodiest battles involving a U.S. division during World War II, Hodges became aware that there was some deeper reason behind why the enemy did not want to leave the village. As long as the Germans controlled the dams, which retained 3.5 billion cubic feet of water, the entire First Army could not cross the Roer. By the time Hodges realized this, so many soldiers had been lost, injured, or exhausted that they were not able to take Schmidt, especially given the arrivals of both winter and Hitler's counteroffensive. All of this happened in October and November; from the perspective of Düren and Jülich, two towns along the Roer, this provided the nonsensical backdrop to their own demise.

Huertgen Forest is dense, murky, rough, wet, and inaccessible by tank. The fir trees are seventy to one hundred feet high, intertwining their lower branches at about human height; streams, ponds, gorges, and ridges divide up the region. The water swells in October and seeps through the morass, dripping from the forest's coniferous crown. The Germans moved about securely in the territory; they had mined it densely and were lurking at all lookout points. They could not ascertain what the Allies were looking for here, especially since they were so clearly at a disadvantage.

Hodges and General J. Lawton "Lightning Joe" Collins, commander of VII Corps, had served in that general area in the Meuse-Argonne campaign during World War I. Hodges had been commander of a machine gun company that was well familiar with death. Positional warfare did not scare these two men much. They kept away from the battle line and obdurately expected the twenty-year-olds to dedicate themselves to purging this wilderness of Germans. They had also risked that in their time. The Aachen operation that demanded this sacrifice ended in the Battle of Huertgen Forest, where the Allies planned to nail the spirited Germans down and wipe them out. But Hodges did not set up a focused attack; instead, up to mid-November, pitiful logistics forced him to gruffly pump more and more of his men into battles that remained permanently stalemated.

Schmidt had become no man's land, passed from one side to the other. During the day, the Americans patrolled the empty buildings along the village's four intersecting streets; at night, the Germans did. Since the Germans controlled the peripheral paths of Huertgen Forest, they were flexible in redeploying their forces. They were thus able to inflict great losses—6,184 casualties—on the 28th Infantry Division in Schmidt and its northern accesses of Vossenack and Kommerscheidt.[120]

What should we make of the number of panic scenes, of the perpetual fear of the German Teller mines that could tear off the leg above the knee, of infantrymen diving into muddy foxholes, exposed day after day to the thunder of shells until, sobbing like children and paralyzed, they had to be encouraged to eat? It was "the saddest sight I have ever seen," reported 1st Lt. James A. Condon about the battle of November 6 at Kommerscheidt Hill.

Down the road from the east came men from F, G, and E Companies, pushing, shoving, throwing away equipment, trying to outrace the artillery and each other, all in a frantic effort to escape. . . . Some were terror-stricken. Some were helping slightly wounded to run, and many of the badly wounded men, probably hit by the artillery, were lying in the road where they fell, screaming for help. It was a heartbreaking, demoralizing scene.[121]

The Germans were on their heels but not in their sights. As the days became dusky, they were always in a cloud, always in the same place, at their backs. Under such circumstances, the decision was made to break out, leave the forest, and head for the Roer, well aware that they would not reach the western bank. Hodges had asked the British to blast the dams from the air. Ever since the dambusting mission at the Moehne dam, Bomber Command was considered the specialist in this discipline. At the Schelde, the dykes of Walcheren Island had recently been breached, putting it totally under water. But in the mist of Huertgen Forest all artistry was for naught.

Failing to either take or blast the dams in a consolidated attack became the next curse after the battle of Aachen. If the Roer had been flooded, the Germans would have been separated from their supplies. Alternatively, taking the dams intact would have made the entire battle superfluous. The Germans got involved in the battle only because they had their enemy in a trap at this point. And so the Allied attempt to advance also got bogged down. Instead, there grew a desire to reprimand this defiant country once again from the air so it would submit to occupation.

The reorganized Ninth Army under Lt. General William Simpson provided Hodges with a peer. Both men would be called upon in the spring to perform great heroic deeds, though this was not at all obvious at the moment. The aim was to leave the forest behind, occupy the banks of the river, retake Schmidt, take the dams, and, in preparation of all this, demonstrate all they were capable of dropping from the sky.

At midday on November 16, heavy bombers of the U.S. Eighth Air Force appeared in the sky to initiate the ground operations for Operation Corona.[122] On this day, four thousand airplanes dropped more than ten thousand tons of bombs on German positions in Huertgen

Forest, including forest villages and cities such as Eschweiler and Langerwehe, as well as three cities on the Roer: Düren, Jülich, and Heinsberg. It was the largest ground support operation of the Combined Bomber Offensive, creating damages equivalent to that of 12,500 V2s. Half the tonnage was dropped on the Roer cities, one-fourth of which fell on Düren, a community of forty-five thousand people. The 4,600 high-explosive bombs and fifty thousand incendiaries meant at least one bomb was dropped for every person.

The Transportation Plan attack on the supply lines to Huertgen Forest bombed Düren with the same tonnage that was dropped on Hamburg, a city with forty times the population. Of 9,322 buildings, thirteen remained undamaged. Düren, Jülich, and Kleve were the cities that suffered the greatest destruction in World War II. In Düren, 3,127 lives were lost. Four thousand tons of bombs were dropped on Eschweiler, Weisweiler, and Langerwehe; 97 percent of Jülich was destroyed. Of 1,700 buildings, 1,400 were completely destroyed and 150 heavily damaged. The five-hundred-year-old bells of the twelfth-century Provost's Church were found melted among the rubble. Only the skull and bones of Saint Christina remained undamaged, in a recess in a wall of the Chapel of St. Christina, as well as the outer walls of the citadel, built in 1548 by Alexander Pasqualini. Because of the citadel, U.S. and French maps had the city marked as a fortification, and the people of Jülich presumed that this error was the reason for the razing—in sixty minutes—of the once Roman settlement in the Roer valley that had been fortified in the sixteenth century by Duke Wilhelm the Rich.

The older masonry in Jülich and Düren was by no means the reason for the raid. They just happened to be situated across the plain that had to become a no man's land so that the attempt to break out of the hell of Huertgen Forest did not simply run into another obstacle. Jülich, at the eastern bank of the Roer, was integrated into a defensive network that extended past Koslar on the western bank, consisting of pillboxes, bunkers, concrete barricades, flak batteries, trenches, "dragon's teeth" antitank obstacles, and mine belts. Ten thousand entrenchments had been built here since September, extending the Siegfried Line to the Roer position. It was three miles deep, with troops entrained at the railroad station. It would have been possible to eliminate the defenses with precision, since there was no antiaircraft artillery. In the raid, the Americans did not lose a single plane and the British lost four. But the Allies had long since stopped taking note of details. There was so much obstructing the Allied forces that clearing everything away seemed the best plan.

Based on information from the towns of Jülich and Düren, the operation took the lives of tens of thousands of residents of the Roer valley and Huertgen Forest. Such a magnitude is hard to believe; in any case, it must have been a great many.

At the time of the attack, Jülich was almost a deserted ghost town. Three hundred corpses were later found in the rubble. There were no coffins, only paper sacks. In the rainy days following the raid, streams of farmers leaving the Roer villages sunk to their ankles in the muddy, rutted, sodden roads. On November 19, during the kermis carnival, all the villagers fled to the western bank and the small animals were slaughtered. Cattle were given ample feed and the gates to the stalls were left open. The bellowing of herds that needed milking accompanied the neverending barking of the German Railroad artillery, which had just been replaced. The Roer front had not moved at all during the mammoth bombardment. The effort to break out to the river got one hill closer near Stolberg, and four villages below the Hamich ridge were cleared. On November 19, the troops had not even come two miles farther. There were still three more miles to the river.

The forlornness of the forest battle remained, but twilight came earlier. The deciduous trees lost their leaves, covering the Teller mines. One mine was buried every eight steps. An attack on Schmidt was launched on December 13 from the Eifel region to the south, already shrouded in snow. The troops had been squeezing themselves through the Monschau Corridor for three days, when German artillery started hammering two hours before daybreak. The Americans, all the way up to Eisenhower, needed some time to realize that this was not at all about the defense of Schmidt and the dams. The fighting there had served as a diversionary tactic to distract the Allies from the preparation of the Ardennes offensive, which was about to start.

Huertgen Forest held out to the First and the Ninth Armies for ninety days. There were 24,000 either killed, wounded, or taken prisoner, and they had come not a bit farther, just as they had not advanced at all in Arnhem, in Aachen, or in Metz to the south. Patton had taken the strongholds at Metz in late November, with a loss of 2,190 men. His Third Army had advanced twenty-two miles in three months, but they were still barely more than six miles from the Siegfried Line, and they had lost 47,000 soldiers since the landing. Now, at the start of the counteroffensive, the Germans had more troops by a ratio of three to one, and their tank advantage was two to one. The artillery was prepared to launch a counterattack that succeeded in penetrating north of Sedan; in mid-January 1945, the front was approximately back where it had been in early September 1944, at the threshold of the Reich.

In mid-December, the western Allies had to ask Stalin to carry out a relief offensive, since the pressure on them was getting too great to bear. Stalin came and stayed, much to the later ire of those who were now despairing about how they could manage without him. Besides that, between February and April, the aerial bombing war once again increased in barbarity. After the Allies had been forced to carry out a ground offensive because the air war was inconclusive, they now radicalized the air war because the ground offensive remained undecided.

After four and a half years of torture, industry and morale managed to establish a western front out of nothing. This left General Henry Arnold, commander in chief of the U.S. Air Force, at a loss. "I don't know the answer," he said, "we have either been too optimistic in our ideas of what we could do with bombing attacks, or we have missed tremendously in our evaluation of the effect that the destruction which we cause would have on the German war machine." Even with "a superiority of at least five to one now against Germany," Arnold continued,

> we have as yet not been able to capitalize to the extent which we should. We may not be able to force capitulation of the Germans by air attacks, but on the other hand, with this tremendous striking power, it would seem to me that we should get much better and much more decisive results than we are getting now.

He hoped in January 1945 for "a glimmer, a light, a new thought, or something which will help us to bring this war to a close sooner."[123]

That "sooner" was not soon enough for the 81,000 U.S. casualties, including the 19,000 American soldiers who died in the Ardennes offensive, the Battle of the Bulge. Eisenhower responded nervously and asked Washington to send all troops available in the United States to the German border, as if the balance of power were shifting. But it shifted elsewhere. Stalin's offensive, which commenced on the morning of January 12 and reached Posen ten days later, had surrounded sixty thousand Wehrmacht soldiers. It took another nine days, until January 31, for them to reach the Oder River. Four days after that marked the commencement of the Yalta Conference, where the Oder was declared to be the Polish border and Soviet puppets installed as the Polish government.

While the western Allies were attempting in the last week of February what they had already intended near Aachen in late September, that is, to cross the Roer, the Red Army had already crossed the Oder and traveled half of the forty miles to Berlin. Eisenhower assisted them by fighting down the consolidated strength of the German army, while Marshals Zhukov and Koniev faced an exposed front defended mostly by veterans and Hitler Youth.

The weapon with which the western powers could assert superior strength through all of Germany from Düren to Dresden and from Kiel to Würzburg was their imposing bomber fleet. By early 1945, the number of available aircraft had grown to more than ten thousand, twenty times the figure of early 1942. Nothing in war history up to that time was even remotely comparable to the annihilating capacity of those hordes in the sky. Henry Arnold's feelings of helplessness were based on misfortune, but it was unfortunate only as compared with the Allies' illusory expectations. The country that had been bombed until it was ripe for invasion did not give itself up into the hand of the advancing invaders willingly. The invaders had to bear the full burden of a ground campaign and continue to wage a war involving considerable losses against an adversary unwilling to yield.

The bomber fleets that in September were again flying over Germany after having accompanied the campaign in France accomplished up to April 1945 what the air-war utopians had been promising the civilian population. They had absolute control over everything that stood or moved on the ground. The demise of the German fighter weapon diminished the extreme vulnerability of the bomber. And once the flak cannons moved from the cities to the front to secure the borders, the bomber fleet was immune. The attackers no longer needed either the cloak of nightly darkness nor the protection of high altitudes. They were masterfully autonomous. In the security of the sky and outnumbering the enemy by an overwhelming magnitude, they lacked only suitable targets, large cities with populations around 100,000. Eighty-nine percent of those were already destroyed or severely damaged. The rest were militarily irrelevant, like the university city of Bonn. Its irrelevance was no protection.

According to the standard procedure of burning out the city center, the Old Town of Bonn died in a fire of eighty thousand incendiary sticks, two hundred high-explosive bombs, and fifty blockbusters. The City Hall and the former residence of the elector, which now housed the university—both examples of the French rococo that had left its mark beyond the Rhine—went up in flames, the former down to its foundations. The minster church of 1070, with the sarcophagi of the martyrs Cassius and Florentinus, suffered heavy damage. On December 21, the destruction continued, this time within the dictates of the Transportation Plan, claiming the clerestory of the central nave. In practice, there was virtually no difference between Transportation Plan bombing raids and other bombing raids, except that in this transportation raid the transportation objective, the railroad station, was not hit. In its stead, however, 486 civilians lost their lives, compared with the 313 who died during the conventional attack in October.

The transportation offensive, as it was staged in Sicily and Normandy by Solly Zuckerman, had received sophisticated analysis during a conference of international transportation experts and intelligence officers, who explained how Germany would collapse in only a few weeks if a transportation wasteland could be created. In a similar manner, promoters of the oil offensive had calculated the point at which the lack of fuel would bring Germany to a standstill. War is movement; movement is oil. The enemy would be paralyzed, but when? In the course of the ground offensive, the pulse of time beat faster. It was not possible to stand and, from Antwerp to the Eifel region, wait for months until the Wehrmacht broke down. The autumn standstill gave Hitler and Stalin their chances to lead a winter offensive. That cost a lot of blood and political clout. No, the western Allies were in a desperate hurry.

The western Allies' air debates always ended by drawing up a carefully mixed list of cities yet to be attacked. If inclement weather thwarted plans, as in the fall of 1944, the impatient Americans abandoned the oil and transportation targets and dropped munitions wherever they sighted a city below. During the deadlocked ground invasion from September to December 1944, the combined air offensive killed 107,000 people. During the same period in the previous year, the figure was only 23,500.[124] On paper, it involved oil, transportation, and "alternative" objectives. The British, too, continued to bomb under the codename of "industrial targets." Railroad yards, marshaling yards, and engine sheds were not particularly prone to fire, but they were usually located in a city center. The massive quantities of incendiary munitions that continued to be dropped suggests that the intention was still fireraising.

The Americans, who two years earlier insisted that their "precision raids" not be confused with British fireraising, now had an army in the field. Protection of that army was an ethics in itself. It demanded that the air forces break the civilian will to resist in the hinterlands of a stormed land front. That saved bloodshed; it was humane. The doctrine dated back to Billy Mitchell, the father of the U.S. Air Force. General Spaatz developed it into the idea of the hedgehopper raid.

The civilian population became aware of their situation more quickly when fighter-bombers started firing their machine guns on random pedestrians, bicyclists, train passengers, and farmers in their fields. From the fall of 1944 until the end of the war, this practice, called "strafing,"[125] was also considered part of the Transportation Plan, since civilians out of doors were usually going somewhere, in vehicles on streets and pathways. A variation of this hunted down railroad workers, to make it a more dangerous job. Dissidents such as Brigadier General Charles P. Cabell, director of plans for the U.S. Strategic Air Force in Europe, expressed his displeasure. "This is the same old baby-killing plan of the get-rich-quick psychological boys."[126] But strafing became a regular tactic of the later air war. The Allies did not get very rich with this tactic, but it was traced back to the fact that they had started out too poor. No psyche would be able to stand up to the present air-force strength—in 1944, the United States produced 35,000 bombers and 38,000 fighter planes.

A new raid tactic was introduced on October 18: round-the-clock bombing. The sorties and drops of the Combined Air Forces were now measured in the umpteen thousands. From mid-August to the end of December 1944, the British released 265,000 tons of bombs in 72,800 sorties, suffering a 1 percent loss rate. In the final year of the war, U.S. air forces dropped one ton of bombs per minute, a total of 165,000 tons between September 16 and December 31.[127] In 1945, Bomber Command ran another 62,824 sorties, dropping a total of about 181,740 tons of bombs.[128] The U.S. forces dropped a record 278,000 tons. This corresponded to a daily average thirty times the volume dropped in 1942.

Transportation routes in western Germany had already endured the tonnage dropped in 1944, but now the repairs had to be destroyed.

Five thousand vehicles of the withdrawing Ardennes army were hit in late January—valuable targets. The rail lines from the Ruhr basin eastward still had to be destroyed, and a handful of oil refineries such as Leuna could not be hit often enough, since they always managed to get operating again. But that would never suffice for such a flood of aircraft and bomb tonnage.

A majority of the air squadrons would have had remained idle in the midst of the decisive battle in the Reich were it not for the psychological targets of staying power and will to resist, which were hard to locate yet presumed to be everywhere. The Allies experienced that will to resist as an amorphous entity, yet it was no less capable of inflicting physical harm in February 1945, when the Allies finally managed to break through the Siegfried Line and were pushing toward the Rhine. Were they waging war against a remnant army, the final contingent of the Nazi party, or an entire people? For an infantry regiment three miles from a town in the Sauerland region of Germany, that was often hard to determine.

In March 1945, every German man was declared a soldier. As members of this militia, called the *Volkssturm*, they wore odd assortments of uniforms but at least they sewed their own caps in the pattern of the Wehrmacht, which identified them as combatants.[129] Members of the *Volkssturm* were not partisans. It was questionable whether they fought as snipers of their own accord or on orders of the gauleiter, the nearest Waffen-SS leader, or an officer. Things were just as vague regarding the civilian population. Tarrying in smaller cities and towns were the elderly, young women with children, foreign or forced laborers, evacuees, and soldiers passing through. Often they themselves did not know whether they had gone underground or were seeking to join a front. This muddled ensemble of people were both the resident population and those on the road fleeing the front, the bombs, and the die-hard Nazis, down to the last Hitler Youth. They all were the "will to resist" in the sights of the mightiest bomb tonnage of all time.

In early February, the Allied forces set off for the Rhine. In the north, the First Canadian Army, which belonged to Montgomery's group, made it to the lower reaches of the Goch-Xanten-Wesel line. This Operation, codenamed Veritable, led a regiment of the 5th Canadian Infantry Brigade to Frederick the Great's summer residence,

Moyland Castle. The Wehrmacht had used the towers as an advance command post and the dungeons as ideal protection from shelling. Families from the neighboring farms and villages also spent time in these cellars to escape the weeks of carpet bombing that leveled the Canadians' route. The Régiment de Maissonneuves washed themselves and shaved for the first time in a week, and they played with the top hats they found in the wardrobes. They threw furniture and pictures out the windows for a bonfire in the castle courtyard. It was still cold, and the Canadians made a pot roast. For many it would be their last meal: experts in forest combat were waiting in Moyland Forest.

On February 9, Simpson and Hodges finally took the Roer dams, which had been flooded by the Germans, thus forcing the U.S. First and Ninth Armies to wait two weeks for the water to recede so they could cross the Roer. Then the war that had been at a standstill for so long was transformed into brilliant movement art. The two armies swept down the western bank of the Rhine. On March 5, VII Corps captured Cologne on the eastern bank, while Simpson was looking for a bridge that the Germans had failed to blow up. Though unable to find it, he did find a good ford near Uerdingen, north of Krefeld. The eastern bank was weakly fortified, and he presumed his men could operate well in the hinterlands.

Simpson's group was attached to Montgomery, who denied Simpson the triumph, since he himself was preparing a grandiose crossing of the river near Wesel. He had already informed the world media about his Operation Plunder. Simpson had to wait two weeks before he was included in the spectacle, because the advance of the Canadians ran into difficulties and the Germans were well entrenched in Wesel. The most capable Allied commander, George Patton, made it across the river in most elegant style. Within three days, he had purged the Eifel region and advanced forty miles with the spearhead of the 4th Armored Division to the western bank of the Rhine. He then followed the river southward toward Speyer and Worms, where he encountered one hundred thousand adversaries, who had been ordered by Hitler to hold the strip along the Rhine's west bank down to the last man, rather than fortifying the east bank as they would have preferred. Patton arrived at two secluded little vineyard towns, Nierstein and Oppenheim, twenty miles from Frankfurt. His engineers built two pontoon bridges in no time and the troops crossed in silence. "Don't tell anyone," Patton reported to Bradley at the top, "but I'm across. There are so few Krauts around there, they don't know it yet."[130] This was very different from the Final Judgment that Montgomery held for the world at Wesel. The whole trek there had been a debacle of the sort of the previous autumn.

Goch, an idyll on the Niers, was a farmers' marketplace and a railroad junction, with a population of ten thousand; the Germans had dug out tank trenches there and laid belts of concrete, barbed wire, and mines. The town was a fortification, but Bomber Command had not razed it to the ground, instead destroying only a few church towers and factory smokestacks. The Scottish highlanders were fired upon from windows. House-to-house combat—from roofs to basements, through courtyards and hiding places in walls—raged in the town; it was a miniature Aachen.

The forest corridor, the two wooded mountain crests along the Goch-Xanten railroad line, became a death trap for the Canadian 2nd and 3rd Infantry Divisions. Snipers hid in the treetops, tanks sank in the mud, and mortars, grenades, and mines claimed their blood tolls. It was the first week of March and Huertgen Forest had returned. Wrath was gathering among the overtired and filthy soldiers heading toward Xanten and the Rhine. They experienced the same thing inside the land of the enemy as they had at its border, but did not want to believe their inevitable fate, prolonging the process of dying infinitely. All the disaster in the world had been wished upon them, and in Wesel that wish was to come true.

Xanten and Wesel face each other where the Rhine takes a bend at the mouth of the Lippe. The latter was a trade center and had been shipping goods by river from the Münster region since the Middle Ages. The former was a Roman veterans' encampment and later became the site of the sojourn of the Nibelung son, Siegfried. Although unconfirmed, the legend had a more powerful effect on Germans than the legend of St. Victor the martyr did, namesake of the most magnificent cathedral between Cologne and Aachen. Under the sign of the cathedral and the sound of its bells, Xanten led a wistful existence in the sweet light of the Rhine valley before it became the headquarters of the First Parachute Army.

In the raids of February 10, 12, and 21, 85 percent of Xanten was destroyed, like Siegfried and Victor in one, by the U.S. Eighth Air Force and, in part, the artillery of the tormented Canadians. Of the forty-two vaults in the five-nave basilica-type church, twenty-seven had collapsed. Both the Carthusian monastery and the Convent of St. Agnes tumbled, as well as two patrician villas that had withstood the changing times along the Rhine since the late Gothic period. But now they got in the way of Montgomery's river crossing.

Eisenhower and Churchill were themselves both in attendance when three armies—1,250,000 troops—gathered at the west bank for the crossing, with sixty thousand tons of ammunition in their baggage. On the night of March 23, two divisions were supposed to cross under a barrage, and on March 24, the Saturday before Palm Sunday, 14,000 paratroopers were to jump from above the mountain ranges north of Wesel to take out the gun emplacements controlling the Rhine. After consolidating the bridgehead, the combined Canadian First, British Second, and U.S. Ninth Armies could advance into the heart of the German Reich's industrial power.

The massive effort of the undertaking alone prevented Montgomery from failing yet again to cross the Rhine. As Kleve and Emmerich had paid for the failure of Operation Market Garden, now Wesel and Xanten were to disappear to ensure success. That is why they had already been destroyed a month earlier, just to be sure. The Germans had recognized that Wesel was a suitable location to cross the Rhine back in September 1944, when the British had tried to cross in Holland; they guessed they would return a bit further to the south. The place was one of the few in the Rhine valley where a lower terrace that was protected from high water extended all the way to the river, making it possible to cross at any time. So the Germans quickly started digging trenches. In early 1945, the site was fortified and assigned a combat commander who committed himself in writing to hold out to the last man.

After the destruction of Emmerich and Kleve, which could be heard as far as Wesel, an oppressive fear descended upon the people there. The authorities urged the residents to leave, but that was not taken seriously until early February, when Operation Veritable launched the battle of the lower Rhine. On a sunny day eight days later, one hundred Lancasters appeared above the town of 24,000.[131] They returned in the afternoon. That evening, black smoke shrouded the town; it was dark, and emerging from the solid cellar vaults, the dumbfounded residents could hardly see the rubble they were climbing on. They were also inadvertently walking on the corpses of men and horses that covered the pavement.

On February 18, the second raid started, with 160 airplanes. Most people had already left the city, but later returned, believing that the enemy would have no further interest in a dying city. While they were busy salvaging what they could of their possessions, they were caught in the third raid. Afterward, a sea of ash and dust blacked out the sun. It was the harshest of the attacks, but it struck mostly stone and found only very few people. The 562 corpses were lined up outside, and the city resolved not to expose them to the bombs any longer but to bury them in the cemetery that very night. That turned out to be out of the question; they had to wait for the full moon, since it was impossible to transport anything through the rubble-filled streets in absolute darkness. The police captain in charge reported:

> Since no stretchers were available, we took planks out of the rubble and used wire or string to hold the corpses in place so they wouldn't fall as we climbed over the bumpy masses of debris. The task was arduous. We never finished because many squads could not find the bodies in the dark. At another location, the corpses were reburied in debris during a later raid and first had to be dug out again.[132]

Local farmers lent horses and carriages to carry the corpses to the cemetery. The horses shied wildly when the raids resumed. It was very difficult to lead them to the cemetery. The funerals took place under strafer fire. Since there was a shortage of coffins, cloth was used. At the entrance to the cemetery, carts were piled high with corpses mutilated beyond recognition, and a handcart carried the bodies of children. On March 10, there were still 1,900 people camping in the town. The formerly densely settled city center at the confluence of the Rhine and the Lippe was deserted, and no streets were recognizable. Only sixty buildings in this important port along the lower Rhine remained undamaged. St. Willibrord, the triple-nave cathedral whose construction started in 1424, stood as a ruin full of holes in a wasteland of debris. The artistic, articulated gabled façades of the old commercial houses at the market square lay in heaps. In view of the fact that 97 percent of the city had been destroyed, residents were at first unable to decide whether Wesel should be abandoned or rebuilt.

The highest number of deaths from the Allied mission to cross the Rhine on March 23 must have been suffered by Dinslaken, a few miles to the southeast. In order to shield the flank of the largest airborne operation of all time, the bombers had showered the town with phosphorus and high-explosive bombs. The residents of the fully inhabited town had not been warned. The first series of bombs fell at around 9 a.m. The streets had been filled with lines of shoppers, and seven hundred people were wiped out, almost exclusively women and children. Fighter-bombers pursued and fired on the people fleeing eastward into the forests.

Starting at 5 p.m., the 3,300 guns of sixty-five artillery battalions supposedly fired two million shells of various calibers on Wesel and its environs. That evening, again under a barrage, the landing mission was started from assault boats and amphibious tanks. It took two hours to fight down the resistance. On the morning of March 25, the airborne landing followed. Churchill and Eisenhower together observed from the church tower in Ginderich what military superiority was capable of. Around noon, Churchill climbed onto the Rheinbaben bridge, which had been blasted by his enemy, and looked out toward Wesel to the razed Watch on the Rhine.

Within a week, every small town within the siege that was to form around the Ruhr basin experienced the same fate. Fanatics dug themselves in everywhere; child soldiers and the dutiful swore to bow to no one but death. In reality, these were self-sacrificing Hitler Youth armed with *panzerfausts*, or bazookas. Commanders who distributed the weapon saw in it the invincibility of their kind. They took the rubble, the fire, and the explosiveness and inflammability of all that existed as proof of the mental granite. There was something that could not be broken. The unbreakable person throws his life away.

Hardly any of the besieged inhabitants along the Ruhr did that. But those who did not want to die lacked any countermeasure. The Allies' goal of unconditional surrender demanded that the populace would be terrorized by all available means for another six infernal weeks.

On March 19, Hitler gave his scorched-earth order. All military facilities for transportation, intelligence, industry, and supply, everything that could be of any use whatsoever to the enemy, was to be destroyed. The enemy had been taking care of that on its own for quite some time; thus the ruination of Germany in March and April 1945 was carried out by united forces. Hitler's Nero-like order was implemented less by demolition and flooding, as he had expected, than by the aimless resistance of the bizarre German troops. The field marshals, at least, led by Blaskowitz, Model, and Kesselring, were perfectly aware that their pinpricks of resistance neither stopped or diverted the enemy nor brought them to negotiate, but instead provoked them to use their overabundant weaponry. And so the Allies managed to scorch earth, village, and city more thoroughly than the SS demolition squads.

Contrary to their military sense of reason, the commanders on the western front left the eastern bank of the Rhine unfortified. The commander-in-chief had ordered them not to retreat behind the river, so it was unnecessary. When the troops crossed to safety, unorganized and sometimes without equipment, their pursuers had an easy time of it. South of Bonn, near Remagen, the German Pioneers failed to destroy the Ludendorff railroad bridge. The load of dynamite exploded, lifting the girders but not breaking them, and the bridge fell back onto the piers. All attempts by divers and even V2s could not splinter Ludendorff's steel. And Courtney Hodges's First Army stood amazed on March 7 at an open passageway to Hesse. But he was no more successful than Simpson had been. Though able to erect a bridgehead at the eastern end, he could not advance before Montgomery began his Wesel operation. Thus Hodges was the first to reach the eastern bank but the last to advance into the interior of the Reich.

The section of the Rhine between Wesel and Remagen borders on the area without which even Hitler could not have waged war: the Ruhr. The Silesian industrial region was already in Russian hands, so the Battle of the Ruhr became the final battle for Germany. The storming of Berlin was still to come, but in Yalta the western Allies had to relinquish Germany up to the Elbe to Stalin, so they did not want to bleed for that. They meanwhile had some experience of house-to-house fighting in German cities and dreaded having to conquer the conurbation between Dortmund and Duisburg, Bottrop and Remscheid.

The combination of factory grounds, mines, and residential communities represented a capital bulwark. Anyone who had to conquer intersection by intersection and block by block did not find the superior numbers of their tanks and bombers to be much help. On the other hand, it is easy to defend rubble. Under the cover of this mass of buildings, it was possible to draw in and wear out division after division, and it did not even require any organized military units, uniformed commandos, heavy weapons, motorized vehicles, or supply lines. The bombing of the aviation industry, refineries, and transportation lines had brought all military operations to a standstill. But everything that was needed for house-to-house fighting—machine guns, *panzerfausts*, land mines, munitions—was lying around piled up in surplus. Field Marshal Albert Kesselring, commander-in-chief on the western front, later wrote that "the Ruhr was an enigma for any assailant, its capacity for resistance being totally incalculable. The Ruhr provided its own protection."[133]

In the so-called Second Battle of the Ruhr, Essen, Duisburg, Dortmund, Cologne, and Bochum had been plowed through again the previous fall. On October 23 and 25, 1944, a total of 1,800 planes dropped more than eight thousand tons of bombs on Essen, a city that according to Bomber Command no longer contained any combustibles. Just in case, though, more than one million incendiary sticks were released; 1,482 people died, including 225 prisoners and foreign workers. On the night of December 12, Bomber Command killed another 463 residents. There was a direct hit on the prison that failed to blast it open. The staff was able to flee, but two hundred inmates in the men's wing were buried in their cells and not dug out alive. The last major raid on Essen was on March 11; the two prongs of the Ruhr encirclement had already been released. Double the tonnage used at Hamburg was dropped, 4,660 tons, and 897 people went to their graves. "The raid on March 11 was like nothing else," wrote young Thekla O. of Essen to her mother, three months later. "That we survived it in the shelters was truly an act of God. There were several minutes between each drop. Then all hell would break loose yet again. No one said a word, but every once in a while I asked during a break if everyone was still there. The end of the world can't be any worse."[134]

The next day, the end of the world moved to Dortmund. Here too the Second Battle of the Ruhr had paved the way. The city center around the train station had already been demolished, according to common standards, on the night of October 6. The 1,148 deaths and 2,451 seriously injured in a partially evacuated city with a well-developed system of air-raid shelters lived up to the name of the operation, "Hurricane," which swept through Duisburg, taking a thousand lives on the night of October 14, 994 in Bochum on the night of November 4, and 1,200 in Solingen the following day. The Battle of the Ruhr from October to December devoured fifteen thousand lives. It merged into the Interdiction of the Ruhr program, from January to February 1945, which cut off all regional connections to the outside and let people inside believe they were being bombed in preparation for an attack. But that attack did not occur until March.

On March 12, Bomber Command sent 1,108 planes carrying 4,158 tons of bombs to Dortmund and pulverized a strip half a mile wide and three miles long, running right through the city center. The bodies were not carried away; there were supposedly too many. The 5 to 10 percent of residences there that had still been intact were now all destroyed.

Italian prisoner of war Father Giuseppe Barbero was in Stalag VI-D near the destroyed Westphalia Hall in the southern part of the city when the raid started. "At 4 p.m.," he wrote in a report in 1946,

> the alarm just sounded and we rushed to our dugout. The infernal four-engine planes were coming. We were caught in a shower of not fragments but exploding bombs of a higher caliber than had ever been dropped on Dortmund. Our air was cut off and at the same moment our lungs were smothered and we were buried in dust. A shelter of the French and Serbs was utterly demolished. All that remained was a pile of flesh where you could make out only arms, legs, and ripped off heads. The Russians again suffered the greatest number of deaths, about two hundred.[135]

On March 21, Eisenhower directed a constantly repeated radio appeal to the residents of cities near the front. He reported that since they were the heart of the war industry, the cities of the Ruhr basin were being relentlessly destroyed. Even the shelters that had functioned well up to then would not withstand the Allied weapons. Then he named a number of cities including Duisburg. These were in the "death zone," he said, and should be evacuated. Three days later, hedgehoppers started chasing down people in the streets of Duisburg, and on March 30, artillery was fired into the city. British radio broadcast that the city of Münster had been totally flattened because it refused to surrender. On a German frequency, in turn, the founding of Werewolf, the partisan army, was announced, which executed traitors who gave up German cities without a fight. On April 1, placards with the same message were posted on walls all over calling for resistance "to the end."

The end came on that very day; the Ruhr cauldron was the largest encirclement ever, enclosing 300,000 soldiers and almost ten million civilians. It was questionable what these civilians' opinions of the militancy of the remnant troops—the *Volkssturm* militias and the Werewolves involved in house-to-house combat—were capable of accomplishing: presumably nothing. But civilians are sensitive to pain, which is why they were the only target of the coercion that could serve to limit the invading army's battle losses. Under a thudding drumbeat, a message was sent through the airwaves that it was better to empty the cities than surrender them as a field of corpses. But where were the millions of urban residents to go in an area where every loco-motive had been riddled through by strafer fire? Out of the cities and into the woods, the fields, the villages, or simply out onto the road.

The encirclement of the Ruhr marked an area on the move, and it was formed by movements. After crossing the Rhine, Simpson's Ninth Army took breathtaking turns as it raced toward Dinslaken, eastward through Hamborn, Ruhrort, and Meiderich, on the north side of the Rhine-Herne Canal. From the other side, Hodges's First Army took off from the Remagen bridgehead, moving up the Lahn valley toward Giessen, Marburg, and Kassel. Past Marburg, the for-mation forked, advancing about forty miles per day with tanks and trucks. The V Corps turned northeastward toward the Sauerland re-gion, Brilon county, meeting up with Simpson near Paderborn. This encircled the entire Ruhr pocket from the Rhine at its base, between the Emscher Canal in the north and the Sieg River in the south, ex-tending to the east to roughly the Kahler Asten–Brilon–Paderborn line. The encirclement covered 2,300 square miles.

In Paderborn, which included the Sennelager military training area and a military airfield, the Germans attempted to prevent the two prongs of the army from meeting. Hitler had declared the min-ing area a fortification to be defended to the end. In a way, he set the pace for the Allies. Finally someone was helping them advance. The entire encirclement of the Ruhr succeeded so quickly because first the west and then the east bank of the Rhine was declared an area to be defended to the utmost. The Führer was the taskmaster of a resistance that did not resist, and each week, the dictator dictated the holding of a different line that could not be held.

The German Fifteenth Army and the 5th Panzer Division did not spread out into the countryside. Instead, they clawed into the ground and let themselves be surrounded. The supplies within the encircled area were estimated to suffice for three weeks, from here to eternity. As the U.S. First and the Ninth Armies approached each other, SS Panzer trainees were doing maneuvers at Sennelager; in their Pan-thers and Tigers they pounced down on the invaders from the wood-ed heights of the Sauerland region three miles outside the city. The well-trained Waffen-SS gunners knocked out seventeen Sherman tanks. Both trainees and teachers ultimately fought on their training field-*cum*-battlefield.

It was one thing to fight the enemy, but they became doubly en-raged over the air preparations of the U.S. advance. Paderborn, a half-garrison and half-diocesan town, was by all standards a defended city. The men of the Waffen-SS had blown up bridges and rail yards to defend it, but that did not stop the bombers. In the manner to which they were accustomed, the 268 Lancasters destroyed the 1,200-year-old city on the Tuesday before Easter between 5:27 and 5:57 p.m. Their fingerprint could be recognized in the 75,000 incendiaries that started three thousand individual fires, in which sparks flew as planned, finally merging into a single blaze. It was not the Sennelager training area that burned but the Old Town.

The half-timbered buildings that were hit painted the air a clay-colored yellow that turned a peat brown once the fires started, ultimately becoming pitch black. Flames stretched sky-high, and no rescue workers could penetrate the large column of smoke coming out of the city center. People who were closed in jumped through a sea of fire that filled the streets as they tried to catch up to the others, who were fleeing to the banks of the Pader, covered in clay dust. The same instinct caused horses, cows, and pigs to rush about on this smoke-filled terrain. A section of street about one hundred yards long was all that remained of the city center; 80 percent of residential housing had been totally incinerated. About six thousand people remained in Paderborn; more than five hundred were killed.

Life left the city; only a few stalwarts continued to live in the ruins whose rubble gradually burned out. No one was left to recover the corpses lying about. The Sennelager troops waited outside town for the Americans approaching via the villages on all roads into the city. SS troops lay in threshing floors and barns; they were often seventeen-year-old recruits transferred directly from the Hitler Youth to the Waffen-SS. They had hardly any uniforms but were equipped with *panzerfausts*. Battles raged at every road entering the village. The small village of Hamborn experienced a veritable tank battle. Stables and homes burned to the ground; panic-stricken cattle and hogs ran around between the Tiger IIs and Sherman tanks.

On Easter night, the SS retreated from Paderborn. As a small congregation was celebrating the Mass of the Resurrection in the crypt of the cathedral, machine-gun fire raked the walls. "Should we stop?" asked the priest from the altar. The congregation members fled to the basement of the general vicarage. Tanks pushed their way into the dead city in a starlike formation. In front of the Church of the Sacred Heart of Jesus, two of them chased a single SS man who zigzagged from bomb crater to bomb crater. Police, Hitler Youth, and SS men engaged in final skirmishes throughout the afternoon. Fighter-bombers fired into the city, partly still aflame, and the final tank tournament took place on an airfield. White cloths hung flapping out of windows where people still lived. At 5 p.m., the weapons went silent. The Ruhr was sealed off and its eastern flank secured.

Eisenhower intended to press the besieged area inward from the north, south, and east, and to split it into smaller enclosures until it imploded. Big city battles were to be avoided. The Ninth Army took thirteen days to carefully isolate and cut off the cities using infantry and airborne divisions. They avoided man-to-man combat and somehow protected their tanks from the flak cannons, which were far more effective against the high turrets of the Sherman tanks than against Bomber Command's Lancasters. But the explosive ventures of the Germans were oddly stifled, as if caught in their throats.

Combat continued for six days in Dortmund, but the battle for the city center lasted only from the evening of April 13 until the following afternoon. A bloody battle among cracked walls and musty cellar corridors flared up in the night ruins; by 2 a.m. it was purged by artillery. Troops reached the center at 6 a.m., and two battalions combed through the mountains of debris until 4:30 p.m. Then the problem was resolved. Absurd duels took place in the sprawling suburbs, such as the three-day battle for the railway embankment between Lütgendortmund Nord and Bövinghausen. In Huckarde, a children's *Volkssturm* militia marched out with the comrades from the Reich Labor Service to protect the tracks of the Emscher Valley railroad. Such gatherings were broken up by the current universal weapon, the fighter-bomber. It also cleared up the situation in Dortmund-Asseln, where worn-out soldiers quickly downed their meal and, before moving out, hastily cut down a tree to obstruct a tank. To prevent that from happening again, the fighter-bombers buried a dozen Asseln residents under their homes. Elsewhere, the Wehrmacht pursued farther-reaching goals and carried off hundreds of civilian suits, for the time when they best shed their uniforms. Castrop-Rauxel surrendered magnanimously; the enemy reciprocated with gifts of chocolate and cigarettes. In Kirchhörde, the residents went to bed in Nazi Germany and woke up the next morning under U.S. occupation. All that had been attacked in the night were minor stores of currant must. At the same time in Hagen, however, German cannons were still firing toward Kirchhörde, but no one knew what they were shooting at.

The German army was comatose. In the veritable arsenal of the Reich, companies wandered aimlessly through the unreal realms, staging bloody farewells. But these were the simply the jerks of fading brainwaves. The army was dead. Commander of the Fifth Panzer Army F. W. von Mellenthin later wrote, "I have seen many battlefields, but none so strange as the great industrial complex of the Ruhr during the final destruction of Army Group B."[136]

Mellenthin wanted to take the battle into the charred ghost towns because they made such excellent terrain. There was an open field of fire, and for people who knew the territory, there were countless possibilities for defense and surprise, much like Huertgen Forest. The Americans had reason to shun the cities of the Ruhr basin; they showed qualities of Stalingrad. But there were no longer any troops to take advantage of them. There were only squads that staged insane battles for a bridgehead. Meanwhile, entire units were surrendering, including their commanders.[137] Every U.S. division took thousands of prisoners. Fifty thousand gave up to the 8th Infantry Division on April 17. A handful of GIs armed with carbines escorted 16,000 Wehrmacht soldiers. The collapse, always falsely prophesied, came precisely when the Germans were thought to have good chances—not of winning, but of inflicting hopelessly deep wounds at any price, as it had been doing since October. The distance from Aachen to Cologne is not far, but what an incredible cost!

A gangrenous waft of annihilation smoldered above the skeletal remains of the Ruhr cities. The army did not see this as a good battlefield; what they saw was that all they were fighting for had long since disappeared. These distorted graveyards did not instill in them the idea that Germany was being defended. The "morale bombing" ultimately did hit morale. Outside the major cities the Allied air war assumed German characteristics: The bomber became a kind of vertical artillery that the tank brought in to resolve its operational difficulties. Nowhere was this connection—bombers clear and armored divisions take over—tighter than in the southeastern corner of the encircled area, in the villages of the Sauerland region.

Until April 1945, the aerial bombing war had touched those villages at most through stray bombs. Since April 1, Hodges's First Army had been pressing into the enclosed region in the ski areas of Meschede, Brilon, and Winterberg, since this was the most probable escape corridor. The closed-in units tried to make contact with the army outside. But here, too, they were no longer the enemy they had been in December. The regular army had lost its bite throughout the encircled Ruhr area. Wherever it was confronted it collapsed. The soldiers were burned out; they knew that no secret weapon or stratagem of Hitler's would hew a way out for them. All that was left to defend was one's own life, and that was done best by turning oneself in.

In the last two weeks of April 1945, the fighting spirit of this monstrous army dissolved. Some commanders refused to take on the replacements offered by the young Hitler Youth soldiers. The berserk SS commanders were not ashamed to stoop so low. This fanatic backbone, along with obedient People's Grenadier Division members and pitiful heaps of an inexperienced *Volkssturm* militia, were supposed to be the masses, with an apathetic army as a façade. It initially managed a ruinous resistance, but was worn away in hundreds of devastating battles in small towns and villages.

The First Army started climbing the winding paths in the wooded heights of the Rothaar Range as soon as the cauldron was in place.[138] Antitank grenades echoed at the entrances to the villages. In order to protect his men, Hodges had the sites fired upon for days by artillery and hedgehoppers before taking the town. Defenders avoided open countryside in order to maintain their cover, and the invaders did the same. They learned how to move in the forest and positioned their artillery there; if they were fired upon, they called for their fighter-bombers to wipe out existing pockets of resistance and anything that could potentially become one, which usually meant the village itself.

Most places had old mining tunnels, slate quarries, or stable beer and ice cellars. The farmers made them inhabitable, and during breaks in the bombing they ran to check if stables were burning, to feed the livestock, or to get coffee and food. As soon as the buildings caught fire, the owners tried to extinguish the flames. They would stand speechless, watching their possessions disappear if the hydrants had no water due to the lines being cut. Dead livestock lay around, as did fallen-down masts. The sick and bedridden waited in the fields on stretchers to be brought back to rooms that no longer existed.

Village after village became the hostages of martial combat commanders who confiscated houses and declared them to be strongholds. They decided it was time for the country folk praying on their rosaries to learn the facts of war, which consisted of, for instance, the sixteen fighter-bombers that disintegrated the village of Bracht with bombs and phosphorus in order to destroy the quarters of a company of the SS Panzer Division Feldherrnhalle. Oxygen in the slate quarries ran out. The people crawled into a tunnel up on Steimel hill and in the Rodbusch. They heard the wretched whinnying of the twenty-four burning horses, the bellowing of the fifteen chained dairy cows, and the squealing of the pigs down in the flame-engulfed town. The Americans set a fog bank and then stormed down from the Wollberg hill into the village hollow with hundreds of vehicles.

On April 7, after the fall of Fredeburg, Berghausen was the re-doubt of the German front. The residents of Berghausen hid in the Niederberndorf mine tunnels. Only the pastor along with eight Fran-ciscan nuns from Aachen endured in the cellar of the parsonage, because he did not want to leave to the flames his precious church, with its Romanesque apse and the beautiful ceiling frescos. The fighter-bombers were above the village, and fifteen bombs were enough to set it on fire. As the Americans marched in, the old and the new schools had been totally destroyed, the parsonage burned, and homes and farms razed to the ground. Those already lying un-derground were brought back to the surface when the cemetery was hit. Nothing escaped the fighter-bombers' war on the villages—not Leckmart, not Schwartmecke, and not Christa Laumann, the seven-year-old girl who had been evacuated from the hell of Dortmund and was found by a grenade in a room in Oberhenneborn. Ten Ameri-cans also lost their lives in Oberhenneborn because a vagabond Ger-man mortar battery fired a barrage. Nothing stopped the occupiers; it merely irritated them. The hour-long convoy of tanks, cannons, and troop carriers would not be retreating to the United States.

On the evening of April 8, the Americans took control of the rub-ble that had once been Meschede, the district seat at the confluence of the Ruhr and Henne rivers. On February 19, 1945, twenty thou-sand incendiary sticks and 250 phosphorus canisters had burned down the town, which, until 1220, was the first and only settlement in the upper Sauerland region, because a convent dedicated to St. Walburga had existed there for four hundred years. The convent dis-trict, the small marketplace with its slated half-timbered buildings, and all the buildings in the city center left this world. When around midday light and dark columns of smoke hid the city from view for eternity, many people of Meschede cried, even though all but forty-five residents survived. But like the Pforzheimers, one-third of whom would be lost four days later, many believed this was the end of the world. The end of the world lasted ten minutes and then it returned on February 28. "It was as if a terrible cyclone, a typhoon rushed through," an air-raid shelter occupant later said, "or a volcano had erupted and the end of the world was approaching. We had to reckon with a sudden, violent death and were kneeled in prayer."[139] A short time later they counted thirty-eight bodies before they congratulated themselves for surviving. A world had nevertheless come to an end, a world in which it had been inconceivable that pilots from America would come to use explosives to hurl a woman into the tree in front of her home on Briloner Strasse and that she would be dead when they brought her down.

The story traveled from mouth to mouth about the demise of the family that burned to death screaming in the cellar of their buried house on Schützenstrasse without anyone being able to come to their aid. Parallels to this were found in the martyrdom of St. Walburga, and in the funeral service on March 5, the Nazi party claimed the incinerated victims as martyrs for its cause. Because the enemies could not win on the battlefronts, they said, the bomber terror raged, and children and their children's children would pay them back for it. The people of Meschede all knew there was not a word of truth in that, because only four weeks later it turned out that the enemies had sent the bomber terror so they could win more easily. They pressed their way from the north and east simultaneously into the city the fighter-bombers had given a real battering just a day earlier. The military had cautiously vanished to Remblinghausen, and all civilians born in 1900 or later were declared a *Volkssturm* militia. They shot apart a few tank crews, but this could not hold off the reconciliation of friend and foe. The Americans were satisfied that much remained intact during the demise of Meschede. "They fried all the eggs I had in the cellar," reported an involuntary host, "and they drank the wine I had been saving in the cellar for when my three sons returned from the war."[140]

An average of 127 people died each day in the aerial bombing war in 1944. From January 1945 until the capitulation, the bombing killed 1,023 people daily, a total of 130,000.[141] The last four months of the war represented the peak of the campaign. The British and American air forces dropped a total of 370,000 tons of bombs; Bomber Command sent its planes on a total of 72,880 sorties against the enemy. The raids included operations to support the ground campaign, oil and transportation raids, and reprisal actions. These distinctions made no real difference to those attacked. Someone from Hildesheim and someone from Würzburg could not say whether the bombs that hit them were part of a transportation raid or one to cause terror.

The twenty-one residents of an old-age home in Paderborn who were killed could not have prevented their deaths by complying with Eisenhower's conditions for closing-up the Ruhr cauldron.

Churchill decided in late March to distance himself from the campaign. On March 28, 1945, he wrote to the Allied chiefs of staff: "It seems to me that the moment has come when the question of bombing of German cities simply for the sake of increasing the terror, though under other pretexts, should be reviewed."[142] Then he proposed the priorities of 1941: military objectives, such as hydrogenation and transportation facilities, which had been objectives of the campaign all along. Churchill's denunciation of "terror and wanton destruction," however, represented a rejection of himself.

Churchill reinterpreted the strategic element of "morale bombing" into a characteristic of his confidant Harris. After the raid on Dresden, there was a general dissociation from Harris, whose horror-filled reputation lived on as a "butcher" and as a partner with sole liability. In the same way that the explanation for five years of polished strategy was reduced to Harris's disposition, the purpose and the course of that strategy got lost, in retrospect, in the question of whether the attack on Dresden involved unjustified use of excessive force. While that might have been true, it should nevertheless be kept in mind that Dresden's casualties made up less than one-third of all the deaths in 1945 raids, and only 8 percent of the total German losses.

Harris calmly noted that until late March there had been a consensus on all decisions regarding bombing strategy. As his biographer has written, "up to this point it was [Churchill] who had been the greatest protagonist of destroying Germany city by city."[143] Harris had not been in a position to wage a private war. The strategy developed owing to his personal verve, imaginativeness, and leadership qualities. That is why he was put in command and, despite passing friction with Portal, maintained his position. There was constant discussion surrounding Harris's authorizations, the selection of urban targets, and the suitability of "morale bombing" in general and its ethical admissibility in particular. There is nothing more normal in war than that a method proves unsuitable, does not work well, and seems morally ambivalent, and that crass personalities have a chance to live up to it. The pros and cons of all of that is normally reviewed alongside the offensive itself.

Churchill viewed Harris as an odd character but one that was beneficial to the cause. The bombs hit poorly what they should have hit better. It was a burden to annihilate innocents and a constant concern whether the bombs were helping the mission. And if not, what else could be done? This normal controversy merely flattened out the breach in civilization marked by the strategic air offensive. Its essence was beyond all discussion. All reasoning fell silent in view of what happened in its breadth and depth.

Five days after the start of the Russian January offensive, the Second White Russian Front liberated Warsaw, which after thirty-one years again came under the control of Moscow. Marshal Konstantin Rokossovsky then divided his troops. The right arm moved up the Vistula River and reached Elbing at the southern end of the Vistula Lagoon (Frisches Haff) on January 26. That surrounded the Army Group North and caught East Prussia in a sack that was open to the Baltic Sea from the Sambian Peninsula to Elbing and extended southward to the lowland plains of the Masurian lakes. The 1,850,000 Germans still living in East Prussia could escape via a land route across the frozen lagoon to the spit, toward Danzig. The Baltic Sea fleet had evacuated a large group of them, about 900,000, as well as half a million soldiers.

In the last week of February, the Red Army spread out to the Pomeranian coast and occupied the section between the lower reaches of the Vistula and the Oder, roughly between Danzig and Stettin. Streams of people escaped by early March along the beach, many headed for Kolberg Fortress, which German troops were defending. When the city was surrounded, there were eighty thousand people inside who during the next ten days of siege tried to catch a ferry to Swinemünde, the airy seaside resort on the island of Usedom. The port there was bursting with refugee ships, and long railroad trains waited at the imperial bulwark to bring the East Prussian, West Prussian, and Pomeranian populations out of danger. People slept at night in schools and on train cars, hoping to be able to travel on to Denmark, Kiel in northern Germany, or even simply to the interior.

Gertrud Thors sensed a thunderstorm in the air:

> The Swina, the river along which I lived for such a long time, on which I went ice-skating and rowing, lay dark, threatening, and ominous before me. The images of the overcrowded port, the refugees camping all around, the many trains with Swinemünde residents dutifully going around with coffee pots and bread, and with that the constant fear of alarms, made for an oppressive atmosphere.[144]

Among the waiting refugees were nine hundred survivors of the *Wilhelm Gustloff*, the evacuation steamer sunk by Russian torpedoes that had been brought ashore at Kolberg, as well as the women who came with the long trains of people who had trekked along the beach, some of whom had asked cadets Wilfried Sander and his comrades from the naval artillery school "to shoot them." They had been raped several times by Russians and their children were lost, "they were utterly demoralized and not responsive. From day to day Swinemünde was getting filled with more and more women who had suffered this tragic fate."

The cadets talked it over and felt it was hopeless from a military point of view, but they decided "to fight to the end if only to protect these pitiable women." Pauline Lenke, who had been evacuated from the Rhineland to Pomerania, was in the Koserow hospital, where she met "young girls, eleven to thirteen years old, who were not only seriously injured, but even before that had been raped by Russian soldiers as they were fleeing. They were children from East and West Prussia who had made a stop in Pomerania."

The Bay of Pomerania was teeming with ships of all kinds. People were packed in the cargo hatches of the freighters. It was cold and stormy, the waves came over, soaking their clothes. Everyone longed for the landing in Swinemünde, where heaters glowed and they could dry themselves. The more comfortable *Winrich von Kniprode*, of the Hamburg-America Line, got stranded at the port on the night of Sunday, March 11, since it had run out of coal.

Christel Bispink did not want to board the ship in Kolberg, "since I was there when the survivors of the *Wilhelm Gustloff* were brought ashore." "Stalin's organs," or the Katyusha multiple rocket launchers, which had shot Kolberg to pieces, were in no way inferior to the torpedo cannons of the Red Fleet. "We endured together shivering in the shelter for five days and then went towards the port, which was under constant fire." Russian strafers attacked the *Kniprode*; now it was stuck there in choppy waters, and Christel Bispink wished she had listened to her intuition.

Pastor Ohse from Virchow in East Pomerania was also stuck without coal on his steamer, with four thousand passengers aboard. "Our eyes wandered far across the bay with its green waves to the bluish hills of Usedom and Wolin; past the numerous ships that were lying with us in the roads." Below deck, straw mattresses one against the other, cowered old East Prussian farmers, injured veterans, and "a woman who was obviously slightly disturbed mentally, who unceasingly continued to sing three or four soft tones." To the right and left, smaller refugee ships steamed on ahead to Swinemünde; half of East Prussia was at sea. Anything that could float was loaded with people. Christel Bispink could take a deep breath early Monday morning: the *Kniprode* was loaded with coal and the huge tub was set in motion. "Hope immediately started budding. But it was totally unfounded. At twelve o'clock the alarm sounded. The deck was cleared. Airplanes had been reported with their course set for the Baltic Sea, Swinemünde."

When the alarm of the Plantage coastal battery reported heavy air units flying in, Cadet Sander was drilling a parade step with his platoon, since a funeral march was scheduled. "Our advance scout on the island of Wolin, a lieutenant, had fallen and was supposed to be buried that day with military honors." The battery manned their three guns right away, but the order was withdrawn, since the approaching units had split up over the water and were now flying much lower than usual. When the bombers were less than twelve miles away, the firing was stopped. "We were too slow, because our First World War–era artillery could only be aimed and loaded manually." The next order had the cadets racing to their one-man foxholes, which had been dug out behind the position in the park.

Most of the refugees were camped along the wide belt of spa gardens that bordered the strip of beach. The U.S. Eighth Air Force knew that, which is why they had loaded a lot of bombs with contact fuses that caused "treebursts"; they detonated as soon as they came in contact with anything, such as branches. The Allies were better informed about Usedom than about any other area of Germany because of the V2 site in Peenemünde.

At 3:00 a.m., Hugo Leckow had arrived with the refugees from Pribbernow in the county of Cammin. They had made their way via Wolin and had to get their carts across the Swina River. Crossing it was an arduous endeavor, because there was only a ferry there—the bridge had been blown up long ago. When Leckow heard the air-raid alarm, he tied up the horse firmly and went back to his cart; a short time later, the bombs wailed down and the airborne weapons hammered. The Pribbernowers crawled under their carts. The hellish noise increased the danger that the horses would bolt and the carts would roll over them. So the men unhitched the horses and held them by the reins, standing behind the carts and hoping not to be hit by bomb shrapnel. "We watched one bomber after another fly over the harbor area and the wagon trains and release their annihilating bomb load. When it got quieter between approaches you could hear the screaming of the injured and the whinnying of the hurt horses."

Pastor Ohse listened to the bombers roaring louder and louder above the ship. "We were all sitting in absolute silence and I imagined what it would be like if right at that moment the bombs hit our ship and it would sink." No one would ever know what had happened to him. "The war caught up with us again," thought Christel Bispink on the *Kniprode*. "The enemy squadron continued to thunder above us, releasing their deadly load onto the city and the harbor. The blazing flames and the black clouds of smoke rose to the sky. We were familiar with this sight from Kolberg." In reality, the war had by no means caught up with her. The lack of coal had kept the ship from entering the annihilation zone.

They distributed life vests on Pastor Ohse's steamer. "There were only enough for a few women and children." Cadet Sander in his foxhole could see how refugees in the park were throwing themselves to the ground "and now their entire bodies were being exposed to the fragmentation effects of the treebursts. The markers had outlined the park clearly with flares," making the carpet of bombs especially dense, "so there was no escaping it."

At the banks of the Swina, in the endless line of vehicles from the trek, Dietlinde Bonnlander was waiting with the people from Fritzow in Pomerania for the bridge to be repaired. She fed the horses; the swaying of the pontoon and the muffled sounds were hard on them. The city was within sight, and through the thin morning mist she could see the bombs falling. When the strafers came, the Fritzowers threw themselves to the ground in horror. They had not yet experienced this "senseless hunting down of people." Isa Berg and the people with her from Labiau who had trekked along the beach from East Pomerania had constantly encountered the bombs. They mowed down the refugees. "Mama yelled 'get down,' and protectively threw herself down on the youngest."

During their rest in Swinemünde the family found a place to sleep in a railroad car.

We children sat on the floor. We heard the prealarm warning, but I don't remember the bomb raid at all. When I awoke, it was dark. People were lying on me, and I couldn't get any air. I wanted the boy lying on top of me to get off, but he just groaned loudly and got even heavier. Wherever I reached out with my hand it felt all gloppy. When they pulled me up I saw my brother sitting there, but the top of his head was gone.

Ten-year-old Martin Krüger and his mother had been waiting for four hours at the train station. They had slept overnight on the road as they walked from East Pomerania and were happy to get something hot to eat in Swinemünde. They had sauerkraut and decided to stay another day. During the air raid's second wave, Martin got hit by a piece of shrapnel that tore open his left carotid artery. "His last words were 'Mama, what's happening?' I immediately applied pressure to the artery, but he had already lost too much blood."

The trek of the Pribbernowers also got caught in the strafer raid at the Swina River. The hedgehopper planes flew along the road to Pritter and attacked people and animals. "Among the dead people lying around and the perished horses, the injured were calling for help and water. Some asked for a cigarette. Our village was hit hard; eighteen dead."

Christel Bispink could make some observations from her spot on the *Kniprode*. "To our amazement we saw far fewer ships. We didn't find out until after the war that thirteen had been sunk in the harbor area." Pastor Ohse was lucky, thanks to thick cloud cover. "We later heard that all the refugee steamers in the harbor had been sunk or transformed into floating coffins." Of the larger trading vessels, the *Jasmund, Hilde, Ravensburg, Heiligenhafen, Tolina,* and *Cordillera* had been sunk, as well as the *Andros,* which suffered the greatest losses.[145] It had put to sea on March 5 in Pillau along the Sambian coast, with two thousand passengers, and was bound for Denmark. On the stormy trip, they ran out of drinking water and food; the freighter docked in Swinemünde on the morning of March 12.

Eva Jänsch came from the besieged Königsberg and had laboriously made her way to Pillau along the road that had been fought open. She thought she had gotten through the worst when the sound of the bomber engines started to swell. "They had dropped their bombs before we even realized what was happening. The firebombs started a fire and in no time the bow of the ship was red-hot." The refugees were split up into two holds. When the ship broke apart in flames the holds were flooded. There was only one ladder to the deck, and hundreds of people rushed to it. It could not withstand the weight and broke. The crew threw down ropes, "but no one made it all the way up. Water was spilling into the ship from all sides. Right after that there was an eerie silence. The icy wave had swept over the people."

The next day, the cadets were divided into groups to recover the bodies from the park. "Among the bodies that our group found in the park there was not a single soldier—just women, children, and a few old men." In fact, however, at another area of the park there were also units of troops headed southward to the front at the Oder River. But the hedgehoppers made no distinctions in the ten seconds of their machine-gun fire. The cadets had performed various drills but had never before heard a bomb drop. And they had never practiced anything even vaguely close to what really happened in a raid. "At first it was as if everyone were paralyzed."

It was often impossible to identify those who had been injured and mutilated. "We had orders to look for identification cards in the clothes of those who had been killed before they were transported off." Those who could not be identified but had usable clothing were stripped, since there was a desperate need for clothing among the refugees. As cadets were recovering the body of a woman who had given birth during the raid, they noticed the uninjured baby hanging dead from the umbilical cord and dropped the corpse in shock.

The raid involved more than one thousand aircraft—671 bombers and 412 escort fighter planes—and 1,609 tons of munitions. Based on the local official count, 23,000 people had been killed, a figure that is hard to fathom. Was it half that amount, or a third? There are few clues. The *Andros* supposedly took 570 people down with it, but there are no further data relating to the harbor. A total of 1,667 victims could be named, but far more were never identified. They were never counted because new waves of refugees continued to come in. The remains were buried in bomb craters or carried away in wagons to mass graves on the hill of Golm. The total number of deaths on ships, in parks, on treks at the banks of the Swina, at the train station, or on hospital trains might be in the five-digit range.

The massacre at Swinemünde is not recorded in the annals of the U.S. Eighth Air Force as a massacre; nor is it recorded so in the annals of world history. The U.S. Air Force listed it as a transportation raid on "marshaling yards."

Right after the country was occupied, a commission of the U.S. armed forces drew up the *United States Strategic Bombing Survey*, summarizing the Allied air war.[146] They were surprised at the number of dead. Such civilian losses were unprecedented, but "far removed from the generally anticipated total of several millions."

3. LAND

"The link back to the Middle Ages has now also
broken off."
———ERNST JÜNGER

*The destruction's scorched trail spreads in a curve from
the coast to the Weser Mountains to the Ruhr valley and
down the Rhine. In 1943, it reaches the south, and in
1944, the east. The people living in the cities settle as did
their predecessors, who had left behind their homes, their
cathedrals, altars, writings, documents. They illustrate
and inscribe the sites as places where something takes
place. The past passed down its sites, and those of the
present stand upon them and see themselves as part of
a succession. History is stone, paper, and narrative, and
largely combustible. Fires, destruction, pillaging, and
massacre are the crossroads of urban narratives. Every
city had been destroyed at least once, but never before had
all the cities been destroyed at the same time. When that
happened between 1940 and 1945, a bridge to a landscape
collapsed, and that landscape no longer exists.*

THE NAME OF THE CITY SOEST comes from "salt," and means "site at the brine well." When in the year 973 the Arab Ibrahim Ibn Ahmed left his Spanish homeland with a delegation of the Caliph of Córdoba to meet Emperor Otto the Great, he gave an account of a castle where salt was extracted from the nearby salt springs. Ibrahim took a route that Drusus had used eight centuries earlier, to march to the Weser with his legions. It was marked out by the Westphalian basin and connected the Rhine with the settlement area of the eastern Germanic tribes.

When Ibrahim's delegation rode toward Magdeburg, the Langobards, or Lombards, who had once settled along the Weser, had long since moved to Lombardy, sharing Italy with the Byzantines. The Saxons, who had once settled east of the Lombards, now controlled the Weser region. After spending thirty years in a fierce feud with the West Roman–Frankish Emperor Charlemagne, they had finally been conquered and Christianized, then assuming the Roman emperorship themselves, after the fall of the Frankish kingdom. The Saxon emperors ruled over a realm roughly between the Elbe and the Maas rivers. The external fate of the empire took place along the east-west axis, across which the history of the peoples is still shunted today. The borders of the north-south axis were clearly marked natural boundaries: the sea's edge and the Alps. The domestic history that took place between these borders was that of the people who over the centuries began to view themselves as Germans. Most of the time, however, domestic and foreign histories could not be distinguished.

The route between west and east followed the route of today's German Federal Road Number 1. At the time it was called the *Hellweg*, the "bright path," referring to its having been cut out of the forest. It was the physical property of the king and included everything that went with it—bridge and mill, forge and farm. The road measured sixteen shoes wide, allowing space for two wagons—or a horseman with a lance held crossways—to pass. According to the custom of the time, a lance held vertically symbolized peace and one held horizontally stood for battle. The king's road served to keep the area in check. The Saxon rulers used the *Hellweg* to connect their Saxon homeland with the Frankish-Rhenish region on which their culture, writing, laws, state of rule, and belief in God were based. The legs of the journey marked out on the king's road have been preserved. Courts grew into cities at Dortmund, Unna, Soest, and Paderborn. The lances and wagons of the *Hellweg* mark the fortified sites and trading posts, the origins of the city.

The region contained iron, copper, lead, tin, and salt, which merchants took with them to trade for wine, spices, and cloth. Soest merchants made it as far as Kiev in 1050, and a long-distance merchants' guild called the *Schleswigfahrer* sought partners in the Baltic Sea region as far as Novgorod. In the mid-ninth century, an exemplary city law was established in Soest that had effects far beyond its borders. It was adopted in Lübeck, a city at the vertex of the Baltic Sea. Lübeck in turn became the model for a string of cities along the Mecklenburg and Pomeranian bays and the Gulf of Danzig all the way to Königsberg and Revel. These ports had far-reaching connections to a base of cities bordered in the south by a line linking Breslau, Erfurt, and Cologne. In the west, Amsterdam was part of this league, which maintained offices in Norwegian Bergen, in Bruges, and in London. It was called *Hansa*, from the Old High German for military troop or band, giving the Old World a northeastern area of civilization that held together for five hundred years, until it destroyed itself in the Thirty Years' War. The shift in world trade to the Atlantic and the rise of the colonial system left the Hanseatic urban landscape and its less-hurried times behind. The town halls, cathedrals, storehouses, cloth halls, and harbor facilities held on to the boldness and brightness of their youth. Its architecture, with its cool, sharply cut facial features occasionally moved by a sated smile, is named after its dark, earth-toned skin of baked clay bricks.

Lübeck was built entirely of this material, which, after the city experienced devastating conflagrations, proved most secure. Its early creations, the cathedral and the Church of St. Mary, wedded the dizzying sandstone fantasies of French cathedral Gothic with the down-to-earth balance of the brick masonry. Derived from the Church of St. Mary are churches in Kiel, Rostock, and Stralsund, dedicated to St. Nicholas, the patron saint of seafarers. Three centuries worked on St. Mary's, the main church in Rostock, consecrating it to eternity.

Lübeck city maps illustrate the common sense of merchants. The market square and the harbor, the two most important sites, were monopolized by the patrician trading families that founded the city, as distinctly shown by the resplendent gabled façades and the richly articulated city halls and warehouses. The elongated central market square marked the festive confluence of streets leading to mighty gateways. The world of the merchant class spread out on modest rectangular plots. One hundred cities in the Baltic Sea region adopted the Lübeck Law as it moved down the *Hellweg*, and their colloquial language was Low German. As the largest of the Hanseatic ports, which also built the cog, the single-masted merchant ship with cargo space for 120 to 200 tons, Lübeck connected the sea trades of the North and the Baltic Seas. It lies back to back with Hamburg, with which it shares the land bridge between the seas.

The Hansa seats freed the city from the castle, which was landlord over the princely tenants. They abandoned the constraints of forest and field, the district of the lance, and received commerce and culture from afar, provided dwellings for strangers, heard their lore, checked their wares, and talked business, negotiating prices and contracts. The city was the present. It was state of the art, and yet it lived in the permanence of stone, changing it over time and passing on what should endure. In addition to the rural cycles within which an exchange with nature and changes in land-held power took place, there was also historical time, an unsettled present, always on the move along the route from somewhere to somewhere. And so Lübeck meshed the bright, modern Atlantic side with the medieval culture of the Teutonic Order of the Baltic Sea. It was the interface of routes from London and Novgorod, and the first city eradicated by Bomber Command. Its Hansa sisters Rostock, Anklam, Wismar, Stralsund, Stettin, Danzig, Königsberg, and even the base of Brunswick, Hanover, Soest, and the others disappeared later.

Lübeck had to fall on the Saturday night of March 28, 1942, within 140 minutes, the crews of the Wellingtons and Stirlings were told, because it was an important seaport that supplied the German armies in Norway and Russia. Lübeck's famous son Thomas Mann spoke to the Germans via radio from California, telling them "there were fires in the city and I shudder to think that the Church of St. Mary, the magnificent Renaissance town hall, or the Old Seamen's Guild House have suffered damages. But I think of Coventry and have no objections to the lesson that everything must be paid for."[1] Hitler also approved of this lesson, and Lübeck's price was paid for with parts of the southern wing of the Exeter Cathedral's choir and monastery buildings of the Canterbury Cathedral. In a letter written on May 4, 1942, Mann reckoned with continued payments to be paid by "the German cities." If you thought of what they were about to face, he wrote, "about to face justifiably, necessarily, indispensably, then a mild fright will befall you."[2]

Thirty-six hours were needed in Lübeck to understand what had been done to obstruct supplies for the German army. "Eighty percent of the actual Old Town was destroyed; cathedral, museum, Church of St. Mary, Church of St. Peter were all destroyed."[3] The Dornier Aviation works, on the other hand, which was important for the war economy, remained intact, because this attack served less as a reprisal than to improve the state of bomb technology used in the Coventry raid. The Germans had demonstrated a model with potential. The Air Ministry in London considered it a secondary success that production in Lübeck had been restricted for six or seven weeks and that 2,600 people had been killed. This was a sevenfold exaggeration, but that was not the point. The fire war, the experiment that had been in hasty preparation since the fall of 1941, had delivered a promising success. The Old Town in Lübeck had withstood far more than had initially been assumed, but the demise of the oldest quarter around St. Mary's, with a majority of the gabled houses, could not be measured by percentage points.

Bomber Command's next station was Rostock. That city paid more dearly, as a special effort was made to continue the raid for four days in a row. The series was flown from April 23 to April 27, 1942. The destruction of most of the historic Old Town came on the third night. The bomb tonnage included the pernicious mixture of two-thirds incendiaries. They devoured the churches of St. Nicholas and St. Peter, a small segment of the library of the oldest university in northern Germany, the metropolitan theater, the Stone Gate, and the dermatology clinic. The raid left forty thousand people homeless. The sea wind helped fan the flames, but the Heinkel aircraft factory, the secondary objective, survived.

Bomber Command did not want to leave the site with two monuments of brick Gothic in ruins and their favorite enemy, Heinkel, intact. Of course St. Peter's, with its 384-foot western tower erected at the crest of a hill, stood out far more clearly against the moonlit sky. The tower was built as a landmark to seamen. According to the new forms of air war, all structures that stood out served more as a signal to be wrecked.

Showing extraordinary determination, Bomber Command returned on April 27 and reached the factory buildings. Heinkel lost a month's worth of production, a fact used to justify the elimination of the seven-hundred-year-old long-distance trade city as a military objective. Although only 216 people perished, far fewer than in Lübeck, the people of Rostock judged the burning of the venerable buildings to be such a heinous deed that 150,000 people fled wildly to the smaller Mecklenburg cities. Gauleiter Friedrich Hildebrandt swore revenge against the Jews and blamed them for the radicalization of the air war. They would soon "gas large areas";[4] anything and everything had to be reckoned with. "It is a Jewish war. Churchill and Roosevelt are only puppets, and they too will be shot if they fail to accomplish the international Jewish mission." If the Nazi party had no means by which to ward off the destruction of the cities, they at least had the means to make someone else pay for it.

On October 9, 1943, the U.S. Eighth Air Force headed for Anklam, near the river crossing of the Peene, southwest of the Bay of Pomerania.[5] For the time being, the Americans were not interested in the fire war; they had set their sights on the aviation industry, and the Arado works were just behind the Anklam train station.

Because the city was smaller it was considered less vulnerable, so many schoolchildren from Stettin had been evacuated there. It had a gridlike system of streets, and a rectangular marketplace in the Hansa style, with a sleepy harbor greeted by the spires of the churches of St. Nicholas and St. Mary. Now it was mostly fishing cutters at anchor that rocked in the water; the heyday of its maritime trade had ended five centuries earlier. Attesting to the lasting influence of burgher affluence were the many sixteenth-century gabled houses of the late Gothic and Renaissance periods and the more comfortable baroque residences of the seventeenth century, as well as the spare half-timbered buildings from the modest eighteenth century. This mirror of the city's history stood polished and displayed most prominently at the Peene River, the Church of St. Nicholas, and Wollweberstrasse.

From an altitude of 13,000 feet, the 1st and 41st Combat Wings of the Eighth Air Force could see at most the spires of St. Nicholas and St. Mary, if the attention of the 1,070 airmen, as they flew over the North Sea, Jutland, and the Baltic Sea and set their course for Stettin-Stralsund, had not been on three hundred German fighter planes. The wings flew at a separation of six miles, but they had closed up by 11:42 a.m., when the first group, with fifty-seven planes and 243 one-ton bombs, aimed straight for the Arado works. Massive columns of smoke quickly shot up and made it impossible for the precision gunners in the second wave to see any more of the small town than smoke, but the town had to be hidden in there somewhere. They dropped their 175 one-ton high-explosive bombs and twenty-two tons of incendiaries into the ball of smoke. That sufficed to eradicate two-thirds of the built-up area, half of the residential and commercial buildings, and four hundred people. The smoke had clearly marked the city center and harbor areas.

Eighty percent of Arado was destroyed and the production had to be taken over by Dornier in Neustadt-Glewe, so the destruction of Anklam was considered extremely successful. The last major city fire had taken place about six hundred years earlier, at which time the robust brick proved to be a tenacious adversary. The Church of St. Mary also held out well in 1943, sacrificing the helm roof of the tower and parts of the vault on the southern side aisle, but generally surviving the war. The Church of St. Nicholas, built over centuries starting in 1300, also survived October 9, 1943, but lasted only another eighteen months. During the fight for the city on April 29, 1945, one week before Germany capitulated, everything was reduced to rubble except for the outer walls, pillars, and partition arches. The group of patrician homes and the marketplace were inadvertently razed by the Eighth Air Force.

Up to three weeks before the end of the war, the seven-hundred-year-old city of Wismar had withstood eleven attacks. Its ghostly, melancholy, Vineta-like appearance perhaps protected it from death, in the way that the eternally ill do not die. Founded on beer export and wool weaving, Wismar had been bled absolutely white during the Seven Years' War. Its three foolhardy, high spires of the St. Nicholas, St. Mary, and St. George churches were disproportionately high in their daydreaming city of red-hot stone and sea-air dampness. The construction of St. Mary's Church, which dominated one of the largest market squares in northern Germany, was started in the fourteenth century and based on the Lübeck model. During the subsequent two centuries, side halls, chapels, a central steeple, and a spire were added. In the interior, a series of six-ribbed vaulted rooms, a meeting of high and late Gothic, dominated the steeply extending central nave. The mighty octagonal pillars supported slender clerestories until the night of April 14, 1945, when American aerial mines tore apart the structure between the tower and the radiating chapels, destroying the designs of works director Johann Grote. The brick vault subsequently collapsed. The collapse of the flying buttresses in turn led to the crumbling of extended sections of the walls of the aisles. The side hall annexes were also doomed.

As in all churches of the northern German seaside cities, the floor was covered with memorial slabs. Prominent families with close ties to the city had the names of their ships engraved between the epitaphs, so that they could sail to the resurrection as surely as they used to sail back into the bosom of the country. The Swedish general Karl Gustaf Wrangel and his wife also lay there in baroque splendor, in one sense in the land of the enemy, but also in the one world of Christian seafaring. The torso of the Church of St. Mary later had to be torn down, for safety reasons. The entire vicinity of St. Mary's, with its brick gables from the late Middle Ages, also disappeared, including the Old School, a delicate jewel with dark green glazes and a longitudinal façade with fifteen axes.[6] The two other major churches, St. Nicholas and St. George, the patron saint of lepers, survived.

In 1234, Prince Witzlaw I of Rügen granted the Lübeck city rights to Stralsund on the opposite side of the Strela Sound. But the city was too successful, so Lübeck, under Admiral Alexander von Soltwedel, invaded its competitor in 1249, seeking to destroy it. That did not prevent Stralsund from becoming a leading power in the Hanseatic League, nor did the city fire of 1271. Its further destiny was intertwined with the area's frequent wars with Denmark and Sweden, the latter of which incorporated Stralsund and West Pomerania into its Baltic Sea empire in 1628. This led to the consolidation of Stralsund as a fortification and subjected it to two sieges. Another fire carried off major parts of the medieval contours; the subsequent reconstruction brought magnificent baroque additions. The fortifications were torn down in 1873. The drama of construction and renovation went on for centuries, which might have stiffened the resistance of the place, for its walls withstood fairly well even the shower of bombs that fell on October 6, 1944.[7] The Church of St. James suffered some cracks, the northern row of pillars shifted, and some of the vaults lost their support and gave up. But the unpretentious main body from the first half of the fourteenth century remained standing, albeit with shaken statics. Some of the beautifully interfaced baroque and brick gables fell, but no more than what had been already ruined. It was the loss of human life that made October 6, 1944, into the most severe raid to date by the U.S. Eighth Air Force. This city of 49,000 was actually not even a target, but it was noted as an alternative objective, mainly in the event that the approach on the regularly attacked V2 test site at Peenemünde proved unsuccessful.

On the morning of October 6, 1944, 447 B-17 bombers left England, headed for the hydrogenation plant in Stettin-Pölitz, a precision target. Because it was concealed by cloud cover, the formations swerved off. In order to get rid of their bomb loads, the pilots were assigned alternative objectives; a city could always be identified by the radar devices despite an overcast sky. Stralsund became the target of 146 airplanes carrying 367 tons of bombs. In twenty-nine minutes, between 12:45 and 1:14 p.m., they emptied their bays. Thousands of Stralsunders died. The military aspect of this operation was, first and foremost, the release of bombs and, second, the release over an enemy settlement. On the ground, the scene was one of absolute massacre. Because of the high water table, it was impossible to lay protective concrete pipes underground, and in small cities, air-raid shelters were considered dispensable. The sheer number of people bombed over the course of the war makes a loss of a thousand lives seem unremarkable, but for a city of 49,000, it is a horrific bloodletting, a ratio corresponding to half of the Hamburg losses.

Stettin was one of the strongest fortresses of Europe. The Swedes, Brandenburgers, French, Russians, and Poles had all either laid siege or been besieged there. Its history was marked not by its buildings but by the shells that cannons outside the city walls had fired into the interior. In 1677, a third of the buildings had not survived the prolonged stranglehold of the Great Elector; none were left unscathed. Following in his footsteps, Russians and Poles only succeeded in destroying 150 buildings, in 1713, but these generals did manage to purge Stettin of its Gothic and Renaissance architecture, except for a few remaining relics. Baroque and classicism brought new creations. Thus the Basilica of St. James, which had been started in the early Gothic style and completed in the fourteenth century, had a completely baroque interior, since the incendiary projectiles of the Elector had destroyed it down to the crypts. A work that emulated heaven in both form and sound was Arp Schnitger's new organ. Twenty years after a direct hit by the Brandenburgers had silenced the previous organ, Master Mathes Schurich of Radeberg near Dresden, along with five journeymen, commenced with the new construction but died in the process.[8] On Dietrich Buxtehude's suggestion, Schnitger worked further on the pipes and the soundboard, taking on his friend Balthasar Held for assistance. The new organ was consecrated on January 11, 1700. Pastor Fabricius's blessing of the royal instrument incorporated Stettin's ability to rise from the dead into his verse:

The organ, which in war
foe's might tore apart,
Schurich, Schnitger, and Held
honored with a high art.

The final besiegers came through the air. The first Wellingtons appeared as early as 1940 and 1941, in search of sites that could do with a load of bombs. The Oderwerke and Vulcan companies built world-renowned ocean liners; three had been awarded the "Blue Riband": *Kaiser Wilhelm der Grosse* in 1897, *Deutschland* in 1900, and *Kaiser Wilhelm II* in 1906. They were truly challenging targets, as were the Kraft ironworks and the hydrogenation plant in Pölitz that started producing aviation fuel in 1940. In 1943, the distinction between industrial and city targets had become irrelevant, so London was very pleased to hear on April 21 that 339 Lancasters and Halifaxes had succeeded in reaching, perfectly marking, and hitting a site over six hundred miles away. The bitter 6 percent loss of aircraft had been worth the sacrifice, since one hundred acres of the city center were reported as devastated. While that assumption was greatly exaggerated, 586 people had definitely been killed.

Bomber Command had chosen an April 20 approach route over Denmark, where the liberation movement took the date as a birthday greeting to Hitler and gloated. The bombs were dropped on the green illumination markers in the southern part of the city. They started 276 fires, with columns of flames extending two and a half miles high. The Stettin fire department could not cope with the blazes on its own, and called for help from Berlin. British Mosquitos had cleverly feigned the launching of a major attack on Berlin, so that city refused to aid Stettin, waiting for the fire that was not to come for four months. The lack of wind that night in Stettin spared the city from total devastation. The following day, there was also no trace of a breeze, giving the city a sixteen-month extension.

The calm lasted until the night of January 6, 1944; the next morning found 244 more deaths and severe fires blazing in the Old Town. Throughout the early summer, German cities had a bit of a breather, as Bomber Command was participating in the retaking of France. On the night of August 16, they returned to commence total destruction. The lot fell to Stettin. Fourteen days later, a follow-up raid was flown, and then the place was history. The city center between the bulwark-fortified banks of the Oder and the Church of Saints Peter and Paul, built in 1124 in place of a Slavic shrine, no longer existed. Of the 400,000 residents, 2,430 had lost their lives. The remaining Gothic inventory that the Great Elector had failed to destroy were blasted apart by Harris's blockbusters and phosphoros canisters.

The most noble brick church in Pomerania, St. James's, took a fatal blow. It had been resting on piles; though supported by iron cross-struts, the pillars had already been thrown out of kilter. The Gothic Old Town Hall, with its wonderfully ornate twelve-star vaults in the wine cellar, burned out totally. The ducal castle of the Pomeranian House of the Gryfits ("Griffins")—started in 1346 by Barnim III, enriched with the Gothic southern wing during the reign of Bogisław X, and rounded off by a Renaissance church by Johann Friedrich— the preferred target of all besiegers, was finally finished off. The Florentine-style castle church with the woodcut tomb of Bogisław, the greatest of his lineage, was also destroyed. And the foe's might devastated the nave of the St. James Basilica, forever silencing Arp Schnitger's organ.

An inexplicable destructive drunkenness must have been what finally reduced old Danzig to ruins on March 26, 1945. Only six weeks later it would become a Polish city, Gdansk. Not one single church remained untouched: St. Barbara's, St. Bartholomew's, St. John's, St. Joseph's, St. Catherine's, and St. Bridget's suffered most. Saints Peter and Paul's, St. Elizabeth's, St. Ignatius's, St. James's, and the Church of the Holy Trinity were severely damaged. The war against Germany's present existence had finally been won. The war against the roots of the past that had borne the disaster still had to be brought to completion, but it was only a matter of days, and the aim was to destroy as much as possible. "Not wanting to die for Danzig" was an inglorious motto at the start of the war; and at the end, Danzig had to die as proof that there was no lack of militancy against Arthur's Court, the Great Mill, the Main Town Hall, the Holy Ghost Gate, and the Great Crane, built in 1444 as both the city's port crane and a city gate, the symbol of the city. The granaries on Granary Island were conquered, as were the wealthy rows of patrician homes, demolished street by street.

Kiel was a military target. It had been a war port since 1871; the eastern side of the firth presented a monoculture of shipyard industries—Germania, Deutsche Werke, Howaldt—and locomotive, train car, and instrument industries. This is where Anschütz and Co. made their gyrocompasses and where, here and there, fish were still being smoked and marinated. A contiguous armaments-spewing belt extended from the southern end of the estuary to past Mönkeberg. At the outer edge, clearly separate, were the workers' residences. The western side, on the other hand, was structured in a totally different way. This was the actual city center with its Old Town and the businesses and administration that emerged from it, as well as mixed industry. A majority of the residents also lived on this side, some in the business and administrative center, most of them in the surrounding blocks. The firth was obvious, creating a natural separation for attackers and distinguishing military and largely civilian targets. Because the industry was waterside, it was possible to use radar that responded to the difference between water and earth to distinguish between industrial works and residential settlements. In view of this, the nature of the bombing of Kiel offers an accurate image of the air-raid objectives. The shipyard industries were among the preferred objectives for bombardment in the early summer of 1940. On July 20, the first reports of total destruction came in. During the twenty-eight operations in 1941, the eastern side remained the main target. But in 1942, the number of raids decreased by 80 percent. The night of October 13, 1942, marked the completed change in strategy. The blockbusters blasted apart sixty-two acres of roof tiles and thirty-seven acres of window panes. The bomb drops were often imprecise, and many hit the small district of Elmschenhagen on the southeastern outskirts. On December 13, 1943, 1,462 U.S. bombers flew a combined raid on Bremen, Hamburg, and Kiel. The Americans, tormented by the losses in their precision-bombing raids, resorted to the British tactics of carpet bombing. Within sixteen minutes around midday, 689 high-explosive bombs and 2,664 incendiary bombs fell on Bremen; at a ratio of one to three they also fell on Hamburg and Kiel. For the first time, not the eastern shipyard area but Kiel's city center was targeted.

The Americans had their own methods of creating the attack zone while they dropped the bombs. Theoretically, a bomber dropped a single bomb to land on a single point. In contrast, the American bomb carpet spread into an area as it fell, covering an area on the ground. All the planes in a unit released their loads simultaneously on the signal of their leader. Such carpets sailed toward western Kiel on December 13. The infrastructure of the city and the population density there were the obvious objectives. After this raid, like the previous ones in 1943, thousands of people were made homeless within only a few hours and evacuated to the nearby counties of Schleswig, Rendsburg, Plön, and Eckernförde. The skilled workers were the troops that were not permitted to desert the production battle. They took up quarters in the communities of Klausdorf/Schwentine, Mönkeberg, and Heikendorf, on the eastern perimeters. What could have been the reason for four-engine bombers to appear over tiny areas that obviously housed not docks but families and so accurately devastate them to the point that half suffered total destruction?

The damage to village land in Klausdorf was so great that in 1948 there were still 1,500 bomb craters more than ten feet deep.[9] The fields could not be cultivated, since 70 percent of the topsoil layer had been blasted away. To prevent the destruction of the working-class families, the Germans had established the "Finnish housing settlements" in 1941 and 1942. These were prefabricated wooden Finnish homes that were placed inconspicuously in the countryside just outside the outlying districts. That alone helped to stem the human losses. Until late 1943, most bomb damage was incurred by the industrial eastern estuary, but this changed in 1944 and 1945, when the large conflagrations burned out the city center. This was ultimately the area of the main damage. The other side of the estuary also exhibited extensive damage, especially in the workers' residential areas. The ratio of damages on the two sides was roughly two to one.

Of the four main attacks in the last sixteen months of the war, the twenty-five minutes on the night of July 23, 1944, represented the highest losses of the war. The 1,500 time-delay bombs greatly hampered the firefighting efforts, but the forty-three air-raid shelters scattered throughout the city provided relatively good protection. Filled to four times their capacity, as proved necessary during the war, half the population was accommodated.

In the total of ninety attacks, there were over 2,600 casualties, or 1 percent of the population.[10] The historic architecture was totally expunged. The area of destruction and damage made up 78 percent of all built-up areas. On the ground lay 6.5 million cubic yards of rubble, thirty cubic yards per resident.

The city of Hamburg, six times the size of Kiel, lay after the 213th raid in a sea of rubble eight times the size of Kiel's. One hundred and twelve of these attacks took place in 1940 and 1941, killing 751 people.[11] The sixty-five raids in 1944 and 1945 in turn killed 5,390.

Excluding the firestorm raid in the summer of 1943, the Anglo-American air forces succeeded in killing only 0.31 percent of the prewar population, an extremely low success rate. If the losses during the summer of 1943 had indeed remained within the framework of what the same volume of bomb tonnage achieved in 1944, then the total casualty rate would have been 0.57 percent. Even then, in view of the 1.7 million bombs dropped—one for each resident—Hamburg air defense should be conceded a victory. Nowhere during World War II was the defense able to improve that ratio. In fact, the events of the five years of the Hamburg air war seem in retrospect to be insignificant, except for three days.

The 40,000 deaths from the July 1943 Hamburg raids, in addition to those of Dresden, Tokyo, Hiroshima, and Nagasaki, are codes for the extremes of what can be inflicted by the force of arms. Not because of the rivers of shed blood, but due to the quick, deadly breath with which life was taken from the world. Little blood flows in a fire or nuclear war. Emergency physicians in Hamburg reported that hundreds of people were caught in typhoonlike drafts of hot air and later found lying naked in the streets. Their skin was a brownish texture, and their hair was well-preserved. The facial mucous membranes were dried out and crusted. Those who had escaped from the cellars to the streets had stopped in their tracks after only a few steps, lain down on the street, and tried to protect themselves from breathing in the hot air by holding up their arms. Children were supposedly more resilient than adults. Dr. Helmuth Baniecki, an anatomist, dissected one of these bodies:

> Corpse of a young man of approximately sixteen years. Right arm held out in a fencing position; found lying totally naked on his back in the street. Scorched head hair; skin on the feet is charred; chin and tip of nose dried up and burned. Superficial charring on the extensor side of the hands. Skin color reddish-brown. Rump muscles appear as if boiled. Tongue surface dry and brownish. Lungs are distended, voluminous, heavy. An abundance of thickened blood in the right heart. The left heart is empty, liver is hard, spleen is melted away. Between dura mater and calvaria there is a large volume of thickened, lubricious, pasty, reddish mass. Cuts through cerebrum and cerebellum without evidence of free bleeding or pathological changes. In the tissue sections, evidence of vital reaction was noted through leukocyte emission. Assessment: The young man was burned alive on the street.[12]

This young man was not incinerated because he was unlucky. He could not have avoided his fate by doing something else or being somewhere else. His organs ceased to function and changed form because the air that life needs to thrive had been exchanged for something else. The firestorm simulated the atmosphere of another planet, one incompatible with life. Gas, uranium radiation, bacteria, or heat do not injure the body through violence; they simply place the body in another place, a place that does not support life. A fatal injury might come from being at the wrong place at the wrong time, but it does not fundamentally change the world. Annihilation, by contrast, occurs when nothing can continue to exist in a certain place. The young man frozen into a fencing position was fencing against the sudden revocation of the world of existence. As if thrown through a revolving door, 4.5 square miles of Hamburg found itself in a room for three hours not where life dies—that always happens—but rather, where life is not possible, where it cannot exist. Hamburg and Hiroshima are symbols denoting a war that isolates certain regions from the world of life.

Most of those who died in Hamburg did not do so on the streets, but in the cavities of their cellars, where sometimes the same and sometimes other laws of chemistry were at work. After a while, the cellars started absorbing the external heat and functioned like crematoria, or they imperceptibly filled with combustion gases. Hamburg authorities listed gas poisoning as the cause of death in 70 to 80 percent of the cases.

The firestorm that developed in the working-class districts of Hammerbrook, Hamm, and Borgfeld barely touched the historic center of the city, between the main train station and the city hall. The center lasted until the 157th raid, on June 18, 1944, in which eight hundred U.S. bombers set their sights on the Blohm & Voss shipyards. The bombs landed about half a mile too far to the north; the Eighth Air Force was bombing from an altitude of 23,000 feet. A few seconds delay shifted the impact to very different targets. In this case, instead of the shipyards, Gotthold Ephraim Lessing was toppled from his pedestal at Gänsemarkt Square and other targets of no interest to the Americans burned down, such as St. James's Church. Arp Schnitger's organ was partly walled in and partly hidden in an aboveground tower bunker, and it even withstood a direct hit on March 22, 1945, which brought down the nave.

Although Hamburg accounted for 56 million of the 523 million cubic yards of rubble that bombs left behind in Germany, the face of the city had not been disfigured beyond recognition as was the case in Cologne, Nuremberg, Darmstadt, Kassel, Würzburg, and Düren. Hamburg's face was marked by the three hours of the first perceived firestorm on the night of July 27. It made the extraterritoriality of annihilation a reality, its exit from place and time, from the trusting protection of the world, so that from one hour to the next it could no longer offer a place for life to dwell. Ever since the period from the summer of 1943 to the summer of 1945, the span between Hamburg and Tokyo and Hiroshima, this kind of annihilation is possible.

The highest number of casualties, 83,000, was recorded in Tokyo. They died on the night of March 8, 1945. Tokyo's population density was five times that of Hiroshima, with its eighty thousand dead. Hamburg's population density was one-third greater than that of Hiroshima, and its death toll was one-third lower. Firestorms occurred in all three of these cities, and most of the victims died in the fires.

Bremen's air-war fate was very different from Hamburg's. The city was 75 percent smaller, but was just as often the target of bomber raids. One hundred and seventy-three attacks leave a different mark on a city of only 424,000. The first two raids took place on May 18 and 19, 1940, each time just after midnight; 214 bombs were dropped, and there were seventeen deaths, along with damage to the Deaconess Hospital.[13] Raids five to nine took place during the week of June 22 to 28. Each of them was responded to with 50,000 rounds from antiaircraft artillery; the raids left ten injured and one dead. On July 2, the Munte 1 garden restaurant was damaged. On July 17, five pilots shot down two days earlier were buried in the Aumund cemetery; they had done their duty. The nineteenth raid, on August 9, hit the industrial port and the psychiatric hospital, but the raid dropped only sixty-six bombs, and the toll was only one slight injury. The year ended with the thirty-sixth and thirty-seventh raids, explosive greetings on the Waller Ring and seventy-eight incendiaries on the Schwachhausen district.

The new year, 1941, commenced with serious intentions. Raids thirty-nine through forty-one dropped 15,000 incendiary sticks on three consecutive days, yielding twenty-six dead. Four weeks later, five hundred children were evacuated to Salzburg because of the air raids. The first aerial mine was dropped during the fifty-sixth raid, killing twenty. The fifty-ninth raid dropped 232 high-explosive bombs and

3,224 incendiaries, hitting the surgical, gynecological, and children's hospitals, the Pathological Institute, a deaf-mute institution, and the State Library. The first raid in 1942, the eighty-seventh, was a direct hit on a family party on Contrescarpe Strasse at the corner of Kohl-höker Strasse: twenty-six dead, ten seriously injured, and eighteen slightly injured. June 1942 brought raids ninety-one through ninety-four, in which 40,771 incendiary bombs were dropped, and raids 102 and 103 in September dropped a total of 37,166 incendiaries.

Harris conceived the ninety-second raid to be "Millennium No. 2," continuing the thousand-bomber attack on Cologne. On the night of June 25, 1942, he wanted to "destroy Bremen's city and port." One thousand sixty-seven airplanes were sent out. The fifth group of 142 planes was to concentrate only on the Focke-Wulf aircraft factory, and twenty Blenheims focused on the Weser AG shipyards. Everything was supposed to be over in sixty-five minutes. The wide Weser River was a good landmark, but it was hard to see under the clouds. This worried Bomber Command, but they counted on the westerly wind to push away the strip of clouds and sweep the sky clear. However, during the night, the wind suddenly stopped and Bremen remained under thick cloud cover. The thousand bombers had to rely entirely on the Gee beams. Consequently, one-third of the fleet failed to find the city. The bombs fell on residential areas to the south and east, burning 572 buildings and leaving eighty-five dead. Focke-Wulf was hit by a heavy bomb, and the Vulcan shipyards, the Norddeutsche Hütte smelting works, and the Korff refinery were also hit. The unit was carrying 1,450 tons of bombs, which was enough to give the city a fate on the order of Hamburg's, but wind and clouds came to Bremen's aid.

The destruction increased. Raid 102 was the hitherto most successful attack, covering all districts of the city and killing 115 people. Raid 103 seriously damaged six schools, two hospitals, the Colonial Museum, and the State Library. Raid 111 also hit a military target, the Focke-Wulf aircraft factory. Ten planes were destroyed and twelve damaged. On Pentecost, 1943, raid 112 left 238 dead, with the usual hits on schools, churches, and the Deaconess Hospital. Raid 117 on November 26, 1943, hit the Deaconess Hospital yet again, as well as eleven schools and the psychiatric hospital, with 270 casualties.

On the night of August 18, 1944, Bremen suffered the most severe attack of the war. It was raid 132, and a firestorm developed. In thirty-four minutes, sixty-eight blockbuster bombs, 10,800 phosphorus bombs, and 108,000 incendiary sticks fell, leaving 49,000 homeless and 1,054 dead. Raid 138 in October, in the industrial area of Hastedt and Sebaldsbrück, was successful: 110,150 incendiary bombs were dropped and 82 people died. Raids 148 to 165 took place between February 24 and March 30, 1945. The State Archives were seriously damaged by the eight thousand incendiaries that fell on the city center. The Vacuum Oil company was hit hard; twenty-two small boats were sunk in the harbor area. Adolf Hitler Bridge was totally devastated, and the girls' secondary school in Langereihe was hit: seventy-five casualties.

The authorities prohibited any privileged treatment of those killed. The edict of April 10 decreed:

> In order to guarantee equal treatment of all segments of the population, the use of coffins shall be prohibited. It is expected that relatives who are able will offer another suitable covering for the corpse, such as a cloth or something similar. Coffins for the purpose of transporting the bodies to the gravesite will be made available. Cremation of corpses shall be discontinued due to scarcity of fuel.[14]

Raids 168 to 171 took place on April 23, at 3:49 a.m., 11:44 a.m., 5:15 p.m., and at 1:00 the next morning. Residents no longer left the shelters, electricity was cut off, and the close crowding of the people used up so much oxygen that open flames guttered and died. The weather outside the air-raid shelter was springlike, but inside, the people gasped for air and shoved their way into the damp concrete blocks when they heard the engines. The last raid, the 173rd, took place on April 24, at 2:00 p.m. It took nineteen people to their deaths. The next day, British tanks rolled into the city.

In addition to the aircraft, shipyards, and oil industries, densely populated residential communities were lost, including the entire western suburbs. The 890,000 bombs that fell on Bremen killed a total of 3,562 residents, prisoners, and foreign workers. Fifty-eight percent of all residential space burned down. The Old Town of the city, which had been registered since the year 787 as a diocesan city, was not destroyed until raid 131, on October 6, 1944. Raid 121 had already torn down the enchantingly ornamented Gothic "Essighaus," and raid 122—together with 137—eliminated St. Ansgar, the willful triple-nave pillar basilica whose construction started in 1229. Number 137 burned down the single-nave brick church in Gröpelingen, whose choir vault had a depiction of the Last Judgment in red chalk.

Bremen is ranked about twelfth in terms of number of air raids. In ninth place was the East Frisian city of Emden, the westernmost of the coastal cities and a prime example of Dutch Renaissance architecture. It was demolished in a single day: Grosse Deichstrasse with warehouses still showing Gothic influence, Grosse Burgstrasse and Grosse Brückstrasse with Dutch corbie-step gables, and the magnificent Old Market from the early Renaissance. Emden was the easiest city for Bomber Command to reach. It was along the flight route, and they saved it for a day such as September 6, 1944. They had not yet completed the return from France, and before facing the new confrontations with Germany's antiaircraft and fighter weapons, Bomber Command got warmed up with coastal operations against Stettin and Königsberg, of which Wing Commander John Woodroffe —one of the most skilled master bombers the RAF had—destroyed 41 percent on the night of August 29. A week later, 181 Lancasters and Halifaxes submerged Emden in a sea of flames. Sixty-six percent of the city would never resurface, including the splendid Town Hall "am Delft," which Antwerp master builder Laurenz Steenwinkel had erected in 1576 on the Old Market square, the heart of Emden. It burned to the ground.

Charlemagne assigned the Anglo-Saxon Willehad the task of missionizing the Frisians and Saxons. The bishopric of Bremen was founded for that purpose, and the bishops of Bremen did in fact control the land between the Weser and Elbe rivers until the time of the Reformation. The Weser was the natural fortification of the Saxons. Forest and mountain ridge became their natural protection. The battlefront lay to the west. The Egge Hills and the Teutoburg Forest arched out against the Rhine. The course of the next thousand years would be fought out against the Franks across the river to the west. The Saxons did not have the Christian scriptures, but they believed in the war god Saxnot, their primary deity. They chose the horse as their totem animal; their symbol, the Irminsul world-tree, told of their invincibility. The other culture across the river, in total antipathy to theirs, lived in churches and monasteries. It wrote on parchment in precious colors, lines, and images. In order to defend himself against a blow of the sword, the apostle Boniface held a book over his head. Although the sword cut through both book and apostle, the sword was still the weaker weapon, as demonstrated alone by the attempt to vanquish books by cutting them in two.

The Saxons carried out raids from the Weser stronghold to burn down churches and monasteries devoted to Scripture and its proclamation. They feared God's might, manifested on the shining gold and purple pages covered with snakelike lines of ink as black as night. These endured and instilled constancy in those who understood them. When the Franks destroyed the sacred tree Irminsul without any response from Saxnot, they knew that he had been unable to do anything, or else he would have. The Saxons pushed on toward the southwest because the space was becoming too crowded for them, and the Franks pushed eastward, because there was no way to maintain neighborly relations with the erratic and unreliable Saxons. When Charlemagne crossed the Pyrenees to set things straight at the opposite end of his empire, where the influence of the caliphate of Córdoba was gnawing, the Saxons stabbed him in the back. They had vowed to be his subjects, but such a promise could not last forever.

Duke Widukind waited for the appropriate opportunity, which came when Charlemagne was recovering from the losses he suffered against the Moors. Widukind led a Saxon uprising and chopped a Frankish army to pieces at the Süntel mountain ridge. A day's march south of Bremen, at Lugenstein, the Saxon site of worship and legal judgment near Verden on the Aller, Charlemagne is said to have beheaded 4,500 Saxon nobles in reprisal, though it has never been confirmed. The remaining Saxons then underwent a forced baptism. They would no longer attack the sanctuaries of the west if they kneeled down in them. This was a doubtful assumption. Saxnot had not been totally exorcised, and he continued to haunt his apostate land and shake it up at intervals.

Charlemagne anticipated that. He set up mission stations in Saxony, dioceses that fostered the fidelity of the Saxon conversion and supervised the subjugation. They were initially in Paderborn, Minden, Osnabrück, and Herford, and new ones were supposed to be added steadily, such as in Brunswick, Hildesheim, and Münster. They firmly looked after the piety of that restless people. Starting in 1940, their conversion was again on the agenda of the western powers. The old bishoprics could not hold off the new paganism, and together they were mercilessly razed to the ground.

Paderborn was Charlemagne's main base during the thirty years of war with the Saxons, opposite the fortress on the Weser. The

Karlsburg fortress, which he had erected where two hundred bubbling springs converge into the Pader River, was destroyed twice by adversaries. Burn layers were repeatedly found in the city. The Ottonian-Salian Palatinate settled on the foundations of the Carolingian Palatinate, the stronghold of rule over the Saxons. Now the Saxons themselves carried the crown of the Christian empire of the west. It was in Paderborn that Charlemagne met with Pope Leo III and resolved the union, which would last a millennium, between northwestern European territorial power and the universal reign of Christ. Paderborn, at the source of occidental thought, had long been the most important residence of the Frankish, then Saxon, then Salian rulers. Henry II had his wife Kunigunde crowned queen here. All of this was turned to stone in the cathedrals, palaces, and abbeys; in their destruction and deterioration newer stones came together for the same prayer.

Ricarda Huch, who saw Paderborn before it was destroyed and described it, called it a sleepy town in which, time after time, fire reduced the tirelessly rebuilt works to nothing. But the cathedral appeared to her like the giant oaks within which the Saxons heard the voices of their gods. The great lines of the first builders, their heroic ground plan, Huch wrote, grew into the ground and helped all later master builders with their works.

> The same greatness of the Romanesque cathedral is in the semi-Gothic Jesuit Church, with its proud ascent and the interior hall that appears gilded in fire, and the Gothic-baroque secondary school and the Franciscan Church with the wide stairway and the fountain. But how much dreamlike, rapt immersion broods over the springs, at the old walls, in the narrow alleyways that lead to the cathedral close. Besides the idea of the all-embracing Holy Empire that set its monuments here, the spirit of the silent savages also reigns, who sat on their estates as lords who honored their gods in the storm and in the rustling of hundred-year-old trees and bowed their blond heads only to the duke they themselves had chosen.[15]

The Jesuit Church was demolished down to the main walls; the Franciscan Church and the Jesuit college were gutted by fire. The cathedral suffered a direct bomb hit in the southern aisle; all the roofs and spires burned, as did the books that the Archbishop's Academy had collected: 70,000 of 160,000 volumes.

Paderborn was the deployment port for the western campaign. Onward from May 10, 1940, bomb-laden aircraft rolled to the front, and on May 21, the opposing side came for the first time; they could hardly believe it. The anxiety was the greatest damage. In 1943, two hundred sirens sounded, but the bombers were usually just flying over, until March 16, when twelve fighter-bombers headed toward the crowded train station in the early evening and dropped sixteen five-hundred-pounders onto the railroad workshops. This ended forty-seven lives, and was the worst until January 17, 1945, when eight waves of U.S. bombers hammered down on the cathedral, the Market Church, the market square, St. Mary's Square, the Academy, the secondary school, and even the eastern cemetery, causing the gravestones, crosses, and bones to whirl through the air. A block-buster blast tore apart a group of young girls and women under the mission cross of the cathedral and a group of French prisoners of war in the Imperial Court. The count was 239 deaths. They were put to rest side by side in long rows, in the Church of St. Meinolf and the Sacred Heart of Jesus Church.

The city's ultimate ruin did not come until March 27, when Bomber Command sent 276 planes to accurately target the Old Town, handing it over to a flaming death in less than fifteen minutes. No disturbances were to come from here when in front of the city's gates the Ruhr basin was closed off. Three thousand fires were set, including one in the basement infirmary of the home for the aged, where the matron and six nurses died. The firebombs had penetrated all the ceilings and vaults and shot a yellowish-blue flame up through the entire facility. In the West-phalenhof Home for the Aged, in addition to the seven nurses, twenty-one residents died. Virtually all the schools went down, as well as the provincial home for the blind and the court prison. Eighty-three percent of the Old Town no longer existed. The rage of the bombs extended all the way to the southern parishland, where it tore apart the seventy-two-year-old shepherd Herdes along with his sheep and dogs.

The sanctum was saved. The archbishop, nuns, and other believers kneeled in a semicircle, thanking God for the protection they had received and remembering all who had burned in the cellars. Those left in the ruined city rummaged through the slowly cooling rubble for their dead. The cathedral vicar Msgr. Caspar Schulte and his helpers personally saw to it that the three hundred corpses were buried. This took weeks, and the gravediggers needed a liter of schnapps a day to numb them to the horror.

At a ford in the river where the trade routes crossed, Charlemagne had established the diocese at Minden, at the rear gate of the Weser fortification, in 800. Henry the Lion, the greatest of the Saxon dukes in the Hohenstaufen period and patron for the Christian merchants in the Baltic Sea realm, married Matilda, daughter of Henry II of England, in the Minden cathedral in 1168. From that epoch the fortresslike westwork of the cathedral of Saints Peter and Gorgonius remained, a divine castle with sections of Carolingian origin. The thirteenth century added first the late Romanesque transept and, toward the end of the century, the High Gothic nave, the most significant of its time. Construction was finally completed in the mid-fourteenth century, with a Gothic polygonal apse. From the tenth to the twelfth centuries, the Saxon and Salian rulers often tarried on the triple-arched emperor's gallery of the westwork. On December 6, 1944, the U.S. Air Force placed a direct hit into the Gothic choir, ripping open the northern wall and causing the vaulting to collapse. On March 28, 1945, they returned. The nave had survived the first raid; this time it received a direct hit. The columns and vault fell, destroying the heart-shaped filigree window tracery. The westwork burned out entirely. Minden had always been a military target, so even at that late date there were troops there. They postponed their retreat until seven days after the cathedral had been destroyed, then blew up two bridges over the Weser, having thereby done their duty. After four raids in 1944, it was the March 1945 attack that made history of the city center, with its market square and Gothic Hanseatic city hall, the large and small cathedral courtyards, and the Königswald, or King's Forest.

The Saxons under Widukind and Alboin had been absolutely crushed in a three-day battle within the Weser fortress near Osnabrück. The battlefield at the River Hase was to lead to their conversion, and Osnabrück became a diocese in 785, and later a city. Charlemagne installed his clerical governors in accordance with sound military considerations; Osnabrück and the Herford monastery made up the central axis between the mountainous flanks and gave the interior region a religious unity. As in Bremen and Paderborn, the bishops here had a terrible relationship with the emerging burgher class. Nowhere did they live out their feud as openly as in Osnabrück. The Roman prayer book, Frankish culture, and baptism, as a consequence of their defeat, remained contrary to instincts. The name of the city alone rebelliously carries the "Os" of the Norse Aesir gods, who were worshipped by the Germanic tribes. In 1241, the pope placed the city under a ban. In return, it burned down St. Gertrude's Monastery, which had stood on a hill once covered by a sacred grove. The monastery was rebuilt, but not out of religious feeling; the motivation was rather to change the pope's mind. A city councilor supposedly burned a picture of the Crucifixion on the open street.

The clergy feared that the townspeople wanted to eliminate them, especially since the city council prohibited their acquiring municipal ground rent in the fifteenth century. In the Saxon manner, the council demanded and was even awarded a voice in selecting the bishop. The citizenry also forced the bishop to deny Jews the right to settle in Osnabrück. The pope declared the people of Osnabrück collectively to be Hussites, and demanded that heresy laws be used against them. The Archbishop of Cologne anathematized them. Of course, the residents of Osnabrück all declared themselves to be Protestants, and so it is not surprising that the city was devastated by a fire in 1613 that supposedly spared only the council school and a small house in which an old man prayed unremittingly. The next blaze was caused by the six thousand tons of munitions dropped from the skies by British and American squadrons near the end of the war.

Osnabrück was one of the most-destroyed cities of the air war. After the final attack on Palm Sunday in 1945, 65 percent of the total built-up area lay in ruins, including 94 percent of the Old Town. None of the historic monuments had been spared devastation. Old Osnabrück, with its winding alleyways, noble estates, town houses, and gabled roofs, was the pyre on which Bomber Command sought to throw the rest of the city. The town was also a primary transportation junction, and it was the home of the Klöckner Works, which produced cannon parts, tanks, and grenade shells. Thus all the requirements and justifications for an annihilating raid came together.

Of a total of seventy-nine raids, the first notable one, on June 20, 1942, dropped nine thousand British incendiary stick and phosphorus bombs. Ten deaths was a low casualty figure, as was the case with Osnabrück in general, due to good air-raid protection. On the other hand, an eyewitness reported: "That night was really horrific. It was terrible since it was so new for everyone."[16] The most severe raid of the early war years, on October 6, 1942, used its 11,000 high-explosive and incendiary bombs to transform entire streets into rows of ruins laconically referred to as "Hermann Göring Square" by the locals. Industrial production was cut down by up to 100 percent over an extended period of time. The U.S. day raid on May 13, 1944, caused the most deaths. Of the 241 casualties, 101 died in a shelter trench whose concrete cover was only two feet thick. Forty-nine POWs died when the Russian camp of the Klöckner Works suffered a direct hit.

Death did particularly good business among prisoners of war, especially the Russian foreign workers. On May 7, 1944, thirty residents of a Klöckner women's barracks were ripped apart. The same raid killed fifty, owing to the lack of space in the Johannis School, where patients from St. Martin's Hospital had been brought. Foreigners were prohibited from using the air-raid shelters, especially since the demand for them started growing in late 1944, overcrowding them to an extreme. Prisoners and inmates of the concentration camp in Emsland, however, were commanded to work building bunkers and streets, as well as removing rubble.

Old Osnabrück went down in a hurricane of fire that was fanned by 181,000 incendiaries and 2,171 high-explosive bombs in only fourteen minutes on September 13, 1944. One month later, another 16,000 incendiaries and 2,616 explosive bombs were dropped, which took the lives of twenty-four prisoners. Their guards had fled to safety, but left the prisoners locked up in their cells. The Palm Sunday attack of 1945 fell from a sunny spring sky, obliterating what was left of the Old Town and new parts of the city.

The September 1944 attack set the train station and its vicinity ablaze. Half-crazed travelers and a number of horrendously squealing pigs tried to escape; a livestock transport had been hit. On November 21, 1944, an unfortunate chance hit broke up an underground tunnel that was considered bombproof, given its cover of muschelkalk twenty-six feet thick. The covering was only half as thick at the entryway, however, which was accessible through the boiler room of a children's home. A bomb hit the weakest point in this tunnel, right in front of the entrance. It exploded inside, behind the heavy iron door that was dented and hurled away. The ninety-six people inside the tunnel were mostly children who lived in the home with their caregivers. Only those in the entrance area showed any signs of injury. The others were squatting and waiting as if they were still alive; carbon monoxide gas poisoned them without leaving a trace.

There were three railroad stations leading out of the Ruhr area. The one heading to the Hanseatic cities on the coast went through Osnabrück, a central marshaling yard. The Allied strategists had been preparing since September 1944 for both the imminent ground invasion of the Reich and its tactical air support, the transportation offensive. The target planners were interested as little in Saxon antiquities, pagan feud, imperial bishoprics, citizens' defiance, and urban history as they were in homes for the elderly or the blind. In addition to "go get 'em" bombardiers who led the weapon along with Churchill's tool Harris, calculating brains such as Solly Zuckerman, creator of the Transportation Plan, were at work. The Americans, even more so than the British air doctrinaires, had economy experts and technicians who viewed the war rather soberly as a modern enterprise. The transportation network was the life support for the upcoming German operations. Oil and aviation industries could temporarily improvise, but troops had to be moved in order to form a front, and they had to receive munitions in order to hold their positions. Neither was possible without the railroad. If that artery were cut, the war would come to a standstill.

Nature gave Germany a geography with three transportation axes, the North and Baltic Sea coastlines, the Rhine, and the west-east land route along the foothills of the Mittelgebirge, the low mountain range, following the course of the former *Hellweg*. Geographically and historically, the west-east tension was concentrated in the Weser hills. Charlemagne's war with Saxony and Churchill's bomber offensive were both concerned with military geography. The Lancasters and Flying Fortresses did nothing to change that. The Reich was defended and conquered from the ground, and ground movements depended on the terrain. The Rhine-Ruhr region was the decisive war-waging realm; from here, train lines fanned out via Osnabrück to the coast, via Hanover to Berlin, and via Soest, Paderborn, and Altenbeken to central Germany. All bombardment of this fan in the fall and winter of 1944 and 1945 was aimed at the railroad network. The cathedrals of Minden, Paderborn, Soest, and Hildesheim went down because of the train stations. Train stations supplied the east-west axis, which connected the three main industrial regions of Germany: the Ruhr, Saxony, and Upper Silesia. The war dramatized this route with the Mittelwerke factories hidden in Nordhausen at the edge of the Harz mountains, where the V2 rockets, aircraft engines, and, starting in late 1944, the Heinkel 162 jet fighters were produced. Resources for this battlefield of the production industries—ores, coke, and coal—rolled up and down the west-east tracks. The same was true for the weapons produced, as fronts, too, had been moving along this line for two thousand years.

At that time, the steam locomotive was dependent on an area's terrain; it could not climb well in the uneven landscape of the Weser fortifications, especially if it had to pull great loads. In order to bridge the unfavorable pitches and slopes of the Egge, the ridge east of Paderborn, two viaducts spanned the Dunetal and Beketal valleys. The larger one, the Altenbeken viaduct, measured a third of a mile long. Three hundred transports crossed it daily during the war; hence it was destroyed in late November 1944 and again in late February 1945. It was one of the most significant strategic objectives in Germany, but was difficult to hit because it was in a cleft and formed a curve. When the two other viaducts leading from the Ruhr basin to the area east of the Harz mountains—at Bielefeld-Schildesche and Arnsberg—were also taken out of commission, the Reichsbahn, the German state railroad, established detoured routes. One ran through Detmold, Herford, and Bielefeld-Ost; the other through Paderborn and Hildesheim. This was easy to anticipate. Without delay, the detours were also bombed, which meant the end of Herford and Hildesheim, two Carolingian foundations, the latter having once been a jewel of the German family of cities.

On November 26, 1944, the day of the major raid on the Altenbeken viaduct, the detour through Herford received seventy-one tons of bombs from the U.S. Eighth Air Force; Bielefeld got one hundred tons. Along the Bielefeld-Herford route, at Schildesche, the viaduct that was constructed for traffic to Berlin became an almost daily target by early 1945. According to the Allied "Ruhr plan," the destruction of the three viaducts and sixteen bridges aimed to totally close off the region. The viaducts alone accounted for half the traffic. Strafers also set their sights around the clock on train stations, engines, tracks, and bridges. On January 27, 1945, for example, two railroad cars and an engine were attacked while stopped at Herford-Stedefreund. On the train were ninety-three Polish prisoners of war and five guards; thirty-one people were killed and twenty-nine injured. On March 7, Rector Vormbrock was taking a train from Bielefeld to Brackwede for a funeral. He got caught in the notorious strafer raid at the Brackwede station that injured a number of people, but he managed to reach the cemetery in one piece. A strafer was already there, and it bombarded the long train of funeral guests in the procession. A train is a train. Consequently, the corpse that the rector was supposed to escort could not be delivered, because the hearse driver was frightened; after receiving some words of encouragement, he finally raced with his guest to eternal peace. The funeral guests snuck to the gravesite along a protected path through the woods. And so in Germany transportation became a funeral, and a funeral, transportation.

The neighboring city of Herford garrisoned two thousand men in *Grenadier-Ersatz* regiments and battalions to defend the autobahn through the Teutoburg Forest.[17] Since February, if the winds were from the west, they had been able to hear the thunder of fire from the approaching front. Morale was a thing of the past. According to the field-hospital doctor, about half the horde was faking their injuries. They were malingerers and kept their wounds open artificially. A boundless will to be sick prevailed. They nonetheless quartered in the town, so although they no longer defended anything, Herford was a "defended" city. If at the time anyone had still been interested in the conventions of war, then the state of being defended would have permitted a bombardment. But the Allies did not bomb when conventions allowed; they bombed because they viewed themselves as in the right, and thus bombed as they saw fit. And they saw that Herford had a shunting yard and a bridge, that the route from Bielefeld passed over a viaduct, and that the detour from the main Altenbeken viaduct passed through there. Under such circumstances, Herford could not remain intact.

Herford, from *Heeresfurt* or "army's ford," had been founded in 790 as a convent for noblewomen. From November 1944 on, it suffered heavy air damage; the heaviest bombing fell on the interior of the rampart on March 3, 1945. The triple-nave minster of 1250 experienced blast damages from a high-explosive bomb on the northwestern corner of the northern tower; the bomb traveled through the entire edifice. Especially after that, the troops stationed there saw no sense in their having it out with the besieging Americans, so they distributed their barracks rations of flour and sugar among the people. On the night of April 2, the *Volkssturm* militia opened the antitank obstacles, so the Americans had no trouble rolling in on April 4. This limited the destruction to 15 percent and was a display of military courtesy, but there were also displays of a different kind. On April 3, the city chronicler noted in concern: "A white flag was hanging out a window on Mönchstrasse. Seeing this tasteless indignity almost brought tears to my eyes."[18]

The Bielefeld-Herford viaduct had still not been hit by March 14, despite considerable effort. A modern method finally proved successful. The British had developed a bomb 26.5 feet long weighing

22,000 pounds. At the start of the war, a number of bombers would have been needed to transport it. The No. 617 Squadron of Bomber Command under Squadron Leader C. C. Calder let this "Grand Slam" bomb drop for the first time on that day. It could create an earthquake. When it was tested a day earlier in Hampshire from an altitude of 14,700 feet, it left a crater 120 feet across and sixty feet deep. The Bielefeld earthquake did in fact dislodge five viaduct piers and twenty thousand tons of stonework. The Grand Slam simply shook up Bielefeld's rubble again, as the city center had already been bombed in the U.S. raid on September 30, 1944.[19] Three weeks later, some of the six hundred casualties were still being pulled from the wreckage.

The first bombs had fallen in June 1940, scattered as usual, so they killed a girl on the Westerwinter farm in the Senne II district of the city. Several days later, the bombs brought down a number of people, including sixteen-year-old Gustav Stolte. He had been fascinated by the planes and was watching the attack from the laundry room door on Wichernstrasse when a sharp piece of shrapnel drilled into his body. The bombing raid profoundly moved people in Bielefeld. It struck the Bethel asylum for mentally ill children, hitting the dormitory and killing twelve of the children. Earlier in the war, Pastor Fritz von Bodelschwingh, director of the facility, had fought for the lives of his charges, who were to be exterminated since they were judged "unworthy of living" by the Nazi authorities. Bodelschwingh was able to ward off euthanasia in his facility, but not Bomber Command. Its bombs hit a second time, killing nursing staff and children. The Nazi party organized a grandiose funeral, castigating the "child murder at Bethel."[20] Bielefeld lost a total of 1,108 people from the 4,400 tons of munitions that had been dropped.[21]

The residents of Hildesheim, like those of many German cities, thought the bombs would spare their city. People there had a great liking for the enemy countries; many emigrated Germans had participated in the American Revolution, and there was a tradition of friendly relations between England and northwestern Germany. And finally, surely no one would intentionally damage Hildesheim, world renowned as a place of interest for medieval culture. For the U.S. Eighth Air Force, however, Hildesheim was a train station that happened to have a city surrounding it.

In early November 1944, the residents shook their heads at the hedgehoppers diving onto areas like the sleepy train station in rural Hönnersum, and were incredulous when bursts of machine-gun fire rained down on Derneburg Station along the train line between Grossdüngen and Derneburg. They thought it must be an emergency reaction of bombers being pursued by German fighter planes. But worse was yet to come. On Sunday, November 26, 1944, the Altenbeken viaduct was attacked, and in order to ruin the potential detour route at the same time, the Eighth Air Force headed for Hildesheim. They flew as a large formation that day, with 1,818 bombers and three thousand tons of bombs, and fought one of the larger air battles of the war. The Eighth Air Force had two primary targets, the Altenbeken and Schildesche viaducts, as well as a handful of alternative objectives, such as the marshaling yards at Hamm, Osnabrück, Gütersloh, Bielefeld, and Herford, and seven targets of opportunity. Hildesheim was a target of opportunity. Many buildings at the Old Market were hit, and, most surprisingly, one bomb had such force that it tore out a heavy tree stump two yards long and weighing two hundred pounds, and hurled it from the Old Market, over the buildings, and onto the cathedral courtyard right in front of the statue of St. Bernward.

Bernward was the thirteenth bishop of Hildesheim and the city's founder. A Saxon of noble birth and a soldier, artist, scholar, and doctor, he fought against the Slavs and Normans at the beginning of the millennium. He collected artwork in Italy and brought back a relic from there, a piece of wood from the Cross of the Redeemer. To give it a dignified place to rest, he had a church built, consecrated to the Archangel Michael. He personally crafted the door to the church, the chandelier that would illuminate its interior, and the sarcophagus that would one day be his own. Its Latin inscription cites the Bible: "I know that my redeemer liveth, and that he shall stand at the latter day upon the earth." Bernward was followed by St. Godehard, who could foretell the hour of one's death and was himself buried in the cathedral crypt that Hezilo, his successor, had built. Hezilo signed the document of Henry IV that deposed the pope. But he put a sign on the document, for the sake of Gregory VII, which made it invalid.

Hezilo was a very belligerent prince, who together with his men conducted a bloody massacre in the Goslar Cathedral against the men of the Abbot of Fulda, for the right to sit next to the Archbishop of Mainz. Because the old warhorses seemed inhibited by the sacredness of the site, Hezilo spurred them on to thrust out bravely, as he would grant absolution to all. The bishop's warriors tied their attack to their belief in miracles. Not conservative but self-assured power asserted itself. In the fourteenth century, Bishop Gerhard sent the burghers and peasants of Hildesheim out against the thrice-stronger alliance of the Duke of Brunswick and the bishops of Magdeburg and Halberstadt. He shoved a relic into his sleeve and swore that this weapon was worth more than a thousand men. The people of Hildesheim believed that too, and were victorious.

The three reverent bishop's churches—St. Mary's Cathedral and the churches of St. Michael and St. Godehard—the wooden-framed buildings of Hildesheim, and the artistic sense that Bernward brought to Hildesheim were described by Ricarda Huch, who visited the town before its destruction:

> Next to and below the cathedral close and its Roman-Catholic though often also diversified forms of life, the German people grew up in stillness. The preference for the vertical drives the walls, poles, gates, and windows ever higher, storming toward the infinite, while the Romanesque church binds the formed symbol to the earth. Just the fact that the people's favorite material was wood brought a profound difference: alive, pleasant-smelling brown wood in which the roaming Germanic imagination could indulge with the woodcarving knife.[22]

The Temple House that was built on the site of the torn-down synagogue, on the other hand, was made of stone. In need of money, the bishop had mortgaged all the Jewish assets to one woman, from whom the city council then bought them. Having been robbed of their assets, the Jews left the city. The Temple House preserves the memory of this event, just as all buildings tell their stories. Ricarda Huch located three hundred half-timbered houses that had been spared from the annihilating rage of the time. There were in fact more than seven hundred that survived.

> In a motherly way these buildings do not want only to give refuge, protection, and warmth. They also want to tell and teach. They show us events from the Old and New Testaments. We encounter the elements, the seasons, the muses, even the so-called Nine Worthies, namely, Hector, Alexander the Great, and Caesar as three pagans; David, Joshua, and Judas Maccabaeus as three Jews; and King Arthur, Charlemagne, and Godfrey of Bouillon as three Christians.

It is unsettling how Ricarda Huch ends her walk through Hildesheim by mentioning the train station:

> Whoever strolls through the streets will notice that nothing was built between 1630 and the end of the century, and that the few baroque buildings are in poor condition. With the Thirty Years' War the great times were past. The ugliness of the modern age is luckily limited mainly to the area around the train station.

The first systematic raid on Hildesheim took place on February 22, 1945, at 1:30 p.m. It was also the date of the second operation against the Altenbeken viaduct. The focus of the raid was the freight depot. "A wild churning up of the destroyed embankments," wrote Hermann Seeland, the cathedral canon.[23] "A chaos of chunks of earth and stone blocks, bare remains of iron rods and iron walls of burned out, overturned railroad cars." The train facilities in the north and southeast were the bomb targets, "but they were certainly not the only ones." He listed the streets that had become one big pile of rubble and mourned the Lamberti church of 1473, of which only the base of the tower and remnants of the nave walls remained. The interior of the St. Magdalena convent church for Augustinian nuns was burned to the ground:

> St. Michael's Church must be mentioned as one of the very badly damaged buildings. Bombs that fell on the former monastery grounds, which were probably intended for the "Ordensburg Germania" established by the Nazi party, destroyed major portions of the northern wing and the eastern transept.

For years, everything still standing in the country had been considered part of the Castle of the Order of Germania. This became true for Hildesheim on March 22, when Bomber Command liquidated the city in eighteen minutes, with 235 airplanes and 446 tons of bombs. Thus in a span of eleven consecutive days, Würzburg, Hildesheim, and Paderborn were razed to the ground in a grand total of fifty-eight minutes.

The American raids of March 3, 14, and 15, 1945, had already dealt with the freight depot; several hundred freight cars were dented up and the surroundings had been plowed. Bomber Command was also in search of undestroyed cities. Until those fateful eighteen minutes, Hildesheim could have been considered among them; afterward, 85 percent of the built-up historic areas of the city had been pulverized. On February 22, the bombers concentrated on the new part of the city, but Bomber Command had firm procedures. An Old Town built totally of wood was part of its repertoire.

Through impenetrable clouds of dust and smoke, Hermann Seeland observed the cathedral, totally ablaze. Direct hits had broken through to the northern aisle and southern transept. The Golden Dome fell, and the statue of the Virgin Mary above the western portal was broken in two at the hip and her upper body came crashing down. Bernward's and Hezilo's works, the Christ Column, the Bernward doors, and the wheel chandelier had been removed earlier, so they were preserved. But the bomb was looking for St. Godehard, and broke through the crypt ceiling to his sarcophagus. The statue of Bernward on the cathedral square remained standing; the old lime trees lay around him splintered and uprooted. Flames entered the bishop's palace from the west and worked their way east. Few walls in the seminary remained standing; the Dark Gate welcomed no one anymore, as there were piles of rubble blocking it. St. Bernward Hospital was lucky. The southeastern wing caught fire and it took firefighters the whole night to contain the blaze to the two upper floors. The patients crowded into the narrow, half-lit corridors on the ground floor and waited for all to go well, because a Tallboy bomb, a 12,000-pounder, had penetrated the main building and landed without detonating in a patient's room opposite the chapel. It was defused the next morning, and eight men carried it out.

From the demolished cathedral tavern, Seeland ran to the St. Anne cemetery. Before he left the city he wanted to check its condition. "What terrible devastation to this once beautiful, restful site, where emperors and kings, bishops and scholars sojourned in reverence for the past."[24] The former chapter authorities had used the high attics of the cloister to store grain. But attics, including this one, had become the most dangerous places of all. His glance scanned upward to the open sky, the source of all the ruin. The graveyard crosses had been loosened by the hail of wooden beams and stone blocks flying through the air, covering the graves in layers. It used to be possible to see the cathedral tower from St. Anne's chapel. But now, "no Golden Dome shines in the sunlight of a spring day! Today, March 24, 1945." It was the Golden Dome that Bishop Gerhard had promised the Virgin Mary if she granted him a victory over the bishops Dietrich and Albert of Magdeburg and Halberstadt, as well as Magnus, Duke of Brunswick. Now Brunswick, Halberstadt, Magdeburg, and Hildesheim had all perished within five months, in the same fire.

St. Michael's was a torn-open ruin. High-explosive bombs had ripped away the northern crypt ambulatory with the vault and the transept gallery, but they could not damage Bernward's sarcophagus. Except for a corner of St. Godehard's church, the wooden ballads of Hildesheim's half-timbering have left the earth, including the "most beautiful market square in the world." The steeply soaring butchers' guildhouse, the *Knochenhauerhaus*, had been praised by Georg Dehio as the most monumental of all wood-frame buildings in Germany; it brought together Gothic and Renaissance styles and it burned down like tinder. The cathedral was one of the most damaged in all of Germany. The scorched thousand-year-old rose bush at its apse soon started sprouting again, which gave many hope. The city of 72,000, built around a train station, was swept away because it was presumed there was a military necessity to shut down the Paderborn-Hildesheim rail line, as it was the only line leading out of the Ruhr valley. And the city around it presented an opportunity that would not exist forty-six days later, to bomb an Old Town one last time—a victory lap, of sorts. The train station was totally demolished; Hildesheim's human losses amounted to 1,736.

On Good Friday, 1945, seven days before the Americans occupied Soest, SS men attempted to destroy the Wewelsburg castle by blowing it up and setting it on fire. It had once been a refuge for the prince-bishops of Paderborn and now belonged to the county of Büren. Büren did not want to sell the fortress, but it leased it to the SS in 1934 for an annual fee of two marks. Reichsführer-SS Himmler had long been looking for a fortified castle "in the land of Hermann the Cherusker" for his Office for Racial Matters.[25] After it was converted at great cost into a leadership school, plans were made to expand it between 1942 and 1945. Around the north tower of the triangular castle, which traced back to a Saxon fortification during the time of the Huns, a castle district was to be built within a radius of a third of a mile, enclosed by a castle wall and looking far down onto the hills and valleys.[26] Wewelsburg was the only fortified height in the area, and the community of Wewelsburg, 1,100 souls in a misshapen scattered village, were to be relocated elsewhere by the Soest Office of Cultural Affairs. Once the village was torn down, a National Socialist village community was supposed to develop in a small, closed facility. The hereditary farms that had been there would have had to be scattered throughout the parish land. The SS started doing just that in the spring of 1945, but the Allied occupation got in their way.

Himmler indulged his Saxon delusions at this site, where he met and meditated with his men in a 115-foot-long dining hall. In a colorful natural stone vault under the dining hall was an incinerator. This was where the coats of arms of deceased SS Obergruppenführer were to be burned and preserved in urns on a circle of pedestals. Himmler expected the magic of the Saxon soil and pagan rituals to give his men moral strength. In the area, the SA had also acquired the Beverungen sports castle, and the Nazi party set up a training school at Erwitte, a moated castle from the seventeenth century; though not an uplifting time for the nation, the rusticity and memory of the old stone masonry was enough to invoke the spirit of the past. National Socialists read this as the first commandment of their Führer. "Die!" And the aura of the stone would add, "and become."[27] Petrifaction facilitates letting go of life. Life gives itself up to the stone's hardness and comes home to the cult of the masonry. And so Himmler wondered in the crypt of the Quedlinburg cathedral if Henry I might not have returned in him. He liked to have secret conversations with him at night, and at the same time he asked himself imploringly if they were not one and the same. Something drew Himmler to the execution site of the 4,500 Saxons, for whom he created a memorial grove near Verden. Their subjugation by "Karl the Frank"—as Himmler called Charlemagne—and his Christian, occidental concept of empire were considered a decline from past strength, and the traces of pagan blood and essence were sought and fostered. Encapsulated within the Christian age, this pagan essence could break out in the presence of certain leaders, especially the present Führer.

The Nazi party nurtured a tactical relationship to history. They invoked those historical scenes that appealed to them because they furthered their purposes; they used them to define their genealogy and appointed themselves as the consummators. The party expressed not its despotism but rather the history of its race. The Saxon masquerade has been scattered to the winds; other historical myths lose relevance and some continue. All generations appropriate history tactically for their purposes. They use those parts of history that help them in their own search for meaning in life. One could almost think that no other history exists than that leading to one's own salvation. That too is an ideology. The destruction of Hildesheim did happen. This city and the others in the Weser region had stored layers of all that had happened up to the time of its destruction. People, buildings, legends. The cities reveal them even today, sometimes as replicas, but mostly as scars, the burn layer of their last destruction. Himmler's Saxon cult is also a fact, as is how it served him. The destruction of the cities in turn stripped all power from Himmler and his kind, who took places, history, people, all of Germany and Europe hostage. At the same time, this seizure of hostages was what Germany was at that time. It came to be with force, with approval or outrage, with indifference or powerlessness. A different Germany is nothing more than a subjunctive mood, a "could have been, would have been," an "if."

Another subjunctive is whether the fires were absolutely necessary. Did Hildesheim have to be wiped out because of the train station? Was that the reason; was there even a reason? Did the fireraisers, in their resolve and rage, want to win at all costs? And is this the price that was paid so they could be victorious? Without a doubt it was an attempt to win, no matter what the price. If Allied history does not depict this as a tragedy, then does German history also have to view it as a total success? Will this simple equating of destruction with success remain when—though things have not yet reached that point—the Germans become aware of their burn layer? The burn layer is a fact without words for it.

Tactical appropriation of history is an empty complaint, though one even lodged by Goethe. Whoever appropriates history is an active subject and thus subjective. There is also a history that no one appropriates, such as that of the great fire. But that nonappropriation and unwillingness is just as active, just as subjective. The not-wanting, the unwillingness of two generations, explains why so much time has passed. It was not the time to appropriate that past. But time changes, and it also changes how the past is appropriated.

Soest was one of the large marshaling yards, 5,500 by 330 yards; other than that, it was a town of 23,000. The officer's camp on Meiningerweg held two thousand French officers as prisoners of war, among them a group of railroaders who in their free time cut engines, train cars, tracks, and switches out of tin cans with shears. On invitation of the management of the Soest train station they exhibited their arts and crafts, along with samples of French train schedules and posters advertising French trains. A general greeted the stationmaster at the entrance, and several officers led the tour through the exhibition. The cab of a French locomotive was set up and not without pride did they demonstrate the safety system of French trains. The Soest station crew was greatly impressed by the artwork and expertise of their French colleagues, and would have liked to have shown greater enthusiasm than was possible under the circumstances. Trains and railroaders belong to an international brotherhood. Extraordinary understanding of all things having to do with railroads was also shown in the expert bombing of train lines and facilities. This expertise was far greater than it was regarding the raids on industry. On December 4 and 5, 1944, the marshaling yard was totally demolished. This cost 250 lives, including a reserve train engineer, a freight workman, a train oiler, and a laborer from the eastern territories working as a cleaning woman at the reloading depot.

On December 5, Soest families were preparing for St. Nicholas's Day. But outside on the train line, there was no rest. The repair crew wanted to get traffic moving again. At 8:55 p.m., the air-raid sirens sounded; 385 Halifaxes and one hundred Lancasters came carrying eighty aerial mines, one thousand demolition bombs, and countless incendiaries. The rail yards had their own antiaircraft artillery set up, operated by twenty-four railroad workers staffing each shift. The battery positions were deployed behind the Osthofen cemetery, at the home for the blind, and on Schwarzerweg. Only two Halifaxes were hit. When the employees left their shelters, they were greeted by a picture of utter horror. The entire station was on fire. The reloading depot, the express freight dispatch office, the freight car barn—it was one giant sea of flames.

The attackers would return, because they knew the railroaders would get things rolling again. In the first few days after the main attacks, thousands of helpers cleared out the train station. These were Soest railroaders, their colleagues from elsewhere, as well as an SS construction train with prisoners from a concentration camp. During the war, the Reichsbahn was often referred to as the "fourth arm of the Wehrmacht." Train stations were the front. When the sirens sent people into air-raid shelters, train personnel had to stick it out, because there were still trains out there on the tracks. Should the trains be allowed to enter the station, or should they be rerouted, or just left on the tracks to be a target? Among the casualties of December 5 were passengers on the evening train from Paderborn, which had left Sassendorf shortly before the raid commenced. As it reached the railroad yard, the train got caught in the shower of bombs. The stoker was among the dead, as were the two conductors from

Paderborn and five passengers. The seriously and slightly injured were recovered from the railroad installations. There was no trace of some forced workers who had not found a shelter to go to, or perhaps they were not allowed into them. They ran right into the open country as the bombs were falling; whether they had run to their freedom or their deaths, no one could say.

The train station was targeted by fourteen raids in 1945, five of them major, and half the city was also destroyed. On March 28, fighter-bombers dove down over the station and the arriving trains all day long. Among them was the train that had come from Hamm and now stood opposite Schendeler Strasse before the station entrance. The cars were full of sixteen-year-old schoolchildren who were to be trained as recruits in the Sennelager training area in Paderborn. From a low altitude, the fighter-bombers could aim directly. Forty dead and seriously injured passengers were carried off the train; the dead were laid out in St. Patroclus's, and the local residents helped the injured with makeshift bandages of linens and towels until the ambulance arrived. The same attack was fateful for a group of *pimpfs*, the young boys of the Hitler Youth, as well as for mothers and toddlers. The train suffered a direct hit just before the train entered the station, near the sugar factory. Of the 108 passengers aboard, thirty-two were killed and seventy-six injured, including many children who were being evacuated from the Ruhr basin to Soest for their protection. It was the set destination for twenty-five thousand people evacuated from Dortmund and Bochum.

Sixty-two percent of Soest was destroyed; 446 people were killed, among them sixty-four foreigners. Thanks to the three aboveground tower bunkers, the air-raid protection was satisfactory. During construction of a bunker, foundations of a connecting building between the Gothic manor house and a Romanesque building were uncovered, as were broken capitals from the late twelfth century. After the fall of the city, the French officers looked for books and pictures of Soest, which had been the first fortified city of the Ottonian era and by the mid-fifteenth century had become the most significant town in Westphalia, with international trade connections. From the officers' camp, for four years the French were able to see nothing but the family of towers: St. Patroclus's, one of the famous Romanesque vaulted basilicas of the twelfth century; the Romanesque St. Peter's Church; and St. Mary of the Meadow, one of the most significant late Gothic hall churches. Now they wanted to have a picture of the lot to take home with them. One of the officers, a department head at Sorbonne University in Paris, tried to prevent the bombardment evacuees and workers from the Eastern territories from taking all the books from the City Hall archives and burning them as fuel; the shelves had already been used for heating and it was still cold.

In 1447, Soest had withstood a heavy siege by the Archbishop of Cologne in the Soest Feud. The city had secured its position by allying with the Hansa and the Westphalian cities, which also had poor relations with Cologne. After the decline of imperial authority in the fourteenth and fifteenth centuries, there was a chain of territorial feuds, during the course of which different groups in Germany mutually crushed one another. And so the Soest feud gave rise to the Münster diocesan feud against the expansive Cologne prince-bishop Dietrich von Moers. In the Battle of Varlar, Münster was seriously threatened, but it was used to that, having already spent much of its history on the brink of disaster. Lothar III of Saxony, grandfather of the rebellious Henry the Lion, had set Münster's fortified cathedral castle on fire and consequently the entire settlement burned down. The circumstances of the blaze remain unclear, but that was one of the military advantages of fire. It just happened. The plague broke out in 1350 and as a result the Jews were expelled from the city. That did not change anything, and the plague returned in 1383. A non-war-related fire had already shaken up Münster sufficiently a year earlier, after commercial activities in the Hanseatic League had helped it blossom magnificently since the previous fire in 1197. Trade with England had proved particularly profitable; the archbishop went so far as creating a currency union, and minted a coin based on the British sterling.

The reformation brought Münster under the bizarre terror of the Anabaptists in 1534. After a sixteen-month siege, their "New Zion" was razed by the Catholics and the strongly Protestant populace was strictly brought back to the old faith. The churches and cloisters devastated by the Anabaptists brought out a need for splendor and ornamentation, a "golden century" that was expressed during the Hanseatic period in Münster's Principal Market, including the interior design of the City Hall, with its dazzlingly beautiful Gothic façade from the fourteenth century. Like other golden creations around the Principal Market, it was destroyed in the baptism of fire conducted by the Allied bomber fleets. The aiming point of the devastation of the U.S. raid of October 10, 1943, was the cathedral's filigreed west portal, situated between two Romanesque towers.

"I was the navigator of the 95th Bomb Group in the Münster Operation," wrote Ellis B. Scripture:

> We were all celebrating one Saturday evening, when we received an alarm around 2200 hours. The orders came by telex. I was shocked to learn that we were to bomb civilians as our primary target for the first time in the war and that our aiming point was to be the front steps of Münster Cathedral. I was very reluctant to fly this mission. In fact it turned me off completely.
>
> I approached Colonel Gerhart and told him that I didn't think I could fly this particular raid and I explained my reasons. His reaction was exactly what one would expect (in retrospect) of a career officer and a very fine Commander.
>
> He said, "Look Captain, this is war . . . spelt W-A-R. We're in an all out fight; the Germans have been killing innocent people all over Europe for years. We're here to beat the hell out of them—and we're going to do it. Now I'm leading this mission—and you're my navigator. You're leading this mission also . . . any questions?" I said, "No Sir," and that ended the incident.[28]

The first bomb landed precisely on the vault of the western crossing.

The Feast of the Motherhood of Mary was celebrated in Münster on October 10. In the autumn sun, believers took a walk in the afternoon to the copper-green towers. It was Sunday, and the candles were shimmering on the high altar. The cathedral canons had just been seated in the choir stalls when the sirens sounded at 2:55 p.m. Since the residents of Münster had gone through four major attacks in July 1941, they swore by their bunkers. The cathedral quickly emptied. Canon Emmerich stayed praying in the northern aisle, and the last of the congregation gathered in the northern tower. From there, stairs led up to the spire and down to the treasure vault. Next to it was the baptistery, which offered protection. When they could hear the roaring of the engines and the first antiaircraft salvos, the cathedral sextons and guards climbed into the treasure vault; others fled up the winding stairway to the seven-hundred-year-old stone tower. For a fleeting second, the howling was drowned out by a detonation; not a sound, but a quake, a thump in the ear. The walls, as everlasting as the firmament, and the Herculean columns wavered. A bomb fragment pierced the iron gate of the treasure vault; the blast tore it off its hinges. The vault of the crossing and the transept crashed down as if the mountains had collapsed.

Those inside the tower and treasury were choking from the swirling dust. Vicar Leiwering granted general absolution. Those who had withdrawn deeper into the tower ran right into the third bomb. Antonius Gerhard, the sixteen-year-old son of the sexton, was a Luftwaffe helper. He was struck on the head by blocks of stone and lay unmoving. The sexton's wife lost her breath from the blast and the sexton himself shouted loudly for help. Leiwering heard the shouts from the tower, hurried to the boy on the brink of death, and recited the prayer for the dying with the boy's parents. Then they all ran back to the tower and treasury, since they heard a rumbling sound announcing the third wave of bombers.

After twenty minutes, the Eighth Air Force left the site, and the bishop, Clemens August Count von Galen, the "Lion of Münster," appeared. His epithet came from a series of sermons he had given in 1941, denouncing the Nazi's euthanasia operations as "pure murder." He preached that from the pulpit on August 3, 1941, declaring he would file a complaint under Section 211 of the German Penal Code. No one else in the Third Reich had dared to utter the word "murder" out loud; only a bishop could hurl such language. Even Hitler did not dare to arrest a man of such status; he swore vengeance, but not until after the war.

Galen saw what the high-explosive bombs had done to the cathedral. The copper roof of the northern tower was lost; its walls were thrown out of kilter. The baptismal font, the Pietà, the Evangelist, pulpit, altars, epitaphs, and wall reliefs were damaged. Vault stones, blocks from the walls, and beams piled up in the west crossing. The second bomb had gone off in the adjacent left transept, so those who fled were able to survive in the northern tower and the treasure vault. Smoke rose from the open, roofless northern tower. In the south tower and the attic of the Old Choir, fires still smoldered. The people there tried to approach with fire extinguishers and water, but rubble blocked the way, so they informed the air-raid protection police. Since open fires were blazing at St. Michael's Square and the Roggenmarkt (Rye Market Square), it took some time for them to respond. In the late afternoon, the fire deceivingly appeared to have calmed down in the north tower. Because the roof had come off, it became a chimney; when evening came, flames shot out glaringly against the sky. The sweltering heat tore off the iron door in a tower chapel along with scorching timber. It fell onto the pile of rubble in the crossing, setting it on fire. The window hatches in the treasure vault also drew in air, endangering the treasures.

While gold, silver, and jeweled Mass requisites were being carried out in laundry baskets, a westerly wind came up and sparked the fury of the fire. Now the flames in the roof truss of the Old Choir were roused. The bishop urged the firefighters working feverishly at the pumpworks at Domplatz, the cathedral square, to direct the water to the cathedral, telling them it was still possible to save it. The firefighters responded respectfully that they could not make such a decision, and that the squad leader was responsible for that. Galen continued walking to Domgasse, but all the water there was being pumped to the Roggenmarkt. The north tower had meanwhile become a torch, and the rafters of the Old Choir were competing with it. The westerly wind was also doing its part. The workers at Domgasse were finished anyway; they rolled up their hose and spread it back out in the western transept. It was 9:30 p.m., six and a half hours after Ellis Scripture had reluctantly but accurately navigated the bombers to the airspace precisely above this location.

The two fires shot out showers of sparks under the open roof of the nave. The exposed timbers of Westphalian oak that had supported the load silently for centuries absorbed the heat. The bishop told the firefighters to abandon the northern tower and direct all water power to the truss above the Old Choir, since under no circumstances should the fire there be allowed to spread to the beams of the nave. After half an hour, the fire brigade realized that they would not be able to alter the cathedral's fate. They packed their things and marched to the side wing of the bishop's close, which could still be saved.

At 11 p.m., the truss of the nave caught fire. In no time at all the flames licked out to the timber, which was as dry as dust. The vaults would collapse—how could they possibly hold? Before that happened, everything movable had to be carried out. The cathedral sexton and two journeymen took down the wings of the high altar and grabbed candelabras, crucifixes, the Beldensnyder reredos cross, and the crucifix against the plague.

The fire brigade from Mühlheim came and were very industrious, but the reservoir at the Domplatz was empty. A sea of flames surged through the cathedral. At roughly 2 a.m., the Lion of Münster entered his burning building. He stood there, thanked the sexton, and left.

The Lord was the last to leave his home. Vicar Holling removed the Sanctissimum from the tabernacle and put it in the basement of his residence. From a distance, young helpers from the flak battery on the surveyors' squadron hill in the suburb of Mauritz watched the burning church towers against the glowing red sky. "A lot of comrades stood as if frozen watching this panorama of horror." Residents tried to evade Colonel Gerhart's punishment by fleeing to the bunkers. A housewife, A. B., was just about to board the 3 p.m. train to Telgte when the first bombs started shattering on the next platform.

> By the time we got to the shelters the heavy bombs were constantly falling on us. We could only move forward in intervals and were scared to death. I got a space in the bunker because I was pregnant. People kept coming who were screaming and had been shot at; some could still walk and some were on stretchers. Next to me a woman collapsed whose back was full of bomb fragments. We sat in the dark for an eternity.[29]

Gerhard Ringbeck, a Wehrmacht soldier, was on his way from the eastern front to France. Like many others in the bunker at the train station, he had not found cover anywhere else. He climbed into the basement of the Reichsbahn office. "What happened next was frightful, it was an inferno, which I'd never before experienced even as a veteran soldier on the Russian Front. . . . All around me I could hear injured people screaming who were trapped under demolished and burning houses."[30]

After four hours, around 7 p.m., the housewife left her shelter. "When I came up in front of the station—what I saw was indescribable! There were masses of dead bodies on the street covered with newspaper. We had to walk around them." It took an entire day to separate the deceased from the survivors. Because the nice weather had tempted many to go on outings, people's locations at the time of the raid could not be verified. One soldier knew that someone out walking had been standing near a wall that collapsed from the blast. From the second they had both jumped behind the wall, only the soldier knew about the otherwise unknown person. He kept insisting until they finally lifted the wall and found the man lying there. No one had expected to find someone under the rubble so no one had looked.

After the raid, the young air-raid helper went out to see the aftermath.

> I can still vividly see the open truck on Groitgasse next to the Town Hall and the bodies piled up on it. Even more corpses were collected from the

pavement and put on top of the pile. At St. Mary's square I discovered a male corpse without a head amongst the rubble. The whole city was covered with the smell of burning. I was stunned and ran back to the flak position alone, because I didn't want to talk with anyone.[31]

He wrote in his diary, "How can this go on? Can such a thing remain unpunished?" Colonel Gerhart had asked Scripture the navigator the same thing.

The pilots punished by the flak helper and strollers punished by the pilots lay side by side in their coffins in the hall in the central cemetery hall of the diocesan city. The raid of October 10 cost the lives of 473 civilians and two hundred soldiers. Another 348 Dutch casualties must be counted as well; the 305th Bomber Group had missed Münster and were flying over the Dutch city of Enschede. They thought it was a German city, in which people lived who had been killing innocent people all over Europe for years, and decided their bombs could not really hit the wrong people.

Münster suffered through forty-nine raids in 1943 and another fifty-three before the war finally ended. The most severe ones were on September 30 and October 22, 1944, when a combined total of five thousand high-explosive bombs and 200,000 incendiary bombs were released onto the city of 66,000. On September 30, the west portal of the cathedral was again the declared target. A direct hit managed to rip open the meter-thick walls and collapse the portal. The November 18 raid raked the Münster environs in a wide circle. Two blockbusters and five hundred high-explosive bombs fell on Telgte; some of them destroyed the St. Rochus Hospital, which housed 150 psychiatric patients. Münster lost 1,294 of its citizens to the air war. Ninety percent of the historic Old Town was razed. The Principal Market, with its rows of arcades, went down on October 28. The fire in the six-hundred-year-old City Hall was viewed by many Münster residents as the epitome of all the plagues that ever befell the city.

The world war chronicles of German cities always declare a "Black Day." Münster's Black Day was October 10, 1943, and Hanover's was the night before. The British fleet of 505 bombers that burned the Old Town of Hanover on the night of October 8 was joined by twenty-six Wellingtons, named after Arthur Duke of Wellington, who, together with Prussian General von Blücher, had defeated Napoleon at Waterloo at the behest of George IV, king of both England and Hanover. For 123 years, the ruler of England and the House of Hanover was one and the same person. This union would have continued had not a niece of George IV ascended the throne in 1837; as a female regent, she was denied the succession in Hanover. Since—and because of—Queen Victoria, Hanover and England have remained separate.

The Anglicization of the city set Napoleon against it to such an extent that he ceded Hanover to the Kingdom of Westphalia after Germany was conquered. From 1807, Westphalia was governed by Napoleon's brother Jérôme from Kassel, and was a further attempt to place the area of Germany east of the Rhine under an exemplary, modern administration. The British-Hanover royal house came from the dynasty of the Guelphs, who inherited the Duchy of Saxony in the twelfth century. Some of the impetuous and shrewd spirit of Henry the Lion must have been transferred to Hanover. In any case, that was what Emperor Henry VI thought, who reduced the place to ashes in seeking revenge against the Lion. Since that time, it was allowed to be referred to as a *Civitas*. Guelph pride did not fare well with the Prussians, which is why the Kingdom of Hanover rejected the founding of the German Empire and allied with the Habsburgs in the Austro-Prussian (or Seven Weeks) War. It knew why. After being annexed by Bismarck, it represented the land bridge to the Rhine area, a function previously served by Saxony. The military sense of the bridge was realized quickly in 1870 and 1871, during another tremor along the east-west track. Hanoverians entered the war reluctantly as Prussians, and secretly as sympathizers of Napoleon III. They were opposed to the Second Reich, Bismarck's German Empire, and in the Third Reich, the Guelph-conservative mayor Arthur Menge still kicked against the pricks of the district leadership of South Hanover–Brunswick.

All of this had nothing to do with the destruction of Hanover, but with what was destroyed. For Bomber Command, three things counted. First, Hanover was the fifth-most important industrial location in Germany. It was here that Continental manufactured tires; Hanomag, motor vehicles; and the Deurag-Nerag refineries, oil. Tanks, artillery, and airplane parts were also made here. Second, Hanover was at the intersection of north-south and east-west traffic. Third, it had a population of 472,000. In a world war, those were three good reasons to destroy it, and Hanover was destroyed three times. In 125 air raids, 6,782 people were killed and more than 300,000 became homeless. The Black Day alone decimated 85 percent of the Old Town and slaughtered 1,200 people. No other city of this significance had its appearance cut away in this way. "The face of the city was permanently marred," declared a publication put out by the city in 1953.[32] And in 1983, the mayor wrote that at the time, the city could be located but was no longer inhabitable.[33] The two cities called Hanover, the one before and the one after the war, had nothing but their name and location in common. In early 1944, the administration considered giving up the city and rebuilding it at the edge of the Deister hills. Transportation would be put underground; the residential areas, with numerous park areas, would be scattered in the countryside; and the city center would consist of high tower bunkers.

Hanoverians went through a six-hour, large-scale raid on February 10, 1941, with 101 casualties. This was followed by six months of quiet, so they assumed that the worst was over, owing to their union with the British royal house. One of the codes the Royal Air Force used to designate their objective in 1943 on the list of cities were two letters, "I/R," for industrial/rubber. The pilots understood the subtleties of that abbreviation. They were not to hit the industrial and rubber manufacturers; instead, they were to hit the city, because it produced rubber and industrial goods. The mission reports note that the raids of September 23 and 28 had "framed" the city first in the south and then in the north.[34] Total destruction was then carried out within the burned flanks.

An odd leaflet, written in German "to the civilian population of German industrial areas," was dropped by the ton over various cities including Hanover during the fall of 1943.[35] In it, Churchill offered a reminder of his appeal of May 10, 1942, at the beginning of the air war. The civilian population in cities with industries necessary to the war effort had been told to leave. But, the leaflet said, the German government had not conducted any evacuations of the industrial cities. It was also unable "to protect the relatively small area of western and northern Germany that can be reached by England during the short summer nights." Now in the longer autumn nights they could fly a hundred kilometers farther each week, the leaflet continued. "All German industrial areas are defenseless. We are firmly resolved to destroy the industries of the German war machine and we have the means by which to carry this out." As long as war production continued in Germany, "all industrial cities in Germany represent a theater of war. Every civilian in this theater of war is obviously at risk of losing his or her life, as does every civilian who trespasses without authorization onto a battlefield. With respect to women and children, they have no business on a battlefield." At the top of the sheet was the royal coat of arms, which had once been Hanover's as well. The population nevertheless did not do what was asked of them, as it is generally difficult for thirty million people to pack their bags and move. To where?

There was an attitude reported in Hanover on the eve of destruction that displayed a mixture of defiance, feelings of attachment to the city, and the will to survive. On October 8, 1943, the prospects were good for a sunny autumn weekend, but writer Eugen Roth was at the main station, transferring to a train to Munich, and he sensed aimless hurrying.

> There were streams of all kinds of figures, encountering and getting entangled with each other. One was always eager to get to where the other was coming from. Hoarders fearfully peering out over bulging sacks, people on business trips, armed soldiers with heavy bags, military police combing through the tumult, and suddenly a chain of deserters is hauled by, shackled from hand to hand.[36]

An hour later Roth watched from the train as the red and green markers started falling. At 12:30 in the morning, the bombs hit the station, and the knot of eight thousand people raced into the train station's air-raid shelter. In the shine of flashlights, Red Cross volunteers moved through the rows, treating smoke poisonings, heart spasms, and fainting spells.

The Pathfinders of 156 Squadron that marked the city wrote in their mission report how they found the "industrial/rubber." "The target Hanover was identified visually by the main train station and other prominent buildings. At 0027 hours the train station was bombed from an altitude of 19,000 feet. The target indicators appeared to be very well placed."[37] The Lancasters of 44 Squadron were able to locate "industrial/rubber" even easier. "The objective was identified through the fires." I/R was burning "about seven miles from north to south and about three miles from west to east."[38]

On the ground, the people of Hanover tried to contain a 1943 raid with the fire extinguishing methods of 1941. They had learned too little in that interval, and proceeded to tear down burning curtains, throw smoldering sofas out of windows, and smother incendiary sticks with sandbags. The new reality, however, asserted itself in the cellars, where preserves in bottling jars started to boil. Before the walls of the buildings blazing above them absorbed too much heat, the people needed to wrap themselves in wet cloth and leave in search of open spaces. Five thousand caught in sizzling cellars were led out by Wehrmacht units.

Interfaces between life and death existed, but they were indistinguishable. There were two residences for tradesmen at Georgstrasse 8 and Bergstrasse 8. A hundred skilled craftsmen were stuck in their air-raid shelters. "When the air in there got too hot," said the report of the municipal office for quarters, "supposedly it was already 185 degrees Fahrenheit, the cellar was cleared to seek rescue out in the open. But the surrounding streets were a sea of flames."[39] Fifty-one craftsmen decided to continue on and forty-nine turned back. "Those who later died"—the forty-nine—"did not venture this single chance to escape, returning instead to the cellar where they presumably suffocated in the heat and smoke."

There are some signs indicating a firestorm, such as a temperature diagram recorded in a weather column that showed a rise in temperature from fifty to ninety-five degrees Fahrenheit during the night hours, holding constant until six in the morning, and then falling around nine o'clock back to the midday temperature of the day before, twenty degrees. The street asphalt later showed impressions of collapsed gable façades, the last trace of their filigreed plant ornamentation.

At Stephan's and Karl-Peter's Squares, total strangers embraced at having survived. Many met at the bank of the Leine River and the Masch Lake. Ten thousand people there experienced the dim light of the dawn. British reconnaissance planes were already underway to record the damages, but they could see nothing. The city was enshrouded in smoke and fumes for another three days. This was surprising: that was two days longer than usual. This was the first time a raid was concentrated so closely on the target, Bomber Command noted. "Hanover . . . had two square miles in its centre devastated in the operation on the night of 8th October."[40]

According to the police president's report, the successful devastation of "industrial/rubber" was double Bomber Command's claim. Four square miles in the center. Of twenty-eight hospitals, three were still functioning: Nordstadt, St. Joseph's, and St. Anna's. The fire brigade failed miserably. Because their chain of command was too centralized and inflexible, the fire trucks did not move. They had received no instructions and hesitated. "The fire engine operators have to be able to act independently," complained the Wehrmacht air-raid protection commander. "While it was burning all around, hundreds of fire engines stood waiting on the access roads into Hanover, blocking them, and they never did anything at all."[41]

In the early morning hours, Walter Lampe of the Lower Saxony Homeland League got on his bicycle to see what was left, but he did not get very far, owing to the chaos of streetcar tracks piled up, broken off overhead wires and street lights, and fallen ledges:

> A steady flow of people in search of open space came toward me, with baby carriages and wheelbarrows, with hair tousled, and pale, distraught, and suffering faces blackened from the smoke and fire. They were all trudging along with the last salvageable remnants of their possessions. Some were ragged, others in their best finery, women that saved nothing but the precious fur coat. The people with suitcases, boxes, and crates looked like gypsies.[42]

Lampe walked his bicycle through the totally ravaged Humboldtstrasse and saw that the Friederikenstift hospital on Dachenhausenstrasse was still standing. "But only part of the beautiful building built by Laves at no. 2 on the same street was still there. That was the case with all the half-timbered buildings, the stunning old Schloss and Hirsch pharmacies with their historically unique furnishings."

Day came, and a caustic, smoldering odor hung over the devastation:

> Your heart just started to freeze and you could only vaguely guess the enormity of the loss. It was not yet possible to fathom it all. I only saw that the old half-timbered buildings across from the town hall were no longer standing, the Aegidien Church was already burned out, the whole area up to the square at the Aegidien Gate was as if swept away, as was the Loccumer Hof hotel. I hurried to the Wilhelm Busch house at St. Georg's Square. There too, the night had done its work. My dear schoolhouse had also been totally gutted; the last pieces of the walls were still burning. Here as everywhere the fires were burning and flickering brightly. You could actually taste the smoke as it wafted over the deathly scene. All you could say, over and over, was, "That too, oh, and that too!" On my way home I looked back on the city as one gazes at the coffin of someone dear.

Hanover itself was a monument to a style of architecture demonstrating austere uniformity and unadorned earnestness. The severity of the form brought together brick Gothic, urban rational burgher-class half-timbering, splendid sandstone of courtly baroque, and medieval monumentality. The vanishing of the old city hall, Leibniz House, Knochenhauer Strasse, and the whole Guelph city with its European windows has left a strip of scorched earth on the old continent.

Bomber Command also took this as the penance for a heinous deed committed by Hanover:

> Aside from the significant contribution to the war effort made by the city's engineering and rubber industry, Hanover also carried sole responsibility for helping the Austrian Hitler to obtain German citizenship. Intending to gain merit in the eyes of a potentially powerful politician, the University of Hanover gave Hitler the honorary professorial title *honoris causa*, which came with a granting of German citizenship, much desired by Hitler. The university and the people of Hanover have learned their lesson.[43]

In fact, Hitler became not a professor but a city councilor, and not in Hanover but in Brunswick. Having renounced his hated Austrian citizenship in 1925 in order to avoid being deported as a burdensome foreigner, he was stateless until 1932. As a candidate for the office of Reich president in 1932, however, he needed German citizenship. Given the political situation at the time, only Brunswick could naturalize him, since that was the only state in which the National Socialists were part of the government coalition. On February 26, 1932, he became a senior civil servant with the Brunswick legation in Berlin and was declared a German citizen at the same time. The first air-raid drills started there that same year.

Brunswick is the city of Henry the Lion. After having been banished several times to England, the country of his wife, he spent the end of his days at the place he had bestowed with a city charter and whose cathedral he had established. He and his wife Matilda were buried there. Hitler returned the favor to Brunswick, the city that declared him to be a German, by making Henry the Lion a National Socialist. His cathedral was profaned in 1935 and declared the nation's holy site, his grave was renovated, and his remains examined.[44] High water in the Oker had continually flooded the grave, and the many Guelph coffins got mixed up when set to dry. The Nazis declared one skeleton to be that of Henry, which could not have been the correct one, since he had limped during his lifetime. Erroneous associations, even here.

His sarcophagus was surrounded with the sgraffito of a Germanic campaign in the eastern territories, and similar scenes were painted on the side walls of the central nave. Henry's eastern colonies, extending at that time as far as Stettin, impressed Hitler. Unlike the

Hohenstaufen emperors, who got lost in Italian fantasies, Henry expanded German *Lebensraum*, or living space, from west to east; Hitler strove for the same. Soon he would march further into the Slavic grounds, past where the Guelphs had stopped. Henry was certainly no less power hungry than his admirer, though he went about it differently. He was totally annihilated, but he bequeathed to his cities his brand of economic sense. Hitler, on the other hand, left them only the destructive revenge for his destructive rage.

Brunswick was once the largest city in the Duchy of Saxony because it was located along the Oker, a river that flowed from south to north. That means it profited not from the west-east military routes but from the domestic trade routes that led southward to Goslar, Nuremberg, and Frankfurt, and across the navigable Oker to the north to international maritime trade. The cities that Henry founded increased his already extensive possessions, but his dealings were based on mutual benefits, not on the lash as with Hitler. To that extent, Henry was the more modern ruler.

Brunswick's heyday and assets as a great center of internal Hanseatic trading between Nuremberg and Lübeck were immortalized in the magnificent buildings of the fifteenth to seventeenth centuries. The *Gewandhaus*, the cloth merchants' house, in the Old Town and the patrician *Mummehaus*, the main work of the Brunswick Renaissance; the *Alte Waage* (Old Scale) weighing house, a mighty, free-standing half-timbered building; the Meinhardshof, a winding, S-shaped, half-timbered street of pure medieval form; the *Lieberei* of St. Andreas, Germany's oldest free-standing library; and the house Lessing died in, at Aegidienmarkt 12.

Ricarda Huch, who was born and raised in Brunswick, wrote in 1927 that the places and names were surrounded by premonitions. Nickelnulk, an alleyway lined with half-timbered houses at the northeastern end of the New Town, "that looked so desolate and forlorn you thought twice before turning into it, sounded like a dark pond inhabited by dangerous water folks; and the *Wüste Worth* that in the Middle Ages had once been devoured by a conflagration seemed burdened with a curse."[45] The boredom of a Sunday afternoon hung over the tastefully fashionable homes on the promenade around the city. "The image of a senselessly repeating cycle of life." The night of Bomber Command, October 14, ended the ennui. It was a Saturday night, and it took away the churches of St. Martin, St. Katherine, and St. Andreas before their bells could call people to Mass.

Until that day, the church towers protected the city: the blunt one of the cathedral, the pointed spire of St. Martin's, the unmatched pair of St. Katherine's, and the slender column of St. Andreas's.

> They appeared to me to be forebears and watchmen, connected to every single citizen by an indestructible band. The stone with which they are built, taken from the nearby Nussberg hill, is gray-brown in color and in the light of the evening sun it blends into a reddish violet, bringing the giants to life.

Early Sunday morning, after the night of the firestorm, fire brigade officer Rudolf Prescher patrolled the Old Town. Residents with meager tools labored away to open their buried and blocked cellars. Were any relatives still alive? Did any of their belongings survive and could they be salvaged before the fire, rekindled by nests of glowing embers in the rubble, reached them?

> The view had become unobstructed from Fallersleber Gate to St. Peter's Gate. The massive tower of the old, twelfth-century St. Peter's Church had lost its baroque roof, yet it continued to dominate the background. The towers of the Church of St. Katherine, whose slender form once rose skyward, had been reduced to stumps. Gone were the pristine, proud buildings once erected by medieval merchants. The cloth makers' house was gutted, but its structure, weakened by the flames, did not burst until a later firestorm. At the Old Town market the destroyed towers of the Church of St. Martin stretched upward and the remains of the Stechinelli House created a smoldering, stinking pile of rubble and ashes.[46]

In 1690, general postal agent Stechinelli built a four-story building at the Old Market, house no. 8, ushering in the enlightened baroque. It had not been long since the last witch, the widow Anna Kagen, whom the people called Temple Aneke, had been put on trial. Aneke healed the lame and the sick and reclaimed things that had been stolen. The court faced the irresolvable question of whether magic came from God or the Devil. No one embraced by magic knew the answer, and they refrained from asking such a question. The results spoke for themselves. The returner might be the thief and the cure might come through suffering; no one cares. The magician's sole concern is the experiment. But the court is forced to fit the facts into categories of good and evil that are out of touch with real life; that is its task. The court received an expert report from the department of law at the University of Jena that documented that Temple Aneke was imbued with the power of Hell, and for that reason she had to burn. The Brunswick court, at the threshold of the Enlightenment, regretted its own verdict. Granting the witch's pleas to be spared the stake, she died by the honest sword.

Brunswick was also among the most-destroyed German cities. Ninety percent of the 370 acres making up the city center were razed. In the eighteen heavy and moderately heavy raids on the city, 2,905 people died, almost half of them foreigners. The penultimate raid, on March 3, 1945, destroyed the Lessing House.

THE WEST

The Rhine is Europe's north-south axis. It is the shortest route for travel between the Mediterranean realm and the North, and Caesar set this line as the base camp from where it was possible to dominate the forested depths as far as the Weser and the Elbe. Based on this view, the banks of the Rhine are the dividing line. People either turn their backs to the river or they face it and secure their crossing. From another perspective, the banks are a unit, connecting the areas to the right and left into a separate land between Germany and Gaul; this is the Rhineland. This intermediary realm was called Lotharingia during the Carolingian partition of the empire. Further south it was Burgundy. Later still it was two versions of the Confederation of the Rhine, and then, to a certain extent, the Federal Republic governed from Bonn. The current version of this realm is called central Europe, and it covers all of Germany and France.

Old Europe was largely the history of the struggles for the Rhine, and in these struggles Europe bled itself white. The battles for the river were fought mostly in the foothills, except for the exterminating battle, the bombardment of Rhine cities during World War II. It began in 1940 with the fall of Rotterdam, to that extent coinciding with England's Rhine policies through the centuries. Lying on the coast opposite the mouth of the Rhine, England was always interested in seeing that no single power dominate the Rhine, especially not at the delta, whether that power was named Napoleon or Hitler. And so the air war started as a war of the Rhine, and it also ended that way.

Twenty-three cities from Emmerich to Breisach were heavily bombed: Emmerich, Rees, Xanten, Wesel, Dinslaken, Krefeld, Duisburg, Düsseldorf, Neuss, Leverkusen, Cologne, Bonn, Koblenz, Rüdesheim, Bingen, Mainz, Wiesbaden, Worms, Mannheim, Ludwigshafen, Karlsruhe, Kehl, and Breisach. Not until their destruction did the Rhine cities totally share the fate of a country from which they never had much to gain. Prior to 1870, they had been Austrians, Württembergers, Badeners, Bavarians, Hessians, Nassauers, Dutch, even Prussians. Most of the time, the Rhine belonged not to one country, but to many, and mostly to the band of its cities.

After World War I, suspicions in Berlin arose that all Rhinelanders were ultimately French. Jules Michelet, a nineteenth-century French historian, returned in 1842 from a trip to the Rhine with the following theory: "The Rhine is a Roman river. Even the Gothic buildings were erected on top of Roman substructures, the fortresses on top of the castra, the churches and monasteries over former temples."[47] To Michelet, the stones were traces of the legions as the "vanguard of the civilized world." It could be that tidings from people who had come from afar also played a part in the spiritual inflammability of the Rhinelanders. Thoughts and fashions, heresy and rebellion, religious rapture and political conspiracies, books and architectural styles, paintings and tastes raced up and down the river faster than anywhere else.

The Rhine was the abode of the Rhine traveler, and the cities were the doors for the welcome guest. The freedom of the city air came from beyond, from business without tolls and roads free of wayfaring bandits, without belligerent avengers and people on the prowl. Trade was cosmopolitan, and along its expansive north-south route, civilization was embodied by the city, not the state. The Rhine of the states was a different one: Not the line that transports and links, but a defense that absorbs the thrust of the vertical, the attack. For the just pursuer, the obstacle of the river is an incentive to seek crossings. These crossings were fortified with bastions and casemates on one side and supported by bridgeheads on the other.

Emmerich could not be bombarded ever since the attack following the Arnhem operation. As of October 7, 1944, Emmerich was nothing but 890,000 cubic yards of debris. At that location, the Allied Rhine crossing near Wesel in March 1945 had been covered only by artillery. The situation was different in Rees, a rural town close to the eastern bank north of Xanten. It had reasonably withstood the third Geldern Feud in the seventeenth century, been in dispute with Emperor Charles V, survived Mendoza's occupation during the Spanish-Netherlands war, helped the Duke of Brunswick to an unexpected advance to the western bank after the Prussian victory near Rossbach, and, having been annexed to the *département* of Lippe under Napoleon, had to endure the French disbanding of the Collegiate

Church of St. Mary, which had been founded by St. Irmgard in 1040, thereby helping Rees come into existence. Rees was a fortified city, and as such it was attacked on February 16 together with Wesel. Eighty-five percent of it was destroyed, the same degree of destruction as in Xanten five days later.

Wesel began as a burial ground in 781, and in 1945, it would end as one. The St. Willibrord Cathedral, the slaughterhouse, and eight thousand books from the scholars' library went down with all the rest during a mild sunny pre-spring day in 1945. After February 16, the city sunk into dark smoke; the residents tripped on the fields of rubble over the remains of bodies. The last major raid followed on February 19, which covered the virtual ghost town of a city with swirling ashes.

Dinslaken, a bit farther upstream, was the flank of the river crossing, and thus got caught under the raid's steamroller on March 23. It was defended by a battalion of the *Volkssturm* militia. The British had dropped leaflets:

> To the mayor: In just a few minutes your town can be transformed into a burning pile of rubble. Airplanes are standing by, their bomb bays filled. Hundreds of towns and villages have been razed to the ground because fanatics tried to continue to resist. Hundreds of other towns and villages have been spared destruction because their authorities have realized that defending them served no military purpose. The decision lies in your hands and you have only a few minutes to make it. You have the choice between surrender or destruction.[48]

No one except the Nazi mayor had any choice. Head physician Dr. Otto Seidel was bandaging patients in the Catholic Hospital "because it was bandage day. A Ukrainian woman on our staff came running to me shouting, 'Doctor! Airplane shot down. I saw.' At that moment the first bombs started falling."[49] Protection at the Catholic Hospital consisted of an operations bunker, a shored-up cellar with a slit trench two hundred feet long. The bombs had no trouble tearing off the twenty-inch-thick cover. Two mothers with their newborns were killed instantly, as was the hospital locksmith. The rest of the bombs then tore away the operating room and that entire wing of the building, including the laundry. Around noon, the operations bunker was entirely demolished, despite its meter-thick walls. The head physician and a Red Cross nurse crawled headfirst through the debris to rescue the trapped postoperative patients.

Here in the ripped open bunker I saw a man; I'll never forget the image. He was sitting on a bench with a block of concrete a meter thick and the size of a desk on his lap. He was still alive and kept shouting, "Doctor, help me!" Another man was hanging by his legs literally in the air. Blocks of rubble had pressed him against the back wall. At once I noticed that all the patients in the blown-up beds were dead. Then I set to work clearing away the rubble and debris to get to those who were still alive. I was able to free a mother with two children; they were the family of Wesel's financial director. The director himself and another daughter died in Wesel. Next I worked to free up a totally paralyzed patient, but she was dead by the time I recovered her body. Lying next to her was a girl of ten or eleven. She was from Barmingholten and had been admitted a short time earlier with several broken bones in her leg. Now she was lying there with a meter-thick piece of concrete on her small head that had been pressed flat like a book.

A short time later liquid-incendiary bombs were dropped, which blocked all the hospital's entrances and exits. Patients were burned alive. Hospitals had the Red Cross sign painted on their roofs, and by 1945, crews could aim precisely enough to avoid a hospital during daylight. None of the 195 Lancasters covering the crossing at Wesel was lost.

A Tallboy, a 12,000-pound explosive that the British called a small earthquake bomb, destroyed the cover of the bunker of the St. Anna Hospital in Duisburg-Huckingen. Tallboys were dropped as of September 1943; they had been developed for dams, viaducts, canal embankments, and expansive building complexes, which included hospitals.

Air-raid shelters, including a hospital bunker, were required to be able to stand up against four-thousand-pound Blockbuster bombs. The Huckingen Hospital was not prepared for the Tallboy. It toppled the four-story building such that the masses of debris caved in the cellar roof. Rescue teams thought they heard some knocking and, using a listening device, could hear calls for water coming from the bunker. An excavator was called in and the area was cleared. Forty-two dead bodies were recovered, including seven kitchen maids, a Red Cross volunteer, the gardener's wife, and nine Ukrainian volunteers. An autopsy conducted by the Pathological Institute in Düsseldorf determined that there was no dust whatsoever found in the upper respiratory tract of the deceased; therefore, death must have come suddenly. The raid on the night of May 21, 1944, was the first major raid of Bomber Command since the Battle of the Ruhr a year earlier. The mission report noted overcast weather, but it said that the Oboe-guided bomb-aiming device enabled accurate color markings in the clouds, so that considerable damage was possible in the targeted southern districts of the city. Huckingen is located at the city's southernmost edge.

Duisburg was bombed 299 times during World War II, an average of once a week. The horror intensified as the intervals became shorter. In July 1942, three major raids took place at two-day intervals and on October 13, 1944, Arthur Harris received the directive for Operation Hurricane: "In order to demonstrate to the enemy in Germany generally the overwhelming superiority of the Allied Air Forces in this theatre . . . the intention is to apply within the shortest practical period the maximum effort of the Royal Air Force Bomber Command and the VIIIth United States Bomber Command against objectives in the densely populated Ruhr."[50] Why "densely populated"?

Duisburg offered military targets like no other city in Germany. One-third of German iron and steel was produced there. In Wedau it had the country's second-largest marshaling yard; its river port supplied the entire Rhine-Ruhr region, and it had a host of shipyards, large coking plants, and coal mines. It was the westernmost industrial location in the Ruhr basin, a stretched-out, long and narrow city, perfectly situated within Oboe's precision radius. Why a massacre in the most densely populated area?

England, the United States, and Canada were stationed at the edge of the Reich with mighty ground forces. The bomber was by no means the only available weapon; the Wehrmacht was hurting from losses in France and had not yet built up a stable Western front. According to the directive, the enemy was not to be hit militarily; it was to be "demonstrated" something. If the enemy saw the superiority of the bombers, as it had been seeing for four years, it would stop doing what it had been doing. The smartest thing to do from its perspective would be to hide beyond the Rhine.

In early October, the Allies still anticipated a rapid breakthrough. They had just fought their way through Aachen but were yet to face the Huertgen Forest. The barrier was presumed to be the river, defended with more blood than anywhere else at the crossover point to the Ruhr basin. The cities east of the Rhine had to understand what would happen to them if their territory became the site of the final battle. And a densely populated area that was utterly destroyed would prove to the German army that the war had been lost. The choice was not between victory or defeat, it was between defeat or annihilation. This had to be demonstrated to the eastern bank; that was the reason for Operation Hurricane on October 14 and 15, 1944.

In the 240th raid, the city was toppled as if a tornado had struck. In all previous raids combined, 1,576 people had been killed, a ratio of only 0.36 percent, a first-class air-raid protection achievement. This protection consisted of thirty-seven aboveground tower bunkers and two underground bunkers, as well as fifty-three minelike tunnels that had been dug into slag heaps. Operation Hurricane started on Saturday morning at 8:45. In twenty minutes, 1,063 British planes dropped 3,574 tons of high-explosive bombs and 820 tons of incendiaries. This was on the order of Hamburg, but the city had one-fourth of Hamburg's population. A second and third raid followed that night. At around 1:30 in the morning on Sunday, 1,005 planes appeared, and at 4:00 a.m. came the third wave, dropping a total of 4,500 tons of munitions.

The three attacks on Duisburg dropped one and a half times the total bomb tonnage of the war to date. The city had to endure nine thousand tons of bombs over twenty hours. No other city in Germany suffered that. "Hurricane" took three thousand human lives, more than half the total Duisburg casualties of 5,730. The map of damages showed only isolated areas as having been left untouched.

The nine-thousand-ton series was continued two weeks later in Cologne, a city almost double the size of Duisburg and spanning both sides of the Rhine. The purpose of the raid suggested a "post-Hurricane." Between October 27 and November 1, a total of 1,900 bombers dropped nine thousand tons. British military historian J. F. C. Fuller wrote that so many planes were being produced that their use had become irresistible, and bombs even rained down on Cologne's rubble heaps. The RAF bombers "were crowding each other so closely that there seemed more danger of a collision than of being hit by flak."[51]

Sixteen months earlier, 1,956 tons were dropped on Krefeld. On June 23, 1943, the *Times* described it as "one of the heaviest loads of bombs ever dropped on a German city. The raid began on June 22 at 12:30 a.m. Four thousand pounds of bombs were released each minute. When the bombs had completed their nightly task, large columns of black smoke rose to a height of three miles above the beaten city."[52] The 8th Squadron, which carried out the mission, recorded in its report that the city covered only a small area. They kept the drops within a concentrated area; "the density of the bombing was kept at a very high standard."[53]

The British air staff occasionally considered whether it might not be better to attack the smaller cities, as they facilitated a far higher intensity of destruction. A fire leaves deeper traces in a city such as Krefeld, which in eight hundred years of history had only been destroyed twice. The first time was in 1584, for a trivial reason during the Cologne war. For contemporaries, the dispute had been bitterly in earnest, because Cologne threatened to fall into Protestant hands. This would have brought confusion to the entire Rhine area, in particular the voting ratios in the Council of Princes that elected the emperor. The war was fought because of the prince-bishop who wanted to force the impossible: to become a Lutheran, marry a canoness, and remain head of Cologne. The cathedral canon ousted Bishop Gebhard, who called in the Protestant cities in the region. The emperor marched to the upper Rhine, Cologne remained Catholic, Krefeld was destroyed, and Gebhard was excommunicated. The passions of the religious wars stopped at nothing, and odd occurrences ignited the fuse.

Krefeld then experienced one hundred calm years within the House of Orange. In 1703, it became part of Prussia, and only fifty-five years later it was near Krefeld that the Duke of Brunswick, allied with Frederick II, defeated the French. Ever since the Austrian War of Succession, the Rhine plain had been France's marshaling zone for battles that were then fought in Westphalia. In the Seven Years' War, Frederick changed this situation, which then held for almost a hundred years. Prussia also became a world power. At its perimeter, Krefeld turned imperceptibly toward its next destruction.

The Krefeld fire-brigade lieutenants and chiefs were Hesse and Brand, Severin, Schwabe, Hölters, Henke, and Gerlach.[54] After the alarm, Hesse went to the staff of the fire-protection police in the Hansa house. Alarms were constantly sounding. "When we realized that this time we were the target of the terror attack, a corresponding atmosphere spread out among us, and everything was still and paralyzed." Brand was the boss and he said to Hesse, "Hesse, actually I should send you out, but then you wouldn't come back alive." So they mounted the motorcycle together and rode off.

The city was already illuminated by the fire. Along the Ostwall people were crowding together in the grassy areas. Terrible screams could be heard. The hair or clothing of some of them was on fire, because they had been doused with sprays of phosphorus. The heavy things from the sky kept striking and the crowd was screaming.

Hesse was hit on the chest by some phosphorus spattering and the motorcycle occasionally tipped over from the thrust of the blast bombs. "Everyone was horrendously confused. They were screaming for help and praying, they stood around confused for a while and then ran again from place to place." The two fire chiefs put handkerchiefs in their mouths, the smoke stung their throats, and the air turned to embers. "I saw the first dead body near Dreikönigenstrasse. It was a child with a crushed skull. Next to it lay the mother; her hair had burned away, leaving the back of her head bald." Brand and Hesse dropped the two off at the doctor's and then continued riding, past blazing gas lines and disconnected streetcar wires hanging down.

Brand thought things did not bode well for him, but he did not want to appear a coward, especially to Hesse. "At Petersstrasse the people ran right into the motorcycle. Since we had to stop for a moment we could hear the loud voices, coming from a cellar, of many people praying in unison. It was high time that they left the cellar, otherwise they would have died." But the thirty people were so afraid that the firefighters had to grab them by the collar and throw them out onto the street. Eight burned to death anyway.

At the corner of Hülsener Strasse a blockbuster threw Hesse and Brand from their motorcycle, hurling them in a high arch into the park at Friedrichplatz, throwing dirt and debris on top of them. Brand had had enough. He did not see Hesse and he did not look for him. Maybe he had been torn to pieces, he thought; he ran through the destroyed Old Town to the main fire department at Hansaplatz and gave a report. Fifteen minutes later, Hesse came in. He was bleeding at the neck; an overhead line had cut a wound close to an artery. "When I saw him alive again it was the only joyful moment of the whole day. We threw our arms around each other."

Hesse also made a report. In response to the question of where the raid's main concentration had been, he said that one could not even speak of a concentrated attack—everything was one big concentration. "I also reported that the Fourth Standby Unit was totally destroyed." Then Hesse grabbed the motorcycle and drove right into the overhead wires, so that the military had to cut him loose. He was surprised at some people's reactions. "It especially upset me that a woman with her two children ran right in front of my motorcycle; in her muddled thoughts she was trying to commit suicide."

Severin was driving around with the smaller fire-engine convoy. He had also been ordered to go to Ostwall, the boulevard along the old rampart, but was not able to make it across Adolf Hitler Strasse. However, he did notice his fifteen-year-old son on Chief Schwabe's fire engine; the boy was in service as a Hitler Youth firefighter. "I took him with me." The crowd of people on the Ostwall median was surrounded by fire and wanted to get out. Severin, his son, and the group drove down Ostwall all the way to the main post office, where there was a reservoir for firefighting. "It isn't really correct to say that we were extinguishing fires here. The blazes were so large and powerful that our bit of water meant nothing. Our spraying of water had only one purpose, and that was to reduce the heat and embers enough to clear a path for the people to escape the sea of flames." And that worked.

The fire drew in gusts of air; the blaze was roaring as it went, pushing ahead the large trash receptacles as if they were toys. It owned the street. Schwabe headed for a public square, Luisenplatz, because he wanted to bring his siphoning pipe to the reservoir. He was wondering how he could get through the ridge of flames. "The absolute absence of people around this time was very conspicuous. We started checking the shelters to see if people were still sitting in them. Almost all of them were in fact still sitting in the cellars of the burning buildings." Severin urged them to go out to Luisenplatz, which became packed with people.

The people who lived around the square had become surrounded by their own burning buildings; their eyes, suffering from the smoke and heat, could make out that much.

So I instructed the women with infants and toddlers to board the closed vehicles. To reduce the heat, I kept spraying water from the hoses over the heads of the crowd; that was appreciated as a true blessing. The heat was so great that we could not touch the metal on our fire helmets. We tried to turn our helmets around to protect our eyes with the neck flap.

Severin sent Fire Sergeant Leygraf to the station with the dispatch that there were three hundred people trapped at Luisenplatz. But first he had to get outside the ring of fire.

"Comrade Leygraf went past the church; the eye injuries he suffered almost blinded him permanently. He had to lie in a darkroom for eight days and was unable to work for two months." Meanwhile, it crossed Severin's mind that people might possibly be stuck in the public air-raid shelter in the Protestant Clubhouse. "With a C-pipe we pushed our way across Neue Linner Strasse to the east. Along that route the burning church was radiating such intense heat that many of us were unable to get past it. We managed only by spraying water at the same time."

Thirty people were sitting in the Protestant Clubhouse. They did not want to leave the cellar because they saw nothing on the streets but smoke and fire. "In reality the heat in the cellar was perhaps even more intense than outside. We were finally able to persuade them. There was great danger that the buildings would collapse and also that the fire would draw the oxygen out of the cellars. Under a constant jet of water, we brought the people to Luisenplatz." The reservoir of water there had meanwhile been emptied. Leygraf's desperate efforts paid off; SA stormtroopers from Mönchengladbach turned up with trucks, cleared the way, and emptied the square, women and children first. "Because the smoke was so thick we couldn't watch the truck driving away for much more than five meters. Our eyes had suffered a lot. Finally the square was emptied of people. By the time we made it out of the worst fire and smoke we noticed that it was morning."

Severin drove to the main fire station to fill up the engine's tank, and there he heard a call for help coming from Schöntgen's butcher shop on Markstrasse. The shop had burned down but they had a cold room in the cellar. The entranceway was blocked by debris, and Severin let himself down on a rescue rope; he cut a few sides of beef for the butcher and transported the meat up through the hatch. "The cold room had long since ceased being a cold room. It resembled more of an oven."

Lieutenant Henke asked fire sergeant Hölters if he was courageous. Yes. "'Then go into the burning church and see what you can do.' There was no one to help me. So I joined together a few hoses, dragged them into the church and up to the organ loft, where everything was in flames. Nothing here could be saved." All of a sudden, Lieutenant Henke was standing there and he noticed a fire in the attic. Up the circular stairway. At the top was a bathtub filled with water, a hand pump, and the chaplain. Now there was threefold courage at work, which saved the attic, the aisle, and the baptistery. "When I was almost done putting out the fires, someone brought over the body of the pastor. He had been struck dead by a burning beam in his apartment." Being courageous was evidently no more dangerous than just sitting around. Foreman Gerlach was sitting in the United Silkworkers plant playing a game of skat when bombs fell on the factory for an hour and ten minutes.

"We all sat there frozen and silent, white as sheets, and we hardly dared to take a breath." What cheered some up was terrifying for others. The gateman's house received a direct hit and people were buried in the cellar below.

> I counted out ten men who were standing near me and told them they had to trot over to the gateman's house. Some people were horrified at the sight of corpses so they took off. With three other men I climbed down into the demolished cellar. Blocks of concrete and iron rods were lying around. We freed the corpses from the rubble and brought them up where the others took them and laid them out on the grass. It was then that we first noticed that two people were still alive.

Enduring the aerial bombing war took a lot of courage. Many of the high-explosive bombs that fell on Krefeld on the night of June 21, 1943, landed on soft ground, which often made them into duds. Special task forces made up of an ordnance technician and several other men defused them. The ordnance man was a Wehrmacht officer; the others were Germans, German concentration camp prisoners, and prisoners of war.

Krefeld was attacked from the air two hundred times. The heaviest bombardments took place in preparation for the Rhine crossing in February 1945. On February 16, 18, and 19, the inner-city area was crushed. There were few losses to the civilian population, since most people had already left the city. The bombs blasted the rubble and injured the corpses that were still lying beneath it. The city lost a total of 2,048 lives to the air war, and 97 percent of the built-up area was destroyed.

On November 17, 1938, Hitler attended a state funeral in Düsseldorf. It was the burial of one of the city's sons, embassy secretary Ernst vom Rath. Vom Rath had been killed eight days earlier in Paris by Herschel Grynszpan, a Pole, in revenge for the fact that his Jewish parents had been forced to leave Germany. In Düsseldorf as throughout the entire Reich, synagogues went up in flames on the pogrom night of November 9, 1938. Into the early morning hours, Nazi mobs demolished Jewish property, apartments, and works of art; eight Jews in Düsseldorf were killed. Three thousand demonstrators converged on the seat of Chief Administrative Officer Schmidt to demand his resignation because he was married to a Jewish woman. Many Düsseldorf landlords evicted their Jewish tenants so the SA stormtroopers would not burn down their apartment houses. In June 1941, the police were granted the right to evict Jews and crowd them into so-called Jews' Houses. Confiscated furnishings were sold dirt cheap to help those who had been bombed out. On the night of June 2, a British raid brought the first five bombing casualties.

The emancipation of the German Jews occurred during the period of French rule. "I was born at the end of the skeptical eighteenth century," wrote Heinrich Heine, Düsseldorf's most famous son, "and in a city where at the time of my childhood not only the French but the French spirit reigned."[55] In 1808, Napoleon himself was the Duke of Düsseldorf, which he administered as guardian for his underage nephew Louis Bonaparte. He had entrusted his nephew with the Grand Duchy of Berg, one of the French protectorates east of the Rhine. France's border was the western bank of the river. There, in the imperial city of Aachen, Napoleon had visited the tomb of Charlemagne in the fall of 1804. The first consul of the revolution took over the empire of a thousand years earlier. As the newly appointed emperor, Napoleon rode past the battlefields of the former emperor, in Italy, Spain, and the eastern campaign. After crossing the Rhine, the Frankish lines, the Weser and the Elbe, attracted him. He continued to be lured farther than Charlemagne had considered possible. After all, he was a revolutionary, and revolution thinks in universal terms. It is meant for all, whether or not they accept it.

Napoleon's fiasco in Moscow—the million human losses of his campaigns—did not shatter Heine's love. Germany had been liberated. They lived under the principles of the Code Napoléon, which according to Heine had been created by "ardent saviors of humanity." When the "relics of St. Helena," Napoleon's mortal remains, were transferred to the Invalides in Paris on December 15, 1840, the emigrant poet dedicated a salute to him. Heine's poetry was banned among the Germans.

> I saw his funeral rites myself,
> Saw the golden hearse go faring
> Bedecked with golden Victories,
> The golden coffin bearing.
>
> . . .

I wept that day. My eyes filled up
With tears, my heart was pounding.
When I heard that long-dead cry of love
"Vive l'Empereur!" resounding.[56]

The German princely family had also once idolized the liberator,
who finally dictated that they follow the administrative order of the
French Revolution and levy a Foreign Legion for his campaigns. A
large portion of the army for the Russian campaign consisted of German recruits. Now there were three German countries. The annexa-
tions of the western Rhineland and the seacoast; the sixteen vassal
princes united in the Confederation of the Rhine, in which Bavaria
and Baden even married into the imperial family; and the protectorates of the Kingdom of Westphalia and the Grand Duchy of Berg.
The capital of the Grand Duchy of Berg was Düsseldorf, administered by highly competent French officials. They asserted tolerance,
supplemented the baroque influence of the capital with French classicist taste, and eliminated the antiquated privileges of the estates
order, giving breathing room to the commercial bourgeoisie. As a
boy, Heine had watched the All-powerful ride into the city, bringing
cultural progress across the Rhine, a river no one still regarded as
German. The hymns to the fatherland did not come until later.

The visitor rode a white palfrey and was wearing a simple green
uniform and his little hat. "The Emperor sat carelessly, almost la-
zily" in the saddle. The boy's eyes settled softly on the emperor's
"sunny marble hand" that was "good-naturedly patting the neck of
the horse." His hands were strong; they had bound fast the hydra
of German anarchy, "the many-headed monster," and had "reduced
to order the war of races." The manner of the horseman was plainly
written on his face. "Thou shalt have no gods before me!" A smile
came over the lips of the only god, thereby warming every heart, "and
yet all knew that those lips needed but to whistle, *et la Prusse n'existait
plus*—those lips needed but to whistle, and the entire clergy would
have stopped their ringing and singing—those lips needed but to
whistle, and the entire Holy roman realm would have danced."[57]

Napoleon "rode calmly straight through the avenue"; behind him,
"his *cortège* rode proudly, loaded with gold and ornaments." Drums
rolled, trumpets pealed, and "the multitude cried with a thousand
voices, '*Es lebe der Kaiser'*—Long live the Emperor!" The liberator
looked down upon the people of Düsseldorf with "an eye clear as

heaven; it could read the hearts of men. . . . The brow was not so clear, the phantoms of future battles were nestling there."

After the Emperor had died and Düsseldorf had become Prussian, Heine returned for a short visit to the city of his youth, taking a seat in the royal gardens. The "enemies of liberty" had been victorious—how could it have come to that? He saw *Le Grand's* eyes open "spirit-like and wide, and I saw in them nothing but a broad white field of ice covered with corpses—it was the battle of Moscow." Heine heard both "a march of victory and a march of death"; "the wildest hurrahs and the most fearful grief were mysteriously mingled." Hobbling through Düsseldorf was the price of the redemption, "these orphan children of Fame." French who had been brought to Siberia as prisoners were released after many years of peace. Stranded at the Rhine, they did not want to return home, instead warming themselves with the pity of the Düsseldorfers. "The poor French soldiers." They seemed to Heine to be dead, arisen in the night from the battlefield and entering the cheerful city. "Through their tattered uniforms peeped naked misery, deep sorrowing eyes were couched in their desolate faces, and though mangled, weary, and mostly lame, something of the military manner was still visible in their mien."

The people of Düsseldorf also felt sympathy for the French foreign workers and prisoners during World War II. They praised their industriousness in their work clearing away rubble, in contrast to the Dutch, who were said to gloat with pleasure at the bombardment of Germany, considered the Allied airmen to be fighting for their cause, and were suspected of sending flashing signals to the enemy aircraft each night. In a show of Rhenish-French tolerance, nine British airmen were buried in 1940 with military ceremonial in the cemetery of honor. Two months later, the first major raid on residential quarters at Friedrichstadt, Oberbilk, Oberkassel, and Königsallee was launched.

This time, the idea of civilization did not come riding in on a white palfrey; instead it steamrolled its way through the streets as a gray-black cloud of dust, smoke, and soot, interspersed with smoldering scraps of files and books. Napoleon's war lasted as long as he reigned, but the battle was quick, thanks to the cavalry, the enthusiasm of the troops, and the unheard-of flexibility of independently operating units. The battles were bloody; the enemy's weakest point was attacked and then destroyed. The air war had similar goals, but how different was the mindless grinding down to the stump of cities such as Düsseldorf and Cologne! The August 1942 police report mentioned many people who were "dismembered beyond recognition and often severely carbonized due to the fires burning beneath the rubble."[58] The rescue and recovery teams needed alcohol to do their job.

In March 1945—two hundred raids later—the same procedure was repeated so often that five-year-old Gerd Fammler and his mother and sister no longer left the shelter; they lived there.

> You entered the bunker through a narrow, barred iron door. Everyone went to "their" floor. The floors were divided into larger niches. There were wooden cots here. It wasn't nice to have to live in such dim lighting, especially for us kids. Whenever I smell damp, musty concrete in old buildings it brings memories of the Second World War to mind, of bombs, bunkers, flames, and pain.[59]

On March 11, 1945, the sun was shining and the bunker folk dared to face the day. In the evening twilight a bomb exploded without warning in front of the air-raid shelter. "I only know that I went flying. I didn't come to until I was back in the bunker. I regained consciousness and saw that I didn't have a left arm anymore. I saw the thick emergency bandage. I was terribly thirsty." Thirty people died right there. Three years and nine months had passed since the first civilians died from the bombing in Düsseldorf. The 120-million-cubic-yard volume of buildings became approximately forty million cubic yards of rubble on the ground. Four percent of public buildings and 7 percent of commercial and residential buildings remained standing and undamaged. Everything else had gone up in flames. Trampling through a network of footpaths past the skeletal façades of the Renaissance-baroque city of Düsseldorf demanded a new sense of orientation, especially in the dark. Children could find their way; adults could not fathom that this was their Düsseldorf. "In the pitch-black nights when you couldn't see your hand in front of your face—the piles of debris, the darting of the searchlights, the roaring of the heavy engines, the howling of the antiaircraft batteries. No! You could often hear people say, no, this is not a life anymore."[60] The people in the air-raid shelters sat pressed crowded together, pulling their children in close to them, putting cotton in their ears. The women tied their headscarves on tightly. No one talked. "When the hellish sirens dropped off, someone said, 'I think it's over.' And we got up to make our way into the burning city." The sun rose as if over Sodom and Gomorrah.

The city endured 243 air raids, nine of them heavy.[61] On the Friday night before Pentecost in 1943, fifteen square miles between the main train station and the Derendorf district were burned to the ground; 140,000 people lost their homes, 300,000 were wounded, and 1,300 killed. Sixteen churches, thirteen hospitals, and twenty-eight schools were devastated. In short, this was a demonstration of the superiority of the British air force over that of the German Luftwaffe, as Churchill had proclaimed.

In 1944, the population in the city dropped to half what it had been. The skilled workers had been evacuated with the industries, as had the women with school-age children. The soldiers were killing and being killed at the front, and 3,500 Jews had been murdered. Remaining in the city were largely the elderly, the foreign workers, women with young children, and the leaders of German industry. Düsseldorf was known as the "desk of the Ruhr basin." Here were the corporations' administrative headquarters, a first-class bombing objective. That is why they continued to bomb in 1944; when everything burned, the offices had to burn too. On the night of April 22, seven industrial plants were obliterated, as well as the zoo and the district around it. And 883 people. On the night of November 2, another seven industrial plants and 678 people. All told, the British and the Americans dropped 18,000 tons of bombs on Düsseldorf, killing 5,863 civilians. When after these operations their ground troops reached the city in early March 1945, they had to besiege it with heavy artillery fire for another seven weeks.

Neighboring Neuss enjoyed a more merciful fate. After 136 air raids, ten of which were heavy, two-thirds of the city remained standing.

Most of the painters of the Cologne School did not come from Cologne. Stephan Lochner was a robust Swabian, Joos van Cleve—the "Master of the Death of the Virgin"—was from Antwerp, Barthel Bruyn from Holland, Pierre de Marres from France, and so on. The mystery of the city instilled in them the very delicate line fantasies, the gold grounds, and the garish, enamel-reflecting colors. Lucien Febvre claimed that this school was founded solely on a similar form of expression that traced its genesis to its original clients, nuns who commissioned mystical paintings for their edification. "They liked the childlike charm of the Rhineland women wearing braids. Painters transformed them into Madonnas. Heavy eyelids covering pupils void of thought, dreamy looks that reflect a thoughtful happiness."[62]

The Cologne form of expression breathed of influences from Flanders and Bohemia, Burgundy and Brussels. The loges of those with great and very great sensibilities crossed paths in Cologne. Processions of pilgrims, called packs, the most indebted ones often barefoot and without a head covering, ended their trip from reliquary to reliquary at the Shrine of the Holy Epiphany in the city with nineteen church parishes and twenty-two monasteries, a city where a thousand Masses were read each day. Cologne was where mystics Master Eckhart and Johannes Tauler preached that in the face of the Crucified the individual shall wish to spread himself into the dust, and the heretics, ecstasized and enraptured, rang precious revolt into the ears of the craftsmen and peasants, until death by fire took them. Karl Marx, editor of the *Rheinische Zeitung*, was the last and greatest of the rousers.

This theater of exaltations, pillory of the topsy-turvy world, pedestal of flight from existence and trading center of European ideas and art trends, was entered for a short time by Hans Memling. Born in Franconia around 1430 and one of the most prolific painters of the time, Memling made his fortune in Flemish Brugge. There he retained the gentle grace of the Cologne School, its gestures, the style of its group presentation. There was an incredible demand for that. Among his special masterpieces is a piece of historic scholarship, the narrative painting of St. Ursula's shrine in Brugge. He knew the story, that of St. Ursula and the eleven thousand virgins, from Cologne, where it is known as the city's quintessential legend.

Ursula was the daughter of Divion, Duke of Cornwall, in the southwestern corner of England. Her father sent her with several thousand maidens to Brittany, on the opposite shore, to wed the French settlers who lived there. A storm came up on the English Channel and the ship was drawn eastward. Divine providence drove it into the mouth of the Rhine. The maidens steered the ship upstream, arriving after a short time in Cologne, which had just been besieged by the Huns. When these savage heathens set eyes on this blossoming host of virgins, they tried to take hold of them. But the heroic young women preferred to resist to their deaths than give in to the heathens. A bloody battle ensued. Led by St. Ursula, the tender maidens fought the infuriated Huns, and fell undefiled on the battlefield. In the most remote reaches of the ship's hull, St. Cordula lay hiding, crying over her cowardliness. Then she stepped out and shared the defiant death of her companions. The Huns were not happy over their victory, however, because suddenly a host of angels approached, as great in number as the murdered martyrs, to avenge these maidens' deaths. Filled with horror, the Huns took flight and Cologne was rid of them.

In gratitude, the people of Cologne buried the martyrs and built a church atop their gravesite. The eleven thousand virgins rested there in peace until May 31, 1942, when British Lancasters set the church's nave on fire. On April 20 and October 28, 1944, and January 3, 1945, British and American aircraft continued to demolish the church. On March 2, 1945, the end of Cologne, a portion of the southern wall of the choir two bays wide was smashed, and the three supporting columns broke. All the vaults but eight collapsed.

The triple-nave gallery basilica had been built in the twelfth century. The eleven thousand maidens had already been dead for six hundred years. It is possible that their remains are actually a Roman graveyard, on top of which the original church had been erected. On the other hand, there was an inscription that mentions the virgin martyrs. The truth of myth, however, does not lie in the chronicle of events.

The Huns did in fact terrorize the Rhine. They were nomads from central Asia who fought as mounted archers. They threw lances when they used stirrups, and in hand-to-hand fighting they used primarily sabers. Having crossed the Elbe and the Rhine, they reached the southern Champagne region, where an allied army including Romans, Visigoths, and Franks defeated them in 451 in the Battle of the Catalaunian Plains. That was also the year of St. Ursula's death. The battle with the Huns left the river basin a permanent melting pot of ancient Roman and Germanic Christian influences. The seemingly hopeless battle of the British maidens against the Asian Huns could in actuality not be lost. Every martyr gives rise to a divine avenger, because innocence in distress is the most just cause. Just warriors are worried neither by their inferior strength nor their self-sacrifice: in fact, unequal odds are a necessary requirement for victory. By killing the innocent virgins, the Huns became an abomination of heaven and earth, and could not hold their power forever.

The Huns remained in Italy another three hundred years, until Charlemagne put an end to them. They were the riders of the apocalypse, the born war criminals. They roamed the land, destroyed churches and chapels, assassinated believers and abducted their wives. They incinerated all the cities of the Moselle region and in the Palatinate. In antiquity, these were not unusual acts of war, but having been committed by Huns, they were feared as a scourge of God, as was their leader Attila. The Huns returned in modern times as a slang term for the Germans. Emperor Wilhelm II, in his brash manner, even referred to himself as one. He was to be feared like the Hun, thus giving his British cousins a rousing epithet. And from 1940 to 1945, Churchill eliminated the people of Cologne, Berlin, and Dresden as Huns. Twenty thousand in Cologne alone.

The first bombing raids in May and June, 1940, lured thousands of curious onlookers to the destroyed buildings. There were six deaths; it was like a crash scene, but in a war. In 1941, there were nonstop light and medium-sized attacks, a constant rain that killed a total of 185 by April 1942. The mouth of the Schelde served as a land-mark for Bomber Command. The estuary was a huge distributor, with branches leading throughout all of Germany's city landscape. For lost pilots, however, it was the nightly bright band of the Rhine that pointed the way northward to the sea. Many routes passed over Cologne, which airmen either coming or going used as a disposal site for surplus bombs. The alarms were certainly not sounded for those, or else the 768,000 people would have lived in a constant state of alarm.

The Thousand-Bomber Raid marked the way into the world of the battle of the Huns. Even the hosts of angels were present. Previously, only the myth could have depicted the 2.5-mile-long wall of explod-ing antiaircraft artillery set for sustained fire, the searchlight cones scanning the sky, the clusters of illuminating colored markers, the bombarded purgatory, the lemures' descent into Hell, the rotting of the bodies. The end of the world stepped out of the wooden-panel painting into that evening in May. Seers and heretics had predicted this as they called down from their pyres that the beginning of the end had come and the thrust of fire would soon envelop the whole depraved world. The world deserved its ruin, and the patience of the Lord had come to an end. The tongues of flame that Bomber Com-mand sent from the sky pushed aside all familiar reality, all false idylls. The fire war demanded an account from the Antichrist who appears before the end of time.

In a transcendental city such as Cologne, the Thousand-Bomber Raid came from the depths of the prophecy of doom. The massacre was the city's oldest myth. In the summer of 1943, the Archbishop's general curacy posted a notice on the churches: "In response to sugges-tions from lay circles, we request that pastors notify the congregations at regular intervals in their proclamations from the pulpit that they can obtain full indulgence during an air raid if they reverently and repentantly recite the quick prayer, 'My Jesus, Mercy.'"[63] There was just enough time for three words. They were necessary between June 16 and July 9, when four heavy raids burned the city center to the ground. The second mission took 4,377 human lives and left 230,000 homeless. In sixty-seven minutes, the substance of 1,900 years was liquidated; it burned for five days. Subsequent attacks continued to plow the ground like a tractor, taking up where the previous raid had left off. On Saturday, July 10, survivors gathered for vespers in the ruins of the Heumarkt (Hay Market Square) to commemorate their bonds with those who died, by ringing all the bells that still existed.

In the spring of 1944, the U.S. Eighth Air Force joined in the elimination of Cologne with carpet bombing. Like the seven plagues, the entire burden of death lowered itself over the city in seconds. In April, Bomber Command flew a thirty-eight minute raid of refined blast-and-burn surgery. Omitting the dead tissue in the fields of rubble, the operators were on the lookout for islands of life, continuing this each month until September.

There were twenty-eight raids in October 1944, making it the most devastating month since the war had started. Over the course of the transportation offensive, sights were set on five precision targets: the Rhine bridges. Barrels of smoke mixture were placed at the embankments and on the streets crossing the Rhine, and when the sirens sounded the bridges disappeared as if under Siegfried's magic helmet. The Rhine districts were transformed into a seething pea soup into which the three raids from October 28 to November 1 pumped nine thousand tons of bombs. St. Gereon's Church was among those destroyed; it had been expanded into a decagon in the thirteenth century, built over the original oval from the fourth century. On October 30, a portion of the northwestern side two axes wide was rammed in from the vault to the base. In St. Pantaleon, the mortal remains of Empress Theophanu, the Byzantine princess who married Otto II in 972 and was regent of the Holy Empire for eight years for the underage Otto III, were desecrated.

Cologne had become a city with few people and many rats scurrying about the mountains of rubble and gorging themselves on the provisions stored in cellars. The rat poison had run out. Debris and timber continued to smolder quietly, and the fires crackled on desolate streets. On March 2, 858 Lancasters and Halifaxes attacked

Cologne for the last two times, killing hundreds of people who remained lying on the streets. Thousands fled the city before the U.S. VII Corps entered it at 3:30 p.m. on March 6. Of the 768,000 residents, only ten thousand awaited the liberators. Five percent of the Old Town had been preserved.

As with most old cities along the Rhine between Basel and Cologne, Bonn is on the western bank and became Prussian; it had been French from 1798 to 1814. The Prussian Rhine University was founded in 1818, leaving its mark on the city. The residents thought they would be exempted from the bombing, since so many Americans had studied medicine and the natural sciences at the university there. The Rhine University was Prussia's reparations for the siege, bombardment, and total destruction that the city had suffered at the hands of Elector Frederick III and twenty thousand Brandenburgers in 1689, in the Palatinate War of Succession. Basically, Louis XIV and England faced off here, since England would not tolerate France's rule of the Rhine. Holland joined in, as did the Habsburg emperor. French control of the river would mean continental hegemony. A number of German principalities joined in as well, including the Electorate of Cologne, which maintained a residence in Bonn.

Cologne as a free imperial city was different from Cologne as an ecclesiastical principality; Napoleon had done away with that flourish of the *ancien régime*. The seat of the bishop of Cologne had fallen to the opposing Bavarian archbishop in the Cologne War. For almost two hundred years, the House of Wittelsbach wore the Cologne vestments; around 1650, it brought the region into the French Wars. England, however, waged the Palatinate War along with Hanoverians, Saxons, Hessians, and Brandenburgers. Bonn had been expanded into a fortress by the French, so the Prussians bombarded the city with cannons until there was nothing left. As punishment for Bonn's Frenchness the fortress was demolished, but in 1941, enough of it still existed underground that the administration and air district command thought it could still be used as protection against British munitions. In July 1944, this was proven to be just as wrong as it had been in 1689.

Bonn built most of its bunkers in the suburbs. In the Old Town, they relied on the firm double cellars and casemates, the provisional air-raid shelters, and the large theater bunker near the Rhine bridge. The city of 100,000 had space for 14,000 in the bunkers toward the end of the war. Since occupancy was commonly five times the intended capacity, there would have been protection for two-thirds of the Bonn population, if they got there in time.

> I saw the airplanes in the sky, a whole swarm of silver birds glistening in the sun. Then I saw the bombs falling. The blast knocked me down the steep stairway to the bunker. I banged with my fists and my feet against the door and they opened up for me. Usually they don't open up the bunker door once the bombs start falling.[64]

When thirteen-year-old Elisabeth Gerstner left the theater bunker, she saw around her a world that the sovereigns of the Enlightenment would have been considered barbarous, even during the most gruesome of the Rhine wars, the Palatinate War of Succession. "I saw a lot of dead bodies. People without heads were lying around, and single arms and legs. They were people who had been rushing to the bunker but didn't make it. Otherwise I couldn't explain why there were so many dead bodies all over." French prisoners of war recovered the bodies of those who died in the cellars. "I heard a French prisoner of war calling to his buddy, 'deux cents des morts,' pointing to a house. I ran away right away and luckily didn't see what had happened there."

The deaths were the result of a test of an improved Oboe radar system called the G-H system. Bonn had no war industries. In August 1943, the Eighth Air Force killed two hundred people in Bonn and Beuel; that was the toll of war there up to that point. Bonn was unlucky in that it had been lucky. Because it was intact, it satisfied the first prerequisite for the test. The second was its location along the ribbon of the Rhine, and the third was poor weather. When the three prerequisites came together, as happened on October 18, 1944, Bonn's Old Town was destroyed.

Bomber Command expected a lot more from the 77,000 incendiaries and 770 high-explosive bombs than what they achieved: three hundred casualties, twenty thousand homeless, destruction of the university, the library, and 180,000 books. "The bombing hit mostly built-up areas," according to the final report. "The result was disappointing for a G-H raid."[65] The test had to be repeated; on November 6, it moved one station up the Rhine to Koblenz.

In January, Bonn was made into a fortress again, not through fortifications but by Hitler's declaration. Other than that, the steadfastness generally declined. On January 6, a tankbuster bomb of the U.S. Eighth Air Force managed to tear the concrete cover off an air-raid shelter under the regional court building, causing the death of 230 people. The raid was targeting the bridgeheads in Bonn and Beuel, but since the clouds were hanging low and blind navigation with instruments was evidently unsuccessful, the munitions landed in the middle of the city, where they could not fail to hit something. Things went similarly during four missions of Bomber Command that had targeted Bonn's main train station and freight depot, under the directives of the Transportation Plan.

The night of December 21, 1944, offered the same ideal conditions of October 18: bad weather, a mostly intact Bonn, and Rhine. The train station was missed nonetheless. On the night of December 27, radar-guided Mosquitos marked out the freight depot many times and in many colors. Seventy percent of the Lancasters were loaded with the heaviest explosives, and they managed a deadly hit not only on the train station, but on Bad Godesberg, the university, and the slaughterhouse as well. On December 29, the munitions were increased to 1,800 blast bombs and twenty thousand incendiary sticks, which fell on the suburb of Endenich-Poppelsdorf and the city center. The heavy bombs penetrated two public air-raid shelters. The two raids took a total of 486 lives. For the third mission, Bomber Command mobilized 238 airplanes and all of its flying and technological capacity to hit the Rhine floodplain and the Siebengebirge hills. Bonn lost a total of 1,569 people. It was destroyed as part of a drill.

The name Koblenz means confluent, those flowing together. Here the Moselle and the Rhine flow together. In history, however, everything flowed apart, starting with the partition of Charlemagne's empire. In October 842, representatives of the emperor's grandsons Louis the German, Lothar I, and Charles the Bald convened at the church of St. Castor, and in six days negotiated the three-way partition that was sealed the following August at Verdun. Koblenz lay precisely at the eastern boundary of Lotharingia, the intermediary realm along the line from the North Sea to the Mediterranean, bordered by the Meuse-Rhone line in the west and the course of the Rhine extending to Italy in the east. Being the eldest, Lothar had picked out his third, which included a connection to the sea, the rivers, and cities, making up the heart of the occident. The brothers reinforced the "bonds of a true and not feigned love."[66] They wished to stand by each other against all "enemies of God and the Holy Church." Then they named the true enemy that made Lotharingia into the site of the drama of Europe: "No one shall attempt through greed to bring chaos to the laws of peace in any of their realms. Whoever tries to do so shall suffer the common punishment."

Greed was inevitable, because the West Frankish and the East Frankish wings were each semicircular territories. As early as 870, the two wing kingdoms that later became Germany and France divided Lotharingia amongst themselves. Through the centuries their relations were marked by attempts by each of them to claim all of Lotharingia, later Lorraine.

Koblenz experienced this intra-German discord in September 1198, at the bloody battle on the shallow banks of the Moselle. There Philip of Swabia and Otto IV feuded as king and antiking. The city was reduced to ashes, and the hegemony of the kingdom in the Christian world declined within fifty years. It was surpassed by the western powers and the pope. The next imperial world power, the Habsburgs, tolerably linked with Germany, lost its cohesiveness during the Thirty Years' War, which brought destructive rage down on Koblenz from all sides. Half of it was ruined. In Louis XIV's Palatinate War of Succession in 1688, the hitherto most violent attack on Lotharingia by the West Frankish brother, two-thirds of Koblenz's buildings went up in flames. During the Revolutionary Wars, the emigrated nobility lived in the area. It was conquered and became the capital of the French *département* Rhine-Moselle. In 1797, the young republican Joseph Görres advocated a Rhenish state supported by France. After seventeen years of annexation, the city's greatest son was then moved to fight against "foreign rule."

From 1815 on, Koblenz was the military and administrative capital of the Prussian Rhineland. In 1914, it became the seat of the Great Headquarters of the Hohenzollern army. The Lotharingian line was then pushed in from the east. After the defeat, the pendulum then swung in the other direction, and the western border was once again back where it had been in 843. Formally, it was temporarily occupied, but in 1923, the French Rhineland Commission recognized a Rhenish state of secession at the Koblenz confluence. It was a German Lotharingia that failed more pitifully than all those previously. On November 6, 1944, Koblenz was destroyed for a fourth time.

This fourth time, the Lotharingian line was insignificant. The border of the Reich was not to shift anymore; no territories were to be distributed, and there was to be neither greed nor hostilities toward false subservience. Koblenz burned without any significant armaments or transportation centers. It had thrived from trade in Rhine wines. The population did not have to be worn down, since most of it had evacuated. The city was destroyed because the destruction of Bonn had not been able to determine the effectiveness of the G-H device. Precision targets were to be hit within an accuracy of 150 feet. The crews received the radar signals on an oscillograph, marked the area, and dropped the bombs faster than usual.

Point targets were blasted. But fire quickly spread out over the surface, uninterested in specific points. The amazing thing about the new precision aiming device was its being tested in a typical fire raid. Bomber Command had loaded twenty-three high-explosive bombs, 120 blockbusters, and 153,392 incendiary sticks, which together composed the epitome of the wide-area weapon.[67] This time, Operational Research was extraordinarily pleased with its success.[68] Half the munitions hit within a circle about a mile across, sufficient for the inner-city area between the Rhine and the Moselle. The Löhr-rondell was at the center of the circle; this round plaza was the intended aiming point, but it was used only for orientation. The tactical objective was to place incendiaries as densely as possible within a compressed area, the Old Town.

In the fall of 1944, Bomber Command tried to increase the saturation level with thermite sticks. Precision was defined as when the entire bomb load landed within a small radius. The flames themselves did the job of spreading the fire, provided it reached an unrestrainable intensity. Up to then, the firestorm had been a puzzling coming together of uncontrollable coincidences, but Bomber Command wanted to ignite one at will, as simply as turning on a lamp. They started with the fuse and increased the volume of tonnage dropped per unit area.

For the Bonn experiment, they had wanted cloud cover, so the bombers would be blind and could not cheat. In Koblenz, they wanted the system to be successful no matter what. The confluence of the rivers made the city an optically identifiable point. The aircrews could recognize the arms of the rivers with their naked eyes. They chose a clear night for Koblenz. The G-H system belonged to a single unit, No. 3 Bomber Group. Twenty-four lead planes took part in the Koblenz raid; half of them could not receive clear G-H signals, and the other half placed their flares and bombs simultaneously at 7:28 p.m. Subsequent waves could clearly see the streets below, and released their loads at 7:50 p.m., in one of the most precise carpet-bombing raids of the war. According to the group report, "the crews were enthusiastic when in the further course of the raid the entire city was in flames and the light from the fires could be seen from as far away as Brussels."[69]

The seventeenth-century façades caught fire slowly; the blaze grew from the back courtyards on Altengraben, Entenpfuhl, Jesuitengasse, and Schanzenpforte. On these narrow lanes, the wooden parts of the buildings were too abundant and fire brigades too few. The thermite sticks had fallen into every corner, igniting curtains and waxed floors. The merging of so many fires into a large conflagration could not be stopped. At around 1 a.m., the three burning areas came together around the electoral castle between Clemensplatz and the Rhine and at the Kaiser Wilhelm Ring. It rained during the night but that did not disturb the fire, and a fresh southwesterly wind that swelled to storm strength in the morning whipped up the flames even more.

The Koblenz firestorm took 120 lives and destroyed 85 percent of the Old Town. Such a ratio occurred nowhere else. The attack razed the historic city without bloodshed. The site of the tectonic fault line of the wars went down without a fight, in an etude of fireraising.

In Koblenz, the factors and coincidences that tragically added up to create a firestorm also helped keep the death toll low. First, many Koblenzers had recently left for the evacuation area in Thuringia or had found a place to stay in the rural environs. Second, the angle formed by the confluence of the two rivers confined the firestorm to a narrow area, making escape routes very short. Third, those in cellars and tunnels felt a lively urge to get out and extinguish the flames engulfing the city with the river water close at hand. Though their efforts were in vain, it served to get people out of the cellars, which became deadly prisons in almost all firestorms. The oldest parish church in the city, the late Romanesque Church of Our Beloved Lady, was near the flaming lane, Entenpfuhl, and it lost its tower and roofs. The curates who defended the fifteenth-century building, by standing on ladders inside the towers with pails of water passed along by a chain of intrepid girls, managed at least to save themselves and the entire firefighting crew. This testing of the G-H systems was entirely superfluous. It was used only a few more times.

On November 25, 1944, St. Catherine's Day, four combat wings of the U.S. Eighth Air Force flew a mission against the port of Bingen and the marshaling yards at Bingerbrück.[70] The target for 120 Liberators was an oil depot in the port, and for 160 others, it was the marshaling yards. This was a textbook U.S. precision raid navigated by G-H radar. There were six hundred tons of explosive and incendiary bombs in the bays, which promised the best possible effect in the depot. The operation was codenamed Golden Brick.

At noon, the leading 2nd Combat Wing accelerated to maximum speed, starting the fourteen-minute approach to the target at Bingen, a distance of eighty miles. All of Bingen and Rüdesheim were already settled in their cellars, since full alarm had been given an hour earlier. Swarms of planes crossed the Rhineland headed toward Saxony. The people received more specific route information via wire broadcasting, a radio announcement of enemy flight movements transmitted via telephone and power lines.

At 11:54 a.m., the wire broadcast reported that three hundred Liberators were crossing over the Trier area. Fifteen minutes later, the one thousand engines could be heard in Bingen and Rüdesheim. Thick clouds covered the towns and a powerful southwesterly wind was blowing, reaching hurricane strength at an altitude of 22,000 feet. It kept pushing the Liberators toward the northeast and the pilots had a hard time staying on course to Bingen. The G-H system sent out a signal that the navigator passed on to the bombardier, who dropped the tonnage by pushing a button. But the navigator of the 93rd Bomber Group erroneously heard a nonexistent signal and a dozen planes released their munitions over a wooded area north of Kirn. At 12:15, the 445th and 453rd Bombardment Groups heard the real signal and the head bombardier, along with all seventy planes of that combat wing, hit their trigger buttons in parallel, as carpet bombing requires. Ten other groups followed over the next eight minutes, until the 560 tons of high-explosive bombs and fifty-six tons of incendiaries were all dropped. There were no bunkers for the residents of the small cities, but there were sometimes air-raid shelters and old rock tunnels, as in Bingen, a city of 16,000. They had connected former wine cellars with vaults under the city center, thus providing a protective space of 4,300 square feet. But even crowded as closely as possible, no more than one thousand people could squeeze in. Most residents of small cities and towns sat in dug-out cellars. As in Bingen.

No cellar could withstand a direct hit. Those in the cellars expected to die from one second to the next. The bombs needed thirty seconds for the 22,000-foot drop from the Liberator. The distance from the roof to the cellar is beyond comprehension by human senses. Upon returning home, the pilots had no illusions about the precision of the raid. Some crews said they had hit a mile and a half northeast of the train station; others had observed through a break in the clouds: "The target was in flames; black smoke rose from both sides of the Rhine. The tip of the cloud of smoke reached a height of 15,000 feet."[71] The result seemed "satisfactory" to the U.S. Eighth Air Force.

As determined by reconnaissance photos, the blast bombs fell from Rupertsberg in the southwest of Bingen throughout the entire city up to the eastern periphery of Rüdesheim. Some dropped into the Rhine. Others felled the trees around the monument in the Niederwald woods. Two incendiary-bomb carpets covered Bingen's city center, and a third ignited a strip between the Rüdesheim train station and the city center. Regarding the precision targets, four of the 2,473 blast bombs hit the Bingerbrück marshaling yard, and nothing happened to the oil depot.

In Bingen, 160 people were killed; in Rüdesheim, on the opposite side of the Rhine, 199. Eighty-seven of the casualties were under eighteen years of age. The youngest was Werner Heinrich Mahn, born on November 24, 1944. The infant had been in the world for one day.

Mainz, situated at the confluence of the Rhine and Main rivers, had always been a strategically desirable place and, accordingly, had massive fortifications. The Prussians laid siege to the city in 1793 and devastated it with a barrage. Even though the French Revolution hanged the Bourbons, it adopted and intensified their hegemonic aims. Danton considered the Rhine, Alps, and Pyrenees to be France's natural borders. Speyer, Worms, and Mainz were quickly occupied. The French knew the territory well, and the Convention of March 30, 1793, declared by acclamation that Mainz was part of the French Republic. A revolutionary club of Enlightenment thinkers from Mainz exercised rule as French vassals, no differently than the German princes did previously and later. The rulers saw themselves as liberators of sorts, but that changed nothing regarding their status as vassals. A majority of the Mainz population was opposed to its liberation.

The Prussians surrounded the city in the spring of 1793, and destroyed it in a way not unlike a bombing war. In the quarters of the Duke of Weimar, Wolfgang von Goethe was among those who participated in the siege. "Terrible bombardment," he noted on the night of July 14. "Firing from the Main Point across the Main sets fire to the Benedictine monastery at the citadel. Firing from the other side of the Rhine sets fire to the munitions factory and it explodes. Windows, shutters, and chimneys on this side of the city break or collapse."[72] As long as he took part in the siege, Goethe was captivated by the aesthetics of fireraising as "a rare and important event in which misfortune itself promised to yield material for the artist."

The eye of the artist, which was startled by the aura of the Kaiserdom, the Imperial Cathedral, started in 975 by Archbishop Willigis, was accompanied by another, which delighted in the outrage:

> 28 June, night. Continuing bombardment of the cathedral; tower and roof burn and many houses round about. After midnight the Jesuit church. We watched this terrible spectacle from the redoubt in front of Marienborn; the night was absolutely clear and full of stars, the bombs seemed to vie with the heavenly lights, and there were moments when it was really impossible to distinguish between the two. The ascending and descending of the incendiary bombs was something new to us; for though they threatened at first to reach the very firmament in a flat circular curve, they always reached a certain height and then fell again on a parabolic path, and soon the rising flames showed that they had reached their target.

The impression of the blazing cathedral was captured by the Briton Mr. Gore, a Weimar painter working with a camera obscura, beside him Councilor Kraus, a landscape painter. "Mr. Gore and Councilor Kraus treated this event artistically and made so many sketches of fires that they were later able to produce a translucent model of this night scene; the model still exists, and when well illuminated it is capable of conveying, better than any number of words, the impression made by the misery of a national capital on fire." Goethe calmed his conflicted senses by considering the military necessity "that in order to save ourselves and more or less to recover our position, we had to resort to such means." But even such means were not able to save the ridiculously antiquated Generals Kalckreuth and the Duke of Brunswick, nor could they reestablish the sterile regiment of Frederick William II and Emperor Francis II.

Mainz fell, the vanquished defenders Adam Custine and Alexandre Beauharnais ended their lives at the guillotine in Paris, and soon General Napoleon had pulled the German-Austrian troops together to such a degree that Mainz was practically forced upon him in the treaty of Campoformio.

Napoleon often went to Mainz, which had become the capital of the Donnersberg *département*, and he took great care in expanding the fortifications that would be of no further use. In the course of the French occupation of Mainz from 1918 to 1930, they were torn down again. The next bombardment of St. Martin's and destruction of the city took place on February 27, 1945. Compared with the mission of which Goethe wrote, at least this one was connected to a historically significant war. The first two major raids by Bomber Command on August 12 and 13, 1942, threatened the symbol of the city with wide-area fires, but firefighting crews were able to keep the conflagration in check. Mainz was left in peace in 1943, and in the fall of 1944, it became the hinterland of the German western front.

Three main railroad routes came together here, and a marshaling yard and two river ports served the transportation needs. "This transportation center," declared the British Air Ministry on February 27, 1945, "is used day and night to move troops and materials into the battle zones."[73] Consequently, Mainz had to be eliminated. That is disputable.[74] After the unsuccessful Ardennes offensive, this section of the front had become absolutely insignificant. It lay within the range of Patton's Third Army, which used its air power only moderately to achieve its objectives in Mainz.

The purpose of specific raids was generally easier to determine by the types of ammunition used than the reports in the bulletins. The No. 4 and No. 6 Groups of Bomber Command carried 935 tons of incendiary and illuminating bombs on that evening, as well as 635 tons of high-explosive bombs, a ratio of three to two. The large numbers of blockbusters among the explosives also says a lot. Blockbusters send out blast waves rather than causing an intense explosion, but train facilities are sensitive only to explosives. And the 500,000 incendiary sticks definitely would not bother them. In short, the bombers were carrying the tried and tested fireraising mixture. The intended firestorm, like the one that had hit Pforzheim a bit further south three days earlier, did not develop, however, because rubble does not burn well. In the precision raid on the main train station in December, the Eighth Air Force missed the station but hit the city center. The devastation it caused created firebreaks and rubble piles throughout the city, which made Harris's fireroller rather ineffectual the following February. But the flames did find some nourishment in St. Emmeran's, a vaulted basilica with five bays built in the fourteenth century; the former Holy Ghost Spital, the oldest German charitable care facility, started in 1236; as well as the market square, which was the heart of the Old Town.

With its storm-tested fortifications, Mainz certainly had enough shelters. The casemates, which had stood up to many a cannonade, also withstood the blockbusters and cookies dropped by the air forces. Newly equipped with ventilators and steel double doors, the casemates with their meter-thick walls gave residents more confidence than the tower bunkers at the freight depot. There were also the citadel, the Bastion Alexander, and the forts of Josef, Philipp, and Karl, which had accumulated through the fear and care of generations of defenders. Designed for a more pleasant purpose, the Kupferberg Sparkling Wine Cellar and the Aktien Brewery had cooling vaults that were also used as air-raid shelters.

At 4 p.m. on February 27, Mainz residents left their stifling dungeons after four hours. Earlier, at noon, the German Aircraft Reporting Service had sent out a full alarm, presumably because of the three U.S. bomber divisions that crossed over the airspace en route to Saxony. Now the sky over the Reich was swarming with bombers. On February 22, 9,788 airplanes sought their target; on February 23 there were 8,400, which flew forty-three raids.[75] It left the Aircraft Reporting Service breathless. The radar installations on the Atlantic coast were lost, which severely shortened the warning time. Around noon on the day of the raid, the reporting service no longer had things under control. At that time, 2,600 airplanes were flying wherever they wanted. The 435 bombers assigned to Mainz slipped through the grid of the reporting service, which believed that all the attackers were on their way home, so the all clear was sounded. When everyone started leaving their cellars shortly after 4 p.m., the Nos. 4, 6, and 8 Groups of Bomber Command were already over Cochem.

People were on their way home, relieved to leave their stuffy quarters, when at 4:25 p.m. the air-raid alarm sounded. The bombs started falling at the same moment. It was too late to return to the fortified bunkers, so they fled into the unstable cellars. In the end, 1,200 died, including forty-one Capuchin nuns, who suffocated in the cellar of the Convent of Perpetual Adoration. The fires had sucked the oxygen out of the vaults.

Besides the city, the train station was also among the targets that were hit. Two months earlier, one of the bomber groups attacking Mainz had destroyed the Bingerbrück marshaling yards with a direct hit. Presumably, they could have accomplished the same in Mainz. In late February 1945, it did not burn as it did during the siege Goethe had described. It was not a matter of hopeless losers acting "in order to save ourselves and more or less to recover our position." It was already clear who the victors would be; all that remained was for them to invest some more blood for their cause and they meanwhile knew how much. The incineration of Mainz could not save them a drop. Victory is both a military outcome and a triumph. Similar to Goethe, Harris had been captivated by the "rising flames" because the bombs that vied "with the heavenly lights," so that "it was really impossible to distinguish between the two," also made the bombardiers become indistinguishable from the Lord of the firmament. His is the revenge.

The Mainz cathedral with its crossing tower, choir tower, and four side towers stood up to the wrong heavenly lights. In three bombardments, on August 12, 1942, September 8, 1944, and February 27, 1945, the roof was burned off, and holes were bombed into the south wing of the cloister and the roof of the Gotthard Chapel, but its majesty remained undamaged. Mainz's city center was 80 percent destroyed by the 1.3 million incendiary sticks and twenty thousand high-explosive bombs that were dropped in 1944 and 1945. The number of casualties in the city of 158,000, with the best air-raid protection, was between 3,500 and 3,800, about double the average.

Across the Rhine from Mainz, on the right bank, lies Wiesbaden, which also had good reason to remain spared from the bombing war. "Wiesbaden they want to spare, because they want to live there."[76] There were several versions to the rhyme, but it always was in reference to a city with a high quality of living. Wiesbaden was the most elegant and cheerful bathing and health resort within the realm of the Hohenzollerns, and before that it was the residence of the Duchy of Nassau. The splendor of the city gave way after the Great War to a patina that meshed most beautifully with the French occupation, which lasted until 1930. But air force staffs do not view cities according to their livability. In the first heavy raid on February 8, 1944, within only a few minutes a carpet of bombs fell on the district of Biebrich, site of the Henkell Sparkling Wine Cellars atop the Adolfshöhe. The carpet extinguished the gallant company and killed the owner, Karl Henkell, as well as a number of employees. No land forces would have done that.

From its industrial staff, the U.S. Eighth Air Force had found out that the Kalle chemical plant was in Wiesbaden, and that made the city a target. Three raids in September targeted the slaughterhouse and the areas of the city where the Kalle and Dyckerhoff companies had their production plants. The three British raids in October were bloodier. With heavy aerial mines, which on the ground were thought to be Vi flying bombs gone astray, they toppled blocks of housing and buried 291 people. From November on, hedgehoppers on strafer raids engaged in deliberate manhunts. From Bomber Command's perspective, these were all raids of opportunity carried out by small Mosquito groups that had not been detailed elsewhere; they were amazingly effective. Not until later did the use of the heavy materials become standard procedure.

In February 1945, Harris was counting up the places that had been spared up to then, and he quickly came upon Wiesbaden. Its population of 170,000 had not yet become acquainted with the power of fire. February was the month of leftover operations. On the night of February 2, between midnight and 12:30 a.m., 495 Lancasters appeared and brought the fire war to the hospitable city. Taking an unusually long time, 27,000 incendiaries and thirty-nine high-explosive bombs fell over fifty minutes, leaving 28,000 people homeless. A large fire spread out across the city center, destroying the city hall, the magnificent Lyceum I, the *Kavalierhaus*, the fountain and theater colonnade, the *Paulinenschlösschen* (the residence of Duchess Pauline of Nassau), and the English-Hessian royal residence "Victoria." Twelve hundred and seventy tons of munitions put a somber end to everything that had been part of the amusing meeting place for nineteenth-century society, leaving nothing but the shadows of a thousand hosts who were killed. As a postscript on March 9, bombers destroyed the municipal nursing home in Biebrich along with forty-one residents, two deaconesses, and three maids.

The house ignited on all four sides and quickly went up in flames, helped along by the wind. Those trapped inside thought they were goners, and prayed to God for mercy. They would have preferred to die in a proper battle. They were suffering an excessive revenge. Someone said they would have to die anyway, no matter what the enemy said. He felt nothing but thirst. Hagen said that whoever was parched should drink the blood over there, and he pointed to a dead soldier on the ground. One of the warriors removed the dead man's helmet, knelt down near the open wound, and drank the blood. The others followed suit and so gained new vigor. Meanwhile, the flames were crackling above them.

> The flaming brands fell thickly / upon them in the hall,
> With upraised shields they kept them / yet scatheless from their fall,
> Though smoke and heat together / wrought them anguish sore.
> Beset were heroes never, / I ween, by so great woe before.
> Then spake of Tronje Hagen: / "Stand nigh unto the wall,
> Let not the brands all flaming / upon your helmets fall."[77]

With their backs to the wall of the hall, and careful that the flames would not burn the straps of their helmets, the Burgundians awaited the Huns.

Aetius, the last notable Roman general, a semi-barbarian, allied himself with the Huns so he would be strong enough to decimate the Burgundians, who in 413 had chosen Worms to be the center of their empire. The Huns devastated Worms; it was the first of four times that the city was destroyed. The Burgundians suffered a lamentable fate. Aetius assigned them to other settlement areas at the Jura Mountain passes above Lake Geneva, and along the Saône River. Some of the Burgundian nobility were forced into slavery by the Huns and abducted to Hungary, to the residence of King Attila. Attila, whom Aetius had wanted only to exploit and pay off, returned a few years later to the Rhine plain, where his style of battle had developed very effectively. When the Huns had pushed forward as far as the Champagne region, Aetius hastily organized a Christian alliance of not only Visigoths, Franks, Alemanni, and Romans, but also remaining Burgundians. That led to a victory on the Catalaunian Plains. The decline of the Burgundians was recorded in the Song of the Nibelungs, and was passed on to later generations as a German myth.

As the divergent parts of the song were rediscovered in the late eighteenth century, it became obvious that the second part, the extermination of the Burgundians at the hands of the Huns, had been altered by court singers. The destruction still took place, but the reasons changed. The Huns now entered the story involuntarily. They still sabered down the Burgundians, but it was not of their own accord. The driving force was now a Burgundian madwoman, the vengeful Kriemhild. The discord between Kriemhild and her own people triggered the self-destruction of the Burgundians. The singers kept switching the events and reinterpreting the story until the context seemed plausible to them. They did not pay close attention to details. Telling a story gives it form. And so the national epic of self-destruction was born.

The devastations of Worms stand like indicators of the chaos of destruction and self-destruction of the empire. The city partook of the imperial splendor of the Salians and Hohenstaufens and experienced the Imperial Diet of 1521, when Luther presented his teachings to Emperor Charles V, in the aftermath of which the religious wars eliminated the empire as an entity of power. France moved into the resulting vacuum. In the Palatinate War of Succession, Louis XIV ravaged a strip of Palatinate-Baden one hundred miles long and fifty to 110 miles wide to secure his retreat. Then he quickly shifted the front in order to be able to cover his Atlantic coastline. The desolation of the Palatinate was a classical application of "scorched earth" policy. The retreating party laid a belt of fire to make it impossible for a potential pursuer to take up its position. After Heidelberg burned, General Melac advised the residents of Mannheim to do basically the same thing that Churchill suggested 250 years later. They should emigrate to Alsace, because the city will be burned to the ground. That applied to Mannheim, Heilbronn, Pforzheim, Rastatt, Baden-Baden, Bingen, Speyer with its cathedral and imperial crypt, Worms with its imperial palace, and hundreds of other towns.

The compactness of this huge historic fire adumbrates the air war and at the same time distances itself from it. The Palatines resisted the burning of their homeland; consequently, the French declared that they were being burned as punishment for Palatinate defiance. "It is absolutely necessary to bring these people to reason," noted War Minister Louvois, "either by hanging them or by burning their villages. Inhumanity against the Germans must be stepped up, if they are not prepared to wage war honourably."[78] One's opponents must be made responsible for the radicalism of one's means—who else? But there was a huge gap between enlightened absolutism and the neobarbarism of modernity, and the devastation of the Palatinate did not include a massacre of the civilian population. Anyone not willing to let their home be burned down would be killed, but the house was not burned in order to kill its inhabitants.

Worms was a city of 58,000 with only one war-related company. Up to February 21, 1945, the city had remained intact. On that day, an ill-tempered raid by 288 Halifaxes, thirty-six Lancasters, and twenty-five Mosquitos dropped 1,100 tons of bombs onto the city center, destroying or damaging 6,490 buildings, making 35,000 people homeless, and killing 239. Part of the bomb tonnage scattered toward the southwest. The cathedral in which Frederick II, Holy Roman Emperor, German king, and king of Sicily and Jerusalem—praised in his day as a heavenly creature—married Isabella, sister of King Henry III of England, got caught under a thirty-pound liquid bomb. The roofs burned, the bells melted, the upper floors of the eastern towers were reduced to ashes, and that was it. Sacrificed to the flames was the Monastery Church of St. Paul, erected in 1002 atop the remains of the Salian castle, the dome-shaped helm roofs of its towers a visible suggestion of Byzantium. The only extant medieval synagogue in Germany was blasted by the Germans in 1942. When they retreated beyond the Rhine on March 20, they also blew up their Nibelungen Bridge, completed in 1900, based on Hohenstaufen models. Something as useful as a Rhine bridge was not touched by Bomber Command. Four weeks earlier, the defenders could have entrenched themselves behind the Rhine. They could have lost just as easily, but at least saved Worms. But this did not correspond to the requirements of the battle of the Nibelungs as depicted in the epic. The Burgundians took their world with them to their ruin; there was no after.

Mannheim was a fortification built by the French in the most splendid, elegant proportions; it was a challenge. Eighteen years after its completion, in 1622, it was destroyed by Catholic League General Tilly, the Hun of his day. Germany descended into the Thirty Years' War and came out of it bled white, mortal enemies with each other, and powerless. France resolved the religious conflict, killed and gagged its Huguenots, established a state religion, and strengthened the nation-state. Elector Charles Louis (also known as Carl Ludwig) of the Palatinate offered asylum to the escaped Huguenots, his coreligionists, and rebuilt the fortifications. The city flourished, and soon the French were standing at the city gates.

In the Palatinate War triggered by Charles Louis's succession, the besieger General Montclar took the fortress with bravura. Before the troops withdrew, they destroyed the city's work of art, just in case. The three major conflicts of the eighteenth century—the Spanish and Austrian wars of succession and the Seven Years' War—left Mannheim intact. The war took place on the stage of the national theater that premiered Friedrich Schiller's *Die Räuber* (The Robbers).

The French Revolutionary Wars, on the other hand, left nothing untouched. The beautifully rebuilt and reinforced fortress was shot to pieces yet again, first by the natural conquerors, the French, and then unnecessarily by the reconqueror, Austrian General Dagobert Wurmser.

Napoleon's Treaty of Lunéville dictated the defortification of the area east of the Rhine, which included Mannheim. Its fortresses had not served any purpose anyway, but it was a shame to lose such beauty. As a state in the Confederation of the Rhine, there was also nothing left for Mannheim to ward off. The next attacker came from the air.

The city was the first to experience a serious fire raid in 1940, so once again it turned to its old project of fortification. No one in Mannheim wanted the ugly fortress of modernity, the bunker, to be visible above ground. Thus underground bunkers were built in the city center and tower bunkers only on the outskirts, and even there they kept within the local taste. The bunkers were built to the specifications of the Siegfried Line fortifications and offered protection for half the population. By the fall of 1943, fifty-one bunkers had been built, with a nominal capacity of 120,000. With a certain amount of crowding, this corresponded to full protection for 284,000 residents. It was the first fortification that served its purpose.

Mannheim lost 1,700 people, or 0.6 percent of its residents, close to half the average. The large number of raids underscores the success of the air-raid protection. In the area of present-day Baden-Württemberg, Mannheim was the city attacked most often. This is apparent from the loss of buildings, which could not be protected in bunkers. The historic city was obliterated. Louis XIV let nothing from the seventeenth century remain, and Churchill, nothing from the eighteenth.

The razing started on the night of April 16, 1943, when the west wing of the castle was gutted. The night of September 5 saw the incineration of the meter-thick oak beams of the artistically adorned Jesuit church and, after a performance of *Der Freischütz* (The Free-shooter), Schiller's National Theater. One in three residences was destroyed. On September 24, the eastern wing of the castle was reduced to rubble. A British leaflet announced in December: "A new airplane is produced every five minutes in America." Since a new castle was not produced every five minutes in Mannheim, the superiority of the side with the airplanes was confirmed. Similarly, the Nazi paper *Hakenkreuzbanner* gloated that every bomb produced a new Nazi.

"The bombs have accomplished what the best and most convincing speech could not. They have unified hundreds of thousands and millions of Germans by making them directly face the shared destiny of the German people. Where the enemies hoped to hit our weakest point, they have hit our greatest strength."[79]

In 1859, *Rheinschanze,* the Rhine entrenchment, Fortress Mannheim's bridgehead on the western side of the Rhine, became one of Germany's youngest cities, Ludwigshafen. The BASF location and the orientation of the eastern Palatinate transportation network along this section of the riverbank drew 124 air raids to Ludwigshafen, leaving the city center, half the residential housing, and ninety of the churches, schools, and factories destroyed in their wake. Despite the city's good air-raid protection facilities, the above-average human losses of 1,778 from a total population of 144,000 illustrate the force of the attacks.

Within the course of three wars in which the world powers of the eighteenth century—England, France, Prussia, and Austria—struggled for control, Karlsruhe was again occupied by Louis XV. The margravates of Baden-Durlach and Baden-Baden, which fought against each other in the Thirty Years' War, were united in the imperial Habsburg camp, which England also joined. Fighting with France were Prussia, Saxony, and Bavaria. Germany was not a side; it was the battlefield for the two sides.

Baden-Durlach had been reunited with Baden-Baden in 1771, after 250 years. A stronghold of enlightened absolutism, it had abolished serfdom and built up a rational city in 1715. Patterned after the star of Versailles, with the castle tower as the geometric center of the circle, twenty-two streets radiated out into the forest, the park, and the city. The city was a segment within the circle, an equilateral triangle with its focus on the baseline. The castle was a throne like a sun on the earth's triangle. The French liked that, especially Napoleon, who made Baden into a Grand Duchy, a pillar of the Confederation of the Rhine. The subjects paid their thanks with both high sums of money and their blood in the Napoleonic Wars.

The first major European war in centuries that was not fought on German soil took place from 1914 to 1918. (The Crimean War, Franco-Prussian War, and Balkan Wars are considered limited conflicts, based on number of participants and the course of the war.) The belated founding of Germany offset the post-Napoleonic balance of countries, resulting in Germany's fighting out the power balance with England, France, and Russia. Military movements were more inflexible, more stationary, and less intelligent than in previous centuries. This time it was the people of Belgium and northern France who suffered the devastation and pillaging. Karlsruhe was a minor exception because, along with Freiburg and Ludwigshafen, it was bombed from the air.

The first massive bombing raid, the turn to modern barbarism, took place on the Feast of Corpus Christi in 1916. That was around the time of the battle of Verdun. Five twin-engine double-deckers of the French flier squadron *Escadrille C6* appeared around 3:10 p.m. in a cloudy sky above the city's radial axes that the people of Karlsruhe call the *Fächer*, or fan.[80] The planes, decorated with the French blue, white, and red cockade, were able to locate their targets using instruments. The copilot quickly lifted the bomb, a two-foot-long steel pear, over the side of the aircraft by the open cockpit and let it fall. Each plane had eight bombs in its bay; thus the entire *escadrille* had forty.

The prelude was enough for the repugnance of the bombing war to become evident, as if it wanted to make it clear to civilization what it was getting itself into. The first five bombs hit next to the tent of the Circus Hagenbeck, which was in the middle of a show for an audience of two thousand people, mostly children. The bang of the explosion caused panic in the circus tent, people leapt outside, soldiers slit open the canvas, people running out trampled those who were slower, and all raced into the next bombs that fell. In the end there were 120 bodies lying in front of the circus tent, eighty-five of them children. The bodies were laid out in the northwestern wing of the train station. For Marshal Ferdinand Foch, then commander-in-chief of the French armed forces, this raid was repayment for the German bombardment of the undefended French town of Bar-le-Duc, where eighty-five civilians were killed. Now the score was even.

Although it was impossible to aim bombs during World War I, the staff bulletins reported that industry and train stations were declared as targets and also hit. Only the pilots, who knew better, admitted that it was mostly the effect on morale that counted, through the stories of bombings that were spread throughout the country.

The residential palace of the Grand Duchy was destroyed in the British fire raid of September 27, 1944. The blaze lasted for two days, and all that remained were the outer walls. The pragmatic castle architects had included a pond in the castle gardens for firefighting purposes. That sufficed for a sudden accident but not for the well-planned pyrotechnics of the Royal Air Force ordnance technicians. The pond was quickly pumped dry, but the castle continued to burn. Firefighting crews tried in helpless desperation to enter the building, as if they could convince the flames to extinguish, but the castle's time was up. Time had also run out for the Catholic Church of St. Stephan, which at the height of rationalism from 1804 to 1814 had been modeled after the Pantheon.

The universe of annihilation does not have direction; it is a blind state, a gate to nothingness. That was what the angel on the castle's church tower, which usually indicated the direction of the wind, seemed to want to say. The conflagration created its own air circulation, and the nine-foot-high figure started spinning on its axis as if struck by madness, until its bearings loosened and it fell to the ground. The warning system had failed. This attack and the next devastating raid on December 4 both came as unexpectedly as had the bombardment of the circus. Bomber Command appeared at 5 a.m., and a short time later the *Fächer* had become a row of flames. It was impossible to do anything. The flames drew the oxygen out of the arrow-straight streets; the people had been caught unawares and tried to run toward the Hardtwald forest or into open space or anywhere that was not aglow. Fortunately, the day before, the castle's cleaning lady, Frau Steinöl, had closed the iron, rubber-sealed doors of the airlock that protected the library, which had been moved to the basement. It did not burn.

Karlsruhe endured 135 air raids (thirteen were major), the heaviest of which was on December 4, 1944. It tore up an east-west strip of land 10.5 miles long and two miles wide, a straight line of desert intruding on the geometry that held the city together. According to a saying of the day, the bombs surely missed what they were supposed to hit. What were they supposed to hit? That is a complex question. In any case, they were not supposed to spare anything, such as a plant that had remained undamaged until the end of 1944. Its name alone was provocative: the DWM German Weapons and Munitions factory. The plant was given a raid of its own in 1942; it missed the works but totally smashed the entire street where it was located. Characteristic of December 4 was that even the DWM factory was destroyed. The city of reason was turned into 3.4 million cubic yards of rubble. And 1,754 of its citizens were lost.

Breisach was built on volcanic rock, about two miles southwest of the Kaiserstuhl mountain. The city was ruled by Rudolf von

Habsburg until 1805, so it was caught up in the drawn-out conflict between France and the world empire of the Habsburgs, the longest-lived of all ruling dynasties, which also administered the German Empire. When France initiated its Rhine policies in the Thirty Years' War, it also turned against Breisach, which linked the Habsburg possessions in Alsace and the Breisgau region. Between 1648 and 1806, the city was French for sixty-seven years. It received the mightiest bastions on the Upper Rhine, built by Marshal Vauban, Louis XIV's ingenious fortress builder. They were ground down to a stump by Austria in 1744, when the Breisgau was ceded back to the Habsburgs after the Palatinate War.

France had overstretched its strength; it took a deep breath and returned in 1793 with new vigor. The revolutionary army set a modern-style fire in the city. The blaze lasted four days and nothing remained standing except for the minster and five city gates. Rebuilt in a long, drawn-out process, the city remained dreaming in the beauty of its local landscape, until another offspring of the revolution, the U.S. Armed Forces, attacked Breisach with bombs, fighter-bombers, and artillery 130 times from October 1944 until April 1945. The sight of the place on the upper reaches of the river resembled the wasteland of Emmerich on the Lower Rhine.

The trail of the air war in the area west of the Rhine went through Aachen, Xanten, Trier, Kaiserslautern, Pirmasens, Saarbrücken, and the villages of the Eifel region. Until June 1943, Aachen could claim that it had not been destroyed in a war for more than a millennium. The ones who last craved it were the Normans in 881, the plundering horde of Vikings who conquered England in 1066. It could be that the empire of Charlemagne, as a fantasy of a harmonious Europe, accompanied the nonharmonious Europe, whose history was that of war with itself. Charlemagne had not been at all concerned with building up a harmonious empire, because the Frankish law of succession provided not for its continuity, but for division of the property among the sons.

The Salian and Hohenstaufen emperors, whose empire was set up very differently from that of the Franks, fed into the Charlemagne myth by being crowned in Aachen. Otto III opened Charlemagne's sarcophagus and wanted to be buried in his cathedral. Frederick Barbarossa had pressed for Charlemagne's sainthood, the Golden Bull of 1356 declared Aachen to be the legal city of coronations, and thirty-seven kings had been crowned there up to 1531. When the imperial power shifted to the south of Germany, the old city of coronation was in the most remote corner and had to give way to Frankfurt. But Aachen remained a pilgrimage site, preserving relics, treasures, and the shrine of Charlemagne's mortal remains. Like a shared cradle, the city possessed an aura of peacemaking. Louis XIV's War of Devolution for the Spanish Netherlands ended here, as did the War of the Austrian Succession, and in 1818, the Holy Alliance reinforced the extremely reconciliatory nineteenth century, in contrast to the previous one.

The two world wars fought over Germany brought twentieth-century Europe back to the low of the seventeenth century and even lower. The parties involved no longer saw any reason to spare Aachen. The decisive part of the Schlieffen Plan, Germany's strategy for 1914, was initiated in Aachen and almost precisely thirty years later, troops moved through Aachen in the exactly opposite direction for the breakthrough into the Reich. Neither plan was either totally successful or a total failure. What happened in each instance was worse than either extreme. Schlieffen's plan ended at the Marne, far too late; and Eisenhower's at the Elbe, also too late, as would soon become obvious—because the strife continued to smolder and a final bang was soon considered possible.

The house-to-house combat in Aachen that the Germans offered in October 1944 intensified the previous destruction from the air raid of April 11 and 12, 1944. The medieval city had been swallowed by a conflagration in 1656, which was a calamity but not an atrocity. The atrocity was carried in the bomb bays of 214 Halifaxes, which appeared as harbingers of the imminent destruction on the clear summer night of July 13, 1943. Massive fires could be ignited right away, which destroyed three thousand structures, killed 294 people, and damaged a series of buildings important to the war effort: the cathedral, city hall, theater, police headquarters, main post office, and prison. Ten weeks before they set foot on the European continent, on April 12, 1944, British forces bombed Aachen to dust, once and for all. The raid churned up the ground in an unparalleled concentration: 42,800 incendiaries and 4,047 high-explosive bombs. There were on average six bomb craters for every thousand square feet, which was unprecedented in such a densely built-up area. Sixty-one percent of the buildings had been knocked to the ground. Not one of the sixty-six churches and chapels remained unscathed; seventeen had been utterly destroyed and twenty-six severely damaged.

The explosives had been calibrated and set so they would penetrate a five-story building with three reinforced concrete ceilings and not explode until they reached the basement. Of 164,000 residents, 1,525 died, including 212 children. Two raids in late May targeted the railway yards and did away with the entire suburb of Forst and 271 of its residents. The Carolingian city center had long since been worn down through time and done away with in the fire of 1656. But precious remnants had survived, such as Charlemagne's coronation chamber, later built into the fourteenth-century Gothic city hall. In the end, the bombs knew how to find it. The exorcism by the bombs uprooted the cities as if they had been possessed by the devil and could be redeemed only through fire.

When Napoleon looked around Trier, he disliked a church that Archbishop Poppo had built around the Roman Porta Nigra in the eleventh century. Poppo had brought the hermit Simeon back from a pilgrimage to the Holy Sepulcher. In his honor and to the glory of the Almighty, Poppo surrounded the pagan monument with a collegiate church. He could have just had the gate torn down, but decided instead to enter into a dialogue with it. Napoleon had portions of the Church of St. Simeon removed so the imperial grandeur of the gate could reappear, since Napoleon saw himself as heir to Rome.

Trier enjoyed the Pax Romana for two hundred years, young and cosmopolitan, raising itself above the aged mother city as the residence of Emperor Constantine. But Trier declined as well, and the successors built their churches and manor houses from the stone of the old Roman walls. Only the Normans, who invaded the city in 882, thought nothing of the crushed stone. They did not take possession of an inheritance, did not use the old stone to build altars to the young gods, and did not want to build anything. Instead, to prove their irresistibility, they burned and crushed everything that was standing.

The later Trier prided itself on its transparency. At its roots lay the Roman city like the sunken Vineta. The imperial baths, the amphitheater, the Porta, the reflection of Rome's geometric array of streets. As with hieroglyphics, an expert could read the image of things past in Trier, wrote Ricarda Huch. Then she added in wonderful directness the reason for the permanence of such shells and remnants. "History has become a picture for other races and peoples to look at."[81] The iconoclasm of the bomber fleets was not an attack on one's sense of art; they took away the representation of history, which had become pale and distant tidings.

The fanaticism of war in 1945 no longer permitted the differential treatment of cities. No exceptions were possible; even the Roman city had to burn. Anyone who could not muster the necessary consistency would just as well have had problems with Cologne, Emden, or Hildesheim. As with so many places that had been blessed by the past and then surrendered themselves to the bombs, in Trier it was about the vital point, the railway yards. The bombing war had meanwhile invented its own geometric formula, which it had been following for three years: point times point equals area. The area target was purely abstract, as faceless as the enemy in the trenches. Both target and enemy simply had to be eliminated.

Napoleon made the distinction that human losses are replaceable, but city and land are the payment for which the blood is shed. And the cities fell under his creative might. In order to bequeath his image to history, Napoleon did not shred the view of history up to then. The reason for his ride through Düsseldorf differed greatly from that of Churchill's excursion to the top of the rubble of Wesel and Jülich. Trier was attacked from the air twenty times, resulting in 730,000 cubic yards of rubble. On August 14, 1944, 18,000 incendiary sticks destroyed a palace hall built by Emperor Constantine in 305. As a so-called basilica, Protestant services were held here. The path of destruction extended to the Imperial Baths in the south, which along with the amphitheater and the Barbara Baths suffered less severe damage.

The third squadron of the U.S. Eighth Air Force, which destroyed the Constantine basilica, could not enjoy this accomplishment, since they cared little for those bricks either way. What they had wanted to hit was the Kürenz freight depot and the main train station.[82] When 1,600 airplanes took off from England early that Monday morning, no one thought of Trier, but right before 1 p.m., twenty-five tons of munitions were to burn there. The squadron simply had this amount left over, since it was supposed to bombard military facilities in France but when bad weather surprised them, they veered off and quickly sought a target for their load. Alternative targets were set for such cases. Trier took the place of barracks in France, and the Roman buildings substituted for the freight depot.

The chance events of August were helped along by the systematic plans of December. The outcomes were the same. On December

19, during the course of an operation in the Eifel region, thirty-two Lancasters undertook a precision raid guided by G-H radar, targeting Trier's railway yards. They dropped 136 tons of explosives on the city center. Among the monuments and buildings damaged was the St. Irmine charitable care facility. Bombs penetrated the ceilings and went all the way through to the vaulted wine cellar, where thirty nurses caring for patients too ill to be evacuated were killed.[83]

On December 19, 21, 23, and 24, more than one thousand aircraft bombed the center of town as well as the part of the city from the Moselle River to Petrisberg, St. Peter's mountain. At 2 p.m. on December 21, British and American planes appeared together. The Lancasters were loaded with 427 tons of bombs; the Thunderbolts as escort fighters had twenty-three napalm and flame-jet bombs on board. The fires ignited were inextinguishable, for one thing, because a heavy frost froze the fire hoses. Trier's Black Day was December 23, when 153 Lancasters dropped seven hundred tons of mixed munitions and aerial mines over the entire area. The center, suburbs, suburban train stations, post offices, marketplace, monasteries, and courts were all evenly collapsed, including a gem of Rhenish Gothic, the "Steipe," a patrician banquet hall at the main marketplace with a pewter-adorned façade and open arcades at the base. More than four hundred of the five thousand residents who stayed behind after the evacuations were killed.

On Christmas Eve, ten U.S. Lightning fighter planes checked whether Trier had really been burned to the ground. Just to be sure, they dropped twenty five-hundred-pound bombs into the conflagrations, which continued to blaze into Christmas Day. They reported to the staffs that "all of Trier is in flames." In view of the forward-pressing Ardennes offensive, the staffs were nervous, so in order to separate German units from their rear lines of communication, anything that *could* be destroyed *was* destroyed. The retreating Germans later blasted a line of communication to the rear themselves: the Napoleon Bridge. Any bridge to Napoleon had meanwhile been ruled out.

Aside from losing the basilica, damages to the Liebfrauenkirche, the Church of Our Lady, weighed the heaviest, as Ricarda Huch, who had seen it prior to the destruction, wrote:

> In the interior the Gothic slimness and the imaginative richness of the individual elements joins the compactness of the whole to give an impression of blissful harmony. When the softly colored light shines through the

window in the evening, one feels secure in the calyx of a heavenly blossom, as the floor plan also resembles a rose. In its perfection and sublime grace the church is characterized as the house in which the Virgin Mother of the Lord is honored. It forms a unique group with the cathedral, the church of God the Father, king of the universe, who leads the fates of the stars and the people with a stroke of lightning.[84]

The incendiary bombs of August 14 destroyed the church of the Father at the helm roof, the belfries, and the main roofs. The December raid decimated parts of the upper floor of the sanctuary chamber, all the windows, and the western and southern wings of the Gothic cloister. The vault of the suffragan chapel collapsed, but the nave was not hit. The church of the Virgin was penetrated through the choir vault, the bombs causing cracks from the roof to the ground. The stairway tower fell, vaults broke, pillars shifted in place, tracery splintered away. Beseler and Gutschow, eminent chroniclers of the architectural damages of the air war, characterized the cathedral, whose construction was begun in 326 under Emperor Constantine, as "evidence of historical continuity since antiquity" and "the most venerable construction on German soil." And they regarded the Church of Our Lady to be the "oldest Gothic church in Germany."[85]

Like all mining areas, Saarbrücken too had excellent air-raid facilities at its disposal. The adit was a bombproof hideout, and there was enough space for almost the entire Saarbrücken population. The city's valley location allowed for miles of drivings, which extended from the Old Town to deep into the rock. There were also the exceptional facilities prepared in advance. In building the Siegfried Line, space had already been created to get the entire population underground. There were also galleries from ancient times, as well as the deep cellars of the beer breweries and a good deal of "communal tunnels" that neighborhoods with mining expertise had bored into the slopes. Inside there was a very cozy atmosphere and little fresh air; it was damp and stuffy.

Although the people of Saarbrücken were better protected, the 1.1 percent human loss rate was within the German average. From a population of 118,000 in June 1940, at least 1,234 people died in the bombings. How should such a figure be interpreted? It was double the losses of Coventry, a city three times the size. The loss rate there was 0.17 percent. The 568 casualties in Coventry were all from a single attack, however, whereas Saarbrücken had been subjected to thirty bombing raids. The fate of German cities was different from that of Warsaw, Rotterdam, and Coventry in the same way that a war is not the same as a battle. London was an exception in that regard.

Two-thirds of the deaths in Saarbrücken were from four raids. The two heaviest ones, on May 11 and the night of October 5, 1944, can show us where the losses came from. May 11 taught the lesson that protection in the Third Reich was a privilege, as can be recognized wherever there was a surplus of it. Wisdom and mobility were rarely the attributes that kept people alive during a bombing raid. Either you were in the right place at the right time, or you were not. The odds of survival depended on serendipity, a happy accident. Some places were never the right places to be, such as asylums, prisons, and foreign workers' homes. The inmates were surrounded by two prisons, the carpet of bombs and the bars. They were protected as little as were wild beasts in the zoo. These animals were shot to prevent them from escaping; prisoners could pray. In Saarbrücken's Lerchesflur prison, fifty-seven people died because they were not worthy of protection. For the same reason, ninety-one foreign workers in the Cecilien School died. There were no tunnels for prisoners or foreign workers, and the cozy comfort of the family tunnel was unattainable. The prison and the Cecilien School cases made up three-quarters of all losses in May. October was a different story.

British and American experts had been telling Arthur Harris for quite some time about Saarbrücken's function as a nerve center for troop movements to the western front. The Air Marshal, who did not care for point targets, decided on a double blow. On October 5, an initial attack wave at 8:30 p.m. was supposed to destroy objective number one, the railway yards, in five minutes. A second wave at 10:30 p.m. was to destroy the city in nine minutes. The purpose of such a magnitude was incomprehensible; in far larger cities, the train station and residential settlements were burned down at once. The dual attack always had a tricky side-effect in well-protected cities such as Duisburg and Mainz. In Saarbrücken, too, it would fail to go as planned. The first wave, Oboe-guided, erred when marking the railway yards, and the master bomber aborted the operation. So they would not have to carry the bombs home, the squadrons released them. They scattered down on the city and were mistaken by the townspeople for a raid. The residents went to their tunnel homes and waited for the all-clear signal, which came at 10:04 p.m. Relieved, people resurfaced and made their ways home, away from the stifling air. Five minutes later, the air-raid sirens sounded; it was the second wave of 325 Lancasters, with 350,000 stick incendiaries. "We didn't have time to go back to the bunker," reported Z——, an old Saarbrücken woman, "so we had no choice but to go to the basement. The whole house shook and clouds of dust and the smell of smoke kept coming through the door. We could hardly breathe and there were no lights either. We were incredibly afraid of being buried alive."[86]

In a 1942 raid, a stabilized house basement was usually a cozy cave. Two years later, the volume and force of the munitions could tear it apart like a cardboard box. "The whole cellar seemed to lift up. The blast from the detonation hit us like a powerful hammer. The wall along the length of the cellar collapsed. The iron air-raid door I was standing next to was torn off its hinges. We could hardly breathe." The cellar exits were blocked with debris; the families sat there captive, banging and knocking, which was exhausting. And the fire heated up the stone. Hundreds died in those hopeless corners, though the Saarbrücken network of adits had been dug out specifically so people could avoid the cellars. "A real masterpiece," could be read in the air crews' report. At 10:45 p.m., the city was enveloped in yellowish red flames. Fuel tanks exploded at the freight depot; objective number one was among the things that burned. Bomber Command's evaluation report noted with satisfaction: "The whole town was ablaze," 50 percent of the residential areas had been destroyed, and "the old town south of the river is almost annihilated."[87]

At some point, all the cities in the country had been destroyed by war once. But only once did one war destroy all the cities. The Thirty Years' War, the great ravager of Germany, had a much smaller range than Bomber Command and the Eighth Air Force. King Gustavus Adolphus of Sweden had gone the longest distance up to that time, reaching Kaiserslautern. Under the circumstances, this turned out to be neither affordable nor really advisable for him. France's prime minister, Cardinal Richelieu, the financial backer and wire-puller, felt uneasy about the Swedish thrust into territory west of the Rhine. France nevertheless held to its agreement and maintained the war, which Germany's princes had already ended among themselves with the Treaty of Prague. Their concern, the dispute with the Habsburg emperor about local authority, was taken care of somehow. Meanwhile, Sweden and France were engaged in continental power

politics, because of which the marches through Germany had to continue. France was at war with the German emperor in his other position as leader of the greater Habsburg empire. It was encircled by
Habsburg-Spain, Habsburg-Netherlands, and Habsburg-Lorraine,
and needed to blast through the ring. Gustavus Adolphus could only
reach for the Baltic Sea empire he dreamed of if he won the strip of
the German Baltic Sea coast and kept Poland down. This extent of
restructuring lay outside the realm of diplomacy; it could only come
about by marriage or by war.

Politics continued within the scope of the war. Gustavus Adolphus
turned to the southern German cities. Larger cities were self-governing under the emperor, not the territorial prince. They basically
needed an authority only in order to keep away other authorities.
Holding to a distant ruler such as the Holy Roman Emperor in Vienna, while refusing entrance to the conqueror at the gates, ran against
a city's nature. As with everyone who had something to lose and was
sensitive to punishment, the cities were prone to collaboration. That
was the foundation of Bomber Command's entire strategy: breaking
the cities off from the Reich. Rebellion was to grow out of the cities'
rubble, and then nothing else would happen to them. In 1633, the
Heilbronn League organized the splinters that broke from Emperor
Ferdinand II in favor of the Swedish occupiers. On the side—but not
on center stage—they all became Protestants.

When the Emperor's Catholic Majesty reconquered Kaiserslautern from Sweden in 1635, it staged an abominable massacre in the
former Palatinate of Frederick Barbarossa. Slaughtering the occupiers after storming them corresponded to the customs of the day, as
did allowing the storming troops to ravage the land. The massacre of
1,500 residents resembled more the conditions created during World
War II. But in this war, however, it was not lustful lansquenets who
were ravaging, but heads of state.

How did the break from the rulers that was demanded of civilians
everywhere proceed in the period from 1939 to 1945? Superficially,
by appealing to political reason. However, not reason but obedience
was needed. Obedience was expected in the view of the master of a
boundless massacre. The master of the raid took advantage of it as
did the master of the defense. Both dictated a call for allegiance on
pain of mass slaughter. Whoever surrendered or did not surrender
suffered, respectively, a guillotine's blade or bombs falling on their
heads. City dwellers could not identify who won in the end, or who

they should bet on; they only knew whose finger was on the trigger at the moment. It used to be that the executors of the respective reprisals came one after another; first Gustavus Adolphus and then the emperor. The innovative part of the air war was the parallelism of the reprisal. The bomber fleets punished the cities from above for belonging to the Reich. And the Gestapo punished them from within their own country, for being war weary. More on that later.

The destruction of the Thirty Years' War left its mark on Kaiserslautern. But this time, it was said, the fires would not make it through to the town because it was in a valley and fog often hid the buildings. Nonetheless, tunnels were constantly being dug out on the slopes, old beer cellars were reinforced, and water from the Siegel stream and the Lauter River was used to fill reservoirs for extinguishing fires. When in broad daylight around noon on January 17, 1944, 116 buildings were destroyed or severely damaged and eighty-one people killed by two waves of American bombers, people realized that it was possible.[88] Numerologists are interested in the number three. Three hundred and three times three years had passed since the last major conflagration, in the Thirty Years' War. That had been the second destruction. Would the third one follow during the Third Reich?

Feelings of insecurity accumulated each time the sirens sounded. People reacted with a start; going to the tunnels became a race for one's life. The notorious "bunker rats" no longer dared to leave the shelters, sometimes because they were homeless, sometimes because they were keen on claiming their regular place. With its sixty-six thousand residents, the city was designated a second-order air-raid protection site, and was thus not eligible for national subsidies to build air-raid shelters. The municipality had as many as their funds would allow and as many as the residents could shovel. Protection had to be fought for. Up to August 14, the air-raid sirens had sounded 328 times. On April 23 they sounded eight times within a twenty-four hour period. The residents were overtired, worn out, and at the end of their tether.

On August 14, 1944, the Eighth Air Force returned around midday and dropped combined explosive-incendiary munitions on eighty streets. The oppressively hot summer temperatures slowed down the dissipation of the smoke and heat from the fire. The Eckel furniture company's huge wood supply in the city center ignited; the flames rose upward, forming a torch that drew in colder air layers from the neighboring forests. The resulting draft fanned the flames; it was that notorious, apocalyptic mechanism. Kaiserslautern was surrounded by wood—the city, church, and Reich forests. The imperial murderer-arsonists of 1635 had already had their fun with the wooden frame buildings. Now the buildings were of stone, but the wood once again stirred up disaster.

Master painter August Nebling observed the bombers' activities from an adit under Betzenberg mountain. As he watched the rain of fire falling, he thought of the three barrels of turpentine he had stored in his house, the three hundred children's beds that had to be painted, and the paint and wood oils. "Spur-of-the-moment I jumped on my bicycle and raced eastward on Barbarossastrasse, where the Lotz wooden shoe factory was burning fiercely." The bike ride ended at the Eckel furniture company.

> Their wood storage yard had meanwhile become a huge sea of flames that spread to the buildings on Schneppbachstrasse. So I rode along Schulstrasse, which was already burning. A bomb exploded six meters from me, throwing me through the air against the iron gate of the schoolyard, where I landed unconscious, lying with my face in the rubble. At the last moment I was still able to see how the corner building with Jung's Bakery had slid rather close to me. The suction from the bomb blast had torn it apart.
>
> After what seemed like a short time I came to and besides my general shock I became aware that I was lying there stark naked and only my shoes were still intact. All that was left of my clothes were narrow strips of fabric. Covered with blood, I got up. All around me was fire and smoke, which darkened what only fifteen minutes earlier had been a sunny summer day. The baker's apprentice from the demolished building next door was lying next to me; only his foot was twitching. I lifted him up and noticed a large pool of blood underneath him. He had bled to death. Three meters away I noticed a dead policeman in the rubble.

When Nebling finally crawled home, the inevitable had already happened. The flames were licking six feet high out of the windows, bursts of fire were shooting from the workshop. "My brother was trying to no avail to extinguish the fire in the shop. Blast bombs suddenly whizzing down from the sky quickly chased us back into the cellar. On the way my brother collapsed. He suffered a stroke from the shock and died the next morning."[89]

Nebling's next thought was of his wife in the air-raid cellar,

> but the entrance was blocked by debris from a demolition bomb. It took five hours to get the thirty people trapped in this shelter out through the holes in the walls between the cellars. I banged on the basement window,

but since the bomb left me totally deaf in my left ear and partly deaf in my right, I couldn't hear any response to my knocking. Extremely weakened, I started back towards Preussenplatz. So many buildings had since caught fire on Schulstrasse that thick mushroom clouds of smoke filled the sky above the city, making it very dark. Dropping to the ground every fifteen steps and taking great pains, I was finally able to get back to the square in safety, where the fire brigade picked me up and brought me to the shelter in Barbarossa School.

Nebling died from his injuries in 1949.

The route that day from Betzenberg to Barbarossa School was like a *Simplicissimus* war novel pressed into one hour. The business that was built up with hard work and whose success was made of wood, the reprisal-hungry bomb mixture, the treachery of cause and effect, the senselessness of any and all efforts, the inevitability of the fire, the dying for naught. The annihilating raid on Kaiserslautern was the third one. It was flown by Bomber Command with 909 tons of bombs in the ninth month of the 309th year after the destruction during the Thirty Years' War. The third destruction of Kaiserslautern during the Third Reich killed one-third the number of victims that died in the previous one. But all that numerology brings to light is that three equals three and destruction can be multiplied. Mystics and historians are driven by the same need to make some sense of things, to uncover some pattern to support what is pointless, to justify the massacre with some logic and give history a reason. History takes a series of paths, each one leading in a different direction. At the beginning and the end an irresolvable fact remains: a wood factory caught fire, the heat drew in cool air from the nearby forests, causing a storm, and in the end, nothing remained standing.

In April 1945, close behind the advancing Allied forces, sociologist Daniel Lerner, a U.S. intelligence officer, had a look at the state of the conquered German cities. He reported that the centers of all of them had simply been razed to the ground. The troops could quarter only in residential districts on the outskirts, Lerner continued. Because the centers also contained the infrastructure and public utilities, the electricity, water, and gas lines were often interrupted and never did all of them function at the same time. He estimated the general degree of destruction to be 75 percent, though in some cases 80 or even 90 percent. Lerner based his observations merely on his external impressions. A month later another Office of Strategic

Services officer, economist Moses Abramovitz, made the same trip and offered more specific findings. In Essen, he noted the total devastation of both center and outskirts. "Many streets are still almost entirely obstructed; some are totally unrecognizable under the rubble."[90] No one at all was still living in the center of Cologne. The industrial grounds, on the other hand, were in better condition.

A survey of companies with more than 250 employees in the Düsseldorf area found that only few had been destroyed and the rest were either damaged in part or not at all. . . . According to officers of Rhine Coal Control the Ruhr mines had hardly been damaged and the condition of the winding gear and hauling winches was such that they could be back up to almost full production in only a few months. Based on the surprisingly good condition of the Krupp works in the center of Essen and the suburb of Borbeck, this appraisal does not seem unrealistic.

In western Germany, industrial facilities were to a large extent still usable, Abramovitz recorded, as it was difficult to destroy pits and steelworks. "Also, the Germans were very successful as regards repairs of the industrial facilities."

The so-called Second Battle of the Ruhr in the fall of 1944 reached its peak in Essen on October 23 and 25. The Krupp works were covered with 1,305 high-explosive bombs and ten thousand incendiaries.[91] In those two days, 1,826 bombers plastered the city center, however, with many times that amount: one million incendiary sticks. The total bomb tonnage of explosives and incendiary devices was 8,200, far more than double the volume dropped during the big raid on Hamburg. Bomber Command continued in November, December, and February. The last raid on March 11 involved 1,079 aircraft with a total bomb load of 4,661 tons, double the amount dropped on Dresden. It was one of the major air operations of the war. Everything done to Essen broke a record. Bomber Command was drawn to that city like a magnet. The heart of the horn-skinned Siegfried beat in the Krupp factory; the smelting plants there had cast the artillery pieces that mutilated the British youth on the fields of Flanders in 1916. Harris mentioned by name only a single factory that he ever aimed at directly: Krupp.

As early as the night of May 11, 1940, at 2:05 a.m.—at that point, general orders did not yet allow any operations east of the Rhine— six high-explosive bombs were dropped on an athletic field and two buildings. Between March and April 1942, a total of 1,555 planes had already flown a six-part raid series. The workers' residential district of Borbeck was already considered obliterated in March 1943. In the night raid of April 30, the mass of munitions dropped on Essen had reached ten thousand tons, the hitherto largest volume dropped on any city. The air war went on for sixty months, and Essen was attacked during thirty-nine of them. Krupp, the main target of 1.5 million tons of bombs, seemed best prepared to withstand the matériel battle. In the city, on the other hand, a mere five thousand of 65,000 buildings remained undamaged. Relative to the deluge of bomb tonnage dropped, death profited only marginally. Nevertheless, 6,384 people died, the ninth-highest number lost by a city in the air war.

Those who managed to escape the 272 raids were worn out alive. A doctor who was thirty-seven at the time described life in the air-raid cellars in the spring of 1943, during the Battle of the Ruhr: Dust, noise, shock, mortal fear, blast wave, shaking building, burning street, the sight of death and dying—all of this left behind emotional wrecks, people as ruined as their homes.

> I embraced my wife and noticed she was trembling intensely and unceasingly. This trembling affected me greatly and transferred over to me. I too started to shiver, especially my legs. I tried with all my will to get the tremor to stop by stamping my feet, lifting my heels, pressing down on my toes, and stretching my legs, but I failed totally.[92]

Tremors were a response to the bombed-out ground, which was no longer a firm base that a mobile person moved about on. The energy from the munitions that was pumped into the earth in excess and converted into blast waves and radiant heat set the surroundings in motion. That was why all the descriptions included the image of the world going down: It was truly active, moving, vibrating, shaking, trembling, breaking, piling up, boiling, melting, falling to ashes. The firmness of the earth's crust makes us feel sure of a continuity. At the end of time, the crust breaks. The elementary fact of a bombing war was that no one could move in it. You crawled around and waited until the blast and heat subsided, until the shaking and melting stopped, until objects could stand and firmness returned.

"Every minute the house was being shaken by an aerial mine, soon everything was quaking down to the cellar. Then our space was full of oven gas so I thought that the boiler had burst. The blast forced smoke down through the chimney, through the flue into the cellar. We prayed and cried." The lava of the melted, dripping, former roofing paper or tar was considered a kind of phosphorus. Phosphorus was used as a general name for anything inflammable and molten through heat.

> The liquid phosphorus had a terrible effect. It flowed through the holes in the cellar walls onto the coal and coke piles. Then the buildings started burning from the top and the bottom. The next day it was over 2,700°F in the cellars and the water from the broken water lines was boiling and seething in the cellars that even today were still radiating horrific heat and stinking of gas.[93]

Six women pressed close together on the ground.

> You couldn't even think anymore, you could just pray. During the first bomb drop all the doors were thrown off their hinges and splintered. We lay there in the dark as if we were outdoors. Deafening crashing and whistling of the bombs. The end of the world certainly can't be worse. The bombardment lasted forty-five minutes. At first we couldn't believe that the house and the whole street were still there. Behind our building there was chaos. Nine huge craters that had plowed up virtually everything. Trees were lying about like big dead bodies. Our old garden was nothing but a crater, huge and deep. All the fruit trees except for the cherry trees had been razed away.

It was midnight. "We all just climbed out of the tunnel. The eighth full alarm since ten in the morning. Yesterday there was another big fight in the tunnel." The tunnel director said, "I don't want to see any more baby carriages brought into the tunnel." The baby-carriage women were at the end of their tether. The day before, one had gotten so upset that she knocked over the carriage as she raced to the adit. "There was a plane in the flak searchlight that was being fired on. She was lucky it didn't have any bombs on board." Without the six-foot-thick reinforced concrete, those who lost the race to the bunker were at the utter mercy of the bombs. "Here at Moltkeplatz there was such a panic that eleven people—seven women and four children—were trampled to death. And not a single bomb had even been dropped in our area."[94]

Air battle units were flying over the Ruhr basin every day. They gave orders to the residents, telling them what they had to do to keep from getting killed. "Countless leaflets were dropped from planes. We were told to leave the Ruhr basin because all streets and transportation lines would be under fire. We can hardly go shopping for groceries."[95] And the other side gave counterorders. "It was the worst raid ever flown over Germany. That night posters were already hung up that no one was permitted to leave Essen. There is nothing left of the city center. Soldiers said that Essen looked worse than Stalingrad."[96] Soon there were counterorders to the counterorders. "They were happy when a lot of women and children agreed to be evacuated. They even paid for their train tickets. Just get out of this hell." But where to?

Tacitus mentions Veleda, the seeress, among the rebels against Roman rule. Veleda instigated her tribe, the Bructeri east of the Rhine, to join the Germanic rebels in the year 69 CE.[97] A superior power cannot be everywhere and is not familiar with the area. Veleda told the Bructeri about a hidden cave halfway between present-day Velmede and Halbeswig in the Sauerland region. The local population did not discover what Veleda's cave was good for until two millennia later. It was bombproof. When the war advanced to that area in 1944, the residents of Velmede set up a makeshift camp at the Veleda cave. When they heard the bomber's engines they slipped next door into the Bructeri bunker. The people of the surrounding villages were all eagerly searching for tunnels and rock cellars; they ridiculed the camp, enviously calling it *Angsthausen*, the "scaredy-camp."

Up to 1943, the inhabitants of the Sauerland region experienced the air war in smaller cities and towns as nothing more than air-raid alarms. If the bomber streams flew out to Berlin or Kassel, the sirens wailed, announcing the imminent death of others. And the farmers out in the fields crossed themselves. After the first Battle of the Ruhr came the evacuees from Duisburg, Dortmund, Bochum, and Essen. Inns and hostels started filling up, and extensions were built onto residential housing. In many places the population doubled. The people of the Ruhr basin brought in their money and bought out the stores. They hired craftsmen and flaunted their fashions. Soon the standard braids or buns that women in the area wore gave way to waves and frizzy curls.

The municipal art treasures preceded the evacuees by a year. As of 1942, the museum of the city of Düsseldorf was in storage in the Adolfsburg castle near Oberhundem. The Sauerland region became a depot for the Aachen city archives, the court files from Essen, the Remscheid savings bank books, and the clothing fund of the Wuppertal office of the Reichsbahn. In the spring of 1945, all of this was smack in the main battle line, along the southern flank of the encirclement of the Ruhr. As of late 1944, Bomber Command and the Eighth Air Force were already leveling the way.

Towns such as Fredeburg, with its population of 3,300, had not experienced any warfare since the Soest Feud of 1444.[98] The people of Cologne were the besiegers at that time; now they cowered together white as sheets with the Fredeburgers in three beer cellars and three slate mines, having fled there in futile hopes of escaping the bombs. Outside, Major Wahle barricaded himself in with his thrown-together troops for the battle of the Nibelungs. The U.S. First Army could assume they would find someone like that in every village along their path—in Kükelheim, Bödefeld, and Westernbödefeld. That is why it sent out fighter-bombers that pounded Fredeburg to a pulp in one hour, just as eight thousand bombers had done to Cologne over four years.

The five hundred people who had been in the slate mine for days did not know what had happened to them. They breathed away their oxygen; not even a match could stay lit in the air. The local Nazi party group leader advised them to sleep and to talk as little as possible in order to save oxygen. The evacuees had brought this knowledge with them from the city bunkers. The young people could not be intimidated and continued to tease one another; the parents said the rosary, and the hearts of the elderly failed. Dean Schmidt gave people the last rites.

Fräulein Blydenstein and her friend Fräulein Lutz forced themselves to get up, and they ran straight to the city commandant, Police Inspector Hartrampf from Dortmund. Blydenstein told him of people's hardship. The Dortmund man had nothing to say to her because he was only in charge of the civilian administration. The combat commandant was Wahle, thirty-five years old and finished with life. "My wife and my children have already been taken prisoner; I'll fight to the last bullet." Fräulein Blydenstein was spokeswoman for those who wanted to surrender and had nothing to counter that with. Major Wahle was happy he no longer had to fight to win, but only to hold off the final defeat as long as possible. He was the Hitler of Fredeburg. "Those saying the rosary should finally wake up." They had never done anything but demand consideration from him in the proper defense of the town. House residents protested against having machine guns set up in their apartment windows. Where else could they go? Twenty-two people were living behind them, including two infants, two pregnant women, and two eighty-year-olds. In their self-pity the civilians demanded to be spared. "The building is not your life insurance! If I want to, I'll turn it into a fortress."

The Reich was a fortress. Harris, Hitler, and the Hitler of Fredeburg had very similar views on that. The ones who were slowly suffocating as they said the rosary in their tunnels were always running into combat commandants on both sides of the lines who had long since abandoned the principle of civil defense. Into the remotest corner, both the fortress's attackers and the besieged agreed that civilian personnel inside were not safe. No matter which direction the fire came from, they were ordered to get out of the way of the war. Sooner or later, all these ways led back to the front. There along the front, from Essen with its Krupp works to the cave of Veleda, the principle of noninsurance applied. "War is tough," Major Wahle replied to Fräulein Blydenstein. "It goes on to the bitter end. We too are deeply upset that the fatherland is being destroyed." At about 2 a.m. on the night of April 8, when Fredeburg was destroyed and the First Army entered the town, Major Wahle withdrew from his command post in the Villa Schmitz and moved to the northwest above the cemetery. There stood the village of Altenilpe, which then became the cornerstone of the German front.

A British leaflet from the early summer of 1943 reported that "on the night of May 23, 1943, within one hour the RAF dropped twice the bomb tonnage on Dortmund that the German Luftwaffe dropped on all of England in the six months from January 1 to June 30, 1943."[99] That amount was two thousand tons, a fraction of what was yet to come to the town. A leaflet dropped a short time later illustrated the magnitude of the endeavor. It showed an aerial photograph of the skeletonized, charred Hamburg, with the heading: "Time for the destruction of Germany." In that line is also the announcement on a 1942 flyer: "German cities, ports, and industrial areas important to the war effort shall be put to such a difficult test in terms of duration, force, or extent as has never yet been endured by any country." That might have been the case with Dortmund. Almost half of the 27,000 tons of bombs that were dropped on Dortmund fell between January and March 1945. Already very little had remained of the city center from the battles of the Ruhr in 1943 and 1944. Only sixty thousand of its previous population of 537,000 were still living in the city.

The major attacks of the Second Battle of the Ruhr in the fall of 1944 took 15,000 lives in the evacuated area between September and December. Among them were Poles who had just been brought to the Hoesch works; the attack on September 12 took them by surprise in the delousing shed. They had no time to get dressed and did not go into the air-raid trenches without clothes. The air defense that had turned the Ruhr into a bomber cemetery a year earlier now left the city of Solingen in the Bergisches Land region to a small unit of 170 British airplanes without putting up any fight at all. Two day raids on November 4 and 5 started a large wide-area fire over about one square mile, in the course of which 1,882 people died. The rest of the population then abandoned the city.

Dortmund was slowly starting to fill back up, but less with Dortmunders than with people from Aachen, Trier, and the area west of the Rhine, who were clearing out ahead of the liberating armies. In Dortmund, they got caught up in the continuation of the battle on the night of October 7, in which the city center around the train station was torn asunder. The train station was the precise radar target. Passenger trains rode right into the center of the attack. The passengers died at the entrances to the overflowing station bunker. "Bunker panic," the crushing and trampling in the few minutes as it filled, repeated itself during every raid in January. A heavy, high-explosive bomb was dropped into the crowd in front of the entrance of the already overfilled Eckey Tunnel in Dortmund-Huckarde. Fifty people seeking protection were left on the pavement, ten yards from underground safety.

Since the beginning of the "Ruhr plan," the closing off of all transportation in the area, residents had been caught in the trap. The night of February 21 let loose 2,300 tons of bombs with 70 percent incendiaries onto the center of the target, the station in South Dortmund. Freight being transported out of the district was blocked due to the blasted bridges and viaducts, so passenger traffic was also blocked. Low-flying strafers hunted down traffic movements by road, rail, or water; they even set their sights on streetcars. On March 3, fragment bombs and aircraft armaments hit a crowded streetcar in Dortmund-Eving. The Thunderbolts of the 373rd U.S. Fighter Group killed forty people. A businesswoman wrote to her husband at the front: "One hundred thousand people have to leave Dortmund because there is no way to maintain a life here."[100] There was also no way to leave. "Absolutely nothing has been left standing. There is no water, no lights, and no supply of food. Bomb craters have made all the streets leading out of the city impassable and all the bridges are down." Two of the heaviest bombardments within forty-eight hours drummed down on those cut off from the outside world. "Ferdi, October 6 was terrible, but nothing compared with March 12. It has been officially announced that this was the heaviest and most brutal raid that any city has ever endured during the war. Five hundred tons of bombs."

The munitions of the 1,100 Lancasters rattled the doors of the air-raid bunker. "The bunker was vibrating the whole time from the heavy and even heavier impacts at close range," wrote Hermann Ostrop, who later became mayor.[101]

> There was so much dust in our room that we could hardly see each other. Despite the angled entrances to the bunker, the doors flew open whenever a bomb hit nearby and had to be desperately held shut by the flak soldiers who fled into our room. In order to reduce the effect of the blast, most of the people in there were lying flat on the ground.

The very area that was lying flat on the ground was spoken to in leaflets circulated in March: "In order to prevent a protraction of the war, which has already been lost, the whole war industry of the Ruhr basin will be subjected to merciless bombardment." Sixteen cities were then named, including Duisburg, Essen, Dortmund, and Bochum. "All residents are hereby requested to leave the Ruhr area with their families immediately and go to a safe region."

THE SOUTH

Between 1633 and 1805, Freiburg changed hands twelve times. Five times it went to the House of Habsburg, five times to France, once to Sweden, and finally to Baden. Between 1677 and 1697, when Freiburg spent an extended period of time under the French crown, Marshal Vauban, the most famous military engineer and builder of his day, fortified the city with state-of-the-art defenses. The Further Austrian university city became one of the best-protected sites in Europe.

The outskirts of Freiburg, which had already been reduced to ruins in the Thirty Years' War, were leveled and replaced by a defensive belt of ramparts, trenches, and bastions, where the Dominican convents of Adelhausen and St. Katharina had once stood. A bit farther away in the Lehen suburb, there had also been a convent of Clarisse nuns. The most elegant was without a doubt Adelhausen, which is said to have housed a relative of Rudolf of Habsburg. Vauban did not care; the cloisters obstructed the fortification and he tore them down without exception: fourteen churches, convents, chapels. The grief-stricken nuns moved to the foreign city center.

King Louis XIV donated sufficient funds for new buildings and a church. Vauban's fortifications were, however, so superb that after Freiburg was returned to the Habsburgs in the Treaty of Rijswijk, the French had a very hard time conquering it in 1713. A year later, the Treaty of Rastatt again returned Freiburg to Austria. In 1744, the French had to storm yet a second time the fortifications they themselves had built, only to cede Freiburg back to Austria for the fourth time in 1748, as part of the Treaty of Aachen. They thus regarded Vauban's fortress to be impractical and, before withdrawing, razed it to the ground, which in turn made it far easier for them to retake the city in 1796.

When the fortification was fired upon in 1744, a number of old cathedral windows were broken, and when it was subsequently blasted, additional ones were obviously shattered. But the dark shimmer of the colored glass no longer corresponded to the tastes of the enlightened epoch, which preferred light. The loss of the mystical glow that came when the sunlight was refracted in the glass was not greatly missed. The Cathedral of Our Beloved Lady, which was begun in 1120 as a Romanesque basilica and transformed over the next three centuries of construction into a cathedral of purely Gothic style, dominated the market square like a high-masted ship anchored in the harbor. It was surrounded by the late Gothic Krebs banking house, the three-story city palace of the archbishop, the late baroque public library, the trim Old Granary with the corbie-step–gabled roof, as well as the street-level grain hall and the Geist cathedral hotel.

For the eastern and western blocs—Austria and France—everything was at stake in the dispute for Freiburg. The city lies before the Burgundy Gate, or "Belfort Gap," the low-lying area between the Vosges and the Swiss Jura. This thirty-five-mile-long pass runs past the Doubs River into the free county of Burgundy, the westernmost connection between the Spanish and Austrian Habsburgs. In 1678, Louis XIV had conquered Burgundy, which led Vauban to fortify Freiburg, the eternally annoying outpost of so-called Further Austria (*Vorlande*): a scattered Habsburg property, with its tip pointing toward France—an intolerable state.

Except for the cathedral windows and the leveled convents at the city's periphery, the town remained well preserved in the battles of the major powers. Vauban's defensive belt long maintained its medieval dimensions and street patterns. When Freiburg was destroyed on the evening of November 27, 1944, there was nothing at stake.

The outward justification was the railroad station and the presumed larger number of troops stationed there.

Freiburg was not a starting point for the occupation of southern Germany because of the Black Forest to the east. The French had already taken Strasbourg about fifty miles to the north. And other than that, the fighting of Tassigny's First French Army was limited to throwing remnants of the German Nineteenth Army across the Rhine. In late 1944, the unit that belonged to Heinrich Himmler's Upper Rhine Army Group still held a bulge in the front around Colmar up to the edge of the Vosges, but it was straightened out the following February.

Train lines led from Freiburg to Breisach and from Breisach to Colmar. The French advance to Strasbourg in the north and through the Belfort Gap in the south closed off the sides of the Colmar pocket. Himmler's army could move in only one direction: backward. It was the most remote corner of the western front.

On November 21, Joseph Sauer, a theologian at the University of Freiburg, wrote in his diary: "Great excitement here, the Burgundy Gate has been breached. The French are said to have reached Colmar already."[102] Three days later: "November 24. Enemy tanks have occupied Strasbourg. That is today's alarming news, accompanied by the music of the roaring enemy planes."

On the evening of November 27 in Freiburg, shellfire could be heard over thirty miles away. It had been a slightly foggy, beautiful day. The full moon appeared in the evening sky, casting a mild light on the busy pre-Christmas streets. Sauer lost himself in the breviary; the bells chimed eight o'clock. Two minutes later, the early warning sirens sounded simultaneously with the crashing of the first bombs. Sauer climbed down into the cellar along with Sister Theresa, who was responsible for the housekeeping, and the owners of the building, Fräuleins Lina and Elisabeth Reich. As they were hurrying down, the roaring swelled and the detonations came ever closer.

"I could feel something in me break down," wrote Sauer, "the confident hope that Freiburg would be spared." The diary entry was dated November 28 and began: "I still cannot wholly grasp what I shall write about yesterday evening. It is hard to think calmly that yesterday evening our beloved Old Freiburg found its demise."

Bomber Command had never appeared there before; the city had no notable industry and it was difficult for the airplanes to reach that distance. The 342 Lancasters that were now headed for the modest railroad yard with almost two thousand tons of bombs on board were guided from France by radar. Vehicle-mounted Oboe transmitters assured Freiburg the most precise bearings that Bomber Command was capable of giving. And besides that, the full moon was shining.

In view of the steady quaking and rattling in the cellar, Sauer granted the nun and the two Reich ladies general absolution. Ten minutes later the lights went out.

> Then all of a sudden there was a terrible, eerie roaring above us, so that all three started to scream as if our building were going to be hit, and at the same moment there was a deafening crashing sound, rattling and shattering and hissing, and a breathtaking sweeping through over our heads and faces from the southern basement windows. It left a cloud of dust that almost suffocated us. My Sister kneeled on the ground next to me and called out for the saints and for God's aid. All four of us were bent over to the left from the enormous thrust.

The neighbors broke open the hole in the cellar wall and asked if we were still alive. "At first we didn't know what happened, and couldn't tell whether the building above our cellar was still standing."

Now the early warning sirens sounded; the aircraft reporting centers had been outmaneuvered. That happened more frequently, now that the early warning stations along the English Channel, in Belgium, and the Netherlands had been taken out.

As a city of siege, Freiburg had an extensive system of old underground escape routes as well as the forest gorges on Schlossberg hill. That was where the residents of Freiburg spent the next few days, standing around in the dampness, listening. Just to be safe, the sirens constantly sounded the alarm: pre-alarm and full alarm. At regular intervals, the time-delay bombs of November 27 exploded. People in their nightshirts and overcoats had been staggering for forty hours through what used to be streets. Cellars were opened up where friends and relatives were believed to be. Flames shot out of the openings and caustic smoke escaped. The weapon was still alive in the cellar vaults; the fire continued to eat its way.

The attack lasted twenty-five minutes; at 8:30 p.m., the bombers withdrew. Professor Sauer climbed into the apartment; the building was still standing. His breviary was lying open in the same place it had been when he left it half an hour earlier at compline, but the Book of Freiburg had been closed. He went up to the high mounds of rubble of the university library and looked out at the theater and the secondary school, the Berthold Gymnasium, blazing brightly. The fires from the city center lit up the walls. "The moon shone so calmly and mildly down upon this wretched sight, but soon it was totally veiled under a solid cloud of dust."

Returning to the cellar, the seventy-two-year-old Joseph Sauer lay down on a cot and heard the lively shouting and movements of people headed for the city center. The redness of the fires there grew. Freiburg was a city of stone with very little half-timbering. That should have slowed down the 500,000 incendiary bombs. But they were left to do their work virtually undisturbed. People ran around with pails of water, but fire brigades were a rare sight.

Some of the people who lived in the center sought refuge from the developing carpet of flames on Schlossberg hill. Women, still recovering from childbirth, ran barefoot from a destroyed maternity home with their newborn infants in their arms. Halfway there, at the Old Cemetery, a group of homeless citizens had set up a night camp. Exhausted, they lay down in the damaged chapel on blankets they brought with them. Those who could not find space indoors lay down wrapped in coats and sheets between gravestones and trees. All eyes were constantly searching for a glimpse of horizon. The minster tower could be seen above the flickering blaze.

The next morning, Professor Sauer set off toward the city center accompanied by Friedrich Hefele, director of the city archives. Not until the early morning hours did the entire archive catch fire. Little remained of the university, Erasmus of Rotterdam's place of study, which along with the Church of Our Beloved Lady had the deepest roots in the city. Every part of the Holy Ghost Hospital was on fire. The Mother Superior, who had gathered together her few belongings to move into the charterhouse, reported that all the patients had been brought to safety—except for one woman who suffered a heart attack and one man who wouldn't get up.

All that was left of St. Martin's, the Franciscan convent church built in 1262, were the containing walls.

All the buildings on the right were nothing but mountains of rubble. You were taking your life in your hands to work your way through to Kaiser-strasse; we had to climb over high piles of debris and stone, beams, and iron and wire mesh. All around us was a new world, a horrid desert of stone, out of which only the minster stood out, having been left unscathed by this spook of hell. Tears came to my eyes and I saw a lot of people who were evidently in a similar state. Not a thing was left standing on Kaiser-strasse. But the minster was intact, its structures totally untouched.

Bricks and splinters covered the minster square ankle-deep. At the northern end, not even ten yards from the building, were two huge gaping craters. The building complex behind the choir had been swept away by an aerial mine. The entire ring of buildings around the square had collapsed. Two days later, the flames were still shooting out of the archbishop's palace. The raid took 2,700 human lives. The entire city area north and west of the minster had been totally destroyed. After twenty-five minutes of Bomber Command's operation, all that remained of the Gothic-baroque Old Town was over 1.3 million cubic yards of debris. None of the railway yards had been hit.

Bomber Command's best squadron was No. 5 Bomber Group. In wide-area attacks on German cities, their target-indicator techniques caused the greatest damages by far. The handiwork of this elite task force was responsible for the firestorms of Kassel, Darmstadt, Brunswick, Heilbronn, Dresden, and Würzburg. The complete incineration of cities did not result from a lack of precision; quite the contrary, it was a job of absolute precision. Also a part of No. 5 Bomber Group was 617 Squadron, which had been set up for the Dambusters' Raid on the Moehne dam. This elite force had tested the accuracy of marking precision targets and was able to transfer the technique to wide areas such that the area burned precisely within the intended boundaries. Strict control of the different colors of illumination flares by the master bomber was an integral part of this precision, as was the assessment of wind values, which was a constant source of error, and joint orientation on a fixed target.

Würzburg is not mentioned in the American-British target selection committee until early February 1945. Primary targets at that time were Berlin, Dresden, Chemnitz, Leipzig, Halle, Dessau, Erfurt, and Magdeburg. The bombs were supposed to strike evacuation movements away from the eastern front and troop movements toward it. Alternative objectives included Hildesheim, Würzburg, Pforzheim, Worms, and Nuremberg. In the British House of Commons, Conservative Party MP Reginald Purbrick explicitly mentioned Dresden, Freiburg, and Würzburg when he addressed the government on February 7, with regard to cities that had not yet been bombed, asking when it would be their turn.[103]

Würzburg was to go down on March 16. No. 5 Bomber Group was told around noon that this was to be done between 9:25 p.m. and 9:45 p.m. The weather was favorable, the sky was cloudless, and there was a slight mist on the ground. The 225 Lancasters and eleven Mosquitos started from different airfields between 5 p.m. and 6:10 p.m., gathering at Reading, the orientation point west of London. They set course for the mouth of the Somme, for Reims, the Vosges; they crossed the Rhine at Rastatt, continuing to their turning point at Pforzheim. Bomber Command never flew a direct line to its targets. At 7:45 p.m., sixteen Halifaxes between Liège and Colmar put up a Mandrel screen, a broadband radar-jamming system, which threw out radio noise that blinded the German early warning system so it could no longer detect any flight movements. Thus No. 5 Bomber Group could be registered at the very earliest at Freiburg. Before the Germans could determine what the raid objective was, the attackers were already there. The residents therefore had very little time to seek protection, and the death toll increased considerably.

The aircraft carried 1,127 tons of munitions, made up of flares, 389 tons of explosives, and 572 tons of incendiaries, which in conjunction with the marking techniques of No. 5 Bomber Group was a recipe for a firestorm. At 9:00 p.m., the unit passed over Lauffen on the Neckar, the marker force at the front, to prepare the target, followed by the main force, to destroy it.

Würzburg was identified using H2S radar. The marker force checked the wind, a westerly blowing at 25 mph. At 9:25 p.m., the blind markers started to frame the city center in green, using two thousand flares. Then the illuminators dropped flaming cascades to provide enough light for the target indicators. At 9:28 p.m., the master bomber decided that the green markings were well placed in the target, so follow-up marking in red could proceed. Those markings drifted three hundred feet to the east, but could still be confirmed by the final yellow marker bombs. The master bomber noticed the three-hundred-foot deviation and instructed the bomber force to keep to the western edge of the red light of the flares. When the clouds of smoke later rose, he had the frame remarked so the bomb drops would not lose their focus. That diminishes the effect.

In order to get maximum destruction out of a certain area, Sir Ralph Cochrane, commander of No. 5 Group, improved the conventional means of bombardment by adding a delayed-release technique. This required additional air training. The annihilation zone was divided into sectors, and the airspace was layered in segments. All aircraft, all squadrons in the group at their different altitudes, crossed a reference point on the ground. The reference point for Würzburg was the old bridge over the Main River. From there the planes spread out, each one with its own course and "overshoot." The overshoot determined how many seconds from the bridge the load was dropped.

The planes, spreading out from the Main bridge in different directions, at different altitudes, and with different overshoot times, achieved an optimized consolidation of time, area hit, and overall effect. Würzburg was marked with twenty thousand colored flares and destroyed by 256 high-explosive bombs and 397,650 incendiary sticks. No. 5 Group arrived back at its airfields around midnight; the pilots sat down together for a cup of coffee and the "postmortem conference," after delivering an outstanding piece of work. "Exceedingly well-marked," nodded a captain in 50 Squadron. The 467 Squadron added tersely that it was now generally possible to destroy a city with well-placed marking. The No. 5 report noted "good fires."[104]

No other city had a similar collection of art treasures within such a small area. The greatest art treasure was Würzburg itself, a creation of Balthasar Neumann. Later on, people asked how it was possible to destroy 90 percent of a city—one with the Main River running through it—in only seventeen minutes. The answer was fate and No. 5. All British bombing techniques were geared to forestall fire-fighting efforts. Fire that achieved its peak intensity in the shortest amount of time could not be extinguished. The speed of ignition depended on the qualities of the object—this one lay in the valley basin—the weather conditions, and the ability of the fireraisers to deal with both of these aspects. According to reports, the flames caught quickly. As the British knew, Würzburg's typical rococo architecture contained large amounts of wood. And the corresponding munitions were concentrated perfectly by No. 5. The result is inconceivable.

The city had previously been left virtually untouched by the bombing war, but its luck up to this point turned out to be its doom. Residents and rescue crews were not familiar with effective air-raid conduct. They had only heard through rumors of the treachery of cellars becoming overheated and the concentration of combustion gases. There were no concrete bunkers; the seventeenth-century fortifications had been last used during the religious wars, and even then only temporarily. The calming corridors in the depths had been left undisturbed and, though damp, were perfectly suited as shelters. But this diocesan city, with its art-blessed interior, believed itself to be free of any profound hostilities. Who could fail to love this baroque fortress crowned with towers? Churchill knew Würzburg; as a young attaché he had entered his name in the Golden Book of the city. There were no warmongering industries here, just spinets and altars. Since the Peasant Wars, which the people of Würzburg fought with their own hands, the worst enemy they faced had been the Swedes, whose most dastardly deed was to steal a library; a compliment to both robbers and the robbed. Libraries were meanwhile treated in a different way. And thus the experienced destroyers of the Royal Air Force met a community very out of touch with reality.

Many Würzburgers followed their instincts down to the Main River as soon as the raid started. Those who went down to cellars and air-raid shelters should have left them right after the all-clear signal, since fires developed quickly. Too many lacked this knowledge. They were afraid, felt safe in the cellars, and later totally lost their orientation when encircled by flames; they wandered around underground through the holes connecting the cellars and never found an exit to the street that was free of fire. Similar groups came from the opposite direction. "There was pushing and squeezing, hurrying and shoving and tripping over one another through ten or fifteen or more holes in the cellar walls. And at the end? Fire."[105] Cathedral curate Fritz Bauer wrote:

> No one will ever be able to describe the scenes that went on. None of the survivors knew how he got out. Later I ran into a woman from Ursulinengasse, who had lost two children in this underground quest for life. They had been torn from her in the crowd, fell underfoot the rushing masses, and were trampled to death. The woman told me that with a dry voice and no tears.[106]

There were seventy to ninety people lying under Ursulinengasse, a narrow lane. Curate Bauer climbed down into this hell to recover the body of the hospital doorman's wife.

> There was an eerie, desolate stillness down there. A woman was lying in a two-meter-long hole in the wall; as far as I could tell with my flashlight, her feet and head were charred, but her torso was fine and still dressed. The knitted vest the woman was wearing was largely undamaged. She wasn't who I was looking for.

It was a body that had suffocated and was then attacked by the fire. There were similar deaths on Domer Schulgasse, where death by heat guaranteed death by gases. The human remains there, Bauer reported, were disfigured by the hyperthermia but looked peaceful. "Some were sitting on their chairs; one woman was holding a child in her arms. Weren't the people afraid of the fire? Why didn't they leave the cellars, but instead remained sitting, literally, around the fire? I presume they were already dead by the time the fire reached them." Next to the shelter Bauer found a smoldering pile of coal.

Thousands died in the air war due to the development of gases in the basements. At Domstrasse no. 9, Bauer found seventy-six of them. "They had no injuries. Some had laid an arm across their face, others lay on their backs with their arms outstretched, and yet others had drawn up their legs. A lot had their mouths slightly open. The eyes were usually closed. Their hair was often wild, standing oddly on end." Foreign workers loaded the corpses onto transport vehicles. "It was a chaotic pile of human limbs, torsos, and heads. When the truck was full, they drove to the cemetery, where they let down one of the sides, grabbed into the mass of body parts with their hands and pulled whatever they got hold of off the truck bed."

On March 16, Würzburg lost about five thousand of its 107,000 residents. Twenty days later, the Seventh U.S. Army took over the city. The last 3,500 German troops entrenched there fought a bloody six-day battle among the ruins; for the American forces, it was the most bitter urban battle since Aachen. In both cases, fighting in the ruins favored the hopeless defenders. If the city had been razed to the ground in preparation for its capture, it would have been a military miscalculation. In the end, Würzburg was destroyed as an alternative target on the February 8 objective list. It did not have to be associated with any military use. The destruction was understood as a brilliant coup in and of itself. "South of the train station," as the British summary of operations of March 18 says, "the old town has been almost completely destroyed."[107]

The same night, while Würzburg was burning, a unit that had started out ten minutes before No. 5 Bomber Group turned southward at the Rhine, and then to the east at Rottenburg, reaching its destination, Nuremburg, at 10:15 p.m. At 8:53 p.m., the air-raid sirens blared out. Because the German antiaircraft was dead set on this fleet of 283 planes, they thought the Würzburg group was a diversionary maneuver and left it totally unchecked. But the Nuremberg mission was a chance for the crippled German fighter weapon to prove its once-feared mettle one last time in this war. Twenty-four Lancasters were taken out, a loss rate of 8.7 percent. In contrast to the No. 5 Group in Würzburg, in Nuremberg, the remaining planes encountered a city that was definitely not untouched. They worked their way through the city and finished off the destruction started the previous January 2 and February 20. On April 5, the U.S. 3rd Division would pour down another thousand tons of bombs.

On Würzburg Day, March 16, housing blocks were set on fire in Nuremberg's south city, in Steinbühl, Gostenhof, and Galgenhof. Not only were 517 lives taken, but fires were raised in the opera house and the Germanic National Museum. The only historic building destroyed was St. Clara's, the early Gothic church built in 1270 at the northeastern corner of the Convent of the Order of St. Magdalena.

At that time, the two parts of the settlement were not yet connected, the Reichsburg fortress and the imperial palace in the north with its estate officials and servants, and the quarters of the artisans and merchants south of the swampy Pegnitz River. Not until 1320 did the Henkersteg, Hangman's Bridge, connect the two worlds. In the Third Reich they were again separated, the Nuremberg of the Nazi party rallies its own entity, distant from the city of the people that opened up to the history of Germany like a window.

This best-preserved metropolis between the Middle Ages and the early Modern Age summarized the course of the centuries in its architecture. The Nazi city, however, had its own hangman's bridge to the stone imagery of the past. The hangman took possession of all that, at first renovating the fortress and fortifications, incomparably monumental structures that were stripped of their nineteenth-century romantic ornamentation and returned to a sparse, well-fortified archaism, ostensibly the rediscovered historical truth. The stone wall ring extending threateningly from the approach to the city once denoted a chilly rejection and unenterability to the adversary. This architecture of power intimidated the bombardier less than it had discouraged the attacking hordes of the past. Now the Nazified fortress served its own sustenance.

Wooden paneling, paintings of the sagas, coats of arms, and all the trappings of the nineteenth-century tale of Hohenstaufen imperial splendor were removed. The imperial stables became the Luginsland Reich Youth Hostel. Field-gray plaster, bare beams, and glaring rock formed a new suggestion of what used to be: not minstrel festival, ladies' grace, and accolade, but stronghold and catafalque, positions held to the last man. Dying generations, one after the other. Only the feud lasts. Of value is only that which is bought with blood.

Even in this front-line soldier version, the Salian royal castle in the Pentagonal Tower, the Hohenstaufen imperial castle in the round Sinwell Tower, the great hall, and the bower silently remained their auric selves. The Italian bastions of 1545 displayed classical fortress architecture that led directly to Marshal Vauban. The Imperial and St. Margaret's Chapels in the castle breathed a Sicilian airiness. According to the thinking of the Nazi gauleiters, however, flak artillery belonged atop the Ahnenburg castle. This led to 70 percent of it being destroyed.

The destruction of the lower city was just as impossible to ward off. Bomber Command considered the castle clearly as a military target and also as a first-class orientation point. The rock refuge originally built as protection from the Huns was ground away starting in August 1942; its present state is largely a replica. The first buildings to catch fire were the Pentagonal Tower and the castellan building. The Walpurgis Chapel was blown up on three sides by bombs, and in 1944, time ran out for the Ottmar chapel and the castle administration. In 1945, the imperial stables, the great hall, and the well house burned. Luginsland, literally, "look into the land," lost its sight, and the bower collapsed.

Nuremberg had stayed clear of the air war until January 1945. Either the navigators could not locate it or the night fighters shot the attackers to bits. Some of the bombs meant for Nuremberg that fell on October 12, 1941, hit the residents of Schwabach nine miles to the south; some hit the city of Lauingen on the Danube, over sixty miles from the target. A third squadron that lost its bearings attacked Lauffen on the Neckar, thinking it was Nuremberg. Lauffen, like Lauingen, are located on wide rivers that the dispersed crews mistook for the Pegnitz. The bombardment of Lauingen lasted four hours; seven hundred firebombs and two hundred blockbusters fell. In the face of his burning village, the mayor, who was suffering from heart disease, fell down and died.

The crews were instructed to fly the first major raid of the night of August 28, 1942, as low as possible. The Pathfinders dropped accurate markings with still-new illuminating bombs, but the munitions fell scattered as far as Erlangen. In Nuremberg, the original windows of the Albrecht Dürer House shattered, the roof of the castle flew off, and a direct hit crushed the castle gardener's house. In a brilliant attack, with planes dropping almost to ground level, the Nazi rally grounds were bombed. The mission's loss rate was 14.5 percent; one-third of the planes reached the intended city.

Southern Germany caused aggravation for Bomber Command all the way up to the Black Night, when the force lost ninety-five planes from a fleet of 795, the largest number that England had ever flown against Nuremberg. In theory, the bombing objective was the main freight train depot, and the creep-back effect, that involuntary tendency for each successive bomb drop to be progressively shorter of the declared target, had been incorporated into the calculations. Based on those calculations, the city center would be directly below the bomb bays. The bomber stream, over seventy miles long, would need seventeen minutes to pass over Nuremberg and destroy it.

At 11:22 p.m., they reached the Schelde River. Lying ahead of the attackers were 420 miles of enemy airspace: with a tailwind, it would take 103 minutes. The Germans had detected the approach over the North Sea and were circling in a holding pattern under a shining half moon. The British were startled to discover the enemy so early along the route. On top of that, treacherous weather caused each plane to leave a contrail. Flight Lieutenant D. F. Gillam of 100 Squadron climbed to 22,000 feet in his Halifax and looked down regretfully at the weighed-down Lancaster comrades flying about two thousand feet below him. He decided against a dogfight with the German fighters.

With their bombs on board, the entire force was too ponderous to pick a fight. They dropped their incendiary and high-explosive bombs, hoping to hit the right city in the right place and that the night sky would let them get away undiscovered.

> I watched fascinated, as a twin-engined German type overtook him, approaching just under the contrail.... The German got underneath the Lancaster and fired straight into his belly with an upward-firing gun. The bomber took no evasive action at all. There was an explosion and it blew clean in half.... My stomach turned over and we tried to get even higher.[108]

One Halifax unable to climb to a higher altitude dumped its load, turned, and headed home. A Pathfinder that could not get above 14,000 feet pressed on, with bombers crashing down past it "like a blazing inferno, some too close for comfort." The last eighty-two were shot down approaching Nuremberg.

Bomber Command lost 545 men in this mission. Those who managed to make it through to Franconia were so miserable that one in six mistakenly attacked Schweinfurt, forty-five miles northwest of Nuremberg, and another group bombed the rural districts east of there. The village of Schönberg, buried away in the forests, was marked and burned down. Livestock raced around the pastures as if mad; burnt pig cadavers littered the farmyards. Fowl flew the coop and the residents stood grimacing before their destroyed homes, the women sobbing helplessly. The fiasco of Bomber Command's Black Night marked the abandonment of all remaining hope that Germany could be forced from the air to capitulate. For the present, the British had had enough of Nuremberg.

The U.S. Eighth Air Force appeared midday on October 3, 1944, with 454 Flying Fortresses. They hit the choir of St. Sebald's Church, the castle, the Dürer House, and landed a direct hit on the Peller House behind it, which had been among Germany's most beautiful patrician residences. The bombs plowed through the four-hundred-year-old St. Rochus Cemetery, slinging around the sarcophagus-like sandstone monuments, uncovering the resting bones. Bomber Command returned on January 2, 1945, guided by Oboe transmitters in France, with 2,300 tons of bombs on board. The drops covered the city center with a concentration of more than fifteen tons per acre. After fifty-three minutes, Old Nuremberg was rubble.

The Tucher Castle, the Hans Sachs and Veit Stoss Houses, the Holy Ghost, St. Aegidius's, and Mastersingers' churches, the entire castle grounds, and a total of two thousand medieval homes were crushed in a vandalistic fit of raving madness, but perhaps that impression is deceiving. Historic shrines such as Hildesheim, Magdeburg, Dresden, Würzburg, and Nuremberg, which had all remained intact throughout much of the war as they were militarily irrelevant, were destroyed in series during the last three months of the war. To all appearances, that is the work of reason. Were not these cities the great symbols, demonstrating to the German people their background? Their past was made of these imperial palaces and offices, workshops and royal residences, cathedrals and markets, cloisters and alleyways, universities and hospitals, bridges and dams. They all existed long before any German state had existed. The state that declared the Thousand Year Reich retroactively confiscated a thousand years of history and turned it into its Nuremberg cult. When history became cult it was leveled. Was that cult not the guarantor of the recently established European Reich of the German Nation? To assure that none of that remained, the rubble was pounded twice more by the Americans and once more by the British.

A total of 6,369 people left their lives under 13,807 tons of bombs in Nuremberg. After the January raid, hordes of rucksack-carrying twelve-year-olds who had been evacuated to a children's camp in Kinding, in the Upper Palatinate, returned to the city to look for their parents. Despite the winter cold, people threw away shoes and clothing they thought had come in contact with phosphorus, fearing they would burn to death. Curiosity drew people from the countryside to have a look at the damage. Many refused to leave the bunkers. When the city was conquered in April, they were still sitting there. Air and water supplies had broken down. Dr. Kurt Bingold, who had been persecuted by the Nazis, became director of the municipal hospital once the occupation began. He had the "bunker rats" taken out. "We were in the Tucher bunker. Everyone was sleeping, whether sitting, lying down, or standing. That night there was a calmness nothing short of eerie."[109]

The raid of January 2 also damaged a company that Allied economic experts attributed with having produced four thousand tanks annually, including the legendary Panther combat vehicle. Weighing forty-five tons and moving at about 28 mph, it was the reason that MAN, the Augsburg-Nuremberg Machine Works, had a "priority 1" rating throughout the entire air war. This rating did not lead to any significant interruption in tank production. In the September 1944 raid, 173 of 233 U.S. Flying Fortresses were given this objective alone. They succeeded in cutting one week of MAN production output by 30 percent. The Panther was still being assembled until January 1945. When on January 2 Bomber Command destroyed "priority 1" along with everything else, tanks were no longer helping the Wehrmacht advance.

The company manufactured a product in their Augsburg plant that was highly alarming to Bomber Command: U-boat engines. They were unmatched in this field in Germany. That is why the RAF commissioned No. 5 Bomber Group in the middle of the Battle of the Atlantic. Sir Arthur Harris had just taken his position as Air Marshal and needed a daring exploit in a barely accessible corner to pep up his profoundly depressed troops. Understanding the psychological effects of bombing on both the bombers and the bombed, Harris added to the orders that visiting a city that had been spared up to now would certainly unnerve the population, "who thought they were still outside the danger zone."[110]

No. 5 Bomber Group chose the twelve best crews from 44 and 97 Squadrons. To make sure that precisely the workshops that manufactured the diesel engines were destroyed, the flyers needed both daylight and the lowest possible attacking altitude. They trained for the mission in their tenacious way, with specially equipped Lancasters and using a map of the facility, presumably acquired by a MAN employee, a German-Canadian, who disappeared in 1938. On April 17, 1942, at 3:00 p.m., twelve airplanes with eighty-five men and forty-eight high-explosive bombs set off for the opposite coast near Le Havre, where they dropped to a flying altitude of thirty-three feet, in order to remain below radar coverage.

A German fighter squadron attacked and downed four Lancasters near Paris. The remaining eight reached Augsburg around 8 p.m., setting their bearings along the course of the Lech River, which led them directly to MAN.

> Our objective was not simply the factory, but specific production halls. We knew what they looked like from photographs and could identify them right where they were supposed to be. The flak was firing at us fast and dense and with a flat trajectory. We were flying so low that the Germans even shot at their own buildings. We later found bullet holes in all of our airplanes. The large halls, which were our target, were right in front of us. My bombardier let the bombs go.[111]

Some of the pilots, however, saw the production halls of the paper factory in Haindl in front of them, or they saw the mechanical cotton spinning and weaving works, accepted that they were MAN, and released the bombs from their bays. The planes got caught in flak fire and crashed. Five set off for home. MAN suffered 2.4 million marks worth of damage, and some of the U-boat engines were delivered a few days late. But that was not how Germany lost the war. For that, cities had to be dealt with differently.

Augsburg had been an international financial center in the sixteenth century. Its magician, Jakob Fugger, financier of the House of Habsburg, invested half a million guilders in the fateful election of the emperor in 1519. A nineteen-year-old candidate who could not speak German, had never seen Germany, never thought of ruling there, and later visited there only once every nine or ten years asserted himself with the help of Fugger's funding, and called himself Charles V. He remained the only German emperor who stepped down due to displeasure with a failure of his, which was called Augsburg.

Between the Augsburg Confession of 1530 and the (Religious) Peace of Augsburg in 1555, the Germans failed to accomplish what the French completed so perfectly a short time later: to create a centralized state out of the decline of medieval authorities. When that state finally came to be in 1871, after a delay of three hundred years, this empire—given its nonsimultaneity with the history of its neighbors—displayed some peculiarities, theoretically of a remediable nature. The excessive destruction of the war from 1939 to 1945, however, meant that in the seventy-four years of this delayed empire, everything that *could* fail *did* fail. It is obvious that in addition to the superficial, tangible reasons, a trend developed in the deeper historical path taken. We can imagine what direction Europe would have taken in 1519 if Francis I of France—young Charles's challenger—had become emperor.

The Diet of Augsburg in 1530 tried to ease religious tensions by bringing together the Catholic emperor along with the guarantor of his universal Christian rule, the Pope, and the German religious reformers and princes, in order to draft a written agreement, the Augsburg Confession. There was nothing they could agree on, however, since the religious questions contained questions of power as well, which divided the emperor from the Estates of the Empire, the princes, and the cities. It was possible to formulate the Christian creed, if necessary, but only arms could settle the conflict of interest between local and central powers.

Things were different regarding the French Huguenot wars. They were fought between the parties of nobles; one of them—the Bourbons—succeeded on the battlefield and made the brilliant decision to adopt the Catholicism of the opposing party. As the new holders of the central authority, the converted king guaranteed tolerance to the steadfast Huguenot masses. After stepwise withdrawal, after coercion and massacre, Richelieu's state church finally became established. By contrast, the Peace of Augsburg stood out from that as humane and reasonable. The religious denominations coexisted and the local lords decided which was valid in their respective jurisdictions. This was agreed upon twenty-five years after the Augsburg Confession, but only because in the meantime armed battle had decided nothing. The side of the princes in the Schmalkaldic War was defeated because Charles V lured renegades from their ranks, and Charles lost because he led neverending wars against Francis I. And so instead of conquering the princes, he had to make concessions to them. The French wars, however, were based solely on the opposition between France and the Habsburg dynastic power. It had little to do with Germany.

The Protestant Schmalkaldic League could have fought off the Habsburgs, and the Habsburgs could have forced the princes into a centralized state. Either would have been conceivable and fruitful. Instead, based on the state of things, the most obvious and, as it turned out, most miserable thing happened: the balancing of two anachronisms. On one side was a shapeless empire of loose titles, retaining the property of a dynasty that fought, alternately, either the Turks or the French. On the other side were the territorial princes who divided Germany into an absurd collection of smaller and smaller states. Religion was a matter of the princes, and the matter of the princes was a matter of advantage. This was a situation that led straight into the horrors of the seventeenth century and the confusion of the eighteenth. The princes inevitably stumbled into the maelstrom and service of the absolutist nation states around them.

After Germany had spent three centuries as an object for the power politics of forces far more powerful than itself, it had bottled up a desire for power that gushed out in two world wars. From 1914 to 1918, it was still within the scope in which the imperial adversaries also fought out their causes. Then, after again experiencing a feeling of powerlessness as prescribed by the Treaty of Versailles, a slave-holder state emerged all around—as in the factory yards of MAN and Messerschmitt—which appeared like a break from the history of civilization. "The natural man," according to the Augsburg Confession, "receiveth not the things of the Spirit of God." His nature is evil. If he is not granted the providence of God, then he will sometimes choose to do evil, "to worship an idol, to commit murder, etc."

As if to prove that, four hundred Jewish women were abducted from Hungary as forced workers. Not unlike Russian prisoners or forced laborers, they were assigned air-raid protection that left them at the mercy of the massacre. "Russian civilians," according to a file memorandum at MAN, "are by no means to be allowed to enter the adit."[112] Outside the tunnel, in the slit-trench shelters where the work slaves hid, life was virtually thrown away under the hail of bombs. On February 25, 1944, a raid of 199 planes of the U.S.

Eighth Air Force on the Messerschmitt works killed 380 people, including 250 concentration camp prisoners. The high-explosive bombs had landed directly in their trench. In the next raid in March, the concentration camp laborers sought refuge elsewhere. "This time the prisoners ran into the forest because they did not trust the slit trenches. And this time the bombs also fell in the forest. The injuries caused by splintering trees and branches were worse than the first time."[113] A Luftwaffe warning squad noted: "The enemies dropped their bombs on this forest. The corpses are lying all around, sown like seeds. Sixty dead have been counted, including fifty prisoners of concentration camps."[114] On April 13, another U.S. raid on Messerschmitt destroyed the satellite concentration camp set up in the suburb of Haunstetten, a bunch of wooden barracks.

The prisoners and work slaves were Russians, Poles, Italians, French, Belgians, Dutch—nationalities among which the Germans had spent the centuries of their history of powerlessness. That history culminated under the bombs. No means of force that either enemy armies or German armies under enemy orders had directed against the land and people resembled even remotely the force of the bombing war.

Cities with strong munitions industries, such as Nuremberg and Augsburg, also had an ample population of slaves. They made up a large segment of the industrial proletariat that Churchill and Harris had set their sights on as a demoralization objective. The slaves were demoralized enough. The Germans kept them in a state of humiliation that was uncommon in the power relations among the European peoples. Such treatment was previously reserved only for colonized peoples. Hitler's regime treated the European victories as colonial conquests, especially in the East. This was propagated broadly and sympathized with broadly. In the colonial age, the master races held sway. A master race requires a slave race, and the Germans set up this antiquated model right in the middle of Europe.

The German war industry could not survive without forced labor. The sick manner of the master race, however, was a drive in itself. Characteristically, its echo came from the older, more experienced master race. The bombing war that brought the fall of the Reich was a procedure developed in the colonial wars. As a young pilot, Harris had practiced civilian bombing against rebelling Indians. His shock psychology, as well, was originally tested as a culture shock. Primitive tribes in thatched huts who were confronted with the weapons arsenal of the industrial empire threw themselves down, dazzled. Their lances and idols were disenchanted; they obeyed.

In the bombing war from 1940 to 1945, each side charged the other with barbarism; in that, they were certainly not wrong. Both claimed that the answer lay in the physiognomy of the enemy. That was an excuse. The master race and those bombing it each followed their own history, had an exchange, retained their dissimilarity, and were the perpetrators of their actions. These were not circumstances of coersion. The bombardment of the slave, however, lay outside this exchange of force. It served no purpose. In the bombing war, a total of about 42,000 foreigners were killed from a total of 7.6 million in the areas that were bombed.

The February 25 raid on Messerschmitt ended the American "Big Week" of February 20 to 25, which was aimed at the fighter production, "and," as the British Air Ministry added, "the towns associated with these key installations."[115] The British flew nightly support raids during Big Week. The Eighth Air Force dropped five hundred tons of bombs around noontime onto the Augsburg suburb of Haunstetten; this was the precision attack. At 10:40 p.m., Bomber Command appeared in the sky above the city center. Tower lookout Böld atop St. Ulrich's Church reported that "suddenly all hell broke loose. In a wide circle all around St. Ulrich's Church came hit after hit of incendiary and high-explosive bombs. After about ten to fifteen minutes the Old Town was a sea of flames."[116]

Augsburg, with a population of 185,000, had not a single air-raid bunker. Public air-raid shelters offered space for 5,500, and then there were cellars that "rocked like a little boat in a storm."[117] The city had not experienced any air raids up to then; the power went out. People stayed sitting underground, listening for the all-clear signal. They never heard it; the alarm system failed. Meanwhile, Air District Command VII, stationed in nearby Munich, had received word of another bomber group approaching. "What would happen," thought duty officer Thomas Wechs, "if the second wave is also headed for Augsburg? The city is burning over there. No one will be thinking about a new threat."[118] Munich deliberated and argued whether it would be better for Augsburg to cancel the alarm or not. Finally it was decided. "Augsburg remained on highest alert." Since the alarm sirens were not functioning, it was all the same.

After three hours, the people in the cellars climbed back out, took care of the injured, helped to free those buried in rubble, and the fire brigade turned out against the main fire. And thus they ran head-on into the second wave, which arrived at 12:55 a.m. "People who were perhaps able to salvage some of their furniture were sitting there; others wandered around panic-stricken, and yet others were pulling a handcart with the remains of their worldly goods, oh it was a picture of misery that I will never, never forget my whole life."[119] That is how eyewitness Herr Bessler experienced it. The people reacted just as Bomber Command had expected: they were in a daze. "Suddenly it all started up again. I simply couldn't and wouldn't believe that it was another attack; I thought instead of time-delay fuses."[120] By the time the Augsburgers got over their incredulity and horror, they were caught up in the second raid. They sought refuge in trench shelters, bomb craters, houses that had not yet caught fire. The canals of the Lech River had meanwhile burst, and icy water gushed into leaky basements. The lookout on St. Ulrich's tower had stuck to his post. "The second attack was worse than the first. Huge shells were falling. We could tell they were blockbusters by the blast that threw us back into the interior of the tower. We stayed up there about another ten minutes but then had to give up due to the heavy smoke and sparks."[121]

After the second raid, the fire department started laying out long hoses and pumping water from the Lech canals; the hydrants had been destroyed, as usual. But the frost made it impossible to fight the blaze. "The water from the Brunnen stream and the pond in the municipal gardens," reported a firefighter, "had a lot of ice in it due to the heavy frost. This caused thick ice crusts to develop in the hose lines, which quickly constricted their diameters. Thus there was less water flowing into the pressure hoses so they too froze in no time."[122]

The fire didn't let the icy cold get in its way. It ignited the pride of the city, the Renaissance City Hall, built by the city's architect Elias Holl. It was the evidence and hallmark of Augsburg's financial power, which once spanned the globe. "The City Hall burned like hell," reported a firefighter assigned to the rescue squad. "Flames were licking out of all the windows and sparks were flying. It made an incredible wind, although the weather itself was actually totally calm—an icy, clear February night."[123] Just as the firefighters had laid hoses across Perlachberg hill from the Lech canal near the mill, Kresslesmühle, and were about to wrench the unique monument from the fire's grip, the second wave struck. They took cover, and when they later returned, the fire engine and pump had been bombed.

All of the splendid merchant city's checks had bounced, and the city collapsed in the sharp frost under the rage of the flames. "Major conflagrations developed after the raid," read the succinct police report, "some of which spread out over entire city districts. Combating fires was possible only to a limited extent because most of the water hoses froze from the icy cold."[124]

Inaccurate marking in the second wave prevented the density of munitions necessary for a firestorm. The following day, eighty thousand Augsburgers fled the city. The air war took 1,499 human lives there, half of them on that night in February.

On the way to the Diet of Augsburg, Charles V made a stop in Munich.[125] He watched military parades and was shown new weapons and the storming of a city. For that, a mock-up of a fortified castle was erected. It did not survive the storm, in the course of which the attackers also lost eight men. It took 102 years before reality caught up with the dramatization. The Swedes stood before Munich, took the ramparts, occupied the city, and were generally accommodating. Extortion was common during the Thirty Years' War; it was the so-called war contribution that allowed the citizens to save their city from ruin by paying a ransom. The Swedes demanded 450,000 guilders.[126] Munich paid 104,000 in cash and 40,000 in jewelry; that made up their liquid assets. For the current expenditures, there was nothing else to do but draw up a bill. The Swedes agreed. They accepted the sum as a down payment, and as collateral for the rest of the debt they took forty-two dignitaries hostage and then withdrew. Two years later, in 1634, the army returned and collected again; this time their bad manners had been radicalized. They reduced the surrounding villages to ashes and brought the plague with them, which killed a quarter of the population—seven thousand people.

When National Socialism entered Munich, an attack was again simulated. On August 5, 1933, between ten and eleven o'clock in the morning, an air raid took place. As bells pealed and sirens sounded, paper bombs weighed down with sandbags fell from the sky. Fire brigades and SA men in gas masks conducted an air-raid drill. The attackers were successful. Entire districts around the train station, Marienplatz, and the Residenz, the huge palace complex, were reduced to rubble.

Nine years later, the simulation became reality. Mostly blockbuster mines and high-explosive bombs were dropped from the eighty-nine Lancasters and Stirlings. All eyes were on them to observe their impacts on streets and housing. The actual blasts were almost playful. Some window fronts were blown in at one fell swoop while leaving the building next door totally unscathed. Old treetops had their necks wrung, and buildings were split in two like sides of beef with their innards hanging out: bathtubs, stovepipes, bed linens. There were 149 lives lost, but the population showed no signs of displeasure. You had to grin and bear it. Young women squealed with delight when a basket of fresh laundry was pulled out of the chaos. The expressions of men who knew the meaning of war became "like suddenly aged faces of sullen, naughty boys," noted art historian Wilhelm Hausenstein in his diary. "The faces seemed to have aged, but were not grown-up. Very unpleasant."[127]

Three attacks from March to September 1943 came closer to the gravity of the situation. It took days to free people buried in the rubble, only one in three still alive. Construction equipment and diggers were blocked by fires and glowing embers under the debris. The residents were incapable of putting out fires themselves; they were too depressed or hectically trying to save their favorite pieces of furniture instead of fighting the fires, which they saw as lost causes anyway. Besides, there were too few men present who could have rolled up their sleeves and helped out.

In early November, Bomber Command punched gaping holes in the cultural buildings. One wing of the Bavarian State Library was hit, the national theater burned down, and eighteen churches recognized as historical monuments were damaged. Hausenstein noted that from an aesthetic perspective, "there is perhaps something trashy (I cannot put it any other way) about the rubble from the destruction. A modern metropolis does not seem able to yield noble ruins. In many places it looks like a garbage heap."[128] The children's asylum on Hochstrasse had also become a target, as did the municipal orphanage, the Home for the Blind on Ludwigstrasse, and seven homes for the elderly. But these events were not truly experienced, Hausenstein feared. It did not penetrate into their minds but was barely just accepted due to a mixture of stupor, sensationalism, and apathy. Around this time, people started trampling one another to death in front of the air-raid shelters.

Before the alarm sounded, eight hundred people were already standing in front of the Salvator brewery's storage basement. When its door was opened, a woman fell, and people pushing in behind tripped over her. The crowd raced in over these people as well; eight people died. On April 25, 1944, No. 5 Bomber Group arrived on the scene. The markers took the main train station as their orientation point; after they dropped target indicators, a few high-explosive bombs and many—870,000—incendiaries were placed. The city went up in smoke and flames; yellow-black vapors surged through the streets. The fires could be seen from as far away as the Alps; four weeks later, a burnt smell still hung in the air. About three-quarters of Munich's monuments were destroyed, according to Hausenstein. "With fateful consistency, I dare to say sinister and ironic regularity, the bombardment spared large buildings that were ugly or insignificant."[129]

In July 1944, the U.S. Air Force pounced on Munich with a million incendiaries in seven raids. The first four killed 1,471 people. Private funerals were no longer possible because of a coffin shortage. The corpses, or parts of them, were given identifying markings and buried in mass graves in the North Cemetery and the Perlach Forest. The Americans made extensive use of time-delay fuses in the July attacks. The bombs penetrated the apartment buildings and got caught in the ceilings between the stories. For days on end they continued to explode day and night with a deafening bang, toppling walls and killing residents in their sleep.

Household effects that could be saved were lying around on the streets: bundled-up blankets, chests of drawers from former days, heirloom paintings that had been passed down for generations. Old women crying to themselves watched over the junk. At the Victory Gate, Hausenstein noted, a bronze lion was left standing on its head for over a month. The city's ruination was so radical that people could not grasp it, even though it was staring them in the face.

> People think they are wandering through an absurd dream. The Frauen-kirche, St. Michael's, and the Theatiner Church are still standing, thank God. The streets are totally dead. The population seems to have melted down to a third or a quarter of what it was in one blow. Gruff girls, in a new manner seemingly whorelike, who are apparently indifferent to what has happened, go about their business.[130]

From September to October, the Americans added another twelve raids. Damage to the sewer system, not to mention the garbage that could not be removed due to all the rubble, made Munich dirty, joyless, and intimidated. On November 22, the Americans landed a direct hit on the high altar of the Frauenkirche; St. Michael's, the largest and most renowned Renaissance church north of the Alps, suffered multiple hits in the barrel vault; and the Damenstiftskirche, the Convent Church of St. Anna, was devastated. On the third Sunday of Advent, Bomber Command dropped four tons of aerial mines and eighty thousand incendiary bombs onto Munich's city center, after having given the city a break from the nineteenth to the fortieth air raid. A bit farther away, the Neue Pinakothek art museum, Glyptothek antique sculpture museum, the Maximilianeum parliament building, market hall, two cemeteries, the Brown House Nazi headquarters, the State Opera, the grounds of the SS Reich leadership, and the Krone Circus were leveled. "The city is in such a wretched state," Hausenstein recorded, "that it is impossible to mention each detail."[131] This was only the forty-second of seventy-three attacks.

After the forty-fourth raid, which sent down 1,040 high-explosive bombs and 400,000 incendiary sticks and killed 505 people, Hausenstein wandered around the snow-covered city for three hours. It was January 19, 1945. The destruction was absolute. Some building façades were still standing; "cracked shells" that would fall within the next two or three attacks. How could the future even begin to build upon such a ruin?

> Assuming the monumental buildings and the best apartment buildings, which share the monumentality and are as necessary to it as the air, as the active element of continuity, without which a city is nothing, so assuming that all these pieces could theoretically be restored: it remains inconceivable that such an endeavor would be feasible.

There was no money to finance a project of such magnitude, "since ultimately it would mean re-creating the work of eight hundred years, at least in its main aspects."[132]

This underscores how reasonable the "war contribution" in former wars actually was. Gustavus Adolphus ruined the city only financially, a method beneficial for both sides. Rebuilding eight centuries, however, surpassed the already unsurpassable question of cost, because "the mere idea of even wanting to do this probably already seems absurd." Perhaps individual pieces which served as an anchor for the city could be "prepared," in order "barely to suggest the tradition in this way." Maybe the Frauenkirche, if her vaults could withstand the wetness, the snow, and the frost; the Theatiner Church, part of the Residenz palace; maybe the State Library, or maybe the Alte Pinakothek. "But heaven knows if it will even be possible to pose these questions at all one or two months down the line."

In the February raids by the American forces, the Frauenkirche suffered another hit. All of the vaults of the principal nave and aisles up to the abutment collapsed. It was partially replicated, as was the Theatiner Church. Munich lost 6,632 people—including 435 children—from its total population of 835,000.

"War contributions" as a line of a business in war continued with the French invasions in the Palatinate and Spanish Wars of Succession. The city of Stuttgart was thus required to pay harsh contributions, which brought the budget in the Duchy of Württemberg totally out of balance, especially since similar ransom money had been paid during the Thirty Years' War to the side of the Habsburg emperor. After a clear imperial victory over the Swedes in 1634 in the battle of Nördlingen, the Swede's tool, the Heilbronn League, also disappeared. The emperor bled the disloyal councilors, and aside from that, fifty buildings in Stuttgart were lost in the Thirty Years' War.

The pressing financial emergency made it necessary to relax the ban on Jews living and doing business in Stuttgart, which had been imposed by Eberhard the Bearded, the first Duke of Württemberg. Despite fierce protests by the estates, Duke Eberhard Ludwig authorized one Jew (in 1710) and later another four (in 1712) to settle in his duchy. These were the court Jews admitted in the interest of balancing the state budget. In 1734, Joseph Süss Oppenheimer worked his way up to become finance minister and confidant of Duke Karl Alexander. The budget did not suffice for his representational needs. Oppenheimer improved the state of the coffers by raising taxes, dealing in offices, monopolies, and minting lower-quality coins.

With the sudden death of the duke, the anger of the estates was turned against his financial juggler. He was taken from the court to Stuttgart, sentenced in a vile show trial, and executed. It was a public festival. The gallows towered high above the execution stand so the crowds could watch; tribunes were erected for the dignitaries. "Süss the Jew," whispered Duke Karl Rudolf, had to "foot the bill for Christian knaves." He himself was a crafty knave who diverted the public anger over the royals' financial tricks to the financier. The estates were not concerned by the dodges, as all they heard was Eberhard the Bearded's malediction humming in their ears, "gnawing worms."

Seligmann, kosher butcher and prayer leader for the Stuttgart congregation, stood by Oppenheimer in his final hour. Consequently, the angered estates demanded that all Jews be expelled from Stuttgart—four families. The court was reluctant to dispense with the Jewish services and contacts to the finance market, and appointed more court Jews, the Kaulla siblings from Hechingen. Their financial institution was given the label "court bank" as of 1802, and had friendly relations with the Rothschild family.

Much to the chagrin of the people of Stuttgart, four male Kaullas and all their descendants were given full citizenship in return. The Jewish congregation had since grown to 109 people in fourteen families. Starting in 1819, Jews were admitted to study at the university; their deceased were buried outside the city limits. The last Kaulla, former director of the regional court Otto Kaulla, emigrated to England with his remaining assets of ten Reichsmarks in the spring of 1939.

One year earlier, German Jews had been fined one billion Reichsmarks as punitive payment for fire damages. The fires had been set on the Reich pogrom night, the so-called *Kristallnacht*. In accordance with the ordinance for the "Restoration of Clean Streets," all Jewish fire-insurance policies were paid out to the Reich. After extorting a wealth tax of 20 percent, the demanded sum was still not accumulated, though according to the Nazi newspaper *NS-Kurier*, the 3,600 Stuttgart Jews alone held assets worth 124 million. A day later, a "Jewish contribution" went into force, which plundered all Jews with property valued at more than five thousand Reichsmarks.

On December 1, 1941, one thousand Stuttgart Jews were carried off to Jungfernhof, a concentration camp near Riga, Latvia. On March 26, 1942, Hilde, a twenty-one-year-old nurse, volunteered for the task of digging out a trench in the forest near Bickern. This was a ploy. She was killed with her parents and relatives, the six members of the Justitz family, Stuttgart jewelers. On May 5, 3,500 incendiaries fell on the city area: it was the beginning of the first series of raids.

On September 12, 1944, from 10:59 to 11:30 p.m., No. 5 Bomber Group engulfed Stuttgart in a firestorm. One thousand people were killed, a large segment of them from carbon monoxide poisoning in the cellars. A woman who lived in the western part of the city escaped the gas cellar at the corner of Traubenstrasse and Lerchenstrasse thanks to a water corridor made by the police. She reported, "We had to climb over the dead bodies to get out of the sea of flames. When I turned onto Faltstrasse, I couldn't help thinking that we had just experienced the Judgment Day."[133]

Heavy thunderstorms had swept through Stuttgart in September. Four British raids on the nights of July 24 to 29, 1944, had torn off the roofs, and now the rainwater flooded the basements that had been set up as makeshift apartments. No. 5 Group came with only a few airplanes. The Judgment Day started when Mayor Karl Strölin told the city councilmen that "the enemy had illuminated the airspace like daylight in a heretofore unprecedented massive drop of target indicator flares."[134] No. 5's specialty, increasing the effect of the munitions through extremely careful marking of the bombardment area, achieved a firestorm here, its ultimate goal. According to Strölin, "on this raid, nothing landed in open countryside."[135]

The seventy-five blockbuster bombs, 4,300 high-explosive bombs, and 180,000 incendiary sticks fell in high concentration in an area of narrow streets and very high, densely built blocks in the general area of Hegelstrasse, Hölderlinstrasse, and Schwabstrasse. Its location in a valley was also favorable for a firestorm, which then spread out over two square miles. The unusual speed with which it developed cut many Stuttgarters off from their way to bunkers and hillside tunnel shelters. The cellars were the only protection they were able to reach in time. "A great many people unfortunately died, evidently from carbon monoxide poisoning from the fumes that developed in the streets when the neighboring ground floors and basements had burned out."[136]

As the pastor of the garrison church congregation explained, still greatly affected by what had happened, people who were elderly, frail, or ill, and could not manage the strenuous trip to the tunnels, just sat down in the basements. "The cellar walls quaked. Every moment—and they seemed to last forever—we thought the end had come; Gethsemane, Golgotha, it seemed so near."[137] The fire in the house next door drove the blaze into the cellar where the invalids were sitting. They pulled themselves together. The entrance to the building was already in flames. There was nothing else to do but climb out the windows onto the street, which was covered with a layer of debris from tree branches and streetcar overhead wires.

Where should we go now? We fought our way up Herdweg, but ran into such a firestorm that it didn't seem possible to get through. So we went back to Hegelplatz. The same horrendous sights! The old slaughterhouse at Hegelstrasse 1–5 was one big enormous bonfire. A man from upper Falkertstrasse told us how he ran through the streets in the firestorm and all around him he heard screams for help coming from people buried in the cellars; for the life of him he couldn't help them in the raging flames.

The night of Stuttgart's firestorm filled with calls for help from people who could not be helped. People were running in familiar areas when all of a sudden there was nowhere to go. A glowing, red pursuer had taken over, letting no one through and coming closer all the time. " 'You can't get through here!' someone shouted to us. We had to get through! A huge burst of fire and the big station concourse collapsed. Even the cemetery wasn't left untouched: The giant stone crematorium was burning." The people ran past those who before them had already tried to find a gap in the fire. "They were lying on the streets burned or charred."

Everyone who tried to run through the lanes of fire was looking for the tunnel. It was the twenty-seventh raid. Even during the horrid twenty-second raid it had still been possible to leave the gas-choked cellars in time. Its location on the slopes of the valley gave Stuttgart plenty of tunnels, often self-made, but they were often hard to bear. "It was terrible," wrote Prelate Wilfried Lempp,

> that in the entire tunnel, with space for about one thousand people, there was not a single toilet. Because the people had to stay inside all night and couldn't be let out until six the next morning, there were major difficulties. In the excitement of the night, a women went into labor and you could hear her screams, and later those of the baby, coming from the medical room. Overnight a corpse was carried in. Because of the heat more and more people left the cellars in the neighborhood and made their way through the streets to get to the tunnel, threatened all the way by flying sparks and the firestorm.

More and more people kept jumping up and reckoning they would make it through. "Wasn't there room in the Wagenburg tunnel? People are already coming toward us who had left the tunnel. It is burning over there too. So let's turn around." The blast waves threatened the entranceway; the biggest problem was the lock on the door. On September 12, the heat radiated deep into the earth. The asphalt from the street burned, "and even in the tunnels it got so hot that you could hardly stand it."

The fact that the Stuttgarters had nowhere to run, that the fire's noose was tightening everywhere, and that everything familiar offered nothing but peril all lent a deeper meaning to this attack by No. 5 Bomber Group. Those stuck in the gas cellars knew nothing of that. With the increase of smoke and hot air, their senses were getting dulled and they did not want to leave anymore. Why had they not left in time?

Indescribable scenes, said the official chronicler, took place in the Russian Church, which was built for the imperial Russian delegation in the form of a village house of God. "The people had to flee through the flames and they hurried to their deaths. There were also cases in which people took their own lives or pushed each other into the flames." According to the notes of Pastor Erwin Issler from the Memorial Church, we will never know the moments of horror of that night. Seven percent of his first congregation district—"three hundred—were dead, most died quietly of carbon monoxide poisoning in the cellars." In the "Bollwerk" (Bulwark) local Nazi party district, 452 of 480 houses were destroyed. "In a cellar on Calwer Strasse," wrote the chronicler, "forty-two people died, thirty-five from carbon monoxide."

Elsewhere, people could not get over their attachment to home. "The Swabian prisoners," reported Martha Haarburger from the Theresienstadt concentration camp,

> share a common homeland. We emphasize that we come from Württemberg and speak in a strong Swabian dialect whenever we meet each other. A Stuttgart attorney, Emil Dessauer, who was later killed in the gas chamber in Auschwitz, once even used the typical Swabian greeting: "Hie gut Württemberg allewege."[138]

Sixty-eight percent of Stuttgart's city center was destroyed in fifty-three raids, and 4,477 residents were killed by the bombs.

Fourteen days after the firestorm in Stuttgart, something inexplicable occurred not far downstream along the Neckar. Without advance notice, the whirring of a plane could be heard in Heilbronn as it glided across the night sky with its engine turned off, almost as if it were aiming to crash. Then came an explosion. The next day, three large explosives were found, along with twenty-two corpses. That night, there were again two powerful detonations, and again, the sirens had not sounded. No one had heard an airplane. All of Heilbronn was puzzled, wondering if the explosives were glider bombs or a stray V2 rockets.

The German Air District command headquarters had no explanation. Such an incomprehensible attack from nowhere led to considerable, vague fear among the people of Heilbronn. As compared to the fate suffered in nearby Stuttgart, the damages here were negligible. But still, groups of people gathered in the early evening at the train station in order to spend the night in the countryside. Some people matter-of-factly nicknamed the phantom *"Bomberkarle,"* "Bomber Charlie." They said it was one specific flyer taking revenge on the city for expelling its Jews. Some even knew his name.

The excessive fear of the amorphous avenger "Bomber Charlie" announced the coming of the Angel of Death, who was already at the door: No. 5 Bomber Group. On December 4, 1944, it entered the city's field of vision at 6:59 p.m., and the sirens sounded. At 7:16, the green-red illuminated frame was set above the city, and one minute later, the munitions began to fall. By 7:45 p.m., 1,254 tons had been dropped.

The time-delay bombs continued to explode for a while, keeping the residents in their cellars. The fires needed that span of time to grow into a conflagration. As the explosions ebbed away and the people prepared to leave the cellars, the firestorm took over. It covered an area of two square miles, continued for four hours, and destroyed 82 percent of the city center. By 8:15 p.m., it was a closed blast furnace without entrance or exit.

Heilbronn, surrounded by hills, is wine country. Unless wine was considered a product for the war, such products were not made in Heilbronn. It did, however, have a railroad connection to a main north-south line. But No. 5 Bomber Group did not want to leave the destruction of the railroad yards up to the whims of the fires engulfing the town, so they carried out a separate, additional transportation attack. The bombing of Heilbronn was a purely civilian massacre. That was also the strategy regarding the neighboring city of Stuttgart, as with all major cities, but they were all somehow within the scope of industrial destruction. Daimler-Benz, Bosch, and Stuttgart and the Stuttgarters were burned because they were a unit of work and workers. According to Churchill's law, anywhere with industry was part of the battlefield; that was a comfortable radius of operation. But Heilbronn was a vineyard, and was incinerated because people lived there.

The place suffered agony of a special kind. With its 74,000 inhabitants, the city was designated a second-order air-raid protection site. Consequently, no bunkers were built; there were tunnels in the suburbs. Fifteen thousand people lived in the city center, some in small half-timbered houses with decrepit basements. There were large, sometimes two-story wine cellars that were equipped with air pumps, dry toilets, and entrances that could be sealed off to serve as public shelters for passers-by. Ever since "Bomber Charlie" first appeared, local residents went to their reserved places in them every evening, with their entire family. The capacity was set for 5,680 people; on December 4, they had a fifteen-minute window of time in which to hide themselves away in there. The larger rooms were preferable, and they filled right away; the smaller ones remained empty. All of them were thoroughly unsuitable.

No. 5 Bomber Group, with the most advanced arson technology of the war, conquered the small-town folks, who had not a glimmer of gas protection. The air pumps, with their filters designed for poison gas, pumped the carbon monoxide—which is heavier than air—through the low intake fittings into the cellars. In the cellar at Klostergasse alone 611 people died; the same fate met audiences in four movie theaters, including doctors and senior medical officers, children on their mother's arms with a milk bottle in their mouths. The cause of death could be read from the cherry-red color of their faces. By the time the sudden and overpowering fatigue of carbon monoxide poisoning becomes noticeable, it is already too late. Once people fell asleep, they would never wake again. Anna Weller returned from this twilight realm because a hand pulled her back:

> My husband was in the field. On the evening of December 4, I was at my parents' house on Sülmermühlstrasse. The basement was a public air-raid shelter, well built and subdivided. When the alarm sounded we went into the cellar where about a hundred people had gathered. We feared for our lives, but the cellar held out. We were able to extinguish burning incendiary munitions that were seeping in. Some of the doors had been torn off their hinges from the blast or the draft. The air quickly became harder to breathe but we didn't think we were going to die. Unfortunately there was a furniture truck ablaze in front of the exit. We wanted to leave to go to safety once the truck had burned itself out. All of a sudden everything got frighteningly still. Frau Drautz under me suddenly didn't answer anymore. My girlfriend Dürolf sank down on her knees next to her air-raid cot and couldn't get back up. At that moment I realized we were all about to die. I was lying on my top bunk with my five-year-old daughter in my arm and then I passed out. On Thursday, December 7, I came to in the Weißenhof hospital. My brother had rescued me after midnight. My child and my mother both died.[139]

The Nazi party and its agency, the Reich Air Protection League, had organized air-raid drills in case of gas attack for years, but had never mentioned carbon monoxide. They spoke of overheating, lack of oxygen, and that you were supposed to leave the cellars after three or four hours. But to where?

No. 5 knew how to create a closed fire zone, and it was hard to defend against it under adverse circumstances. A number of adverse conditions came together in Heilbronn: a perfected annihilation machine and a remote objective with few bunkers and tunnels. Heilbronn had not spent a lot of money on bunkers. What could have been the purpose or benefit of cremating a little wine city on the Neckar River? The annihilation principle did not ask such questions. Not until it is too late does everyone know that they too can be struck. Terror does not seek to achieve anything; its regime is absolute. It comes out of the blue, needs no reasons, atones no guilt. Its success might be unconditional subjection, but even that does not end the horror. It makes no deals; its resolve is inscrutable and its aim, absurd. If there were any sense to be discovered, any purpose reckoned, then its law would be broken. It is subject to no rules; it is the rule. Everything that can be destroyed knows that it is the target. That suffices.

"Bomber Charlie" was a rather telling hallucination: an inverse terror that struck down its initiator. But there was no correlation between the annihilation of the Jews and the annihilation by bombs. And no analogy. And death by gas will not create one. Suffocation in the cellars from combustion gases was a remote variety of the airborne gas attacks that interwar-period strategists expected. "Strategic bombing" viewed itself as terror, and could be adequately described using such a definition. But inverse terror is an internal settlement, from "Bomber Charlie" to today. It was the morality of the observer that construed the connection between genocide and punishment by bombardment, but it was a correlation that never existed. In reality, the phenomenon of "Bomber Charlie" consisted of high-flying Mosquitos guided by Oboe transmitters from France that dropped bombs on settlements to distract fighters or keep themselves busy. In Heilbronn, 6,530 people were killed, including one thousand children under six years of age. On the night of December 3, 1944, 8.3 percent of the population was lost.

THE EAST

When Napoleon returned from Russia in defeat, he was confronted by a Prussian-Russian army of enthusiastic young nationalists and flexibly operating leaders. They no longer resembled in any way the dismal lot he had driven before him for years. "Ces animaux ont appris quelque chose,"[140] mumbled the Emperor, and lodged a complaint with his territorial rulers, the princes of the Confederation of the Rhine, demanding more troops who could pound to pieces the contingent of Prussian youth eager to fight for liberation. Theodor Körner, their minstrel, called out to them: "It is not a war known to the crowns. It is a crusade; 'tis a holy war."

The crusade got bogged down in the four Prussian provinces. The subjugated Germans did not feel the same as the Prussians; they had themselves been conscripted by the Rhine Confederation princes and put under French supreme command. Bavaria wavered briefly since it had lost thirty thousand men in Russia. Saxony tried not to get involved owing to its proximity to Berlin. It was conquered from there, and King Frederick August fled to Prague, made ties with the Prussians, but immediately blanched before the Emperor, who reconquered Saxony and made his allies face battle outside Leipzig.

The location was unfavorable for Napoleon, and his main concern was to maintain a line of retreat to the West. The singing in the enemy camp bothered him less than its sheer size. Austria had joined up with Prussia/Russia, and Sweden and England were also part of the league. It could be politically divided but not militarily defeated. The Germans, as usual fighting on both sides, were well aware of the balance of power, and the princes kept an eye out for the right moment to switch fronts. They also knew what they would offer the King of Prussia, aside from their treason: the elimination of Napoleonic liberalism and the return of their divine rights.

The Saxons expected the Battle of Leipzig to go awry. The troops of the Confederation of the Rhine had so far maintained their oath of allegiance; the king alone could release them from it. For some reason, the officers thought the king might be unfree and that his words might not be in keeping with what he knew and thought, and that he might even want to change sides, but for some unfathomable reason was unable to order it. They could not at all imagine that their king was no longer able to escape the snares of his scheming and was ignoring reality.

The fighting developed to Napoleon's disadvantage, and the Emperor ordered his army to retreat to the city. The Saxon generals requested that their king release their contingent from the loser. He rejected the notion brusquely and so they defected with three thousand men on the open battlefield. And besides them, the Württembergers.

The French were long aware that without a triumph in Leipzig the Confederation of the Rhine would dissolve. During the battle, General Auguste Marmont kept close watch on his Saxon cavalry.

> At first I thought they wanted to take position filling one of the many spaces that formed within our troops. But their intention soon became clear to me. Lined up in columns with the led horses in front, they rode quickly past the French line of troops and were taken in by the enemy ranks. Infantry and artillery followed their example in great haste. But once the artillery had reached a certain distance they made a treacherous stop, unlimbered to load, and shot at us. This decrease in our numbers forced us to shorten our lines.[141]

Napoleon managed to flee the city with ninety thousand Frenchmen. He left it up to the Confederation mercenaries to cover his escape. Thus all those who had no opportunity to defect were left to fight a losing battle. However, when on the same day even the Czar and the King of Prussia rode in, everyone cheered and shouted, except for Frederick August of Saxony, who was taken as a regular prisoner of war. With half a million participants, the Battle of Nations in Leipzig was the largest battle thus far in history. The city was strewn with 100,000 wounded and fallen. Prussian corpses lay rotting at the ramparts for days. In the concert halls of the Gewandhaus, the dead were not isolated from the injured. From morning to night, carts were loaded with anything that no longer moved; bodies had been thrown from the houses onto the street like rubbish. There were too many bodies for the civilians to handle. The farmers who had cleared the battlefield laid friend and foe on top of each other in mass graves. When the next war started moving toward Leipzig, no one wanted to let the same thing happen again.

In contrast to many cities that thought they would be spared by the air war, Leipzig reckoned firmly with being targeted. As early as 1934, twenty-seven corpse-recovery crews were established.[142] In July 1942, a mayor's task force commenced its work; the first air raid was still a year and a half away. Forty-six reception centers were set up, which could provide room and board for twenty thousand homeless. Arrangements were made with institutional kitchens to be able to provide ten thousand portions at once. Rice soup in the mornings, a rice meal for lunch, and potato soup for dinner. Notices were printed for those who might later be bombed out, telling them not to leave the city except if in possession of a travel permit, in which case they would receive a free ticket.

The task force sent delegates to bombed cities in the west—Mainz, Düsseldorf, Karlsruhe—to study their local disaster procedures, and improvements were discussed. After the catastrophe, it would be necessary to distribute special rations of coffee and tobacco immediately; hospitals also needed sufficient reserves of windowpane glass. The thirty thousand forced workers and prisoners would have to go under immediate observation. Patients with infectious diseases would be taken to quarantine wards in the hospitals or to Hitler Youth homes. After a short time, the reception centers were able to accommodate 300,000 people, half of Leipzig's population.

In August 1943, as a measure responding to the raid on Hamburg, ten athletic fields throughout the entire city were selected "for temporary laying out of the dead."[143] "It has been seen to that the selected athletic fields are behind hills or shrubbery and are not in the direct vicinity of residential housing." Transport biers and burying the dead had already been discussed among all competent authorities in 1934; the preprinted ID cards to fill out for casualties of the air war was something new.

At the first briefing in 1937, Mayor Rudolf Haake complained of problems with the water supply to extinguish fires, but there was nothing that could be done. Unfortunately, all the hydrants had nonstandard hose couplings, and their special gauge made them incompatible with all other fire departments. Nevertheless, crews from fifty neighboring fire departments were reserved in advance. The iron shortage made it impossible to replace the hydrants. Another problem was that the bunker situation was very meager. In 1943, there were ten bunkers with a total capacity of 7,500, enough for 1 percent of the population. Eighteen other projects were never completed due to shortages in materials. Mounds of earth were deposited at the base of 26,000 buildings, at least, to protect against shrapnel. More was not necessary, since in other buildings cellars were either nonexistent or unserviceable.

Evacuees spread a feeling of the certainty of disaster. Since 1943, Saxony had been the district designated to receive the throngs of people fleeing Cologne, Aachen, the Weser-Ems region, and Berlin. They painted a vivid picture for the incomparably better-off Leipzigers of what they had to expect. Unlike Dresden, for example, Leipzig was home to armaments giants such as Heinkel, Messerschmitt, and Junkers, as well as MiMo (Mitteldeutsche Motorenwerke) and Erla plane-engine plants. It was world famous for its trade fairs, and there was no way around its getting destroyed. The war outside the city would, as in 1813, penetrate to its center; the Führer had far fewer options for action than the king had. There was no switching sides to the alliance of the liberators, no matter what absurdities the British leaflet propaganda had to say about it. No one can defect to an air force. The people stood on the doomed side, which had already selected the monument to the Battle of Nations for the magniloquence of its burial rites.

The autograph collection of the municipal library was in fireproof storage inside the monument. The air-raid protection staffs did not waste a word on the unique features of the fireraising methods recently experienced in Hamburg and Kassel and the conclusions to be drawn from that. They also failed to inform the residents about them. People were instructed to stay in the cellars until it was all over. That was the most certain way to die. So they prepared for the worst of cases and then took every measure except that which would avoid it.

On the night of December 3, 1943, squadrons from all six RAF Bomber Groups set out on one of the most successful fire raids of the air war. No. 5 Group with its 619 Squadron made up the largest aircraft contingent. At 3:50 a.m., Leipzig's city center was clearly illuminated and marked, despite thick cloud cover. By 4:25 a.m., almost 300,000 incendiaries and 665 tons of high-explosive bombs and blockbusters had been concentrated onto the target. Just a week earlier, the Leipzig fire department had sent more than half its fire engines, the best equipped ones, to help out in the Battle of Berlin. The fire brigades of the surrounding towns were alarmed immediately; they already arrived at 3:45 a.m., but could not use their equipment at all. Although couplings for the incompatible Leipzig hydrants existed and every police department had them on hand, in the rush they could not be found. There were ten fires for each firefighter, who could do next to nothing to stop them.

There had long been plans to overhaul the water lines;[144] 90 percent of all reserves were connected to a single elevated tank. The pipes did not generate enough pressure; they should have been thicker. Because the city had been cost-conscious, they erected economical cisterns; because there were only a few of them, the hoses had to be correspondingly longer. They were nowhere near sufficient. Leipzig was particularly sensitive to fire. In addition to the densely built Old Town were the extensive inventories stored in the trade-fair city, especially those of the book publishers. Fifty million books caught fire.[145]

Two hours after Bomber Command departed, block after block of the city center went up in flames, and a firestorm rose up. According to firefighting officers, it attained Hamburg proportions.[146] Many of them were sucked in by the vacuum, hurled about over streets and squares, and killed. The rate of destruction testifies to the fire's hunger; 41 percent of all housing was wiped out. The 140,000 people rendered homeless confirmed the previous estimate. Only the number of deaths remained below expectations. The attack cost an unusually high number of lives: 1,815, but this is low with respect to the magnitude of the firestorm.

Though Leipzig reckoned with all kinds of catastrophe, it was not protected from them. The residents, too, acted in a way totally contrary to air-raid conduct rules.[147] Victims of the firestorm usually died in cellars surrounded by flames. Anyone who attempted to leave the underground shelters had drawn a lot that could bring either life or death. If the Leipzigers had obeyed their air-raid protection leadership and stayed in the cellars until the all clear came, thousands would have burned to death and suffocated, as in Kassel, Heilbronn, Darmstadt. When the all-clear siren sounded at 5:23 a.m., the ring of flames had closed. But Leipzig residents acted in an unusual manner. While everything was burning, they climbed out of the shelters to extinguish the fires. It was impossible to put out the blaze but their plucky move outside gave them one last chance to run through the gaps in the flames before the conflagration closed up around them. The pervading spirit of the city assured an escape at the right time, as it had in 1813.

The curse on the city prevailed in Magdeburg; since it was stormed in 1631 by Tilly's and Pappenheim's imperial troops it was the epitome of the war-ravaged city. Tilly, who did not leave a single wall standing, shied away only from the cathedral, which was built starting in 1209 around the tomb of Otto I, and the church of the Our Beloved Lady Monastery, 130 years older. The setting of the atrocities became a site of ignominy when in November 1806, Prussia's strongest fortification surrendered to seven thousand French besiegers without siege artillery. Twenty thousand men with eight thousand cannons and a million pounds of gunpowder gave up the position to the French marshal Michel Ney without a fight. The looting that soon started brought old pictures back to mind.

Marshal Ney knew that. But the campaign against Prussia had to feed itself. It had begun with only 24,000 francs—virtually empty coffers, as was common in that army. Victories financed themselves. On October 15, after the battle near Jena, Napoleon declared himself the victor, though he had by no means reached Berlin, and he imposed a contribution of 159 million francs on all the Prussian provinces. Confederates and Prussian vassals quickly switched to the emperor's camp, thanking him for their liberation. Magdeburg's capitulation on November 11 sealed the defeat, and the Magdeburgers thanked Marshal Ney with 150,000 talers so he would stop the vandalism by his troops.

Magdeburg fortified itself to the teeth in the hundred years after it was raped by Tilly. Entire districts of the city gave way to ramparts, bastions, and redoubts. When the "unbeatable" Prussian Army rotted away at Jena in 1806, the residents engaged in undirected and chaotic agitation. They had not expected in the least that the exposed city would now have to defy the besieger.

The fortress commander and generals were old men who knew enough about war from their youth to see that they could not turn the tide with their fortifications. They could offer an example of being unyielding, defending themselves to the last man and permitting the French to take the place only by storm. Without a field army for relief, and isolated by the secession of Hanover in the west and Saxony in the southeast, the outcome was not in question, only the honor.

When the aged generals laid down their arms in the common interest—they had come from the prerevolutionary period, which budgeted its strengths—they were the first to suffer the complaints of the residents. The subsequent lot of Magdeburg as the capital of the Elbe *département* in Jerôme Bonaparte's kingdom of Westphalia disparaged the capitulators even more. They were crassly taxed; terrorized by Police Commissioner Schulze, the creature of the occupiers; corralled into occupation troops of one Frenchman for every two citizens; and economically ruined by the forced affiliation with France's anti-British economic bloc.

The two diametrically opposed conquests of Magdeburg purported that no matter what decision was made, it was wrong. During the third siege, there was nothing more to decide. Magdeburg had ten concrete bunkers and thus better air-raid protection than Leipzig, twice its size. Magdeburg had experienced thirteen raids in the year prior to its destruction on January 16, 1945, but the experience did not help at all. The human losses on the night of the firestorm exceeded those in Leipzig threefold, though the severity of the attack was similar. Leipzig lost 0.25 percent of its population; Magdeburg, 0.75 percent.

In the late afternoon of January 16, the U.S. Eighth Air Force attacked the Krupp-Gruson works and the BRABAG hydrogenation plants. Bomber Command converged on Magdeburg in the evening with six subunits, coming from six different directions.[148] Before entering the Reich, it put up the Mandrel radar-jamming screen, and then the aircraft approached the city from over the coast, from the North German lowland plain, and from southern Germany. The aircraft-warning center thus could get no clear picture of the target. Between 9:23 and 9:26 p.m., twenty-one Lancasters dropped tinfoil strips and magnesium flares. At 9:28, the master bomber, his second in command, and three visual markers reached the city. They marked a frame in red and green. At 9:30 came the target illuminators, who released cascading flares for the following bomber stream. A minute later, ten Lancasters at low altitude raced over the city center and set a central orientation marker in red; a minute after that, the munitions were dropped. At 9:28 p.m., the air-raid alarms had sounded. Everything else in Magdeburg was decided by the events of the next 240 seconds. "When the sirens blasted, we quickly got ready to go down to the air-raid cellar."[149] Hedwig Behrens's daughter was ailing and bed-ridden; the illumination flares were already visible in the sky; the bombs were falling blow after blow; dear, get dressed in the stairway!

"All of a sudden the entire house shook and our eyes were filled with dirt." Was the house going to collapse? "Everyone was in a panic." An aerial mine had shaken up the building and hurled the father against the cellar column. He lay there on the ground with a gash the size of a hand on the back of his head. A splash of water roused him. "I said to my daughter, can't we still save some down comforters; it isn't burning here yet." The daughter tied the comforters together and threw them out the window. Husband, wife, and daughter, each with a blanket bundle, ran in search of shelter. "There were already so many people in the buildings that were not on fire that we weren't allowed in."

It was already "lights out" in the women's prison. When the sirens started wailing, the guards ran into the air-raid cellar. "We three cellmates got up to get dressed; outside it was light as day. The building trembled and rocked like a ship on high seas." Several hundred women, locked in, begged and screamed to have the doors opened. "They took their wooden slippers and were banging in helpless desperation against the doors." Meanwhile, the bombs started falling, and the alarm prompted Dr. Sandmann to go to the bunker at the northern cemetery. "The frightened people were pushing their way through the small opening to safety and blocked it totally." An aerial mine fell and the blast pressed into the bunker and set it quaking. The people inside wanted to close the bunker door; "the bunker was closed without any consideration to the people outside, who either burned to death or were killed by flying fragments." It was unbearably hot in the bunker. Dripping with sweat, the occupants cranked the emergency ventilation.

Sophie Pasche, who had already gone to bed, got dressed in a flash, "one last gaze at my deathly ill husband." He did not want to go to the cellar. There, the building residents were sitting and listening to the crackling of incendiary sticks as they fell. "The lights went out and we could hardly breathe; that's how powerful the blast from the explosions was." Someone called out that everything upstairs was burning. Frau Pasche thought about her husband, "but they held me back with force."

In the Home for the Aged on Stiftstrasse the cellar was overcrowded. The frail were carried in, "but four others and my paralyzed husband died of smoke inhalation." The lights went out, there was a lack of oxygen, and "then a man went crazy and started thrashing about with his chair until he passed out and collapsed." Someone said that five women and a man were caught in the courtyard. "We opened up the corridor to the Reuter passage but it was already obstructed by dead bodies, people who had wanted to reach us from the other side." The inspector instructed the men to finally help the people locked in the courtyard. "But they refused since they didn't think there was any point anymore." Wilhelmine Becker, the inspector, and a woman they did not know tried to do it alone. "We had barely entered the courtyard when a large phosphorus canister exploded. It struck the woman in such a terrible way that she burned like a column of fire." The people locked in the courtyard were also beyond help.

Even after the bunker at St. James's Church was filled past capacity, there was still a crowd of a hundred jammed up in front of it, vehemently trying to get in. "So now they closed the bunker doors and the people were so afraid they threw themselves on top of each other." On Blauebeilstrasse people decided, well before the building collapsed and many were buried, to flee into the infernal flames. They squeezed up through the basement window, which they enlarged with a hammer and chisel. "Except for one, a salesman who was unnaturally fat from a disease. He went back, sat down quietly in the corner, and waited for death." In the house next door, someone who had been buried in rubble and lost his sense of direction worked his way from cellar to cellar with a hammer until he made it, thirty-six hours later, to the next cross street.

"My flatmate and I went down to our basement corridor. Unfortunately we didn't have an air-raid cellar." Because of the blast from the explosion "we were now all standing in a circle and had linked arms because we were stumbling back and forth. Then we had to kneel down or else we would have fallen." Franz Freyberg and the other residents of his house had just lain down on the floor. "In candlelight we held on to each other in silence and waited for what was to come. The building shook with each bomb that fell." In the corridor, a woman sat down calmly on the stairs, "dressed only in a shirt. Shivering from the cold and holding a pair of socks in her hand, she asked me to put them on for her."

It was about a hundred yards to the bunker. "But it is impossible to get through." A jump to the house across the street: Everyone who did not make it to the bunker was sitting there. "They are standing along the walls with eyes wide open, hanging around unmoving, holding their belongings pressed against them, or else holding hands somewhere in the dark. Stale and mephitic air."

Outside, the icy cold continued. "The water cisterns out on the streets were still frozen despite the heat." The wet blankets people wrapped around themselves against sparks and embers froze right to their bodies. "The air draft ripped off my kerchief." Many fled on the street, which was covered with black ice, "including the amputee patients from the Blenkesche Hospital in the Reformed Church in their pajamas. They limped and slipped and slid and fell on top of one another. Among them was a young woman running barefoot through the icy rubble in a thin silk nightgown with a naked child in her arms."

"For the fire department, January 16 had actually started early in the morning." The Eighth Air Force bombarded Krupp-Gruson. "Our instructions were firefighting and rescue at a bakery on Planetenhügel." Dieter Becker was fifteen; he was holding his permanent post, the lookout stand on the hose-drying tower of the Ottersleben fire brigade. U.S. munitions exploded starting at Salbker Chaussee and the hill Planetenhügel, in the direction of the Krupp-Gruson plant.

> Those were my first corpses; we had to collect them from the field and along the avenue: young French women, foreign workers at Krupp who were refused entrance to the air-raid bunkers in the plant, especially Krupp's Aschenberg bunker, and so they sought protection from the bombs on the open field. We were busy on the hill until it got dark. On the way home to Ottersleben the alarm sounded again. It suddenly became light as day.

Magdeburg lost four thousand lives that night; about 6,500 all together during the air war. It holds a leading position among major German cities with respect to degree of destruction. The 7.8 million cubic yards of rubble amounted to twenty-six cubic yards per resident.[150] In the cathedral, 8,600 square feet of masonry was destroyed in the western façade and the vault.[151] The bombs hit Our Beloved Lady in the roofs, the choir, and the western cloister wing.

On April 5, 1945, Harris complained that "it was already extremely difficult to find suitable targets."[152] In east central Germany, Chemnitz was bombed on March 5 by 720 British planes carrying 1,100 tons of bombs; one-third of the city area was burned down. Two days later, 84 percent of Dessau, the old royal residence, was destroyed; on March 12, Swinemünde experienced its ruin; on March 31, 1,100 tons of munitions shattered one-fifth of the houses in Halle. Zerbst, Frankfurt (Oder), Nordhausen, Potsdam, and Halberstadt went down in April.

On April 7, the U.S. First Army had reached the Weser River, and together with the Ninth Army they continued marching on to the Harz Mountains. To scare the local population, Gauleiter Lauterbacher told them on April 7 that "all males between fourteen and sixty-five in the enslaved western regions of the Reich were brought together in assembly camps and are guarded by Negroes and Jews. Our women were abducted and taken to Negro brothels."[153] If that were true, it would still be a preferable fate to what the British No. 5 Mass Destruction Group did in Nordhausen—six thousand dead, including 1,300 concentration camp prisoners[154]—and what the U.S. Eighth Air Force did in Halberstadt.

Since January, the Americans had been attacking, without much success, the train station and the Junkers plant at the outskirts of the city. Within the scope of the raid on 158 railroad objectives on February 19, Halberstadt was back on the list. Not only was the train station devastated, but also the tax office and the Wehrstädter Church, including 146 people who had sought refuge inside. Strafer shelling of a passenger train traveling between Halberstadt and Wegeleben also killed fifteen British and two American prisoners of war that day.

In April, 65,000 people were living there, four thousand of whom were sick and wounded, spread out over fifteen military hospitals. Opinions diverged on whether Halberstadt should resist and stop the U.S. Ninth Army. Local district party head Detering swore to fight; the mayor made reference to the architectural beauty and cultural and historical significance of the city and refused, as did the local officers, out of concern for the hospitals. The heated debate remained in a stalemate. The American spearhead tanks were about forty miles away; the *Volkssturm* militia meanwhile started digging trenches; it was the weekend of April 7–8.

On Saturday afternoon, fighter-bombers appeared in the sky, dropped a few incendiary sticks, and the air gunners aimed for pedestrians on the streets. There was a flak train at the main railroad station. From there someone unfortunately fired back, which drew the fighter-bombers to the tracks. A munitions train standing on track 9 was not hard to hit. The explosion tore a crater covering over 120 acres. The signal towers, engine houses, switch units, quick repairs unit, freight dispatch, and entrance and exits were in ruins. "Many railroaders," reported the train newspaper *Fahrtwind*, "lost their lives in this raid while on the job."[155]

The blast blew out windows throughout the city. In the evening, residents nailed shut the openings with boards and cardboard. Nazis stalked the streets with paint cans, painting "We will never surrender" on walls. They did not really have to do that, because the issue was decided on the following night, when half of the 19,000 dwellings no longer existed.

Halberstadt enjoyed renown as a half-timbered city in Lower Saxony, with 721 preserved buildings, the oldest of which was the three-story Ratskeller, eleven panels long and nine wide, decorated with Gothic tracery.[156] The shape of a praying knight was carved in a stone plate at the base. Carved human and dragon heads looked down through foliage from the sill over the ground floor.

As in Hildesheim, the half-timbered houses in Halberstadt were eloquent—telling more stories the older they were. The "Stelzfuss," the building of 1576 with a stilt foot at the corner of Schmiede-strasse, wore masks at the beam-ends; above the oriel lintels there were long inscriptions informing passersby of the status and significance of the builders and residents. Mayor de Hetling pleased his two wives by hanging their coats of arms at the fish market square; at the Old Council Scales, a dwarfed sinner knelt at the abutments in front of the bishop. Two men were lying down and showing their puffed sleeves; two fishwives, their scaly dress. Two birds contented themselves with a mouse. Stork, frog, dragon, and dog ignored the man at the main sill with the flag. At Martiniplan all four seasons slipped into busts of women with various degrees of charm. Behind the Town Hall at no. 17, St. Anna lived one story up; Sebastian identified himself with his coat of arms; a female figure held a crown and the church; another held a small man. Another man was hanging over to a beer barrel and glass.

Great men bestowed hard times upon Halberstadt, starting with Henry the Lion. In a feud over disputed fiefs he was defeated by Bishop Ulrich in the Battle of Langenstein. Having been placed under a ban, he then went to Halberstadt, the seat of his conqueror and proscriber, where the Lion prostrated himself before Ulrich, paid a penance, and was in turn forgiven. Neither of them took it to heart; it was the protocol of war at that time. The feud continued, as did the bans and absolution. Henry, who made more enemies than he could defeat, needed peace in Saxony, since Emperor Frederick Barbarossa was pressuring him from the front. Nothing helped; he was beaten at this front as well, and was again placed under imperial ban and divested in 1180 of all fiefs and his duchy by the Imperial Diet in Würzburg. Ulrich took advantage of the opportunity, proclaimed his ban, and performed a trial invasion of Henry's territory.

On a Sunday, September 23, Henry responded by destroying Halberstadt. The citizens, who favored Henry only because he chastised the bishop, fled to the churches. The wooden town was soon ablaze; the flames surrounded the cathedral, the third of its kind on the site, where the pagans had already made towers of sacrificial stones. St. Stephan was incinerated. The remains of the saint were charred, a sacrilege that made Henry blanch in Brunswick; he had not been present. A thousand residents were slaughtered. The number is not known, but certainly a large segment of the Halberstadt population had been exterminated. The bishop came to Brunswick in fetters, but he did not release Henry from the ban until Christmas, and he died a short time later from his venom.

Bishop Christian was a figure of no less vigor. He drew Halberstadt into the cauldron of the Thirty Years' War. Sacking and pillaging by Tilly and Wallenstein were roughly the same as being saved from it by the Swedes. In the grimaces and the dragons, the storks and the dogs, the bishops, supplicants, knights, and saints, the feud of Halberstadt was carved into the beams of the buildings—combustible material. Especially common among these motifs was the fan: It told nothing of the past, but only of the future.

On Sunday morning, the residents of Halberstadt had fifteen minutes to take cover from the 218 Flying Fortresses of the U.S. Eighth Air Force. Not in the cathedral; it was safer in the caves. After the alarm sounded, thousands ran out of the city to the Spiegelsberge mountains, where natural rock caverns had been set up to serve as air-raid shelters. Some of the hospital patients could even be carried to the "long cave." Eyewitness Krause reported in 1946 that from there "you looked into hell. Here and there magical carbide light peered into the darkness and illuminated the groaning of the injured, the dying, the mothers with young children crying who had silently yielded to their fate."[157] The hell was something called the "fan."

At 11:25 a.m., four U.S. squadrons with 550 tons of bombs were in the air, en route to Zerbst and Stassfurt. The industrial haze obstructed their vision there, which was a problem since they were testing the "fan," a new British bombing method, which required good visibility. They took a sweeping turn toward Halberstadt, which was enjoying sunny spring weather.

The fan was precision bombing that combined a point target with a wide-area objective. The old opposites were reconciled. The point was a large, easily visible school, the Auguste Victoria secondary school; the area was the city center. Point came before area. Point was precisely marked and area was bombed precisely with reference to its distance from point. The geometric shape through which the point developed into an area was fan-shaped. The pivot point was at the bottom; the area fanned out from there. All the planes passed over the point from the south and flew at different angles toward the north, northwest, and northeast. That was the most exact way of destroying an area on the ground. Almost all of the half-timbered buildings in the city went down. The motif of its ruin had been carved on its face.

Five hundred and fifty tons of munitions served to destroy three-quarters of Halberstadt. The human losses were as difficult to estimate as they were in 1180, but were probably somewhere between 1,800 and 3,000.

In early February 1945, there were about 800,000 people living in Dresden, perhaps a million. About 640,000 of them were regular residents; the rest were refugees. The two groups sacrificed a total of forty thousand people on February 13 and 14, 1945. Next to Hamburg, this marked the highest human losses of a German city during the air war. The outcome of the Hamburg mission resulted from, along with Bomber Command's efforts, a rare combination of factors. That July success clearly stands out from the preceding results of the Battle of the Ruhr. Such a density of destruction exceeded the weapon's potential; there had to be an unforeseen booster factor, such as Kassel's firefighting problem due to its isolated location.

The Dresden raid was different, which harkened back to Allied plans to carry out a "thunderclap" in the summer of 1944, a colossal massacre with more than 100,000 casualties. They had been thinking of Berlin. This in turn was a moderate version of the gas and germ-warfare attack that Churchill had wanted to impose on sixty German cities.

The Eighth Air Force would find out just how hard it is to kill 100,000 people when they hit Berlin with half a thunderclap in February 1945. Instead of the planned two thousand aircraft, only 937 participated; instead of five thousand tons of bombs only 2,266 were dropped, and they killed only 2,893 civilians instead of the projected 110,000. Even a miserably defended metropolis with totally insufficient air-raid facilities resisted total destruction by virtue of its sheer volume. The Allied principle of closed zones of annihilation could be best implemented on areas of under two square miles. Small and medium-sized cities with a densely built historical Old Town were vulnerable to firestorms. And only fire could seal the death zone.

The tighter the dimensions, the more complicated the hit accuracy. No. 5 Bomber Group had become expert in precision annihilation and it led the Dresden mission. The "thunderclap" was to come to a city so remote and insignificant for the war effort that it had been ignored for four and a half years. It was a long distance away, but no farther than the Brüx hydrogenation works, where the Eighth

Air Force had dropped four thousand tons of bombs, and they had dropped eight thousand tons at the Leuna plant, still farther west.

While Churchill, Eisenhower, Harris, and Portal were writing down thunderclap ideas, No. 5 Group was methodically testing all that could be achieved with the available means. By the fall, this group had forged the summer's destruction plans into a murderous weapon. In contrast to Hamburg and Kassel, five-digit casualty figures did not merely come to be, they were created. On September 11 and 12, 1944, No. 5 Group kindled a firestorm in Stuttgart and another in Darmstadt. Stuttgart was consumed by fire, but its inhabitants were protected, thanks to its tunnels. Darmstadt was 75 percent smaller, but suffered thirteen times the human losses. From then on, that became Bomber Command's reference raid. It served as a model for Dresden. Darmstadt was the rehearsal, and Dresden, the performance. Because the rehearsal stage was so tightly built up, the impact there was more intensive. The rate of annihilation there was 10.7 percent, more than double that of Dresden. Only Pforzheim was bled whiter.

The attacks against Darmstadt and Dresden used No. 5's own procedure, the fan. The fan was a quarter of a circle. Its vertex in Darmstadt was at the parade ground; in Dresden, it was at the soccer stadium of the Dresden Sport Club, within the expansive Ostragehege fields. In both cases, the approach was divided among a number of routes, misleading the aircraft-warning center. In Darmstadt, there were ten minutes between alarm and bombs; in Dresden, twenty-five, but in Dresden, the distances to the shelters were also greater. Darmstadt did not mark the escape routes to the shelters with arrows. Neither of the two cities had bunkers.

At 10:03 p.m., the illuminators began to light up the Elbe Valley and the city with white cascading flares. Two minutes later, green markers were dropped on the DSC stadium.

In Darmstadt, the white parachute flares floated down to the parade ground at 11:35 p.m.[158] The marker aircraft dove down to 3,300 feet, outlining the gleaming, bright square first in red and then green. One target indicator went astray, to the main train station. The master bomber raced in and annulled the green with yellow, as if with a highlighter pen. Then he climbed up and called in his bomber squadrons.

Dresden's master bomber swooped down, penetrating the thin cloud cover, and eyed his target.[159] It evidently lacked flak defenses, so the high-flying Lancasters could drop down to ten thousand feet, and the visual markers down to nine hundred feet. The stadium was marked in red. It was 10:13 p.m.; after ten whole minutes of undisturbed illumination and marking, not even a searchlight flashed on.

In Darmstadt, too, the plans were being calmly carried out without any disturbance. At its pivot point, the fan spread out to 45 degrees. The master bomber first called the three squadrons from the west. The overshoot was six seconds from the pivot, and then the bombs dropped down along the left edge of the fan. In the city, this was the line toward the slaughterhouse. Then the bombers in the second wave marked the right edge toward the southern access to the city center. The third wave, with four squadrons, flew between the two legs of the triangle and rolled the carpet of death and ruin over the wide inner area.

On February 13 in Dresden, the course of events was more routine. It worked in Heilbronn, in Freiburg, and would soon raze Würzburg. The plan could not be delayed at all in Dresden because the planes started with 2,200 gallons of fuel in their tanks and had no reserves. There was a twenty-five-minute window of time, from 10:03 p.m. until 10:28 p.m., then the planes had to begin the nine-hundred-mile flight home. The master bomber, the first to arrive, had only twelve minutes once target indication had been completed. Instructions over VHF radio announced: "Controller to Plate-Rack Force: Come in and bomb glow of red TIs as planned."[160] Then the fan opened up. The left leg crossed the bend in the Elbe twice; the right leg ended at the train tracks at the Falkenbrücke overpass. The connecting arc was completed in front of the train station.

The quality of the bombing involved covering the entire fan area equally with fire, blast waves, and explosions. Fire was spread like a paste. The master bomber and the marker leader made sure that no gaps remained that the fires could not close up. It was a matter of the exact angle taken by each plane within the fan and the precise overshoot, the distance between pivot and bomb release.

The master bomber's eye was glued to the fan. "Hello, Plate-Rack Force. Attention, one dropped too late. One went down too wide. . . . Good work, Plate-Rack Force. That's nice bombing. . . . Hello Plate-Rack Force, the bombing is getting wild now. Pick out the red glow if you can."[161] Mass destruction was precision work, down to the millimeter, and it would not occur if tons of bombs were randomly dropped on a town; a town could cope well with that.

In Darmstadt, the flames worked their way into a firestorm within an hour. The local fire department's thirteen fire engines extinguished the burning firehouse. It took until 3 a.m. for their colleagues from Mannheim, Frankfurt, and Mainz to arrive via the autobahn; at 6 a.m., there were three thousand firefighters with 220 engines. By then, the blaze had been sated for two hours. The fire must work faster than the firefighters. Otherwise it would just be a lot of fires, not an annihilation raid.

In Darmstadt, fate wanted to outdo the part of the time-delay bombs, which usually kept the cellar dwellers from climbing out of their shelters at the end of the raid and escaping through the gaps that initially existed in the fire. That would prevent the 100,000 deaths the general staffs had dreamed of. Three-quarters of a mile south of the Darmstadt main train station, a munitions train was waiting on the tracks and caught fire. The shells on board continued to fire into the air for an hour, giving the people in the cellars the false impression that the raid was still in progress.

By the time the thunderous banging of the munitions train died down, the firestorm had sealed all exits from the cellars. The heat and gas turned the shelters into execution sites. One in ten residents, a total of 12,300 people, died. This outdid the rate of killing of the gas attack that Churchill had projected in July. But the 12,000 deaths did not satisfy the objectives of Operation Thunderclap at all. Based on the million people in Dresden at the time, this corresponded merely to the average losses in all German cities.

The fan of Dresden created the expected firestorm within half an hour after No. 5's departure. Although the bombs fell slightly off the intended target, the effect was precisely as planned. The group's method kept the fan from spreading out too much; at its widest point it was 1.5 miles across. It covered three-quarters of the Old Town. Owing to the substantial weight of the airplane fuel, only 877 tons of bombs could be loaded, which was exactly the tonnage dropped on Darmstadt. Harris therefore ordered a double attack, which had been tested in Duisburg, Cologne, and Saarbrücken. The double attack did not merely double the devastation, it multiplied it because it struck just as the people in the city thought the worst was over. Ninety minutes after the all clear, Dresdeners barely had time to drag themselves to the Great Garden or the wide, grassy banks of the Elbe before the sirens howled again, this time only in the suburbs. The alarm systems in the city were no longer functioning. The "double blow" reckoned with such defects; it helped increase the human losses.

As expected, there was no longer ground visibility when the second attack fleet arrived at 1:16 a.m. The firestorm shot a mile-high cloud of smoke into the air. The Old Market was nevertheless the designated point target, in the middle of the fan. This corresponded to the purpose of the double blow; it delivered a knock-out punch. The first attack chased the people into shelters and the second attack hit those leaving their protection with feelings of relief. The protective effect of cellars was exhausted after two hours. After that, under a blazing city district, the basements no longer preserved life. Whoever let themselves be chased back into the cellars during the second attack rarely emerged alive. Those who hid outdoors, like the refugees in Dresden's Great Garden, also failed to survive. The logic of the process was geared toward inescapable mass extermination.

When the master bomber saw the situation in the fan below him, he considered it deadly enough and had the area to the side of the quarter circle marked, to open the fan wider, in both directions: toward the left across the Elbe, which the fire could not jump across, into the new part of the city, and to the right toward the main train station and into the Great Garden, an easily recognizable, nonflammable area.

The left bank of the Elbe is bordered by a strip of meadow a third of a mile long. That February, an icy wind was howling across it, and it had started drizzling overnight. The people in cellars near the river hurried to the cooling morass after the first attack of smoke, flying sparks, and scorchingly hot air, which were all being sucked toward the brewing firestorm. The nursing staff of the Johannstädter Hospital carried the patients in their thin, striped hospital gowns and laid them down there. Women who had just given birth were running out of the polyclinic. That was the first group that the double blow had lured from their hiding places and now held caught, defenseless.

On the other side, by the train station, was another island of refuge, the expansive Great Garden, a park area with a stand of trees. This was where the second group of Old Town refugees fled. The meadows along the banks of the Elbe and the Great Garden gathered up tens of thousands. They had no other choice. The way the fan was spread, the city geography offered only these two sites. The conflagration area of No. 5 Group squeezed the people caught there as if into a bag held open. And that was where a large portion of the munitions of the follow-up attack were pelted down.

The main train station was outside the fan. It was packed to the brim with refugees from the eastern front. The first raid had left open a chance to shunt a large number of passenger trains out of the city area, which were brought back once No. 5 had completed its work. That made the train station a preferred target for the second blow. Thus three extermination centers had been established: the cellar landscape below the Old Town conflagration, the grassy areas, and the train station. However, the blazes of No. 5, coupled with the double-blow method, created only a fraction of the numbers of deaths that the thunderclap bosses had commissioned.

"The sky arches over Berlin with a blood-red eerie beauty," Goebbels entered in his diary for Saturday, November 27, 1943. "I can no longer stand to look at it."[162] In the preceding week, the government district around Wilhelmsstrasse had burned, including the Kaiser Wilhelm Memorial Church in the west and the zoo. It was the third major raid in five days. This opening offensive of the Battle of Berlin killed 3,758 people, and 500,000 were rendered homeless. The main part of the bomb load on November 27 hit the northern working-class district of Reinickendorf. Goebbels went to view the aftermath on Monday morning.

> Male and female workers here received me with an enthusiasm that was as incredible as it was indescribable. . . . Everyone addressed me in the familiar and called me by my first name. . . . Women embraced me. I was forced to give out autographs. Cigarettes were handed out; we smoke a fag together. In short, everything was as jolly as an amusement park.

There was incredible destruction spreading out around the amusement park, "but as far as the public themselves are concerned, they are taking it in great humor. . . . Tobacco is now the most approved luxury; a Berliner will stand on his head for a cigarette."[163]

The Nazi party had expected something else from the Berlin population and had formed "SA raid patrols for special duties." "I can hardly believe that this city led a revolt in 1918," noted Goebbels.[164] The November Revolution was for Goebbels, as for Churchill, the point of reference. The rebellion would be bombed to its knees for the proletariat of the capital. The leaflet that was dropped along with the bombs conveyed regrets that the bombs were hitting. "Where is the Luftwaffe?" it asked in March 1944. "Masses of American bombers are now flying over Berlin in broad daylight. Today they were over the capital of the Reich five times. Of course you are now asking, 'Where is the Luftwaffe?' Ask Göring; ask Hitler."[165]

6. Dresden.

Source: Bildarchiv Preussischer Kulturbesitz.

The obvious group that should have asked questions, the Berlin populace, was not moved to do so by 45,000 tons of bombs. The Americans continued to attempt to provide that incentive until February 3, 1945, when they thought they killed 25,000 people. That corresponded to 0.9 percent of the people in the city at that time, who then would truly have had reason to ask questions. The official history of the U.S. air war, however, had reported the figure with one too many zeroes.[166] The bloodiest raid that the city had to cope with resulted in 2,893 deaths, far fewer than half the Heilbronn casualties. Based on the city's four million residents, the total of 11,367 tons of bombs corresponded to one-third of the average loss ratio.[167] But dead people do not rebel. Berlin endured more raids than any other city and thus had to defend its life as hard as Essen and Cologne did. The fates of the nearby Magdeburgers were sealed within four minutes—not much time to deliberate. Berlin fought for four years.

The people living in Berlin had their own unique and crafty character. Berliners believed nothing, absolutely nothing, that they were told. That was why Goebbels was surprised that they trusted him here, of all places. "I would never have believed it possible for such a change in attitude to take place."[168] And in fact it was not possible. The internal situation in Berlin during the bombing war has been described more accurately in the notes of the foreign correspondents on the ground than by Goebbels. A people consisting of Nazi martyrs does not appear anywhere in their accounts. Hitler maniacs, whom Goebbels evoked and Churchill's bombs reeducated, were not really of any concern in an air war. Anyone wearing such a mask got it blown away by the blockbusters. The political stature of civilians and their encounter with the means of destruction had little to do with each other. A cluster bomb and a phosphorus cascade penetrated deeper into people than their political views did. To that extent, the psychology of morale bombing was relevant. But the consequence was not that people would incite a political upheaval. Nothing was further from their minds; bombs tend to privatize.

Swiss correspondent Konrad Warner wrote:

> The people on the streets, in stores, and on public transportation looked terrible, in this gray November in the fifth year of the war. They were pale, their eyes sunken, skinny bodies stuck in shabby clothes. They were tired and yet driven by a constant hurrying, by the unhealthy haste of excessive existential fear. This haste was of necessity: you couldn't get to the store too late or the goods would be sold out; you couldn't get to the stop too late or the streetcar would be gone or the seat grabbed up by someone else. You couldn't get to work late or you risked having your wages cut; you couldn't get to the restaurant late or there would be no more food; and you had to get home on time or you would be caught by surprise by the air-raid alarm somewhere along the way. In addition, hurrying and haste were remedies against self-reflection and brooding.[169]

People in a bombing war waited it out in the cellars, or were out getting things done for hours and hours. Destruction forced you to take care of errands: finding protection, a roof over your head, family members; filing for government aid; arranging to get what is constantly lacking; and buying and selling on the black market. In Berlin, everything was out of the way.

The trains overflowed with people who didn't know up from down, letting out gasps of despondency; worried and distracted women with lips pressed together; the wounded with blood-soaked bandages. "People's faces are pale, unhealthily white as flour, except for red rings around their tired, lifeless eyes." Due to the lack of vitamins in the food; "teeth are decaying fast and obviously. My dentist said they are decaying all at once almost like cubes of sugar dissolving in water." Strong odors lingering in the cars could knock the feet out from under the passengers. "Sometimes you just have to get out at some station halfway to your destination to take a breath of fresh air between trains."[170]

The crowding came to a head at the subway tunnel:

> The stairs leading down to the station were blocked by a mass of people. People wanting to go up and pushing their way down got wedged into one another and were stuck fast. You would've had to break them apart with a crowbar like pieces of coke. Left and right along the two walls a thin thread of bodies made their way up and down.[171]

Lines were interrupted, trains came less frequently, every trip took five times as long as it should. For those who lost everything—housing, job, breadwinner—there was compensation from the authorities. You had to go there and wait in line, listen and tell, everyone had a story. Someone's apartment exploded from a blast bomb, and they lost everything; someone's home burned down, he was lucky to escape with his bare life! "Someone told of burst pipes and flooding, someone else of mutilation and being buried alive. And all these accounts spoke of war, death, and destruction."[172] But worst of all was the pushing and shoving, "so that finally you could forget the war and start arguing and complaining." The train dispatcher explained in detail why the trains were late, which made them later. Now there was a relief ID card, also called a "bomb passport," for people completely bombed out. There were also ration coupons somewhere else, one station farther, in the store, but there were no rations left, so you went to the black market trader.

Keeping busy was the medicine against depletion for the body of three million. Too many air-raid alarms, too much was wrecked; too much worrying about the children, the next night, intact limbs. The bomb was an axe that cut into the gray elephant skin until the thousands of wounds festered. The axe struck unceasingly, because it was a small weapon in comparison to the monster. A metropolis did not topple from one blow; it leaned on the wideness of its streets, the waterways, the parks. It had room, lungs, air.

The pressure was also cushioned by the Berlin *esprit de corps*, which did not like to be fazed. The cardboard sign in front of the authorities commented on that: "Business is continuing as usual,"[173] and it had nothing at all to do with staying power.

The flak bunker at the Zoo train station had a capacity of 18,000. Through the meter-thick reinforced concrete you could hear the muted air-raid alarm; in the living room of the bombing war you were cut off from the outside. "Lined up like in church were the rows of benches where people were sitting who had been caught by surprise by the alarm. Soldiers regulated traffic, distributed people to the different floors and rooms; electrical lights made it possible to read or do handicrafts."[174] Window shoppers from the exclusive Kurfürstendamm slouched against the wall, conversation was lively, the antiaircraft artillery unexpectedly fired from the roof, aha, so it was not a diversionary raid after all!

> Then all of a sudden there was a hard impact and the massive building shook down to its foundations. Somewhere there was a loud metallic sound, the lights went out in the bat of an eye. The conversations went down to a whisper. One woman passed out, someone shouted for water, then everything was quiet again. "Is it you or not?" asked a girl's voice and three or four men responded at once. Laughter.[175]

The way home from the bunker led through a shower of sparks. "People called to each other: 'You're on fire, pat it out!' I kept running, patting out the sparks on my coat and hat."[176] The walls to the right and left were disintegrating. Flames devoured; tractive and shearing forces wrestled. "Up above a tower-like oriel slowly started to come free. I felt like I was watching in slow motion. And at the same time I saw the elderly people below who had just put down their suitcases to take a deep breath." But before the scream formed in my throat, the old people emerged from the cloud of dust in one piece. A fire engine drove by slowly to get a better view of the situation. "A woman ran behind it screaming 'Come to me, it can still be extinguished. Please come, please, you can still put out the fire.'" The firefighter did not let himself be grabbed by the arm. "No one turned around to her; she waved her handkerchief. At that moment the sirens started sounding again." Everyone went back to the belly of the Zoo bunker.

The city wore down. You had to know your way around; street signs were brought down by fire and blasts. "The burned-out rows of buildings all looked the same."[177] There were the flat, indented façades where aerial mines hit; there were those riddled by fragments. "I came through streets where not a single building showed even a trace of life." Along the way you swallowed vast amounts of dust, smoke, and soot; handkerchiefs were pitch-black by evening, and you could not get the fine dirt out of your eyes. Millions of glass shards became the pavement, cutting into the soles of shoes.

Work at the rubble lots resembled that at a field hospital. "Listening devices were used to get a fix on any signs of life such as knocking. Oxygen equipment was used to try to aerate spaces where people were trapped." Berlin's housing blocks were nested, consisting of a front house facing the street, a connected side building and back house facing the first courtyard, a second courtyard with its own side building, and back house, and so on.

> When there is a direct hit, you can imagine what a mountain of debris a five-story building creates. The people lie within the mountain; some were never found. Russian prisoners of war carefully cleared away one stone after another and they were getting nowhere. Down in the cellar the people were banging and not a single one of them could be rescued.

In early 1945, thousands were jammed in front of the Zoo bunker when the alarm sounded. Fearful people circled it for the whole day. Being granted entry was the ticket to survival; getting there early was a way to ensure a place.

> The feeling of security inside the heavy concrete bunkers brings out a kind of everyday atmosphere. Quiet chitchat and humming, the ladies sit around and talk about the food prices. You hardly sense any sadness or a tragic feeling about Berlin's fate. The store counter and the workshop, the dining table and the bed at home are the main things; if they are still standing, then all is well.[178]

Reevaluating what are major and what are minor things serves to seal the psychological bulkheads. Beds and dining tables can be saved; Berlin cannot. Inflating the value of beds, dining tables, workshops, and store counters led into postwar Germany, which was made up mostly of such concrete things. People could work with that. All that was reconstructed consisted of dining tables and other practical things by necessity, but people liked dealing with things they could understand. The actual main thing continued to be quoted far below value, or else it would all not be as simple as it was.

Berlin's Neukölln district dealt dryly, bone-dryly, with the human losses after the raids of February 1945, as witnessed by Danish correspondent Jacob Kronika.[179] Doubt arose among some women in the bunker regarding the invoices of the Baumschulenweg crematorium:

FIRST SPEAKER. We're getting cheated with our dead.

SECOND SPEAKER. The same coffin is used for all funerals in the chapel. But there is no corpse in the coffin.

THIRD SPEAKER. The dead are all cremated together and a share of the ashes are put into each urn. Whoever wants can take one.

SECOND SPEAKER. If we don't count for anything in life, then why should the dead?

THIRD SPEAKER. Too many people are dying. Who has time to give each one a proper funeral?

FIRST SPEAKER. Something must be done. There are limits.

There *are* limits. But when Berlin approached the limit, the limit moved as well. A businessman saved two suitcases from a residence that burned to the ground. A friend had a heart attack trying to put out the flames, and the second friend got struck by a piece of burning wood. "I've had enough," said the burned-out person to Swiss correspondent Warner before he left. He wished the wood had struck him as well. "I am worn out." The psyche steps out of this world with one foot and lies down to sleep. Some peace and quiet certainly would not hurt. Either you fought or you let it be; the drama about the whole thing waned. In the Adlon Hotel, everyone spoke in whispers. The revolving doors turned incessantly, "but still, everything is quiet, very quiet in the lobby." Soot-covered faces, everyone carrying a suitcase, a package, a bundle, like in a refugee camp. "Everyone seems dead tired; everyone has gone through the same thing; no words or explanations are necessary. Truly, a cosmopolitan city is perishing before our very eyes."[180]

In Berlin, which was pumped with fewer munitions than Magdeburg and Dresden, a strange lifelessness settled in; it stiffened and turned to stone. "On one of these indescribable days" following a night raid,

I walked down Uhlandstrasse. The people were huddling over their rescued pieces of furniture and possessions in snow and rain. Some were sleeping as they stood, by leaning against something. They were frozen in a dulled desolation and looked apathetically at the remains of their homes, where flames shot out of the basements.[181]

Kurfürstendamm was swarming with people, "dark shapes without any contours that were carefully reaching out with their hands in order to find their way. You get startled if someone laughs." People moved through Berlin as if they were on the ocean floor. Drifting by wrecks and lifeless bodies everywhere. After the war, the term "emotional paralysis" was tailored to this twilight realm. The flow of sensations came to a standstill, because the soul could not manage it. It scabbed over and became numb. Business went on, the next step was taken, a bundle of salvaged items was tied: for that a cloth and a cart would help.

4. PROTECTION

"This civilian casualty total is far removed from the generally anticipated total of several millions."

—THE U.S. STRATEGIC BOMBING SURVEY

The annihilation zone is both temporary and localized. It can be endured in protective spaces, if they are sealed and numerous, or in remote refuges that are made inhabitable by means of transportation, logistics, and supplies. Almost half the population needs bombproof quarters. Only the government can make such spaces available; the state is the guarantor for the protection of life. It also provides substitutes for the rapidly dwindling consumer goods and residences. The bombing war fetters people to the government. As a state, the Nazi regime organizes survival; as a regime, it organizes terror against the capitulators. In this way it protects itself, though already halfway wrested of sovereignty over its territory. The only choice the population has between bomb terror and regime terror is to save itself from both. Based on the annihilation energy expended, the protection of life is enormously successful, with only 0.75 percent losses. The regime, too, remains undefeated from within.

IN WAR YOU TAKE COVER. The city used to be a fortified realm, protected from cannons by its walls. When the cannons blasted through, the ramparts were reinforced. The art of fortification consisted of placing a series of barriers between the city and the enemy, who approached along the ground. As long as the enemy attacked from the horizontal plane, the city was protection. Once artillery started being fired parabolically into the city, the besieger gained the advantage. Although a city possessed ordnance and fired back, it was isolated from its supply lines and its populace remained highly vulnerable. The bomb from the air can better be resisted by the horizontal plane of the earth. Those seeking protection must head underground.

When the city of Nuremberg started building bombproof air-raid bunkers in the fall of 1940 as per the Führer's orders, it recalled the system of catacombs that the Middle Ages had driven into the sandstone rock upon which the castle, the imperial fortress, stood. The vaults had access to ventilation shafts, and in times of conquest and fireraising they served as both abode and escape. In April 1943, they were networked by means of crosscuts, insulated against moisture, and faced with clinker. That yielded protection for 15,000 people. All kinds of long-forgotten underground facilities were opened up in Germany: abandoned pits, secret passageways connecting buildings, mines, natural caves, adits and shafts, storage vaults, and the abundance of former beer cellars.

In addition to the labyrinths that frightened generations had dug into the ground, a less prestigious site came to life: storage spaces for potatoes, preserves, and coal, for barrels and bottles—in a word, cellars. The musty world of house basements became human hiding places. The bomb no longer allowed living room and bed, restaurant and street to be places of peace and quiet. Within fifteen minutes, that environment could become a boiling death zone intensified by blast waves, sparks, and shrapnel. This was not some farfetched nightmare; in 1944, the air-raid sirens blared it out almost daily.

Infantry combat had been industrialized to such an extent in 1914 that ground troops could no longer advance by marching. The firing

7. Entrance to the shelters.

Source: Archiv Michael Foedrowitz.

density left no room for that, so the army disappeared into the trenches. The battlefield remained empty until the tank arrived. When the city became a second front, the civilian, too, had to either be armored or go underground. The population was instructed to go to bed with their clothes on if possible, with their air-raid shelter suitcase at hand. It was supposed to contain their ID card, stock and bond certificates, contracts, family documents, jewelry, linens, towel, and cash—and a steel helmet, gas mask, and warm clothes. Ears were tuned to the air-raid siren's sine wave, oscillating between 300 and 400 Hz, a howling sound of constant volume; it was the most penetrating acoustic tone. Then there were ten minutes to get to safety.

The sirens were the disguised voice of the government in war; it had arranged with the citizens a series of signals that represented the situation in the air. They sounded over a radius of about 1,600 feet; a major city required hundreds or thousands of them. Warning stations triggered the alarm after being informed by the aircraft-warning centers that were linked to the radar stations. Radar and warning stations signaled the anticipated time of the danger. The message was transmitted via a code consisting of tones. It was a message of state. Increasingly complicated and finally very difficult to understand, the signals reported roughly: first, that a bomb raid could be imminent, but that nothing should be done except to remain alert; second, that a bomb raid was imminent and everyone should be in the shelters within ten minutes; third, the raid might be over, and everyone should leave the shelters; and fourth, the all clear, the danger has passed.

The bomber squadrons selected approach routes that would make it difficult for the enemy to recognize the target. They took bizarre detours, raced past the target and then returned. If Bomber Command crossed over Hanover, then everyone in Berlin who was able went to the cellars. And then there was Brunswick, Magdeburg, Leipzig: which one was the intended target? From the point of view of the attacker, a false alarm was the correct one, since it wore out the object, constantly hearing false alarms, and ideally hearing none at all at the proper time.

Over the course of the air war, the regimen of people's response relaxed. The immense and unobstructed number of bomber planes flying over the Reich confused all predictions. The danger of attack was far more frequent than the attack itself. In order to not constantly interrupt work and daily routines, the danger was endured without triggering a response. It was internalized. One could not give in to the reflex to flee; thus one lived in acute fear. Shutting out real fear for years was, in a way, the shadow cast by destruction. While few people were annihilated, most stood in the shadows of annihilation most of the time. The "public aircraft warning" siren code introduced in August 1942 announced possible attacks but did not authorize civilians to leave their homes or work to seek shelter—thus the alarm simply transformed fear into a public state. The fear was not private chicken-heartedness. The bombers were on the way and they were unpredictable.

From 1943 on, the movements of the swarms that were constantly crossing the sky were reported in an endless announcement from the "wire radio," a radio network set up over telephone and power lines. Many people in cities at risk started spending every night in the shelters. Toward the end they stayed during the day too. They lived there.

In August 1939, the ninth Implementation Order to the Air-Raid Protection Law required all homeowners to upgrade all basements to serve as air-raid shelters. The cellars had to be able to absorb the force of the collapsing building, they could not let any splinters or gas enter through windows or hatches, and there had to be a second escape route. That was a lot to demand of buildings from the late nineteenth century or earlier, whose builders had no idea that these mouseholes would one day be the fortresses in which the residents hoped to survive the collapse of their buildings. The older barrel vault proved to be the sturdiest of all basement ceilings, as in Frankfurt am Main, where medieval half-timbered buildings with multistoried basements had first-rate vaulted cellars. They were built with a mysterious mortar that was harder than cement. No one knew its composition, but the residents in the Old Town section trusted it and sought no other shelter.

Modern basement ceilings were usually able to hold up the debris of the building if they were supported by iron or timber props. Rooms were not supposed to have a capacity of more than fifty people, or else they needed thick interior walls to help stiffen the exterior walls. In order to fend off the thirty-pound incendiary bombs that were designed to penetrate interior floors, an additional casing was advisable.

In Hamburg and Düsseldorf, the outer walls of 90 percent of the buildings extended far above ground level, owing to the high groundwater table, and thus too much surface area was vulnerable to blasts and air suction. This could destabilize the basement ceiling supports. As a precaution, rubble was therefore piled up along the outer perimeter and stuck together with sand, clay, and cement. The cellars were then capable of withstanding the concussion. Even if the earthquake of a major raid made all the walls rock like a boat, and dozens of men had to brace themselves against the props to hold them upright, the cellar proved not to be particularly challenged by the mechanics of a general collapse. The stabilized cellar ceiling settled into the earth's crust, and the earth does not topple over.

The danger lurked elsewhere. The trauma of the cellar lay in being buried. The debris from collapsing buildings blocked the exits and turned the refuge into a tomb. Then the last resort was to go from cellar to cellar, continuing until at some point there was a clear way out. The construction of these passageways of underground corridors, linking together a large number of buildings, made people uneasy. They feared that thieves would come. This was why the separating walls, which were usually firewalls, were broken through and then loosely bricked up. The hole was marked with red paint. In an emergency, only a few blows of a hammer were needed to knock out the provisional masonry. This was required by law; in major cities, the costs were borne by the government.

The holes between the cellars saved many people, especially when the paths crisscrossed, forming a grid of escape routes, as the Frankfurt magistrate ordered constructed underneath the Old Town. The 36,000 Frankfurters who took cover under their apartment buildings could flee the three-quarters of a mile from Eschenheimer Gate to the Main River if they had to. There were just as many cellar chains in Kassel, but these always ended at the end of the block. If caught within a wide-area conflagration, such a corridor was usually too short, and all the exits led into the flames.

In the fire war, the caves in the ground did not provide protection very long, because the flames poisoned the air. Combustion generates heat and gases, the main agents that attack the body. But the body was rarely ignited by the fire; instead it was subjected to radiant heat or carbon monoxide. From a certain but unpredictable moment on, the cellar ceased to be a safe place. People inside the cellars had to abandon them or else be asphyxiated or die of heatstroke. The cellar retained a deceptive coolness, even when the house was in flames. People felt safe there. Outside, the explosives were detonating, sparks were flying, and boiling magma from buildings was racing through the area. Just when all instincts were advising you to stay, you had to abandon the escape hole. The stone gradually absorbed the radiant heat, glowed to the core, and turned the cellar into an oven.

The basic rule was to leave the cellar as soon as the building started burning and smoke was drawn in. The basement was not sealed against the combustion gases. They were odorless; smoke offered a warning, but not a reliable one. Innumerable cellar dwellers fell into their eternal sleep next to smoldering coal piles. The fumes often streamed through precisely those holes in the walls that allowed escape. Sometimes the holes were hammered open out of anxiety as soon as the first bombs started falling. That cleared the escape route for an emergency, but it also cleared the way for the carbon monoxide. Someone's stored coal, somewhere not far away, absorbed heat, started smoldering, and soon was emitting gases that spread throughout the block. The chemistry of combustion generated these gases from many sources. Such a fire source had never existed before: smoldering items in storage with the building above it ablaze. The draft of winds tearing through the streets and drawn into the fire lowered the air pressure in the cellars, which in turn drew in the gases from the fires above, causing the "injector effect."

At its peak, fire created two insufferable spaces, the blazing exterior and the gas-filled interior. In Kassel and Hamburg, 70 to 80 percent of the fire casualties had been gassed to death in the cellars. American researchers calculated the causes of death of the bombing war as 5 to 30 percent due to physical injuries from explosions, blast waves, and falling debris, 5 to 15 percent due to burns and inhalation of superheated air, and 60 to 70 percent from carbon monoxide poisoning.[1]

Kassel's police chief stated with regard to carbon monoxide: "This imperceptibly lethal gas can develop in any fire and will therefore always appear in major conflagrations even if no coal ignites."[2] He also said that the gas entered the cellars through the holes broken through the cellar walls. Anyone who escaped from it into the streets of the Old Town could run about one hundred feet if they then reached an open space more than three hundred feet in diameter where there was fresh air. "In narrow streets it can be assumed that some people were incinerated without a trace. The air was so hot that you felt as if you could no longer breathe." There were constant "life-threatening situations created by burning timber and pieces of masonry falling from collapsing buildings." People were deceived into

wandering from one cellar hole to the next, only to finally find what seemed like a secure air-raid cellar and to sit there crowded together and await death. For many people it would have meant being saved from death by asphyxiation if the system of passageways through the cellars were extended through underground tunnels leading out of the Old Town area to the Fulda River and the park side.

That was the failure of Kassel's police chief, who acted as the local director of civil air defense. He had nine thousand cellar holes made, most of which ended at the same place: the fire. The events of the night of October 22, 1943, were included in the reports of 120 survivors, recorded five months later by Kassel's missing persons office:[3]

> On the night of the bombing I was at home with my wife. We were alone because our son is a soldier on the eastern front. After dinner I listened to the radio, but there was interference around 7:40 p.m. For the first time during the war I brought my suitcase and other belongings into the cellar of the four-story apartment house. It was very difficult to carry my things downstairs since one of my legs had been amputated.

His wife dismissed his worrying. "The things you keep hearing!" The factory owner and his wife observed the southwestern sky from their balcony. It was dark and cloudy. Steps of the last pedestrians could be heard on the pavement late that evening; it was time to go home.

When the radio went out, it was a sign also for housewife Dorothea Pleugert née Herzog. "We got dressed and dressed the kids. We were making jokes. I said I cleaned up because today the Tommy is coming." That's what the British were called. Glazier Ottilie König from Pferdemarkt (Horse Market Square) celebrated her fiftieth birthday and sat down at the table, which was already set, "when the sirens sounded. So we took the suitcases we kept ready and the wardrobe that hung in the closet and went down to the cellar." At its base, it was twelve feet below the street. A hatch led to the garage; it was closed with a cover. "The cover kept flying up from the blast and then setting back down firmly. We kept ducking and thinking, now it's coming down."

According to the observations of the man with the amputated leg, the recent terror raids on other cities all took place shortly after dusk. Sounds of propellers hummed in the air; it could also just be planes flying over. The sirens called from the school building. There were no antiaircraft searchlights, "but I still had an eerie feeling. 'Come on, let's go to the cellar. I can feel that something's wrong.'" The couple were the first to enter the cellar. As soon as they arrived, "the gates of Hell opened, making you think the end of the world had come. The other tenants came dashing into the cellar. Most of them had very little with them and some were not dressed warmly enough."

Elisabeth Schirk, a soldier's wife, had not heard the air-raid warning right away. "My husband was home on leave; things were pretty lively here." They were the last couple from their building to go down to the bomb shelter; all the other residents were already there. "We heard hit after hit. We thought everything was collapsing above us. No smoke got in, and there was no smell of lime, but it did smell of dirt. And then we went through the hole in the wall and through number 7 through to number 5. And we stood there a while, walked around into this corner or that corner."

Just as the alarm sounded, Gretel Simon, young mother of Irmgard and Brigitte, observed the direct hit on the Sommer Inn. "And then I said to my Grandma, 'look, the people look all black, coming out of the passageway.'" Then she hurried with her grandmother and children to the well-built air-raid shelter in the Pinne Inn. "If I had stayed home then everything would have been fine. What was going on in the Pinne, I can't really explain all that well, because I blacked out. And when I came to, my daughter was screaming 'Mommy, I can't breathe.'"

The air-raid shelter of the amputee

> was well-prepared by all standards. When the first bombs hit around 8:25 p.m., the bricks around the hole through the wall were flying around like pieces of rubble. After every close hit there was such a churning of dust and air through the cellars that you thought the building would collapse at any moment. The sound of buildings crashing down nearby was so dreadful, as was the terrible thunder of two factory chimneys that collapsed, both landing right next door. Peeking out through the cellar hole you could see only a sliver of the sky, glowing red.

After three-quarters of an hour things got quieter; two men climbed out, "but they came back down immediately with the terrible news: every building, the entire neighborhood was in flames. But our building was not yet on fire."

Dorothea Pleugert, who had no cellar in her own building, had gone down to the street, to Wildemanngasse no. 30, where the residents of no. 32 were already assembled,

> since everything there was on fire. Then our building caretaker came and said we had to leave, that the whole building was already burning, but

don't get excited. A man went through the hole in the wall to find a way out. He called out, "It's impossible. Everything is in flames." Then we wanted to go out to the street through Frege's place, but the phosphorus started coming down the stairs. So we went back.

Ottilie König, the glazier, didn't know what to do; the fourth floor of the building was burning. "The men were trying to put out the fire, but when they looked out the window they saw that the Old Town was already a sea of flames. They came down to the basement and warned us to be prepared to leave, because the fire was working its way down." People came from the cellars at Pferdemarkt and asked what they could do. They had come through the holes connecting the cellars looking for a way out. "We told them that the best chances were by us, because you could run diagonally across the street to Kasernenstrasse and then to St. Martin's Square. But most of them didn't listen and continued to crawl through the cellars."

Soldier Schirk and his wife were not very lucky:

> Then the men tried to see if there was some way we could escape, but when the lights went out my husband said I should just sit down with the little ones. He was running around looking for some way to save us. Finally, when he couldn't keep going anymore he said, "Come on, let's lie down. It's no use." The people in the room were rather calm; only the young children were crying terribly.

The parents, their twelve-year-old boy, and the little girl lay down to sleep.

The screams of her child pulled Gretel Simon back to consciousness. "She was lying under dead bodies in the cellar. And I had my youngest on my arm and she survived until six in the morning." Gretel Simon blacked out again from the gas. "The older one kept screaming, so I kept waking up. That was good." Her youngest child lay at her feet. Because there was no light, she could hear her older daughter Irmgard, but couldn't see her. "And I wanted to ask a neighbor if she had any matches, but the woman was already dead and cold."

In view of the increasing heat of the fire, the amputee factory owner was determined to leave the cellar. "When I expressed my opinion, a sense of general disquiet spread throughout the cellar. My wife also said 'we have to get out of here, the firewall is coming down on us.'" The neighbors lay down flat on the ground, one woman held her head with both hands and pulled her jacket over her ears. "Little Marga kept calling out 'are we getting dead?' Someone said, 'We'll never get out of here; it's burning everywhere.'" Those who wanted to leave soaked blankets, coats, and hats in water, and everyone took a gulp of cognac from the factory owner's bottle. "It was French Hennessy that we had been saving."

When they were standing outside, the group was taken aback. "The first sight of the street was a gaze into hell. Every building, almost every cobblestone was burning as if driven by a blowtorch." Some wanted to go back to the cellar. "Then we can die just as well on the street," said the amputee, "if only the wooden leg doesn't catch fire." He couldn't make it over the piles of rubble with the leg.

Meanwhile, Dorothea Pleugert and the people from Wildemanngasse had found a way out and had wandered aimlessly through the fire for half an hour before finding refuge in a cellar of the Department of Sanitation, since they could not keep going anymore.

> Then the police and fire department came. We had to leave or else we'd be stewed! A lot started saying: "We want to wait until a car comes by." "Then you'll be waiting a long time." There was another woman in this cellar who was about to give birth. And since there was no one there who could help her there was a man who washed his hands and was going to try. I don't know what happened to that woman.

The glazier was encouraged to flee the cellar around 9:30 by her daughter and her daughter's friend. "Now come on, we don't want to suffocate." Ottilie König gave her the shopping bag with "our cutlery with bread and butter." They were supposed to run to St. Martin's Square where there would be enough air. "And that was the last we saw of them." The mother took her mother's hand but soon lost her. "I myself was pushed by the firestorm into St. Martin's Church, where three hundred people had gone for shelter, until it burned above our heads. The organ burned, the choir, the roof, and the big bell fell down." A Wehrmacht unit brought the people outside. "Now I am alone with my husband; that was our only daughter."

Dorothea Pleugert, still waiting in the Sanitation Department's cellar with Frau Pfarr and her three children, was afraid to come out because the children were wearisome. "Someone came and said she had to go out right away, that he would bring the other child who was standing at the back of the cellar. But she refused, saying 'I won't leave here without my child.'"

The man with the amputated leg had chanced upon a wide street with his group,

or else we would not have been able to save ourselves. It led us to the Lower Town station where a lot of people were already gathered. We thought, first of all we could get some air. Air, air, air. All around us was a picture of horror. Mothers with their small children squatted on the bare ground and dropped from exhaustion. One woman called out looking for her husband, "Have you seen my husband?" "My dear woman, how should I know who your husband is?" "Well, a man all by himself." Another woman kept screaming, "I've lost everything. I've lost everything." "Oh, don't drive us crazy. Be quiet, we lost everything too." We had filled our pockets with apples. I had an apple in my hand and gave little Marga one too. And a woman came and said, "oh, let me have a bite." And she just about grabbed the apple away from me. The thirst was unbearable. And then there was Herr Lingens. He laid down on the ground and cried. We asked, "Where is your daughter and your son?" "I don't know anything. I don't know anything. They were able to save themselves but have serious burns." We hoped that at least our things in the cellar were safe. We had carried everything down there: dishes and linens and blankets and clothes and hats and shoes and furs and all the bookkeeping and the cash box. Churchill took everything, the bastard.

Dorothea Pleugert made it to the Fulda bridge with her girlfriend and the three children. "Then we turned onto the Schlagd promenade. When we made it up to the old fortification tower, the Rondell, there was a woman standing there with a child in her arms. 'Someone handed me the child; it wasn't mine.'" As Dorothea Pleugert went by the Pinne Inn the next morning looking for her mother, they were carrying out both the living and dead on stretchers. "The children they were carrying out of the Pinne were mostly wrapped in cloth, so we couldn't recognize them. Their faces were also mostly disfigured."

It was soldiers who dug out Gretel Simon and others at the Pinne at 7:30 in the morning. "I woke up and called out, 'Dear man, please help me pull out my child.' I couldn't even stand up since the dead bodies were lying all around my feet. Two soldiers came and got out my older child and myself. The little one was already ice cold."

Elisabeth Schirk woke up early Saturday morning on Jägerstrasse, lying on the pavement, after having lain down to sleep the night before with her family. She was taken to a Red Cross camp.

The next morning I felt so wretched about my loved ones and I tried to see if I could walk. I walked from the Red Cross back to Jägerstrasse all by myself, only semiconscious. And my husband was lying there dead in the street. Then they said it was an air-raid alarm and we had to leave. I ran to the bunker at the Schlagd. And when the alarm was over I went back and as I got to Jägerstrasse my son was lying there; in the meantime they had just carried him out. I screamed so terribly, they sent me away. A woman told me she saw my husband die on the street; why had they not gotten them out until Sunday? My husband was young and strong; he certainly would have survived.

Because the cellars were both shelter and grave, there was a lot of discussion about the point of transition between those two states. It was important to leave the basements in time. When this point came depended on the outcome of the raid. What was happening outside? Visibility was poor. Concrete blinds guarded the cellar windows against shrapnel and debris fragments; and delayed-action bombs might be exploding in front of the doors. The situation invisible from down below was confusing up above; it changed from one minute to the next. The survivors had done something right; the dead, something wrong. There was no other way to see it. Also, one's understanding blurred the more one thought about it. As the oxygen supply diminished, so did one's insight. A leaden fatigue settled on the brain. Those who understood better tried to pull along those who were totally apathetic or for whom the effort was too great, the decision too difficult, or the risk too high. Advice and persuasion became a matter of life and death. Some husbands could not get their wives to break out of the cellars, neither by pleading nor by force. Older children left behind timid mothers; the former ran to their ruin and the latter suffocated. The majority survived by good luck alone; the bad luck of the losers was reported by the recovery teams and anatomists.

Inhaling the gases accelerated one's heart rate. An uneasiness developed before consciousness sank into a bottomless ravine. The lack of oxygen functioned differently; people searched for it and slurped it up laboriously, finally lying down on the ground, since that was where the last remaining bit hovered. The Hamburg anatomists Siegfried Gräff and Helmuth Baniecki examined the cellars when they were still warm and made detailed descriptions of the human remains they found.

They were often sitting on chairs or on the steps in rows or individually on benches. Yes, I could even find a corpse standing, leaning against the wall; others were lying in all kinds of positions on the ground. Often they were covered with cloth or they had some kind of object on their heads, a steel helmet or woolen things, and some of them also had put a gas mask over their face.[4]

The descriptions often repeated the comment "as if sleeping." In Darmstadt, there were reports of opening up cellars "in which coke had burned." Wehrmacht recovery teams "needed alcohol in order to be able to work." The bodies they recovered "were sitting there like ghosts; their faces masked with blankets and scarves with which they sought protection from the smoke."[5]

The cellars were used as a refuge for human bodies in the fire war because there were so many of them to begin with. How else could fireproof auxiliary accommodations suddenly be acquired for one and a half million Hamburgers? Not until the summer of 1943 did it sink in that there was nothing else available. The bomber swarms were undaunted by both fighter attacks and flak artillery. The Germans wanted to endure the war from the air, but most of them were left with no better protection than their basement cellars. The trusted vault turned into a hostile enemy during a fire raid. Constant warnings to remove the coal stored in the cellars were met in part with compliance and in part with the question: and put it where? No one thought they would be gassed to death by their own bricks of coal. Owing to people's inertia, the matter was never resolved. But the problem of the drafts of air, on the other hand, was not in their hands in the first place.

Residents were instinctually drawn to the basement if something outside exploded, splintered, or burned. But the underground coolness merely postponed the inevitable. The cellar was a cold oven. The burning housing block transferred the glowing heat to the cellar stone, where it was stored. Rescue teams could not enter buried cellars for days or even weeks because they remained too hot. If not touched directly by the flames, the fire casualties were mummified, and not until an autopsy was performed could it be determined whether the cause of death was gas, lack of oxygen, or heat, but people wanted to know. In order for a chamber to become an oven, there had to be a draft, a flow of air.

After gaining experience from the Kassel firestorm in late 1943, Dresden's air-raid protection agencies started interlinking the cellars under the Old Town with passageways that had been dug out and bricked up under the streets.[6] The cellars and passages created a meshed network. Whereas in Kassel escape to the Fulda River had been blocked, in Dresden every corridor was supposed to lead either to the Elbe River to the north or the Great Garden to the south. There were large exit shafts on the Elbe side at the New Market and at Schlossplatz and Postplatz, the squares at the castle and post office. On the opposite side, toward the main train station and Ammonstrasse, Wiener Strasse, and Lennéstrasse, there were no special exits, but any entrance to an apartment building could serve that function.

Dresden did not have bunkers. The network of catacombs of the basement cellars provided cover, and the banks of the Elbe and the Great Garden offered cooling and air. But this system failed. The cellars held their occupants tight, and thousands died in them due to the air draft.

The corridors under the Old Town served as an entrance and exit. According to the plan, people entered when the bombing started, protecting themselves from fragments, shrapnel, and flames, and left when the bombers withdrew after thirty to sixty minutes. During that time, the cellars remained cool. As the stone gradually started absorbing the heat of the fire, people were supposed to move to the natural escape zones outdoors. The concept failed to consider both the ovenlike qualities of the cellars and the behavior of the people who became aware of those qualities.

There was a differential of up to five feet in the cellar levels under Dresden's Old Town. The network was not on a single level: there was an upper and a lower section. Also, if an entire city district went up in flames, the fire also penetrated downward into the ground, igniting stores, storage shelves, slatted partitions, and coal. Individually, they were isolated, extinguishable occurrences. In addition, the masses of people seeking refuge did not all enter the passageways at the same time. Pedestrians came running in somewhat later, and were relieved to find a door or a hatch to what they believed was safety. The higher entrance was not sealed properly; there were open gaps, and a chimney effect developed. The small fires were fanned by drafts from numerous sources, and the flames blazed up. Hot air rises. The element of fire did not tire at turns and corners; it swept through the grid of corridors to its destination. On the way it hurled embers and sparks into all the cellars adjoining the higher corridors. The people in more than a hundred cellars there were steamed and roasted by hot air.

The agitation of the cellar dwellers had them opening up almost all the holes in the walls within a few minutes, which multiplied the draft. Heat, gases, flames, and smoke whipped though the entire labyrinth. The people trying to flee filled up the passageways, which were blocked by luggage, baby carriages, and people waiting. The entire Old Town was running around down there, narrowing the diameter of the already tight corridors. Computations reckoned with the gradual emptying of the cellars. But a panicked mass that fights its way through will hit, squeeze, or trample to death anything in its path. And that was just what happened. Several horror stories were reported: fifty people got so wedged in a corridor that they got stuck like a plug. They died together, and when their bodies were recovered, they had to be separated by force.

The tightly meshed underground construction was a landscape of insanity. Underneath the intersection of Margarethenstrasse and Marienstrasse, across from the Drei Raben Hotel, a suspended door connected two passageways that came together at a right angle. The inhabitants of two cellars bolted for the door at the same moment from opposite directions, which kept the door from opening at all. Since they themselves were the obstruction, they were unable to remove it, and they died together from the heat.

There was a steel door underneath Moritzstrasse measuring only twenty-three inches by thirty inches, which closed off an exit shaft. A group raced toward it and the man in front opened it. Those behind the first man pulled him back because they wanted to get out first, and he was killed. Two hundred people were pushing from behind, so the dead man's body could not be moved out of the way. Instead, the pressure pushed it into the shaft, blocking the outlet. It had to be moved either forward or back, but there was no leeway because of the pushing from behind. The corpse could not be budged, and it took everyone with it to their deaths.

The tightness of space, heat accumulation, combustion gases, lack of oxygen, and the draft in the cellars all contributed to making the closest escape route into a crematorium. That was where most bombing victims died. However, the vast majority who climbed out of them unscathed would probably not have survived outside the cellars.

The Germans tried quickly to build something better. Shelters that were stronger than the explosions and conflagrations, indestructible and nonflammable, that would remain standing when everything else collapsed and burned to the ground; fists of reinforced concrete; manifestations of their staying power.

There was a hierarchy of protective structures. Similar to the basement cellars but better fortified were the "Public Air-Raid Shelters," which were simply larger cellars under administrative buildings, department stores, train stations, museums, schools, or banks; in other words, under more solidly built buildings. People at busy locations who were surprised by the air-raid alarms were to go to these shelters. There were thirty-two square feet allotted per person, with a maximum capacity of four hundred people. The reinforced ceiling, fans, airlocks with gas-tight doors in case of chemical warfare agents, blast-proof metal doors, and emergency exits were highly appreciated. According to regulations, they had to withstand direct hits by one-ton bombs; that had been the standard size of the attackers' bombs, until newer developments weighing three to six tons. The asylums that were most resilient to blasts and detonations were fatefully also highly fire-prone. Department stores burned best of all; they went up like torches, quickly igniting the wider surroundings. No cellar could withstand the heat of a glowing, red-hot department store, such as the Karstadt store in the Barmbek district of Hamburg. The 370 lifeless bodies found there as if they had fallen asleep, however, had been poisoned from gases from the coke pile.

Suburbs, smaller towns, villages, parks, and foreign-worker barracks had to be content with the weakest of all protections, the slit trench, which was a ditch with a concrete slab cover. It measured seven feet deep and six feet wide, with wood supports on the sides. Galleries for about fifty people each were offset to hinder the progression of a longitudinal blast. Adaptation of the trenches from the previous war offered some protection from shrapnel fragments and blast damages. It could not withstand a direct hit, however, which brought down the earthen covering. In smaller towns, residents of homes without basements protected themselves in ditches they dug and maintained themselves. That was the extent of the air-raid protection in Herford, for instance, where half of the residents lacked adequate cellars. At least people in ditches could not be buried by rubble; they were spared this ever-present fear, which traumatized cellar dwellers. Nothing remained after a direct hit. The slit trench gained new renown starting in the fall of 1944. It did its job passably well when strafers started chasing down anything that moved.

Underground cells of medium quality, the pipes, were lowered about six feet below street intersections, bus stops or tram stops, and in crowded areas outside the city center. The human-sized concrete tube was between sixty and 260 feet long, and offered short-term refuge. Other than that, it collected too much water at the bottom, and the mold and mustiness were depressing. Fifty people usually sat on benches facing one another; there was forced ventilation, electricity, dry toilets, and neighbors in the pipe "next door." Up to five of them were laid parallel or sometimes stacked on top of one another in the ground. Larger systems of them could pack in more than one thousand people. If heating and folding cots were added, people referred to "pipe bunkers," but that raised false hopes. The pipes could protect against falling rubble and bomb shrapnel, but nothing else. At the time of the firestorm, Hamburg had 370 of them, with room for sixty thousand.

The best protection the ground could offer were the "underground tunnels" dug about thirty to forty feet into the ground, which were surpassed only by the "slope tunnels" in mountainsides. The recesses of mountains and hills provided the best possible protection against direct hits of any caliber, all incendiary weapons, and even firestorms. These caves were dug into rock and earth like mining adits; lined with concrete or supported by steel arches, they offered refuge for up to 1,500 people. For higher capacities, common rooms were required with 3.5 square feet of floor area and 26.5 cubic feet of air space per person.

Slope tunnels were preferred because they required minimal construction and less time to complete. Types of slope tunnels were also built in the flatlands in mining waste mounds and blast furnace slag heaps. The facilities had electricity and were drained, ventilated, and—thanks to the excrement disposal lift—hygienic; porous building materials worked against condensation. Once "earthquake bombs" started falling, a sixteen-foot-thick protective cover was added if the stone was crumbly, and the entryway was fortified. The excavation work was done by young people; blasting and drilling was supervised by older pit workers. Cities with a mining tradition, such as Essen, built their own air-raid tunnels, with a total capacity of 58,000.[7] Existing mining adits accommodated another 27,000. All in all, 136,000 people went down into the underworld of shafts and eighty thousand into tunnels, flak towers, and bunkers. About 40 to 50 percent of the population that remained in Essen had access to a safe asylum from bombs. Nearby, Dortmund dug out a system of deep tunnels up to the end of 1943 extending from the main train station to the West Park; there were nineteen entrances to the system, and new side tunnels were constantly added, for a total capacity of eighty thousand.[8] The walls were lined with benches. Visitors sat facing one another in the cylinder like train passengers traveling through the bombing night.

The city of Osnabrück extended tunnel protection to almost half the residents.[9] Toward the end of the war, the system was three and a half miles long and accommodated 45,600 people, who were crowded in seven per yard. The incredible congestion under the Kalkhügel, a hill with two longitudinal tunnels and numerous cross-cuts, increased to two thousand visitors in the densely built-up area when the alarms sounded. Army families set up the Barbara tunnel, with entrances on Mozart Strasse and Johann Sebastian Bach Strasse. A tunnel grid with space for eight thousand was set up in the rock of the Klushügel. The hospital tunnel at the Wiener Wall embankment was the largest, offering space to 12,000 people. City-center residents and people caught out on the streets found refuge there, beneath more than eighty feet of rock. Residents living near the Schinkelberg hill drilled out 266 protective passageways themselves.

A ring of hills usually spurred residents to seek protection in their interior. The Stuttgart valley basin was interspersed with concrete tunnels and 115 U-shaped Pioneer tunnels braced with mining timber, which attracted groups of house residents to the hills in the evenings. Anyone who helped build was guaranteed a permanent admission ticket. The twenty thousand people who fit inside had thus completed a Pioneer engineering achievement. In early January 1943, there were 481,000 people living in Stuttgart; in January 1945, only 282,000.[10] During those two years of heavy raids, 200,000 had left the city for the rural environs; those who remained shared the 410,000 places in air-raid shelters; it was a first-class ratio.[11] Far more than half were residential basement cellars; 25,000 found refuge in public air-raid shelters, 4,500 in slit trenches. Bunkers and adit tunnels offered protection for 102,000 Stuttgarters; during the most dangerous period, that was roughly one in two. The armaments industry drew fifty-three air raids to the city, which was hit by a total of 27,000 tons of bombs—about twenty thousand high-explosive bombs and 1.3 million incendiaries. On top of the constant raids came the intensity of the impact; one in three homes was completely destroyed. Its unfortunate location in a valley basin led to the firestorm of September 12, 1944. Stuttgart lost 4,477 people; based on the lowest figure of inhabitants at the time, that represents 1.56 percent. Osnabrück had offered 100 percent of its citizens place in a shelter, half of which were bomb-proof. The roughly ninety thousand residents of Osnabrück who remained there were subjected to ten thousand tons of bombs, 220 pounds per person; 1,434 people died, or 1.59 percent. Stuttgart and Osnabrück touched on the upper limit of what was possible in German air-raid protection during World War II.

Refuge in bunkers was available for 68,000 Stuttgarters, almost 10,000 in the two-story, five-door Wagenburg tunnel. The titanic bulwarks of the bombing war assembled the German people, except for those fighting at the front. But there were also always a few dozen front-line soldiers home on leave who said how good it was to go back to the front. The cellar was a place of drama. It was in direct contact with the annihilation going on outside. The house residents were either silent or they prayed, screamed, and cried, or wrestled with the question of whether fleeing or waiting would save them. In the bunkers, this was out of the question. The bunker occupants were prepared for the ruin of it all: city, property, state, nation—everything except for their bare skin. Sheer life was saved; existence deteriorated. The bunker was the venue of the "we." With very few words—since the Gestapo had ears everywhere—the "we" came to an understanding of the state of affairs.

The state of affairs of the bunker itself says it all. Between walls made in accordance with the *Braunschweiger Bewehrung*, the "Brunswick method"—that is, structural steel beams, steel wire mesh with concrete three meters thick, with a greater percentage of metal toward the inside—three thousand people can survive in a multi-story cube. Survival was questionable outside the cube, but its walls marked the absolute limit of destruction, which could not overcome the Brunswick method. Its walls surrounded a fictional place that did not participate in the demise of the world. Krefeld building officer Werner Jansen, who was responsible for air-raid bunkers in his city, called them Noah's Ark.[12] Because it stayed afloat, the Flood was not absolute. Life continued.

Hitler, as an amateur architect, by no means regretted the burning of the cities. "We'll rebuild our cities more beautiful than they ever were," he swore to Albert Speer, "I shall see to that. With more monumental buildings than they ever had."[13] Guarantor of the "afterward" is the first of the monuments: the bunker. Afterward, the occupants come out, Germany is gone, and they build a new one. Did any concept of that remain, except in Hitler's fever? The cellar dwellers shared the destruction of existence, as was summarized in the stereotypical sentence: "I lost everything." The bunker dwellers also lost everything, but the bunker told them that that was not the main thing. As long as the bunker kept them bunkered, they could apply for replacements. So the bunker fed the notion that Germany could be replaced. You just had to come out alive.

In reality, cellar dwellers and bunker dwellers were the same people. People took cover in one as well as in the other. The difference in the security they offered later led hordes of people to move from the cellars to the bunkers, which were filled to three or four times their capacities from 1943 on. This movement kept the human losses down to an average of 0.7 percent, based on the total population. Wehrmacht losses were ten times that amount. The rapid increase in human casualties followed the multiplied volume of bomb tonnage; deaths and tonnage both increased, but not to the same degree.

Air-raid protection was highly effective in two ways: it could ensure the survival of the people and the survival of the regime. In view of the 50 to 90 percent destruction of the cities, the 1.5 percent average rate of urban casualties must be viewed as a success. The difference between the two losses diverged though they were mutually dependent. Because the intensity of destruction increased, Germany went to the bunkers. And because Germany was sitting in the bunkers, it was not as bothered by the destruction. Continued survival was relatively certain, so Bomber Command and the Eighth Air Force were able to ablate the urban landscape little by little without their really moving very much. According to an old saying, the air war was fought between British bombers and German concrete. The opposite was just as true. The bomber-versus-concrete war was ineffective except for the fact that it did not cease wrecking everything outside the bunkers.

Göring banked on the active air defenses, namely, fighter planes and flak. Hitler, on the other hand, disliked the whole idea of protection, because terror could be broken only through terror anyway. He insisted on attack. All that was lacking was an offensive weapon. All the more astounding was the Führer's emergency program of October 10, 1940, for the construction of "bombproof air-raid shelters" in seventy-nine cities. Accordingly, 5.3 million cubic yards of concrete were to be used by the following summer to provide protection as fast as possible for a half million people. The list mentioned primarily industrial cities, including some smaller ones, even some that

Bomber Command had not yet attacked: Wülfrath, Neunkirchen, Oberwesel. This demonstrated certain sensitivities.

The Germans feared—at a time when the British were having trouble finding enough to eat—a systematic attack on the key sites of weapons manufacture. Because factories could not go into the bunkers, Hitler's program protected the working-class families, a group whose morale was considered questionable since 1918. They were the first to need support. Armaments minister Fritz Todt, who, as the chief civil engineer in charge of public works, had already built the autobahns and the Siegfried Line, saw his new concrete battle as a successor to the ramparts, trenches, and fortifications of earlier days. Now he saw the inextinguishable emerging, the "defense for all time." In practice, it referred to more pressing matters such as the four-thousand-person-capacity container for the sulfuric-acid-producing proletariat at IG Farben in Uerdingen near Krefeld. Militarily more dispensable were the residents in the vicinity of the imperial cathedrals in Worms and Speyer, which were not on Hitler's list. Plain and simple, the bunker construction program was the answer to the British plans to bomb the workers' rebellion into existence.

After a year, 4.5 million cubic yards of concrete had been used in construction, more sluggishly than intended; the next million took longer. On May 7, 1943—during the first Battle of the Ruhr—the 6.7 million cubic yard mark was reached. In between, in September 1942, the decision to build the Atlantic Wall was made. According to German predictions, Churchill's bombing war would fail, a ground offensive on France's northwestern coast would follow, and the beachhead area would have to be fortified. The 13.6 million cubic yards of concrete in this structure was no longer available for bunker construction, which otherwise could have increased to three times the volume.

When the Atlantic Wall was completed in May 1944, just in time for it to fail, the bunker capacities flowed into the industrial relocations. Now the subterranean bunker worlds emerged in remote forests and saved the factories. The Reich was stingy with the building materials that it allocated to the cities and communities that administered their own air-raid matters. Less threatened cities—so-called second-order air-raid protection sites—bore the burden themselves anyway; from 1943 on, even the "first-order air-raid protection sites" did not have much of a choice. Mayors and police chiefs—like all of Germany—proceeded to arrange the bare necessities. A barge load of cement or a train-car load of iron rods was trafficked like black-market butter; highly punishable, but it helped.

Once the central authorities withdrew from protection construction, all imaginable organs started improvising. The Nazi party dug out twenty-three thousand slit trenches in the late summer of 1943; the SS formed construction brigades made up of concentration camp prisoners; cities such as Mainz reactivated ancient stronghold vaults. Construction companies called on communities for help, and offered everything: equipment, hands, materials. Starting in December 1943, residence groups in southern Westphalia raced to dig tunnels. Wherever it worked, air-raid protection was a self-help project even regarding its leading product, the bunker supply. The quality varied from place to place; average figures said nothing about the actual conditions. A well-equipped air-raid protection site was one that lost only between six and sixteen human lives per hundred tons of bombs. A poorly equipped one yielded 1,200 to 1,700 deaths.

Like all figures and facts about the air war, blanket statistics are uncertain and disputable. The Reich auditing office accounted for two thousand bunkers, but credible officials have said that three thousand were built. A small one measuring 22 x 33 x 33 yards needed a maximum of eight thousand tons of reinforced concrete, for a total of twenty thousand tons of building material. Such a mass countered the blast of a blockbuster with an inertia that could easily absorb it within the short duration of the detonation. The prescribed cube strength was 4,250 pounds per square inch.

A direct hit caused a very loud, metallic sound on the outer shell. The upper floors got covered with dust, and the entire bunker shook, not in its structure, but rather because it rocked on its sand or clay base, even given the wide screening around the foundations, to fend off bombs impacting at an angle. In exceptional cases, bunkers cracked, as on Körnerstrasse in Cologne, in Hagen, where four hundred people were killed, and in Bonn and Münster. A bomb believed to be a special model penetrated the Schützenhof bunker in Münster and detonated; blocks of concrete broke off and struck sixty-eight occupants dead. Admittedly, the roof was only 4.5 feet thick, half of what was prescribed for a 1,500-capacity bunker. News of the new "bunker-buster" bombs was the impetus for eight thousand people, more than 6 percent of the population at the time, to flee the city, which had enough space in bunkers for one in five. This cracked bunker did not lead to any above-average casualty figures in the city's total of 102 air raids and 1,400 dead, but it did shatter people's trust in the bunker as a final protection. It was feared that the bunker-buster bombs could someday split the eternal concrete of the Reich.

The fact that his bunkers held out at home corresponded to Hitler's orders to hold out on the front. They were the "last man" in the incinerated city and at the same time his domicile. The leadership knew this. While new construction generally decreased, they did not stop reinforcing the walls and ceilings of their strongholds. The roof strength was increased to almost fifteen feet in areas worthy of great protection. The war continued "the undecided race between bomb-resistant structures and bombs that constantly increased in penetrating force," wrote the United States Strategic Bombing Survey in 1947.[14]

Construction of a large bunker took nine months, cost 700,000 marks, and was, according to the USSBS, "Germany's great experiment. No shelter buildings exist in the United States or England similar to these so-called 'Bunkern.'"[15] The adversaries assessed the structures for air-raid protection more positively than later voices in the Federal Republic of Germany, which thought the effort had been too little and too late. The USSBS referred to "the most tremendous constructional program in civilian or passive defense for all time."[16] By that they meant the endeavor to accommodate, according to a hierarchical security concept, Germany's urban population, in cellars, adits and tunnels, bunkers, and trenches; to bunker hospital patients, artworks, files, libraries, and archives; and to provide everyone with more or less protected, often gas-proofed shelters that were accessible within ten minutes.

Subterranean bunkers, which were favored at the start of the initial construction phase, were quickly abandoned in favor of the more economical tower bunker. While its mammoth size appeared to proclaim the greatness of its originator, it was actually only a sign of financial difficulties. The Nazi party felt uneasy about assemblies of three to five thousand people and, regarding the flak bunkers at Heiligengeistfeld (Holy Ghost Field) in Hamburg, up to even thirty thousand. But it was less expensive to build one mammoth than six buffaloes for five hundred people each.

The party was suspicious of public gatherings in the bunkers, because this had been their very own specialty. This time, however, the master of ceremonies was the air war, and it placed the facts of the devastation of existence into the midst of life. These could be balanced out only with counterfactuals, not with speeches. The Nazi party could not offer any facts; all it had were words that everyone was tired of hearing, now that they had proved to be hollow. The bunker gatherings were also interested in news, another commodity of which the party wanted to protect its monopoly.

News during the air war was transmitted by rumor, and the bunker was its marketplace. What had really happened at the landmarks of Cologne, Wuppertal, and Hamburg was passed along only by stories, hearsay. Neither Goebbels nor the London radio spoke of the realities of a firestorm, the number of dead, and the circumstances of death. The rumor—as imprecise, exaggerated, and bizarre as its nature was—was closer to the events than the propagandists. The bunker dwellers, as the party verified, were avid listeners; they believed everything and quickly passed it on. Germany had become one huge rumor mill. The scarcity of official news and facts confirmed for Hitler loyalists that everything was going well, and for skeptics, that one had to reckon with the worst. The worst circulated as rumors and jokes.

As more and more residential housing was destroyed, the bunker became an abode. Several wide stairways and an elevator led to the corridors, onto which rooms for six or more people opened. The interior was supposed to be attractive; the bedrooms had bunk beds. Rooms with benches were added as needed. There was a shared toilet and washroom for every twenty-five people. A first-aid room for three hundred people was the minimum standard; the maximum equipment included complete hospital facilities. The forced ventilation system had to accomplish an enormous task: It had to pump out the carbon dioxide that was released by so many people in such close quarters, as well as their odors. Filters against combustion gases were necessary, as were others for poison gas, in case the Allies used chemical weapons. Eleven cubic feet of air was planned per person per minute; the temperature had to remain within the range of 62 to 75 degrees Fahrenheit; the relative humidity between 25 and 75 percent. The motor for the ventilation and heating could be operated in three ways: with electricity, diesel fuel, or by hand. The oil supply had to suffice for at least eight days.

Air conditions became precarious if the bunkers were crowded beyond capacity; oxygen masks and smelling salts were available for people who passed out. One room in every bunker was reserved for pregnant mothers and newborns. Home births were too risky due to the perpetual danger of air raids, and there was no longer any space available in hospitals. Bunker delivery rooms were set up. People carried their sick to the medical rooms in the bunkers, and the physician in charge gave them first aid.

Because of the mortal anguish suffered by residents in cities that were repeatedly attacked, many refused to go into basement cellars and public air-raid shelters. Only those obsessed with their possessions still stayed in their apartments defending their property, because the barricades to keep out looters were inadequate. The residents of entire streets moved into the bunkers. The daring part of the neighborhood banded together to form patrols that guarded the deserted districts. Between 4 and 5 p.m., the subways were jammed with suitcases and baby carriages; workers who could not get on the trains became annoyed and raised hell. It was the hour of the "bunker broads," who set out early to secure their space.

The working-class population got annoyed with "idlers" who claimed their bunker places in the late morning hours. Over the course of the day, several hundred people gathered in front of the two narrow entrances to the bunker at Hermannplatz in the Neukölln district of Berlin, including many mothers with children. Waiting rankled. Some women who had already secured spaces were not from the area. They had time and could wait for hours to be the first to scurry in. The "folding-chair squadrons" were constantly marching to the bunkers. The Neukölln bunker did not open until five minutes before a full alarm. The "national comrades" opened up their chairs and sat in the corridors, blocking the way. As a result, it was impossible to fill the bunker quickly, and there was no room left when the regular arrivals finally got there. The bunker in the Friedrichshain district was just about stormed because one section was not opened. There, people tried to avoid the policeman standing at the door. Nazi party monitors, sometimes the local group leader, took their posts inside. They shouted and gave confusing instructions. People came in with heavy suitcases that they placed on the seats, which were then unavailable for others to sit on. They got nasty when reprimanded. "Will you replace my things if they get blown up?"

It took fifteen minutes to fill a large bunker with a capacity of twenty thousand people. People entered through four five-meter-wide doors. Then the doors were closed once and for all. There was an average of ten minutes from the alarm to when the bombs started falling. After that, the police repeatedly stressed, no one was supposed to be on the streets. Getting six people with luggage to pass a five-meter entranceway each second requires military discipline. The fear and shoving, with children and the elderly, with the bombers threatening, led regularly to infernal incidents.

Three thousand people could fit in the lower level of a subway station converted to a bunker in Berlin-Neukölln. Once, in August

1944, the alarm sounded too late. By the time people seeking refuge reached the tunnel, the flak were already firing salvos into the sky. The entrance stairway was blocked and a triangle of people that gradually made its way through the doorway got stuck due to latecomers pushing from behind. Because they were afraid that the gates would be shut in their faces, they forced their way in until no movement at all was possible. The hurrying suitcase-carriers got stuck like a cork in the stairway bottleneck and were unable to enter. Soldiers tried to pull people out from above in order to allow passage, but some people below fell and were trampled to death. After ten minutes, the entrance was clear again, but ten women, children, and elderly people lay lifeless, lined up on the platform. Not a single bomb had been dropped in the area.

The same scene played out in virtually all of Germany's major cities. In the raid on Magdeburg on January 16, 1945, bombs started falling at 9:30 p.m. At the bunker at St. James's Church, three blocks from the Elbe, the blast doors made of double steel plates closed tight on the rubber sealing gasket. After the firestorm, the secure doors could not be reopened, due to the mass of dead bodies lying in front of them.

In Hanover, on the night of July 14, 1944, a father and his two daughters were standing in line in front of the bunker at Klagesmarkt Square.[17] The red markers fell from the sky and the iron door shut. Monitors pulled one of the girls into the half-empty bunker. "In their panic and their fear, the people pressed even more down the stairs. They didn't know the doors had already been closed. Consequently, especially the elderly and children were crushed and trampled. Some men jumped into the melee from the railing." The second girl was halfway down the stairs, carrying her belongings in a backpack. "She was pushed up, so she could breathe and she survived. After the all clear it was impossible to open the bunker doors since so many dead and injured were lying in front of them. The monitors exited through an emergency shaft and saw to it that the doorway was cleared."

The advantage of bunkers over other air-raid shelters led to their overcrowding by four- or fivefold the official capacity. The flak tower at Berlin's Zoo train station, with room for twenty thousand, filled with thirty thousand people. Statistically, Berlin had enough air-raid shelter space for less than 2 percent of the population, making it one of the most poorly equipped cities, after Dresden and Leipzig. Because the city was so spread out, the death rate still remained below that of

Ruhr cities, which were far better organized as regards air-raid protection. But that did not mean that people didn't pant to get a space.

Over greater distances, the subway and commuter trains were crammed with protection seekers. The battle for a bunker space was occasionally preceded by the battle for a space in the subway to get there. On February 3, 1945, the day after the 2,200-ton raid by the U.S. Air Force, residents ran around the streets wildly, not paying attention to the unexploded and time-delay bombs. At 11 p.m., the sirens announced an air raid. A hectic mass of people awaited the last subway on the line from Memeler Strasse to Alexanderplatz. There were fights at every station. "The people literally ripped clothes from each other's bodies," reported a Wehrmacht account.[18] "They totally forgot themselves in their panic and were hitting each other." The passengers could have used the subway tunnels for cover, as the London underground was, during the autumn nights of 1940. But Berlin's subway tunnels are very close to the surface. Those who had sought cover in the Nollendorfplatz station during the first Battle of Berlin in January 1943 felt what a direct hit could do. It was a deeper section, which had been considered absolutely safe. They were in the target area, and a heavy bomb burst the water main, which flooded the tunnel, creating a terrible panic that caused more damage than anything else.

From the standpoint of the bombing war, the subterranean part of modern, urban civilian life is rubbish. What held up were the walls of Pasqualini's Renaissance citadel in Jülich. But securely bunkering even one-third of a city of four million would have required 260 mammoth bunkers. Nowhere in the world did that exist. But Berliners were more annoyed by something else.

Entrance to a bunker was in principle a privilege, because a majority of city dwellers did not find a space in them. But the scarcity of bunker spaces was less the problem than suspicions that the available space was allotted unjustly. A large inventory of artworks was stored in the Zoo bunker; this stole space from people and was thus disliked. People said it was as if the people were expendable as long as art remained, which turned everything upside-down. Even more bitter were markings in the bunkers: "Only for railroaders." Looking for a safe place was a depressing and life-threatening endeavor in Berlin, and refuge seekers were constantly encountering reserved seats. Shelter spaces for war invalids and the frail and infirm, as at the Gesundbrunnen subway station, were quickly returned to general use.

Entrance to the public yet highly guarded shelter of the German national bank, with its extremely solid vault, had to be stormed. Breaking into the bank paid in this case, since only two soldiers and twenty prisoners of war had been sitting around where there was space for three hundred. The scandal spread throughout the entire city.

In May 1944, the Air Ministry had proposed the distribution of bunker tickets. Entrance was selective anyway. Men between sixteen and sixty-five were temporarily barred from using the shelters in Hanover. People with contagious diseases were refused access across the board, as fear of transmission was rampant. Bunkers transported everything, including infections; they were considered breeding grounds.

Prisoners of war and foreign workers, whether forced or voluntary, were not admitted into the bunkers. Since these groups made up a large proportion of the urban population, it was difficult to separate them out, and this gave rise to constant friction in the bunkers. After Rome defected from the Axis in the fall of 1943, "Badoglio Italians" were considered traitors and had to forfeit their seats in the bunkers; now they had to share the slit trenches with Russians and Poles. Labor from the east and the west were treated differently based on a racial hierarchy, but life was full of exceptions, whether it concerned vulgar remarks about the Germanized Dutch or the attachment that a gauleiter's wife felt for her Polish maid. The bunker community weighed the pros and cons of entry ad nauseum, because they thought in egalitarian terms within the inner, family circle of acceptees. Their distrust of privileges for bigwigs and officials was profound, which is why the bunker-ticket plan failed in a storm of indignation.

Germany survived and was defiant in the bunker, having been rammed in, dripping with the sweat of fear, deaf from the din of the blockbusters that crushed the market squares, libraries, castles, concert halls, and cathedrals. What the nation experienced from the very bottom of its soul in the four bunker years became part of its character. The social analysts of the USSBS, who directly took up this psyche empirically and theoretically, came to a memorable conclusion in their "Morale Division Study." More so than hastening the defeat, the inner effects of the bombing had caused a farewell, a "denazification of Germany,"[19] but not immediately.

Under no circumstances whatsoever would the bunker community tolerate Jews in their circle. Frankfurt had deported 9,339 of its

Jews by early October 1943; seventy-six more were to follow. Excepted from this was a group that included an old, established Frankfurt resident Sigismund Singer, World War I veteran, bearer of the Iron Cross 2nd class, the Hessian medal of bravery, and the Wehrmacht Badge for the Wounded; he was married to a Christian woman.[20] As a husband in a mixed marriage, he was spared deportation and the gas chamber; as a soldier on the front lines, he more or less avoided constant harassment by the Gestapo, but he did forced labor in a brickyard and at the East Cemetery. On the morning of October 4, 1943, he sought cover during a bombing raid in a small shack where he sometimes ate. He was slightly injured, but the medics called in refused to help him. His Jewish coworker Fritz Stolz lifted him onto a wheelbarrow, and the two men, wearing Yellow Stars, were cursed by passers-by as they made their way to a Jewish doctor.

After finally getting home with his head in a bandage, Singer heard the sirens announcing the second part of the raid. Because he was not allowed to seek protection in bunkers or public shelters and the couple wanted to stay together, Singer and his wife went down to their basement cellar, where their apathetic neighbors were gathered.

The thirty-eight bunkers in the city excluded more than 400,000 people; that is how many did not fit in. This excluded group, the cellar community, numbered four times that of the bunker community, and they in turn closed their doors to Jews. Singer's enemy was the air-raid warden, responsible for the house residents; it was a preferred position for the boastful. On October 4, however, the air-raid warden, who otherwise chased the Jew "onto the dunghill," could not assert his wishes. The neighbors decided the Singer couple could stay. No one could go anywhere anyway, because they were all trapped by fire: the Jew, the anti-Semite, and also a leper, the foreign wife of a Wehrmacht deserter, who huddled in a dark corner with her child.

Singer looked after her; she cried and her strength was spent. The hole to the next cellar led into a sea of flames. The deserter had been slain by his comrades; his wife was from Norway and sat, ostracized, with the child of the ostracized, in the corner of a Frankfurt cellar, above and next to which the buildings were aflame. Singer, who had seen worse, grabbed the child and pushed the woman. There was an escape to the inner courtyard, which was already surrounded by flames. They made it through to the street and from there into another cellar, a large crowded one, in which the danger Singer faced once again came from the cellar occupants.

But there was always a kindly soul or two who helped, in this case two friendly women who shooed Singer and a man who shared his fate into the darkest corner of the cellar where there was a large manual air pump. The two Jews faced the other way and worked the pump for two hours, so the cellar, where no one wanted to see them, would not smother. The two wives shielded their husbands from looks with their bodies. The rage that haunted the scene ultimately settled on Orenstein, an old Jew who had been pulled in by the two women because he had a large gash in his head inflicted by two soldiers on the street during a break in the bombing. The air-raid warden did not allow his wounds to be treated. Singer survived; Orenstein died from his injury.

The bunkers fell from the inside. When the cities had become uninhabitable, the people who were bombed out moved. Sixty percent of the population in Bottrop took up residence in the bunkers; in Kassel, 21 percent; in Mönchengladbach, 20 percent. In Essen, it was several thousand; in Dortmund and Hanover on the other hand, the move was not at all common. Some cities did not allow it; others permitted mothers with children or the elderly, or those who could prove they were homeless or without means. The bunker was now open, except during the air raid. In the Nuremberg train station bunker, homeless wives waited for their husbands, who worked out of town.[21] In February 1945, a week after the 2,800-ton raid by the U.S. Air Force that shut off the power and water supplies, the foreign workers took over the bunker. These women had been assemblers at the recently destroyed Siemens-Schuckert transformer plant. They had become acquainted with a squad of flak soldiers, who "sleep in the same room on the same benches as the women," as the Wehrmacht services observed. A large segment of the company stayed there all the time.

The severe overcrowding during the raids, many times the official capacity, caused the hygienic conditions to take a turn for the worse. The fans could not handle the increased carbonic acid level and the moisture in the air. There was sufficient oxygen, which had been calculated meticulously, but it was the exhaling of the occupants, the perspiration on bodies and clothing, and the rise in temperature that caused nausea and vomiting. Toddlers took ill. People opened the doors after waiting for or declaring a break in the bombing. The crowd cut off the air; somehow there had to be some ventilation. Because the occupants did not move, the situation did not get put straight. "Bunker fever" abounded. Spending only a few days there made the bunker dwellers dulled, coarse, and indifferent. At first over-wrought, the men became grumpy and monosyllabic; they tampered with things that were not theirs and were inconsiderate of women and children. All sense of order and cleanliness disappeared. People who used to be well-groomed failed to wash themselves, brush their hair, or shave, and they let their clothing become shabby. Mothers neglected their children; men became brutish toward women seeking protection. No one prepared any meals; they ate what they got from the public welfare agency and then complained about the bland taste. Seventy percent of the bunker occupants suffered from "bunker sickness," scabies. There were no delousing facilities.

"A horror comes over me," reported someone from the air-raid protection medical services in Hamm in late January 1945,

> when I see how children with scarlet fever and diphtheria wrapped in blankets and cloths keep being found in the bunker rooms. Hopefully we will be spared typhus this time. This description might seem exaggerated, but I can name bunker doctors who observe how otherwise orderly people gradually become brutes and animals, all of a sudden turning into cave dwellers after all their belongings have been destroyed.[22]

At that time, 60 percent of Hamm had been destroyed in fifty-five raids. The last major attack in February took only four lives; there had been sufficient space in the bunkers. But since September, the broken water facilities had been rusting. The city arduously kept the supply going using wells and tank trucks. Where munici-pal utility grids had not been patched, the bunker was also out of commission. Emergency generators were lacking or insufficient; in Gelsenkirchen, the bunker doctors worked by kerosene lamp. People with injuries lay three days waiting to be transported to hospitals. Lack of lighting made it impossible to find the toilets, which could not be flushed due to a lack of water and were therefore clogged. The occupants relieved themselves in dark corners. Emergency toilets and latrines set up outside were not used. To prevent the spread of disease, Hamm and Gelsenkirchen cleared the building each morn-ing and had the fire department clean and disinfect it.

Those who survived thanks to the bunkers suffered psychological damage. Even if everything was intact on the outside, inside, they fell apart. Bunkers and their occupants lost their strength and stability to-gether. Neither the depth of the shelter nor the strength of the concrete could save a life from the complete ruin of its world. And when it was ruined, the owners of those lives could no longer stand it. They did not push toward the end as in 1918; they had already reached the end of their tether. The players had bet everything on one card: their refusal to yield. As long as they lived—and that depended on the bunker—they would keep their chins up. The stake in the contest of bombs versus concrete was the cities, which the centuries had given them for safekeeping. When the cities were reduced to ashes, the occupants climbed out of the cellars and bunkers to surrender. There was no other way anymore.

Air raids were designed to kill people by the millions. As far as can be discerned from archives, there was no lack of willingness on the part of the Allies to do just that. Hitler, on the other hand, was a thwarted destroyer of cities. He loved to watch the film of the bombardment of Warsaw in September 1939, and fantasized about toppling the skyscrapers of New York. He considered war the natural law that put the weaker at the mercy of the fittest, and that subjected acquiescent races to the tenacious. So he was a born bomb strategist—albeit one without bombers. Germany's war objectives were the eastern territories, so it mustered a conqueror army in 1935, which gained speed with the use of the motorized weapons—tanks and airplanes. Hitler appreciated the theory of strategic bombing, as Trenchard termed it, and—putting it even more spectacularly—the theory of Italian fascist Giulio Douhet, namesake of the Douhetist school. Hitler was a Douhetist through and through, though a passive one. He never achieved a decisive air offensive, though he did have to endure one.

His 1938 memorandum on fortress construction contained the key idea that security was by no means the purpose of a fortification. "It is not the purpose of a fortress to guarantee the lives of a certain number of fighters under all circumstances, but rather to warrant the maintenance of overall fighting strength."[23] Neither were cellars and bunkers meant to help the civilian population make it through the war safe and sound. The difference between soldier and civilian no longer existed; everyone was a warrior. With that, Nazi party philosopher Alfred Rosenberg had made explicit allowances for the air war in 1934: It reconnected the people to the war, he said.[24] Up to now, citizens had let soldiers die for them, bathing all the while in love of peace. But the same military tactics that had so far girded civilian life with a military defense broke them apart again. The war of the future would be carried out under the banner of the air fleets, Rosenberg went on, and would involve the whole nation in the struggle for survival.

When the war had flared up fully, Hitler added the psychology of increasing combat strength: Fighting strength was not secured by the person concerned with self-preservation. "People fight fanatically only when they have the war at their own front doors. That's how people are. . . . Now even the worst idiot comprehends that his house will never be rebuilt unless we win."[25] Over the course of the air war, struggle and loss became one. But first, Rosenberg the ideologue was proven right: in the air war, the civilian population became combatants. They defended the territory on which they lived.

In Germany, a party that marched in uniforms and used a military "Sieg Heil" greeting had seized power. The state was then tidied up according to the military law of command and obedience. The chain of command was led by the Führer, but not openly. Life functioned according to the principle of leaders under the Führer, subordinate leaders who both obeyed and commanded. To do so, they each needed a unit of their own. Factories, professional associations, youth organizations, and the SA and SS elite units all had their strict leader-retainer hierarchies. In times of peace, that might have appeared as an authoritarian masquerade. However, the substance of the military commands was not about demonstrating authority, but about mandating a combat mission. Orders are given when something is not done voluntarily, since it runs contrary to the principle of self-preservation: laying down one's property, life, and limb. An army is an association regulated by this understanding; the German people, too, were to be accustomed to doing this through the air raids. The orders were to defend that which the air force destroyed—the material substance of the cities, the authority of the state, and the social process.

People going to war because of the bombs dropping overhead was largely a suggestion of the Nazi party that did not jibe with reality. The civilian warriors were defenseless; they had no weapons and were highly amazed that the Luftwaffe was unable to accomplish anything against the bomber swarms. The sense behind tarrying in the battlefield of modernity, countering attacks with nothing but a water hose, had to be instilled gradually. Air force and civil-defense experts, on the other hand, had reckoned with high initial losses, but were wrong. This befell the people of London. The Germans temporarily improved their airspace position by conquering France and Holland; they put men along the ground front of the air war, and now had two years' time before the soldierlike aspects of it became obvious to the civilians. That was when the massive losses started. The civilians viewed this as the slaying of the helpless. The enemy was dastardly enough to attempt it, and the government was weak enough to let it happen. The first thing this new people's war had to explain was in what role the people died. As innocent victims or as soldiers?

Goebbels referred to the dead as "fallen" who had given their lives in the field. They were buried with military honors staged by the party, with a dull drum roll as musical accompaniment. The Führer himself sent a wreath—actually, the Führer sent just the ribbon; the local authorities provided the garland. The adjutant's office footed the bill. The Iron Cross decorated the graves of those who fell in the air war, survivors received the War Service Cross, and those who were injured received the Wounded Badge. A "grove of honor for air war victims" was established in Leipzig's south cemetery.[26] Unusual was the "burial service for fallen European foreign workers," attended by Polish, French, Belgian, Czech, Lithuanian, and Ukrainian delegations. Hans Fritzsche, plenipotentiary for the Political Organization of the Greater German Radio and head of the Radio Division of the Ministry of Propaganda, proclaimed at a mass funeral in Schweinfurt in October 1944 that the dead had died so Germany could live. In July 1943, he spoke on the radio of "those millions in the bombed areas, the great heroes of this war who wear the invisible oakleaf and before whom entire generations of Europe will sometime bow."[27]

Goebbels praised the home front as "iron which is hardened, and not softened, by blows."[28] In his first proclamation to the soldiers at the eastern front—which at that point ran through Berlin—Hitler cited the civilian defenders as soldierly models: "The regiment or division that abandons its position behaves so disreputably that they should shame themselves before the women and children who are bearing up under the bombing terror in our cities."[29]

Twenty million helpers reported to fight the damages of the air war, more than a fourth of the population. By the end of the war, a majority of them were women. The original idea of German air defense was that cities should be defended only by their residents. The Air Ministry, an umbrella organization, formally gave the air district commands responsibility for carrying out the air-raid protection, though in fact the city police authorities assumed the task.

The fire departments and technical repair services were under them. But they were in no position to protect 100,000 buildings. That required a company in every building: the tenants, a company leader, drills, and an air-raid warden, who could exercise police authority in an emergency. The next-higher unit was a battalion of ten to fifteen buildings or a block controlled by a block warden. Six to ten blocks formed a subgroup, and fifteen to twenty thousand people, a division, who composed an air-raid protection precinct, identical to the lowest level police precinct. This militia of the air war had the mission to set up their respective positions.

Basic training at the *Reichluftschutzbund*, the Reich Air-Raid Protection League (RLB), included procedures to protect a building and shake off a raid. The league was a public body on par with the Reich administrations, but in actual fact, it was a club supported by its members. During the war, the RLB had twenty million members who showed personal interest in air-raid protection issues, paid one mark annual dues, and wore a badge, an eight-pointed starburst on white metal.

The residents of an apartment building made up an air-raid shelter community. Like any group, it had to level out social contrasts as well as conflicts between the generations and the genders. The air-raid warden, with the stature of a sergeant, vouched for that. The war dealt primarily with taking possession of territory. The territory of the bombing war was the sea of buildings, to which Bomber Command devoted in-depth territorial studies. The territory was conquered if the building was incinerated, and this happened mostly due to the wood in the floorboards, roofbeams, and rows of shingles on the roof. Furthermore, the only territory that can be attacked is one that can be seen. From a great height and in the dark, a building complex was given away by its light. It behooved the air-raid warden and his company to black out the object and defend the attic.

All unnecessary wood and junk had to be removed; the essential beams were impregnated with fireproofing agents: lump lime, slaked lime, quicklime. Carpets and rugs in the apartments were to be rolled up, curtains taken down, and all doors left open. In case the incendiary sticks hit an attic or upper floor, the damages were minimal for the first three minutes. Ample containers with sand and water were available to smother the incipient fire. If a fire started in the roof truss, action had to be immediate to be of any help at all. If the residents could get the fire under control with a stirrup pump, fire flail, and shovel, it would not spread into a major conflagration.

The water was mixed with cattle salt so it would not freeze in the winter. The less robust women serving as air-raid helpers filled bags with sand. Two or three of them thrown correctly could thwart Churchill's efforts. The magnesium alloy–thermite incendiary stick was actually a quite harmless weapon in and of itself. If discovered right away, it could even be grabbed by its iron base and hurled outside into an open space. Dropped by the hundreds of thousands, they were among the most ruinous combat weapons of the world war.

The more massive the drop of incendiary sticks and the more tons of explosives dropped along with them, the riskier it became to wrestle with the fire face-to-face. In order to detect the ignition, at the very least one had to hang around in the house, if possible not in the cellar. The female element made the stay there nicer; "sometimes it was almost cozy," said a man from Bonn who experienced them as a boy, "because almost the entire neighborhood gathered in the cellar during an air-raid and treated us children with tender loving care."[30] Comfort and coziness were also mentioned in reports from Hanover. "Some women brought down cakes or meatballs, and the men brought beer. People played skat, and I always felt very good."[31] Ladies' fashions were taken to new heights with the previously very uncommon "new, chic air-raid slacks."

The air-raid warden meanwhile patrolled the building. The entire attic was supposed to be covered with eight inches of sand, which was distributed free of charge at central locations. Upholstered furniture was not allowed to be placed near windows, but had to be moved into the interior of the room. Fittings and connectors for any garden hoses had to be the right gauge. Hoses and fittings would grow to be one of the greatest technical challenges of the air war. There was water everywhere in Germany, but taps and hoses, while all complying with a DIN standard, did not all comply with the same one.

The patrol ended with the air-raid protection readiness of the building and extensions, stalls, and warehouses, and was frequently repeated for the duration of the attack. The command post of the helmeted warden was the cover shelter in the roof ridge with an observation slit. It was a metal or concrete shield that repelled small fragments. If a high-explosive bomb hit, the outcome would be fatal; it took considerable courage to hold out there very long during a heavy raid. Holding a position at the roof was not for everyone. According to the report of Dortmund's Fourth Air-Raid Protection Precinct, it was more obvious from the raids of May 1943 that many men, including Wehrmacht soldiers home on leave, behaved like sissies. Instead of remaining in their buildings as the fire-watch, they crawled into the bunkers like scaredy-cats, taking space away from women and children, and had to be picked up by police and SA patrols and reminded of their duty.[32]

The soldier's reflexes made him take cover when fired upon. Soldiers on leave from the front often found their world turned upside-down, when the air war caught them by surprise at home. They advised staying in the cellars instead of fleeing to the burning streets. Throwing themselves directly into the enemy attack seemed to them like very unmilitary, dramatic heroism. "I want to remain a soldier," admitted someone who escaped from an air-raid cellar in Cologne, "and I will be returning to the front in the morning. My God, do we have it good out there!"[33]

In contrast, the air-raid warden was thought to be like a Nibelung character who lets himself be cut into pieces at the threshold to his home. He was usually a responsible and tough elderly citizen. "A spirited man draws people to join him," the Hamburg Chief of Police exhorted the house guardian, "in protecting our residences from destruction."[34] Göring furnished him with a helmet, fireman's hook, and whistle; after the danger was over the warden directed his workforce in the tasks to be done: forming a bucket chain, saving threatened furniture, asking higher offices for disposal of unexploded and time-delay bombs; rarely did anyone come, and he had to try to do it himself. No man in the building was permitted to leave the attack vicinity; everyone was under orders—including women and young people—to defang the bomber weapon. "I had to do it," said a Cologne woman to the medic bandaging her charred hand. "What would my husband have thought of me? He's in Normandy. I couldn't let the house burn down, we'd saved twenty years for it."[35]

There was an odd contrast between the light of the flames in the kindled cities, which could be seen from miles away, and the ordered blackout of cities. All artificial lighting had to be turned off and any light that was absolutely necessary for life, industry, and transportation had to be dimmed, colored, or filtered with close-meshed wire netting or screens. No light that could be perceived on a clear night from an altitude of 1,600 feet was allowed to leak out of windows, doors, skylights, or glass roofs. Advertising in storefront windows, movie houses, and theaters was switched to dark blue lighting.

According to a scientifically unproven notion of the Führer, the shorter wavelength blue color was more difficult to see, which is why existing light bulbs were dipped in a colored solution that was developed by the Luftwaffe and available in stores. Hitler personally oversaw the blackout procedures, and had the gauleiters informed that people were turning on their night-table lamps when the alarm sounded and were endangering themselves by such carelessness. Violators of blackout regulations were to be punished with having their electricity cut off for eight days. Negligent municipalities were threatened by the district authorities with a week's power outage. Hitler's informant on the ground, the air-raid warden, observed the transgressors, confronted them with their wrongdoing, and imposed sanctions; otherwise he was liable. Loudspeaker trucks patrolled the streets commanding "lights out" whenever they discovered cracks of light from windows.

Curbs were marked with phosphorescent paint interrupted every 160 feet, stairs received a zigzag marking, and parts of buildings that jutted out, poles, pillars, bridge rails, barriers, riverbanks, and curves in streets were marked with lime. Street lamps were turned off at 10 p.m., and people moved around carrying flashlights with colored filters. Weakly luminescent stripes and arrows on building foundations provided information about the distance to and location of the closest air-raid shelter. People liked to wear small fluorescent badges so they would not run into one another. Car headlights and bicycle lights were covered with a mask with a horizontal slit. Windows were covered by dark shades that were pressed against the wallpaper by a clamp screwed onto the wall, so no edges of light leaked out.

A shocking technical discovery was made in 1942. All mechanical shields, Venetian blinds, and cardboard served no purpose whatsoever if the enemy could monitor the infrared radiation emitted from the heat of the lit interior rooms. The Germans had an experimental device called "Seehund," or seal, that the navy used to convert infrared emissions into visible light. Now Seehund had been developed into the "Spanner," or "Peeping Tom," apparatus, which rendered all blackout efforts utterly useless. The enemies also developed infrared detection devices toward the end of the war. Meanwhile the Germans started treating their blackout fabrics and blinds with Spanner-proof chemical additives.

Blackout procedures diminished the efficiency of industry, whose moonlight-reflecting glass roofs, blast furnaces, and coking plants with glowing slag heaps already helped point the bombers in the right direction. Slatted grates helped some, as did covered ladles that transported the molten iron in the dark, tapping shields, and protective hoods for burning off excess gas. To neutralize factory lighting, complementary colors were used, which did not let certain colors pass through filters. Industrial crews could work in red-yellow lighting that was filtered by a blue-green film. But this had negative psychological effects.

White towers, bright concrete streets, polished granite, and corrugated iron roofs all reflected the moonlight, and all of them were homing points for bombers. People living along the Rhine loved their bright, whitewashed houses. "People really shouldn't be surprised," remarked the local Nazi party office, "if the British find them without a problem every time and plaster them."[36] So architects and painters devised encasements and washable camouflage coatings. The effect of all this is uncertain. In the first two years, visibility on clear moonlit nights was most important, but with the development of radar navigation and carpet-bombing techniques, this became secondary. The bombardier oriented himself by the flare markings of the pathfinders. The target did not have to shine; it was illuminated. The H2S screens were difficult to read, so visual sighting of course contributed somewhat to target identification.

The blackout might also have been a tranquilizer. Children cover their eyes with their hand to be invisible. Reversing seeing and being seen gives them power over something that is actually out of their control. Putting out lights was normal military camouflage procedure. When all of Germany put great effort into immersing itself in darkness, it reclaimed control of something it had lost: being a target or not. With its omnipresence in the sky, the enemy had unobstructed visibility. Like God's punishing eye, it saw everything, mostly with a flash and a camera. This was hard to withstand; sinking down together into absolute darkness presumably gave Germans the illusion of being alone, among just themselves again. It was generally agreed that the feeling most difficult to endure was that of being totally helpless and at the mercy of others, hoping and trembling with fear. Hiding oneself was at least a way of being active.

All these efforts to hide were proved inadequate in the spring of 1942, with the Thousand-Bomber Raid on Cologne. The blackouts did no good because the planes oriented themselves along the silver ribbon of the Rhine. They approached from the north and followed the moonlit river southward. The first wave set its illumination flares and dropped incendiaries into the outlined square; the second and third attack waves already saw the city in flames from miles away. The wonder of the tiered bomber stream that kept up dense waves of attack for twenty minutes, thundering down 1,397 high-explosive bombs and 153,413 incendiary sticks, checkmated the Germanic tribal defenses.

The current method of attack allowed the bombers to do their work unhindered for a period of time, letting the effect accumulate through the mass of hits. During this time, all air defenses were forced to take cover. Breaks in the bombardment were eliminated; twelve planes flew over the target every minute. Squadron after squadron dropped their tonnage into the illuminated sector and not, as was previously the case, scattered over the city. The bomb mixture was now geared entirely toward starting fires, and its effect was intensified through the new thirty-pound liquid-incendiary bomb. It carried a charge primer that hurled the burning mass out over an area of three hundred square yards. Each phosphorus cake lit a fire of its own; water simply evaporated and did not extinguish the flames.

When the people of Cologne climbed out of their cellars and bunkers once the all clear came, they found themselves standing on a new battlefield, that of the fire war. Twelve thousand individual fires had merged into 1,700 major torches that could not be put out with stirrup pumps and sand bags. No municipal fire brigade knew how to subdue such a beacon of fire. The air-raid protection control center had called on 154 fire departments from Bonn, Düsseldorf, Duisburg, Essen, Bochum, and Gelsenkirchen to race to Cologne. A fire engine that set out too early from the fairgrounds in the Deutz district was stopped by a direct hit on the bridge. Huge pipes were submerged into the Rhine to siphon out hundreds of tons of water with each stroke. The hoses, stretching for a mile or more and branching into the buildings, were connected to sixty-six motor-driven fire pumps to increase the water pressure. But even the benevolence of the Rhine and the aid from neighboring cities could not stop the destruction of one out of every ten residences. Hundreds of bakeries, butcher shops, and restaurants were taken out; 4.4 million pounds of potatoes wrapped in bales of straw burned in the covered market.

Cologne was a deployment zone with packed barracks. Twenty-five hundred soldiers marched to do clearing work, along with two thousand prisoners of war and 1,650 specialized workers. The "overhead wire crew" from the Rhine-Ruhr cities came out with a shop truck to get the streetcars going again. Four cranes in the port felled by direct hits had to be taken apart underwater and lifted, since they blocked the entrance. Thousands of craftsmen and skilled workers, including two thousand glaziers, set off for Cologne. Tank trucks filled with milk rolled in. Transports rained down sandwiches. Overflowing supplies of food, 6.5 million pounds of rice, and 5.5 million pounds of pasta were brought in. Trucks were parked on the access roads, waiting for their loads to be taken into the city. Germany had become a veritable warehouse for Cologne. The volume of clothing, linens, and furniture delivered to the city overwhelmed the local retail stores, so emergency sales centers were set up; weapon shops sold stockings. Aside from food, soap was also in demand; the air war was dirty business. Seven hundred thousand bars of soap removed the dust and soot.

That Thousand-Bomber Raid marked the collapse of the cellars. In the Blaubach district, a large housing block caught fire. One hundred fifty people in the air-raid shelter yelled for help since the exits were blocked. The occupants were able to work their way from cellar wall to cellar wall with a pickaxe, until they finally made a hole that led out into the open. But the entire block of houses near Rheingasse had collapsed. Nothing could be done from the inside to get out. Police drove an air shaft into the rubble, expanded it, and propped it up until fifty-one sobbing, upset people wiggled their way out. One threw his arms in the air in relief, then fell over, dead. The cellars themselves were well built and properly supported. In Cologne, the ceilings were braced with efficient T-beams, cast in concrete.

In comparison with the 1,460 tons of bombs dropped, about five times the average up to then, the human losses were not high: 469 people. A year later, it took five days to put out the fires in the city and dig 3,460 bodies out of the city center. They were laid out in rows to be identified. Often there were pails next to the corpses, like the one on Weissbüttengasse labeled "building residents, 36 people, July 3, 1943." Another year later, they used bulldozers in Cologne for the first time, very carefully—so the cellar roofs weighed down with rubble did not collapse—digging 1,200 people out alive.

Heavy equipment, risk, strenuousness, and disgusting work brought about a professional, quartered home-front unit in air-raid protection, and for the less physical jobs of social work, a rear echelon consisting of the entire population. The Security and Assistance Service was affiliated with the police department and was later termed the air-raid protection police. It comprised fire protection carried out by the professional and volunteer fire departments, the repair service made up of utility company personnel and technical specialists, the medical service, the decontamination service made up of city department of sanitation personnel, and the rescue and recovery teams, including larger groups of prisoners and concentration camp prisoners. The Luftwaffe contributed motorized units that were joined by the technical Wehrmacht reserve forces such as railroad and fortification engineer Pioneers. On top of that were the Technical Troops, a special unit of the army composed of production engineers, works managers, and older officers no longer fit for active duty. They performed the miracle of undauntingly getting vital facilities and services going again. The motorized troops, in turn, were the backbone of town-to-town assistance.

Damages from a major raid could no longer be handled by local reserves, so immediate aid by forces from neighboring towns was provided, transported via the network of autobahns. Effective aid had to arrive within an hour; the range was between one and three hours, but up to six thousand workers were brought in for the effort. A medium-sized city with a population between a quarter and a half million had about one thousand regular police at its disposal, three thousand from the affiliated Security and Assistance Service, six thousand auxiliary helpers, and a few hundred men from Wehrmacht relief units. The main area of attack in present-day North Rhine–Westphalia was defended by 22,500 units of firefighting, repair, and medical teams. Three-quarters had equipment; their physical fitness corresponded to the average age of fifty-four years.

Water had a hard time keeping up in a fire war. All the elements favored the fire. The water had to be brought in with vehicles, fire engines and extinguishers, and fragile pipes. The public water supply network was a primary bombing target and was turned off during all major raids. When a building collapsed, the pipes broke; under the debris cone the water flowed into the ground, which killed the water pressure. The air war needed a second water supply, from canals, rivers, lakes, ponds, and reservoirs. The smartest thing to do was to draw the canals into the cities. The Reich could not afford the expense and instead prepared water towers, fountains, rainwater collection tanks, vats, barrels, and public swimming pools. The cellars of previously destroyed buildings were coated with concrete and filled with water; the people collected water for extinguishing fires in bathtubs and garbage bins. Heilbronn even built thirty-two sunken cistern bunkers for firefighting purposes. The water was siphoned out using hoses and galvanized quick-coupled pipes with parts shaped to fit the terrain. A large number of power pumps forced the water over the long distances, and others then ultimately transported it to the fire. Before that, the site of the fire needed to be localized, a fire engine had to be assigned, and a route through streets blocked by craters and rubble had to be scouted out. The professional fire brigades in a major city of 380,000 such as Stettin had only 140 full-time firefighters plus four hundred members of the volunteer fire department at their disposal. In the twenty-one most-threatened cities in the Rhineland and Westphalia, there were a total of 750 power pumps for their own use and to assist their neighbors. This was what was to counteract the 100,000 or 200,000 incendiary bombs of a heavy raid.

The tower lookout reported when the blast bombs hit and when fires started. Situated at the highest point atop schools, churches, and city halls, the observer followed the events of the attack from a location weakly protected from flak shrapnel. Like the tower guard of old with his horn, the air-raid protection police—later young women served as fire watches—informed the control center via a dedicated line or through signals. Smoke and clouds of dust obscured the view, but detailed data was superfluous during a wide-area conflagration anyway. Fighting a lost cause, the fire watch struggled for an overview, sought a way to somehow be of use, and held the position. The one in the tower of the New City Hall in Munich was advised to keep his mouth open all the time to prevent eardrum damage. During the attack on Osnabrück in September 1944, which ravaged the Old Town, St. Mary's Church with its tower also went up in flames. The four women standing watch—Ostholt, Telljohann, Lewonik, and Meyer—submitted their final damage report at a point when their own location was worthy of inclusion. They managed to get down safely.[37]

In the field of rubble, pathways were often only a matter of memory. The bashed-in façades made the streets unrecognizable, and knowing a place meant comparing the current stumps with yesterday's picture. It was not only difficult to pass through streets buried in debris—it was also difficult to know where the streets even were. The firefighters, especially those helping out from other towns, had to be piloted to the fire or else they could not find it for all the flames. Sometimes lost firefighters stood still in front of blazing buildings, with the residents pleading for them to help, but the fire engine was waiting for driving instructions to the assigned site. Fires were not extinguished by shouting.

The common bottleneck facing auxiliary fire departments called in from other areas were the access roads to the city. The fire engines parked there and waited for instructions and driving directions. The command bunker had no idea where individual actions still made sense; it usually was better to set up a concentrated joint action, but no one had experience with something like that. The fire brigade was a doctor who visited single patients. No one had ever had to get a fire epidemic under control. At the access road, the fire engines from out of town were greeted by the guide. It was usually a Hitler Youth, the regime's perpetual reserves. He knew his sector even at night, had checked out road damage and detours, and could give directions and make reports. All telecommunications were based on runners, motorcyclists, and bicyclists.

Damage reports, orders, couriers, and fire engines confronted a reality that was rarely related to the job of firefighting. It still applied to some extent at the fringes of the raid, where small groups of eight people extinguished fires to save ten buildings on their street. They were the hedgehog positions of the early tenant groups. What overwhelmed them could be taken care of by huge pipes. The wide-area conflagration, however, was conceived by the enemy's fire engineers to be inextinguishable. Their counterparts in the Reich understood that right away. So they concentrated on what few advantages they had.

First, German fire engineers knew the city structure better than their enemies, and, admittedly as commanders of retreat, drew the line of defense at a point where it would hold. The flames were abandoned and closed off at the technically correct location. Only a strong phalanx of workers could establish a fire break that could successfully check the fury of the flames, and they often did. Second, amidst the sea of flames, there were also islands, squares, parks, embankments, fountains, bunkers, and free-standing housing blocks where everyone had fled, helped along by presence of mind and a good dose of luck. Spirited attempts to get people out were made; the most common means was by laying a water corridor. Two parallel columns of water spouts shot up every fifty feet at an angle to form a colonnade, a curtain of water cutting a lane within the sea of flames. This was the final escape route from certain suffocation, even if many of those caught inside doubted it. The sudden blazing heat that people faced when climbing out of cellars or bunkers clouded all judgment. If they had not been forced out, they would have died.

In 1944, Bomber Command tried four times to destroy Brunswick. The Oker River flows through the city limits from the south, splitting in the middle into two arms that arch apart only to come back together a mile farther down. This forms a circular island that contained the historic Old Town. It grew in a medieval and early modern half-timbered building style, richly ornamented with woodcuts. Surrounding the center were residential areas that included three industrial sites, a textbook example of a British fire-raid target.

Early in the morning of October 15, 1944, 233 Lancasters appeared and dropped their twelve thousand explosives and twenty thousand incendiaries precisely onto the Old Town in the Oker ring and the surrounding residential area. During the forty-minute break in the attack, fire protection police officer Rudolf Prescher noticed the extremely high density of incendiaries that had been dropped. They sounded like flittering sheet metal as they fell; the explosive bombs whistled.

> The incendiary stick bombs that burn with a white flame are clearly distinguishable from the hissing and smoking blow of the flame jet bomb. During this time it was impossible to drive a vehicle through the streets. The tires would have ignited immediately from the incendiary bombs, which were lying around in such great density that you could not even have avoided them driving slowly with a light motorcycle.[38]

The flames raced as intended through the Old Town buildings, small streets, and alleyways. There were not any wide streets that could have divided the fire into sections. Consequently, the fires quickly merged into a wide-area blaze. About forty thousand people lived within the ring. Because of the high groundwater level, many buildings lacked a usable cellar, or even any cellar at all, which is why six major bunkers and two public air-raid shelters had been built. On the night in question, they housed 23,000 people. The conflagration enveloped the entire Oker ring, and the strong draft created threw people's coats over their heads and carried away tables and chairs. A gust in the other direction rushed into the glowing debris and chased a dense rain of sparks through the burning district. "Whatever got in its way," Prescher wrote, "was scorched, roasted, or incinerated. And the 23,000 bunker occupants definitely got in its way."

The air-raid protection police took it for granted that a firestorm of medium intensity would develop in the area around Wollmarkt,

Lange Strasse, and Weberstrasse. Although the people in the massive bunker were safe from explosion and fire, the engineers were suspicious of the overcrowding. The twenty-four bunkers in the city were intended for a total capacity of 15,000. But now there were 23,000 people sitting in just six of them. "The horrendous heat of the fire would not yet have penetrated through to them, but would there have been enough air to supply the overcrowded air-raid shelters with sufficient oxygen?"

The bunker was supplied with outside air through its air-intake fitting at the top. The oxygen consumed by the firestorm and the rising hot air, however, did not leave much oxygen for breathing. And the half-timbering of the buildings would continue to feed the firestorm for hours, suffocating the occupants. Around 5:00 a.m., enough auxiliary fire brigades and equipment had arrived to lay a water corridor.

The fire area was supposed to be breached in the northwestern part of the city center. There were actually sufficient water reserves nearby, but they were within the area consumed by the firestorm. Consequently, long hose lines had to be laid and pressure had to be pumped in. The firestorm also kept shifting its direction due to local winds, which had an unpredictable effect on the fire.

> As soon as the people prepared themselves for the radiant heat to come from one direction, it changed and they had to adapt to the new situation. As protection against the blaze, the pipes had to be constantly sprayed with a water film before being shoved into the oven. The range of the individual jet pipes overlapped, so a closed zone of artificial rain was established.

Around 7:00 a.m., workers had reached the bunkers.

> When the rescuers opened the bunker doors they were greeted by the muffled sound of many subdued but nervous people talking. They were all still alive. Most of them were not even aware of the imminent danger. The streams of people were led out without any losses. Minor outbursts of panic could be dealt with by the rescue crews. They succeeded in avoiding a catastrophe.

The firestorm in Brunswick took 561 human lives, ninety-five of which through carbon monoxide poisoning in the air-raid shelter on Schöppenstedter Strasse. No damage could be detected in the shelter. The obligatory candles were lit to monitor the oxygen content, and they also indicated any inflow of gas. When the candle flames turned a blue color and then extinguished, the occupants knew they were inhaling gas. Their only choice at that point was between two forms of death: suffocation or burning. The death rate within the area of the firestorm was an unprecedentedly low 0.28 percent, thanks to the meshing of the two protective shields: the bunker and the fire brigade's water corridor.

The shelters that did not hold out contained living or dead, usually both. Survivors had withstood the attack but were trapped by rubble. They did not have much time. Those who had died needed a proper grave. The most pressing task was also the most painstaking: to uncover survivors. People in Cologne received leaflets preparing them in the event of their being buried. They were advised to refrain from doing the most obvious thing, as "shouting and yelling use up an excessive amount of oxygen, which is usually scarce."[39] More effective was "banging with a hammer or other hard object against the wall or ground. Even scratching with a fingernail could be perceived by a sound-detecting device." The sound locator was the contribution of the Air Force Ministry. It was used once the heavy equipment—tractors, grippers, excavators, drilling machines, trough scrapers, and jackhammers—went silent. People who were buried were supposed to wait until then, as they were instructed in Munich, and then begin scraping and scratching. Whistles were ineffective because the frequency was drowned out by the humming of the sound detector's amplifier.

Teams trained to hear banging and scratching noises sat shielded off in a vehicle that received via cable whatever was picked up by the diaphragm at the location where people were presumed buried. Wherever a beam, a pipe, or a piece of iron led down into the ground, the listeners banged an SOS into the metal and waited for a response.[40] If people had been buried alive, they had to do something. If they were not able to respond, the search and rescue team moved on until they heard something in their headphones. Then they began to dig.

If possible, the teams searched where people were reported missing, so everyone's place of residence needed to be known. The air-raid warden was in charge of that; everyone was required to report as they came and went. Nothing unreasonable for troops.

Sometimes people appeared to have been swallowed up by the earth during a raid. Bombs falling during the American raid on Münster in October 1943 stopped a resident of Aegidiistrasse on his way to the air-raid shelter on Grüne Gasse. The blast wave hurled the man through a hallway, and that was it. When he came out, he could not find his wife, daughter, and neighbor who had accompanied him. The rescue and repair crew proceeded to search all the rubble in the vicinity but found nothing. The man insisted on his story. He indicated the distance to the people who disappeared, which coincided with a bomb crater on the street, so they started to dig it up. About five feet down the body of the neighbor was found, another ten feet deeper, the daughter, and at a depth of twenty feet they found his wife's body.

Rescue and recovery operations in the unstable ruins demanded a lot in terms of technical capabilities as well as endurance and disposition. Wherever miners helped out, the time-consuming task of clearing away the rubble could be dispensed with in favor of driving tunnels under the cellar floors and pulling out the people who were trapped. Crawlspaces were dug out at about twenty-five to twenty-eight inches per hour. If this was done unprofessionally, the crumbling earth would bury people up to their necks. Since the buildings were so shaken up, nothing was supposed to be touched without consulting architects—otherwise generally underemployed at the time—who decided which structures should preferably be torn down before they collapsed on the heads of the rescuers. That is what building contractor Schorn of Münster recorded, who spent four weeks searching for people and human remains after the October 10 raid, with at first with fifteen, and later only four, auxiliary repair crews from Osnabrück, Hamm, and Gelsenkirchen.[41]

Two of the most unfortunate hits destroyed the St. Clemens Hospital and the house of the St. Clemens nuns on the very day the hospital matrons were allowed to have their relatives come to visit. Digging out the nuns and their guests "was only possible by driving a tunnel through or under the mass of rubble. Even after combing through the entire building for days, it was not possible to find everyone who was missing." Of fifty-two nuns, including the superior general, not one was recovered alive. The most difficult job turned out to be recovering the bodies of those who had been missing from under the gutted St. Clemens Hospital.

The fire found abundant fuel in the wood, beds, etc. When clearing out the debris it was necessary to set some of the rubble under water since part of it was nothing but a mass of embers. Under such circumstances a power shovel could not be used because it would have destroyed any clues as to where it would be possible to rescue people. So the entire mass of rubble had to be moved with a hand shovel in order to find the people who were lost; it took fourteen days.

All aid was too late for the patients. "What we were able to find of the individual people needn't be mentioned in detail."

How many people might have spent days in buried cellars waiting to be rescued and gradually giving up? The air-raid protection police had to weigh where life could still be presumed and where it could not. Some errors were undoubtedly made, many owing merely to the sheer number of lots that were nothing but rubble. In Hamburg, 135 miles of street frontage burned. Postal Senior Secretary Julius Zingst of Kaiserslautern lived through being buried after a fighter-bomber raid on December 27, 1944.[42] The city with a population of seventy thousand was attacked eight times that month. From the kitchen of his house on Pfaffenberg hill, Zingst felt the low-flying planes approach. He and his five housemates leaped down to the cellar; they heard the high-explosive bombs whooshing overhead, followed by a powerful quaking, and then a dull detonation. "Simultaneous to this dreadful din, a building collapsed above me, and part of our air-raid cellar was blown in." It was the building next door that was hit, but the blast threw his house off its foundation so that nothing remained but the blown-in cellar.

> To our horror we realized we were totally cut off from the outside and even getting a flow of fresh air proved impossible. Since we knew the neighbors had to presume we were in the cellar, we held out in total darkness even though the air was getting increasingly scarce; we mustered all our energy, encouraging each other, and from time to time we made signals by knocking and calling out.

After four hours, two neighbors noticed the signals and did the right thing. They pounded a hole underground into the foundation. That brought the half-suffocated cellar occupants back to life. An hour later they were free. "The neighbors said the Technical Emergency Corps had gone by while we were buried. Looking at the pile of rubble they had given up all hope with the comment, 'nobody could still be alive under all that debris.'"

Since rescue was always a question of time, Bomber Command used time-delay fuses set for thirty-six, seventy-two, or 144 hours after the bomb drop. That kept rescue crews at a distance, which let the powers of destruction proceed unhindered. Firefighters were unable to disarm the time-delay bombs as they did unexploded bombs. Involved experiments were attempted using household items such as balls of paper or peat and bundles of branches, but the only alternative turned out to be simply cordoning off the vicinity and refraining from all rescue operations. Disarming a dud frequently cost a firefighter his life. "Often we had to disarm bombs hanging head down by our feet," wrote Karl Nakel of Munich, then a twenty-six-year-old bomb ordnance officer. "Then there were also loamy areas where the bomb penetrated more than four yards and we had to disarm it in absolute darkness. We were already in our grave. With each bomb we took off our ID tag and wedding ring and left everything in the car. Then we set to work on the bomb. It was a conscious form of dying."[43]

It was possible to divide up the process of dying. The outrageously dangerous work was not done only by the responsible Wehrmacht ordnance specialists. "We used concentration camp prisoners for our work. When I went to the Dachau camp early in the morning and said I needed twelve prisoners, a hundred stepped forward. I was regarded as an ordnance specialist to whom nothing ever happened." The cities also recruited prison inmates to be volunteers, "to gain freedom by doing a brave deed." In Siegen, they got volunteers for an even lesser prize. The fire department took twenty convicts from Werl and had them disarm thirty-five tons of unexploded bombs under police supervision. As a reward for their effort, they got to live in a remand center. The fire department would pick them up there in the morning and bring them back every evening.

Prisoners and foreign and forced workers were also used as reserves for the most nauseating part of recovering bodies. For immediate aid in the post-raid phase, air-raid protection units recruited any civilian from the street. First they had to clear the way, then pull people out of the rubble. The order of these tasks was disputed but constant. Paul Körner of Saarbrücken, then a Hitler Youth head messenger, remembered recovering people who had just been buried; it was the first major raid on the city on the night of July 29, 1942:

> We tried to clear away boulders, ceiling beams, and supports, sometimes with our bare hands, in order to reach the people who were buried as quickly as possible. Many of them were already dead and in really terrible

condition. It was a shock whenever I recognized someone I had known. We lived right next door, around the corner.[44]

Buildings that were gutted in the fire and rubble in the conflagration areas continued to glow for weeks. During that time, the rubble was too hot to handle. The radiant heat in the cellars had to cool down before the job of recovering dead bodies could begin. The repair and rescue services could not deal with the physical state of the bodies, so squads of Russians were formed for this task. The cellars revealed stages of decomposition that were quickly covered with chlorinated lime.

The transformation of the body back to matter is a horror to the eye; only in war does this happen in the light of day. The clearing of the battlefield is a job in itself and must be prepared for in advance. According to the ordinance of the Interior Ministry of August 28, 1934, the welfare police, health department, cemetery office, and medical services were responsible for clearing away the carnage after air raids.[45] In September 1934, Leipzig had twenty-seven body-recovery teams, each one made up of a directing police officer and four assistants. In 1936, church halls had space to lay out 1,034 corpses; mass graves were designated in the Trinitatis, South, and West cemeteries, despite firm assumptions that Saxony was beyond the reach of the air war. That was merely the administrative scheme of a reality that assumed a form that no longer appeared compatible with any state order.

The infernal scenes that were revealed when cellars were opened challenged any and all public authority. What were the reasons of state when things were permitted to happen as they did in Darmstadt? Heating pipes burst in the buried cellars and the occupants were boiled in the outflow. People trapped in the cellars' escape routes under the apartment building blocks hurried higgledy-piggledy, and a bottleneck always formed at the holes in the walls to the next cellar. Knots of human beings were found stuck together, needing tools to separate them. Some of the bodies showed cuts and bruises that they must have inflicted on one another in their mortal fear. According to reports on cleaning out the cellar of the Café Hauptpost at the main post office in Darmstadt, the bomb blast killed the occupants, including a woman in labor. "Those were cellars where coke had been smoldering. Either the people boiled to death in water or they were charred. Or else they just sat there like ghosts, their faces covered by blankets and cloth, as they tried to protect themselves from the smoke. That's how the asphyxiated people were sitting in the cellars. The stench was ghastly."[46] The candle that registered the oxygen content indicated to the Darmstadters that gas would be their end. The physical gestures of fighting the suffocation were preserved in the rigor mortis. The Russians, Ukrainians, and Poles who gathered up the tormented bodies could only go down into this Hades under the numbing influence of alcohol. "For these people it was just as horrific. They vomited over the edge of the vehicles, had perpetual sickly, discolored faces, and looked worse from day to day. Packed full, the carts and trucks then started rolling with their unfortunate cargo."[47] In Stuttgart, the saying went, "There is no time for piety." Disgust and fear of contamination by touching the human remains deadened the senses. The uncovered scenes of dying, however, caused the rescue and recovery teams, who had little reason to feel sympathy, to burst into tears, again and again.

Recovering bodies was just as much an air-raid protection task as it was a family matter. After the raid, people were concerned first with their own survival, and then with that of their relatives. Corpses picked up on the streets were laid out on sidewalks and in open spaces; the living walked hunched over along the rows of deceased, fearing they might see a familiar face. The rows multiplied as search and recovery efforts continued. After the cellars were opened, the teams removed the upper, loose layer of debris. The bodies of the slain worked their way up to the surface—or at least, that was often reported.

Six days after the February 1945 raid on Dresden, Theodor Ellgering, head of the interministerial committee on air-war damages, saw body parts, heads, and arms poking out of the rubble as he monitored the repair work. He joined a young woman's search for her parents. A rescue team lifted the debris from the holes in the cellar walls and "you could literally feel the hot air escaping from the cellar."[48] With a flashlight and guided by the marking arrows, they entered the air-raid shelter where the residents of the building were sitting

exactly the way people always sat in air-raid cellars, one next to one another on benches with their so-called air-raid luggage beside them. About thirty to forty people, mostly elderly, women, and children were dead, sitting on the benches against the wall. Only a few had fallen to the ground. It was so shocking that the young woman almost collapsed at the sight.

Her parents were not there. The family had separated in the network of passageways under the Old Town because the daughter found the development of smoke to be suspicious. The father had a weak heart and wanted to wait until the smoke died down a bit; the mother wanted to stay with him. The two of them pressured their daughter to fight her way through the billows of smoke to the Great Garden. They were later found in the back rooms of the cellar, in a pile of 108 corpses. This group had wanted to escape the smoke by going into the nearest inner courtyard, but they had trampled one another to death.

Russian laborers and prisoners excavated ditches at Dresden cemeteries to bury ten thousand who had fallen. Then mild pre-spring air came, accelerating the decomposition process. "We no longer had any choice," wrote Ellgering,

> but to authorize the incineration of the corpses. They were cremated at the Old Market, where iron girders were built into huge grates on which roughly five hundred bodies each could be stacked into a funeral pyre, drenched with gasoline, and burned. These funeral pyres at the Old Market in Dresden represent a blemish in the history of our century that we will hard put to find another example of in the future. Whoever witnessed it will never forget that horrible scene as long as they live.

At the same time in Pforzheim, the Wehrmacht had offered to get rid of twenty thousand corpses using flamethrowers. The city was one-tenth the size of Dresden, but had to bury half as many casualties. The residents brought their dead to Friedhof auf der Schanz, the main cemetery, in handcarts, cattle trucks, and hay wagons. When the hall was filled, and mountains of mutilated and charred bodies began growing next to it, no one had any better idea than the flamethrower. Then the mayor of Heilbronn offered a power shovel. The same piece of equipment had been used eleven weeks earlier to put the six thousand Heilbronn victims of the December 4 raid into the ground. In the eastern section of the cemetery, three fifty-yard-long ditches were excavated. "We had to lay 3,500 dead in each ditch," recalled Arthur Kühn, who was there at the time, "with ten to fourteen on top of each other. We made steps out of the bodies in order to manage it. We had become so unfeeling. Our work had to be done, as difficult and horrid as it was."[49] In cities such as Pforzheim, Darmstadt, and Heilbronn, one had to go back to the time of the plague to find similar monthly death tolls of one in four, ten, or eleven residents.

8. "Gruesome details from the Dresden catastrophe. Russian troops are still busy burning the charred corpses on large wooden pyres in the center of the city." —Horst Lange, diary, March 10, 1945.
Source: Bildarchiv Preussischer Kulturbesitz.

As late as February 1944, Hitler had still strictly prohibited mass graves for the burial of the bombing victims. That resembled fates of annihilation that were meant for others. A Streibel squad had participated in erecting the grates on Dresden's Old Market square, which burned for five weeks. SS-Sturmbannführer Karl Streibel, commandant of the Trawniki units made up of Ukrainians, Latvians, and Lithuanians that also served as guards in the extermination camps, learned of cremation procedures from Treblinka. There they used six railroad tracks on concrete pedestals.

The recovery of the corpses corresponded to the killing procedure. The exterminated did not receive an individual grave or an individual death, because they did not have a right to live. They had been stripped of it as if it were a jacket. The one thousand children under ten years of age were not bombed as punishment. Bomber Harris did not presume they were in any way guilty. Churchill merely claimed that they could not assert any rights from him. In World War I, they would have had such rights, but not in World War II. Hitler, Churchill, and Roosevelt took the rights from them. The urban population that had to take leave of the light of day precisely because they belonged to the urban population did not need a soldier's grave that was an individual one.

The soldier remained a legal entity even if he could be killed. This was only permitted to continue as long as he himself continued to kill. If he laid down his weapon, he enjoyed a pardon. Things often did not go that way in the Russo-German war, but that war, too, ultimately ended in prisoner-of-war camps. The children of Heilbronn could not lay down their weapons because they did not have any in their hands. Consequently, they also received no pardon—and how could they have been taken prisoner? They were neither legal entities nor individuals; they were a group defined by virtue of their residence in the target area. The rights of the bomber pilot were regulated by the Geneva Convention. If he bailed out by parachute, he was to be taken prisoner.

Hitler's prohibition of mass graves aimed to secure individual graves for the German national comrades as some final personal protection. It ultimately failed due to the incapacity of the cemeteries. Frankfurt am Main decreed in October 1943 that up to one thousand corpses were to be buried in complete coffins, between two and six thousand in half coffins with a paper covering, and more than six thousand in paper bags. "The paper and suitable cord have been made available."[50] Leipzig was still able to bury the 1,800 from December 4, 1943, in row graves.[51] That kept 250 soldiers with extra rations of cognac busy for three weeks. When another 972 people were killed in the next raid, on February 20, and the Johannis Cemetery in Leipzig had to close because it was heavily hit, the people of Leipzig became so panicked at the thought of mass graves that the authorities declared: "The death of all these men, women, and children are self-sacrificial and heroic deaths." Each one received its own coffin and was laid to rest in the South Cemetery; the dead were honored at the monument to the Battle of Nations. The 368 foreigners among the fallen were given a place in a pit in the East Cemetery. In Würzburg in late March 1945, there was not enough time or energy to separate the five thousand dead.[52] Ninety percent of the population had been evacuated; for every two people who remained there was one death. Soldiers and foreign workers managed quickly to put three thousand bodies into mass graves in front of the Main Cemetery. Eight hundred of them were identified by name.

The families all made a great effort to ascribe the remains to the people they wanted to commemorate at the grave. Two widows whose husbands had indistinguishably burned to ashes divided up the ashes to bury them as their mortal remains. The people of Darmstadt gathered the human remains in crates, pails, and washtubs and then carried them to the cemetery. Those who had a family gravesite buried the parts in it. Those who did not labeled the containers and left them there. Where nothing remained but a number of charred bones, the sign read, "twenty-eight people from the building on Kiesstrasse."[53] This had at least been a group from one air-raid cellar, and as such, there was something personal to it. In Pforzheim, some bodies lay on the pavement with labels stating "Please do not put in mass grave. Will be buried privately."[54]

The last recoverable dignity is the name; the identification services worked on that. Whoever was known by name to be dead was no longer looked for. The surviving family members were released from the uncertainty. Above and beyond that, there was something unsettling about burying anonymous remains. If no physical characteristics were extant, in Heilbronn, an "identification bag" was made, containing jewelry, keys, and remnants of hair or fabric. The police chief's report on the firestorm in Kassel stated:

> It is particularly difficult to identify women because the lack of pockets in their clothing means they normally do not carry their identity papers directly on their person. Regarding female corpses, therefore, it is especially important to secure any jewelry. As a foresight, identification squads are recommended to carry strong pincers to remove rings and scissors to take dress fabric samples.[55]

Identification was the responsibility of criminal investigators, who separated known from unknown dead, attached identification cards to the unknown, and left them under guard at the place they were found, so any information nearby residents might have could be entered. Nuremberg set up such a site at the foot of the monument to Martin Behaim. In Kassel it was decided "to leave unknown dead where they were found for as long as the decomposition process allowed. Demands of piety must be deferred to the more important task of identification."[56]

A report from Pforzheim read:

Many names are written in chalk on walls of building ruins. Most of them are followed by a cross. Sometimes there is also an address. "Where are you?" was once written in Pforzheim dialect. Following in block letters was: A L L D E A D. There were rows of dead on Luisenstrasse whose features could still be recognized. A lot of acquaintances among them. Almost all of them in Sunday dress, fur coats, carrying handbags. The air-raid goggles over eyes wide open don't fit the picture. The bodies at Reuchlinplatz look the worst. The blue-black flesh is incredibly swollen; legs are fat as if all of them had been wrestlers. The bodies are bloated, heads like pumpkins, lips like Negroes, arms rigid and stretched out. Two women look at a large torso with a tiny little piece of fabric on it. "It could be Emma," says one of them. "Yes, she was wearing that dress in the cellar," replied the other in heavy dialect. Then they wave to a man with an official cap: "Write down that that was Frau Emma F."[57]

Identification crews in Kassel continued to work at the cemeteries, writing down physical descriptions. The search for names went on in the personal effects collection center. The city of Hanover encouraged residents to carry "a piece of tin can with them with their name and address scratched into it."[58] The municipal medical officer recommended in March 1943 to the Reich Health Commissioner that the German people should be furnished with identity tags like the ones carried by members of the Wehrmacht. This might unsettle the population, the recommendation continued, but the people were fully aware of the effects of major raids. The situation now was different from that of three months earlier. Every such measure would actually be welcomed as "helping to alleviate" the situation.

Surviving family members of someone who fell in a raid received a burial fee of 210 marks from the German state and another forty from the local government. The public health insurance funds, which paid their members a similar amount in the case of natural death, wanted to balance these two sums, but they confronted

9. Hamburg, August 1943.

Source: Archiv Michael Foedrowitz.

resistance from the Reich insurance office. Bombing victim benefits could not be offset against claims from other sources. This was justified on the basis of the principle "that the burial assistance provided by the Reich is primarily a form of welfare payment. Cutting a welfare benefit in favor or because of an insurance benefit would not be in line with the nature of welfare."[59]

The Reich had three faces. As a political organ, it waged war and was responsible for the exchange of hostilities. As a military organ, it failed in the most sustained and difficult battle, the one in the air. As a welfare organ, it accommodated the German people in their time of need. The people were well aware that the helper had caused the need in the first place. Churchill's leaflets reaffirmed that the need would end when the helpers were defeated; he too was a rescuer from an evil that he himself sent out. But before all the ifs and thens came the need. For the person who had to suffer, the bombing war triggered not political reasoning but the need for a bowl of hot soup.

In the winter of 1940–1941, when the Reich was preparing for an extended air war, the Air Ministry, the Interior Ministry, and the Nazi party reckoned with a mass exodus of the population from the threatened cities. In order to keep such movements in check, barriers and reception posts were set up at the town limits. As it later turned out, the German state and the Nazi party had to use persuasion and force to get residents to leave the cities and move to rural quarters. The welfare state and the needy nurtured their social relations more closely than ever before.

Reception centers at the outskirts of the cities were established, but not as a police cordon. After major raids there were the expected aimless movements out of the fire areas into the open spaces. In some locations, this took place in a disciplined manner. In Stuttgart, for example, people wandered directly to the suburban train stations and bought tickets to Bad Cannstatt, Esslingen, or Vaihingen. Of the twenty-two peripheral reception centers, four placed themselves discreetly near train stations at the edge of town. They were instructed by the regional authorities of Württemberg-Hohenzollern:

> Psychological assistance for national comrades is the duty of the political leaders. The citizens are to be accommodated as far as possible in halls, barns, and similar quarters, where they have an opportunity to sit or lie down. Temporary care of people who have lost everything, who are sparsely dressed or whose clothing was greatly damaged during their escape, is

among the tasks of the National Socialist Public Welfare. People who are homeless must be made aware that citizens whose job binds them to Stuttgart need to stay in Stuttgart or its direct proximity. Only those whose job does not bind them to Stuttgart can be placed in more remote counties. Heil Hitler (signed) Murr, Gauleiter.[60]

Around the reception centers set up in all cities, welfare personnel on bicycles combed the area, gathering up people who were confused and despairing and treating them to something to drink, "since fear and anxiety make people thirsty."[61] After thirst was quenched, desperation was assuaged and morale stabilized.

The same refreshment posts also hurried to the damaged areas; loudspeakers and rumor announced the locations. As soon as bombs started falling, people there started making sandwiches and tea: "A warm drink and tasty bread and butter are a great help after such an upsetting night." In November 1944, Duisburg distributed a total of 220,000 slices of bread and butter after the three major raids. In the final two years of the war, growing homelessness in Cologne made part of the population into boarders of the city administration. The meal center served 7.3 million cooked meals and several million slices of bread and butter in thirty-four days in the summer of 1943; up to 300,000 meals were served on individual days. On top of that, tank trucks came through the cities after raids with drinking water, since taps were not functioning. The water-treatment equipment yielded five liters per hour. After it was filtered, clarified, and decontaminated, any water that was not too salty or toxic was distributed.

The welfare part of air-raid protection was organized by the Nazi party. In December 1943, Hitler appointed propaganda minister Goebbels to be the Reich inspector for civil air-raid defense. Deeds were the only kind of propaganda that still counted. So something was done for the bombing victims. The National Socialist Public Welfare agency, the League of German Girls (Bund Deutscher Mädel), and the National Socialist Women's Organization looked after those who suffered damages. The social welfare offices were confronted by a flood of neediness, which was absorbed by an army of conscripted emergency service employees from all branches of the public sector, including teachers, librarians, lay helpers from the Red Cross, and nursing students. The social welfare offices and the Nazi party set up "assignment folders" with arrangements as to who would treat whom. The party used the solidarity efforts to show its true colors.

It was called the "second seizure of power." Keeping the hardship under control cemented the bonds between people and regime as never before.

The most comprehensive damage of the air war was to the apartments. Each medium-sized raid on Cologne obliterated 10 to 12 percent of the residential housing. When the heaviest bombardment began in 1944, 62 percent of the housing was completely destroyed or severely damaged. The final year of the war left only 19.6 percent in a damaged, albeit halfway usable, state. The homeless supported whomever could give them a roof over their heads, and that was the Nazi state.

In the back rooms of restaurants, the regime set up rendezvous points for the homeless. They procured temporary mass quarters, usually in schools identified on the outside with a yellow and blue banner marked with an "N." These included gender-separated sleeping and common rooms for up to three thousand people. After six raids in the Battle of the Ruhr in 1943, for example, more than forty thousand homeless in Duisburg registered such a need (May 13), more than fifty thousand in Dortmund (May 24), eighty thousand in Wuppertal (May 30), 140,000 in Düsseldorf (June 12), 72,000 in Krefeld (June 22), and thirty thousand in Mülheim (June 23). Offices were already active in the emergency lodgings, issuing certificates for family support, cash advances, and, later, compensation for lost clothing, linens, and everyday consumer goods, as well as coupons for food, clothing, and meals at soup kitchens. A milk can proved to be the most desirable and therefore most scarce item. Aside from the elderly, mothers with young children were the most-represented population group in the war-struck cities. School-age children had largely been evacuated starting in 1943.

The special department for housing welfare found a temporary abode for the homeless, at first on the housing market and later through confiscation. In Soest, the municipal administration required Jewish residents to leave their homes and make them available for bombed-out families. Homeless bombing victims, who were often inadequately dressed, were also given emergency clothing; this was recorded in their *Fliegergeschädigtenausweis*, which identified them as having suffered bombing damages. This ID card contained an exact description of damage to their windows, doors, curtains, and household items. These things were either replaced or indemnified; to prevent abuse, all benefits were recorded in the

Betreuungsnachweis, the welfare care card. Health issues were taken care of through the *Heilfürsorgeausweis*, the medical care identification card. Medical care was supposed to follow seamlessly after raids, which caused many eye injuries.

Eyes were the most threatened organ in the air war. Blindness was caused by phosphorus clouds, soot and gas particles, smoke, dust, and especially by perforation of the eyeball by minuscule glass splinters. The condition was treatable, but the people affected did not know that yet. They only knew their vision was gone, and assumed it was gone permanently. They remained immovable at least for the duration of the raid, the fire, the danger of time bombs. In apartments, cellars, and streets, numerous people who were temporarily blinded wandered around not knowing whether they were coming or going. Even later, they could not find their way to receive proper care. Helpers patrolled the buildings, gathering up these people.

Faces were also lost through particles of walls, lime, plaster, and earth forced into the head by the high explosive pressure, causing a "dirt tattoo." Rapid swelling and crusting of the facial skin could cause an eyelid edema that blocked vision. It was not possible to treat it on the spot. Red Cross workers calmed the injured party, who was not to try to open the eyelid with their hand nor squeeze it shut. The person was to be taken for treatment in a sitting position with the eyes slightly closed. Glass splinters generally caused serious eye damage and needed to be removed by a surgically trained physician in a hospital. But the hospitals were seriously damaged by bombs. The greatest gap in care was caused by the lack of sufficient alternative facilities.

At first, people believed that painting a red cross on hospitals would keep them out of the attack zone. Later, they had the impression the adversary actually preferred to destroy cathedrals and hospitals. The cathedrals were simply a good orientation point for the Old Town quarters built around them. And hospitals fell faster because they were large and resembled factories. Their cellars had been converted into hospital dormitories, operating rooms, and delivery rooms, as well as isolation rooms for quarantining contagious diseases. They were secure from poison gas, splinters, and debris. And they could be used for another twelve hours after water and power supplies were cut.

As soon as the sirens sounded, the nursing staff carried down to the basements the patients who could not walk. The available cellar space, however, was not at all in the proper ratio to patients needing to be relocated. The head physician allotted the space. When the cellar was filled, the ground floor was packed even fuller; when the ground floor was overcrowded, the corridors were filled; and when the corridors were full, the rest of the beds were rolled away from the windows and placed against the wall. Huddled under their blankets, the immobile patients saw the incendiary sticks whoosh past, saw the fiery glow on the horizon, smelled the burning through the shattered panes, and clung to the power of prayer.

No one had reckoned with such a great need for auxiliary and additional beds in the air war. In June 1939 one bed per one thousand residents had been calculated for cities designated "first-order air-raid protection sites." Youth hostels and boarding schools sufficed as provisional hospitals. In late 1940, shortly after the bunker construction program had been announced, the situation was already viewed more realistically. On December 4, 1940, the Reich Health Commission ordered "all health facilities to be cleared of all seriously ill, bedridden patients." At that time, however, Berlin refused to permit the "elimination" of chronically ill patients. As the degree of hospital outage in 1943 approached a final balance of 55 percent for Nuremberg, 57 percent for Augsburg, 81 percent for Munich, and 82 percent for Stuttgart, there was little else that could be done besides sending the incurably ill home and in turn refusing to admit any hopeless cases, in accordance with the Interior Ministry—that is, Himmler's—edict of February 11, 1944. Death was everywhere.

Efforts to organize transfers to remote hospitals were not very promising, since there was a more pressing demand to treat the wounded Wehrmacht soldiers. A rivalry for alternative options in homes for the infirm or aged and for the necessary beds, blankets, and medical equipment developed between the front lines and the home front. What became of the previous patients? Hospitals in Düsseldorf had to turn away injured parties after air raids due to overcrowding. The mentally ill had been moved from their asylums to restaurants in the Neander Valley near Düsseldorf; in seven hundred cases, beds in the Grafenberg psychiatric hospital were freed up through poison injections.

"As the increased destruction in the Rhineland through air raids also increased the need for suitable space for military and civilian hospitals, space was continually made available, especially in psychiatric hospitals," according to a ruling of November 24, 1948, by the Düsseldorf regional court, in a case of killings.

In the fall of 1942 the damaged Riehler Sanatorium for the elderly in Cologne was supposed to be moved to the Hoven convent. In order to free up the necessary space, 370 psychiatric patients had to be brought away. Because there was no satisfactory space within the facilities of the Rhine Province, defendant Dr. Walter Creutz had the Reich Interior Ministry inform him about empty space elsewhere. From there the Hadamar facility was specifically named.[62]

In the case in question, a total of 946 adults and thirty children, most of whom were schizophrenic, were murdered in Hadamar and Waldniel. The care offered by the Nazi state for some involved terror against others. Both served to secure the nation's cohesion and readiness to fight.

The contents of the vast number of households destroyed by fire needed to be replaced. This could not be accomplished by German production, which had not only been geared to the war economy but also had suffered serious bomb damage itself. The necessary metals, textiles, and labor could not be found. In January 1944, Hitler's secretary Martin Bormann encouraged private industry—since they understood the situation better—to buy up textiles and household goods within the occupied areas of Europe. But the market remained tense, and occupied Europe too had started producing for the German armaments demand. So replacements were taken from what already existed. One of the inventory sources was property stolen from Jews who were then exterminated. No cutlery or tablecloth from this source failed to be channeled for reuse.

People who lost objects in the bombings received generous compensation, albeit in cash and ration coupons. For this type of compensation, there had to be something to buy or ration out; over time, that became difficult. Initially, however, the bombed-out population had hardly any time to be needy, as gratification was sought with verve. As soon as they had money or coupons in their hands, they were busy. In Cologne after the May 1942 raid, 28,000 cash-payment orders were issued for clothing and commodities, 55,000 for food and lodging, 100,000 for reimbursement for damages, and 300,000 for additional expenditures.

Compensation for loss of living space was made in the particularly exemplary Stuttgart by filing an application for assessment with the mayor. The assessment agency sent an appraisal commission that prepared an inventory of damages at the site. In Munich, however, a thousand-mark advance on expected benefits was paid. In cases of excessive demands, the standard administrative procedure was usually to recognize the claim rather than provoke the petitioner. About 50 percent of damage reports on personal property were usually approved, so people always applied for double what they needed. In the arbitrariness of the air terror, an orderly administrative process proved most efficient. The aftermath of the bombing was administered in a German way; the state could cope with that. The most nightmarish external violence in one's own home was always followed by some calm, official regulation.

After major raids, white bread, meat, schnapps, wine, and tobacco were distributed. Front-line soldiers were inclined to receive extra rations. Germans viewed with satisfaction the fact that the state continued to function. Surveys showed that 58 percent were satisfied with the care they received; they said that everything possible was being done. About 56 percent assessed their quarters as satisfactory, and 44 percent found them unsatisfactory, which, considering the unpleasantness of extreme overcrowding, was viewed by the authorities as a highly tolerant attitude. Medical care received the highest approval rate; more than 85 percent judged it as satisfactory.

There was some displeasure from feelings that the state was too generous. Employers complained that people who received compensation refused to work because they did not need the money. By standing up for the damages suffered, the state claimed the air war for itself. As long as it footed the bill, things could continue. The air war created need; the Nazi state declared itself in charge of dealing with it. That had a unifying effect.

The regime ultimately mobilized people to support one another. People who offered lodging were supporting those who needed it. Roughly ten million children and adolescents between ten and eighteen years of age were registered starting in March 1939 for compulsory youth service. They toiled away for the ailing parent generation. It was as if the women's organization, the Drivers' Corps (NSKK), the SA stormtroopers, the Public Welfare, the party officials, and the entire fabric of society were made for the air war. That was also what the Douhetists proclaimed. Totalitarian society was the civil form of total war, so now they were one with themselves.

Applicants took compensation for damages literally. The authorities conferred as to how immaterial values should be compensated. Artists registered the loss of their own works according to collectors' prices that only future fame could have procured. Of course they wouldn't have sold for a lower price! Someone who lost a Biedermeier sofa did not file for a sofa but for a piece of period furniture. The antiques market grew and prices mushroomed. Resistance to the unprecedented destruction of property meant having everything replaced: the sofa, the watercolors. It was not right that everything was taken from them.

All prices for new merchandise were fixed and all purchases rationed. That is why the vast amounts of money distributed, which was not backed up with an increase in goods, were not subject to inflation. So another outlet emerged: the black market. Articles that disappeared from storefront windows returned as profiteer's wares at market prices. Bartering flourished in the same shady atmosphere. A report from Stuttgart mentioned a black market operating in Cannstatt that was started by foreign workers trading bread for cigarettes, cigarettes for shoes, shoes for pants, and pants for bread. Bartering was kept moving by the cleverness of the hoarder. Everything for everyone at any time. One could acquire whatever was available at the moment and get enough for a reserve supply. And that was how the market ended up swept clean. And one had a currency with purchasing power!

The police tried in vain to control the circulation of food and clothing. In Wetzlar, people said, so many bartered goods were going around that for every resident, one police officer was needed, and for every policeman, a second one. Even the authorities themselves joined in on the marketeering. In October 1944, a hint of Rhineland separatism surfaced. The invading army of the Allies was not far away, and voices intimated that the Reich had already written off the Rhineland. When the city of Bonn was hit hard by a raid on October 18, 1944, it confiscated a shipment of salt from a barge on the Rhine because the city quickly needed something to barter with other cities.

The black market, like other iniquities, was attributed to the foreign workers. Their connections with their home country did in fact facilitate deliveries of rare goods. But all of Germany hustled goods, especially the party bigwigs. Hawkers were often apprehended in the cellar ruins—the bazaar of the black market—but never the wholesalers. That suggested where they were hiding. In Dortmund, the Nazi functionaries, businesspeople, and well-paid laborers were considered the main profiteers.

Though encouraged by the destruction-and-replacement system of the bombing war, profiteering was nevertheless an economic crime. People participated in it, yet they considered the air-raid shelter community an egalitarian one. A lack was easier to endure than a privilege. Price control and rationing were cooperative ways of budgeting the shortages. The black market, on the other hand, divided people into those who could raise the bid and those who had to pass. The most common wares were food, such as the legendary black-market butter. There were accounts of a virtually perfected black market in Hamburg with house-to-house delivery. Someone spending five hundred marks a month was considered affluent here. People applauded when a cigarette depot in Cologne valued at 1,600 marks was confiscated, even though the public had nothing to smoke. On the other hand, there was nothing more profitable than a cigarette stockpile. Such opposing aspects were reconciled in people's conceptions by simply agreeing that participating in the black market was a crime typically committed by foreigners.

The sentence "Germans don't loot" took on a similar kind of regulation. It was an imperative that the judicial system bloodily refuted. Between 1941 and 1945, fifteen thousand citizens of the Reich were sentenced to death for misdemeanors on the Home Front:[63] looting, "undermining the military morale," or listening to enemy radio broadcasts. A tailor shop for uniforms in Hamburg-Wandsbek was totally destroyed in a major raid on July 27, 1943. After moving into emergency lodgings with an elderly widow, the owner went on an extended looting spree in bomb-damaged buildings. She acquired clothing, food, and basic consumer goods worth several thousand marks, as determined by the Hamburg Special Court.[64] On October 18, 1943, she was sentenced to death, as was a bombed-out couple that dug through rubble in search of their relative's property. They failed to separate out other peoples' possessions they also picked up and therefore, as the chief of police noted, "exploited out of greed the catastrophic conditions in an irresponsible way."[65] The case of Friedrich Bühler, an office clerk, was similar. On July 28, the day after the firestorm, he was observed rummaging through property that was salvaged, from which he took a large basket of linens, a radio, and several packs of cigarettes. He gave a fireman two winter coats and two suits. A week later he was sentenced to death, a German postscript to the forty thousand deaths of July 27. On August 30, the seventy-one-year-old pensioner Schmidt picked up two pairs of shoes, five ties, and two silver women's watches from the debris and paid for it with his life, just like the thirty-nine-year-old office clerk Maier, who on the morning after the raid took off with a crate from a wine cellar. He was stopped by police at the exit to the cellar.

In the friendly tone of the early postwar period, Dr. August Schuberth, then a public prosecutor in Hamburg, described what was going on inside the bombing victims from a criminological perspective:

> Air raids of the type of the attacks in July 1943, causing total destruction of large parts of the city, change not only the structure of the city as a whole but also the individual human being subjected to the catastrophe. Such destruction not only provides ample opportunities for criminal acts, but also lowers the moral code and changes the social position of the victims of the attack. One who experiences the loss of all and everything for which he has worked and slaved for many years, perhaps all of his life, and sees bursting into flames all of his dreams of home and future, becomes indifferent to the law and order of government actions.[66]

At the time the crime was committed, no one was concerned with the criminal liability of the ruined or thirsty looters in cities filled with rubble. What counted was protection of the scorched belongings that piled up on the street in front of the debris-filled lots, which represented life as it had once been. Given life at that time, one life more or less did not matter, as the *Hamburger Anzeiger* newspaper of August 19, 1943, threatened:

> In an unceasing effort, the tight grip of justice and police manages more and more to justly punish all who have taken advantage of the plight of our national comrades for their own benefit by looting. Anyone who has plundered and thus offended the community in a most severe way shall be weeded out! May this be another warning to those elements who are inclined to steal in our hard-hit city or to gain any other unjustified advantages at the expense of society. They can be certain of ruthless extermination.[67]

The *Verordnung gegen Volksschädlinge*[68] of September 5, 1939, defined "crimes during air-raids" as an offense. It was basically petty theft in blacked-out cities, called "blackout crimes." The lightless cities offered all-night opportunities for crime and stirred up insecurity. The repair and recovery squads pulled not only the dead and injured but also their households out of the rubble. After a night of bombing, there might be nothing in the world more valuable than sturdy children's shoes, and a mattress is a precious possession in times of scarcity, not only for the owner. The objects waited amidst the piles of debris to be picked up, while the people bombed out of their homes waited for housing in emergency shelters, worrying the whole while about their belongings. The state kept an eye on them.

Work crews put the possessions in warehouses within the program to "secure household items." Cologne had 150 such storage spaces, comprising almost 350,000 square feet. Each household was stored separately. In the first eight months of 1943, 11,700 people worked in this salvage department, which salvaged very little. All the warehouses went down in subsequent bombings; hardly anything survived.

Until the possessions could be transported away, the damaged areas remained closed off, but not for the victims. They continued to scavenge through the bricks for their missing belongings and anything else they lacked. As long as they kept digging, no one unauthorized did, like the invalid Eggebrecht of Berlin, who took nine pairs of shoes from a burning building for himself and paid for them with his life, the sentence imposed by the Special Court in Berlin.

The salvage teams, which sometimes came together spontaneously, were met with just as much gratitude as mistrust, especially when the foreigners outweighed the Germans. Eighteen-year-old Marius Carpentier, a Frenchman who went to Germany of his own accord in search of work, met his end on a work crew, when he fished a belt, a pair of binoculars, a pair of gloves, a jar of jam, and a game of dominos out of the rubble. The Special Court in Berlin ruled that this proved "such a high degree of reprehensibility that he herewith expelled himself from the community of all upright and just-thinking people. He was therefore to be sentenced to death."[69] Being a foreigner was always judged as aggravating evidence, though the courts were not much more lenient with Germans.

On March 24, 1944, the U.S. Air Force bombed Weimar.[70] The bombs fell on the northern district and set houses on fire, including the one at Riessner Strasse no. 11.[71] Only a few hours earlier, thirty-nine-year-old office courier Georg Hopfe; Private Fritz Gerlach, home on leave; and the laborer Fritz Nauland met in the Gambrinus restaurant. After a stimulating conversation and a few beers, they moved on to the Scharfe Ecke bar for another beer before returning to the Gambrinus. They downed their last beer in the Kloster-

Kaffee restaurant; it was their seventh glass, and when they set off homeward, they got caught in the bombs. At Riessner Strasse no. 11, the air-raid wardens and a few officers and soldiers were waiting for the fire department. The beer-happy trio now thirsted for action. Nauland kicked in the door of Frau Hopfgarten's apartment; Hopfe and the soldiers followed. They looked around and decided to salvage the living room. Hopfe and the soldiers carried the furniture into the building across the street, then turned their attention to the bedroom. While the soldiers were carrying out the bed and wardrobe, Hopfe's eye caught the resident's set of perfume bottles, and he pocketed an opened bottle of cologne as a thank-you for his effort, along with a half-pound knockwurst from the bureau, to eat along the way. The fire engines had meanwhile arrived, and the three cheerful, helpful spirits moved on. Each of them had a souvenir with them: Nauland had two bars of toilet soap and Gerlach, a pair of leather gloves. Hopfe's sausage was eaten in Gerlach's apartment, and because it was so salty, they went to the train station restaurant and ordered three beers. Meanwhile, Frau Hopfgarten discovered her losses and reported them.

Hopfe and Gerlach, who fell under the jurisdiction of the Special Court, were sentenced to death. Hopfe excused his actions by saying that he took the sausage only because he had been out since 7 p.m. and had not eaten anything for hours. The Special Court in Jena responded on April 11, 1944:

> If that had been the case he would certainly have consumed it immediately and not secretly put it in his pocket. That in particular proves his base intentions. Anyone acting in such a way is a looter, as defined by the law and according to public sentiment, and must be punished under article 1 of the Decree against Public Enemies.[72]

This decree of September 5, 1939, did in fact call for the death penalty for anyone "found looting in . . . buildings or rooms voluntarily vacated." However, it lay totally within the discretion of Regional Court Judge Blankenburg to rule according to public sentiment that eating the knockwurst was payment for services rendered. After seven beers, Hopfe could have been too drunk to know better, or the report of the expert witness could have been taken into consideration, which declared Hopfe's to be a borderline case between slight moronism and general stupidity. But Blankenburg decided that Hopfe deserved to die "because of the despicable and hostile attitude demonstrated by the deed and the baseness of his character. Whoever commits such an abhorrent crime sets himself apart from the national community."[73]

The ruling characterized a terror justice that did not allow the guilty to atone for a crime but rather simply attempted to eradicate a type, that type being someone who made himself independent in the midst of the rubble's chaos. Law and order maintained its existence in the insanity of destruction both by saving lives and by killing. When entire residential areas disappeared in flames in half an hour, the ownership of a jar of jam was no longer all that important. More important was whether or not state power still existed when all military power came from the enemy's hand. What does such a state still have the power to do? Make an example of fifteen thousand poor devils.

The Nazi regime pronounced one thousand death penalties from 1933 to 1941. That was a bloody figure when compared with Mussolini's Italy, which imposed a total of 130 death penalties. The fifteen thousand death penalties imposed in the last four years of the war, however, did not render judgments on actions; instead, they exterminated little by little those personality types that might have doubted the authority of the order. It did not have to be true; it worked because it was asserted. Terror was not a punishment for those involved; it was a lesson for the bystanders. The Nazi regime that distributed a million slices of bread and butter at the homeless rendezvous points was the same one that beheaded someone for stealing a knockwurst. Power over life and death. That was precisely what the air bombardment so conspicuously called into question. Rescue and destruction were both evidence of Hitler. Just as not welfare was his concern, but the solidarity it mobilized, the terror was especially his, by inciting destructiveness.

Judicial terror that threw itself on countless trifles could not be set in motion by the eye of the police. But people in general were invited to become criminologists and informers, to attend both to the property getting dirty on the pavement and to the increasingly porous state authority. A segment of the population became the hunters, and they were on the lookout for "pests harmful to the people" and those who undermined the military morale.

According to section 5 of the Decree on the Special Wartime Penal Code (KSSVO) of August 17, 1938, any attempt to publicly paralyze or undermine the will of the German people to assert itself was punishable by death. This referred to the will to fight that Churchill attacked from the air in order to undermine, and the undermining of which Hitler avenged from the guillotine in order to maintain. Churchill imagined the German people's undermining act as a popular revolt, like the one of November 1918. So did Hitler, but he knew that then it would be too late for him. The memorandum of June 26, 1944, by Dr. Vollmer, undersecretary in the Reich Ministry of Justice, clearly defined the regime's moral line of defense:

> The following types of utterances shall no longer be tolerated and are fundamentally deserving of the death penalty: The war is a lost cause; Germany or the Führer senselessly or frivolously started the war and must lose; the NSDAP [Nazi party] should or will step down and like the Italian example make way for a negotiable peace; a military dictatorship must be established, which will be able to make peace; we have to work slower so the end will come; Bolshevist infiltration is not as bad as the propaganda paints it and will hurt only the leading National Socialists; British and Americans would bring Bolshevism to a halt at the German borders; word-of-mouth propaganda and letters to the front calling upon soldiers to throw away their weapons or turn around; the Führer is sick, inept, a human butcher, etc.[74]

Vollmer saw the threat posed by words as directly proportional to the prestige of the speaker, "for example department heads or authorized officers, physicians in consultation with their patients, clerics working in their congregations, public transportation employees."

Professor Walther Arndt was just such a person.[75] The fifty-three-year-old curator of the Berlin Zoological Museum ran into his childhood girlfriend Frau Mehlhausen and her mother on the platform of the Landeshut train station in Silesia on September 4, 1943. Just the previous night, 316 Lancasters had flown over Berlin, causing destruction in the residential districts of Charlottenburg, Moabit, and Siemensstadt, killing 422 people, including 123 foreign workers. Arndt reported to the two women that this had been the worst raid on Berlin up to then and that it was terrible that everyone had to suffer because of what a few had started. Frau Mehlhausen responded: "We aren't responsible for the war." Arndt's reply: "Of course we are responsible for the war," but now the guilty parties were being called to account for it. The German armies were giving way at all fronts. Mussolini had been taken care of in three days and that was what would happen in the Reich as well. "In four weeks it'll be all over for the party." Before that happened, Mehlhausen thought, it will be all over for her childhood friend. She went to the district directorate of the Nazi party and then filed a report with the People's Court in Berlin.

"Looking at her in the main proceedings," wrote presiding judge Roland Freisler in his decision, "one could see how heavy-hearted she was, having to incriminate Arndt, she surely did not say a single word more than corresponded to the truth." Because Arndt gave the struggling German people, as represented by Mehlhausen, a stab in the back with his discouraging words—"she suffered greatly from these statements"—he was hanged.

Two Nazi nuns filed a complaint against Ludwig Mitterer, pastor in Otterskirchen. He was executed for undermining the military morale because he had said that the Hamburg firestorm was the total war that everyone was crying out for. "We started it and it looks to me like 1918." And the pensioner Wilhelm Lehmann had written on the pissoir at Mariannenplatz in Berlin's Kreuzberg district in blue chalk: "Hitler, you mass murderer, you must be killed, then the war will be over." Laborer Max Willi Karl Reiche read the sentence, wiped it away, but then hid waiting for the writer to return. Lehmann did return, wrote again, and that was his doom.

Based on a complaint filed by crane operator Fritz Hoffmann, the People's Court sentenced Konrad Hoffmann to the gallows, but not before instructing the denouncer that he was not obligated to testify against his brother. "People like him should be eradicated," shouted Fritz into the courtroom. "We don't want to experience another 1918."[76] Herr Münter, a locksmith from Wuppertal, who had reported his coworker for saying "The bombs will get through the Third Reich," boasted in the plant about the death penalty that was issued: "That was my doing!"

The judge was his tool, just as the Gestapo was the tool of the sixty-six-year-old businessman Herr Paasch, who, in early March 1944, denounced the "Jewess Paasch" with whom he had been married for thirty years.[77] In the course of a marital dispute, Amalie Paasch had said that the war could no longer be won, the German soldiers were murderers, Hitler himself was the murderer of the Hamburg children killed in the air raids, and the day of Jewish revenge would come. Paasch and his sister mentioned this to the Nazi party block leader, who sensed that this was purely a family matter being shifted onto a political track. After conferring with the local chapter director, it was decided that they would take no action against Amalie Paasch. When no one reacted, Herr Paasch went to the

Gestapo office at Rothenbaumchaussee no. 38; he asked if a complaint had been filed against his wife. The Gestapo official said no, and warned Paasch that false accusations against Jews were punishable. He responded by writing a detailed report and submitting it formally to the Gestapo. After Paasch confirmed the contents upon intensive questioning, Amalie Paasch was picked up and taken to the Fuhlsbüttel police prison, and was later sent to Auschwitz.

On July 21, 1942, the People's Court passed a death sentence on philosopher and theologian Alfred Kaufmann and artist A. Will for an offense that half of Germany could have been charged with, namely, violating the regulations of September 1, 1939, regarding special measures pertaining to the radio. Sections 1 and 2 declared that listening to enemy broadcasts was punishable by prison sentences. "Whoever deliberately spreads news of foreign radio stations that are suitable to threaten the strength of the German people's resistance shall be sentenced to death in especially serious cases."[78]

Kaufmann and Will ran the so-called Friday Circle in Giessen. Among the women in the group were a teacher, a student, a branch manager, a professor's wife, and the housewife Dagmar Imgart, who worked as a liaison officer for the Gestapo out of a desire for adventure and recognition. The Friday Circle regularly listened to London radio, and then discussed how the war was going. The People's Court sentenced Kaufmann and Will to death, claiming they had contaminated with defeatism the German women they listened with. "Enemy propaganda is a means of warfare; the broadcasts must be viewed as acts of war. Anyone in the country who incites others to listen to his reception of news of enemy propaganda is participating in these acts of war and promoting them."

Pests harmful to the German people, people undermining military morale, and radio-broadcast criminals were all put down as promoters and beneficiaries of the enemy, and their denunciations came from their neighbors, colleagues, and relatives. The People's Court, the major Special Court for war-related criminal cases, condemned to death half of all those accused between 1942 and 1944. When the fire war from the air began in 1942, death penalties increased tenfold. This sudden killing rage, however, remained far behind the number of denouncers. In the three years from 1942 to 1944, the People's Court held trials against 10,289 defendants, but 25,297 complaints had been filed.[79] The year with the greatest increase in denunciations was 1944, when the number rose to 13,986, double that of the previous year. That was also the year the country was given up to unleashed round-the-clock bombing.

The Gestapo recruited informers such as the saleswoman Marianne Koll of Remscheid, who put the heads of her friends and even her fiancé on the block for a monthly bounty of eighty, and later sixty, marks. Capitulators frequently kept their undermined morale for themselves; often they had to be made to talk. Hans Wiehnhusen, an agent provocateur working for the Gestapo in Trier under the code-name "7006,"[80] summoned two detective superintendents to the cafeteria of the Goeben barracks so they could listen to him at the next table as he got his boss, a beverage manufacturer, to talk.

"I'm convinced," began 7006, "that we will win the war."

Boss: "I don't want to rob you of your faith."

7006: "The Führer will run the show fine."

Boss: "You're all so fanatic that you can no longer tell the difference between propaganda and reality."

7006: "We'll swing it somehow."

The conversation was interrupted by the cafeteria manager, who was suspicious of the people at the next table. "They are surely from the Gestapo. They are listening to what you are saying."

7006 and the boss: "Oh, don't be ridiculous."

The cafeteria manager: "I have better intuition about these things than you two."

The detectives left, and the boss felt free to speak his mind. Three sergeants joined him, one of whom was missing his left leg. "You assholes," said the boss, "you let them shoot off your bones out there and you don't even know why."

"For Germany," said the one-legged man.

"You lost your leg," countered the boss, "not for Germany, but for Adolf Hitler."

"I'll get through it all right," said the sergeant.

"My, you are a happy optimist," called out the boss.

He himself did not get through it all right, because his employee Hans Wiehnhusen denounced him to the People's Court. Judge Freisler liked the boss and tried to get around the death penalty, so he asked Wiehnhusen, the main witness for the prosecution, if the accused was intoxicated at the time; after all, there was a bill for sixty-nine glasses of schnapps. The boss had been in full command of his mental faculties, Wiehnhusen answered, and had said even worse things.

The beverage manufacturer was executed because he got into a conversation. The Nazi party could hardly prevent all unfavorable talk in Germany, but it could create a climate of feeling forlorn, because people tended to live bitter and alone. No one could be trusted except for the party, if one was blindly committed to it. The Nazi party always mistrusted urban residents. Cities bred vice, decadence, intellectuals, politicization, and rebellion. In the future, the settlement form of the German people had to be a more healthy one. The air war alone showed that the metropolis of the nineteenth and twentieth centuries had become as obsolete as a knight's castle. It was no longer possible to defend. The proximity of industry and workers' quarters, the mass of houses, the tenements, and the chaotic jumble of the Old Town all just tempted the fire war. Ever since the air became an operational area, the conventional city became military insanity.

Hitler, a politician by profession but an architect by avocation, long had plans to overcome the gap between city and countryside. The air war made it necessary, earlier than presumed, to alter the German pattern of settlement, in the form of the emergency evacuation program. Germans could not survive in the cities, and neither could the regime. The cities were not bombproof and never would be.

After the Hamburg firestorm of July 1943, about a million people left the city. "After their experience," wrote the chief of police, "people are going as far as they possibly can by foot. The places where they stop have to prepare themselves for the growing demands on them for assistance."[81] The communities were obliged to arrange room and board, and "sending homeless people haphazardly back and forth is especially to be avoided." Transportation was organized to more remote placement areas.

Long waits for transportation led the refugees to wander into the woods and sleep outdoors. The rural communities they passed through were shocked by the impression the refugees gave. Some wore sweatsuits; some were barefoot, in shirtsleeves and underwear. People wondered how these wanderers stayed so calm and collected in their situation. As far as the police could manage, they directed the flow to the intact railroad stations at the outskirts of town, where special trains stood waiting. Fifty thousand people were transferred to ships on the Elbe. All police and Wehrmacht vehicles, every bus, and every car and horse-drawn cart that could somehow be acquired shuttled back and forth to wharfs and train stops. About 786,000 people were transported on 625 trains.

The district assigned to receive people from Hamburg was Bayreuth. That happened during Bayreuth's annual Richard Wagner festival, and the Nazi party donated opera tickets to wounded and decorated soldiers. Soldiers on leave wearing their dress uniforms had been brought with special trains from field hospitals or the eastern front and were greeted on the train platform with military marches. The ragged, disturbed Hamburgers arrived on the next track with fear written on their faces. A large number of frail and infirm people could not participate in the Bayreuth transport. Men who had accompanied their families returned to Hamburg to go to work. After the rather unregulated escape, many went home "out of loyalty to the terrorized city," as the police chief believed. They settled in peripheral city districts that had not been destroyed.

The Reich leadership had been preparing for a larger evacuation of people from the cities since early that year. More than anything else, Bomber Command destroyed residences in mass housing projects. The alternative abodes for the homeless were running out and space was needed. "Placeholders" had to be evicted. Whoever was not crucial to the war effort was urged to move to Thuringia or the Allgäu region. That also unburdened the air-raid protection and relieved pressure on the overall mood. A rough calculation in June 1943 showed that of the twenty-six million residents in cities with populations over 100,000, those over sixty-five years of age or under fifteen did not perform arms-related jobs. This corresponded to about 6.5 million people, or one-quarter of the total. It was thought that the best thing would be to send them elsewhere. This was an unprecedented effort with respect to both logistics and care, but that was not the problem.

By July 3, 1943, the Reich was divided up into evacuation and placement areas. According to the statistics, about half the Essen population was to be housed in Württemberg, Tyrol, the lower Danube, Styria, Carinthia, and Swabia. The party would manage to carry it out, but they did not know how to persuade the families to leave. The regime had been pressing for about three years to thin out the urban population, with moderate success. In October 1940, Hitler had recommended that children under fourteen in Berlin and Hamburg be put up in rural school retreats. Children were evacuated by grade, starting in 1941. By August 1943, 300,000 children had been removed from the major urban centers; by the end of the year, most schools in areas threatened by air raids were closed. But there were

935,000 children living in Berlin and Hamburg alone. The government estimated that perhaps one-sixth of Berlin's children, about 100,000, came under its custody. The parents tried to get around this by asking cousins and aunts in the countryside for accommodations.

The program to evacuate children from the cities, *Kinderlandverschickung* (KLV), was the most unpopular measure of the entire Third Reich. Parents feared they would lose legal guardianship of their children. From the bosom of the family, the children were given into the care of the Hitler Youth, which ran the KLV and taught slogans rather than prayers. Think of the moral neglect! In the depths of Alpine valleys, in Silesia, in Baden, school instruction was still conducted by the regular teaching staff, but camp life became an experimental stage for adolescent Hitler Youth leaders. The food tasted good and no Lancaster bombers would find the retreat, but parents could die in the bombing raids, leaving their children alone in the world. Heart-rending farewells took place at the departure of the overcrowded evacuation trains. Ten percent of the 40,450 children evacuated from Munich returned home by October 1943, because the parents could not bear the separation. Right around that time, Munich was targeted by heavy raids that killed 435 children.

The city school buildings had since become indispensable emergency hospitals and assembly camps for the homeless. All institutionlike facilities—homes for the aged, infirmaries, psychiatric hospitals, orphanages, homes for the blind—were moved in 1944, because the buildings were needed for air-raid protection. For the residents of the home for the blind on Oranienstrasse, it was no longer possible to stay in a Berlin that suffered ninety-four air raids that year anyway. The blind were taken to the Sudetenland to work in armaments production.

Severing families, over which Goebbels's agitation failed, was accomplished by the propaganda of Bomber Command's actions. From March to August 1943, the Battle of the Ruhr and Hamburg's Operation Gomorrah killed roughly sixty thousand people. The mood changed to utter horror in early August, when Goebbels sent a letter to all Berlin households, urging them to leave the city. People feared that the leadership evidently reckoned with the Hamburgization of the capital! So they evidently do not have anything to stop the British from doing so.

Up to September 25, 720,000 people were evacuated from Berlin. Together with those who left earlier, Berlin had thus lost 1.1 million residents, about 25 percent. At first there was tumult in the train stations; many camped in the forests outside the city. The evacuation plan provided for only 300,000 spaces in Brandenburg, East Prussia, and Posen. Things were also getting too hot for hundreds of thousands of people in the Ruhr basin; Rhinelanders and Westphalians stormed trains to Main-Franconia, Upper Bavaria, Baden, Saxony, and the Sudetenland. Aside from the hardship of being in a strange place, the separation hurt. Some could not handle the worry about their homes and family being bombed, so they returned to share the fate of their hometowns. Another group spent their time going back and forth, and the third group led a safe and secure existence among the evacuated population. For the regime, however, the situation changed yet again.

The city was also an inappropriate place for industry, especially since the British and Americans started hitting it hard around the clock, as ordered in the Casablanca Directive. Rather than evacuating cities to make space for industry, it was smarter to evacuate the industry and house the people somewhere nearby, where things were less risky. When the transportable manufacturing industries and their workforce relocated to open areas, they ran into the evacuees, who were now in the way yet again, taking away the terrain from the armaments battle.

The Reich Interior Ministry decided to discontinue further transfers, which were at first haltingly accepted, then regretted and dodged. There were other ways to group people. Bombing methods had meanwhile become standardized, which led to graded danger zones within the city limits and new prospects for the always preferred model of scattered settlements out toward the open countryside. Whoever felt uneasy about going to the Allgäu region was sent by the gauleiter to a nearby recreation area.

In a mirror image of Bomber Command's bombing scheme, with its core of city center and surrounding residential blocks, the residential scheme was to be centrifugal. Extending out from the market square, a system of concentric circles would lead to the rural outskirts. Zone 1, the area of the city center, with a dense built-up area and a residential density of more than eighty people per acre, was to be emptied of all nonworkers. The only employment there would serve to maintain facilities essential for survival. Danger of wide-area conflagration was unavoidable. Zone 2, the less-dense periphery of the city, had a residential density of eight to twelve people per acre; it needed to be cleared of all nonworkers and used to house the labor force for zone 1. Zone 3, the close commuter region, with gardens and agricultural areas and sixty minutes' travel time to work, would be filled with the families of people in zones 1 and 2. There would be additional relocations to the "weekend commuter zone" 6 and the "remote 'homeland' zone" 7, which was a four-hour train ride from the center. This was reserved for all nonworkers with no links whatsoever to the inner zones.

This dispersal plan followed and supported the Reich relocation plan. Only about half of the initially estimated evacuation volume of 11.77 million people was actually relocated, to parts of the country far removed from the bombing and to the rural outskirts of the cities. Especially as regards the conurbations of Berlin, Hamburg, and the Rhine-Ruhr valleys, there were not enough scattered weekend and "homeland" zone areas available. The families there were broken up and distributed as necessary. This took attack areas away from the air war in two ways. The target to be destroyed shrunk. The cities offered up fewer people to the incredible bomb tonnage of the previous nine months. Also, the relocation of the population relieved the regime. The urban population was no longer a functioning social organ; it was now a stringy, amorphous heap: splinters of families, garrison troops, prisoners, foreign workers, and nothing that would confront the gauleiters as a united citizenry.

What used to be a family might have become this in 1944: The father worked in Dortmund, the mother lived with a toddler in the Allgäu region, the twelve-year-old daughter was staying in Thuringia through the KLV program, her fourteen-year-old sister was in Franconia at a training camp run by the Public Welfare, and the nineteen-year-old son was besieging Leningrad. All of them thought of nothing else but getting back together again. The Führer paid for free train tickets, so they were constantly on the move. In such a state of affairs people did not make trouble—they made travel plans.

In principle, every evacuation area had its own placement district with a rural periphery. The placement district closed ranks and made room. The party set up a branch welfare office, offered childcare, and ordered a handful of people in uniforms who patrolled and registered complaints, since the atmosphere was charged and the mood larmoyant. The German tribes experienced one another closer up than they would have liked. A woman from Bad Tölz whined,[82] "Even if the war is lost, we have gotten to know exactly what Prussians are like and that too is worth something." On August 19, 1943, one Hamburger wrote to another: "No one here in Austria is very understanding. I wish they would get some bombs too. You all cannot imagine the suffering of the refugees. Better to hold out in Hamburg; staying there cannot be more ghastly!"

Munich was annoyed that Hamburg's "upholders of North Germanic civilization" were chauffeured more than six hundred miles to southern Bavaria, where there was no longer any room for the people of Munich. The people of Bayreuth, in turn, whose district bordered on the gates of Nuremberg, by no means wanted any evacuees from Nuremberg, especially since they were already bursting at the seams, with 500,000 Hamburgers.

Rural meals seemed like pig's feed to the urbanites. The Alpine villages had no cooking gas or movie theaters. The evacuees in Ratibor pulled out their ration cards for real coffee. "Don't have any!" Raised eyebrows. "What primitive, lowbrow people!" In the Bayreuth restaurants, Hamburgers felt deceived, wrote one on September 27, 1943: "The vermin here eats and drinks to their heart's content, while we who have lost everything don't get a drop of wine to drink anymore."

The countryside was boring. If a movie was finally shown, then it was only old films. The evacuees did not greet people with "Heil Hitler," but instead grumbled their dialect versions of "Evenin'" and "G'day." The hosts were Catholic and their language was incomprehensible. "Never again Bavaria." The Bavarians were also sick and tired. "If that's the future, then I'd prefer an independent Bavaria!"

The refugee women refused to make the beds, and they did not have any linens with them. The hosts ran out of towels and flatware. People who were bombed out took advantage of the better shopping options in their new surroundings. There they acquired articles such as women's coats and redirected them to the black markets of the shattered west. Warehouses in Breslau, Danzig, Königsberg, Stettin, and Weimar were soon emptied of women's underclothes. There were also no more shoes available, because the footwear of the city dwellers was worthless in the eastern districts, and the refugees equipped themselves with sturdier galoshes instead.

The social gaps also caused some distress. Better-off families who put up the poorer classes from Cologne's Old Town were shocked at their lack of cleanliness. For the first time, an official delousing action took place in their homes, which did not make them feel particularly hospitable to their guests. The evacuees, on the other hand, saw themselves as martyrs and wanted to be treated accordingly. Their basic condition was depression, and they expressed it by complaining.

They complained from dawn to dusk about the inadequacy of their assigned accommodations. The Nazi party leadership informed its local groups "that these national comrades need constant care and attention; August 28, 1943, signed [Martin] Bormann." Guests and hosts were given prudent rules of conduct to help alleviate the friction. Goebbels suggested delicately cushioning the psychology of living together with strangers in the closest of quarters. Forcing it won't help! The party had delegates from the evacuated regions appear, who were greeted by people deeply touched. "Our home will not give us up for lost." When the Hamburg State Opera came to Bayreuth, the cheering went on forever.

Whoever did not want to deal with the incompatibility of the tribes tried out their relatives in the countryside. Private quarters with family or later even with good friends were authorized, and people taking advantage of such options were entitled to evicted family benefits, free transportation tickets, compensation for double rents, and so on. The only ones who received no support were people who moved without notice or authorization, for example, women who left on their own, without a departure notice, without being homeless, who simply took off to areas safe from air raids. There were fewer and fewer of those. Eastern and southern Germany, in the end even small towns and villages, were subjected to massive bombing in 1944 and 1945. The organization gradually slid into chaos. Transports were turned back; districts said they were not the designated district or that they were full. "Go somewhere that still has space!"

The refugees moved from place to place, getting sent from pillar to post; people did not understand why. They clogged railroad lines and highways and were often hindered from moving on. Flows of Esseners, Düsseldorfers, and Cologners roamed the Weser-Ems region, south Hanover, the Moselle region, Hesse-Nassau, Hesse-Kassel, and Main-Franconia. At most they found unauthorized lodging, where the board had not been arranged. Many preferred to stay home.

After the Cologne raid of May 1944, which left in its wake 25,000 homeless and 664 dead, including 411 women and children, virtually no one registered for evacuation. Married couples decided they would rather stay together in times of need, and people were afraid of leaving their apartments and felt attached to their local area. Evacuees returned to Dortmund in droves in order to live normal family life again. The greatest problems in organizing the evacuations were posed by the separation. Bonds to the sinking city caused more people to return than did grievances about the evacuees' lot.

Considering the burden placed on the host counties and towns, they brought the urbanites out of harm's way with equanimity. The complaining was background noise. According to police survey data, one-third of the hosts tolerated the evacuees out of necessity or did not like them. Two-thirds endured them with a sense of fraternity, with reservations against their arrogance, laziness, and regional haughtiness. Some said that food and space were tight. One in nine considered the evacuations to be poorly organized. But they brought one-quarter of the 19.1 million residents of the most severely threatened cities out of range of the bombs.[83] That was double the available bunker capacity in those cities, even taking into account the most extreme overcrowding.

Bunker and evacuation programs combined provided one-third of all people at risk with cramped but absolute protection. Limited protection in cellars was available for 11.6 million people. In view of this, the high esteem that the air-raid protection, which had been quickly thrown together in 1940, enjoys even today by the air-war enemies, appears to be well-deserved.

The evacuees involved all of Germany psychologically in the air war. They knew everything and they knew how to report it. It was essential that the hosts learned why the evacuees were burdening them. What it really looked like in the front cities! The rest of the Reich had absolutely no idea what the war conditions were like. They did not know that people went to work without public transportation over mounds of rubble and through clouds of dust; that they neither cooked nor washed, since water, gas, and electricity were cut off; that there was no food to buy because of the damaged stores; that every bowl and every spoon that could be salvaged was a treasure; that time-delay bombs were constantly exploding and walls collapsing. That was roughly what it was like. When recounting the bombing nights, the stories were vividly embellished.

The Gestapo informant from Main-Franconia noted morosely that Hamburg eyewitnesses reported half a million dead. Besides that, they said that the government did nothing to ensure the safety of the national comrades. No one could withstand an attack in the house without being blown to bits, but if you ran out onto the street it rained burning phosphorus. The air-raid cellars long since stopped offering fire protection from the phosphorus. Fire no longer started in the roof trusses; it started in the cellar and ate its way up. It was smarter to stay in the apartment than to burn to death in the cellar. People ran through the streets like flaming torches, and women drowned burning children. Whoever was injured beyond remedy was shot by the SS.

The evacuees' accounts, the informants summed up, led to paralyzing horror. The stories were enthusiastically sucked in and the hair-raising exaggerations were believed unconditionally. The evacuees were not tough as nails in bearing their fate, as the newspapers wrote. Women who lost children trembled as they accused Hitler of not setting up protection. In Frankfurt (Oder), where Berlin women and children steadily arrived in August 1943, a rumor made the rounds that lime pits were already dug out in Berlin for the next victims of the terror. The informants feared that this would trigger an anxiety psychosis.

The reports of the evacuees, the informants continued, disclaimed all propaganda.[84] All of it dealing with the air war was said to mention the destruction of well-known cultural monuments extensively. But the loss of thousands of civilians and the eradication of entire cities were not reported. The arrivals were scantily dressed, and it was obvious from looking at them that Hamburg had been razed and that disease was rampant there. Compared to Hamburg, Cologne was a piece of cake, they said. And today, each attack took 15,000 lives. Silesia's turn would be coming soon. A "pathological anxiety of air raids" prevailed. The rural cities by no means calmed themselves with the fact that they lay far from the battlefield. They felt uneasy, saying it would reach them too. People got the impression that Germany had no means of countering the terror from the air; they were sold on revenge but were disappointed when that revenge never came. The informants considered the evacuations the epitome of morale depressants.

5. WE

"People complain, but they do their part."
— SS SECURITY SERVICE

German civilians know that they are the target and are supposed to submit to the will of the enemy. The German cities are competing against the British cities: Who can suffer the most? The bombing war puts national cohesion to the test. Holding out is like a game at first. The damages are tidied up; you don't let them get you down. But then gradually, a general shock develops at how utterly permeable the air defenses are. They can riddle the bomber stream with shells but cannot prevent the planes from dropping their bomb loads. The full impact of the weapon can only be passively endured; that indignity is harder for the civilians to bear than the casualties themselves. The helpless regime launches the slogan Vergeltung, "reprisal." The prospect of making the British pay would bring back some semblance of a battle, instead of the current slow ruin. Reprisal becomes the narcotic and mantra of the bombarded community. But the German Vergeltung, their V-weapons deployed after the Allied ground invasion, kills fewer people than the raid on Pforzheim did. Other than that, the "reprisal" consists of lynching bomber pilots who have bailed out.

AT THE TIME OF THE DEFEAT of the Sixth Army in the Stalin-grad pocket, Goebbels summoned his press aides and told them that since the start of the war they had been steering their propaganda on the wrong course. The motto had been:[1]

FIRST YEAR OF WAR: We have won.

SECOND YEAR OF WAR: We will win.

THIRD YEAR OF WAR: We must win.

FOURTH YEAR OF WAR: We cannot be defeated.

"The German public must understand not only that we want to and must be victorious, but also that it is possible."[2] Their basic defensive position was an utter catastrophe, he emphasized.

In early 1943, the situation was asymmetrical. The German public could not win, but in the air war they very well could lose. The army on the other hand, the only institution capable of winning, could—based on the progress on the fronts—hardly be defeated for the time being. That would take another two and a quarter years. Over that time, the people in the country would have enough reasons to collapse. They were the weakest link in the chain. Whether it would break or hold at that point would determine the course of the world war. Goebbels remarked, "Getting through this difficult period is primarily a psychological problem."

Propaganda would not win the war, but psychology could inadvertently lose it. "We have to extrapolate six months down the line," noted Goebbels in his diary in early March, after hearing news of 468 deaths in the last Berlin raid. "Then we will be facing an expanse of ruins in many cities, thousands of dead, and a somewhat shaky attitude among our people. We cannot afford that under any circumstances."[3]

The next day, he prohibited use of the word *Stimmung*, mood, in the propaganda ministry.[4] You could not speak of "mood" when buildings were burning and cities were being devastated, he said. After that, of course no one would shout hurrah. Instead, the positive attitude should be underscored. The mood in the air war was necessarily miserable. But attitude was something else, a military virtue that proved itself in the throes of depression. There was a silent capacity to persevere, an obduracy of the Germans as of future targets of air war. Civilians are stubborn. That was to be focused on.

The air front moved over the Reich in the opposite direction to the land front. In May and June 1940, when the army quickly conquered

10. Crosses planted in the rubble of Pforzheim.
Source: Stadtarchiv Pforzheim.

Holland, Belgium, and France, the adversary appeared in the sky over the homeland. No weapon stopped it, as was incredulously noted. On May 22, two hundred bombs rained down on the Aachen area. Bombers circled in the glare of searchlights for three hours and none of them were successfully shot down. People had firmly believed that such attacks would be countered quickly and effectively. In Cologne, Koblenz, Dortmund, Düsseldorf, and Darmstadt, too, there was heated discussion about the lack of flak defenses. There were no fighter planes in sight, and not even the alarm sirens worked. In the second week of March, the people of Düsseldorf received incessant warnings and all-clear signals for half a day, until everyone was thoroughly confused. In Hamburg and Bremen no warnings were given at all; the bombers were flying over the city for an hour before antiaircraft positions reacted.

Because these raids led to no major fires or damage to property or people, few were fazed, but many were outraged. The night raids were demonstrations of cowardice and the air-raid protection was one big blunder. No one was surprised that almost only civilian targets and hardly any military ones were hit. Timely warnings gave people a sense of relief, demand for the "people's gas mask" rose dramatically, and everyone reckoned with further raids. Leaflets dropped in late May promised that "from now on we will continue to come every night until we break you down." Other leaflets were busily circulated in trains and trams, in stores and on the street, but were never found by the police. The flyers claimed that five thousand aircraft were standing ready to attack the Ruhr area and the public was instructed to leave within three days. They had felt only the beginning, the flyers warned, and massive gas bombs would be falling soon.

In June 1940, Bomber Command flew regular raids in the west, randomly dropping small amounts of bombs and causing minimal damages, but they circled more extensively over the cities night after night. The warning centers still could not keep up; industrial plants with night shifts independently informed their workforce. The general population now felt all the more unnerved. Residents of apartment buildings organized wake-up services; some set the alarm clock for midnight and climbed down to the basement, at the latest when flak shelling started. In the first two weeks of June, wild rumors circulated about enormous human and property losses elsewhere. The increase was nevertheless scant. In 1940, human casualties averaged 143 per month.[5]

Because the all-clear signals were just as unreliable, cellar dwellers spent restless nights underground. Half of Jülich's factory machinery was at a standstill due to the extreme fatigue of the personnel. Women and girls in a needle factory in Aachen fell asleep on the job. The victory of the troops in the west brought Germany's mood to a peak; the war was over. Victory! After the night of June 18, Düsseldorf lamented ten deaths from 130 bombs, due in part to a premature all-clear signal. Anger toward the air-raid protection efforts was assuaged only by the belief that it would all be over soon.

The night raids of June 17, 18, and 19 were met with amazement. The die had been cast, the battlefields of the west were conquered. Why the bombardment? Over the course of June the Germans grasped that there had definitely been no cease to the fire. The battlefield had not gone silent. It stretched through their streets and apartments; that was the only battlefield that remained. Late that month, the British dropped a satirical German "Official Announcement," topped with the Nazi party emblem, over all of northern, western, and central Germany.[6] It said that air raids could not be stopped by the fighter planes and flak. "In or near virtually every city, as every national comrade knows, there are installations that must be regarded as military objects." Inevitably, "almost all German cities will be affected." Everyone could "draw the conclusions they deem necessary." People drew the conclusion not to be intimidated by "such pranks."

The British propaganda notice of the first week in August declared "Hamburg pulverized," which greatly amused the people of Hamburg. In any case, people there mistrusted the propaganda of both sides. They presumed that German news was not telling them everything. Hamburg lost sixteen lives on July 4, twelve of whom were children. On the same day, there were eight dead in Kiel. Ten days later, anxiety psychosis became widespread, when a rumor circulated in the city that a major raid would begin within an hour. Dortmund panicked from news that a paratrooper had landed and was preparing a gas attack. People doubted that there were enough gas masks. And airplanes were supposedly scattering potato beetles in an attempt to destroy the harvest. After an avant-garde attack on the health resort Bad Lippspringe—time-delay bombs and twenty flame cones on parachutes turned the night of July 14 into the day—1,200 concerned spa guests left within a few hours. Towns that were attacked discussed nothing else but the bomb drops. Women and children were tormented by headaches, colds, exhaustion; no one felt like working anymore. It was August 1940; the air war had been going on for ten weeks.

In Hamburg the mood changed. Words could not chase away the British airplanes. Thousands of dead were presumed so far, reason enough for reprisal. Scattered actions did nothing; it had to be a great big strike. In July, the papers had already cited the imminent revenge, but without approval. On the one hand this, but on the other hand that. Just don't throw oil on the fire!

The Battle of Britain was launched in August, and grandiose leaflets floated down on Berlin:

> Do you finally understand? Have you forgotten about our Air Force flying around over Germany doing whatever it wants, which in July dropped 37,000 bombs on military targets in the Ruhr region and the Rhineland alone? We are the ones who will decide when and how this war will end, we and the whole world with us.[7]

Goebbels imagined the great big strike that was desired in Hamburg to be within reach. It had to be considered from the political standpoint "that the destruction of London would represent the greatest disaster in the history of humanity, so that such a measure would have to appear somehow justified to the world."[8] He said there had not yet been the electrifying British attack that they could respond to "with a shout of outrage." In Berlin, only trifles were smashed, as foreign correspondents were shown based on a model of the city. The widely publicized damages were insignificant considering the city's size. The regime regarded the number of bombing deaths as tolerable, since they remained within the range of traffic mortalities. On September 11, Goebbels informed the press that since May 10 there had been not 1,500 but only 617 bombing deaths, but that number was kept secret because the same number died daily in London.[9] The 2,871 deaths in Berlin that the British claimed in late October were corrected down to eighty-nine by the propaganda ministry, which also proposed publicizing totals in the killing competition between London and Berlin. That was deemed too flippant in the Führer's headquarters.

Both sides twisted figures and events in the interest of stimulating the public imagination. The British boasted of 43,000 German civilian deaths, which was forty times the actual, inglorious result. The Germans awaited the carnage in order to be able to retaliate. The propaganda effort on the bombed Bethel children's psychiatric hospital was met by those in party circles with a roguish smile, since we "discovered our heart for those with hereditary abnormalities."[10] It was not worth making such a fuss over a few idiots, they said. The "child murder at Bethel" sufficed as "fodder for America," serving "to justify to the world our own, heedless actions in England." It would also close up the inner ranks. The Christian community dropped their reservations against raids on London. According to the consensus, "this new turpitude could only be compensated for by the heedless destruction of English residential districts."[11] The population around Bielefeld was disappointed only with the funeral speech that Pastor von Bodelschwingh held for the eleven children who had been killed. No word of reprisal, victory, not even the cause of death. The closing prayer united the government representatives in attendance with the request for a speedy peace.

Throughout the fall, people gobbled up headlines of pulverized London. Just to be certain, they wanted close-up photographs of the destroyed streets to be printed, to draw comparisons with Warsaw and Rotterdam. The results were actually no worse than there, they decided. The photos of Londoners camping in the subway tunnels showed how little Germans had suffered so far. They started viewing the hardship competition as a sport, praising the perseverance of the British. Would they be just as tough in withstanding such tests? The German press's artificial indignation over British raids that aimed exclusively at hospitals, children's homes, and allotment gardens no longer got people riled up. "It is war, and we are doing the same thing." Total war must be fought much harder, people said.

The Nazi party complained that the German people had misjudged the dimensions of the British capital and that their views on the effective strength of the German Luftwaffe were illusory. But the public noticed just as quickly as the Luftwaffe that something was not working properly. Why did cities have to be bombarded more than once, even if after the first attack they were already reported as a "dead city"? How did Londoners manage to get their groceries if they supposedly never left their cellars owing to all the bombs and alarms? Had they been evacuated and were long since safe, or did they simply ignore the alarms and go about their business?

The Coventry operation was met with a breeze of delight. That was what reprisal had to look like. All the more puzzling was that London, even after having been bombarded for weeks, still did not look as "plowed" as Coventry did after one night. December brought cheerful news of direct hits in Britain's government district; hopefully Churchill got his share. Publication of the monthly tallies of bombs dropped was met with widespread expert interest; more could be read out of those figures than from the perpetual fires that started and the January note that said "hardly a single house is still intact" in London. No one believed that, but British staying power enjoyed unrestricted admiration. Relative to that, the bombardment of the Reich barely counted. "Compared with what our planes are chopping up in England," it is "hardly worth mentioning."

The West—Aachen, Bielefeld, Brunswick, Düsseldorf, Koblenz—became accustomed to the night alarms. People rarely went to the air-raid shelters. The risk of catching a cold from the chilly, damp rooms was greater than the tiny chance of getting hit by a bomb. Whoever was that unlucky was insured with the Reich. The system of compensation and air-raid ordinances started to roll; people adapted themselves to the air war. Problems arose that had not been anticipated. If the residents of only 44,000 buildings in Frankfurt went to the cellars as recommended when the sirens sounded and then turned on their electrical heaters, peak usage jumped to 12,000 kilowatts in one fell swoop, shaking the entire grid. A dispute arose in the compensation offices as to whether a radio was absolutely vital and thus guaranteed replacement. It was even more difficult to prove that it was truly destroyed. The officials did not know how to deal with bomb damages of two pounds of bacon and five pounds of flour. The bombed-out petitioners could not be convinced to refrain from filing those kinds of losses. And then there were the couples pulled from the rubble barely clothed, who went from the Public Welfare Office to the Ration Book Office and back, and still had no clothing because there was none to be had.

The administration started by working out the regulations; the decree on the authorization to enter streets and public squares during an air raid was changed ten times. Certain occupational groups were permitted, but only slowly did it become clear which ones. The status of the regulations had to be sent to all county offices; millions of letters circulated, creating chaos. Relief was received faster from the collection that Bishop Clemens von Galen made in the Münsterland area, for aid to the damaged cathedral and people who were bombed out. The rural population donated generously. It blamed the Nazi party for the fires in Münster: it was revenge for the prohibition of the fire processions that had been held each year to ask for protection from that destructive element.

The first instance of systematic arson went beyond what Lübeckers were able to handle. The old men of the Security and Assistance Service could do nothing against it, but the Hamburg colleagues arrived, bringing their experience of 117 raids. Luckily, many Wehrmacht soldiers were on weekend leave there, because on Saturday evening the residents were out and about and unsuspectingly did not happen to have fire tools handy—hoses, water, sand, picks, shovels, crowbars—so that only the dauntless hands of the soldiers managed to contain the flames. Boys from the Hitler Youth and girls from the League of German Girls (BDM) ran around helping out with the injured and homeless; amidst their disaster, the Lübeckers were dumbfounded. "The national comrades' sense of community and belonging has never before been put to a test like it was on that night."[12] On Sunday, the merchants defiantly opened up their stores. A sign in a store window announced: "Disaster butter sold here." The only annoying thing was that the Wehrmacht report was not at all concerned with the trials and bravery, and succinctly reported "some losses."

The population that had been imagining the horrors of the gas war for years viewed the dropping of incendiary munitions containing phosphorus as the commencement of the "aerochemical war." Fire, gas, and bacteria were all classed in the same category of warfare. After the Thousand-Bomber Raid on Cologne in May, warnings about the drinking water circulated faster than lightning. Did the British contaminate it with typhoid fever? The police had to use a sound truck to quash the rumor. The panic was not totally unfounded. In the Manchurian War in 1931, the Japanese had poisoned wells with cholera, typhoid fever, and dysentery. Germany's enemies did not choose the water—they chose the mail. In December 1942, the Gestapo found a germ-warfare arsenal of typhus bacilli in a four-room house in Warsaw. In 1943, the Polish underground movement sent seventy-seven "poisoned parcels," which they claimed infected 426 people within four months.[13] Germans assessed the aerochemical war differently than the bombardment thus far. Before it even broke out, there was already a "general feeling of helplessness" and the "certainty of being at its mercy without any defenses."[14]

In the year between the attack on Lübeck and the first Battle of the Ruhr, the air-raid shelter community took great pains to maintain a sporting attitude. The Augsburg mission of No. 5 Bomber Group earned soldierly respect. Everyone was impressed by the gutsy approach to the target, the concentration on an armaments plant, the dive into the blind spot of the flak artillery, the precisely calculated drops from a 330-foot altitude. Their own team inspired a feeling of trepidation. Why did Augsburg, renowned the world over as a producer of fighter planes, not have any fighter cover? The antiaircraft artillery was either unmanned or asleep! People wanted the fighter cover to be stretched over the city like an umbrella. Since it was shifted westward toward the Kammhuber line, it was all the more puzzling that for hours bombers got through all the way to Augsburg, over territory controlled by the Reich.

To the citizenry, the front used to be an area beyond the horizon. And the army there made sure that it held. If it broke down, then the army was beaten and the war about to end. The realization that the front was above their heads and there was nothing between them and the enemy took their breath away. Two basic head-shaking facts of modernity continued to be noted from 1940 to 1942. How had the enemy gotten above our roof? And why can he fire vertically down on us without any payback?

When the flak shot down twenty-nine bombers over Hamburg in July 1942, no one could believe it. There were no night fighters; the city felt totally abandoned, counted 337 dead, and was bitterly disappointed. The raid had long been expected and was not ignored; the air defenses would take care of it. The 7.2 percent shootdown rate was quite a success, militarily speaking. But it would not be a psychological success. Deep dejectedness spread, but it did not affect the people's attitude. The "Overthrow Hitler and you will have peace" leaflets were read as a "dumb and idiotic attempt to sway opinion."[15]

All of Hamburg showed solidarity. Everyone helped everyone else out of the debris, cleared out endangered apartments, sprayed water, threw sand, and tore down sheds and fences, the notorious fire bridges. Women and girls distinguished themselves, daring to take anything on; women workers prepared their entire supply of instant coffee. Afterwards, applications were filed for compensation for a total of 250 million marks.

"We could learn a lot from the British," advised Goebbels. "During the heavy raids on London they lionized the attitude of the British population and made a legend of London."[16] The Wehrmacht reports would just once have to present the drama of the air raids colorfully. In August, he excused the scant presence of the Luftwaffe as owing to their missions in the Russian campaign. At that time the war was being decided on the eastern battlefields. "We will beat England in the East." The slogan held for about three months; that was how long the West clenched their teeth.

At the Saar and in the Palatinate, the only topic of conversation was which city would be bombed next. Familiar with the British habit of repeating attacks in one place several times in a short series, many people there immediately started leaving each evening and returning at daybreak. Even in Main Franconia, people in the big cities stored their valuables in rural depots, just to be sure; Würzburg textile companies relocated their storage inventories. The German army in Russia meanwhile thrust out toward the Don River and received innumerable telegrams from home saying that the enemy ruined the vitrine. Cologne needed replacements for 35,000 broken living room sets; they were gathered up from all corners of Europe. In late June 1942, in the party headquarters, Martin Bormann instructed the gau, county, and local group leaders to choke off the growing flood of private telegrams to the fighting troops. The news undermined the spirit. Post offices were to accept a telegram request only if it could

be shown to be urgent. Members of soldiers' families could, if necessary, turn to the local military district commands. Muzzling was not
an effective way of getting the subject under control, as Goebbels
knew. Millions of people were concerned daily with the precarious
air situation in the West, asking themselves how things would end
and when things would be different. Was it better to raise hopes or to
depict the graveness of the situation? "We have still not been able to
catch the proper tone for the air war."[17] The German populace could
not be left to itself to discuss the subject. But in September 1942,
they expected something else besides the proper tone.

A sense of rage toward Berlin slowly developed in the Rhine-Ruhr
cities. The different authorities sent study commissioners to the
bombed-out cities in September, but they were received with great
reservation. People did not want bureaucrats talking to them. They
stole time and created false sympathy, and no one wanted anything
except help. In early January 1943, the main topic of conversation
in Krefeld was the bombing of Berlin.[18] Without exception, the
Krefelders showed profound satisfaction. It was high time the big-
mouthed Berliners got what was coming to them. They were rather
callous there as regarded the suffering of the Rhinelanders. Retaliatory strikes followed right on the heels of trifling attacks on Berlin, but not a single airplane from the eastern front was freed up to
punish the British for the incomparable damages in Cologne, Düsseldorf, and Duisburg. On top of that, people claimed that after the
bombardment, Berlin started receiving extra rations of coffee. It was
whispered that it would be fine "if the British flew more frequently
to Berlin so that the inhabitants there would get a taste of how we in
the west are feeling . . . we in the west are regarded as second-class
people and the whole Rhineland has already been written off."[19]

The mood crumpled in the First Battle of the Ruhr. In the spring
and early summer of 1943, everyone's eyes were on the western cities. Neither the tank battle in the Kursk bulge nor even the Allied
landing in Sicily distracted attention from events in Wuppertal and
Remscheid. Rows of smashed blocks, seas of flames extending for
miles, and bomb craters twenty-eight yards across and nine yards
deep, shrouded in smoke, all put an end to the game of holding out.
The spry, do-what-needs-to-be-done attitude faded; it made no sense.
Those suffering the damages were beaten, happy to have saved their
skin, and nervously awaiting the clean-up squads. Once the essential remnants had been salvaged from the rubble, they stretched out

in the grass and expressed their skepticism. "The Führer lied to us through his teeth." They should stop, they said, if lazy reprisal was all they could think of to do. "They want to get it through reprisal, but Churchill is sticking to bombing." Verve was mustered only by the Hitler Youth, the Nazi party, and the SA men doing rescue and recovery work. Nothing mattered except "where they [British bombers] were last night." That much was announced in the Wehrmacht report, and the radio did not have to broadcast anything else. When German radio broadcast the hit "Ich tanze mit dir in den Himmel hinein" ("I'll Dance with You to Heaven") while Essen burned like a torch during the second major raid, it was viewed as utter mockery. Listeners hectically tuned the dial to receive air warnings and came across the enemy frequencies.

The year 1918 stirred in people's memories. By the time the Americans entered the war, it was all over. We have been "encircled, after all, yet again." A threefold offensive front: "East—Sicily—Air" cannot be maintained. "It was all for naught again." Talk about the invincibility of Fortress Europe sounded like a joke. An Allied foothold in Sicily would mean the end for Italy. Germany fought the war in the summer of 1943 passively, for the first time. The Reich Security Main Office reported to the party chancellery on June 25 that voices were becoming loud, saying that "our weakness no longer allows for any offensive. To an extent never before considered possible, an absolutely clear superiority of the enemy has developed on all fronts: land, sea, and air."[20] People waited with tormenting anxiety. The will to hold out was unbroken, the report continued, but due to a lack of great events, rumors got the upper hand. People's pessimism made them susceptible to any and all negative views that were introduced. Propaganda and announcements by the leadership could not turn that around. Caught up tightly in the events of the war, "the people are waiting, on the one hand, for the catastrophe that could befall them any night, and on the other hand, for reprisal."

By orders of the party chancellery, all German air strikes were to be referred to as retaliatory measures, never as terror raids. The term *terror raid*, according to the directive, mirrored the criminal conduct of the enemy, whose disposition led it to favor attacking cultural monuments and civilians. Those were the pillars of air-war propaganda. Because "cultural barbarism" prevailed, those who were bombed out were quickly fed up with the "fuss about the Cologne cathedral." The hole in the façade hurt Rhenish Catholics deeply and truly. "The Lord would not allow this to happen if we were on the side of right."[21] His blessing had abandoned us.

Details on air raids that circulated constantly and everywhere contained drastic fantasies. For example: the July raid rendered half of the Cologne population homeless, the families were sleeping on the banks of the Rhine, 25,000 people lay dead or buried in rubble, riots broke out, stores were stormed, troops were instructed to shoot. They were said to have thrown away their guns, but the SS came in and put things back in order. Reconstruction of the Rhenish-Westphalian cities would take thirty to fifty years. "To start with, it is impossible to imagine what to do with all the rubble."

The regime avoided the most pressing question of the German people. "Where did the enemy attack; how high are the losses?" Newspapers disguised the Battle of the Ruhr in boilerplate. "Steadfastness versus Murderer-Arsonists." "Tough and resolute against British terror." The information gap was filled in with rumors. Rumors exaggerated, but reality followed in their footsteps, just one step behind. In early July, rumors about "innovative warfare techniques of the enemy powers" abounded. The fires spread too quickly. "The number of fire casualties predominates among the total dead."[22] After giving the "ruined cities in the Ruhr basin" a working over, the air terror spread to all of Reich territory. Berlin, Munich, and Nuremberg were "razed like Stalingrad." The deployment and combat zone formed in the west. Thousands of unidentifiable bodies ended up in mass graves. The phosphorus caused them to shrink into small mummies. They were burned alive in the cellars. At one o'clock in the morning, people were lining up in front of the bunkers.

Confidence in victory melted away in the Hamburg firestorm. The feeling of security "collapsed suddenly." A tormenting feeling said that an opponent who wages such attacks is invincible. "They'll trounce us." We should "end it at any acceptable price," since "the sacrifice is growing from day to day." Compared to Hamburg, Cologne was child's play. "You can't fight it." Despite all the announced countermeasures, "we have to watch helplessly how one city after another is destroyed." The British came whenever they wanted. "They literally strut through the air day and night." "The air war will finish us off," the women thought, and were "done with life."

As the strength of the raids increased, the defenses decreased. The flak managed to shoot down only isolated planes, although the night echoed for hours with the humming of the engines. The aircraft

definitely did not fly very high; they swooped low enough to practically tear the roofs off. "Scarcity of munitions has always been the German fate." Those who still hoped for victory were considered idiots and incorrigible optimists. "How do you imagine that we can win the war?" Soldiers on leave from Russia were the only ones who were still positive. Without the occupied Ukraine, maybe the Bolshevists would be brought down by a famine. "If we were to make grimaces like you then the war would have been lost long ago, and you would already be rotting away, hanging from the next tree."[23] Farmers shook their heads incredulously.

The general view was that the Russians were stronger economically and in numbers, but the war would be decided in the air. Until the Battle of the Ruhr, hopes were placed on the defenses: Fighters and flak would cause the bomber fleet to flee. In the fall of 1943, the fighter weapon came close to doing just that, but public opinion said that no chances remained. "It doesn't help at all, no matter how many are shot down. They bombard one city after another. Either we have the weapons to hit England in a sensitive spot or the complete annihilation of the Reich is imminent." Then, said the women, "we will just have to die." What could we do? "We will not calm down until the reprisal comes." That was the pivotal point of all conversations, "from our side absolutely desirable." And the only thing that kept people going. "Our mourning will end," read an obituary in the *Rhein-Mainische Zeitung*, "on the day when the death of our child is avenged." The depression came from the puzzling question of "why the German leadership is letting this go on for so long." People used to say, "the others talk, we act." Now it was just the other way around. "Comforting words" did nothing but make people angrier. "It is simply impossible to watch how thousands of people are killed almost daily." At first, they bit off more than they could chew, but were supposedly prepared for any eventualities. Now defense was impossible because German engineers were still at work.

Goebbels launched the rumor about a reprisal weapon in the early summer of 1943 to distract people from the fiasco in Russia. It bridged a year of the most bitter of bombing wars. In September,

11. Air-raid poster, 1940: "The enemy sees your light! Blackout!"
Source: Bildarchiv Preussischer Kulturbesitz.

rumors already spoke of a rocket-driven projectile of incredible force with "guiding beams" steering it to its target. The rumors knew a lot: Only a few such missiles were needed to totally destroy London, but the problem was the accuracy, with a tolerance of over fifteen miles. England already had an antidote with which to intercept the rockets in midair and cause them to explode. The production sites on the island of Usedom in the Baltic Sea had already been destroyed by bombs, which was why the reprisal had been delayed. People tried to read information about the supposed Reprisal Day from the lips of the evasive leadership. *Vergeltung*, reprisal, was the vote of confidence per se. Goebbels rambled, they are almost finished, slowly but surely, and people were able to hold on to the "surely" for a while.

On November 8, 1943, Hitler held his last public speech, to the veterans, the "old fighters." It was recorded on magnetic tape and broadcast on radio at 8:15 p.m. He spoke mostly of the strength of sacrifice. Whoever has paid with their property, he said, could expect to recover what was lost only through victory. "Hundreds of thousands of people who have been bombed out are the vanguard of revenge." The industrial damages were inconsequential, the two or three million ruined residences could be rebuilt in no time at all, "let them destroy as much as they want." He was pained by the anguish of women and children, but he bowed down in gratitude before the Almighty that he sent no more difficult trials, like the battle on German soil, "but rather that he let this struggle against a world of superior strength be successfully fought far beyond the borders of the Reich." Germany would never repeat the errors of 1918 by laying down its weapons at fifteen minutes to midnight. "You can count on that. The last one to lay down his weapons, that shall be Germany, and it will be five minutes after midnight."[24]

In passing, Hitler mentioned that the war criminals from the other side would be enlisted for reconstruction efforts: "that is the first thing that I must say on that account, and the second thing, may the gentlemen believe it or not, the hour of reprisal shall come." In the previous year, words like "it doesn't matter" and "don't let it get you down" expressed exactly how the public felt; now the public could detect in his words what it was interested in hearing. If the Führer spoke of reprisal, then reprisal will come. On the other hand, he must not know what to do either—otherwise he would not start invoking the Almighty. "Hardship has taught him to pray." At least he mentioned the torment of women and children and not the cathedrals. Totally contrary to his usual manner, Hitler had less to announce about what Germany would deal out than about what it could take.

Comparisons of staying power in the last war and this one were not appreciated at all. The Nazi organ, the *Völkische Beobachter*, wrote on November 14 that sometimes more people in the cities burned to death within hours than soldiers died back then in four years. People saw no sense at all in that kind of pride in their sacrifice. Hitler also boasted of how much others could withstand. "Could you imagine, my party comrades, that in the World War we could have suffered and withstood for even only a month what we have now been enduring for years?"[25] That was a credit to his educational effort. But the Germans did not want to be taught how to burn to death. The bombings had caused a seething hunger for revenge to build up in them that found no reference or outlet in Hitler's speech.

Feelings of hatred rolled over the entire population. "There is almost unanimous agreement among the national comrades in their demand that the British people be exterminated. Revenge against England cannot be strong enough." Not even a Christian's duty muted this wish. Believers spit out biblical curses. "The brood must be eradicated root and branch."[26] Fear of gas turned around into active voice; Göring wanted to respond to the bomber terror with gas. People either longed for reprisal or fell into despair; there was nothing in between, only a transition from one to the other. "If we could strike back, we would have done it long ago, before the Cologne cathedral was destroyed, but we can't."

Crouching acquiescence of the attacks consumed all confidence. The "purposeful propaganda" angered people, and "no longer ensnarls anyone." In central Germany in December, people repeated the couplet "*Leipzig, Magdeburg und Halle / und der Krieg ist alle*" ("Leipzig, Magdeburg, and Halle / and the war is over"). If the reprisal was going to wait until the Saxon industrial centers were all finished off also, then they could spare themselves the effort. "Bitterness from the senseless destruction is eating itself deeper and deeper." Details about the imagined miracle weapon were uttered "with love." The east was still hoping for it, since "they are coming closer all the time." At the North Sea and Baltic Sea coasts, closed American B-17 formations were cavorting during the day. The American nimbus of 1918 shrouded the real-life disaster of the Eighth Air Force in 1943. They paraded their formations in German airspace "like at the Nazi party rally." The Flying Fortresses, which Goebbels called "Flying Coffins," were being shot down by fighter planes in large numbers, yet their numbers did not seem to be diminishing. "Before the reprisal comes we will all be six feet under."

The largely depressing mood did not change the attitude. After the major raids in the winter, hundreds of thousands of people who were homeless and injured wandered the streets of Berlin; they complained less than they did under normal circumstances and gave "an incredibly disciplined impression." Behind this impression was a trance. The zestful offers of aid started to dwindle; people vamoosed when heavy furniture had to be salvaged. The zeal of the Hitler Youth remained unbroken. They threw themselves into fighting the fires, keeping it up for twenty-four hours at a time; they "were black as Negroes, had neither slept nor eaten a square meal." They were second to none as messengers, dragged carts of household items to the evacuation trains, and gave their lives at the flak artillery. There were still 120,000 children living in Berlin for whom there were no evacuation sites available. The schools were closed; tens of thousands of schoolchildren loitered on the streets and formed gangs.

Christmas of 1943 went by "with an unsurpassable, profound longing" for speedy reprisal.[27] Those who suffered bombing losses "carry the idea around with them constantly." They ran from store to store looking for shoes. Women's and boys' shoes were virtually impossible to find. In Hamburg, stovepipes, washtubs, and children's bathtubs were scarce. There were loud scenes in offices and stores when in mid-November only twenty thousand of the 400,000 people burned out of their homes in the firestorm received a cooking pot. Frying pans and irons were issued only to households of four or more. Bedsteads, mattresses, and pillows confiscated from Jews in France and Holland were auctioned off in the free port. The SS thought the old, extremely worn furniture was not worth the effort in terms of time, transport, or logistics.

People's skin got thinner as the Battle of Berlin continued in 1943. "When someone has endured these strikes, then only an idiot can tell me he'll win the war." People demanded germ warfare after the Frankfurt raid on January 28; they said you should not wait until the enemy used those weapons against us too. "This sentimental humanitarianism we have displayed up to now must end, once and for all."[28] The leadership was making a mistake "by continuing to watch the population get murdered." In Munich and Nuremberg, the foreign workers were reviled after air raids: "You too are responsible."[29]

12. Berlin.

Source: Bildarchiv Preussischer Kulturbesitz.

French prisoners of war on leave to volunteer to help extinguish fires were later chased from their private quarters. Russian forced workers and prisoners jumped out of their slit trenches even before their teams of guards did, and, without orders, rushed into the burning factory hall to fight the flames. The company distributed schnapps and sausage. "The brave actions of our workers from the East must definitely be acknowledged. They show unparalleled courage; it has been observed that eastern workers threw themselves on the incendiary bombs in order to extinguish them with their bodies."[30] A large number, on the other hand, were not fazed by anything. They did not care about airplanes, bombs, fires, and flak, and instead eyed the foreman with greater reticence the next day.

The forced workers from Holland "enjoy a certain amount of malicious gloating." The Germans, they said, could not treat the British and the Americans the way they had treated Holland. As far as the Dutch were concerned, if the bombs kept falling, they would get to go home sooner. To show their support for the bombing, 95 percent of the Dutch forced workers in a camp in Wesermünde near their homeland did not go to the air-raid shelter. In Berlin, people said they saw Frenchmen grin and smirk; in the Rhineland one heard only praise. In Düsseldorf and Duisburg prisoners impulsively offered their services. "This is not war anymore, it is murder." Others said, "our friends are here!" The Italians were frightened and "it is hard to get them to leave the cellars," but they were reliable, "positive workers" when manning fire-watch posts.

Poles and Ukrainians were considered the most loyal workers. Poles, marked with a "P" on their clothing, showed great attachment to their farmsteads and the livestock they cared for. Near Cologne, "two Poles rescued the livestock out of burning stalls despite the flames; they had to be protected all the while by the spray of the water hoses." For workers from the eastern provinces, the strict surveillance lessened during the bombing. They went about their business, since the Germans were concerned with their own safety. Men found opportunities to make contact with other national groups, as did the women. "There are more than enough guys here," a young Russian woman in Cologne wrote back home. "French, Dutch, Poles, and Russians. We don't have any free evenings, but during the air-raid alarm is the best time to get together. When the shelling is very intense, we go into the cellar and after the all clear we are together for thirty minutes."

Germans viewed the foreign workers with suspicion. Perhaps they would exploit the chaos during an attack to escape. The Dutch supposedly gave the airmen blinking signals, or maybe they were intent on theft. The beaten master race knew that they too were being watched, especially by the alert Frenchmen. The latter knew what defeat was and made observations: The Germans' attitude was always to "live for the moment."[31] Shortly after the bombing they would collapse in pain and despondency, saying the war should stop at any price.

About a week after a raid, the perpetual fatigue and apathy returned. They blamed the lack of sleep and long work hours. They said the Germans constantly repeated the word *Arbeit*, work. As soon as something fell down broken, there was some work to do. Work served the country, and the reprisal weapon served the victory. Everyone clung to this promise. Filled with reprisal rage against the "terrorists," there was no anger left to attack the powerless government.

The workers said Germans were not at all affected by the destruction of cities other than their own. The Ruhr workers were amused by the raids on Berlin. In Berlin, in turn, the residents of the Tempelhof district did not care what happened to the Charlottenburg district, and vice versa. The destruction was not all that bad anyway, since everyone hoped to get a nicer apartment. All the family members felt like they were soldiers and considered their suffering to be a soldier's sacrifice. No one in Germany went into mourning. The German women would wear a narrow black armband for a few days. In the big cities, the dead were forgotten incredibly quickly after heavy raids. The workers said that was inconceivable in a Romance country.

In May 1944, the Nazi party was worried about their national comrades who heard nothing but sirens wailing, engines roaring, flak shelling, and bombs crashing and could not get the sounds out of their heads. "Especially the women drive each other crazy." Radios were on from morning to night in order to catch any news of approaching planes. Even radio announcers tripped over their words when they warned of approaching aircraft, passing their nervousness on to listeners. More and more women broke down during the newscasts. They started to tremble and were unable to work; with tears in their eyes, the "running for one's life" went on. Country women working in the fields thought about nothing but their children, out playing on the streets strafed by hedgehoppers. Now, with attacks on trains and people on outings, evacuees felt as insecure as they did in the city. "When will this terrible plague finally end?" The air war was talked about, compulsively, always; it did not leave people's tongues. "Will it be our turn tonight?"

Another subject came up alongside it: the invasion. Since January 1944 at the latest, it was regarded as an established fact. Right after the landing in Sicily in July 1943, the skeptics knew "soon they will be coming to us." The invasion was linked to the promise of the reprisal weapon; it started with the attempt to land. Once the landing was underway, a tension that had become unbearable dissolved. The decision was made: "The invasion is the trump card." There were immediate outbursts of delirious joy in response to the Wehrmacht report of June 16, which announced attacks on southern England and London with an innovative explosive device. That might lead to "counter-reprisal." The enemy supposedly had ordnance at its disposal that would end the war in no time. "What else could that be besides gas?" The presumption was not wrong.

In early July the euphoria leveled off a little. The V1 needed some time to have an effect. There were positive signs: the British lamentation that the weapon violated international law, the evacuations in London. Reports of direct hits in the center were cause for rejoicing. All technical details about how it worked were devoured by the public, but little was revealed. Of course it could not be discussed: there was "protective secrecy regarding the new weapon." The projectile supposedly totally leveled three-quarters of a square mile. There were stockpiles of one million of them, and five hundred were fired each day. None of that was true.

The missiles raised questions. After three weeks of V1 firing, nothing tangible had changed. Between July 11 and July 19, the U.S. Air Force dropped more tonnage on Munich alone than the V1 did over England in three months. Bomber Command dropped roughly the same amount in four raids on Stuttgart and Brunswick. The Munich raids were assessed as the answer to the V1, and they were sobering. Were it the final stretch, then everyone wanted to do their share and stick it out for the remainder. However, the day raids by the Americans were an unchanging fact, and maybe the V weapon was not going to change the course of the war. The few planes shot down over Munich were due to the flak artillery. Nothing could be expected of the fighter defenses, since the enemy was "far superior." The blind optimism subsided; "what good is reprisal if the air war continues?" The housewife quoted by the SS put it well: "I expected more from it."

The enemy's fast movements and the fall of Paris were the center of attention in August. Older people suffered their own grief when the battlefields of World War I were taken. After losing Cherbourg, the last bastion at the English Channel, everyone sensed that the enemy would also get through by land. "They have great losses, but they achieve their goal." Here and there people broached the question of what they would do if the invasion penetrated into northwestern Germany. In Sicily the year before, it had not been received in an unfriendly way, as Germany disdainfully noted. The party issued a slogan in the fall: "Scorched earth and flight." Only a minority still believed that new weapons would turn the tide. Workers in the armaments plants found the air strikes so destructive that they thought the production sites would be destroyed by October, and thus even the most miraculous inventions would be for naught. In Wuppertal, there were hopes in October that a compromise with the enemy would bring an early end to the war. "Too much has been demanded of the people; everything humanly possible has been tried." Hardly anyone even noticed the deployment of the V2 rocket in November. Rumors said that England had a similar weapon. Once again, the rumors raced ahead of reality, but they only had a four-month lead: the people of Cologne were already leaving the city!

Ten days before the first V1 was fired, Goebbels recommended that the Germans take reprisal into their own hands.[32] In the *Völkische Beobachter* of March 28 he wrote that hedgehoppers firing salvos into harmless groups of people, "with such criminal combat techniques, are acting outside of all internationally recognized codes of war. This has nothing to do with war anymore; it is sheer murder." Parents of children who were shot killed the pilots who had performed emergency landings or bailed out. "Police and Wehrmacht could hardly intervene against the German people when they give child murderers what they deserve." The party chancellery instructed the gauleiters not to obstruct the "people's justice against Anglo-American murderers." The license to lynch encompassed strafers and bomber pilots to the same degree. No rules could be laid down for excesses. "American airman shot down," read the entry in the diary of a Mainz fireman. "He was beaten to death on the market square with wooden slats. Children also participated in the action."[33] In late August, three Luftwaffe soldiers led the eight-man crew of a Liberator shot down near Hanover through Rüsselsheim. The train tracks had been bombed and were unusable, so the group was marched through the center of town to reach a passable line. They were headed for the airmen's reception camp in Oberursel. News traveled quickly of the prisoners' march through town. Men and women flocked together armed with clubs, iron bars, broomsticks, shovels, and fence slats, and they flailed at the prisoners. The guards watched calmly. When the Americans were already lying on the ground, a Nazi party leader added a blow with a hammer and fired shots. The bodies were loaded onto a hay wagon and carted to the cemetery. In the meantime, air-raid sirens started blaring and the torturers raced off to the bunker. Two of the men who had been lynched were still alive; they crawled from the bloody cart and fled toward the Rhine. Discovered by a policeman, they were brought to their original destination, the camp in Oberursel. The six who didn't survive were put in the ground in Rüsselsheim.

More than one hundred pilots were lynched in the last year of the war, sometimes in complicity with Wehrmacht institutions, and sometimes police and soldiers saved the prisoners from such raging vengeance. In Essen, two members of the Luftwaffe escorted three Bomber Command pilots through a street of rubble to their inter-rogation. Soon they were surrounded by a horde of agitated civilians who belted, stoned, and bludgeoned the British pilots. When the procession crossed an overpass, the crowd threw the prisoners over the side. One of them broke his neck; the people raced after the two survivors and trampled them to death.

Knowing that all means of defense and reprisal were for naught because the fighters were all destroyed, the flak unmanned or relo-cated, and the rockets as ineffective as clubs, the Germans found themselves in the flaming torch of the last eight months of the air war. In Duisburg, the sirens never stopped wailing. "I lost the desire to live. The smut and dirt covered everything and it was impossible to keep anything clean. . . . Life was no longer beautiful." There was no time anymore between the warning and the full alarm.

> My sister and I put our babies into their carriages and ran with my father
> to the bunker. Many phosphorus bombs were dropped, and everywhere
> houses were in flames. . . . Finally, I took my baby out of the carriage and
> ran on with him in my arms. By the time we reached the bunker, bombs
> were falling on all sides. I was completely exhausted and said I could never
> go through this again. . . . All that day we were running from the house to
> the bunker and from the bunker to the house.

People could not go to work anymore because of their nerves. "Bun-ker fever" drove them into the run-down concrete dungeons. "The milk soured in the bunker and my child was often sick." There were now four thousand people in a bunker built for eight hundred. "In there we were so crowded and hot that one after the other vomited and the air became all the worse on that account. We just took off clothes without shame because of the unbearable heat. Most of the time I did not use the public shelter anyhow." The walls and ceilings in the cellar quaked from the blast bombs; the men braced them-selves against the supporting beams. "People were crying and pray-ing. They said that we had to thank our Führer for this."[34] In late March, people in Hamburg were afraid that an air disaster was im-minent, "since the western German cities are no longer available as targets."[35] That was something good about the occupation: it brought an end to the bombing raids. In the pubs at the port there was no heating, no lights, no electricity, and no gas. There was beer, but no one wanted to drink it in the cold. "The Brits should come and bring this to an end." March 11 brought the 197th of 213 raids. Ten thousand bombs were dropped, killing ninety-seven people. "If only it would hit," said a middle-class Hamburg woman into the whistling sound of bombs falling. "What should I do in this world anymore? I lost my children; my husband fell as a soldier, and now all this sacrifice for nothing. That is the worst of all."[36]

6. 1

"You didn't feel how horrible the experience was.
That was switched off."

—— M E D I C

The physical pressure of the bomb blast is absorbed by people individually. Nerves and blood vessels gear up for the moment of detonation. The bang is anticipated and expands into a continuous presence. During the actual raid, the inner realities of the self are altered. It falls out of the time frame of its internal clock, compresses the duration of events, and mentally lags behind the actual course of the attack. One's personal sense of time shrinks; actions are taken under erroneous assumptions. A psychological filter reduces the duration and the shocks conveyed by the raid scenario. Perception of the fire war is numbed, both in the moment and afterward.

IT HAS BEEN SAID that men and women in Aachen danced unceasingly, with passion and rapture, in churches and on the streets,
during the plague of 1374. Similar reports also exist regarding the air
war. After the raid everyone talked about it, immediately and in great
detail. "The whole thing was like being inebriated."[1] Humor came
through, people were excited and went for a stroll to look at the damages. "In the presence of nurses, even the head nurse, I made jokes
that were really meant only for men's ears."

The nurses were not overly sensitive. They worked with rescue
crews dragging dead and injured out of the cellars. The former
ended up on biers in the lobby of Munich's east train station, and the
latter were bandaged up in the hospital. "Later I ran home and as I
entered the house I saw that it was one big pyre and everything was
in flames. I was so at my wit's end that I got up on the pile of rubble
and laughed a pathetic, godawful laugh."[2] One doctor said that after
the attack it was "like after a war that has been won," when everything was managed well.

After the destruction of the house, "we celebrated pretty boister-
ously that we had gotten through this Christmas disaster and were
still alive. My husband was so jovial that Frau Krüger teased, 'Do
you have some damage upstairs?' pointing to her head and twirl-
ing her finger." In the general merriment, real coffee was brewed
and they felt ravenous. "Afterward I was really full of vim and lit
up a cigar, with a clearly elevated self-esteem that now I could talk
with the rest of them." The furniture was gone but one felt "unburdened," lithely jumping over unexploded bombs and "the whole day
feeling as if I were reborn."

For every case of euphoria there were two of apathy. "I felt incredible pressure on my chest. It was somehow hard to speak. Even afterward I was still very agitated and I trembled." That person's mother-
in-law, on the other hand, had more of a "couldn't care less" attitude.
It "all just doesn't make sense," and once home, "I was even more
afraid than during the raid. I got a really eerie feeling. I had to lie
down. I felt like I had walls weighing down on my body."

The regime noticed with concern in October 1944 that the wom-
en's nerves were "strained to the limit." No one ever got a night's rest
anymore; many never even got out of their clothes. No one felt safe
at home with fifteen alarms each day. "The people live like hunted

deer." They no longer read newspapers, and movie showings were constantly interrupted by air-raid alarms. It wasn't worth going in the first place.

Expecting the alarm was worse than the alarm itself, because at least during a raid one had something to do, bags to pack. "I slept partly on my back so my right ear was completely free. Even in my sleep I always had a sense of listening." Women woke up in the morning with stomachaches. "What is going to happen today?" One was in a constant state of anticipation, "at the early warning signal my whole body was already trembling."

Forget about sleep. The night in bed was spent listening for sounds. "After this raid I became more sensitive to air threats. I had become so fearful that my wife, who had never experienced anything like this before, almost made fun of me." Being in the cellar was like being buried alive. "After the heavy raid I didn't go into the cellar anymore. When the alarm sounded I ran out into the open and lay down in a shelter trench." The initial wail was what was unpleasant about the sound of the sirens; it was like a scream of fear in a dream, starting low and growing to a loud shriek. "That ultimately filled me with such rage that I would have liked to smash something." Every swelling sound, the roaring of a car starting up, the whistling of a train engine, or the initial sound of a cow's moo all triggered, "at the very same moment, pounding of the heart right up to the throat." Vibrations of windows in the wind, roaring thunder, shrill telephone rings, "those are all such familiar sounds." Chilling were words such as "train engine shed," "signal tower," "freight dispatch." The mood changed. "It was something you could not escape, could not get rid of." Everyday life was constant wincing. "Dammit, pull yourself together, the others are coping too." Even if it was not in accordance with air-raid protection regulations, "during alarms and when plane engines are roaring, I like most to be outside in open space. In the cellar I pace back and forth like a wild animal, to try to get some air."

Danger in war was recognized by sounds. Once you could see something, it was too late to act. Shells and bombs were not visible, but they could be felt. People listened into the void to hear what was coming. When it was there, the sense of hearing was the first thing to shut down. "Because of your nerves, you have to cover your ears." The acoustics of the bombardment were worse than looking at it. "My father is very hard of hearing. He remained incredibly calm and composed; a woman said 'it doesn't faze him because he doesn't hear anything.'"

The horror started with the whooshing of the bomb drop. The raid affected all of the senses. The nose registered the fire and odorous gases, and the skin felt the temperature and the blast of air, the build-up of the blaze and the wind that carried it. The blood vessels ultimately either absorbed the blast waves or they burst. The suction ripped clothing from the body.

The self in conventional war was active. It showed strength, skill, and courage, but transferred to the group. The corps was not a body, and it asserted itself not physically, but in cohesion and solidarity. We operated, our tanks broke through, the artillery protected us. The target of the bombardment was the individual corporeality. The war was not fought, it was absorbed; the senses withstood it with each individual's own constitution. If I were deaf, then I would enjoy an advantage, because the sense of hearing could not be attacked.

"I assumed a crouched position although I was convinced that I was not in direct danger. Others also stood as I did: standing bent over with our hands on our knees and our heads pulled in a bit." The impulse to duck reduced the area of the body that can be attacked. "You automatically get smaller and smaller," the head bent away. "I pulled the hood of my nurse's cloak over my head. In my fear I clawed into the shoulders of the medical sergeant and buried my head in his shoulder." The instinct to cling did not offer the least bit of protection; it was the futile flight to the herd. "There we were standing pressed together into a human knot with handkerchiefs in our mouths, clinging tightly to each other." Couples embraced, children and parents, women and men, neighborhoods. "We all had our arms around each other and waited anxiously to see if more bombs would fall."

The knots let go of each other again, the bombers left, but the war has worked its way into the senses and will not leave. Not for the children or the children's children. "It is most scary before it really gets going. Once the bombs start falling, you get much calmer."

The attack was anticipated internally. The nerve tracts broke down the subsided pressure and inculcated reflexes, even in reaction to things like the telephone ringing. Fear—the instinctual, primal companion of living beings—turned to dread. Dread knew what was threatening and drew a membrane over the human being that was tuned to the frequencies of the danger, and continued to react to it all day and all night.

The physical matter, without any intervention by the person, absorbed the attack in the limbs and entrails. "After the fifth wave we had several hits in the building. I thought I had trouble getting air. And then I felt as if my stomach hurt and as if I had diarrhea, my intestines were getting all churned up. I also couldn't stand any more and sat down involuntarily on the ground."

The body wanted to get off its feet and get in contact with the ground over an increased area. One thus became a larger target, but standing took too much energy. Once it started outside, all one's strength might already be used up. "My knees conked out totally and threatened to collapse. Although we were at most two minutes from the bunker, I could not go another step." The plight of adolescence was shed. "My legs started trembling terribly as if a little boy were really afraid. I fought against it, but to no avail." Finally, even words were too great a burden. "When I spoke I noticed that my lips were trembling." Speaking was a form of translation. The force of this sensory impression, however, could not be translated, "and I could not get words out the way I usually could." The organ stopped functioning in order to avoid the profanity of speech. "My aunt could no longer speak. She lost her voice."[3]

Some wanted to deal with what was happening all by themselves. "During a raid I preferred to withdraw to my corner, and I sat there by myself. I kept thinking, 'Now it's coming. Now it's all over.'"

Muscles and tongue gave in, and the heart, vessels, and secretions had to work all the more. "I got a feeling as if a whole lot of blood was flowing to my heart and as if the heart was blown up like a balloon." The bomb that fell close to the body and was meant for me caused the heart to skip—it switched over. "It often took only a fraction of a second. And then I got powerful heart palpitations beating up to my throat. Then I started sweating such that I wiped my forehead or blew air into my face. The warm perspiration quickly turned into cold, clammy sweat." Blood vessels contracted abruptly and expanded just as suddenly. "In any case I got spider veins in my cheeks like you get when you go pale." The cellar was cold, but the pulse raced and sent warm sweat, which alternated with cold shivers. "I was shivering, had goose bumps on my entire body," like when one is not dressed warmly enough. "I felt incredibly cold. I was shivering as if I were getting a fever" and "my teeth were chattering."

Time crawled into the beat of the pulse. The self lost its sense of the passage of time. It remained spellbound in the "now"; before and after ceased to exist. "I didn't have just any old thoughts. All I thought was: now, now it's going to hit us." When four days later another raid came, "I could not control myself and I screamed, 'Hans, something is going to happen to us now; it's our turn!'"

The "now" was absent of fear. Fear prevailed in view of what was to come in the future. "The feeling of fear was gone. It was a kind of resignation: 'Now one will get you and you're gone.'" The "now" was the most intense exchange between the weapon and its addressee. They had been synchronized. As soon as one perceived the whooshing, "it is as if you hold your breath, with your hands on your ears to muffle the noise, and then 'now, now, now it's coming again!'"

There was an eerie counterpart to the dissolution of time in the "now" of the impact: the swaying of the ground. Usually, time moves on and the ground is firm. Now time stood still and the ground was set in motion. It was no longer permanent; there was no ground anymore. "The ground started clearly shaking, which I found very unpleasant, and I thought I could see the walls breaking apart, and I thought 'it isn't all that terrible when you bite the dust.' At that moment I had forgotten my worries about my children."

Many people yielded to the pact between the organism and the bomb; others did not. And a fire raid was rarely about suffering a direct bomb hit. That was only part of what happened. The main event was a short bombardment followed by the hours-long battle by people buried in the rubble, caught in the fire, or seeking a way out of the annihilation zone. First and foremost was the urge to do something and then the horror of discovering that nothing could be done. In between was the illusion of doing something. "I spent the raid with my hands flat against the wall. I gauged the time with the utmost concentration. I got a very clear and levelheaded feeling 'this is it; now it's over.' I had the feeling that time was shorter than it was in reality." Holding on to the wall and to time, the subjective, congealed body time of "now" felt like fifteen minutes. In reality, forty-five minutes had passed.

The self could react only in real time. Instincts drew it into the protection of the places, bunkers, or cellars. The bunker sealed out the present; in the cellar, the temporal order from outside prevailed. The raid was directed down to the minutest detail. It was based on the temporal structure of the frequency of drops per minute, the span in which the fires merged, the bombs' time-delay settings, down to fractions of a second. This clockwork of annihilation cost the enemy the sense of time. His inner clock moved too fast. "I had the feeling of maybe sitting in the bunker all of two hours. But in reality it was already light when I left, so I must have spent twelve hours inside." A doctor observed a state in himself during the tumult of exploding bombs and collapsing walls. "I'd call it 'shut down.' It was the consciousness that 'any minute it will break through' and a matter-of-factness that one could call submission or fatalism. I don't have any particular memory of physical paresthesia." The compressing of real time meant that it was always later than it seemed. There were no reports of "too late" cases; people evidently simply misjudged the time. "What should I say, how long it lasted? I couldn't say. It could have been ten minutes, or an hour. I just don't know."

Contact with the course of outside events blocked off the internal events. Defense was a sensible action even if it did no good.

> I heard the formations approaching and the two of us rushed down to the basement. The infernal concert had already started. I got very frightened. I wanted to try to prop up the ceiling—it was a narrow corridor—and I stretched up my arms. I didn't tremble. You try to calm yourself down, even by doing nonsensical things. Afterward you have the feeling the nightmare is past and it's good to laugh.

When the alarm sounded, Draeger wanted to go to the cellar, but Heckmann wanted to keep working:

> I was thinking that the window could fly out against me. The flak were shooting and Draeger said "They're already dropping." I got as far as the door to the hallway which was hard to open because of the blast. I braced myself against it, but it immediately flew shut again. Heckmann shouted "Get down" and pushed me and Draeger to the ground. Heckmann shouted "Open your mouth!" I had a vague impression of roaring but I can't say I heard a bomb. Heckmann was the one with a presence of mind; he shouted "Up and out." Then there was another powerful hit and the windows rattled. I stayed standing there perplexed and looked around helplessly. Down in the basement I saw the patients and civilians running around and praying. Heckmann prodded them into the air-raid cellar. I made it to the entrance to the cellar. Herr Bender came toward me, hugged me, and said "It's all over." At that moment I didn't hear anything but I saw smoke and dust in the cellar and it smelled like sulfur. Heckmann said "Stay calm, nothing happened" and ran back out.

Heckmann was the man of the hour, the subordinate leader who rose to the occasion. His effectiveness was based on his refusal to perceive the situation. That would not have helped. Whoever let the situation have an effect on them had already lost the game. There was always a most obvious thing to do in a situation, like opening your mouth during a blast. But one could not pay attention to the most obvious things and at the same time reflect on the larger context, as the twenty-year-old stenotypist did. "I couldn't understand the sense of the whole war and that we had to endure and suffer so much." Consequently, "my legs stopped working and I remained lying there in the middle of the street. I said I wanted to die right there on the spot. I did not care what could still happen. They just dragged me by the arm another hundred meters. Two sergeants guided me. In the cellar I sat down on the ground and trembled." A realist in some sense.

The subordinate leader thought realism was useless if you were gobbled up by reality. "I tried to calm people down by saying banalities." The well-supported cellar was packed full with mothers and children.

> I myself was as scared as a schoolboy, but I couldn't let that show. My gall bladder reacted suddenly. My mouth was full of water and I secretly took some atropine. All of a sudden there was a powerful blast. It tore the strap on my steel helmet. A brace came flying at me; there was terrible screaming. In that second I felt neither my gall bladder nor my body. I had only one thought: Keep your poise and help. Now I had a feeling of unshakeable composure; the most insane pressure was suddenly lifted. I could think things through calmly and clearly.

Thinking clearly did not help much, because the façade had collapsed onto the entrance, and the ceiling had dropped five feet. People were injured, "and so we came to the realization that we were trapped. The women got terribly frightened again." The most obvious thing to do was to tell the children fairy tales, which also calmed down the mothers. After three hours of waiting, helpers pounded a steel pipe through the rubble so they could at least communicate. By ten in the morning everyone had been freed, "I was so happy I drank a cognac, and it did me good."

In the bitter position of being buried in debris, holding on to a possibility of the improbable—that the outside world will pound a pipe through the rubble—is the only rational thing to do. If you have nothing else to do but hang on, sink your claws into your luck. The air war created its own sense of reason and did not bring about storms of emotion commensurate with its horror. These had been filtered out by a psychological immunity shield. A sixty-one-year-old woman who had been trapped by hot debris in her cellar for eight days suffered from diarrhea, cried, and dozed for five months in a depressed void, and that is how she got back on an even keel. There were no psychiatric patients whose minds had been as mutilated as the limbs of others. Even the mentally ill conducted themselves in a composed and disciplined manner during the air raids. The military hospital in Cologne that registered eight thousand neurological patients from late 1939 to late 1944 had only soldiers; there were no patients from the air war. "I can remember only three acute psychological reactions to air raids," wrote Dr. Friedrich Panse, who worked there. "One soldier had been buried in the air-raid cellar with his wife and children, and over the hours he could feel his wife's body underneath him gradually turn cold. His children had also died. Shortly after he was freed he attempted suicide once and then he stayed with us another few weeks in a depressive state."[4]

In addition to feeling composure, increased suggestibility was reported. "I thought the door frame was the safest place; then I observed the faces of the others there, to see if the danger was really that great." Calmer people knew that they transferred their calmness to others. "The women in the cellar were very agitated; they talked loudly and screamed. So I slowed down because I had the feeling I should not unsettle the women even more. And then I went slowly to the two airlocks."

Nothing was more moving than prayer, the transfer of responsibility for one's fortune to a higher power. People felt a need to be one of God's children. "My grandmother had a great influence on us. She is very religious and she calmly and earnestly instructed us to pray with her." The murmuring of the nurses' prayers in the stillness infused the patients with a sense of peace.

Resolve was contagious. "As soon as one of them started, the others also grabbed hand extinguishers from the walls. Then they sprayed wildly all over. It was like an electrical spark that spread to all of them. Everyone thought that whatever the others were doing must be right and then they joined in." People infected one another with the measure of how much one could take; they picked it up from others and passed it on. I obliged myself to withstand what others could withstand, and I found I could do what I couldn't, and it worked.

Everyone absorbed the bombing war in his or her own way, but always incredibly flexibly. "From the cellar we could hear that people we know were killed by falling debris. Although I normally cannot stand the sight of blood and some of those who were buried—seventeen in all—had been seriously injured, it did not matter to me at all. I could actively help out and bandage the injured, together with a Red Cross nurse."

I do what needed to be done as if outside of my self. The sensory skin, however, was numbed. "All at once the fighter-bombers that had long pursued us turned back." The medical orderly felt a jerk, threw himself down, and the door of the hospital train car flew far away onto the tracks from the blast. The injured who could still walk raced out of the car. "The amputees screamed from their cots. I stood up quickly and went over to them, lifted them hastily out of their cots—there were about twelve of them—and laid them down on the floor of the car." While the medic was still moving the amputees, the fighter-bombers began their second of six approaches. One of the wounded yelled "'Send greetings to my wife and children.' A short time later I saw him pass away. I believe he died from the fright." The medical orderly stayed lying on the floor. The amputees clung tight to him and screamed, "'Medic, what are we going to do?' I tried to calm them down; said we have to keep down." At that very moment the senses blacked out. "It was as if my body had no feeling anymore." The limbs became stiff, "as if they were somehow blocked." His cocoon isolated him from the situation. The increased pressure from the distress engaged an interruption in perception. The medic had shut down.

After the direct hit in the bunker, the soldiers on the third, military level tried to open their compartment door, which required a firm push. The stillness in the building and the air draft coming from the darkness were bad signs. The wind could not be coming from a fan, because the power was out. "The bunker must be out of order." With matches and a flashlight, they set out to investigate what happened. Individual voices could be made out, including a girl's voice droning a high-pitched "la, la, la." "Then we discovered that the corridor was full of dead bodies lying on top of each other." Shadows of civilians flitted past to the exit, which was also blocked by corpses. "A comrade says that we have to help out here." The comment was met with uneasiness. "I initially had inner reservations about rescue operations because I felt uncomfortable touching all the corpses." Starting reluctantly,

I then gave myself a moral shove; "you have to." Two comrades were rougher and simply pulled at the bodies. I couldn't stand to watch the pulling and we tried to sort out the bodies calmly and orderly. In doing so I realized that although I am otherwise not the strongest, I had unusually great physical strength. I lifted a child's body easily with one hand. Mentally I was totally absent.

There were 150 dead bodies and twelve injured on the ground. "I saw a comrade start to take jewelry, but with a short comment I got him to put it—it was a necklace—back on the body."

Reports that were put to protocol after the fact sometimes depicted the self of the air war as an alter ego. This other self differed from the initial self because of its armor around sensation and feeling. It let shock and horror penetrate only in a muffled form. The initial self would not be able to cope with the flood of dreadful images.

Several bombs had exploded in front of the train station bunker. Because a lot of people had still been standing in front of the bunker there were several hundred deaths. The wall of the bunker was totally plastered with body parts. In the tunnel within the station that leads to the tracks there were groups still standing, who had been holding on to each other. Railroaders, civilians, and soldiers, standing there as if they were still alive. But they were dead. The most horrible image was an older woman standing in a corner, upright with very swollen eyes, with a young boy pressed against her, also still standing, who had dust-covered, dried foam around his mouth. I felt as if it wasn't me looking at them but a stranger. I didn't feel like I participated actively in the whole experience.

Who did experience the air war? Diminished emotional investment, coupled with industrious helping hands, made it easier to get through it all. It also helped when dealing with memories of it later. Emotions did not further reflect on actions such as gathering up body parts from family members in tin pails. This was calmly done and was a general form of rescue and recovery. The containers were labeled and carried to cemeteries or placed on sidewalks. "I saw a man dragging a sack with five or six bulges in it as if he were carrying heads of cabbage. It was the heads of his family, a whole family, that he had found in the cellar."[5]

Herr L. and Frau F. from Pfauengasse came to me in the morning in the cathedral. He had his deceased wife and she her deceased husband with them and they wanted to have them buried. Herr L. carried the remains of his wife in a sack: a pelvis and a segment of spine with the tops of the thighs. Frau F. carried her husband in a preserving pot: the completely preserved buttocks and a piece of the spine. The pants around the buttocks had been baked into the flesh. In the pocket was a railroader's watch, which was burned out totally but still easily recognizable; this was how the woman had identified her husband. We dug out two holes, I recited the burial prayers, and then we closed the graves.[6]

The clergy in Würzburg were asked to perform these services so the victims of March 16 "would not have to be put under the ground like animals."

Photographs of the pails are not part of the iconography of World War II. The families also did not pass down this image. But it cannot be struck from memory, which overflows with scenes that the memory-self preserves as unforgettable. The experience-self endured them in a state of local anesthesia. According to clinical findings of postwar psychotherapy, emotional paralysis warded off the air war. Civilians withstood a mental trauma considered impossible. It does not seem like the numbness later gave way. Speaking out from the transfiguration of the cities was an abandonment of the scenarios in which the atrocities happened. It made no sense to look back upon this head of Medusa. It is still too close for that. Numbing does not eliminate the pain, it only blocks the perception of it. But it exists nonetheless. The remembered scenes hand down a torture that will not always remain unspeakable. Furthermore, the cellar, the bunker, the radiant heat, the gas, the blast wave, the mutilation are afflictions of modernity. They are both memories and warnings. The place that still protects, the blast that the unfortified self can absorb, the molten mass of physical bodies, these are all acute subjects. They have a beginning and thus at the same time an unsurpassed rage.

In the bunker, "the situation was horrific. Injured people lay on the benches and screamed for water and medical care. On the ground the condensation was inch-deep."[7] When there was a direct hit, "the bunker rocked back and forth. Women came down from upstairs with their heads bandaged. Concrete had fallen on their heads. We were down in the bunker. One woman kept screaming for her child who had stayed in the apartment. She just wanted to go shopping!" When there were constant air-raid alarms, people moved into the bunkers. They were overcrowded. "We spent eight days in the corridor. I washed the diapers out in the toilet. They were always dark and dirty. When there was a pause between alarms I went to the next house and asked if I could wash my baby for once."

Self-dug tunnels were cool and damp. Tunnel communities could not seem to get them dry. The wetness ran down the walls and a slippery morass collected on the ground. It was cramped; the occupants sat along both sides, knee to knee. The infants came down with "bunker disease," a serious intestinal infection. Diphtheria, scarlet fever, and tuberculosis broke out. Those who were infected had to leave the tunnel, otherwise they could cause an epidemic. Families held fast to their regular spaces; no one wanted to stay near the doors. Everyone pressed toward the middle of the tunnel. Life there proceeded as if in a stupor; breathing used up oxygen, the flames from the carbide lamps and candles extinguished in the haze. If things weren't so restless one could fall asleep, but instead, people sat knitting and complaining, singing and praying. The children whined.

The impact of heavy blockbusters set the bunker in motion. It swayed and quaked, the lights went out. "The people started praying and bawling. The air was getting worse all the time. A totally disturbed young woman pressed an infant into my mother's arm and disappeared in the chaos." It got very dusty when there were major concussions. Destruction of the indestructible triggered uncontrollable outbursts.

> Suddenly panic broke out in the jam-packed bunker. The screaming sounded like animals; we huddled together into a group of five soldiers. It gave you some feeling of security. When the quaking was very powerful, I felt like I was floating for a short while. I know that from the chloroform inebriation when anesthesia is starting to take effect. You didn't feel how horrible the experience was. That was switched off.

In poorer-quality protective spaces, the occupants were "like out of their senses." Even in a deep, vaulted wine cellar,

> these sounds are indescribable. The walls shook and one wall started moving toward us. A blockbuster had fallen. But then the wall moved back because another bomb fell on the opposite side and pushed it back up. We were crouched in the middle of the cellar with our arms around each other.

The girls apprenticing at the municipal savings bank did not have enough time to get to the air-raid shelter. They ran downstairs into the cloakroom. "The blast ripped us back and forth. Many prayed; many screamed. None of us was killed, but one apprentice lost her entire family."

The first bomb fell in the yard and all the windows rattled at once. The second one was a direct hit. It was a hard strike, splitting the house in two. Down to the cellar each half of the house slanted to the side. "Right above us the steel beams held and the cellar ceiling hung like a tent above us. There was danger of asphyxiation. Then we got some air through the hole to the next cellar that I had broken open the day before on a hunch. Then we heard voices: 'Is anyone alive in there?'"

The collapse of the cellar started with the support column breaking off in the middle of the room. "Then all I saw was a flash. When I came to, I could move my head only a little bit to the side. It took a while before I realized that I was totally trapped under the rubble." Tap water was streaming out into the cellar vault; it was chest-high. Below mother's head her red coat was shining. Father got people from the repair crews. "By their calling and asking questions I could confirm to these people that more must have survived, that they are very far away from me. . . ." Karin, the neighbor's daughter, was lying in the next cellar. She was also trapped. Everything took so long because one gable end threatened to collapse and had to be propped up. "I was complaining to these people, since I didn't know what was taking so long." The hole between the cellars was enlarged to the side and they kept bracing it. "Karin's upper body was already in the hole but her legs were still caught by fallen rubble. Now the hole had been opened up enough that my head was free. I realized that my mother was underneath me, dead." The rescue operation took fourteen hours, because the mass of debris had to be continually braced or else it would slide back down, burying the people trapped below. Karin was the only person in her family to survive. In the hospital, she was washed and given tea and zwieback.

You can be freed from brick debris, but burst concrete required equipment that was unavailable. A U-shaped concrete pipe had been dug into the ground, a tunnel bunker with a double-door airlock at the exit. Just as someone opened the first door, an aerial mine struck. The blast traveled through the pipe, lifting it up and letting it fall and break. The meter-thick concrete shells were immovable, impossible to chop, impossible to saw. The people who were trapped inside were alive and could speak. "Clergymen came who gave the buried people spiritual support, the last rites and absolution. A lot of them were screaming terribly from pain." Doctors injected morphine. "That was my worst experience in the war."

A protective space with more than thirty feet of earth above it was a bombproof shelter. A connecting door led from it to a second chamber that had a thinner covering, which broke. Fire and smoke traveled from the second room to the first. Someone opened the door and the smoke rushed in. Panic developed at the doors. One, at most two, fit through, and people pushed from behind. "Maybe four or five meters from the door I could feel how my child was getting pushed down farther and farther. It was all very loud and from outside you could hear the crackling of the flames. But I summoned all my strength and shouted as loud as I possibly could, 'Help, my child.'" The man next to her realized the seriousness of the situation and threw himself back with all his might, "so that I could quickly pull my child back up, who had already been pushed down to my stomach. That was the most horrible moment of my life. Outside I looked for my baby carriage, which was filled with milk powder, children's flour, and diapers. The carriage had been crushed and had lost a wheel."

Bold help was double-edged. Professional helpers stayed away from doubtful cases. The steel beams in the air-raid shelter had come down, the people who were trapped screamed for help, the fire department was there but they decided not to enter the building because too much burning rubble was still falling. "I walked by. I asked the fire department to keep spraying me with the hose and I tried to free the people caught in the entranceway. One of those trapped screamed 'You're standing on my face.' We cleared away the smaller pieces of rubble and this man could be saved." A glowing anchor bar flew into a woman's face, but it could be removed by spraying the helper's hand with a steady stream of water. A total of three could be pulled out. From below some were yelling "help us," because they were drowning in the water from the hoses, but there was nothing that could be done. Attempts were made elsewhere with more people.

The main water pipe was broken and the water in the cellar rose quickly. "We tried to form a chain in order to bail the water out of the cellar," but the pails had to be shoved through a narrow hole in the cellar wall. "We couldn't deal with the water; the people drowned that night. Their screams haunt me still today, and I'll never get rid of them."

The ones who survived to tell their tales were the ones who could still move after the bombs caused their damage. They could remember the immobile ones who were left behind after the explosion. "The flames licked out at us. I had my child on my arm. With the other hand I tried to rip out the slats from the basement window in order to get to the street. I soaked a bedsheet and wrapped it around my whimpering baby." Not everyone ran onto the pavement; some stayed where they were.

I could see the people very clearly, because the walls were gone. The small, only five-feet-tall Herr Kieselstein came shouting loudly for the fire department. His wife had been paralyzed for thirteen years, which is why he didn't go into the air-raid shelter. I couldn't see his wife. Then the flames totally enveloped the short little man and he burned alive with his paralyzed wife. I can still hear his screams today.

Elsewhere, a wiry air-raid protection helper appeared at the last second in the middle of the night, jumped over a stone wall, and groped around in the frame of the ruins.

I couldn't see a thing but I heard whimpering somewhere in the dark and then I found the old woman lying on the ground. "This way, Granny, over the wall!" Because she couldn't walk I grabbed her by the shoulders and dragged her out. She was moaning without end that her handbag with the diamonds was still inside.

Things went worse for "my pregnant sister, who was pretty far along, she was expecting her eighth child," and the soldier who wanted to pull her out at Dransdorfer Weg. "Run outside," said the neighbor to her children, "to Neumann Meadow." Then she looked into the burning shed where the pregnant woman had to be. She was lying between the kitchen and the bedroom underneath a cabinet.

Then burning tar came down. A soldier came in and called to her "Get out of here or you'll burn too." She could not get out that easily and the soldier had to help and he burned too. The story is interrupted—no one saw what happened—and continues when the neighbor's husband says, "All of Dransdorfer Weg is gone and the coffins are already out on the street." At this point in time I still didn't know what had happened to my sister.

The neighbor interrupted her husband. "'Be quiet. You know that her sister lives there with her family.' I was totally upset and frightened."

For the new mothers in the state obstetric hospital, it seemed "as if the floor and walls are made of rubber. Everything stretches and seems to sway when the dull strikes shake the building."[8] Mortar and pieces of masonry flew through the room, thick smoke made its way in, and the nurse "implores us to stay calm."

Patients with common maladies had long since been released. The hospitals were full of people injured from the bombings. "They fastened a board to my mother's arm and she could hardly move." Husband and child made the daily visit. Bomber alarm! "The nurses opened the doors to the individual rooms and shouted 'Everyone down to the cellar.'" Luckily, the husband of the woman with her arm on a board managed to get her out of bed and dress her. "She would not have been able to leave the room on her own." A short time later, the ceiling collapsed. "We stood in a protected corner on the basement floor. The kitchen was there too. The cook was sitting in the kitchen and had just prepared the meat for Christmas. The patients were writhing in pain on the floor, screaming. Our legs were injured from doors, windows, and kitchen utensils that were flying around." In the deep cellar, the nuns were praying; the nurse thought of the blackout regulations and called out: "The fuses should be switched off. Lights are burning in the whole building." Soldiers dragged dead and injured people into the hospital from outside. "While the raid was still going on, Prof. Steinhauer and Dr. Militor started operating in the coal cellar. The hospital was partly destroyed."

The gynecological and surgery wards were safe from destruction, hidden away in an H-shaped air-raid tunnel that had been dug into the mountain. The city archives were also stored there. People injured in the train raids of December 1944 and farmers from the surrounding villages who were shot by hedgehoppers were put in the hospital section. The bunker lay so deep in the rock that sirens and the noise of the raid were inaudible. When trucks brought in injured bedded down on rags and straw, the personnel knew what had happened: "I had had training as a Red Cross helper so I could stay in the bunker. Operations were performed under the light of kerosene lamps. At night we went from room to room by candlelight." Water was tapped from a well branch; it was only available during the day. "The used bedpans were stacked in one room. They could not be immediately emptied and washed. Outside next to the transformer was a small room where the corpses were placed. The water flowed out of the corpses like rainwater over the curb into the canal." The motor pool picked them up each day, stacked one on top of the other. Later, there were paper bags for them. "There were many seriously injured children in the bunker. Once I could go home in between and made some candies out of sugar, butter, milk, and vinegar. Our ward nurse Helene had given me the ingredients."

The air war killed about 75,000 children under fourteen years of age—45,000 boys and 30,000 girls—and injured 116,000. Fifteen percent of the total deaths were children.[9]

> I huddled up with Grandma. Suddenly I felt a powerful blast. Then I realized that my lower body was caught. I was stuck in the mass of stone. In the background I could hear my grandmother groaning. At the same time I noticed that water was flowing and I could feel that it was getting deeper. I was buried in past my chest in rubble; one arm was free. I hadn't been told for a year that my sister Uschi had died. My mother died along with the newborn. Little by little they told me that my whole family was killed. At the time I couldn't register it.

Karin Melchers lay with paralyzed legs next to the soldiers in the hospital. She learned to walk again with crutches.

The children of the air war perceived it in a child's way. Siblings without heads, strangers with burning hair, charred corpses shrunken down to the size of a three-year-old. "The man was covered with cardboard. Looking closer I could see that his head was missing. The head of my best friend was lying about ten meters away. His name was Paul Sauer and he lived on Kesselsgasse." Lacking any shyness around the corpses, the children observed the grimaces of death brought about not by the bombs themselves but by indirect effects of the bombing. "A soldier was standing by a destroyed villa. He was leaning against a wall and was dead. His lungs had burst." People got caught in the indirect effects of the bombing, like the woman standing at the window when the bombs were dropped. "Her head just flew away." They could not find it. Remains were often lost as if they had been hidden. "My father and my brothers spent eight days digging out my uncle."

The organisms that were recovered were not corpses but states of matter. "They were lying next to each other and were bloated." Astonishing was the doll size of those who died from the intense heat, "so unbelievably small that you could hardly fathom it."[10] The violet-blue skin of women with a child in their arms looked like colored masks. "Mama, why is that child so black?" The children witnessed the identification efforts among the rows of bodies lined up in Darmstadt. "Is that Papa?" The sons dug out bodies. "Stay calm Mama, we'll get you out."

"A boy in a Luftwaffe uniform came out of the cellar crying, carrying a covered enamel pail in his hand. Someone asked him what was the matter, to offer some comfort. It was his parents." Young children who had been orphaned did not even know who they were, so signs were hung around their necks with their names and those of their relatives.

Sister Agnes at St. Mary's Hospital: "I will never forget the two children, maybe nine and ten years old, who were looking for their Papa in our basement and in the morgue. 'We have been everywhere already.'"

"One day I saw a retarded boy on the street in the smoldering ruins. He stumbled forward with unsteady steps and a shrill laugh. The game of destruction seemed to delight him." In Darmstadt's late-summer descent into Hell, the annihilation contrived freaks of disembodiment. Heat, blasts, and falling debris did not cut the bodies, as was the case with bullets or a blow; they scrapped them. The metaphors of these deaths extolled the cosmic forces of radiant heat and shock wave, that invisible crusher of veins and stone. They rejected the decrepitude of the tissue, whose decomposition already denoted it as waste. The pail acknowledged that. "It must have been about four o'clock. Disturbed, soot-covered, deathly pale people, all in an unreal and dull silence. The most horrid moments; there were hands and legs protruding out from the mountains of rubble on Ludwigstrasse; and the head of a man buried up to his chin, with glassy, staring eyes wide open." His route took him to the semicircle of casks, preserving pots, and crates at the entrance to the cemetery. "All day long the people of Darmstadt brought their dead in old pails. A whole family in a washtub."

Like the house lying on the chest of its resident, reality was topsyturvy. Dead people appeared as the living. An elderly man sat leaning against a tree. "I wanted to start a conversation but he didn't answer." Two women in advanced pregnancy gave birth at the moment of their death. The birth of a child was its death. "I counted 192 people I knew who were killed." But nothing was known anymore; there were only identifying features.

Through the smoke I could see a charred body right in front of my house. Convinced it was my wife, I picked her up and held her for a long time in my arms, carefully removing the wedding ring and watch and then I suddenly noticed a gold filling in the front teeth that was foreign to me. Then I was certain that it was not Martha.

Incineration forced the body to make expressive gestures that the beholder tried to decipher.

A young woman was lying there like a sculpture that didn't come out very good. The legs with charred high-heeled boots were stretched out high backwards; the arms raised as if in defense. The face was still preserved in outlines; the mouth with brownish rows of teeth wide open, so that you could not tell if the face was laughing or screaming.

The laughing was not funny and the scream was not painful. This creature was an expression not of feelings, but of its creator. It was a sculpture of the fire war.

7. STONE

"saxa loquuntur." Stones speak.

The munitions that are dropped become one with the materials of the city—stone, wood, and interiors—and so they have a devastating effect as a weapon. Movables, such as people and objects of art, can avoid the impact; that depends on how much effort is expended. Buildings cannot be removed; they become the bearers and transporters of the blaze. With them, Germany loses its external and inner possessions. Artworks, archival materials, and books take flight, at first behind remote, sturdy walls and finally in deep, solid rock. Otherwise almost all of the culture would have been destroyed. The libraries could preserve within stone most of the books from what was still the largest book burning in history.

ON APRIL 9, 1943, Hitler ordered that artistically precious ceiling and wall frescoes be photographed in color. They started in the western administrative districts of Cologne, Düsseldorf, and Aachen, and included sculptures, choir stalls, and furniture as well. A year and a half later, Hitler decreed: "In view of the steadily growing losses in irreplaceable artistic and cultural assets through the air war, I consider it urgently desirable that valuable monuments and other unmovable works of art be photographed to the greatest extent possible—that is, in detail."[1] In December 1944, the photographers also prepared pictures of the small and medium-sized cities. In Frankfurt, the daily *Frankfurter Zeitung* suggested in the spring of 1942, after the attacks on Lübeck and Cologne, that the nineteenth-century patrician town houses be photographed, because "who knows how long this Frankfurt will continue to stand."[2]

The Old Town stood until the March 1944 attacks. On March 22, the anniversary of Goethe's death, the house he was born in at Am grossen Hirschgraben no. 23 went down. People had kept night watches to protect the house. Through holes in the cellar wall it was linked with the Frankfurt catacomb system and served as an intact exit to the street when people in the neighborhood were trapped by rubble. On March 18, the mansard roofs caught fire, but it was gotten under control, right above the room in which Goethe was born. Four days later, nothing could be done: Hirschgraben burned from both ends and was impassable, as were the intersecting streets. The residents lost their orientation in the hurricane and wondered where they were. Between March 22 and 24, the building whose cornerstone was laid by the young Goethe when it was expanded in 1755 slowly burned to the ground. The walls were damp, so it took a long time. Damage was caused by water used to fight the fire as well as from the fire itself. On the morning of March 23, the gabled room disappeared; at midday, the stairwell collapsed. The next day, all that remained were the cellar and cellar stairs, the sandstone posts of the door and windows, and the window arches. In September, a blockbuster toppled the last remaining walls on the ground floor. It was one of the older town houses, of which Frankfurt had maintained two thousand. Ten remained undamaged; a few others saved parts of their ground floor.

The March raids, with two million incendiary sticks, razed the ring of medieval buildings around the Römerberg main square and the cathedral hill, including the Gothic town hall with the Kaisersaal (Imperial Hall), the Old Mint, Paulskirche (St. Paul's Church), and the Schopenhauer House. The sofa Schopenhauer died on and his desk chair were removed from the ground floor in time. Explosives struck the southern transept of the cathedral, where from 1356 on the German emperor had been elected and, since 1562, crowned. The Stone House, the most beautiful patrician town house from the Middle Ages, with corner towers and crenellations, was lost. A replica was later built from photographs.

The Stone House was one of the most vulnerable of all targets in the fire war. Residents proved to be more tenacious than anything, industry reproduced itself, and 80 percent of the archives of books and works of art could be saved due to their mobility. However, the hardest, oldest, most permanent material, though it had bridged the ages, lacked any power of resistance. Stone was immobile. That which gave it firmness over centuries, its anchoring in the ground, had now fettered it, rendering it unbudgeable. In October 1943, one in five Frankfurters could be evacuated; industry found accommodations in monstrous bunkers one hundred feet high, 1,600 feet long, and 650 feet wide. The Frankfurt town hall, the Römer, on the other hand, stood in the same place for five centuries and was not portable. Because the fire war created a realm of destruction, stone was at a disadvantage.

The bomber circulated everywhere, but the bomb was fixed on a certain segment of ground. It could not reach the greatest part of the country, so an alternative area existed. Only stone, with its weight, confronted the bomb, with its destination, on the same exact piece of ground. Destructive force and inertia met eye to eye. From the bombardment perspective, there was not much to do if not for the stone house and its inventory. An air offensive could do little damage to a rural population. Its violence unfurled only in collapsing that which was firm and solid, in burying people and property in rubble, in creating fire bridges and draft conditions in the buildings. Stone and weapon merged. The air war was not the tonnage dropped but the blazing city thereby created. The dwellings of generations did not merely split in two, they became masses of stone that struck people dead, glowing ovens that asphyxiated, dungeons that gassed to death. Its final face was that of fury. The stone was broken and dispossessed at once. It was the main tool of the enemy, its most pernicious aggregate.

When stone and weapon became one through the sixty-eight thousand blockbusters and eighty million thermite sticks, it spoiled people's images of the city's landscape that was rooted in history. Later on, people did not want to rebuild the prewar structures for several reasons. There was only weak support for the idea of restoring the unity of space and history. It would cost too much money and effort. This venue had been discredited by the horrors of the fire. And the newly built cities would have to be more comfortable, have better transportation, and, most importantly, be better bombproofed. The residents ultimately tore down more stone than the bomb did. They could no longer stand to look at those fateful shells.

In the summer of 1942, after the raids on Lübeck and Rostock had just inaugurated the fire war, a conference of cultural and air-raid protection officials discussed how they would deal with monuments, museums, and libraries. The danger of a direct hit by a high-explosive bomb was minimal. But a complex such as Berlin's city palace, with its huge top floor and barely accessible false floors, would require an extensive fire-watch contingent with knowledge of the building. It was as if a castle were built to burn down, as had been confirmed in the demise of Kassel's residential palace. The water supply and fire-fighting crews were nowhere near adequate in containing the flames that leapt over from the neighboring department store. Interior walls lined with silk, gilded woodcuts on the doors and sills, parquet floors, and red sandstone offered a wealth of combustibles. It joined the swarms of incendiary sticks; no one could interfere with that mutual attraction. The Johannisburg Renaissance castle in Aschaffenburg, one of the most beautiful of its kind, was gutted in several raids between November 1944 and April 1945. Castles have roofs that simply could not be saved.

The Air Ministry recommended covering the attics with a thirty-inch-thick layer of sand. The small diameter of the four-pound incendiaries helped it attain a considerable final velocity and penetrating strength. Sand could have stopped them, but the suggested depth weighed 330 pounds per square foot, and ordinary ceilings could not withstand such weight. Two layers of hard-burned brick or eight inches of reinforced concrete slab would also have hindered the impact, but it was impossible to furnish all German buildings with that.

After experiments performed by the Bavarian Palace Department, the attic floors were insulated against flying sparks and the impact of isolated hits. In May 1943, at the threshold of the firestorms, Göring and Himmler started immunizing the Old Towns with a white lime and saline solution.[3] Thousands of buildings steeped in tradition were limed, including the Wartburg Castle. This disintegrated the treated wooden parts, but by no means made them fireproof. In the fall, a list of buildings to be protected was published, but the guards were helpless in the face of the fires. Islands within wide-area conflagrations could only be saved with luck.

The raid on Bonn in October 1944 started at 10:30 a.m.; the attackers were gone within thirty minutes. Dr. Franz Rademacher hurried from his place of work in the Rhenish State Museum to the monuments in the Old Town.[4] From the train overpass at Poppelsdorferallee, he could already see everything ablaze. The southern tract of the university was on fire all the way to the Rhine; nothing could be done about that. Schinkel's Academic Art Museum had so far caught fire only at a corner of the roof. Professors Richard Delbrueck and Ernst Langlotz just formed a bucket brigade; Rademacher joined them. While they were extinguishing the fire, the air-raid sirens sounded. The helpers fled to the museum basement, the flames continued their work. False alarm; the follow-up raid did not happen. Rademacher left the museum to the professors and ran down the blazing rows of houses on Remigiusstrasse to the market square. The wall of fire closed behind him. Up ahead at the Old Town Hall there was not a single person who was concerned about the already gutted building, which dated from the time of the electors. "My next destination was Beethoven's birthplace. I got there about noon." The house was undamaged except for shattered windows. Danger threatened from the building next door to the north, which was burning from the roof to the floorboards. Hasselbach the castellan opened up when he heard the loud shouting. Some soldiers were standing around in the corridors; they had no idea it was a memorial, but for thirty minutes helped carry some pictures into the cellar, then disappeared. The main inventory at the Beethoven house had long since been put in storage elsewhere.

Hasselbach and Rademacher decided to defend the building at three points: no more sparks could be allowed to hit the rotting roof truss, the window openings had to be cleared of shutters and curtains and watched, and the cellar was unpredictable. The tobacco stores from the Quantius company in the cellar next door were smoldering. The usual hole had been broken open in the thick wall separating the cellars, so the fire could spread through at any time. Small explosions sounded constantly next door. Hasselbach closed the hold with an iron plate and kept it wetted down with water from tubs kept nearby. Quantius was burning away on its own, but not far away to the north a conflagration was roaring. "You could see a huge glaring wall radiating tremendous heat." It moved forward to the Adam furnishings store, diagonally across the street. There were piles of mattresses in there.

Rademacher broke into Adam's, threw mattresses and blankets out the window, which attracted an audience. He called to them to bring the things to the Jesuit church as a night camp for the homeless. "Unfortunately, one teenage boy was the only one who seriously helped out." Hasselbach had a bad heart and was exhausted. The fire sprang over to the furniture storage, from there to the warehouse, and from there to the old roof trusses at Bonngasse nos. 21 and 23 across the way. At the northern end of Bonngasse, the blaze was already arching out the windows over the street. Only a fire engine could protect the Beethoven House from that. At the nearest fire-protection reservoir at the marketplace, Rademacher found a fire-brigade crew with an available pump, but it broke apart as they were transporting it.

Major Brandt at the air-raid protection control center yelled that no fire engines were free. "I retorted: 'To save the Beethoven House it must be possible to free up a fire engine in Bonn.'" A fire captain put in his two cents; yes, he could make one available. "Where is the Beethoven House?" asked Brandt. The captain said he knew and he could be there in fifteen minutes. Rademacher ran back and cleared the furniture from the street. At five o'clock, the fire engine arrived and hoses were laid to the reservoir at the market. When the pumps started, the building next to the Jesuit church collapsed, burying and tearing the hoses. They were dug out and patched, but now the water pressure was insufficient to reach the attics at house numbers 21 and 23. "The hose lines were pulled up two flights in the Beethoven House and the fire was fought from the windows there." After an hour the fires in the buildings were extinguished. From the glowing stumps of the ceiling beams, firefighters quickly wet down the Beethoven House, "and after seven hours I could go home, relieved knowing that in the severely damaged Old Town of Bonn, the birthplace of its greatest son could be saved." All because of a serendipity named Rademacher.

In Stuttgart, the house that Eduard Mörike died in burned down; in Bayreuth, the tomb of Franz Liszt; in Hanover's St. John's Court and City Church, the grave of Leibniz; in Hamburg, the birthplace of Johannes Brahms; in Frankfurt on the Oder, the birthplace of Heinrich von Kleist; in Hanau, the birthplace of the Brothers Grimm; in Eisenach, the Luther House.

The regime could not expend the effort necessary to save monuments and building complexes given the sparse teams available even for the protection of life and limb. So protection of stone remained limited to memorabilia. Portals, figures, monuments, Roland's columns, and fountains were wrapped up and enclosed in walls. The Bamberg Horseman was surrounded at first by a wooden structure filled with sandbags and later replaced by an octagonal brick tower, encased in plaster, and covered with a conical block of reinforced concrete. Angled, broken channels were cut for ventilation purposes. The tomb of St. Sebald in Nuremberg received a similar shell. A forty-six-foot high stamped concrete wall protected the west portal of Nuremberg's St. Lorenz Church.

Relics were thought to have a perpetual guarantee, such as that provided by steel mattresses in front of the Tiepolo frescoes in the Würzberg residential palace. But such coverings could no longer be supplied by as early as mid-1942. The burlap for sandbags was in short supply, and there was no wood for the formwork for concrete screens. Paper sacks with lean concrete were used instead to pack the portals of the cathedrals in Cologne, Freiburg, Xanten, Münster, and Paderborn, as well as for the Beautiful Fountain in Nuremberg and the equestrian statue of Frederick the Great along the boulevard Unter den Linden in Berlin.

If an explosive entered such a casing, the protective effect became destructive instead. Pieces of stone were hurled like shells into the artworks. The stone remained ambivalent. Church windows that were walled up warded off flying sparks, but it hindered the air circulation that the frescoes needed to keep mold from destroying them. Church paintings faded away gruesomely. Without any packing materials, it was also hard to help the sculpture and relief ornamentation. Improved explosives made it necessary to have secure encasements shaped like the objects to be protected, with reinforced concrete. There was nothing of the sort available. At their last meeting in Eger, the Luftwaffe and police representatives could not offer the curators of the monuments any blastproof, fragment-proof walls. By the summer of 1944, the immovable cultural assets were virtually undefended in face of the finale of fire. They had been abandoned.

The photographs were their death masks. At least we know roughly what Ulm once looked like.

Hirschstrasse, with its steep gabled, narrow patrician houses leading to the cathedral, was completely destroyed in December 1944, as were the seats of the guilds from the sixteenth century, the *Kornhaus* (granary), and the *Zeughaus* (arsenal). In the fire raid of December 17, which blotted out two-thirds of the city center, the *Seelhaus*, founded around 1400, could not be protected separately. This early evidence of Christian devotion was founded by nuns as an asylum for people with infectious diseases. The city hall and *Schwörhaus* (Oath House) were both destroyed. Despite the fifty individual fires on its roof, the cathedral could be saved by its own firefighting squad, thanks to the iron roof truss that was added in 1880. It now stood out tall like a bare trunk, having been robbed of its "foliage" at its entrances on Walfischgasse and Hirschstrasse.

Potsdam's historic constructions, the works of Schlüter, Schinkel, and Knobelsdorff, were reduced by 47 percent in the evening hours of April 14, 1945.[5] To that end, Bomber Command needed five hundred airplanes and 1,700 tons of bombs. It was its last major raid, with an impressive target and an aftermath of five thousand dead, more than the total dead in the years 1940 and 1941 throughout all of the Reich. The court and garrison church where Frederick the Great was buried burned, as did the Potsdam city castle, a specimen of Prussian baroque.

The bomber hammer struck down on the strict stateliness of entire streets and building ensembles because the stone had a soul. The building structure was an educator that silently taught beauty and form, measure and aim. The bomb was also an educator, and it judged power and powerlessness. Someone without a defense who cannot appeal the verdict is powerless. If he is defeated then he is subjugated. The subjugator cannot be made accountable in the name of a religious, legal, or moral obligation. Because he *is* the religion, law, morality, *iustus iudex ultionis.* He shares his authority with no statutes; he is the ruler of the ruled. Potsdam was destroyed in order to annul the history of Prussian militarism.

England was often and willingly allied with Prussian militarism, but that is not the point here. It waged war against the demon. The demon was an extremely difficult target. A monster and his tools of power had bodily contours, whereas a demon was a spirit, a jinn hidden in some vessel. Whoever destroyed the vessel did not necessarily hit the jinn; it was flexible and moved on. Each and every vessel that could offer the demon a future abode had to be broken in an attempt to track him down. With Potsdam's ruin on April 14, the bombers were hot on the demon's trail. The mythical stone of Potsdam and Nuremberg was triumphantly toppled. Its leveling spoke to the attacker: the enemy had been edified by it, but would no longer.

The bombardment of Giessen meant absolutely nothing to the bombardier. He filed down the town of 47,000 in twenty-seven raids from September 1944 to March 1945 and did not in any way imagine that the Hessian half-timbered town was a Nazi shrine. A small city was simply swept away, because the bomber was a sweeper. One-third of the 250 Lancasters of No. 5 Bomber Group aimed for the railway yards on December 6, 1944, and two-thirds worked on the Old Town, which was lost a short time later.

In contrast to the artful countenance of Potsdam, façades such as the Hirsch apothecary with the strange corner oriel; the old-fashioned professors' house; and a box with many windows that had once been the Paedagogium, a preparatory boarding school, were a family album. Nothing but the stones have passed on the familiarity of distant places. They were found, transformed, left behind, and they set—in addition to a lifespan—a second measure of time. History is that second time. Stone gave it a physicality and structure. The fifteenth-century city hall, with slated Renaissance gables and set on angular columns; the Old Castle at Brandplatz, the castle of the Hessian landgrave with a keep from the fourteenth century that became a royal court in the nineteenth century and was later covered with Renaissance elements; the Burgmannen House of 1349, one of Hesse's oldest half-timbered buildings; the classicist Old Clinic of 1819; the art nouveau theater of 1906—they all communicated their origins. Forms and patinas were communicative even before any academic interpretation. They generated a sound the people could simply hear. Bomber Command eliminated this resonance in the stone all across the country. Now it is missing.

Remote monuments and stone caves sheltered the movable art treasures. Without these evacuations the cultural history stored in paper, wood, and canvas would have survived the air war only in fragments. It was not always easy to determine what was stationary and what was portable. The Gothic sculptures on the pillars in the high choir of the Cologne cathedral were not put there with any intention of their changing locations before the Last Judgment.[6] Those finely modeled figures weighing a ton held themselves up, along with baldachins and consoles, with rusty old doweled joints that could not be

13. Peller House, Nuremberg.
Source: Stadtarchiv Nürnberg.

undone without breaking them. The sandbag packing that towered up on wooden supports was both effective protection against fragments and a fire hazard. Replacing the planks with correspondingly steep, massive walling risked overloading the ground, which was hollow with crypts and vaults. A cathedral can be neither armored nor dismantled.

The monumental furnishings of the baroque organ fronts, high retables, heavy pulpits, and pews refused to be transported. That which served worship was as firm as the firmament and sought no other abode. The doweled joints and timbering of the parts were built for eternity, and the totally rusted iron nails from the Middle Ages in the tannin of the old oak wood made it possible only to remove individual figures and triptychs, whereas the main structure was as immovable as the pillars and arches. Its stability also resisted being walled in. The wood required air circulation, but airholes drilled in the walled-in protective spaces created an oven effect. There was also a scarcity of work crews and experts to carry out these complex rescue operations. The call to arms left only aging guards at these sites; nightly transportation or firefighting actions in burning church wings were beyond the realm of what was possible. In Dortmund, on the other hand, a seventy-year-old cabinetmaker appeared at the Church of St. Peter and knew how to dismantle the five-ton carved Flemish altar. Before the First Battle of the Ruhr could destroy it, the altar traveled to a remote corner of the Weser valley and, as luck would have it, the Weser was not flooded when the Eder valley dam was breached. In the Church of St. Peter, built in 1353, the direct hit, which ripped apart the northern wall of the choir and all the vaults, would certainly have destroyed it.

The most endangered elements were the stained-glass paintings in medieval churches. They shattered even if a bomb hit a great distance away. At the cathedrals in Cologne, Xanten, and Altenberg, as well as in numerous city and village churches, glass painters removed the old panes from their fittings and packed them in crates to be brought to dry cellars, first those from the Middle Ages and then those from the Renaissance. Having been made for the light, they turned milky and disintegrated at the slightest dampness. In all of the Rhineland by the middle of 1942, there was hardly any original glass still in its original fittings.

At first, remote areas were sought to store the artwork, open countryside far from military and war-relevant facilities, from prominent points on the ground, and as close as possible to mountains and forests. Isolated fortresses and castles with solid outer walls and massive, vaulted rooms were well-suited as storerooms. Castles became less suitable after the beginning of the fire war because of their enormous roof areas. Moated castles, on the other hand, had fabulous fire-protection reservoirs, though the dampness of their valley locations damaged the stored items. The optimal site, a high fortified castle on steep cliffs, let bombs slide off and had good air circulation. Less useful were the lower ground floors of larger hospitals and nursing homes, because the heated rooms were bad for panel paintings and furniture accustomed to the cold. Concrete bunkers were useless because of condensation.

When the air war extended to rural quarters, it forced the objects of cultural value to travel even farther, into subterranean stone, casemates of fortresses, and mining shafts and adits. When necessary, people managed to cope with dampness and lack of ventilation. But carpets, tapestries, paints, and paper would never adapt to such a climate; they rotted away from mildew, mold, moths, woodworms, and flies. Paintings that had spent years protected from daylight lost their color. In order to stack artwork underground, humidity and ventilation had to be strictly controlled. The Ehrenbreitstein fortress near Koblenz had already been set up for archival storage before the war; on top of that came the inventories of the Berlin museums. Similar services were provided by underground installations in the Nuremberg castle. Berlin had originally planned to build subterranean bunkers for its inexhaustible assets, but followed the better advice of the general director of the Prussian State Archives in 1943. Disused salt and potash mines proved to be excellent sites for the storage of endangered cultural treasures. They were dry, clean, deep, and extended for miles. There were sufficient areas available in Württemberg-Baden, in Austria, and in the "potash triangle" in central Germany between Hanover and Magdeburg.

In 1943, the Prussian State Archives was the first to start storing its documents in the salt mine near Stassfurt, just in time for the Battle of Berlin. The Berlin museums followed suit. Stuttgart's museums found huge, bombproof subterranean rooms without bracing supports in the Kochendorf salt mine. But the entry shafts and drawing cages had not been built with the winged altarpieces in mind. In Bavaria, the only means of transportation large enough was the Bavarian State Theater's trucks for transporting backdrops. The usual vehicle used was a well-sprung furniture truck. Shipping personnel and curators emptied out the cultural landscape until it was as bare as a house ready for demolition; then the bombers could come. Very large paintings were removed from the frames, wrapped in tissue paper, and carefully rolled onto wood rollers.

In order to limit losses, the collections were decentralized. The Rubens paintings should not all be stored in the same place, nor under any circumstances should too many of the highest quality works. The most valuable pieces were always placed near the exit. A reliable guard lived as close as possible to the exiled inventory, counted it daily, rotated the batches so they would get air, opened the packaging at regular intervals, monitored the conditions, and filed reports.

Experts thought the artworks were not robust enough to withstand the move to inadequate storage sites, so even transportable works were kept in one location. In the haste and shortages of the bombing

war, thousands of tons of cultural assets were set in motion on barges or horse- and cattle-drawn carts, wrapped in wool blankets and
loosely thrown together. Traffic bottlenecks led to utterly intolerable,
draining delays. In the haste of flight, with makeshift coverings and
crashing about on precarious routes, the cultural legacy of a nation
made its way underground. The only alternative was phosphorus and
explosion. This weapon divided the world into combustible and non-
combustible. People were too mobile to burn. Technology and nature
had tenacious ways of resisting. Railroads and tool machines, forests
and harvests did not respond the way the magnesium-thermite sticks
and blockbusters wanted. Culture burned better than anything else.

Older history manifested itself in stone and paper, wood, glass,
cloth, leather—in other words, kindling. Stone was its venue and
paper, its memory. In Frankfurt, a third of the municipal archives
burned, but not the Golden Bull of 1356, Germany's oldest written
imperial constitution. If it had been lost, its contents would have remained. Still, the document was its own vault and final evidence.
Regarding most documents, no one knew what they contained. Families had collected bundles of manuscripts, files, letters, and pictures
over the course of generations. They often packed what they considered most important into their air-raid suitcases. Churches, industry,
and the nobility hoarded papers and lists that along with state and
local archives stored information that will never be deciphered; they
remain mummified pieces of time. The fire war's eradication of this
testimony is immeasurable.

Since time immemorial, people have removed what could be
saved, the public and secret archives, in times of war. Files are booty.
As early as the summer crisis in 1938, institutions west of the Rhine
had considered storing selected items. As enemy forces approached,
politically and historically sensitive archival materials were to be evacuated. Materials from upper floors could be relocated, thus rendering
them immune to dangers from the air. As soon as the war started,
church records, registers of vital statistics, and official files of communities beyond the Siegfried Line were brought behind the line.
After the early victories on the western front, the authorities took a
deep breath—nothing more could happen to the Rhineland. Based
on the experience of German archivists regarding the large-scale relocation of French materials, the damages that had been incurred
from the transport made it clear that this time the assets should not
leave their safe storage. The experts' reservations against scattering

everything without a custodian were again confirmed. The only thing that helped against the danger of bombs was to fortify the stacks.

Modern archive buildings offered the greatest security; that remained the motto even after the Lübeck raid. Wall up the windows, put in shrapnel-resistant walls, cover the stairwells, employ guards, divide up large rooms with firewalls, install fireproof doors, and eliminate the grated, chimney-forming floor structure.

The larger part of the Reich believed they were unaffected by aircraft approaches, and only the most suspicious complained that they would not be able to counteract the destruction by improvising when necessary. They were not prepared. But no building could have been prepared to hold out against the blast of shock and fire waves. Even archival stacks made of steel and concrete could not protect paper from fire. If locked in safes, it would simply roast and char. Even the vaults of the Reich bank in the Berlin mint did not stand up to a direct hit; they were not built to do that. Stored museum pieces were simply smashed. On the other hand, the basement vault of the German Ministry of Economy withstood the raids, although the massive building was gutted by fire from the roof to the basement. A mound of dirt several yards high managed to preserve the catalog of the Prussian State Library. A bank safe in Giessen's city center protected a jewel of the city, the "Giessen Papyri" of the university library, including a parchment with a segment of a Gothic Bible translation, the oldest in Germany.[7] A nearby hit cracked the safe, which allowed groundwater to seep in, and the papyri were severely damaged.

On September 3, 1942, the Karlsruhe State Library was hit and lost almost all of its 360,000 books; only five thousand survived. Doubters felt confirmed that the bombs created total destruction. The archives located exclusively in major cities were at great risk, which was temporarily averted only by dividing up the materials. They were distributed to alternative sites in the parish; the normal risks of getting caught in ground combat were another question. That problem did not come until 1945.

After the night of March 8, 1943, when Nuremberg suffered its third major raid, the Bavarian State Archives decided that "our inventory can only be saved in hiding."[8] On March 15—there had been no major losses up to then—Commissioner for Archive Protection Ernst Zipfel, director of the Reich Archives in Potsdam, decreed that materials should be evacuated as a precaution. Eight months later came the first massive damages, in the Hanover State Archives, which lost the old core holdings and all of the finding aids and indices to the archival materials. From that point on, the institutes were in a race against time.

By March 1943, the Secret State Archives in Berlin had relocated 8.5 percent of their huge inventory. The top sixth floor of the stacks was empty. Once the major raids of the Battle of Berlin started, the fifth level was also evacuated. Anticipating fire, the archivists worked doggedly to clear out levels three and four. On December 29 the bomb hit, but found only part of one neglected set of shelves. The mountains of rubble made it increasingly difficult to move things out. Sixty schoolchildren were brought in and they worked without a break. The feared direct hit struck the massive building on February 15, 1944. Its upper tracts were blown away, but they no longer contained any archival materials. Forty-eight percent of the total inventory was in storage elsewhere. Archive asylums were set up in remote castles, monasteries, manor houses, forest wardens' homes, water towers, churches, parish houses, schools, rock tunnels, wine cellars, mines, and fortresses.

The commissioner for archive protection relocated state and municipal reserves and advised the small, nonstate collections. The army and the churches hid their own historical materials, the latter rather successfully. Starting in the spring of 1944, a veritable hiding fever became widespread. It even reached the small and medium-sized towns, causing extreme shortages in crate-slat wood, string, and sacks, and there was much daily bickering over transport space and fuel. As of June 1, 1944, 80 to 90 percent of the total holdings of twenty-seven of the ninety-six archives under the auspices of the commissioner for archive protection, and half the holdings of fifty-three of them, had been brought to safety. By November 1944, 2,250,000 documents, 500,000 manuscripts and official records, and 1,750,000 file bundles had been relocated.[9] At that time, the archives had an average staff of four or five people.

Once the process of bringing the materials to their remote homes had been halfway successful, there was no such thing as "remoteness" anywhere in Germany. When the Swabian town of Löwenstein in the Löwenstein mountains was destroyed, for example, Stuttgart's city archives burned. On the threshold to the ground offensive on two fronts, all terrain became a potential combat zone. The pretreatment during the transportation offensive forced re-storage underground, in rock, salt, and potash mines. The records from the eastern front that had been stored in the state archives in Marburg were then relocated to the Grasleben salt mine near Helmstedt. In seven train cars the Königsberg State Archives arrived with the papers of the Teutonic Order and the dukes of Prussia. They were joined by five cars of the Reich Archives of Danzig, which had formerly been stored in the Marienburg castle and at the Bismarckian estate in Varzin. In February 1945, the Secret State Archives in Berlin recalled their possessions from Lübben, which was near the front, and transported them to a shaft near Schönebeck on the Elbe. The archives from southeastern Germany moved from their alternative locations deep in Burgenland and Styria to the caves of the Salzkammergut. Prussian archives in western Germany from Kiel to Wiesbaden saved themselves in the final months in the Grasleben and Salzdetfurth salt mines; southern German holdings hid in the Kochendorf mine near Heilbronn. In December 1944, relocation began from the largest safe place, the Ehrenbreitstein fortress. Stored here were handwritten manuscripts; official documents of emperors, kings, and popes; apographs of documents and letters; medieval and early modern rural customary law rulings; and cadastral registers, which now made their way through railroad blockades and on freight barges to Salzdetfurth and Grasleben. The adit tunnels of the Hain iron and steelworks near Siegen had been provided with heat, ventilation, and humidity control in August 1944, so they could be used to store the relics of Charlemagne and the cathedral treasures from Aachen, Essen, and Trier.[10] At some places, the tunnel ceiling was raised so the flags of the Hohenzollern army from the Tannenberg cenotaph would fit. But the transport of the flags could not be carried out, because of the danger of air raids.

About half of the German archival records were removed from the impact of the fire war; the other half faced it, and four-fifths burned. The Army Archives in Potsdam died along with the German army in April 1945, including all the files on the wars of 1864, 1866, 1870, and 1871, and both world wars. The March 1945 attack on Würzburg eliminated the files of the electorate of Mainz and the prince-bishopric of Würzburg, which had been stored in the castle. The Darmstadt firestorm took with it the documents of the central Hessian authorities of the nineteenth and twentieth centuries. And Munich lost the records on Bavarian history of the Ministries of Finance, Justice, and Culture, as well as twenty thousand bundles of files on the Bavarian army; Hanover lost almost all its inventory on the history of the kingdom of Hanover in the nineteenth century, most official documents including the world's last papyrus, a papal certificate of 1026 for the bishopric of Hildesheim. In the Prussian Secret State Archives in Berlin, a large portion of the files on Brandenburg-Prussian history were lost. A freight barge carrying the files of the Lower Rhine Archives sank in the Mittelland Canal and remained underwater for five months. The archives of the Augsburg trade association were lost, as were the bishop's archives of Osnabrück. Dortmund lost three-quarters of its city archives. The archives of the Friedrich Krupp works suffered serious losses; the Protestant parish archives in Bochum-Langendreer burned, as did the Catholic parish archives in Dinslaken, and so on.

Munich's fame as an artistic city was founded by Albrecht V (1550–1579). He placed Johann Jacob Fugger in his services, who moved to Munich along with two librarians, a Belgian and an Italian. Fugger's book collection was made up largely of handwritten manuscripts and books published prior to 1500, which were later called incunabula, "from the cradle." Forty thousand were passed down, giving an impression of what the late Middle Ages considered worth reading and pondering. About two hundred copies of each work were printed, and roughly half a million survived in all.

The printers did not want to demonstrate the advances and advantages of printing; instead, they imitated the handwritten character and the ornamentation of drawn handwriting. At first, a rubricator marked the print with chapter and page headings or initials. Wood or metal cuts illustrated the text. The fonts used, especially Gothic ones, were varied, and expressed the taste of the bookmaker, who, like the hand scribe, liked to add the place of printing, year, and his name at the end, as a colophon. The incunabula were inventoried starting in 1904; since 1925, an overall catalog of the incunabula was printed. The first type register was published between 1905 and 1924 in five volumes, so that incunabula printed without a company name could be identified according to the respective master printing workshop. Most of these early books were kept in public libraries.

Johann Jacob Fugger laid the foundation for the court library in Munich, which Elector Maximilian I, a friend of historiography, transformed from a collection into a source of scholarship, a place to store the knowledge of the age and all ages.[11] That required a central catalog. Maximilian ordered the monasteries of the land, the oldest places of study, to submit a description of their manuscripts, to create a general index of all his libraries. As of 1663, a copy of every book printed in Bavaria or by a Bavarian author found a place in the court library. By around 1800, it contained about 100,000 volumes. Three years later, the monasteries were suppressed and their book and manuscript collections were carted to Munich, which soon also attracted the inventories of the cities that had previously been self-governing under the emperor and now belonged to Bavaria. Consequently it became the largest collection of books in the German language.

In the eighteenth century, the court library was located in twenty-four rooms of Fugger's palace. When new arrivals brought the total above the one million mark, the hall library was abandoned in favor of stacks, in a monumental new building on Ludwigstrasse. It survived the first nine bombing raids on Munich without a scratch. On the night of Tuesday, March 9, 1943, Bomber Command dropped seventy thousand incendiary bombs.[12] The attack started around midnight, the guards patrolled the attic storage space and removed about thirty magnesium alloy–thermite sticks, almost as if they were performing a drill. At the same time, news came in that a large fire had started in the central building. They could hardly believe it, since observers had gone through there two minutes earlier; in that time a fire fifty feet across had developed. A little later, the entire area was in flames. The column of heat shot through the glass roof, creating a chimney, and a flame darted up 150 feet into the night sky. That was the work of liquid incendiaries at the most vulnerable point, where old-fashioned wooden structures and the glass roof virtually invited a major conflagration.

A strong southwesterly wind bent the flames from the central building toward the northeast wing. The six defenders did all they could to keep a connecting line open between the two wings of the building and to block the flames from the northeastern tract. That meant sacrificing the theology room and its precious Bible collection at the axis of the complex. At one o'clock in the morning, the first fire engine arrived from the National Theater. The staff escorted firefighters through the labyrinth of stairs and corridors and then turned their efforts to saving books.

From two o'clock onward, a growing troop of civilians and military gathered at the State Library, and by morning there were about a thousand people. Thanks to these helpers, the manuscripts and incunabula, the music collection, and the catalog were removed in time. They were placed in the nearby St. Ludwig's Church. In the early morning hours, the blaze seemed quenched. Dawn had not yet broken. The inner courtyard was filled with a chaos of hoses, pumps, and lines leading into the building and crawling up the stairways. The flames came to life, rebelled, turned against the northwest wing, and eradicated the whole second floor. The central section was still smoldering; black clouds of smoke raced through the courtyard, the northwest wing was a torch glowing blindingly. The blaze of the library loomed up from Ludwigstrasse into the dark sky. The south wind increased, sweeping down the breadth of the blaze and picking up burning and glowing scraps of books; a snowlike flurry of glowing bits of paper floated through the air.

Down the street, between the library and St. Ludwig's, the book carriers scurried around with their arms full, all the while taking care that their clothing did not catch fire. In the dim aisle of the church, in nooks and altars, the mountains of rescued books grew. Around 8:00 a.m., the fire died down a second time, but it fooled the firefighters yet again. A fire had lodged unnoticed in a false floor and it flared up in the afternoon, took sudden hold of two rooms on the third floor in the northwest wing, and devoured the North American collection and all the holdings on non-European geography, all of which had been considered perfectly safe.

The last embers went out after four weeks. The inner courtyard had a mountain of 45,000 cubic yards of rubble reaching up to the second floor. The Bavarian State Library lost half a million books on the night of March 9, which was 23 percent of the total inventory. The subject areas affected were classical philology, archeology and art history, theology, and non-European geography. Irreplaceable was the complete collection of the Academica, the publications of scholarly societies and academies. The total losses were comparable to the burning of the library in Alexandria in the third century. Only four months later, the state and university libraries in Hamburg lost 625,000 books. Never before in the history of humanity had so many books burned.

On August 28, 1939, the Heidelberg university library had already moved the medieval *Codex Manesse*,[13] which was sent east to Erlangen in inner Franconia, a region considered rather safe. That would change, so the Heidelberg stores left the Erlangen cellars to move yet deeper into the natural rock under the Nuremberg castle. The Prussian State Library in Berlin entrusted their treasures to the vaulted safe of the nearby Reich Ministry of Economy, but they kept the library open and functioning until 1943. Not until after that time did the entire inventory go on the lam. One-and-three-quarter million books were hidden in a potash mine on the Werra River; another part went to the Tepl monastery in Bohemia and the salt well near Schönebeck on the Elbe. Three hundred tons of books were packed loosely onto barges that traveled along the Spree River, headed for southern and western Germany; they were transshipped six times in the process. The most bitter losses were in the Berlin incunabula section; 2,150 books were destroyed, which was the greater part of the collection, including all of the section on the Orient.

Of the forty million books in Germany's scholarly libraries, thirty million had been relocated during the war.[14] They took the same routes as the archival materials. Manuscripts and incunabula were first sheltered in basements. When on September 9, 1941, the Kassel State Library burned down along with 350,000 books, the path of the books that could still be saved led to rock cellars of breweries, manor houses, mountain castles, or back to the monasteries. Leipzig opened a depot in the Battle of Nations monument. Bad luck struck Heidelberg's university library; after it had evacuated fifty tons of books to Mentzingen Castle near Bruchsal, the castle was shelled by fighter-bombers and caught fire. The main Heidelberg library building was left unscathed. The Saxon State Library in Dresden lost the mathematical manuscripts of Albrecht Dürer and the score of Bach's *Mass in B Minor*, due to a broken water pipe at their evacuation site.

Coal and fruit barges, trucks, and—for the most precious, hand-carried treasures—passenger cars all led to the books' final station under the ground. Salt and potash mines offered the most favorable air; sandstone caves were too damp. Half of the possessions of the German Society of Oriental Studies (DMG) in Halle were ruined. Book crates made specifically to fit in the salt mine lined the tunnels for miles. When no crate wood remained, the books were stacked as high as people could reach, with a makeshift covering of linen cloth, tent tarpaulins, packing paper, or nothing at all. But the books needed oil paper that kept away the problematic salt dust. When the books were returned to the light, the hygroscopic particles sucked in moisture and smeared. Only after undergoing an extensive restoration process were the books readable again. Damages were also caused when unpacked inventories were transported. Some books fell in the water when hurriedly loaded onto boats, or they slipped out of train cars and were never recovered at all. When stored in damp places, mold was rampant; elsewhere, they were ravaged by hungry mice.

In order to reduce risk, the institutes divided their collections among a number of locations. Freiburg's university library was split up among eleven shelters.[15] Twenty-three crates of manuscripts and incunabula were taken in by the Pfullendorf prison; eighty thousand volumes were held for safekeeping by the St. Trudpert Benedictine abbey in the Münster valley. The Hirzberg tunnel at the eastern outskirts of the city, a heated and concrete-lined dungeon dug deep into the rock, took the incunabula when doubts were raised about the prison. The tunnel in turn had to be made available to military offices, so the early books went far into the high Black Forest. At the malt threshing floor of the Rothaus state brewery, a deep cellar was previously available to safeguard the works. The synagogue in Sulzburg, which had already been abandoned in 1933, protected thirty thousand books as well as scientific and medical journals.

Freiburg's worst damages proved to be a mold that grew on the thirty thousand books from the section on dogmatics and pastoral theology, which had been stored in a malt factory near Lahr. Direct bomb hits on the office of the archbishopric in Freiburg and in the Löwenbräu brewery, with its cellar twenty-six feet below the street, threw the shelves holding six hundred theological incunabula as well volumes of archeology, music, and Anglo-American literature to the ground, but damages were limited to disorder.

Books that remained at their original sites largely burned. The German Library in Leipzig stored 1.6 million books at ten different places for safekeeping in the Ore Mountains and the Unstrut valley, but retained 400,000 in its basement corridors, of which fifty thousand burned on December 4, 1943. Trusting in good fortune, on December 11, 1944, the Giessen university library lost nine-tenths of its inventory, which had comprised 520,000 books and 300,000 doctoral dissertations. The catalogs survived. Münster, which evacuated its libraries too late, lost 360,000 books, two-thirds of the university holdings.

Without the mass flight of the books, not much would have remained in Germany. Even considering all the effort that was made, two million of the 3.5 million books in Hessian libraries did not make it through the attack. The number of books lost from public facilities is estimated at eight million; private losses are unknown. The fire war did not prevail over paper to the extent that paper's flammability might suggest, even though fire eliminated more paper than had ever been destroyed before. But paper has prevailed in the end. It lasts longer than fire.

EDITORIAL REMARKS

A LOT HAS BEEN WRITTEN about the air war, but for a long time that included nothing about the suffering on the ground. Cities published chronicles with figures and testimonies over the last fifty years that seldom corresponded to scientific standards. The author has used official records and, with caution, these publications also. It would be a public project to critically review the inventories of the city archives and reconstruct the history of the bombing of German cities. Up to now, there is not even a reliable estimate of the number of casualties. The five-digit figures in Pforzheim and Swinemünde, for instance, put them among the greatest tragedies of World War II, yet they are virtually absent from historiography. A review of the existing statistics is a pressing desideratum. The best available eyewitness accounts, those that Anneliese Barbara Baum compiled in the mid- to late 1980s regarding the Bonn air raids, show how much has been saved in the memories of the generation who experienced the raids. This knowledge should be recorded without delay.

In certain areas, our knowledge of the air war is based on the achievements of historians who dedicated a life of research to the task; in particular, Horst Boog and Olaf Groehler should be mentioned. The author is indebted to their work. As a scholarly zenith he acknowledges the major documentation published in 1988 by Hartwig Beseler and Niels Gutschow, *Kriegsschicksale deutscher Architektur*. It is limited to the former area of the Federal Republic of Germany (that is, former West Germany) and is supplemented by the work by an East German writers' group, *Schicksale Deutscher Baudenkmale im Zweiten Weltkrieg*, published in 1980.

The Anglo-American part of the Strategic Air War has been outstandingly documented in the official historical works by Webster and Frankland, Craven and Cate, the *United States Strategic Bombing Survey*, and a continuous stream of sound monographs.

Finally, thanks are due to my assistants, sponsors, and those institutions that made this work possible. The generosity of the Berlin Senate Library, the library of the Academy of the Bundeswehr in Strausberg, the German Federal Archives in Berlin, and the Military Archives in Freiburg paved the way to the corpus of sources. The English version benefits from the care and art of its translator, Allison Brown.

AFTERWORD

FOR AMERICAN AND BRITISH READERS

THE STORY OF *Der Brand* (*The Fire*) is a 500,000-fold journey. That is how many readers have made their way through the seven chapters. They have by no means all arrived at the same picture of the events because every imagination reconstructs them in a different way and every heart gives rise to its own feelings. Since *Der Brand* deals with the manner of mass dying of German civilians in a world war, the echo of emotions cannot remain neutral. The reader is biased and so is the author.

The book aroused the passions of Germans in early 2003, at the same time as the public eye here was on the war in Iraq, which I supported. My readers, however, asked me if the Americans had still not learned anything. But had Dresden been bombed with the same result as Baghdad, there would have been no story for me to tell of the intentional mass killing of urban residents. No air force chief of staff today would command the annihilation of 900,000 enemy noncombatants, as Sir Charles Portal did in 1942. One of my most highly esteemed British colleagues reminded me on television about how many Germans had voted and cheered for Hitler. Did every one of them therefore deserve the death penalty? If so, there would still be many in the world to punish for their "sympathies for political monsters." The judges at the International Military Tribunal at Nuremberg, especially the Soviets, would in any case have gone pale in view of such justice by bombing. And how could the bomb distinguish between Nazis, anti-Nazis, and the 70,000 children who were killed, who did not even know what a Nazi was?

No interviewer with the English-language press failed to ask if it was not Hitler who started both the war and the bombing of cities. "They that sow the wind shall reap the whirlwind." If only that were true! A characteristic of air wars is that those who sow the wind do not reap the whirlwind and those who reap the whirlwind did not sow the wind. One of the sowers was certainly Field Marshal Hugo Sperrle, who as commander in chief of German Air Fleet 3 led the bombing of London and Coventry. Tens of thousands of British citizens died by his hand. In 1948 he stood before the U.S. military tribunal in Nuremberg. His prosecutor was the great American international law scholar and historian Brigadier General Telford Taylor. But Taylor did not even charge him with that bloody act—though 40,000 victims were a lot even by Nuremberg standards. That act did not appear in the proceedings; the charges included only the Russian prisoners of war allegedly assigned under Sperrle's command to build military facilities. That is prohibited by the Geneva Convention. The judges acquitted Sperrle due to insufficient evidence. Why was his documented annihilation of London schoolchildren, hospital patients, and churchgoers not consider a wrong? And why were the firestorms that consumed the schoolchildren of Hamburg, Dresden, and Cologne their proper punishment for Sperrle's unpunished attacks? Why was every soldier in the Nazi Wehrmacht—even the Waffen SS—who was captured in the invaded countries of Poland, Russia, or Belgium taken into custody and treated and protected according to the Geneva Convention while his wife and child at home were outlaws? The enemies could do what they wanted with them, albeit only if the attack came from the air. If Charles Portal or Hugo Sperrle had run amok through Berlin or London with a machine gun, then Taylor would of course have charged him for the action. At least that is what he later wrote. According to the legal position in Nuremberg, it was not the willful killing of noncombatants that determined the crime, but the direction of fire. The horizontal fire of a machine gun is illegal; the vertical direction of the bomb munitions, on the other hand, is legal.

A major Egyptian newspaper did not support this legal perspective but instead commented on *Der Brand* by demanding that Churchill's mortal remains be exhumed and chopped up as punishment for his air war. With their moderate disposition, many Dutch people told me they felt the Anglo-American bombardment of German and Japanese cities was barbarous—and that of Dutch cities too. Citizens of

Rotterdam, the Hague, and Nijmegen burned and bled to death from aerial bombs. These were dropped from the planes of their German attackers and tormentors, as well as from those of their Allied liberators. Five times as many Dutch people were killed by the bombs of the liberators than by those of the subjugators. It could be that both kinds of death were equally tragic and cruel. But if a patient bleeds to death on an operating table, it still makes a difference whether the surgeon wanted to operate on him or strike him dead. Thus many readers viewed the operations described in Der Brand as a cure for the world and the victims as its "military necessity."

In an interview with a major Israeli newspaper, I described Churchill's situation in the years 1940 through 1943, when there was only one way left for him to hurt the Third Reich. Invisible and protected by the cover of night, bombs had to be dropped with lightning speed in the most inflammable residential areas of the cities. This had nothing to do with punishing Nazis; there is no evidence of that in the archives. Churchill had no opportunity to carry out "surgical strikes" on military objectives, so he destroyed what he could: civilians. "That," the Israeli interviewer said, "is what our suicide bombers also say."

I am familiar with the interpretation of mass annihilation as a "military necessity" from my earlier research on the Nuremberg trials. All of the Wehrmacht generals who were charged there defended themselves by saying that the enemy's killing of German civilians was a legitimate means by which to wage total war. In total war, the battle is waged not against the enemy armed forces, as was previously the case, but against the enemy population as a whole, they stressed, and in any case they had not done anything different.

There are records documenting German people's support for the killing of British civilians. I told my readers in Dresden that a V2 raid on London in February 1945 with 30,000 deaths would have had people in their city dancing in the streets. Civilians do not show mercy to civilians; pain comes from the destruction of my body, my loved ones, my city. Total war consumes the people totally, and their sense of humanity is the first thing to go. Everyone wishes the worst on everyone else, and it is not my profession's to judge who deserved or did not deserve what. Whoever opts for the "military necessities" can read what these looked like "on the ground." The story of this book is an international chain of passionate judgments. In Spain, a country in which the passions of the civil war that raged seventy years ago are cooling down, in which families are tired of asking if the fascist uncle or the Bolshevist cousin was rightly and necessarily massacred, I heard a six-word commentary of *Der Brand:* "It is an encyclopedia of pain."

JÖRG FRIEDRICH
BERLIN, MAY 2006

NOTES

1. Weapon

1. Krüger, *Die Geschichte der Bombenangriffe auf Wuppertal*, 41–42.
2. Here and following cited from Pogt, ed., *Vor fünfzig Jahren*.
3. Ibid., 47.
4. Ibid., 156ff.
5. Ibid., 89.
6. Ibid., 137.
7. Ibid., 118.
8. James K. McElroy, "The Work of the Fire Protection Engineers in Planning Fire Attacks," in *Fire and the Air War*, ed. Bond, 122–134.
9. MacBean and Hogen, *Bombs Gone*, 135.
10. Ibid., 135.
11. "Over-All Report (European Report #2)," in *United States Strategic Bombing Survey*, 1:2.
12. Middlebrook and Everitt, *The Bomber Command War Diaries*, 707.
13. Vogt and Brenne, *Krefeld im Luftkrieg*, 182ff.
14. Middlebrook and Everitt, *The Bomber Command War Diaries*, 240–256.
15. On statistics, see also ibid., 241, and *The Strategic Air War Against Germany: Report of the British Bombing Survey Unit*, 40ff.
16. Middlebrook, *The Schweinfurt-Regensburg Mission*, 243.
17. *The Strategic Air War Against Germany*, 36.
18. Middlebrook and Everitt, *The Bomber Command War Diaries*, 708.
19. Price, *Instruments of Darkness*, 191.
20. Crane, *Bombs, Cities, and Civilians*, 57.
21. Middlebrook, *The Schweinfurt-Regensburg Mission*, 228.
22. Middlebrook, *The Berlin Raids: RAF Bomber Command*, 58.
23. Ibid., 80.

24. Cooper, *Air Battle of the Ruhr*, 108.
25. Ibid., 61.
26. Middlebrook, *The Berlin Raids*, 26.
27. Cooper, *Air Battle of the Ruhr*, 44–45.
28. Garrett, *Ethics and Airpower in World War II*, 81.
29. Cooper, *Air Battle of the Ruhr*, 41.
30. Garrett, *Ethics and Airpower in World War II*, 82.
31. Crane, *Bombs, Cities, and Civilians*, 58.
32. Garrett, *Ethics and Airpower in World War II*, 82, citing Middlebrook, *The Battle of Hamburg*, 349.

2. Strategy

1. Hampe, *Der zivile Luftschutz*, 14; Groehler, *Bombenkrieg*, 316ff.
2. "Beobachtung von Bombenwirkung in Warschau," BA-MA RL 4, 335, 188; here: 199–200.
3. Churchill, "Shall We All Commit Suicide," in *Thoughts and Adventures*, 174–181.
4. Terraine, *The Right of the Line*, 9–10.
5. Colville, *Forges of Power*, 229. The number of airplanes mentioned is erroneous.
6. The number of bombers is erroneous, as is that cited in Saundby. See note 24, below.
7. PRO AIR 14/775, Air Ministry Directives, vol. 1, cited in Irving, *Churchill*, 406–407.
8. Irving, *Churchill*, 406–407.
9. Fröhlich, ed., *Die Tagebücher von Joseph Goebbels*, 4:296.
10. Liddell Hart, *History of the Second World War*, 103.
11. W. Hays Park, "Air War and the Laws of War," in *The Conduct of the Air War in the Second World War*, ed. Horst Boog, 341 (which cites Webster and Frankland, *Strategic Air Offensive*, 4:72, 4:78).
12. Fröhlich, ed., *Die Tagebücher von Joseph Goebbels*, 4:296.
13. Irving, *Churchill*, 406–407.
14. Domarus, *Hitler: Speeches and Proclamations*, 3:2086 (September 4, 1940).
15. Groehler, *Geschichte des Luftkriegs*, 264, 271.
16. Irving, *Rise and Fall of the Luftwaffe: The Life of Luftwaffe Marshall Erhard Milch*, 102.
17. Fröhlich, ed., *Die Tagebücher von Joseph Goebbels*, 4:318.
18. Ibid., 320.
19. Ibid.
20. Ibid., 363.
21. Ibid., 367.

22. Ibid., 402.

23. Ibid.

24. Saundby, *Air Bombardment*, 96. Erroneous figure regarding number of aircraft.

25. Liddell Hart, *History of the Second World War*, 106.

26. Hillgruber, *Hitlers Strategie*, 96.

27. Clark, *The Rise of the Boffins*, 86–87.

28. Ibid., 66.

29. Colville, *Forges of Power*, 194.

30. Ibid., 192.

31. Ibid., 194.

32. Terraine, *The Right of the Line*, 261.

33. Ibid., 259.

34. Ibid., 263–264.

35. Webster and Frankland, *Strategic Air Offensive*, 4:135ff.

36. Garrett, *Ethics and Airpower*, 91.

37. Webster and Frankland, *Strategic Air Offensive*, 4:205ff.

38. Boog, "The Anglo-American Strategic Air War Over Europe and German Air Defence," 516.

39. Webster and Frankland, *Strategic Air Offensive*, 1:323–324.

40. Harris, *Bomber Offensive*, 76.

41. Terraine, *The Right of the Line*, 476.

42. Cited in *The Cork Examiner* (June 3, 1942), translated from *Dokumente deutscher Kriegsschäden*, 2nd supplement (reports in the neutral press), 105–107.

43. Ibid.

44. Cited in *The Irish Independent* (June 1, 1942), translated from *Dokumente deutscher Kriegsschäden*, 2nd supplement (reports in the neutral press), 94.

45. Gilbert, *Second World War*, 352.

46. Terraine, *Right of the Line*, 505–506.

47. In Rumpf, "*Bomber Harris*"; first part cited from Harris, *Bomber Offensive*, 191–192.

48. BA R 19/34a, BL. 4L 134; *United States Strategic Bombing Survey*, vol. 2, therein: "Civilian Defense Division—Final Report (European Report #40)," 3–4.

49. Here and in the following: Verrier, *Bomber Offensive*, Appendix, doc. 2, "The Pointblank Offensive," 330–338.

50. *Handels- och Sjöfartstidning* (Göteborg, Sweden, March 13, 1943), translated from *Dokumente deutscher Kriegsschäden*, 2nd supplement (reports in the neutral press), 153–154.

51. Krüger, "Die Luftangriffe auf Essen 1940–1945," *Essener Beiträge*, 262, 275–276.

52. Cooper, *Air Battle of the Ruhr*, 55.

53. Hastings, *Bomber Command*, 202.
54. Ibid.
55. Hasenclever, *Die Zerstörung der Stadt Remscheid.*
56. Vogt and Brenne, *Krefeld im Luftkrieg*, 233.
57. Ibid., 228.
58. Garrett, *Ethics and Airpower*, 89–90.
59. Ibid., 99.
60. Ibid., 111.
61. Ibid., 113.
62. Ibid., 64.
63. Ibid., 71. See also Clark, *The Rise of the Boffins*, 84, 157, 219, 211–212, 226ff.
64. Ibid., 72.
65. Euler, *Als Deutschlands Dämme brachen*, 218–219.
66. PRO PREM 3/65, cited from Harris and Paxman, *A Higher Form of Killing*, 100.
67. Harris and Paxman, *A Higher Form of Killing*, 101.
68. Ibid.
69. PRO AIR 20/341 (London).
70. Hampe, *Der zivile Luftschutz im Zweiten Weltkrieg*, 147.
71. Statistics from PRO AIR 22/341 (London), CAB 66/65, CAB 66/63, CAB 66/64, AIR 40/781–848, cited from Groehler, *Bombenkrieg*, 393.
72. Harris, *Bomber Offensive*, 237–238; see also Rumpf, "*Bomber Harris*," 115–116.
73. Schmalacker-Wyrich, *Pforzheim*, 229. Cited is the final figure from the Pforzheim Office of Statistics from April 1954. This is a correction of the preliminary estimated figure of 17,600 published by the same office in 1948, which has been cited in literature by Brunswig, Middlebrook (citing Brunswig), and Groehler.
74. Schmalacker-Wyrich, *Pforzheim*, 154.
75. Ibid., 151–152.
76. Ibid., 127.
77. Ibid., 150.
78. Ibid., 105–106.
79. *Zentraler Luftschutz* 17, nos. 7–8, 197ff.
80. Brunswig, *Feuersturm über Hamburg*, 272ff.
81. Ibid., 270–271.
82. Losses in Hamburg amounted to 41,000 people. See comments in Groehler, *Bombenkrieg*, 119. I base the rate of 2.73 percent on the roughly 1.5 million people who were in Hamburg at the time of the raid. Based on the peacetime population of 1.7 million, this would represent 2.41 percent losses. My calculations regarding Berlin are based on the four million people who were in the capital in the summer of 1943.

83. *Hiroshima and Nagasaki*, 364. Joint Japan–U.S. Survey Report of 1951 mentions 64,602 deaths. The maximum estimate of the Japan Council Against A and H Bombs of 1961 refers to 119,000 to 133,000 deaths. I used the widespread estimate of 80,000 deaths.

84. Irving, *Rise and Fall of the Luftwaffe*, 230.

85. Bond, ed., *Fire and the Air War*, 125, 129.

86. Middlebrook, *The Berlin Raids: RAF Bomber Command*, 307, 321.

87. Groehler, *Bombenkrieg*, 141.

88. Dettmar mentions 10,000 deaths (Dettmar, *Die Zerstörung Kassels*, 141); the city of Kassel refers to "more than 8,000"; Groehler mentions 6,000; Hampe, 13,000; Middlebrook, around 9,000.

89. Verrier, *Bomber Offensive*, 192, citing Webster and Frankland, *Strategic Air Offensive*, 2:51.

90. Milward, *War, Economy, and Society*, 80–81.

91. PRO PREM 3–14–1; PRO AIR 14/3507, cited from Horst Boog, *Das Deutsche Reich und der zweite Weltkrieg*, 7:67–68; Webster and Frankland, *Strategic Air Offensive*, 2:47–48, 2:192.

92. Boog, *Das Deutsche Reich und der zweite Weltkrieg*, 7:99.

93. Galland, *The First and the Last*, 290, also 243.

94. Ibid., 250 (quote), 269–270.

95. See also Zuckermann, *From Apes to Warlords*; Rostow, *Pre-Invasion Bombing Strategy*, 527–530; Lytton, "Bombing Policy in the Rome and Pre-Normandy Invasion Aerial Campaigns of World War II," 54; Schaffer, *Wings of Judgement*, 40–43.

96. Schaffer, *Wings of Judgement*, 40–43.

97. Ibid.

98. Ibid., 40.

99. Ibid., 44.

100. Ibid., 42.

101. Gilbert, *Second World War*, 548.

102. Ibid., 587.

103. Ibid., 440–441.

104. Schaffer, *Wings of Judgement*, 56.

105. Ibid., 39–40.

106. Gilbert, *Second World War*, 546.

107. For all quotations in this paragraph: Gilbert, *Second World War*; see also Gilbert, *Auschwitz and the Allies*, 307–308, 315–317, on a U.S. raid on the synthetic oil plant in Monowitz.

108. Calder, *The Peoples' War*, 648.

109. Gilbert, *Second World War*, 557.

110. Figures from Bode and Kaiser, *Raketenspuren*, 118.

111. Gilbert, *Second World War*, 557.

112. Hastings, *Bomber Command*, 343.

113. Bode and Kaiser, *Raketenspuren*, 218.
114. Gilbert, *Second World War*, 601, 613.
115. Piekalkiewicz, *Arnhem 1944*, 9.
116. Liddell Hart, *History of the Second World War*, 566.
117. Liddell Hart, *The Other Side of the Hill*, 429.
118. Ambrose, *Citizen Soldiers*, 151.
119. Ibid., 154.
120. MacDonald, *The Battle of the Huertgen Forest*, 120.
121. Ibid., 113.
122. The bombardment itself was carried out under the codename Operation Queen. Rahier, *Jülich und das Jülicher Land*, 27–45; Thömmes, *Tod am Eifelhimmel*, 116–117.
123. Craven and Cate, *The Army Air Forces in World War II*, 3:716 (citing Arnold's memo to Bissell of Jan. 8, 1945 and his letter to Spaatz of Jan. 14, 1945).
124. *United States Strategic Bombing Survey*, vol. 2, therein "Civilian Defense Division—Final Report (European Report #40)," 3–4; Groehler, *Bombenkrieg*, 319.
125. Translator's note: From German *Gott strafe England* ("May God punish England"), a German propaganda slogan during World War I.
126. Crane, *Bombs, Cities, and Civilians*, 111.
127. Middlebrook and Everitt, *The Bomber Command War Diaries*, 704; *The Strategic Air War Against Germany*, 56ff.
128. Ibid., 704.
129. Seidler, *Deutscher Volkssturm*, 208.
130. Gilbert, *Second World War*, 651.
131. Richard, *Der Untergang der Stadt Wesel*, 107.
132. Ibid.
133. Whiting, *Battle of the Ruhr Pocket*, 38; see also Kesselring, *The Memoirs of Field-Marshal Kesselring*, 252.
134. Krüger, "Die Luftangriffe auf Essen," 325.
135. Barbero, *La croce tra i reticolati*, cited passage translated from Sollbach, *Dortmund*, 52.
136. Whiting, *Battle of the Ruhr Pocket*, 101.
137. Ibid., 140.
138. Description that follows cited from Huyskens, *Der Kreis Meschede unter der Feuerwalze des Zweiten Weltkriegs.*
139. Ibid., 26.
140. Ibid., 60.
141. Groehler, *Bombenkrieg*, 320.
142. Saward, *Bomber Harris*, 290–291.
143. Ibid., 290.
144. Interessensgemeinschaft Gedenkstätte Golm, ed., *Das Inferno von Swinemünde*, 48.

145. Brustat-Naval, *Unternehmen Rettung*, 146.

146. *United States Strategic Bombing Survey*, vol. 4, therein "The Effects of Strategic Bombing on German Morale (European Report #64b)," 2 vols. (1946–47), 1:9.

3. Land

1. Mann, *Zeit und Werk*, 655, cited in Groehler, *Bombenkrieg*, 43.
2. Mann, *Briefe 1937–1947*, 270, cited in Groehler, *Bombenkrieg*, 43.
3. ZstA Potsdam, no. 14659, cited in Groehler, *Bombenkrieg*, 42.
4. City archives of Plauen (Central State Archives of the GDR), no. 35, cited in Groehler, *Bombenkrieg*, 59.
5. Roger A. Freeman, *The Mighty Eighth War Diary*, 123–124, cited in Groehler, *Bombenkrieg*, 134–135; see also Eckardt, *Schicksale deutscher Baudenkmale*, 57ff.
6. Roger A. Freeman, *The Mighty Eighth War Diary*, 85–86.
7. Groehler, *Bombenkrieg*, 374.
8. See also Gelinski, *Stettin*, 54.
9. See also Voigt, *Die Veränderung der Großstadt Kiel*, 45.
10. Ibid., 19–20.
11. Brunswig, *Feuersturm über Hamburg*, 450–451.
12. *Dokumente deutscher Kriegsschäden*, 1st supplement, 137.
13. Figures taken from Peters, *Zwölf Jahre Bremen*, 194.
14. Ibid., 278; the chronicle of the Bremen raids was also taken from this source.
15. Huch, *Im alten Reich*, part 1: Der Norden, 244–245.
16. Spratte, *Im Anflug auf Osnabrück*, 27.
17. Pape, *Bis fünf nach zwölf*, 199.
18. Ibid.
19. See also Sax-Demuth, *Weiße Fahnen über Bielefeld*, 34.
20. bid., 26.
21. Hampe, *Der zivile Luftschutz*, 166.
22. Huch, *Im alten Reich*, part 1: Der Norden, 141, 143, 152.
23. Seeland, *Zerstörung und Untergang Alt-Hildesheims*, 13; see also for the continued history of events.
24. Ibid., 35.
25. See also Höhne, *Der Orden unter dem Totenkopf*, 143–144.
26. See also Scheck, *Denkmalpflege und Diktatur im Deutschen Reich*, 103–104.
27. Translator's note: "Die and become," in the German *Stirb und werde*, comes from Goethe's poem "Blissful Yearning (from the West-Eastern Divan)."
28. Stadtmuseum Münster, ed., *Bomben auf Münster*, 44; cited in part (in English) in Hawkins, *Münster: The Way It Was*, 90–91.

29. Stadtmuseum Münster, ed., *Bomben auf Münster*, 56.
30. Hawkins, *Münster: The Way It Was*, 159.
31. Stadtmuseum Münster, ed., *Bomben auf Münster*, 58.
32. Stadt Hannover, ed., *Tod und Leben Hannovers*, 61.
33. Grabe, *Unter der Wolke des Todes leben*, 7.
34. PRO AIR 14/3766, translated from ibid.
35. Facsimile, in Dettmar, *Die Zerstörung Kassels*, 54.
36. Roth, *Spaziergänge mit Hindernissen*.
37. PRO AIR 27/1041; translated from Grabe, *Unter der Wolke des Todes leben*, 73.
38. PRO AIR 27/450; translated from ibid.
39. Ibid., 79.
40. PRO AIR 14/3766, as cited in Webster and Frankland, *The Strategic Air Offensive Against Germany*, 2:161. See also Grabe, *Unter der Wolke des Todes leben*, 74, 77.
41. Grabe, *Unter der Wolke des Todes leben*, 76.
42. Stadt Hannover, ed., *Tod und Leben Hannovers*, 40–44.
43. PRO AIR 14/3766; translated from Grabe, *Unter der Wolke des Todes leben*, 80.
44. See Jordan, *Heinrich der Löwe*, 232–233.
45. Huch, *Im alten Reich*, part 1: Der Norden, 40.
46. Prescher, *Der rote Hahn über Braunschweig*, 95.
47. Febvre, *Le Rhin: histoire, mythes et réalités*, 147.
48. Cited from Dittgen, *Der Übergang*, 46.
49. Otto Seidel report, cited in ibid., 53–54.
50. Middlebrook and Everitt, *The Bomber Command War Diaries*, 601.
51. Fuller, *The Second World War, 1939–45*, 316; cited (in German) in Vogt and Brenne, *Krefeld im Luftkrieg, 1939–1945*, 295.
52. Translated from Vogt and Brenne, *Krefeld im Luftkrieg, 1939–1945*, 233.
53. PRO AIR 25/155, translated from ibid., 234.
54. Ibid., 340–357.
55. Heine, *Werke und Briefe*, 7:185.
56. Heine, *Germany, A Winter's Tale*, 49–52, 65–68.
57. Heine, "Ideas. Book Le Grand [1826]," in *The Prose and Poetical Works of Heinrich Heine*, vol. 4: *Pictures of Travel 1825–1826*, 321, 329–331.
58. Hüttenberger, *Düsseldorf*, 3:634.
59. Landeshauptstadt Düsseldorf, ed., *Erlebtes und Erlittenes*, 307.
60. Hüttenberger, *Düsseldorf*, 3:636.
61. See Weidenhaupt, *Kleine Geschichte der Stadt Düsseldorf*, 170–171.
62. Febvre, *Le Rhin: histoire, mythes et réalités*, 168–170.
63. Cited in Fischer, *Köln '39–45*,' 133.
64. Vogt, *Bonn im Bombenkrieg*, 224, 217.
65. PRO AIR 25/79; translated from Vogt, *Bonn im Bombenkrieg*, 68.

66. Grewe, ed., *Fontes Historiae*, 482–483.

67. Schnatz, *Die Luftkrieg im Raum Koblenz*, 283.

68. Ibid.

69. PRO AIR 14/3074; translated from ibid., 285.

70. Described in Busch, *Der Luftkrieg im Raum Mainz*, chap. 14.

71. Eighth Air Force Mission Reports, Albert F. Simpson Historical Research Center (Maxwell, Ala.), microfilm B5005; translated from Busch, *Der Luftkrieg im Raum Mainz*, 200.

72. Here and below, from Goethe, "Siege of Mainz," in *Goethe's Collected Works*, vol. 5, *From my Life*, 757–763.

73. Air Ministry Bulletin No. 17700, 27–2–45 no. 41; *United States Strategic Bombing Survey*, Mainz Damage Assessment Folder (NA RG 243); translated from Busch, *Der Luftkrieg im Raum Mainz*, 321.

74. See ibid., 321, 357–358.

75. PRO AIR 40/809 (London), 810, cited in Groehler, *Bombenkrieg*, 423.

76. For this and other information, see Müller-Werth, *Geschichte und Kommunalpolitik der Stadt Wiesbaden*, 200–204.

77. Anonymous, *The Nibelungenlied*, trans. George Henry Needler (New York: H. Holt, 1904). Adventure 36: How the Queen bade set fire to the Hall, verse 2118–2119.

ORIGINAL TEXT:
Daz fiuwer viel genôte   ûf si in den sal.
dô leiten siz mit schilden   von in hin zetal
der rouch und ouch diu hitze   in tâten beidiu wê
ich waene der jâmer immer   mêr an héldén ergê.
Da sprach Hagen von Tronje: "stêt zuo des sales want!
lât niht die brende vallen   ûf iuwer helmbant!"

78. Sorel, *Europe and the French Revolution*, 77.

79. Cited in Walther, *Schicksal einer deutschen Stadt*, 2:275.

80. See Kranich, *Karlsruhe*, 69–70.

81. Huch, *Im alten Reich*, part 2: Die Mitte des Reiches, 30.

82. See Thömmes, *Tod am Eifelhimmel*, 271–272, 278.

83. See ibid., 71; Middlebrook and Everitt, *The Bomber Command Diaries*, 634.

84. Huch, *Im alten Reich*, part 2: Die Mitte des Reiches, 32.

85. Beseler and Gutschow, *Kriegsschicksale deutscher Architektur*, 997.

86. Cited in Eckel, *Saarbrücken im Luftkrieg*, 161–162.

87. Ibid., 168.

88. Statistics cited in Braun-Rühling, *Eine Stadt im Feuerregen*, 57.

89. Ibid., 79.

90. Borsdorf and Niethammer, eds, *Zwischen Befreiung und Besatzung*, 29, 47–48, which cites the original sources; on Abramovitz: NA 740.00119 Control (Germany) 5–2345; on Lerner: NA RG 226, OSS 123864.

91. Statistics and the following quotations cited in Krüger, "Die Luftangriffe auf Essen 1940–1945," *Essener Beiträge*, 159–329.

92. Ibid., 285.

93. Ibid., 287.

94. Ibid., 306.

95. Ibid., 310.

96. Ibid., 325.

97. See Huyskens, *Der Kreis Meschede unter der Feuerwalze*, 19.

98. Ibid., 78–79.

99. Facsimile in Dettmar, *Die Zerstörung Kassels*, 55.

100. See Sollbach, ed., *Dortmund*, 53.

101. Ibid.

102. Sauer's diary, in Vetter, *Freiburg in Trümmern*, 24ff.

103. Mainfränkisches Museum, ed., catalog, 54.

104. PRO AIR 27/1931, in ibid., 74.

105. Bauer, *Würzburg im Feuerofen*, 19ff.

106. Ibid.

107. PRO AIR 24/312, cited from Mainfränkisches Museum, ed., catalog, 74.

108. Middlebrook, *Nuremberg Raid, 30–31 March 1944*, 140–141.

109. Nadler, *Ich sah, wie Nürnberg unterging*, 125.

110. See Pöhlmann, "*Es war gerade, als würde alles bersten ...* ," 94–95. The following quotations also taken from Pöhlmann.

111. *The Times* (London), April 20, 1942, translated from ibid., 96.

112. Pöhlmann, "*Es war gerade, als würde alles bersten ...* ," 86.

113. Ibid., 84.

114. Ibid.

115. Webster and Frankland, *Strategic Air Offensive*, 4:162.

116. Pöhlmann, "*Es war gerade, als würde alles bersten ...* ," 101.

117. Ibid.

118. Ibid., 102.

119. Ibid., 103.

120. Ibid., 102.

121. Ibid.

122. Ibid., 105.

123. Ibid., 104.

124. Ibid.

125. See also Bauer and Piper, *München*, 87–88.

126. Ibid., 112ff.

127. Bauer, *Fliegeralarm*, 44.

128. Ibid., 67.

129. Ibid., 80.

130. Ibid., 100.

131. Ibid., 131.
132. Ibid., 135.
133. Bardua, *Stuttgart im Luftkrieg*, 147.
134. Strölin's report in ibid., 270.
135. Ibid.
136. Ibid., 273.
137. Quote from September 12, 1944, in ibid., 144–156.
138. Zelzer, *Weg und Schicksal der Stuttgarter Juden*, 237.
139. Steinhilber, *Heilbronn*, 99.
140. "These animals have learned something."
141. Wincker-Wildberg, ed., *Napoleon*, 289.
142. Statistics here and in the following are cited from Horn, *Leipzig im Bombenhagel*, 41, etc.
143. Ibid., 40.
144. Groehler, *Bombenkrieg*, 208.
145. Horn, *Leipzig im Bombenhagel*, 87.
146. Ibid., 78.
147. Groehler, *Bombenkrieg*, 208.
148. See Wille, *Der Himmel brennt über Magdeburg*, 31.
149. Summary of various eyewitness accounts from the year 1950 in ibid., 58–83.
150. Ibid., 45.
151. Eckardt, *Schicksale deutscher Baudenkmäler*, 249ff.
152. PRO AIR 37/1129 (London), translated from Groehler, *Bombenkrieg*, 433.
153. Hartmann, *Die Zerstörung Halberstadts*, 10.
154. Groehler, *Bombenkrieg*, 432.
155. Hartmann, *Die Zerstörung Halberstadts*, 17.
156. Eckardt, *Schicksale deutscher Baudenkmäler*, 226ff.
157. Hartmann, *Die Zerstörung Halberstadts*, 39.
158. Schmidt, *Die Brandnacht*, 5–6.
159. Groehler, *Bombenkrieg*, 406.
160. Bergander, *Dresden im Luftkrieg*, 127.
161. Ibid.
162. Piekalkiewicz, *Air War 1939–45*, 278.
163. Ibid.
164. Ibid.
165. Schäfer, *Berlin im Zweiten Weltkrieg*, 267.
166. Craven and Cate, *The Army Air Forces in World War II*, 3:726.
167. Groehler, *Bombenkrieg*, 319.
168. Piekalkiewicz, *Air War 1939–45*, 278.
169. Schäfer, *Berlin im Zweiten Weltkrieg*, 112.
170. Smith, *Last Train from Berlin*, 162, cited in ibid., 122.
171. Schäfer, *Berlin im Zweiten Weltkrieg*, 122.

172. Warner, *Schicksalswende Europas?* cited in ibid., 155.
173. Schäfer, *Berlin im Zweiten Weltkrieg*, 184.
174. Warner, *Schicksalswende Europas?* cited in ibid., 144.
175. Schäfer, *Berlin im Zweiten Weltkrieg*, 145.
176. Ibid., 148.
177. Ibid., 158.
178. Findahl, *Undergang; Berlin 1939–1945*, cited in ibid., 274.
179. Jacob Kronica, *Berlins Undergang*, cited in Schäfer, *Berlin im Zweiten Weltkrieg*, 294.
180. Schäfer, *Berlin im Zweiten Weltkrieg*, 168–169.
181. Warner, *Schicksalswende Europas?* cited in ibid., 192.

4. Protection

1. *United States Strategic Bombing Survey*, vol. 5 (1976), therein "Physical Damage Division Report (ETO) (European Report #134b)" (1947), 1, 50.
2. Dettmar, *Die Zerstörung Kassels*, 120–121.
3. Ibid., 218–224. Names have been changed by the present author.
4. *Dokumente deutscher Kriegsschäden*, 1st supplement, 132–133.
5. Schmidt, *Die Brandnacht*, 101.
6. See Feydt, "Betrachtung zur Frage der Rettungswege im baulichen Luftschutz," *Ziviler Luftschutz* 5 (1953): 139–140.
7. *Dokumente deutscher Kriegsschäden*, 2/1:348.
8. Sollbach, *Dortmund*, 20.
9. See also Spratte, *In Anflug auf Osnabrück*.
10. Bardua, *Stuttgart im Luftkrieg*, 200.
11. Ibid., 97.
12. Vogt and Brenne, *Krefeld im Luftkrieg*, 78–92.
13. Speer, *Spandau, the Secret Diaries*, 200.
14. *United States Strategic Bombing Survey*, vol. 2 (1976), therein: "Civilian Defense Division—Final Report (Eur. Rep. #40)," 151.
15. Ibid., 157.
16. Ibid.,150.
17. Narrative of Lisa Bachmann, cited in Grabe et al., eds., *Unter der Wolke des Todes leben*, 153.
18. Wette, Bremer, and Vogel, *Das letzte halbe Jahr*, 203.
19. *United States Strategic Bombing Survey*, vol. 4 (1976), therein "The Effects of Strategic Bombing on German Morale," 1:1.
20. Schmid, *Frankfurt im Feuersturm*, 55–56. Names have been changed by the present author.
21. Wette, Bremer, and Vogel, *Das letzte halbe Jahr*, 365–366.
22. BA-MA (Freiburg), RL 4/448, report January 21, 1945. On Hamm, see also RL 4/445.

23. Domarus, *Hitler Speeches & Proclamations 1932–1945: The Chronicle of a Dictatorship*, vol. 2 (1935–38), 1123 (June 28, 1938). See BA-MA (Koblenz), H 10–38.

24. Rosenberg, *Mythus des 20. Jahrhundert*, 557.

25. Speer, *Spandau, the Secret Diaries*, 200.

26. Horn, *Leipzig im Bombenhagel*, 154.

27. *United States Strategic Bombing Survey*, vol. 4 (1976), therein "The Effects of Strategic Bombing on German Morale," 1:74.

28. Goebbels, "The Soap Bubble," in *Das Reich* (December 12, 1943), cited in ibid., 74.

29. Domarus, *Hitlers Reden*, 4:2223. See "Soldaten der dt. Ostfront!" Proclamation, German News Agency (DNB), text of April 16, 1945.

30. Vogt, *Bonn im Bombenkrieg*, 121.

31. Grabe et al., eds., *Unter der Wolke des Tode leben*, 118.

32. Sollbach, *Dortmund*, 33–34.

33. Fischer, *Köln "39–45,"* 139.

34. *Dokumente deutscher Kriegsschäden*, 2/1:311–312.

35. Fischer, *Köln "39–45,"* 58.

36. BA-NS 19/14.

37. Spratte, *Im Anflug auf Osnabrück*, 71–72.

38. Prescher, *Der rote Hahn über Braunschweig*, 94–95.

39. Fischer, *Köln "39–45,"* 128.

40. Krämer, *Christbäume über Frankfurt*, 115.

41. Stadtmuseum Münster, ed., *Bomben auf Münster*, 59.

42. Braun-Rühling, *Eine Stadt im Feuerregen*, 83. Name has been changed by the present author.

43. Berthold and Materna, *München im Bombenkrieg*, 105.

44. Eckel, *Saarbrücken im Luftkrieg*, 41.

45. Horn, *Leipzig im Bombenhagel*, 41.

46. Schmidt, *Die Brandnacht*, 101.

47. Ibid., 80.

48. *Dokumente deutscher Kriegsschäden*, 2/1:443.

49. Schmalacker-Wyrich, *Pforzheim*, 103.

50. Schmid, *Frankfurt im Feuersturm*, 62.

51. See also Horn, *Leipzig im Bombenhagel*, 155.

52. Domarus, *Der Untergang des alten Würzburg*, 236.

53. Schmidt, *Die Brandnacht*, 26.

54. Schmalacker-Wyrich, *Pforzheim*, 79.

55. Dettmar, *Die Zerstörung Kassels*, 130.

56. Ibid., 130.

57. Report by Wilhelm Riecker in Schmalacker-Wyrich, *Pforzheim*, 156.

58. Grabe et al., eds., *Unter der Wolke des Todes leben*, 63.

59. *Völkische Beobachter* (January 30, 1945) in *Dokumente deutscher Kriegs-schäden*, 2/1:488.

60. *Dokumente deutscher Kriegsschäden*, 2/1 (August 23, 1943), 70–71.

61. Ibid., 106.

62. Rüter-Ehlermann and Rüter, eds., *Justiz und NS-Verbrechen*, 3:465–529. The quotation is from 486.

63. Vieberg, *Justiz im nationalsozialistischen Deutschland*, 54.

64. *Dokumente deutscher Kriegsschäden*, 2/1:474.

65. Ibid., 475.

66. *United States Strategic Bombing Survey*, vol. 4 (1976), therein "The Effects of Strategic Bombing on German Morale," 1:91.

67. *Dokumente deutscher Kriegsschäden*, 2/1:476.

68. Translator's note: The title of the decree of September 5, 1939, was translated for the Nuremberg Military Tribunal as "Decree against Public Enemies"; the Nazi term *Volksschädling* literally means "pest or vermin harmful to the German people."

69. Friedrich, *Die kalte Amnestie*, 381.

70. Ibid., 384.

71. Ibid., 383.

72. Ibid.

73. Ibid., 384.

74. BA-R 22 Gr5/457.

75. Friedrich, *Die kalte Amnestie*, 391.

76. Friedrich, *Freispruch für die Nazijustiz*, 575.

77. Friedrich, *Die kalte Amnestie*, 149–150.

78. Friedrich, *Freispruch für die Nazijustiz*, 551–552.

79. Wagner, *Der Volksgerichtshof*, 876–877.

80. Friedrich, *Die kalte Amnestie*, 151.

81. *Dokumente deutscher Kriegsschäden*, 2/1:109.

82. Boberach, *Meldungen*.

83. Groehler, *Bombenkrieg*, 246.

84. BA-NS 6/823.

5. We

1. Boelcke, *Wollt ihr den totalen Krieg?* 417–418.

2. Ibid., 418.

3. Ibid., 450.

4. Ibid., 452.

5. Figures of the General Wehrmacht Office cited in Groehler, *Bombenkrieg*, 317. BA-MA (Freiburg), RL 5/649.

6. Boberach, *Meldungen*, 5:1413–1414. Quotations in this chapter not otherwise referenced have been taken from this collection.

7. Ibid., 5:1504.

8. Boelcke, *Wollt Ihr den totalen Krieg?* 128 (September 7, 1940).

9. Ibid., 133.

10. Boberach, *Meldungen*, 5:1605–1606.

11. Ibid., 5:1595.

12. Ibid., 10:3597.

13. Harris and Paxman, *A Higher Form of Killing*, 89, 249, citing NA CCS.381 Poland (6630–43) Sec. I.

14. Boberach, *Meldungen*, 14:5311.

15. Ibid., 11:4019.

16. Boelcke, *Wollt Ihr den totalen Krieg?* 353.

17. Ibid., 366.

18. *United States Strategic Bombing Survey*, vol. 4 (1976), therein: "The Effects of Strategic Bombing on German Morale," 1:18.

19. Ibid.

20. Boberach, *Meldungen*, 14:5402–5403.

21. Ibid., 5449.

22. Ibid., 5355.

23. BA-NS 6/411, 62.

24. Domarus, *Hitlers Reden*, 4:2055–2058.

25. Ibid., 2058.

26. BA-NS 6/411, 56–57.

27. Boberach, *Meldungen*, 16:6205.

28. Ibid., 16:6299–6300.

29. *United States Strategic Bombing Survey*, vol. 4 (1976), therein: "The Effects of Strategic Bombing on German Morale," vol. 2, "Pilot Study on French Escapees," 58.

30. On the conduct of foreign workers during air raids, see Boberach, *Meldungen*, 13:5295–5301.

31. *United States Strategic Bombing Survey*, vol. 4 (1976), therein: "The Effects of Strategic Bombing on German Morale," 2:58.

32. See Friedrich, *Das Gesetz des Krieges*, 310–311.

33. Busch, *Der Luftkrieg im Raum Mainz*, 104.

34. *United States Strategic Bombing Survey*, vol. 4 (1976), therein: "The Effects of Strategic Bombing on German Morale," 2:113–118.

35. Wette, Bremer, and Vogel, *Das letzte halbe Jahr*, 401.

36. Ibid., 390–404.

6. I

1. Unless otherwise noted, quotations up to page 448 (at the space break) have been taken from Panse, *Angst und Schreck*.

2. Berthold and Materna, *München im Bombenkrieg*, 78.

3. Vogt, *Bonn im Bombenkrieg*, 269.
4. Panse, *Angst und Schreck*, 17.
5. Schmidt, *Die Brandnacht*, 65.
6. Bauer, *Würzburg im Feuerofen*, 35.
7. Unless otherwise noted, the quotations, here and in the following, have been taken from Vogt, *Bonn im Bombenkrieg, Zeitzeugenberichte*, 116–320.
8. Kiepke, *Paderborn*, 52.
9. The author's estimates are based on figures from Hampe, *Der zivile Schutz*, 176 and 142, and the 500,000 total deaths were estimated as in chapter 2 of this volume.
10. Quotations from here to the end of this chapter taken from Schmidt, *Die Brandnacht*.

7. Stone

1. Goehler, *Bombenkrieg*, 313.
2. Schmid, *Frankfurt im Feuersturm*, 25; Dolf Sternberger to editor-in-chief Wendelin Hecht, June 12, 1942.
3. Groehler, *Bombenkrieg*, 312.
4. Rademacher report, cited from Vogt, *Bonn im Bombenkrieg*, 100–101.
5. Eckardt, *Schicksale deutscher Baudenkmäler*, 147.
6. *Dokumente deutscher Kriegsschäden* 2/1:383.
7. *Gießen 1248–1948*, 61.
8. Wilhelm Rohr, "Die zentrale Lenkung deutscher Archivschutzmaßnahmen," *Der Archivar* 3, no. 3: 111.
9. Ibid., 116.
10. *Krieg und Elend im Siegerland*, 144.
11. Bosl, "Die Bibliothek in der Gesellschaft," 7–8.
12. Halm, *Die Schicksale der Bayerischen Staatsbibliothek*, 3–8.
13. Translator's note: The *Codex Manesse* is the most comprehensive collection of Middle High German songs and poetry, transcribed and illustrated in the early fourteenth century.
14. Hampe, *Der zivile Luftschutz*, 525.
15. Leyh, *Die deutschen wissenschaftlichen Bibliotheken*, 84–85.

BIBLIOGRAPHY

TRANSLATOR'S NOTE: Every attempt was made to cite the precise original English wording and sources for passages that had been cited in German translation. This was not possible for the U.S. National Archives and the British national archives (Public Records Office); in those cases, direct citations were translated from the German sources, but the archival references indicating where the original wording can be found were included in the backnote. Additional sources that were consulted for English citations have been added to the author's bibliography, and, wherever possible, German editions have been replaced by English-language sources. Original sources in languages other than German or English have been listed under their original publication information instead of the secondary references in German.

Archives

The following citation forms are used in the notes.

PRO = UK National Archives (Public Records Office)
> Department codes:
> AIR = Air Ministry, Royal Air Force
> CAB = Records of the Cabinet Office
>> Divisions within CAB:
>> CAB 66 = War Cabinet and Cabinet Memoranda
>> PREM = Records of the Prime Minister's Office

NA = U.S. National Archives
> RG = Record Group
>> RG 226 = Records of the Office of Strategic Services
>> RG 243 = Records of the U.S. Strategic Bombing Survey

BA = German Federal Archives (Bundesarchiv)
> MA = Military Archives

H = Heer (Army)
RL = Reich Luftwaffe (Air Force)
R = Deutsches Reich, German Reich/Empire 1495–1945
NS = National Socialism

Books and Articles

Aders, Gebhard. *Die Geschichte der deutschen Nachtjagd 1917–1945.* Stuttgart, 1977.

Allen, Hubert Raymond. *The Legacy of Lord Trenchard.* London, 1972.

Ambrose, Stephen E. *Citizen Soldiers: The U.S. Army from the Normandy Beaches to the Bulge to the Surrender of Germany, June 7, 1944–May 7, 1945.* New York, 1998.

Barbero, Giuseppe. *La croce tra i reticolati. Vicende di prigionia.* Turin, 1946.

Bardua, Heinz. *Stuttgart im Luftkrieg 1939–1945.* Stuttgart, 1985.

Bauer, Fritz. *Würzburg im Feuerofen. Tagebuchaufzeichnungen und Erinnerungen an die Zerstörung Würzburgs.* Würzburg, 1985.

Bauer, Reinhard, and Ernst Piper. *München. Die Geschichte einer Stadt.* Munich, 1993.

Bauer, Richard. *Fliegeralarm. Luftangriffe auf München 1940–1945.* Munich, 1987.

Baumeister, Werner. *Castrop-Rauxel im Luftkrieg.* Castrop-Rauxel, 1988.

Bekker, Cajus. *Angriffshöhe 4000. Ein Kriegstagebuch der deutschen Luftwaffe.* Oldenburg, 1964.

Bergander, Götz. *Dresden im Luftkrieg.* Cologne, 1994.

Berthold, Eva, and Norbert Materna. *München im Bombenkrieg.* Düsseldorf, 1985.

Beseler, Hartwig, and Niels Gutschow. *Kriegsschicksale deutscher Architektur.* Neumünster, 1988.

Best, Geoffrey. *Humanity in Warfare: The Modern History of the International Law of Armed Conflicts.* London, 1983.

Blumenstock, Friedrich. *Der Einmarsch der Amerikaner im nördlichen Württemberg im April 1945.* Stuttgart, 1957.

Boberach, Heinz, ed. *Meldungen aus dem Reich. Die geheimen Lageberichte des Sicherheitsdienstes der SS 1938–1945.* Herrsching, 1984.

Bode, Volkard, and Gerhard Kaiser. *Raketenspuren.* Berlin, 1999.

Boelcke, Willi A. *Wollt Ihr den totalen Krieg? Die geheimen Goebbels-Konferenzen 1939 bis 1943.* Munich, 1969.

———, ed. *Deutschlands Rüstung im Zweiten Weltkrieg. Hitlers Konferenzen mit Albert Speer 1942–1945.* Frankfurt/M., 1969.

Boog, Horst. "The Anglo-American Strategic Air War Over Europe and German Air Defence." In *Germany and the Second World War.* Vol. 6, *Global War,* edited by the Research Institute for Military History (Potsdam, Germany), translated by Ewald Osers et al. Oxford and New York: Oxford University Press, 2001.

———. "Strategischer Luftkrieg in Europa und Reichsverteidigung 1943–1944." In *Das deutsche Reich und der Zweite Weltkrieg*. Vol. 7, *Das Deutsche Reich in der Defensive*, edited by Militärgeschichtliches Forschungsamt. Stuttgart, 2001. (Not yet translated.)

Bond, Horatio, ed. *Fire and the Air War*. Boston, 1946.

Borsdorf, Ulrich, and Lutz Niethammer, eds. *Zwischen Befreiung und Besatzung. Analysen des US-Geheimdienstes über Positionen und Strukturen deutscher Politik*. Wuppertal, 1976.

Bosl, Karl, "Die Bibliothek in der Gesellschaft und Kultur Europas vom 6. bis zum 18. Jahrhundert." In *Schöne alte Bibliotheken*, edited by Margarete Baur-Heinhold. Munich, 1972.

Braun-Rühling, Max. *Eine Stadt im Feuerregen*. Kaiserslautern, 1953.

Brunswig, Hans. *Feuersturm über Hamburg*. Stuttgart, 1981.

Brustat-Naval, Fritz. *Unternehmen Rettung. Letztes Schiff nach Westen*. Berlin, 1998.

Busch, Dieter. *Der Luftkrieg im Raum Mainz während des Zweiten Weltkriegs 1939–1945*. Mainz, 1988.

Calder, Angus. *The People's War 1939–1945*. London, 1973.

Carter, Kit C., and Robert Mueller. *Combat Chronology 1941–1945 (The Army Air Forces in World War II)*. Washington, D.C., 1973.

Churchill, Winston S. *Thoughts and Adventures*. London: Cooper, 1990.

———. *Second World War*. 6 vols. Boston: Houghton Mifflin, 1985. First published in 1948.

Clark, Ronald W. *The Rise of the Boffins*. London, 1962.

Colville, John. *Forges of Power: 10 Downing Street Diaries 1939–55*. New York: Norton, 1985.

Connelly, Mark. *Reaching for the Stars: A New History of Bomber Command in World War II*. London, 2001.

Cooper, Alan. *Air Battle of the Ruhr*. London, 2000.

Crane, Conrad C. *Bombs, Cities, and Civilians: American Airpower Strategy in World War II*. Lawrence, Kan., 1993.

Craven, Wesley Frank, and James Lea Cate. *The Army Air Forces in World War II*. Chicago, 1965.

Czasany, Maximilian. *Europa im Bombenkrieg*. Graz, 1998.

Demps, Laurenz. "Die Luftangriffe auf Berlin. Ein dokumentarischer Bericht." *Jahrbuch des Märkischen Museums* 3 (1978): 27–68 [part 1]; 8 (1982): 7–44 [part 2]; 9 (1983): 19–48 [part 3].

Dettmar, Werner. *Die Zerstörung Kassels im Oktober 1943*. Kassel, 1983.

Deus, Wolf-Herbert. *Soester Chronik: Zugleich Bericht der Stadtverwaltung Soest über die Zeit vom 1. April 1942 bis 31. März 1948*. Soest, 1951.

Dittgen, Willi. *Der Übergang. Das Ende des Zweiten Weltkriegs in Dinslaken und Umgebung.* Dinslaken, 1983.

Dokumente deutscher Kriegsschäden. Evakuierte, Kriegssachgeschädigte, Währungsgeschädigte. Die geschichtliche und rechtliche Entwicklung. Edited by Bundesminister für Vertriebene, Flüchtlinge und Kriegsgeschädigte. Bonn, 1962.

Domarus, Max. *Der Untergang des alten Würzburg und seine Vorgeschichte.* Würzburg, 1955.

———. *Hitler Speeches and Proclamations 1932–1945: The Chronicle of a Dictatorship.* Vols. 1–3. Translated by Mary Fran Gilbert. Wauconda, Ill.: Bolchazy-Carducci Publ., 2004. Volume 4 has not yet been translated.

———, ed. *Hitlers Reden und Schriften.* 4 vols. Munich, 1965.

Douhet, Giulio. *The Command of the Air.* Translated by Dino Ferrari. Washington, D.C.: Office of Air Force History, 1983. First published in 1942.

Dreyer-Eimbke, Erika. *Alte Straßen im Herzen Europas.* Frankfurt/M., 1989.

Dyson, Freeman. *Weapons and Hope.* New York, 1984.

Eckardt, Götz, ed. *Schicksale deutscher Baudenkmale im Zweiten Weltkrieg. Eine Dokumentation der Schäden und Totalverluste auf dem Gebiet der Deutschen Demokratischen Republik.* Berlin (GDR), 1980.

Eckel, Werner. *Saarbrücken im Luftkrieg.* Saarbrücken, 1985.

Eisenhower, Dwight D. *Crusade in Europe.* New York: Da Capo Press, 1977. First published in 1948.

Euler, Helmut. *Als Deutschlands Dämme brachen.* Stuttgart, 1975.

———. *Die Entscheidungsschlacht an Rhein und Ruhr 1945.* Stuttgart, 1981.

Febvre, Lucien. *Rhin: histoire, mythes et réalités.* Paris: Perrin, 1997.

Feuchter, Georg W. *Geschichte des Luftkriegs.* Bonn, 1954.

Feydt, Georg. "Betrachtung zur Frage der Rettungsweg im baulichen Luftschutz." *Ziviler Luftschutz* 5 (1953): 139–140.

Findahl, Theo. *Undergang; Berlin 1939–1945.* Oslo: H. Aschehoug & Co. (W. Nygaard), 1945.

Fischer, Josef. *Köln '39–45'. Der Leidensweg einer Stadt.* Cologne, 1970.

Foedrowitz, Michael. *Bunkerwelten. Luftschutzanlagen in Norddeutschland.* Berlin, 1998.

Freeman, Roger A. *Mighty Eighth War Diary.* London, 1981.

Friedrich, Jörg. *Die kalte Amnestie.* Munich, 1995.

———. *Freispruch für die Nazijustiz. Die Urteile gegen NS-Richter seit 1948.* Berlin, 1998.

———. *Das Gesetz des Krieges. Das deutsche Heer in Rußland 1941 bis 1945. Der Prozeß gegen das Oberkommando der Wehrmacht.* Munich, 1996.

Fröhlich, Elke, ed. *Die Tagebücher von Joseph Goebbels.* Munich, 1987.

Fuller, J. F. C. *The Second World War, 1939–45: A Strategical and Tactical History.* New York: Da Capo Press, 1993.

Galland, Adolf. *The First and the Last: The Rise and Fall of the German Fighter Forces, 1938–1945.* Translated by Mervyn Savill. New York: Holt, 1954.

Garrett, Stephen A. *Ethics and Airpower in World War II: The British Bombing of German Cities.* New York, 1997.

Gelinski, Heinz. *Stettin. Eine deutsche Großstadt in den 30er Jahren.* Leer, 1984.

Gießen 1248–1948: 700 Jahre Gießen in Wort und Bild. Prepared by Karl Glöckner for the City of Giessen in commemoration of its 700th anniversary. Giessen, 1948.

Gilbert, Martin. *Second World War.* London, 1989.

———. *Auschwitz and the Allies.* New York: Holt, Rinehart and Winston, 1981.

Girbig, Werner. *1000 Tage über Deutschland. Die 8. Amerikanische Luftflotte im Zweiten Weltkrieg.* Munich, 1964.

Goethe, Johann Wolfgang. *From My Life.* Edited by Jeffrey L. Sammons and Thomas P. Saine. Translated by Robert Heitner. New York: Suhrkamp, 1987.

Golücke, Friedhelm. *Schweinfurt und der strategische Luftkrieg 1943.* Paderborn, 1980.

Görlitz, Walter. *Model. Der Feldmarschall und sein Endkampf an der Ruhr.* Frankfurt/M.–Berlin, 1992.

Grabe, Thomas, et al., eds. *Unter der Wolke des Todes leben. Hannover im Zweiten Weltkrieg.* Hanover, 1983.

Grewe, Wilhelm G., ed. *Fontes Historiae Iuris Gentium.* Berlin (FRG), 1984.

Groehler, Olaf. *Bombenkrieg gegen Deutschland.* Berlin, 1990.

———. *Geschichte des Luftkriegs.* Berlin (GDR), 1975.

———. *Anhalt im Luftkrieg: 1940–1945. Anflug auf Ida-Emil.* Dessau, 1993.

Halm, Hans. *Die Schicksale der Bayerischen Staatsbibliothek während des Zweiten Weltkriegs.* Munich, 1949.

Hampe, Erich. *Der zivile Luftschutz im Zweiten Weltkrieg.* Frankfurt/M., 1963.

Harris, Arthur. *Bomber Offensive.* London, 1947.

Harris, Robert, and Jeremy Paxman. *A Higher Form of Killing: The Secret Story of Gas and Germ Warfare.* London: Chatto & Windus, 1982.

Hartmann, Werner. *Die Zerstörung Halberstadts am 8. April 1945.* Halberstadt, 1980.

Hasenclever, G. *Die Zerstörung der Stadt Remscheid.* Remscheid, 1984.

Hastings, Max. *Bomber Command.* London, 1981.

Hawkins, Ian. *Münster: The Way It Was.* Edited by Richard H. Perry. Anaheim, Calif.: Robinson Typographics, 1984.

———. *B-17s Over Berlin: Personal Stories from the 95th Bomb Group.* N.p.: Brassey's Inc., 1995.

Hays Parks, W. "Air War and the Laws of War." In *The Conduct of the Air War in the Second World War: An International Comparison,* edited by Horst Boog. Oxford: Berg Publishers, Ltd., 1992.

Heimatbund Niedersachsen, ed., in collaboration with the Presseamt der Hauptstadt Hannover. *Tod und Leben Hannovers. 9. November.* Compiled by Heinz Lauenroth and Gustav Lauterbach. Hanover, 1953.

Heine, Heinrich. *Werke und Briefe.* Berlin and Weimar, 1980.

———. *The Prose and Poetical Works of Heinrich Heine.* Vol. 4, *Pictures of Travel 1825–1826,* translated by Charles Godfrey Leland. New York: Croscup & Sterling, 1900.

———. *The Complete Poems of Heinrich Heine.* Edited and translated by Hal Draper. Boston: Suhrkamp/Insel, 1982.

Henke, Klaus-Dietmar. *Die amerikanische Besetzung Deutschlands.* Munich, 1995.

Herbert, Ulrich. *Fremdarbeiter. Politik und Praxis des Ausländereinsatzes in der Kriegswirtschaft des Dritten Reiches.* Bonn, 1985.

Hillgruber, Andreas. *Hitlers Strategie: Politik und Kriegführung 1940–1941.* Munich, 1965.

Hinchcliffe, Peter. *Luftkrieg bei Nacht 1939–1945.* Stuttgart, 1998.

Hiroshima and Nagasaki: The Physical, Medical and Social Effects of the Atomic Bombings. Edited by the Committee for the Compilation of Materials on Damage Caused by the Atomic Bombs. New York, 1981.

Höhne, Heinz. *Der Orden unter dem Totenkopf. Die Geschichte der SS.* Munich, 1967.

Horn, Birgit. *Leipzig im Bombenhagel—Angriffsziel "Haddock."* Leipzig, 1998.

Huch, Ricarda. *Im alten Reich. Lebensbilder deutscher Städte.* 3 vols. Bremen, 1927.

Hüttenberger, Peter. *Düsseldorf. Geschichte von den Anfängen bis ins 20. Jahrhundert.* Düsseldorf, 1989.

Huyskens, Albert. *Der Kreis Meschede unter der Feuerwalze des Zweiten Weltkriegs.* Bielefeld, 1949.

Interessengemeinschaft Gedenkstätte Golm, e.V., ed. *Das Inferno von Swinemünde. Überlebende berichten über die Bombardierung der Stadt am 12. März 1945.* Iserlohn, 2001.

Irving, David. *Rise and Fall of the Luftwaffe: The Life of Luftwaffe Marshall Erhard Milch.* London: Weidenfeld & Nicolson, 1973.

———. *The Destruction of Dresden.* New York: Holt, Rinehart and Winston, 1963.

———. *Und Deutschlands Städte starben nicht,* Augsburg, 1989.

———. *Churchill's War.* 2 vols. Bullsbrook, W. Australia: Veritas, 1987.

Jacobsen, Hans-Adolf. "Der deutsche Luftangriff auf Rotterdam am 14. Mai 1940. Versuch einer Klärung." *Wehrwissenschaftliche Rundschau* (1958): 257–284.

Janssen, Gregor. *Das Ministerium Speer. Deutschlands Rüstung im Krieg.* Berlin, Frankfurt/M., and Vienna, 1968.

Jordan, Karl. *Heinrich der Löwe.* Munich, 1979.

Kesselring, Albert. *The Memoirs of Field-Marshal Kesselring.* Translated by Lynton Hudson. London: Greenhill, 1988.

Kiepke, Rudolf. *Werden, Untergang, Wiedererstehen.* Paderborn, 1949.

Kluge, Alexander. "Der Luftangriff auf Halberstadt am 8. April 1945." In *Chronik der Gefühle*. Vol. 2, *Lebensläufe*. Frankfurt/M., 2000.

Koch, Horst-Adalbert. *Flak. Die Geschichte der deutschen Flakartillerie und der Einsatz der Luftwaffenhelfer*. Bad Nauheim, 1965.

Kock, Gerhard. *"Der Führer sorgt für unsere Kinder . . ." Die Kinderlandverschickung im Zweiten Weltkrieg*. Paderborn, 1997.

Krämer, Karl. *Christbäume über Frankfurt*. Frankfurt/M., 1983.

Kranich, Kurt. *Karlsruhe. Schicksalstage einer Stadt*. Karlsruhe, 1973.

Kraume, Hans-Georg. *Duisburg im Krieg. 1939–1945*. Düsseldorf, 1982.

Krause, Michael. *Flucht vor dem Bombenkrieg. "Umquartierungen" im Zweiten Weltkrieg und die Wiedereingliederung der Evakuierten in Deutschland 1943–1964*. Düsseldorf, 1997.

Krieg und Elend im Siegerland. Prepared by Adolf Müller. Siegen, 1981.

Kronika, Jacob. *Berlins Untergang*. Copenhagen: Hagerup, 1945.

Krüger, Norbert. *Die Geschichte der Bombenangriffe auf Wuppertal im Zweiten Weltkrieg*. 1967. Unpublished manuscript.

———. "Die Luftangriffe auf Essen 1940–1945." *Essener Beiträge* 113 (2001).

Landeshauptstadt Düsseldorf, ed. *Erlebtes und Erlittenes. Gerresheim unter dem Nationalsozialismus*. Düsseldorf, 1993.

La Farge, Henry, ed. *Lost Treasures of Europe*. New York, 1946.

Lauenroth, Heinz, and Gustav Lauterbach. *Tod und Leben, Hannovers 9. Oktober*. Hanover, 1953.

Ledig, Gert. *Vergeltung*. Frankfurt/M., 1999.

Leyh, Georg. *Die deutschen wissenschaftlichen Bibliotheken nach dem Krieg*. Tübingen, 1947.

Liddell Hart, Basil. *History of the Second World War*. London: Cassell, 1970.

———. *The Other Side of the Hill*. London, 1983.

Lindkvist, Sven. *A History of Bombing*. New York, 2001.

Longmate, Norman R. *The Bombers: The R.A.F. Offensive Against Germany 1939–1945*. London, 1983.

Lytton, Henry D. "Bombing Policy in the Rome and Pre-Normandy Invasion Aerial Campaigns of World War II." *Military Affairs* 47, no. 4 (1983).

MacBean, John A., and Arthur S. Hogben. *Bombs Gone: The Development and Use of British Air-Dropped Weapons from 1912 to the Present Day*. Wellingborough, 1990.

MacDonald, Charles B. *The Battle of the Huertgen Forest*. Philadelphia, 1963.

Macksey, Kenneth. *From Triumph to Disaster: The Fatal Flaws of German Generalship from Moltke to Guderian*. London, 1996.

Mainfränkisches Museum, ed. Catalog to the special exhibition on the occasion of the fortieth anniversary of the destruction of Würzburg on March 16, 1945, March 10–June 5, 1985, "In stummer Klage, Zeugnisse der Zerstörung Würzburgs." Würzburg, 1985. Includes Heinrich Dunkhase, "Würzburg

16.3.1945, 21.20–21.42 Uhr, Hintergründe, Verlauf und Folgen des Luftangriffs der Nr. 5 Bomber Group." Reprint from *Mainfränkisches Jahrbuch für Geschichte und Kunst*. Vol. 32. 1980.

Mann, Thomas. *Zeit und Werk. Tagebücher, Reden und Schriften zum Zeitgeschehen*. Berlin (GDR) 1956.

Messenger, Charles. *"Bomber Harris" and the Strategic Bombing Offensive 1939–1945*. London, 1984.

Meyer-Hartmann, Hermann. *Zielpunkt 52092 N 09571 O. Der Raum Hildesheim im Luftkrieg 1939–1945*. Hildesheim, 1985.

Middlebrook, Martin. *Nuremberg Raid, 30–31 March 1944*. London: Allen Lane, 2000.

——. *The Battle of Hamburg: Allied Bomber Forces Against a German City in 1943*. London: Allen Lane, 1980.

——. *The Schweinfurt-Regensburg Mission: American Raids on 17 August 1943*. London, 1985.

——. *The Berlin Raids: R.A.F. Bomber Command Winter 1943–44*. London, 1990.

Middlebrook, Martin, and Chris Everitt. *The Bomber Command War Diaries: An Operational Reference Book 1939–1945*. Leicester, 1996.

Mierzejewski, Alfred C. *Bomben auf die Reichsbahn. Der Zusammenbruch der deutschen Kriegswirtschaft 1944–45*. Freiburg, 1993.

Milward, Alan S. *War Economy and Society*. Berkeley: University of California Press, 1977.

Mues, Willi. *Der große Kessel. Eine Dokumentation über das Ende des Zweiten Weltkrieges zwischen Lippe und Ruhr/Sieg und Lenne*. Erwitte, 1984.

Mühlen, Bengt von zur. *Der Todeskampf der Reichshauptstadt*. Berlin, 1994.

Müller-Werth, Herbert. *Geschichte und Kommunalpolitik der Stadt Wiesbaden*. Wiesbaden, 1963.

Murray, Williamson, and Allan R. Millett. *A War to Be Won: Fighting the Second World War*. Cambridge, Mass., 2000.

Nadler, Fritz. *Ich sah, wie Nürnberg unterging*. Nuremberg, 1955.

Neufeld, Michael J. *Die Rakete und das Reich*. Berlin, 1997.

Nossak, Hans Erich. *Der Untergang. Hamburg 1943*. Frankfurt/M., 1948.

Overy, Richard. *Why the Allies Won*. New York, 1996.

Panse, Friedrich. *Angst und Schreck in klinisch-psychologischer und sozialmedizinischer Sicht, dargestellt anhand von Erlebnisberichten aus dem Luftkrieg*. Stuttgart, 1952.

Pape, Rainer. *Bis fünf nach zwölf. Herforder Kriegstagebuch*. Herford, 1984.

Pape, Robert A. *Bombing to Win: Air Power and Coercion in War*. Ithaca, N.Y., and London, 1996.

Patton, George. *War as I Knew It*. New York, 1947.

Peters, Fritz. *Zwölf Jahre Bremen 1933–1945*. Bremen, 1951.

Piekalkiewicz, Janusz. *Air War 1939–1945*. Translated by Jan van Heurck. Poole, Dorset: Blandford; Harrisburg, Penn.: Historical Times Inc., 1985.

———. *Arnhem 1944*. Translated by H. A. Barker and A. J. Barker. New York: Scribner, 1976.

Pieper, Hedwig. *Der westfälische Hellweg, seine Landesnatur, Verkehrstellung und Kleinstädte*. Münster, 1928.

Pogt, Herbert, ed. *Vor fünfzig Jahren. Bomben auf Wuppertal*. Wuppertal, 1993.

Pöhlmann, Markus. *"Es war gerade, als würde alles bersten . . . ." Die Stadt Augsburg im Bombenkrieg*. Augsburg, 1994.

Poll, Bernhard, ed. *Aachen, Herbst 1944*. Aachen, 1962.

Prescher, Rudolf. *Der rote Hahn über Braunschweig*. Brunswick, 1955.

Price, Alfred. *Instruments of Darkness*. London: Kimber, 1967.

———. *Battle Over the Reich*. New York: Scribner, 1974.

———. *The Bomber in World War II*. New York: Scribner, 1979.

Rahier, Josef. *Jülich und das Jülicher Land in den Schicksalsjahren 1944/45. Kriegsgeschichtliche Ereignisse der Stadt und des Kreises Jülich nach authentischen Berichten*. Jülich, 1967.

Renz, Otto Wilhelm. *Deutsche Flugabwehr im 20. Jahrhundert. Flak-Entwicklung in Vergangenheit und Zukunft*. Berlin and Frankfurt/M., 1960.

Richard, Felix. *Der Untergang der Stadt Wesel im Jahre 1945*. Düsseldorf, 1961.

Rosenberg, Alfred. *Mythos des 20. Jahrhunderts*. Munich, 1934.

Rostow, Walt W. *Pre-Invasion Bombing Strategy: Eisenhower Decision of March 25, 1944*. Austin, Tex., 1981.

Roth, Eugen. *Spaziergänge mit Hindernissen. Anekdoten*. Munich, 1982.

Rumpf, Hans. "Bomber Harris." *Ziviler Luftschutz* 17, no. 7–8 (1953).

———. *The Bombing of Germany*. Translated by Edward Fitzgerald. New York: Holt, Rinehart, and Winston, 1962.

———. *Der hochrote Hahn*. Darmstadt, 1952.

Rust, Kenn C. *The Ninth Air Force in World War II*. Fallbrook, Calif., 1970.

Rüter-Ehlermann, Adelheid L., and C. F. Rüter, eds. *Justiz und NS-Verbrechen. Sammlung deutscher Strafurteile wegen nationalsozialistischer Tötungsverbrechen 1945–1966*. Amsterdam, 1969.

Rüther, Martin. *Köln, 31. März 1942. Der 1000-Bomber-Angriff*. Cologne, 1992.

Saundby, Robert. *Air Bombardment: The Story of Its Development*. New York, 1961.

Saward, Dudley. *"Bomber Harris": The Story of Marshal of the Royal Air Force Sir Arthur Harris*. London, 1984.

———. *The Bomber's Eye*. London, 1959.

Sax-Demuth, Waltraud. *Weiße Fahnen über Bielefeld*. Herford, 1981.

Schäfer, Hans A. *Berlin im Zweiten Weltkrieg. Der Untergang der Reichshauptstadt in Augenzeugenberichten*. Munich, 1985.

Schaffer, Ronald S. *Wings of Judgement: American Bombing in World War II*. New York, 1988.

Scheck, Thomas. *Denkmalpflege und Diktatur im Deutschen Reich zur Zeit des Nationalsozialismus*. Berlin, 1995.

Schmalacker-Wyrich, Esther. *Pforzheim, 23. Februar 1945. Der Untergang einer Stadt*. Pforzheim, 1980.

Schmid, Armin. *Frankfurt im Feuersturm*. Frankfurt/M., 1965.

Schmidt, Klaus. *Die Brandnacht. Dokumente von der Zerstörung Darmstadts am 11. September 1944*. Darmstadt, 1964.

Schnatz, Helmut. *Der Luftkrieg im Raum Koblenz 1944/5*. Boppard, 1981.

Schramm, Georg Wolfgang. *Bomben auf Nürnberg. Luftangriffe 1940–1945*. Munich, 1988.

Sebald, Winfried Georg. *On the Natural History of Destruction*. Translated by Anthea Bell. New York: Random House, 2003.

Seeland, Hermann. *Zerstörung und Untergang Alt-Hildesheims*. Hildesheim, 1947.

Seidler, Franz W. *Deutscher Volkssturm*. Munich, 1989.

Siedler, Wolf Jobst, and Elisabeth Niggemeyer. *Die gemordete Stadt*. Berlin, 1993.

Smith, Howard K. *Last Train from Berlin*. New York: Knopf, 1942.

Sollbach, Gerhard F., ed. *Dortmund. Bombenkrieg und Nachkriegszeit 1939–1948*. Hagen, 1996.

Sorel, Albert. *Europe and the French Revolution: The Political Traditions of the Old Regime*. Translated and edited by Alfred Cobban and J. W. Hunt. Garden City, N.Y.: Doubleday, 1971.

Speer, Albert. *Spandau, the Secret Diaries*. Translated by Richard and Clara Winston. London: Collins, 1976.

Spetzler, Eberhard. *Luftkrieg und Menschlichkeit. Die völkerrechtliche Stellung der Zivilpersonen im Luftkrieg*. Göttingen, 1956.

Spratte, Wido. *Im Anflug auf Osnabrück. Die Bombenangriffe 1940 bis 1945*. Osnabrück, 1985.

Stadtmuseum Münster, ed. *Bomben auf Münster*. Münster, 1983.

Steinhilber, Wilhelm. *Heilbronn. Die schwersten Stunden der Stadt*. Heilbronn, 1961.

Strategic Air War Against Germany, The: Report of the British Bombing Survey Unit. London, 1998.

Terraine, John. *The Right of the Line*. London, 1988.

Thömmes, Matthias. *Tod am Eifelhimmel. Luftkrieg über der Eifel 1939–1945*. Aachen, 1999.

Ueberschär, Gerd E. *Freiburg im Luftkrieg 1939–1945*. Freiburg and Würzburg, 1990.

United States Strategic Bombing Survey, The. 10 vols. Introduction by David MacIsaac. New York and London, 1976.

Verrier, Anthony. *Bomber Offensive*. London: Pan Books, 1974.

Vetter, Walter. *Freiburg in Trümmern 1944–1952*. Freiburg, 1982.

Vieberg, Gerhard. *Justiz im nationalsozialistischen Deutschland.* Edited by the German Federal Ministry for Justice. Bonn, 1984.

Vogt, Hans, and Herbert Brenne. *Krefeld im Luftkrieg 1939–1945.* Bonn, 1986.

Vogt, Helmut. *Bonn im Bombenkrieg. Zeitgenössische Aufzeichnungen und Erinnerungsberichte von Augenzeugen.* Bonn, 1989.

Voigt, Hans. *Die Veränderung der Großstadt Kiel durch den Luftkrieg.* Kiel, 1950.

Wagenführ, Rolf. *Die deutsche Industrie im Kriege 1939–1945.* Berlin (FRG), 1963.

Wagner, Walter. *Der Volksgerichtshof im nationalsozialistischen Staat.* Stuttgart, 1984.

Walther, Friedrich. *Schicksal einer deutschen Stadt. Geschichte Mannheims 1907–1945.* Frankfurt/M., 1950.

Warner, Konrad. *Schicksalswende Europas? Ich sprach mit dem deutschen Volk . . . Ein Tatsachenbericht.* Rheinfelden, 1944.

Webster, Charles, and Noble Frankland. *The Strategic Air Offensive Against Germany, 1939–1945.* 4 vols. London, 1961.

Weidenhaupt, Hugo. *Kleine Geschichte der Stadt Düsseldorf.* Düsseldorf, 1983.

Werner, Wolf. *Luftangriffe auf die deutsche Industrie.* Munich, 1985.

Westphal, Siegfried. *Heer in Fesseln.* Bonn, 1950.

Wette, Wolfram, Ricarda Bremer, and Detlef Vogel, eds. *Das letzte halbe Jahr. Stimmungsberichte der Wehrmachtspropaganda 1944–1945.* Essen: Klartext, 2001.

Whitaker, W. Denis, and Shelagh Whitaker. *Rhineland: The Battle to End the War.* Toronto: Stoddart, 2000.

Whiting, Charles. *Battle of the Ruhr Pocket.* New York: Ballantine Books, 1971.

Wille, Manfred. *Der Himmel brennt über Magdeburg. Die Zerstörung der Stadt im Zweiten Weltkrieg.* Magdeburg, n.d.

Wincker-Wildberg, Friedrich, ed. *Napoleon. Die Memoiren seines Lebens* Vol. 13. Vienna, n.d.

Zelzer, Maria. *Weg und Schicksal der Stuttgarter Juden. Ein Gedenkbuch.* Edited by the City of Nuremberg. Stuttgart, n.d.

Zenz, Emil. *Rauch und Trümmer. Trier 1944/45.* Trier, 1962.

Zuckerman, Solly. *From Apes to Warlords: The Autobiography, 1904–1946.* New York, 1978.

IMAGE SOURCES

INDEX

Page locators in italics indicate photographs.

THE

Jörg Friedrich

TRANSLATED BY ALLISON BROWN

COLUMBIA UNIVERSITY PRESS   NEW YORK